CW01476539

Aldo van Eyck

Aldo van Eyck
Works

Compilation by Vincent Ligtelijn

Birkhäuser Publishers
Basel • Boston • Berlin

Colophon

This publication was made possible by the provision of subsidy from the Dutch Foundation for Architecture.

Stimuleringsfonds voor Architectuur

First published in the Dutch language 1999 by THOTH Publishers, Bussum, The Netherlands
Original Dutch title: Aldo van Eyck, Werken
© 1999 The concerned authors and THOTH Publishers, Prins Hendriklaan 13, 1404 AS Bussum, The Netherlands

International distribution (except The Netherlands and Flanders) by: Birkhäuser – Publishers for Architecture, P.O. Box 133, CH-4010 Basel, Switzerland
Telephone: + 41 61 2050 707
Fax: + 41 61 2050 792
E-mail: sales@birkhauser.ch
http: www.birkhauser.ch

Translation from Dutch into English: Gregory Ball (part of the projects texts, the articles of Vincent Ligtelijn and the appendix), Victor J. Joseph (the article of Henk Engel) and Aldo van Eyck (the article of Herman Hertzberger)

A CIP catalogue record for this book is available from the Library of Congress, Washington D.C., USA

Deutsche Bibliothek Cataloging-in-Publication Data
Eyck, Aldo van:
Aldo van Eyck, works / comp. by Vincent Ligtelijn. [Transl. from Dutch into Engl.: Gregory Ball ...]. -
Basel ; Boston ; Berlin : Birkhäuser, 1999
Einheitssacht.: Aldo van Eyck, Werken <engl.>
Dt. Ausg. u.d.T.: Eyck, Aldo van: Aldo van Eyck, Werke
ISBN 3-7643-6012-7 (Basel ...)
ISBN 0-8176-6012-7 (Boston)

This work is subject to copyright. All rights are reserved, whether the whole or part of the material is concerned, specifically the rights of translation, reprinting, re-use of illustrations, recitation, broadcasting, reproduction on microfilms or in other ways, and storage in data banks. For any kind of use, permission of the copyright owner must be obtained.

Printed on acid-free paper produced from chlorine-free pulp. TCF ∞
Design: Studio Hans Lemmens, Ilpendam
Printing: Mart.Spruijt bv, Amsterdam
Binding: Van Mierlo, Nijmegen

Printed in the Netherlands

ISBN 3-7643-6012-7
ISBN 0-8176-6012-7

9 8 7 6 5 4 3 2 1

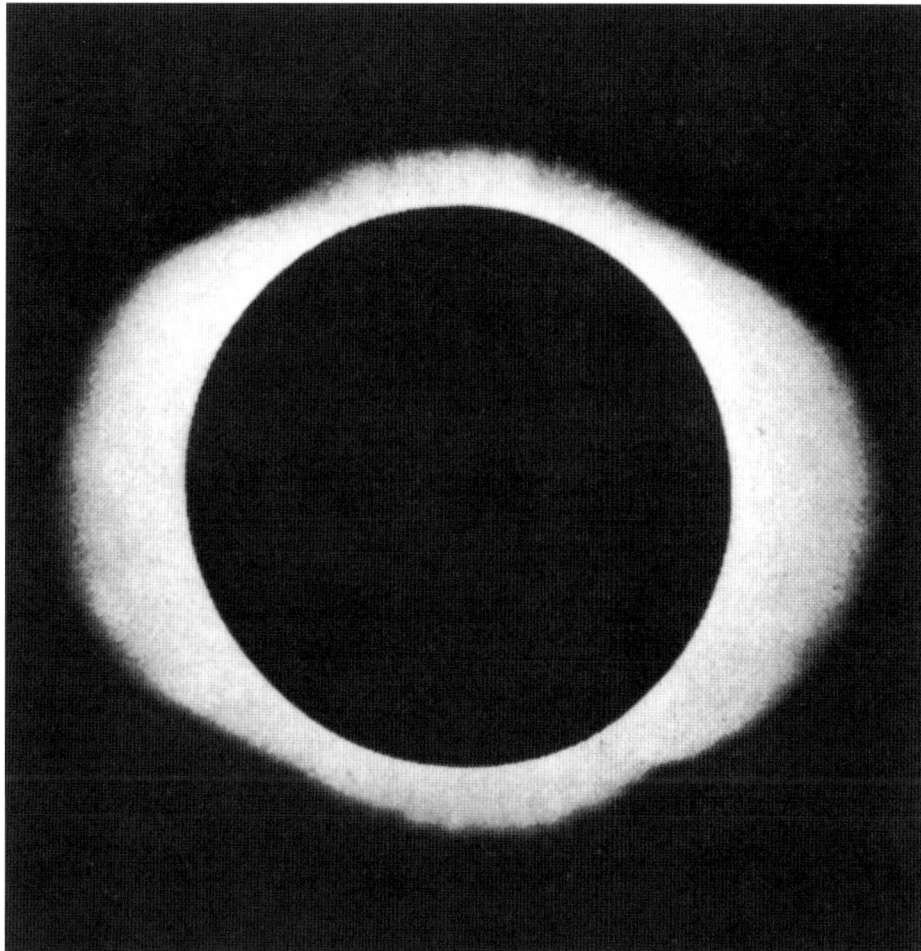

Moon's gnawed out in normal course,
What imprecise force
Swallows the sun?

Ezra Pound

Contents

Vincent Ligtelijn

The Paradox of Responsibility

8

A building in the form of an illustration on a flat plane often offers no more than an indication of its qualities. In order to experience it spatially it is more or less essential (but often impracticable) to stay in it for some time. Aldo van Eyck shared this opinion with Adolf Loos. But unlike Loos, who distrusted drawings and photos as a means of communication, and replaced them with his own written and spoken words, Aldo van Eyck – following in Le Corbusier's footsteps – was interested precisely in evoking the meaning of architecture in the combination of word *and* image. This applied equally to his descriptions of his own work. He linked

considerations that had led to the creation of a specific design to statements of a general nature. In so doing, his rhetorical points kept to the rules of the paradox, for the sake of clarifying the essence of the 'story of the other idea'.

Van Eyck's story has been a very consistent one. While selectively tied to architectural traditions, he kept his distance from passing fashion. His ideas were all informed by the need for an unconditional identification and equality between maker and user. This is indicated in the title, *by 'us' for us*, of his manifesto for a timeless experience of architecture – the Otterlo circles as well as by his definition of space, as simple as it is fantastic: 'space is the experience of it'. Conversely, his work displayed a number of remarkable changes architectonically speaking. Although, in terms of development, it can be formed into several groups, each work is different again. In each project he sought an architectonic order that responded to the specific circumstances of the assignment and the context, but with no tendency towards the idiosyncratic. Particular architectonic themes were referred to and explored depending on the circumstances.

Van Eyck saw practice and theory as extensions of each other. The majority of his theoretical articles were written as a reflection on a particular design. With a view to demonstrating the coherence of his ideas, some of these articles have been included in this book in addition to the 'Otterlo Circles' (among them 'The Medicine of Reciprocity Tentatively Illustrated', 'City Centre as Donor' & 'Transparency and the Gift of Colour', which were written in connection with the Orphanage, the reconstruction plans for the Nieuwmarkt area and the Hubertus House respectively).

As far as the project texts are concerned, we have taken the original versions as our basis. Since at the time they had to fit in with specific and changing editorial requirements, van Eyck himself has to a great extent adapted them for this book. Those who compare the Dutch version with the English (or the German version based on it) will discover that several of these texts have not been translated, but rewritten by Aldo, who was of course bilingual. His desire to achieve precision and refinement in his ideas made no distinction between writings and buildings. This book only includes those designs that are illustrative of his ideas. Several projects are accompanied by design sketches to indicate the way they evolved.

Van Eyck's works are prefaced by several essays by architects and architectural historians who have an intimate knowledge of Aldo and his work. Each considers the work, or aspects of it, from the point of view of his own understanding and interests. The aim of these articles, which are complementary to each other, is to sketch a picture that matches Aldo's 'inclusive' approach – for which my thanks to Joseph Rykwert, Peter Smithson, Herman Hertzberger, Francis Strauven and Henk Engel.

This book, on which I have been able to work as part of a research programme at the Faculty of Architecture of Delft University of Technology, draws much support from the mass of work done by Abel Blom, a member of staff at Aldo and Hannie van Eyck's practice. His contributions involved the arrangement and adaptation of the material as well as the necessary drawing work. Yvonne Kiers and Marianne Nuberg did sterling work behind the (PC)scenes, as editor Wim Platvoet looked after both the tranquility and the continuity of the project, while Hans Lemmens took great pains over our layout desires. From the start publisher Kees van den Hoek has been interested and willing to publish this specific Aldo van Eyck-book.

Without Hannie van Eyck, who was a tower of strength in all of this, the book would never have appeared. It is for this reason that I would like to dedicate *Aldo van Eyck – Works* to her.

'You can always get round one of your buildings, but not your book!' was what Aldo van Eyck impressed upon me when we started on this work. In this paradox he reflected the responsibility he has taken for his work throughout his life. But Aldo died before his buildings were finally handed over. All at once he became a memory and his work history. Let us hope that this collection of his work and accompanying texts, with a lay-out based on his own idea, will contribute to the continuation of the inspiration his ideas bring us.

Joseph Rykwert

Preface

The death of C.I.A.M., after the Otterlo-congress, 1959
above l. to r.: Peter & Alison Smithson, John Voelcker, Jaap Bakema and Sandy van Ginkel
under l. to r.: Aldo van Eyck and Blanche Lemco

How will Aldo van Eyck's contribution to the architecture of his time be assessed? He started working during the great euphoria at the end of World War II, when the coincident CIAM victory was presented at the same time as the final conquest of academic reaction by modernity. Though the nature of that minor victory was not clear at first, it soon became evident that the new architecture which would be produced by those local or central government offices engaged in reconstruction would not follow the poetic direction of Le Corbusier, to which Aldo was committed (as was I), but the somewhat different and much 'drier' team-work mode of Gropius and Mies. This official, diagrammatic modernity soon moved out of government offices to become the dominant manner of the anonymous commercial and corporate practices, so that team-work came to imply the homogenized production of an office that could be floated on the stock market as a limited liability company.

Early in the sixties, before any of this had become quite clear, I invited Aldo to lecture at an institution in which I was working. A senior architect there (an excellent draughtsman himself, incidentally, which makes the story more poignant) discussing the problem of getting good draughtsmen as assistants for his office, asked:

- and how many people do you have drawing for you, Mr van Eyck?

to which Aldo answered:

- I will not have people doing drawings for me. I enjoy doing them myself too much!

He may have been overstating his case, of course, but it was a case that needed pleading. The architect who does not take physical pleasure in mastering the means by which he translates his concept into material reality cannot – even now, when he manipulates lines on a screen – be said to be a true architect.

This physicality marks all Aldo's teaching and writing (as well as his projects). He always appeals to direct, sensory examples, as when he urges his readers to walk barefoot along the sea's edge, tramping the firm strand as it is constantly moistened by the withdrawing and returning eddies, a space neither sea nor land, where neither zone draws you, where you accept the pleasure of the in-between. Aldo keeps on returning to this key notion. 'In-between' is the zone about which he has thought a great deal, since it is there that your body – your hand or foot – will touch a building directly: threshold, doorjamb and windowsill. You can only reach shelter, the interior, by passing through them.

This in-between realm dissolves the narrow borderlines which he finds so intolerable in the work of some contemporaries. In the in-between zones the borders can be cajoled to 'loop generously' and these generous loops can be read in his own drawings, since he has always maintained mastery over the pleasures of representation; he uses his drawings to pass messages to clients and to his friends, as well as to the contractor. His assertion of that pleasure and that mastery has been an important if – in the short term – a losing battle, since architects have sold out to the anonymity of corporations.

The lesson of the in-between realm is rooted in his insight that anthropologists could offer a new understanding of the architects' task. It is an insight which offers another benefit – it returns architecture to the humanities. Aldo's commitment is treated sometimes as an eccentricity, like collecting antique motor-cars or following some picturesque guru. In fact it is central to his whole enterprise.

In the fifties and sixties, when he started his practice, architects were supposed to be not only rational, but also 'scientific', which – as far as the humanities were concerned – meant sociology of that most empirical kind which relied on direct market surveys to find out where people wanted to park their prams and where they wanted to hang their laundry to dry. Or, translated to an urban scale, it could answer questions about what could be the most efficient form of public transport in a given city, or where to locate a successful supermarket. Aldo's teaching was that the builders in an African village might know something we had forgotten about the nature of their skill and about what their society expected of them – it was an insight hidden from their more sophisticated European and American colleagues. This required a

new orientation of architectural thinking which went against prevailing attitudes and therefore required not only intellectual conviction but also great courage.

Of course he was an intrepid traveller, and his trips to Africa – particularly to north Africa and later to the Dogon – have often been recorded. That he brought back beautiful objects and powerful impressions is almost incidental. For him the urge to undergo the hardships – and run the very real dangers these trips involved – was driven by the sense that he was returning to the sources of a visual and plastic language. Where traditional crafts have been maintained for centuries, and the forms of building and of occupation are closely bound to the customs and the patterns of movement in a community, there is an understanding of built form which more 'advanced' societies seem to have lost. In particular, Aldo believed that craftsmen, but builders perhaps more emphatically than the others, have a clear sense of the social value of their work.

When he took over the editorship of Forum, the most important (certainly the most influential) Dutch architectural periodical at the time, this was a lesson he hammered home constantly. He determined that his editorship would champion a view of architecture and its role which would be 'The story of another idea'. 'The other idea' offered an alternative understanding of modernity whose simplicity was not schematic like that of many of Aldo's contemporaries, but rich and multi-layered – a poetic modernity which drew on Picasso, Joyce, and Stravinsky, but perhaps even more on Brancusi, whom he liked to quote: *on arrive à la simplicité malgré soi en s'approchant du sens réel des choses.*

To heal the rifts between a hostile environment and the community, he offered 'the medicine of reciprocity'. That became his watchword, almost his slogan. Architects, he thought, had to be persuaded to realize the importance of those tangible elements modernity had neglected – and most of all regain the sense that buildings should welcome the touch of and handling by their users, that they would also be 'read' by them. Of the Dogon and of other such peoples, he says that their '...cities, vil-

lages and houses – even (their) baskets – were persuaded by means of symbolic form and complex ritual to contain within their measurable confines that which exists beyond and is immeasurable: to represent it symbolically.'

Such a profession would – and of course did – set him virulently against the prophets of the death of architecture and the exquisite emptiness of built form. But it also made him utterly hostile (and he is not one to dampen any hostility he may feel) to any attempts at mitigating the terrible damage teamwork-architecture has done to our cities by dressing up standard commercial buildings in diagrammatic bits of the past, a movement that used be labelled 'post-modernism'. This was a repugnant attitude to someone who loves the plastic elaboration and poetic modelling achieved by Francesco di Giorgio or Palladio or Borromini.

But his love for the buildings of the past, like his love of those in remote places, is also very much part of his modernity. He wants his own building to *be* like those of his heroes, not *look like* them. And he is familiar and passionate about the best contemporary architects. The revival of interest in the work of Johannes Duiker, for instance, is in part at least due to his enthusiastic advocacy. Nor is he any less generous to younger architects. I knew nothing about Herman Hertzberger when Aldo insisted on showing me over Hertzberger's Students' House in Amsterdam – which was then quite new (it must have been in the mid-sixties) and I remember with grateful pleasure the enthusiasm with which Aldo pointed out its excellencies to me. And he introduced me early on to the work of Piet Blom. His ideas and his formal inventions will live on not only in his own work, but of the many architects, anthropologists and historians who have learnt from him.

Van Eyck has never been a man of half measures and he never was mealy-mouthed. Those of us who were lucky to share most of his tastes and his *parti-pris* know that his loyalty to causes was unflinching, even if the slightest *salonnier* indulgence of the enemy might bring down his ire. I have many reasons to be grateful for nearly forty years of friendship.

Aldo van Eyck

The Otterlo Circles

BY US?

The diagram contains the following labels arranged around the circle:

IMMUTABILITY AND REST

concepts of the mind

CHANGE AND MOVEMENT

to bring together opposite quali...

extensions of collective behaviour

VERNACULAR OF THE HEART

when is architecture going to bring together opposite quali...

we can discover ourselves everywhere – in all places and ages – doing the same th...

to discover anew implies discove...

12

The Otterlo Circles: Each culture stresses specific aspects – fundamental solutions – which are universally relevant but which, for various reasons, particular and random, are emphasized whilst others are repressed. Ultimately man suffers from these limitations, from what is overemphasized at the cost of what is omitted and often forgotten. Now, today, what is specific, what gives meaningful identity, should no longer depend on what is thus arbitrarily omitted or stressed, but on how these specific aspects are absorbed, adapted, and combined for the sake of more inclusive solutions which can respond to the nature of the human person as a whole instead of in part.

The three little images united in the first circle hide no real conflict; nor are their properties incompatible. They com-

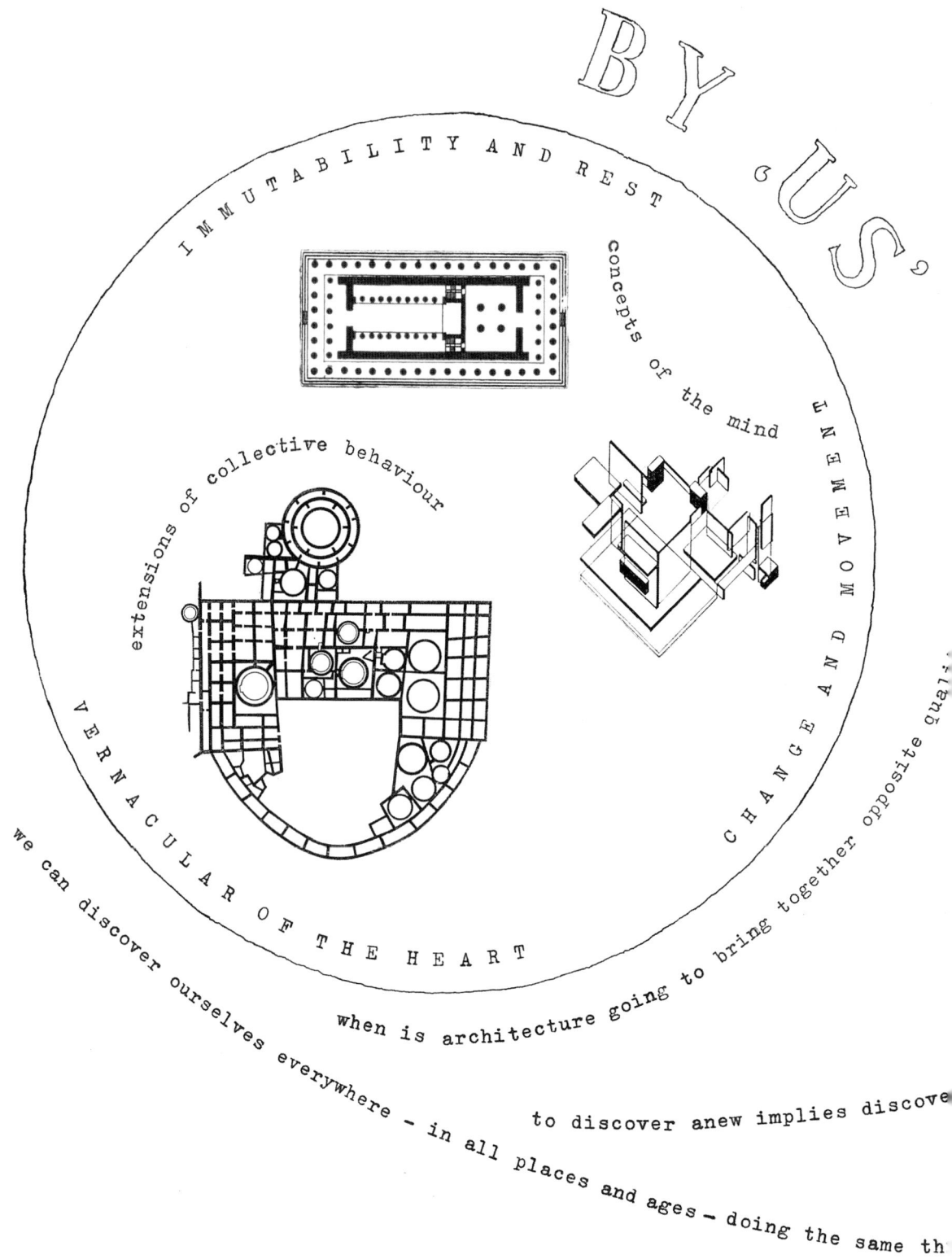

FOR US

FOR EACH MAN AND ALL MEN

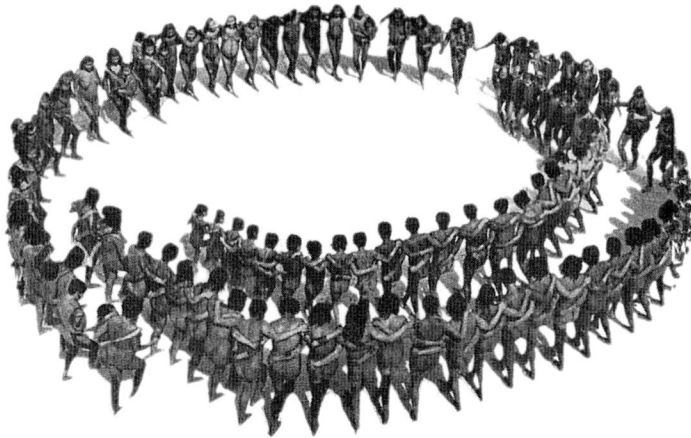

close to the center - the shifting center - and build.

...hing new.

different way, feeling the same differently, reacting differently to the same.

plement each other, belong together, and reflect equally valid aspects of the human personality. If they are allowed to interact, if their properties are brought together, it should no longer be difficult to resist the lure of false eclecticism – false regionalism and – false modernism – three kinds of shortsightedness which continually alternate.

The three images in the first circle do not exclude others equally essential. No limitation is implied. Add San Carlo alle Quatro Fontane or Vierzehnheiligen and we can start reconciling them – the essence, not the form – in a wonderful sequence of possibilities that would really fit man. This is our job: *by 'us' for us*. For us implying each man and all men, the individual and society – hence the second circle.

Get close to the shifting centre of man and build!

The Greek temple represents an order that rests within itself, one that is valid whenever we deal with the singular or with limited multiplicity. Theo van Doesburg's drawing – a 1911 cubist painting or Duiker's sanatorium would be equally appropriate – represents plurality and relativity. The one stands for classical harmony, the other for what I call harmony in motion (the aesthetics of number). House and city can only be understood in terms of both these images today – these two and a third! The third image, an Indian pueblo for example, represents what I call the vernacular of the heart – the extension of collective behaviour into built form – limited multiplicity successfully tamed.

13

Second version of the original design for the CIAM-congress, Otterlo, 1959.

Vincent Ligtelijn

Introduction to the Work of Aldo van Eyck

'Space is the appreciation of it'[1]

Aldo van Eyck looked not only to the left and right, but also, and more especially, all around. On the basis of his appreciation for all architecture as built meaning, and inspired by modern art and non-Western cultures, he has been able to develop his own vision of contemporary architecture. In this vision he broke away from the polarisation of traditional and modern as inward-looking phenomena. This open attitude was sufficient to make him an unusual representative of Nieuwe Bouwen,[2] and an architect who wanted to combine opposites.

Van Eyck saw his share in this as the continuation of what has already been accomplished in the past. As far as the contemplation of existence is concerned, the combination of polarities had already emerged in pre-Socratic times (Heraclitus). In his familiar metaphor, in which the part and the whole are seen in each other's light, Alberti also referred to the ancient philosophers.[3] The 'duo phenomenon' developed by van Eyck – after his travels to the Dogon and under the influence of their twin cosmology, called the 'twin phenomenon' – is an extension of this. In the same way arises his need to link the written and spoken word to design practice. That means many things in one, but also one among many: Aldo van Eyck.

His writings, intended to address the individual's sensitivity to form without propounding all-embracing theories, have appeared in various publications. Forum magazine, from which the functionalist certainties of the time were beleaguered, even served as his mouthpiece for several years.[4] Using architectonic concepts like 'place, doorstep and the in-between', and qualities like 'ambiguity, reciprocity and reversibility', van Eyck approached architecture in a poetic language at odds with the usual barren jargon. The anonymous 'users' were reborn as 'people' with a heart, as were the architects, in the realisation that architecture is all about the everyday surroundings of one and all. This had already led to 'the story of another idea',[5] which was not highly appreciated by the lackeys of the establishment.

A new space opened up, architecture was a

realm of emotional dimensions, and this is what van Eyck demonstrated: ideas, concepts, linked to images of every continent and age! This had a stimulating effect on those who wanted to develop their own, more inclusive attitude towards architecture. In the sixties and seventies, the manuscript of his *The Child, the City and the Artist*, which was never published, rolled through the duplicators at schools and universities from Europe to America. His professorship at Delft University was inevitable, as were many guest professorships in places all over the world. He liked to have kindred spirits around him, but his attitude and contribution were not intended to form a 'school'. In the same way he was averse to the idea that modern architecture is a universal language. Everyone has their own space and responsibility.

Aldo and Hannie van Eyck surprised many people with their work. Their indefatigable wish to experiment means it remained unpredictable, and they were always reviving not only things that had got into a rut, but also those that had been forgotten. For a grand old man and trendsetter of modern architecture, documentation of his work is still too fragmentary and therefore essentially underexposed. This undoubtedly has something to do with the fact that he could be very demanding and difficult, but this did nothing to diminish the need for documentation. Not only because his design work was the source of his writings, which played their part in the general change of mentality, but above all because there is a great deal to be learnt from and enjoyed in his work. This book of his collected work aims to redress the balance somewhat. The intention of each of his works can be read even without his writings to hand, which is a positive quality in independent architecture.

Van Eyck's career was as long as it was intensive. He started in 1947 as a designer of children's playgrounds for Amsterdam city council, and was till his death active on several fronts in the profession. And with the same dedication, as militant as ever and ready to take full responsibility for his work. Just before his eightieth birthday, not long after his scintillating building for the Court of Audit in The Hague was finished, he rebutted criticisms of it made by a number of journalists only vaguely concerned with the profession, partly by referring to the necessity for architecture to be linked to social, human and practical motives.[6]

Status was alien to him, but paradoxes were his friends, and assertions were tested for their tenability by means of their possible reversibility. He approached architecture as a non-conformist with a conscience, it being only a meaningful bearer of culture if it does not become estranged from its original aspirations, in other words if 'the architecture is presented as more complicated than we are ourselves – which is complicated enough.'

In the course of time his concepts were tightened up but remained essentially unchanged. Although his work is recognisable by means of his personal style and themes, no two projects are the same in terms of form. Superficially, his work is meta-stylistic rather than stylistically pure. But van Eyck's style, even more so than is usual in modern architecture, lies not 'on' but 'in' his work. His criticism of certain contemporaries is also an extension of this. He accused colleagues in CIAM of a lack of attention to the autonomy of architecture and of ignoring the past, while he charged the Postmodernists with the opposite: 'Both then and now, the same mechanical clockwork notion of time prevails, the same awkward posturing vis à vis the past. It is still history "OUT" or history "IN". In the minds of architects this all too often means IN and OUT of ROME – or YES or NO to classicism alternating every 30 years or so. Why this constant and unnecessary choosing between imagined alternatives... Team 10 – that is certain – behaved far less pathologically towards the past and history than either CIAM or RPP.'[7]

As a counterpart to thinking in terms of mutually exclusive alternatives, van Eyck employed the dialectics of reciprocity, which encompasses the fundamental equality of differences. In the elementary text accompanying the Orphanage, 'The Medicine of Reciprocity Tentatively Illustrated',[8] he explores in great depth the twin-phenomenon that makes opposites qualitatively recordable and measurable without neutralising each other. In his work he let the complementary aspects (individ-ual–community, order–chaos, one–many, etc.) form a non-hierarchical fabric of twin phenomena, that forms a constituent part of the configurative process.

Van Eyck's desire for horizontal equality was fed by the members of the avant-garde from the beginning of the century. They were artists and scientists who, each from their own specific medium, made a contribution to the establishment of the relativity world view, a culture which, according to van Eyck, might be the myth of our age. Arp, Brancusi, Miró, Mondrian, Bartók, Joyce, Heisenberg and many others united in his 'Great Gang' gave van Eyck a dynamic view of things: 'After all, by way of the subject, science has brought much of the essence of the object to the surface, provided new and deeper understanding of the world inside and outside man, in that it finally became clear that inside and outside form a twin phenomenon, object and subject too.'[9]

His examples were independent figures like Aalto, Le Corbusier, Duiker, Loos and Rietveld, all architects who were able to incorporate the new awareness into their work. Not on account of the forms they employed, but of the spirit they expressed – a spirit that was by no means to be found in the work of Gropius, Mies and Oud, the darlings of the 'international style'.

It was van Eyck's intention to turn the ideas of the Avant-gardists, which were pulverised in the practice of technocratically-oriented architecture, into the starting point of a contemporary architecture by confronting them with tradition, their original 'opposition' – to use the word with the meaning Theo van Doesburg gave it. Van Eyck saw tradition as retaining its value as an expression of the human identity which, although it has manifested itself in different forms in other ages and cultures, has essentially remained constant. In this light he wanted to understand the architectural heritage in order to be able to reconstruct it.

There is a great difference between CIAM and De Stijl, but their similarity is that they both turned their backs on the past. But Le Corbusier, Sert and Giedion provided evidence of the opposite. Like van Eyck they were steeped in history. Van Eyck's work still forms a bridge between past and present – the past stripped of any hierarchies and assimilated without leaving any sentimental or eclectic traces behind.

The 'Otterlo Circles' represent this pursuit of a timeless experience of architecture. This 'manifesto' presented during the CIAM congress in Otterlo in 1959 embraced his vision of the new architecture and tried to strike at CIAM's pride in Western culture: the applied images are in an early phase of development, where they are not archaic. Both circles, which, as each other's counter-form, sym-

ivity. The one stands for classical harmony, the other for what I call harmony in motion (the aesthetics of number). House and city can only be understood in terms of both these images today – these two and a third! The third image, an Indian pueblo for example, represents what I call the vernacular of the heart – the extension of collective behaviour into built form – limited multiplicity successfully tamed.'[10]

Van Eyck set the trend for his later work in his early designs for playgrounds in Amsterdam, and the Cobra exhibitions in Amsterdam and Liège:

panding, linear character (see sketch below). He recognised this quality in the work of artists in and connected with De Stijl, and also in artefacts from archaic, so-called 'primitive' cultures. They tempted him and his wife Hannie into going on distant travels, and also into continually extending their collection of ethnographic objects. These things form as it were their 'specimen room', an inexhaustible source of inspiration in whose midst they lived together in Loenen.

The thing that especially fascinated him in the decoration of these objects was both the attach-

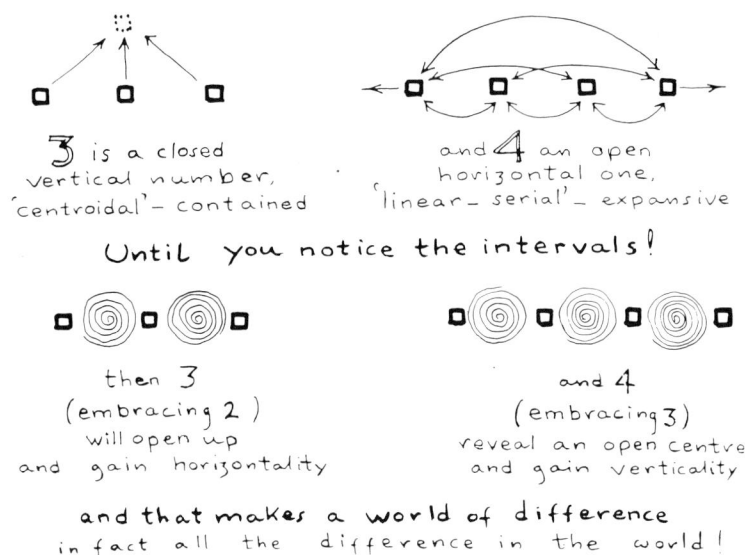

Aldo van Eyck: Until you notice the intervals!

bolise architecture and society, are connected by linking lines of text and by the headings "by 'us' – for us", emphasising the unconditional identification and equality of the maker and the user. In the architecture circle the elementary values from various cultures can be seen, and their connection is considered essential to meeting the totality of our identity: 'The Greek temple represents an order that rests within itself, one that is valid whenever we deal with the singular or with limited multiplicity. Theo van Doesburg's drawing (a 1911 cubist painting or Duiker's sanatorium would be equally appropriate) represents plurality and relat-

both lively and elementary. The play equipment was given primeval shapes, while the etchings were exhibited in the position in which they were made: horizontal. Both the children and the paintings tumble through space. Their direct spontaneity and liveliness are set in a state of tension, their arrangement based on De Stijl's universal 'aesthetics of relations'.

Van Eyck became increasingly convinced of the significance of the interval which – depending on the attention devoted to it – is able to transform 'vertical' formations with a central and closed middle section into open, 'horizontal' systems with an ex-

ment of equal value to both the object and the background, and the rhythmic arrangement of 'the large number'. To this is linked his appreciation of the artist Richard Paul Lohse, with his linear and serial experiments following on from the work of De Stijl. He had this to say about what Lohse's work might signify in urban planning: '...Lohse proves this – what is individual, less explicit, will arise once more, as the universal, the recurring, brought into balance, to a harmony in motion...'[11] It is characteristic of van Eyck that he also made this outlook into the starting point for his buildings.

Van Eyck saw architecture as a problem of 'the

greater number', which he wanted to approach in the framework of a pragmatic, geometric vocabulary. The three schools in Nagele, his first major brief in the Netherlands after his studies and stay in Zurich from 1938 to 1946, were the first finger exercises in his so-called 'aesthetics of number' within this compositional technique. The highly rhythmical ground plans display an alternation of openness and closedness, moving away from the idea that everything in modern architecture has to be in glass. He also distanced himself from organising on the basis of classical symmetries with a single

nisation started with his contributions to the town plans for the new village of Nagele and continued by way of the Buikslotermeer housing plan and the Congress Building in Jerusalem. In the meantime, the Orphanage had made concrete Mondrian's words 'the culture of particular form is approaching it's end. The culture of determined relations has begun'. The building changes as you change, the centre moves along with you, it is polycentric. The twin phenomena blossom, and part and whole interlock at every level, even as far as the directions followed, as appears in the forked articulation of

In his poetic text 'Place and Occasion'[12], van Eyck elucidates this ambivalence: 'Man still breathes both in and out. When is architecture going to do the same? There is a kind of spatial appreciation which makes us envy birds in flight; there is also a kind which makes us recall the sheltered enclosure of our origin. Architecture will fail if it neglects either the one or the other – labyrinthian clarity, at any rate, sings of both. Birds nest, bird-flight, bird.' This expressly created a relationship between 'place' and 'space', one over which many epigones have flown unawares.

Bakuba weaving (raffia), Congo

Aesthetics of Number

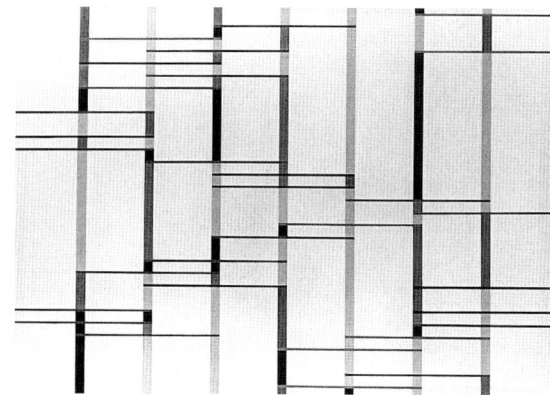

Richard Paul Lohse: Composition 1947

17

dominant centre or direction. By applying asymmetric shifts and rotations, means that had already been tried out by the Nieuwe Bouwen architects, van Eyck allowed an order to arise in which part and whole define each other reciprocally at every level and in which several and different centres, axes and directions of visual attention are present on an equal footing. This is a working method that van Eyck described as 'the configurative process', and in which is incorporated his criticism of the prevailing practice of conventional site planning techniques.

The turn away from additive principles of orga-

the building. This is an articulation that latches onto the situation and finds its answer in the diagonally developing internal streets and pavilions. As can also be read in van Eyck's sketch for the pavilion for the smaller children from 4 to 6, in which is indicated how the small, eccentric play-house, which makes tangible the large domed space, becomes the source of the diagonally directed focus on the outside. The essence of this serial-form connection between spatial extremes is clear: from the intimacy of the small, round house, the child is able to feel involved in the world outside the building, which borders on the road to the town.

Van Eyck saw the Orphanage as a metaphor for the city: 'Make of each house a small city and of each city a large house.' His own 'Four Tower House' in Baambrugge, which was never built (rejected by the provincial planning authority) which was to be one house and four houses at the same time, was an extension of this outlook, in which architecture is considered in the light of the city. As well as the superb Sonsbeek pavilion which, in terms of density and tension and the way man and sculpture were faced with each other, is very urban. The step towards an architecture as an active and structural complement to the city was taken in the design for the competition for a town hall in Deventer. This was unfortunately never built, but the contextual approach was continued on an urban planning scale in the plan for the restructuring of the Nieuwmarkt area in Amsterdam. By means of this plan and the many articles, including *City Centre as Donor*,[13] he and his staff forced a breakthrough in favour of the more cautious handling of old city centres, partly by their participation in action committees.

The many housing projects that followed, in which the configurative method was abandoned in coming literally and figuratively more colourful and transparent. The configurative method also reappeared as if reborn, which can be seen in, among other things, the wonderful house in Retie and the Hubertus House in Amsterdam. The Modissa fashion shop can be seen as a predecessor to the Hubertus House. In this competition design from 1963, whose asymmetrical setting on a corner site in Zurich formed the link between two streets, the building and its three main volumes are just as important as the space between, the interval. Crosswise relationships from the inside out are opment. In its sideways continuation, as a 'delayed entrance', the interval also unites the old and new Hubertus buildings. From the inside, the area round the interval offers a view of both the outside of the building, and of the more distant spaces of both the interior and the exterior. The modulation in depth so created intensifies the feeling of place by means, paradoxically enough, of the transparency created: 'what is at stake... is a kind of openness in which enclosure is, as it were, innate – included *a priori*.'[14] To this end the street front, with its slender metalwork and the constant reflec-

Hans Arp: Mountain, Table, Anchors, Navel
(oil on cardboard with cut-outs), 1925

"So here Hans Arp fraternally brings together the most diverse things: mountain, table, anchors, navel; 1925.
One can only deal with it reduced. Not even Kafka could take it on easily. By saying 'and walked the sideways grass' instead of 'and walked sideways in the grass' – i.e., by using the adverb as an adjective – the subject and object come so close to each other that the distinction between the two is absorbed through the equivalence, and the old hierarchy conquered."

Aldo van Eyck

the face of realistic considerations, had a great influence on the architecture of urban renewal. However, in the development of the projects, which was for a large part appropriated by his partner Theo Bosch, playing with tradition more than once led to references to historical forms, which led to a great many misunderstandings. Semi-professionals among the critics even thought they had found a precursor to Postmodernism in van Eyck! After this period he once more oriented himself towards the Moderns. His wife Hannie van Roojen, with whom he collaborated officially in 1983, was a great support to him. The tone of his work changed, be-

formed with the adjacent spaces in the street across this ambiguous interval, especially from the peripheral outside space on the ground floor.

In the new vertical building of the Hubertus House (1973-81), a home for single parents and their children, the game played round the interval is extended. It distinguishes and connects not only the various adjacent volumes, but also the spaces in front of and behind the building, so that even the children's accommodation, which is situated deeper in the enclosed street block, can still orient itself towards the street. The transparent interval gives the building a significance in terms of urban devel-

tion of its glass, had to be stripped of its spatial indeterminacy. His solution was paint. The colours, which because they are all experienced at virtually the same time – at least in the 'high-rise' section – are set in a spectral series, and in their cyclical unfolding across discernable sections of the façade force back the plasticity of the volume to a number of planes of colour that permeate each other. In this figurative transparency the building seems to dissolve in colour and thereby rid itself of its actual material. In this building, active colour makes its riotous but irreversible entrance into van Eyck's work. The serene psychiatric clinic in Boxtel, the

18

dazzling Moluccan church in Deventer and the festive restaurant and conference complex for ESTEC in the dunes near Noordwijk would be unthinkable without colour, which has become a defining element in their spatial quality.

In these low-rise buildings the roofs also became more active, as ceilings. It was no longer possible to read the designs fully from the ground plans alone. Both the church and the ESTEC complex are essentially all roof! Just as the ESTEC office is all window, with iridescent weathering by way of fine eye make-up for the cantilevering in the façades. The van Eycks were hereby turning in a new direction:

by the nature of the brief. This is certainly the case when compared to those works that show up the only relative importance of the boundaries, where they appear as a single thing from both inside and outside. This is the case with the Orphanage, the Hubertus House and the house in Retie, all open though finite structures. As far as this is concerned, the Court of Audit is a classical building, with an independent, though related, interior and exterior. But van Eyck paid that much more attention, both in the ESTEC offices and the Court of Audit, to those areas where the interior and exterior space meet: the windows. The tapering columns of the

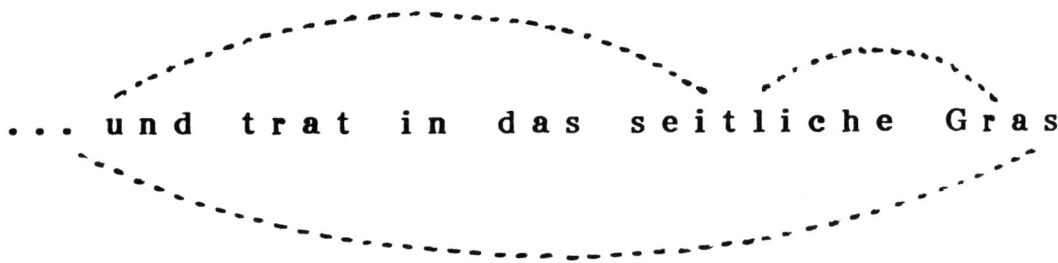

... und trat in das seitliche Gras

the building was clad (in untreated iroko wood) to protect the concrete structure. The cladding only gives a veiled image of the structure of the building, but is given an active visual role, in relation to the surroundings too. The same applies to the polycentric building for the Court of Audit in The Hague. It is a scintillating and colourful building, concealed behind a stately avenue, and has a surprising presence, reached by way of an old brown gate. It is an enrichment of the old city centre, also because of the varied public spaces the building creates. The structural heterogeneity between its interior and exterior intensifies the spatial tension between the two, whose presence is determined

latter make the windows at the top wider, so that they have a slightly different appearance on each storey. They are designed and finely detailed in such a way that they mediate in the spatial break between interior and exterior. By which means van Eyck listened to his own call, made at the start of his career, to 'make a welcome of each door, a countenance of each window'![15]

This seems to bring us full circle, but is it not so that 'the circle is actually a very generous square', and has been for the last fifty years?

Notes

1. From the introduction to the 'Adolf Loos' exhibition in Delft, *Delftse School* (April 1965, no. 12).

2. 'Nieuwe Bouwen' is a Dutch term for the Modern Movement, covering works with names like De Stijl, Functionalism, Nieuwe Zakelijkheid, de 8 and Opbouw, etc.

3. Alberti, *De Re Aedificatoria*, I, IX, 4-5: 'And if, as the philosophers assert, the city is a large house and inversely the house itself is a little city, why should one not then regard the parts of a house as little dwellings?', English translation in: Francis Strauven, *Aldo van Eyck. The Shape of Relativity* (Amsterdam, 1997), footnote 384, p. 300.

4. Van Eyck was a member of the editorial staff of *Forum*, together with Apon, Bakema, Hardy, Hertzberger and Schrofer, from 1959-63. First issue: 1959, no. 7, the last: July 1967 (extra publication).

5. The title of Aldo's first Forum publication as editor: *Forum* (1959, no. 7), 196.

6. Aldo van Eyck, 'Lured from his den', *Archis* (1998, no. 2), 19-26.

7. Aldo van Eyck, 'R.P.P. (Rats, Posts and other Pests)', Annual Discourse, in *AD News Supplement* (1981, no. 7).

8. Aldo van Eyck, *Forum* (1960/61, no. 7); also p. 88 in this book.

9. Aldo van Eyck, from a reaction to the Faculty of Architecture, TU Delft, in the late seventies.

10. Aldo van Eyck, 'Is architecture going to reconcile basic values', in O. Newman, *CIAM 59 in Otterlo* (Stuttgart, 1961), 26-35.

11. Aldo van Eyck, *Forum* (1952, no. 6/7), 186.

12. Aldo van Eyck, *Progressive Architecture* (Sept. 1962), 155.

13. Aldo van Eyck, *TABK* (1970, no. 20), 469-70.

14. H. Hertzberger, A. van Roijen-Wortmann, F. Strauven, *Aldo van Eyck* (Amsterdam, 1982), 81; also in this book, page 201.

15. *Forum* (1960/1, no. 4), 154.

Peter Smithson

Church at The Hague by Aldo van Eyck

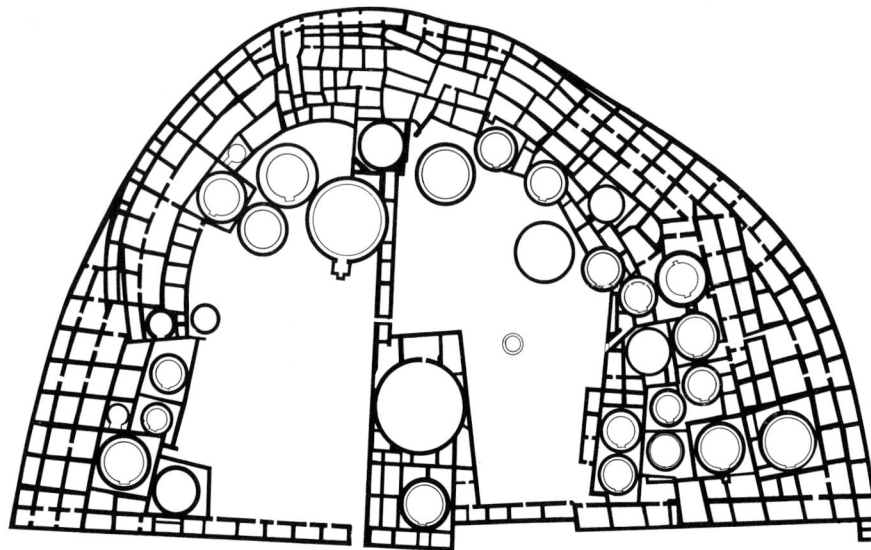

Pueblo Bonito, New Mexico

Aldo van Eyck has been preparing himself to build this church for a very long time.

The immediate feeling one has on entering is of being in a church; the place induces silence, produces a change in awareness of self... it even smells like a church. Now, according to Aldo van Eyck, the architecture of the present period should be able, as a conscious act, to gather into its language an understanding of the languages and the meanings of the architectures that preceded it. This anyway is my interpretation of what he meant when he said 'the time has come to gather the old into the new, to rediscover the archaic qualities of human nature'.[1]

Aldo van Eyck's life over the last twelve years, it would seem, has been spent confirming the architectural language that he had chosen by instinct, and the church at The Hague is his affirmation of that choice. For he has used an architectural language of circles, and parts of circles, and rectangles – including the square – from his earliest working years.

Am I wrong when I remember his old room in the Binnenkant as a round stove in a round hearth with a round flue in a rectangular room? Certainly, in the first publication which includes his work, which I now possess – Dutch *Forum* 6/7 from 1952 – there are playgrounds which use this language. He used it (with van Ginkel) in the three schools at Nagele published in 1960[2] and his Orphanage – the Kindertehuis in Amsterdam – intensifies and extends this language into a notional Order. His travels, to the Pueblos (winter 1961–62) and to the Dogon (published in 1967), were made after this building was completed; and these journeys, I am saying, were part of a process of confirmation of the idea of the Kindertehuis – 'As for this home for children the idea was to persuade it to become both 'house' and 'city'; a city-like house and a house-like city'[3] – and confirmation also of the adequacy of his chosen language to body-out that idea. In both groups of villages studied on these journeys, the plan shapes are predominantly circles and rectangles; and, amazingly, in the Dogon appear those pierced lintels or over-lintel slots, which device is the essence of the extension of Aldo van Eyck's architectural language, which had taken place at the Orphanage, and

Dogon, Mali

through which that architectural language had become recognisably in Order.

'All external and internal walls, as well as all major elements built within their enclosure, terminate at column height. The space between here and the roof is either occupied by horizontal precast reinforced concrete architraves – intermediary elements that bind and enclose, form an extension of the walls upwards, an extension of the roof downwards – or is filled in with glass. Sometimes it is left open.'[4]

The church at The Hague uses the Order established at the Orphanage, more densely worked but more coolly stated. It has gathered the old into the new more completely than I had believed possible. And it never quotes... not even from Mackintosh!

One problem for me remains: the church on its wooded islet seems to be profoundly isolated. It is not that I want it to be one of a 'bunch of places' (which would insult one of the least literal buildings, I know), but I regret that it provides no hint of the kind of connectivity – an aesthetic of connectivity in isolation (!) – that it seems to me we must somehow learn to achieve. You can imagine

that I am not talking about attaching the church to another building, but of quality of connection.

Visiting the Orphanage again fifteen years after first seeing it... what uninhabitable gulfs lie between the built-events of the modern city! Not that the problem was neglected here in the first thinking... 'It seemed best to anchor the children's large house – little city – to the street, i.e. to the public sphere, there where they enter and leave it, by introducing a large open square as a transition between the reality outside and that inside.'[5] Its very success within its own territory makes us aware that we really have no effective vision of a new sort of urban space. We can view the Orphanage, with hindsight and through the images that Aldo van Eyck has himself brought to our attention, as a kind of Pueblo in a sparsely inhabited terrain. So it almost really was in 1959; but today it is in a city, a form amongst other forms, a human group among other human groups.... So also the church, from its inescapable very beginning.

First published in *AD* 1975, no. 6, 345-350

Notes

1. Aldo van Eyck from *Team 10 Primer*, edited by Alison Smithson, published Studio Vista, 1968 edition, page 20 line 37. (*Team 10 Primer* was first published in *AD* (1962, no. 12) and subsequently as an *AD* book)

2. No trace of the language appears, however, in the published projects for the Village of Nagele in Dutch *Forum* (1952, no. 6/7). These were prepared for the 7th Congress of CIAM in Bergamo in 1949, so were made presumably in 1948. At some time therefore between 1948 and 1952, Aldo van Eyck settled on the language which would enable him to build.

3. Aldo van Eyck, from Dutch *Forum* (1960-1, no. 6/7), page 237, starts line 32 from bottom.

4. As above, but page 238, starts line 23 from the bottom.

5. As above, starts line 2 from the top.

Herman Hertzberger

The Mechanism of the Twentieth Century and the Architecture of Aldo van Eyck

Picasso, *Tête d'homme*, 1910

I am not an historian, and can only place van Eyck and his work with reference to myself, by making a very personal selection of the moments which were especially significant to me because of the associations they evoked. My perception of them, my private collection, in fact is only a criticism of myself.

In Nagele, the rudiments of the Orphanage – for me the masterpiece in Aldo's oeuvre – were already present, but here the plan has developed into a full-fledged settlement. The organization of this building, with its 'streets' and 'squares' and independent building units, is like a small self-contained city. It evokes these associations even if one is not familiar with the exhortation 'Make of each...'.[1]

This identification with a 'small city' is perhaps in itself the most creative step, and a highly significant breakthrough. In the design phase, once this 'connection' has been made, a train of further associations is released, adding a new dimension to the quality of the communal, 'public', places. Corridors become 'streets', interior lighting becomes 'street lighting' and so on. Although a building can never be a city nor anything between the two, it can still become city-like and thus become a better house.

This reciprocal house-city image leads to a consistent articulation of large and small both inside and outside in sequences of contingent units which interlock without stress or effort. When this articulation is carried through to the smallest dimension, not only buildings and cities acquire reciprocal meaning, but buildings and furniture also, because large scale pieces of 'built' furniture are like small houses in which one feels yet more interiorized than in a large room. Thus each part is given the dimension which suits its purpose best, i.e. the right size through which it comes into its own.

All this has become common knowledge by now, so I wonder if there is anybody who believes not to have been influenced by it. But what I always found the most amazing is that no matter how absorbing the elaboration down to the smallest part may be, the essence of the larger whole remains as powerful as ever. The whole radiates the calm of an equilibrium which encompasses an extraordinary intricacy of form and space in one single image.

It seems to me that the secret lies in the inexorable unity of material, form, scale and construction combined in a building order of such clarity that I have always associated it more with classical order than with the casbah. (I know, Aldo wants both: clarity, but labyrinthian, and casbah, but organized. Neither one nor the other, but both at once, which calls for a more inclusive mechanism. By now we should be in a position to achieve this, with all the means at our disposal in the 20th century.)

Perhaps the lintels have something to do with it also, marked as they are by the horizontal openings placed in such a way as to give the impression of a widening of the columns at the top, capital-like. The continuous lintel zone forms a horizon throughout the entire building, both inside and outside. What thus became clear to me was that the way a landscape is set free by its horizon is akin to the way the cohesive potential of a building order can give a building a horizon from which – strange paradox – it likewise draws its freedom.

It is the dome-like roof units, the round columns and above all the lintel chain which make the penetrability of the building's perimeter from both outside and inside reciprocally possible. They invite, as it were, a play of walls around them, letting outdoor areas in and interior areas out. Duiker's open air school comes to mind. There the glass skin around the classroom's outer edge, by turning inwards away from it, leaves space for the ample loggias (outdoor classrooms), whilst the concrete frame continues allowing you to 'read' the entire building mass. Through cantilevering, the way only Duiker knew how, the corners are rendered even lighter and more transparent.

In the Orphanage the outer skin also turns inwards to form either porch, loggia or verandah within the periphery, but the opposite occurs as well, for there the interior breaks out in three places, doing away with the internal corners which otherwise would have constricted both movement and view of these particular places. Solutions of

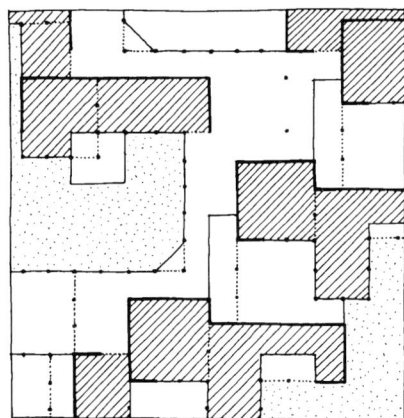

Orphanage, 1955-60

this kind are certainly astonishing.

My very first cursory confrontation with the Orphanage, still under construction at the time, was enough to convince me that this wonderful new building, only partially built, was going to be of an entirely new kind, based on a different mechanism and heralding another kind of architecture – one which was to keep me in its grip. The strange thing about the Orphanage is that it gives you the feeling of having been seen before. This is probably because, whilst evoking a host of associations, it does not really look like anything else and certainly shows no more than a vague resemblance to African villages! No, if anyone influenced van Eyck then it must have been Le Corbusier: the same

intense concentration, the same self evident solutions. Then there are traces of Stravinsky, and quite unmistakably Picasso. Here again forms suggest a lot without being altogether explicit, thus representing a kind of collective unconscious and resounding what is stored deep in the mind of all people, whether archaic or modern. That is how it must have been: Picasso, Stravinsky and all those others, who during the first decade of the century, became fascinated by the forms and rhythms produced by primitive man, which, polyvalent as they are, and apparently unfettered by worn meanings (from which one wishes to escape), opened the door onto a store of new associations and formal possibilities.

After the Orphanage came a fallow period of many years. Aldo van Eyck remained unused precisely when people were ruthlessly making the Netherlands even less habitable, and architects lending a professional helping hand to 'organize the meagre'. Le Corbusier died during the same period and it slowly dawned on us that we would have to carry on without that source. It was seven years before the Sonsbeek pavilion appeared, in 1966. Its dimensions were modest, but it was another genuine van Eyck building, full of new surprises.[2]

The previous pavilion had been built in 1955, when the great Rietveld himself made a brief appearance with a minimal construction of quite substantial planes which, although not actually 'occupying' space, provided no more than a vague suggestion of an interior. It was impressive, all the same, if only because of the achievement of having knocked something together in an almost shoddy manner that still managed to evoke completely the spirit of the Heroic Period. Sculptures probably did not feel very much at home in it, though. They stood around everywhere looking a little lost, but anyway...

Van Eyck's pavilion was also made of rough walls, though of equal height, and forming parallel streets (what a housing scheme!) and populated by both sculptures and people. Height is employed as a kind of serene constant, with even and diffused light coming from above (another constant) through reinforced nylon. It holds one's attention

within a horizontal world in which curves, hollows, shiftings and all kinds of inversions constantly narrow and widen one's field of vision, resulting in alternate openness and enclosure from place to place. One might say that where it took the Baroque three dimensions to achieve this, van Eyck managed in two – thus gaining a dimension!

If it is true that space in van Eyck's work is there contained in the plan, then the Sonsbeek pavilion exemplifies this very clearly. It was often regarded as a kind of sculpture itself, though for me it was far more like a painting. After all, are not painters always striving to render surface somehow spatial? They tend to manage better than architects who are granted one dimension more.

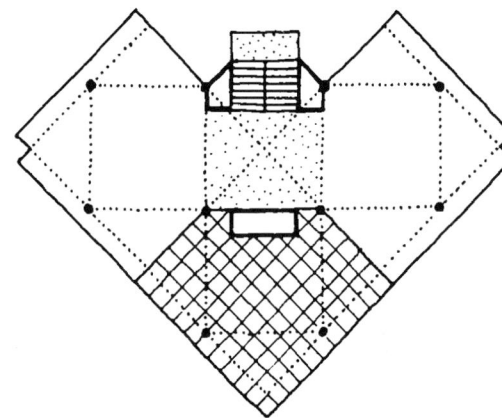

J. Duiker, Open Air School, Amsterdam 1927-8

If it were possible to walk through an early cubist Picasso or Braque, one from around 1911, or a Max Ernst 'Interior of Vision', it might well be that associations of this sort (in which case they are perhaps too literal) derive primarily from the strong image of the pavilion's plan which survives as a lasting reminder of the short while it stood there, and one was actually able to walk around in it, interpreting the space as an architect.

Rietveld and van Eyck who succeeded each other in Sonsbeek (with several years between), and remained close together in Bergeyk where Rietveld had built a house for the art collector Martin Visser in 1955, the very year he built Sonsbeek. Although not a typical Rietveld house, it was a Rietveld house none the less! Though for once neither intense nor really relaxed, it also provided little space and practically none for paintings and sculptures.

We can only guess what van Eyck must have gone through not only to accept but also to fulfil the request to alter and extend this particular house. A single masterstroke here, however, dispels all doubts.

The circular wall is placed in such a way that the rather weakly determined openness on the obtuse garden side is compensated by its counterform within the circle. New external and interior spaces result between the two components, between what was already there and what was added: the rather indistinct terrace acquires shape, the undefined obtuse angle makes sense all at once and

G. Rietveld, Pavilion Sonsbeek, 1955

the orthogonality of the existing living room is extended into the drum and thus reinforced.

That the house was little more than a trunk until it was given a head now became apparent. Van Eyck, in completing Rietveld's house, incorporated what was weak as a component into a new coherent whole, thus turning it into something positive. The way a good reply can render a feeble question meaningful. In music this is called counterpoint.

The circle (insofar as it is one) is, in fact, wonderfully square, 'really just a gentle square', as Aldo van Eyck described it himself. It is the curved termination of an orthogonal space system which is also continued in the roof construction.

The secret of this perhaps most balanced and

relaxed space he has made, in my opinion, surely lies in the complete absence of the dominating central point so often present in circular spaces, due to the practically unavoidable identical and fixed relationship of every point within them to that point.

Aldo talks about the difference between a circle drawn with a compass and one drawn around a saucer. What he is saying is that one is never free of the centre when relying on a compass: the circle continues to cling to it 'like a wheel or clock'. If it needs to be divided up this is done the way a circular cake is cut up. But the circle around a saucer has no marked centre. It defines a circular surface which one feels free to divide up in other undoubtedly more suitable ways than into sharp angular pieces of cake. Were not round spaces always chosen, consciously or unconsciously, to stress a central point, thus establishing a spatial hierarchy and subordinating what is there all round? In the early 20th century architecture shook off the bonds of rigidly centred spatial systems, the way Schönberg freed music from the burden of tonality.[3]

Circles and, where they become larger, portions of them, abound in van Eyck's work. The loveliest in my opinion, apart from the Visser house one, are those in the church in The Hague – the skylight drums in particular. The originality here – definitely a breakthrough – is that, instead of being placed in a passive area from a construction point of view, between the horizontal roof beams – the usual and obvious solution – they are placed over them. This divides them in two halves which come together as one cylinder higher up above the beams. The structural members are emphasized through this shift due to the light which now falls onto them from above. In addition, the tendency to interpret the two semi-circles turned away from each other as a form is just as strong as the tendency to interpret the two semi-circles facing each other around and above the beams.

The result of this ambiguity is that the areas between the skylights become just as pronounced as the skylights themselves, even though the latter are bathed in light. Instead of breaking up into active beams and passive areas between them, the

ceiling becomes a single whole – a single dome, as it were, over the entire space.

The church, with its exceptionally sober rectangular exterior, is like a box full of circles, one of which (apart from the skylights) struck me in particular. It bulges outwards next to the main entrance, where it forms the only articulated exterior place. Actually, the chapel within the hollow of this three-quarter drum is partially situated outside the perimeter of the church, although, like the circular wall in the Visser house, it faces inwards. The exterior glass drum in the Schmela art gallery in Düsseldorf may have been conceived at the same time, for the two are almost identical, except that there the exterior space breaks into the interior, literally allowing those outside to see what is inside.

The associations these two examples call to mind make their affinity even more intriguing. I mean the round external staircase on the south side of the main building of the Zonnestraal sanatorium and how it penetrates the building's perimeter. The other example which still excites me each time I see it is the staircase, likewise curved, breaking out of the north façade of the Van Nelle office block. When compared with the two van Eyck examples, there is affinity in pairs with regard to aspects such as open/closed, view inwards/view outwards; and finally the question whether the circular form penetrates or emerges from the building sideways.

Now for the home for single parents and their children. This recently completed building closes the gap left in the street front after the demolition of an old synagogue next to the existing houses already in use by the Hubertus Association for the same purpose and in conjunction with which it now forms a whole. It would in this situation have been quite normal to have headed towards either a self-contained more or less autonomous building or else one subordinated to those already there.

Nothing of the sort happened here. Contrary to all expectations, both the new and old houses terminate facing each other, leaving an intermediary open space between them just where one would expect to find a dominant volume. It is here that the tall glass staircase serves as a vertical pivot con-

24

necting the various split-level building elements. And looking right through it into the backyard, one discovers the children's wing. Nor should one assume that the main entrance is to be found at this pivotal point, however obvious a place this might appear to be. The intentions are affirmed even more surprisingly by the way entry into the new building takes place via the old one. Could it have been otherwise?

More to the point is how a solution of this kind enters one's mind and what van Eyck's motives were.

One might say that the division into two building elements, each leaning against the one next to it on either side, creates a sense of ambiguity as in syncopation. The emphasis lies on each of the building elements, though also, and no less, on the

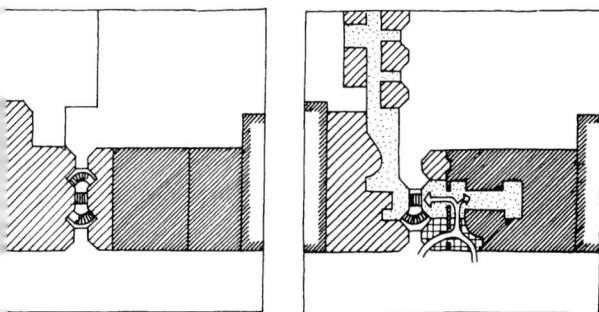

Hubertus House, Amsterdam, 1973-81

space left between them – depending on where one's attention happens to be focused. (The interesting thing about syncopation recurrent in 19th-century music, is not so much the shift of accent as the tension between the anticipated beat present in our heads and what is actually heard.)

When looking at a still life, force of habit leads us to attach particular importance to the objects depicted – for example fruit – and to pick them out from the rest. But with a Cézanne, the question arises whether it was just the apples which occupied the painter primarily, or the space between and around them in equal measure.

With the cubists every doubt on this score is soon dispelled owing to the basic equality granted all component elements, so that things of major or minor importance become interchangeable – everything is at once subject and space between, depending on which one's attention is focused.

With Max Ernst the space in between acquires articulate shape – it even becomes a figure in its own right. Such things belong to the game in both music and the fine arts, but in the realm of architecture I have, so far, never come across anything built along these lines. It was van Eyck and, as far as I know he alone, who kept pointing to relativity as the true constituent pivot of 20th-century thought. So continually shifting attention away from where it is usually focused as a matter of course and on to what is contingent is to be expected in his case, though not less surprising for all that.

Aldo van Eyck's work shows again and again that it is not a matter of choosing between inside and outside; between enclosure with solid walls once and openness with lots of glass now, but of employing both in conjunction in such a way that the right reciprocal effect is obtained.

What the 20th century has really revealed is, far from abandoning either gravity or the horizon, that our attitude towards both can be quite a different one and freer relative to ourselves, our place and situation. I was not there at the time, but I can well imagine van Eyck harrassing those gentlemen during CIAM meetings about this sort of thing!

Yes, he manages to turn walls into entrances and entrances into places, thus rendering accessible what is solid. Transitional places which invite people to stay.

In fact, what actually happens is that familiar ingredients and shapes are brought together in a particular way which releases them from their established functions and fixed meanings. Thus relieved of this load and in a new setting, they evoke fresh associations. By shifting the point of focus, portions of what was thought to constitute an indivisible whole assume other meanings and characteristics and thus are free to fulfil other functions.

This brings us to the cubists again, and in particular to the early collages of Picasso and Braque; to the way everyday objects and materials are taken out of their accepted context and placed in a new one, altering their significance, which in turn sets off sequences of new associations.

It is through eyes adjusted to 20th-century painting that the Hubertus House becomes more readily intelligible. Painted as it is in a collage-like cohesion, it is to me like a translation of a Picasso or Ernst into space (the image is a risky one because so much in this building is coloured). To me the colours accomplish what the lintels in the Orphanage also accomplish: they form a horizon for the building as a whole and, finally, they are a simple means of allowing the entire building to become a complex kaleidoscopic whole.

Aldo never tires of telling us that it was the painters, sculptors and poets of this century who opened his eyes to that 'great kaleidoscopic idea' as he calls it. Picasso's words often quoted by him could well have come from van Eyck himself. Since I cannot think of a better way to summarize his intentions in architecture, I shall quote them again for the sake of the essential equality they exemplify:

'L'artiste est un réceptacle d'émotions venues de n'importe où: du ciel, de la terre, d'un morceau de papier, d'une figure qui passe, d'une toile d'araignée. C'est pourquoi il ne faut pas distinguer entre les choses. Pour elles il n'y a pas de quartiers de noblesse.'

Shortened version of the introduction to the book published on the occasion of the completion of the Hubertus House in 1982.

Notes

1. See Forum (1960-1, no. 4), 154.

2. The Sonsbeek pavilions which were built in 1955 by Gerrit Rietveld and in 1966 by Aldo van Eyck, were designed as open-sided sculpture galleries. These temporary structures formed the core of the regular sculpture exhibitions in Sonsbeek Park near Arnhem.

3. In tonal music the tensions between the various tones are unequal; their arrangement in a hierarchical system means that the ultimate relaxation is provided exclusively by the keynote. All tones play second fiddle to this 'tonic', as if driven by a gravitational force. It was Schönberg with his dodecaphonic music who, around 1914, committed the revolutionary act of making the tensions between all twelve tones fundamentally equal. With that, he was able to do away with the hierarchy of tonality, and the tonic was ousted from its focal position.

In our time, each work of art has to stand on its own. Certainly Neoplasticism's complete realization will have to be in a multiplicity of buildings, as the c i t y. But to reject Neoplasticism because it cannot be realized today is unjustified. Today, even Neoplastic painting has to stand on its own – but this does not make it individual, because of its determined 'plastic' character.

The practice of architecture today is generally not f r e e – as Neoplasticism demands. Today freedom is found only through individuals or groups who wield material power. One is therefore limited to t h e individual building, which opposes itself to its environment – to nature, to traditional or heterogeneous building. It is nevertheless a 'plastic expression', a w o r l d i n i t s e l f and thus can realize the Neoplastic idea. The Neoplasticist must a b s t r a c t the environment, for he recognizes that there can only be harmony through e q u i v a l e n c e; for him, harmony between nature and the man-made is f a n t a s y – u n r e a l, i m p u r e.[1]

Piet Mondrian

Words and Things in the Work of Aldo van Eyck

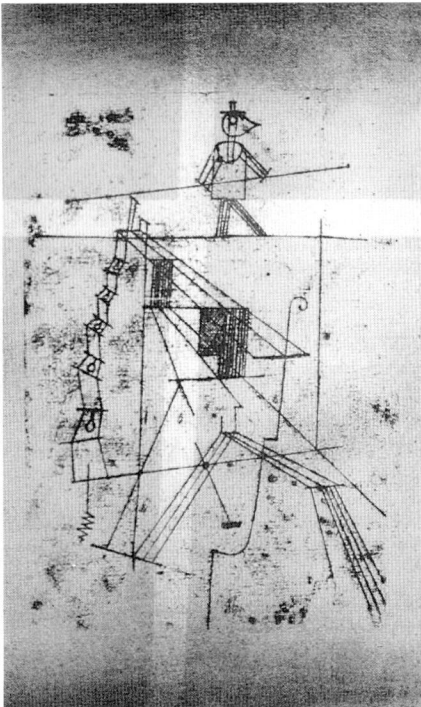

Paul Klee, *Tightrope Walker*, 1923

Aldo van Eyck is a great architect and is thus public property. He belongs to us all and all of us benefit from him. The completion of his Court of Audit in The Hague and the celebration of Aldo and Hannie van Eyck's eightieth birthdays gave occasion for a debate about the importance of Aldo van Eyck's work to present and future generations of architects. Architectural critics have voiced their dissatisfaction with the current architectural culture. One of these awaits 'a new chapter', while another presses for a 'follow-up project' in which 'van Eyck's insights and achievements will be turned to account'. Both seek leads in the work of van Eyck for a more 'heroic' approach to the present moment.[2]

The first question that arises is thus, do these times, do we at this moment, need heroics? I think not, but opinions on this may differ. It cannot be denied that the heroes of architecture, especially the young heroes, enjoy exceptional popularity in our present culture and that the architectural critics are partly responsible for this. But if we must go in search of heroics, have we come to the right man in Aldo van Eyck? This is the second question and it merits an unequivocal answer, for it is crucial to the general perception of van Eyck's work and of his exertions as an educator.

One of the critics believes the answer must be yes. We must look to van Eyck for our heroics – and heroics in depth, at that. This he considers is wholly justified by 'the kind of artistic standpoint and architectural role that Aldo van Eyck pursued all his life: that of the avant-gardist'. But isn't this a serious misapprehension?

Athwart the times

Avant-gardes make a clean sweep and establish a new beginning. There is nothing in van Eyck's output to indicate that he saw this as his vocation. On the contrary, the new beginning had already been launched by the avant-garde movement of around 1920. As van Eyck wrote in 1958, 'In the Beginning there was a "De Stijl" idea, but this genesis is now far behind us.' He also wrote, 'ten times thirty years may be needed to match a new outlook to the reality of everyday life and vice versa.' *This* is van Eyck's project, one to which also tried to win over his students; a project which is in line with the avant-garde but not avant-gardist in its own right.

Aldo van Eyck saw that a beginning had already been made. But in the interests of his project's success, he also taught that before this beginning, and in parallel to it, there existed worlds that must provisionally be recognized as much greater and much richer. He thereby opposed the arrogance of modernism towards the past and the still non-Westernized world (as though we, here, constitute the peak of civilization). This project may be seen as a way of giving a place in education to the experiences of the avant-garde. A real avant-garde does not belong in education, for its device is the *tabula rasa*. This is a little unfair to the students because avant-gardists do actually go to school themselves even if afterwards they demolish what they have learned. They know what they are doing and in any case leave just enough standing to carry on. Without that knowledge, the student could do no more than blindly follow his teacher. This is totally opposite to what van Eyck strove for in education; or at least it was so in Delft where I myself studied. He opened up a world of knowledge to his students and only with great difficulty could he be persuaded to talk about his own architecture. I am thus wholly unsurprised by the observation there is 'no longer any successor whose work resembles what the master himself would have done'. There has been no prospect of the formation of a school in this sense because van Eyck continually discovered new paths in his architecture, and in certain respects succeeded in surpassing himself every time.

To some of his assistants and students in Delft, van Eyck was an outstanding stimulus for research into modern architecture and the avant-gardes. I myself have had to accept that van Eyck's position in this area is not easy to trace. Perhaps it is in the 'Otterlo Circles' that he comes closest to the standpoint Mondrian formulated in 1920, in a short passage of 'Natural and Abstract Reality'. X, a representational artist, and Z, a Neoplasticist (Mondrian) are swapping some ideas:

'X: Presumably you wish to build different buildings for every generation?

Z: That is the idea of an architectural Futurist. But wouldn't it be a better solution to make buildings so that they are suited to many different generations?

X: But what if all generations are "different", as you have said?

Z: It is nonetheless possible, or it will at least become possible, by making the buildings a pure manifestation of the unchanging; that is, that which is the same for every generation.'[3]

Mondrian considered that the architecture of the future should not have to rely on the *Zeitgeist* or any other temporal phenomenon, but should

unite and obviate all periods within itself. In the context of modernism, this is a singular standpoint. It bears a close similarity to the position taken by van Eyck, although I would not be immediately inclined to describe the upshot as a timeless architecture. Van Eyck's work might best be described as *'Unzeitgemäß'*, as a critical commentary athwart the times. The primary butt of his criticism was the professionalism that had crept into modern architecture following the Second World War. For this purpose, van Eyck resorted to 'De Stijl' and the whole 'Great Gang' of the avant-gardes.

'Ideology and Métier'

A striking feature of Aldo van Eyck's work is the connection between design practice and verbal praxis; with the spoken word, lectures with slides, the written word, short texts and collages of text and photos. General statements are attached to commentaries on designs. The texts condense into aphorisms, which combine with photographs of van Eyck's own work and works from diverse cultures to produce concrete concepts. The architecture is absorbed into the praxis of the word. It figures as a vehicle for the argument.

The compactness of the aphorism gives the texts the tenor of general, timeless wisdom. It is easy to forget that the texts are embedded in the general problematic situation of modern architecture. The essence of compact formulation is paradox. Concepts such as form and function or time and space are extracted from the conventional theory of modern architecture and given a paradoxical twist. The paradoxes are dynamite. They explode the arguments of modernism. They derail the lines of reasoning which would reduce form to function, which equate time with linear motion and space with extension, and which cannot see style as anything but an expression of the times. What the paradoxes reveal are unexpected, largely forgotten connections. Destruction is a constructive act. Van Eyck aims to overturn the negativeness of modernistic thinking by shifting the focus of the critical debate about 'modern architecture' from the first word to the second: the object of reflection is not what makes modern architecture 'modern', but

what makes it 'architecture'.

Van Eyck's buildings and designs show the same characteristics as his writings. At first sight they are hermetic constructions. It is very tempting to regard his designs as a direct interpretation of his writings. The designs have their own material, however, and it is a resistant one. Like the aphoristic texts, they draw their artistic material from the tradition of modern architecture. Just as the argumentation of the moderns determines the context of what is thinkable, the works of modern architecture form the horizon of what is imaginable.

The 'tradition of the moderns' is, in its own right, a paradox, which at least implies that 'tradition' is not something that contemporary architecture simply has on tap, but implies rather a choice that finds its justification only in the work. Van Eyck, like a true gold digger, sank his teeth into the heritage of the moderns from the outset. In his designs, he measured himself directly against what he regarded as the great – Le Corbusier, Rietveld, Duiker, Aalto. This did not take the form of the now-familiar flirtation with visual quotations assembled into an idiosyncratic collage. In the first instance, the image played scarcely any part in his assimilation of the modern tradition. Essential is the plan, the composition. Just as the rhetoric of paradox fulfils a critical purpose in his writings, so does composition in his designs.

It is precisely in the decompositions of Neoplasticism that van Eyck found the tools to break open the typological conventions. In the aesthetic experience as described by Theo van Doesburg, the 'normal' organization of visual experience is based on concepts and labels.[4] Labels determine identities; they create caesuras in the continuous field of visual impressions and they pick out objects. The naturalistic conception of the object-world depends on an intimate interaction between the world of language and the world of visual impressions: the process of recognition. In the 'aesthetic reconstructions' of Neoplasticism, naturalism is breached. The frontiers between objects are erased. A field of autonomous relations opens up – not only between objects and their environment but also between elements that belong to distinct objects.

Identifying devices

One of the illustrations in the 'Otterlo Circles' is a drawing of the 'Maison Particulière' by Theo van Doesburg. But if van Eyck's work has any connection with the experiments of De Stijl, it is not with the works that typify the general picture of 'De Stijl architecture': the models made for an exhibition in Paris in 1923 by van Doesburg and van Eesteren, and the Red-Blue chair and the Schröder House by Gerrit Rietveld. It is the procedure of Neoplastic decomposition from the earliest period of De Stijl and the principles of 'Concrete Painting' that are most relevant.

In the Paris models, van Doesburg presented his as an architect and declared Neoplasticism old hat. In its place he proposed Elementarism; plastic decompositions were replaced by elementary compositions. Elementarism opened up the way for what van Doesburg called a 'formless architecture'. Despite van Eyck's considerable esteem for van Doesburg, especially his Dadaistic activities, the architecture and planning experiments of the Elementarist period appear to have offered him no points of contact for further development. Such points of contact were however present in van Doesburg's last works which he presented as 'Concrete Painting'. The subsequent refinement of Concrete Art by the Swiss artist Richard Paul Lohse particularly suggested ways of 'creatively conquering the tyranny of numbers' to van Eyck. He regarded that as the main problem facing contemporary architecture.[5]

In his article 'De straling van het configuratieve – Steps Towards a Configurative Discipline', van Eyck developed the impulses he had found in Concrete Art into a design theory that forged all scales of architectural and urban design together. Eight years later, in 'Stadskern als donor' ('City Centre as Donor'), he tackled an entirely different subject. This latter text can easily be seen as confirming a breach in his work that must have started in 1966 with his design for a town hall in Deventer.[6]

'Steps Towards a Configurative Discipline' does however introduce the concept of 'identifying devices', a concept which at first sight contradicts the configurative method, but which in my view is essential to the whole of van Eyck's oeuvre. It is this concept that separates the 'formless architecture' van Doesburg had in mind in 1923 from the 'concrete architecture' of van Eyck.

The discussion that took place in Team X about Blom's design and about the import of van Eyck's entreaty to 'make of each house a small city and of each city a large house' coincided almost exactly with the publication of 'Steps Towards a Configurative Discipline'. This text makes it clear, particularly where it refers to 'new identifying devices', what the real area of discussion was: the problem of the large urban extensions – an issue that was especially urgent in the early sixties. The concept of 'identifying devices' implies that it is necessary (in analogy to city structures from the past) to establish 'meaningful structure-defining features' for major urban extensions, which can either be natural features such as 'a mountain, river or seashore' or artificial ones. In the latter case van Eyck considers, in full agreement with the prevalent opinion among Team X members, that the most appropriate point of departure would be the new artifacts engendered by the explosive increase in mobility. The artefacts concerned here are the 'large elements' which are still capable, even at the highest stage of multiplication of the configurative process, of structuring the surface area of a large city in a meaningful way (i.e. a perceptible and comprehensible way from the point of view of the everyday life of the modern citizen). The 'fugatic' procedure of multiplicative levels, which was based on the principle of the house-city analogy, clearly met its limitations at the scale of the 'large city'.

'City Centre as Donor' goes on to explain that in the large urban agglomerations the role of the identifying device has fallen to the old city centres; in such measure, indeed, that they threatened to succumb under the concomitant demands.

The article, written in 1970 in the context of far-reaching changes to the centre of Amsterdam (underground railway construction, road widening and multi-storey car parks) which the city council considered necessary precisely because of one of the large urban extensions (Bijlmermeer), amounts to a plea for the preservation of inner cities. 'We believe that today old city centres – both their spatial reality and their content – are psychologically indispensable for their own sake, simply because they exist in all their multicoloured intensity and enclosure, and because so far no newly-built districts possess these essential qualities in the least, not even in a contemporary version. They are rigid, empty and sterile and are therefore inadequate as places to live. As long as they remain this way, the city centre will continue to function as a donor. Nowadays, however, its donor task is too great for its size. It is therefore absolutely essential not only to keep its size as large as possible, but to ensure that the addition of certain quanta does not have the effect of losing precisely those qualities that, owing to the sterility of the suburbs, make it into a donor.'

The thinking in 'City Centre as Donor' continues the line taken in 'Steps Towards a Configurative Discipline'. The concept of the identifying device is the key to diagnosing the architectural and planning mishaps which are likely to occur in large cities undergoing expansion. But the identifying device is not a central category to the designs, to which these articles are in a certain sense explanatory notes. It has a non-central function, which is peripheral to the design process but relates rather to the context of the design task. This emerges clearly in the notes to the town hall design for Deventer.

The central category of the design is the 'configurative process'. The identifying device imparts a means of orientation – not only to the city dwellers but to the architect and to the design process. This is true for van Eyck at least, in my understanding. From the point of view of the design process, it is thus senseless to regard van Eyck's buildings as 'identifying devices' in their own right, although in the physical context they may well come to acquire that significance to the spectator. If one takes it that van Eyck intends the object of his design work itself as an 'identifying device', then the 'configurative process' becomes a hermetic, self-contained procedure that can only produce 'autistic' results; a problem that clearly figures in much structuralist work.

Configurative discipline

The relation between the 'configurative process' and the 'identifying device' outlined here is in my opinion essential to understanding van Eyck's work, certainly so when one recognizes that in his designs the concept of the 'identifying device' is relevant not only to 'the highest stage of multiplication of the configurative process' but also to the 'lower' stages. It is an essential concept because it introduces a finiteness, an external relation, into the 'configurative process', which van Eyck describes as a process of multiplication of basic units. It is this that makes the 'configurative process' a procedure that generates form: 'The secret of form is that it is a boundary; it is the thing itself and at the same time the cessation of the thing, the zone in which the thing's being and non-being are one and the same.'[7]

The finiteness of the work of art is at stake here. In painting, this is determined by the frame. In Lohse's art this was the structural point of departure. He articulated his painting surface in relation to the edges of the canvas. In architecture, however, the boundaries must be produced by the structure of the building.

This analysis is connected with another feature of van Eyck's approach to architecture, one which is arguably typical of all modern architecture: the absence of a predefined form language. The form is the result of the design activity.[8] Granted, van Eyck appears to have a number of compositional devices at his disposal, such as the use of a module and its repetition by addition, axial disposition, asymmetrical shifting, rotation etc. But the actual formal elements from which the composition is made up are undefined and must be discovered independently for each project. A particular characteristic of van Eyck's work is that in each design he does not so much seek after forms appropriate to the various requirements of the task, but after a coherent formal language – a tectonic order – which is capable of expressing in a single movement both the extensiveness and the finiteness of the architectural object.[9]

Once an architectural order has been found, it applies exclusively to the project at hand. The process starts all over again in the next project. In this he is exceptional compared to other modern architects; the absence of a predetermined formal language is in van Eyck's case not nullified by the fostering of a personal style. This is certainly true of his pre-1970 projects. Subsequently, with his growing volume of commissions, several series of formally related features become identifiable in his work. This does not alter the fact that the relative durability of certain of his concepts and ideas has been attended by some striking changes of architectural tack.

In this light, the shifts in van Eyck's architecture are evidently explainable not by changes in ideology but by differences in the tasks and in the specific opportunities they have offered for grappling with and exploring new architectonic problems. In short, the explanations reside in the development of the métier. An architect does not always have a free choice in this respect. For van Eyck, however, there is no sharp distinction between ideology and métier. It is not so that he has taken up a fixed theoretical position since the start of his career. If there is any such thing as a van Eyck ideology, it consists of a whole series of notions he has explored in his writings in the course of his development, notions which show the clear imprint of the tasks and discussions to which he addressed himself. He wrote, for example, several important articles about his work after the completion of the designs.

'Transparency' and 'The Gift of Colour' are as far as I know the last of van Eyck's texts to be occasioned by a design which introduces a new motif into his work (the Hubertus House). As to the projects which he completed after the Hubertus House and which similarly show striking architectural mutations, the critics have found themselves empty-handed. This is notably so for the series of office buildings, ESTEC, Tripolis and finally the Court of Audit. These buildings were never to receive a text from Aldo van Eyck's own pen. In my view, such a text would have enlightened us about *the boundary, the non-tectonic aspect* and *the surface treatment* of the building, for it is in these respects that the Court of Audit stands out significantly from his earlier work.

Notes

1. Piet Mondrian, 'The Realization of Neo-Plasticism in the Distant Future and in Architecture Today', De Stijl, V, 5 (1922), 66. In Hans L.C. Jaffé, De Stijl, (New York, 1971), 168.

2. Bernard Colenbrander, 'A tradition resumed. Rethinking Aldo van Eyck', Archis no. 11 (1997). Aldo van Eyck, 'Lured from his den'; Henk Engel, 'The irritant principle of renewal'; both in Archis no. 2 (1998). Ed Taverne, 'Vicissitudes'; Bernard Colenbrander, 'In and around the minefield'; Hans van Dijk, 'Eighty years in the avant-garde. What now?'; all in Archis no. 3 (1998).

3. Piet Mondrian, 'Natuurlijke en abstracte realiteit', De Stijl, III, 3 (1920), 31.

4. Theo van Doesburg, 'Grondbegrippen van de nieuwe beeldende kunst', Nijmegen 1982. For the application of the principle of decomposition to the work of J.J.P. Oud and Gerrit Rietveld, see respectively Henk Engel and Jan de Heer, 'Stadsbeeld en massawoningbouw', O no. 7 (1987), 10-22. See also Henk Engel, 'Het verlangen naar stijl, tussen de biologie van een rechthoek en de geometrie van een kreeft', Oase no. 26/27 (1990), 26-45.

5. Aldo van Eyck, 'Over Lohse', Forum no. 7 (1959), 223. See also Henk Engel, 'Compositie en stad', Plan no. 5 (1983), 22. On the application of the principles of Concrete Art to architecture, particularly of Max Bill, see Hans Frei, Konkrete Architektur? (Baden, 1991).

6. Aldo van Eyck, 'De straling van het configuratieve', Forum no. 3 (1962), 81-94; 'Stadskern als donor', Forum no. 4 (1970), 20-7.

7. Georg Simmel, Zur Metaphysik des Todes, Logos 1, (1910). According to Hannie van Eyck, 'When Aldo's buildings carry a suggestion of repeatability, they are always simultaneously characterized by a self-contained form. They are finite and open at the same time.' In 'Niet om het even, wel evenwaardig, by and about Aldo van Eyck', (Amsterdam, 1982), 140-1. Comparison with the fractal geometry of Mandelbrot is inapplicable to van Eyck's work precisely in this respect. See L. Lefaivre and A. Tzonis, 'De Draak in de duinen', in Aldo en Hannie van Eyck. Recent werk, (Amsterdam, 1989). See also F. Strauven, Aldo van Eyck. The Shape of Relativity, (Amsterdam, 1998), (footnote 488, 373).

8. John Summerson, 'The case for a theory of modern architecture', RIBA Journal, June 1957, 307-10.

9. 'We do not seek forms, we discover style; this is at least our goal', is the concluding sentence of 'Wij ontdekken stijl', Forum no. 2/3 (1949), 115-6.

Francis Strauven

Aldo van Eyck and the City

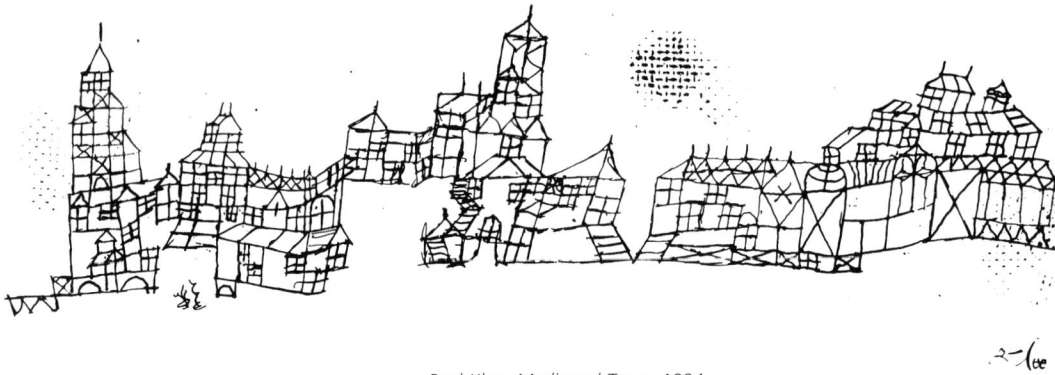

Paul Klee, *Mediaeval Town,* 1924

Aldo van Eyck has always nurtured a particular interest in traditional cities, the historical towns of Western culture as well as the vernacular settlements of archaic cultures. Unlike his functionalist colleagues of CIAM, he did not consider the traditional city as a residue of an outstripped past, doomed to disappear in order to make way for new rationalist structures but as a precious heritage, as a thesaurus of environmental experience. He recognised traditional cities and settlements as concretised patterns of human interrelations, as built expressions of human values. He felt that all valuable building experience of the past, from the Dogon village to the Palladian church, from Fatepur Sikri to Zonnestraal, should be gathered into the present in order to be implemented in contemporary design thinking. The present must embrace the achievements of the past in order to acquire temporal depth and associative perspective. Yet this does not mean that van Eyck ever aimed at an eclectic reproduction of historical forms. He always dealt with history from a definitely modern point of view. The heritage of the past has to be understood in a structural way, it has to be recreated with a view to the anticipated future.

Notwithstanding his interest in the past, van Eyck's cultural view is firmly rooted in the ideology of modernity. He is convinced that contemporary culture has to be developed in accordance with the new world view that was disclosed by avant-garde art and science at the beginning of the century – a world view which he holds to be grounded on one fundamental idea, the concept of relativity. This concept implies that reality can not be considered as having an inherent hierarchical structure, subject to a privileged absolute frame of reference or to an intrinsic centre. It means that the coherence of things does not depend on their subordination to a central dominant principle but on their reciprocal relations. In the new culture, every frame of reference must therefore be regarded as equally legitimate, standpoints are relative and as such all are equivalent. In other words, relations between things are as important as the things themselves. This concept of modernity can be related to the past in the sense that classical and archaic cultures, despite their hierarchical character, offer various onsets and anticipations of non-hierarchical structures.

Van Eyck's design attitude towards the urban heritage has been twofold. On the one hand some of his major projects were based on the structure of the traditional city, on the other he always conceived his urban projects as a constructive contribution to the existing city.

The most eloquent outcome of the first attitude was the Amsterdam Orphanage he built in 1957-61, a 'large house' which he conceived as a little ogy of part and whole. Both the building as a whole and the 'houses' of which it consists turn their back to the north and open through complex indentations to the south, both are conceived as clusters of places which are linked to the outside world by centrifugal squares. In the Netherlands this 'configurative' design approach inspired a new architectural current, known as Dutch Structuralism (Piet Blom, Herman Hertzberger, Joop van Stigt, Jan Verhoeven and other Amsterdam architects).

Another instance of the first attitude was the Sonsbeek pavilion van Eyck realised in 1966. From inevitably'. So he designed a little city for sculpture and people, a 'bunch of places' intended to make the visitor approach and appreciate the works of sculpture from various points of view.

The second attitude appears from the beginning of van Eyck's practice, notably in the numerous playgrounds he realised in Amsterdam. These were simple, carefully designed urban places, which were laid out on waste lots in the old city, in the interstices of the urban fabric. Composed of elementary forms inspired by Constantin Brancusi and Sophie Täuber-Arp, they were cheerful spots in

As the past is gathered into the present and the gathering body of experience finds a home in the mind, the present acquires temporal depth – loses its acrid instantaneity, its razor-blade quality. One might call this: the interiorisation of time or time rendered transparent.

city. Rejecting the rationalist solutions of CIAM he designed a complex configuration of interior and exterior places, clustered along sinuous internal streets. The interweaving of inside and outside, open and closed, small and large, public and private, results in a truly urban fabric, a polycentric tissue of equivalent places interlinked by 'inbetweens' or 'doorsteps'. The archetypal language of columns and domes evokes the image of an archaic settlement. Yet the interior space breathes the dynamics of De Stijl. Moreover the coherence of this 'little city' is confirmed by a structural anal- the outside a simple construction of parallel walls, at the inside this building unfolded as a whirling maze of streets and squares, a labyrinth of straight and round, convex and concave, traversed by oblique views. The dynamics of the interior space were produced by a succession of curved walls which burst through the basic structure of parallel walls. Van Eyck wished this small building to possess, like the Orphanage, 'something of the closeness, density and intricacy of things urban'. He wanted it to be city-like, 'in the sense that people and artifacts meet, converge and clash there public space. As literally hundreds of them were executed, they formed a kind of network within the urban fabric, a network of places which the child could recognise as his own territory. Nonetheless, since they were furnished with tectonic archetypes such as arches and domes, parapets and benches, they constituted places of a distinct urban character which made sense for the adult as well as for the child.

This contextual approach gained importance during the sixties. The more van Eyck saw his premonitions about the deficiencies of modern town planning confirmed, the further he distanced himself from the functionalist ambition to design new towns, and the more he became interested in the qualities and the potential of historic cities. He actually was one of the first moderns to regard the historically grown city as a constituent standard for true urbanity. He came to consider the old city centre as a 'donor' for new town planning developments, as a source of energy for the reanimation of contemporary urban thinking. He concretised this view in the urban projects he carried out from the mid sixties onwards.

very form, acknowledge and show appreciation for the specific qualities of its context. This in no way means that it must imitate its neighbours. It has to legitimate itself by the new meaning it introduces.

Aldo van Eyck first carried out this approach on the scale of a building in his prize-winning competition project for the Deventer town hall (1966-7). From the first sketches onwards, it is apparent that the new building was not conceived as an autonomous entity but as a cluster of differentiated units imbedded in the existing urban structure. The units were articulated in accordance with the historic

rately describes what he achieved in this 1966 design. The project was not executed, but it proved to be of considerable importance in the development of post war architecture. It was one of the first modern designs for a public building not to be conceived as a negation but as a conscious contribution to the existing historic city. It lay at the root of the urban housing projects which van Eyck evolved during the seventies in association with Theo Bosch, projects which were diametrically opposed to the prevailing modernist urbanism. Particularly their project for the Amsterdam Nieuw-

It seems to me that past, present and future must be active in the mind's interior as a continuum. If they are not, the artifacts we make will be without temporal depth or associative perspective.

In these projects he recognised the urban context as a basic component of the design concept, an attitude which implied increased attention to the specific character of the project area. For every urban project he closely studied the structure of the site, not only in order to preserve its qualities but also to determine its amenability for other, complementary qualities. He developed the simple but pertinent rule that a new design is not allowed to take away existing quality but must add to it. A new urban project must behave properly in the context it joins. A new building should, through its

fabric of oblong parallel lots and were covered with open mansard roofs. The components of the plan were grafted onto the existing streets and alleys. Towards the public square the building presented a low volume which didn't compete with the adjacent old town hall, a 17th-century building reserved for formal and ceremonial functions. From the River IJssel it appeared as an ensemble of gabled houses inserted into the riverbank façade. He accommodated his design to the urban morphology by reinterpreting the existing typology. Although he didn't use this terminology, it accu-

markt renovation (1970) was conceived as an alternative to the official plan which involved the destruction of the existing quarter and the construction of an urban motorway on top of the new metro line. The concept they proposed and succeeded in carrying through consisted in the reconstruction of the original urban fabric, including traditional city streets and differentiated blocks of houses. The project for the Amsterdam Jordaan quarter (1972-80) comprised the reconstruction of four blocks along the existing street. These blocks, which consist of row houses and shops, are opened up at the street corners by means of stairs which lead to terraces looking out onto the backyards.

Van Eyck's contextual approach reached maturity with the Hubertus House, a home for single parents and their children which he designed and built in Amsterdam between 1973 and 1981. The brief for this building was comparable to that of the Orphanage but the context was in this case a 19th-century street. To shape this contemporary institution van Eyck did not resort to the symmetrical model of the conventional institutional building. He conceived the building as a transparent link in typal connections, a shifted centre, a spiral and a transverse axis. The shifted centre, which is marked by a recess in the street front, forms the pivot of an asymmetrical equilibrium. It is situated between the new building and the new extension of the old one, an extension in the form of a large oriel executed in the same new functionalist idiom. The glazed recess does not lead to an axial entrance, as might be expected, but exposes the winding stairs which join the different levels of old and new in a suggestive spiral. The new entrance is actually located in the extension of this spiral. It twists in a version of the well known urban building type. Their lodging is conceived in the form of five little row-houses which places them, despite their unusual situation, in a familiar pattern of dwelling. Each of the little houses accommodates ten children and features a double height stairwell with kitchen, a living room with veranda, a bathroom with toilet, and a bedroom. On the whole the Hubertus House thus does not constitute a homogeneous unity, based on an overall geometry, it embraces several components with a different character. Just like the real historical city it joins, it

This is not historic indulgence in a limited sense; not a question of travelling back, but merely of being aware of what 'exists' in the present – what has travelled into it: the projection of the past into the future via the created present.

the urban fabric, as an opening in the existing block giving access to the inside of the city. Far from copying its eclecticist neighbours, he confronted them with a lucid functionalist idiom of concrete, steel and glass – not to take delight in their conflict but in order to reconcile them. The building was not conceived as a discourse on a future, entirely new 'open' city but acts as a new component of the existing city. It appears as a refreshing renewal grafted into the old urban fabric. The junction of new and old was realised by the imaginative non-hierarchical application of arche- loop through old and new. Thus the visitor does not reach the interior of the new building directly but via a small detour through the old one – a pattern that is intended to unite also mentally the two counterparts. On the inside the old is linked to the new by a new transverse axis, parallel to the street, a clear cut view which takes various shapes on the different floors.

The building is not only carefully attuned to its urban surroundings, to some extent it is also conceived as a little city. The children's wing is reached via a top-lit arcade on the first floor, a miniature acts as a kaleidoscope, it displays a complex pattern of various elements, developed through time, which reveal more aspects as one moves about. The building shows how modern architecture can be a positive component in the variety of the historical city. It demonstrates that functionalism doesn't necessarily need to transform this variety into a monotonous isotropic universe. It makes clear how functionalism can be or become a contextual idiom; how, without denying itself but precisely by returning to its origins, it can learn the language of the city and enrich the urban context with new meaning.

33

Vincent Ligtelijn

Table, Zurich

Coatrack, Zurich

Flat, Zurich

A Closer Consideration of the Built Work

Aldo and Hannie, Amsterdam, 1948

'Reciprocity belongs to my credo'[1]

Aldo van Eyck's credo, which was first expressed in the late fifties both in the design for the Orphanage (1955) and the accompanying text 'The Medicine of Reciprocity Tentatively Illustrated', developed into a manifesto in the 'Otterlo Circles' (1959) and to which he remained true in spoken, written, designed and built form, was not insignificantly influenced by his experiences during his Zurich years (1938-46). In the avant-garde climate of that city, where 'dada' started life in a small café and where several years later many artists of necessity sought asylum, Aldo van Eyck became convinced of the significance of relativity to cultural renewal. The elements that played a very stimulating part in this were his direct contacts with the world of art, first in Zurich and after the war in Paris, his

encounters with Arp, Lohse, Tzara and Brancusi, among others, and in particular his friendship with Carola Giedion-Welcker, one of the first classically-trained art historians to concentrate on the meaning of modern art. He later said of Carola, 'She opened my windows – and I haven't closed them since; she tuned my strings – nor did they ever require retuning', and continued with 'She loved the Great Gang and joined their Riot, understanding completely what the gang was up to and the Riot was all about.'[2] Carola Welcker's insights, certainly those concerning the connection of opposites, were essential to the formation of van Eyck's ideas on twin phenomena, balances by which means the old hierarchies were overcome.

Van Eyck had little affinity with the Swiss architecture that surrounded him. With a few exceptions it backed away from the cultural innovation that was taking place everywhere. His Swiss friend and fellow student at the ETH, Felix Schwarz, made him familiar with the Dutch pioneers Duiker and van der Vlugt, in whose work he recognised the spirit of the avant-garde.

It comes as no surprise that in his first pieces of work, the **furniture for his flat** in Zurich – the 'flying' coatrack and 'spidery' table (1943) – he looked chiefly to the weightless and immaterial character of Nieuwe Bouwen. Van Eyck used several similar

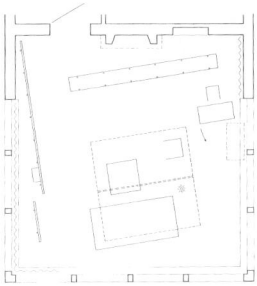

Tower room Loeffler house,
Zurich / **p. 52**

Playgrounds, Amsterdam
p. 68

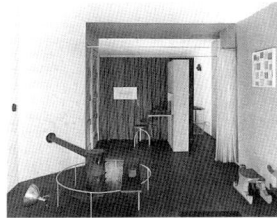

Own apartment, Amsterdam
p. 54

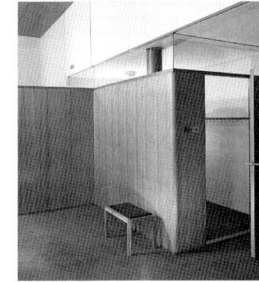

Heldring & Pierson bank,
The Hague / **p. 56**

Cobra exhibition, Amsterdam
and Liège / **p. 60**

constructions to delineate a transparent space within the existing boundaries of the **tower room at the Loeffler house** (1944) in Zurich. It is striking that the old space and the new put each other into a dynamic perspective without any building changes having to be made to the old shell. All that was removed was a central chandelier, and this was replaced by an eccentric floating horizontal plane which, as a reflector for the standing lamp, stated the quite relative significance of the geometric centre. This piece of work, in a house designed by his teacher Friedrich Hess, van Eyck clearly turned the spotlight on the difference in mentality between the two generations.

After the war van Eyck and his wife Hannie van Roojen moved from Zurich to Amsterdam, where he got a job as an architect in the Public Works Department. With his design for the Bertelmanplein, a start was made on carrying out the initiative put forward by Jakoba Mulder at that department to give every neighbourhood in Amsterdam a public playground. The plan is simple: an eccentrically positioned sand-pit bounded by a broad concrete rim on which can be played – enclosing an iron climbing arch and four round concrete disks – is surrounded by five benches and a small group of acrobatic frames. This project was such a success that in the course of thirty years (1947 to 1978) van

Eyck was able to design about 735 **playgrounds** in Amsterdam. These playgrounds were an ideal laboratory in which to develop his syntax. He designed countless variations on his first play elements. His formal language drew inspiration from the work of Hans Arp and Sophie Täuber and from artefacts from primitive cultures, while the way they were organised was linked to classical equilibria and Mondrian's aesthetics of relations.

Although, as far as the significance of the elementary was concerned, van Eyck felt a kinship with De Stijl, his objects had not been 'purified' of associations. The first playgrounds already indicate this. The same goes for his **apartment**, on the Binnenkant in Amsterdam (1948), with its freestanding round iron stove with a six-legged iron ring with a wooden board on it. This composite piece, which is a stove, bench and table all in one – and as such is as simple as it is complex – forms, as a place with a closed nucleus, the counterpart to the place with the open nucleus in the middle of the house. The two places make the living room into a multiple unit. The conversion of the **Heldring & Pierson bank** in The Hague (1948) was also stripped of every superfluity, in connection with the desired working atmosphere, the main requirement for which was a high degree of spatial continuity. To this end one of the walls perpendicular to the

façade, which supported five floors, was replaced by a portal construction. The only sign of this major intervention is a single column clad in black granito, which stands there shining casually like an umbrella in a corner of the cloakroom. The concealed construction, the sheets of glass mounted cold against each other while cutting through the walls and ceilings, the mahogany on both the walls and the ceilings, as well as the curtain running through the room, were at that time as modern as they were curious.

The drawing by Paul Klee suspended in the room, against the backdrop curtain in the middle section of his house, is in a certain sense the herald of the open arrangement of the **Cobra exhibitions** in Amsterdam and Liège (1949 and 1951), where van Eyck radically distanced himself from positioning the works of art at equal distances from each other and at eye-level, like washing on the line. He used a varied and mutually dependent positioning of the works of art in order to try to bring about reciprocity between object and space, a relationship intended to do full justice to both the spectator, the space in the room and the works of art. The combination of the expressionist Cobra works and an arrangement in the spirit of De Stijl, typifies van Eyck's desire to see opposites in each other's light, so that, as different expressions of the same reality,

1950

Landmark Ahoy',
Rotterdam / **p. 58**

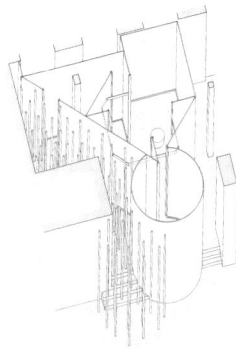

1951 and 1968

Triennial (sketch 1968),
Milan / **p. 162**

1951–4

Damme house, Amsterdam
p. 64

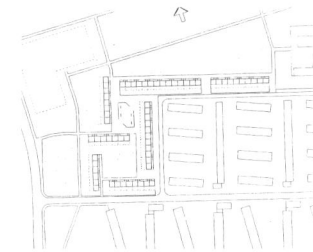

1951–4

Dwellings for the elderly,
Slotermeer / **p. 66**

1952

Blue-Purple room,
Amsterdam / **p. 82**

36

they will enrich instead of exclude each other.

His contacts with Cobra led to later collaboration with Karel Appel on the Middelburg visual arts centre (1990) and with Constant in the experiment of the **Blue-Purple room** at the Stedelijk Museum in Amsterdam (1952). In this exhibition room designed for the 'Home and People' foundation, in which the L-shaped parts of the room formed by the two colours were extended into the flat plane of the painted surfaces, the experience of the architectonically three-dimensional space is confronted with that of a highly compressed short space. Within this tense relationship, in which colour is used on an equal footing with the architectonic form, Constant's enlarged painting sprouts not as a mural but as a freestanding painting, due to the white wooden frame.

The experiments with the 'compression' of the plasticity of the volume by means of colour could only be continued years later in the exterior of the high-rise section of the Hubertus House (1973-81), where the planes of the façade, fragmented by the colours of the rainbow, dematerialise the building by letting it dissolve into colour. After the design of the **landmark** to indicate the entrance to the **Ahoy' marine exhibition** in Rotterdam (1950), in which the different logics of art and of construction meet, there followed a period in which Aldo van Eyck col-

laborated with Jan Rietveld. Rietveld, who was always able to produce little models out of his hat, had a completely different way of working from van Eyck: 'The concept comes to me very quickly... and then I work backward, then I have to incorporate the demands and wishes of the client into it, and that can take a very long time.... Aldo works constructively, he gets there slowly, step by step.... He starts at the beginning, while I start at the end. That's a big difference. That's why I have always been able to get on with Aldo so well.'[3]

Their entry for the ninth **Milan Triennial** (1951) was followed by the dwellings for the elderly in Slotermeer (1951-4) and the **Damme house** in Amsterdam (1951-4). In this house the division between the two floors was removed by means of a void. This double-height space, with a high glass wall facing south, also enables the living room to be oriented towards the canal to the north. In terms of form, the house consists of two different L-shaped volumes arranged in opposite directions around an open entrance court and intersecting each other at the void. Entry into the house, first through the low and then the high volume, gives this intersection an actual spatial form.

The interior staircase, on the street-side of the void, branches off as an exterior staircase at the landing. In a turning movement, in the opposite

direction to that of its lower section, the staircase ends up on the garden side of the house via the roof terrace: the bed is thereby linked to the garden. The house becomes a place where one finds oneself between differences: front-back, above-below, orthogonal-diagonal and light-shadow are brought into relation with each other. Just as architecture and urban planning are linked together in the **dwellings for the elderly** in Slotermeer (1951-4). These houses, grouped together round two squares of different format and arrangement, in patterns like interlocking windmill sails – each with its own direction of spin – form a configuration distanced from the abstract 'land division' as proposed in the original plan to a design by van Eesteren. The doorstep in front of each house, with its horizontal iron pipe and partly extended, and lower, sheds with roofs projecting on the entrance side to form a canopy, heightens continuity between the interior and exterior more than the terrace on the garden side.

The Damme house, the houses for the elderly in Slotermeer and the three **schools** in Nagele (1954-6), with their cube-shaped volumes and flat roofs, display a formal language closely akin to the architecture of the Nieuwe Zakelijkheid. In terms of their interiors, however, the schools follow a course of their own. Van Eyck's ideas about 'the aesthetics of

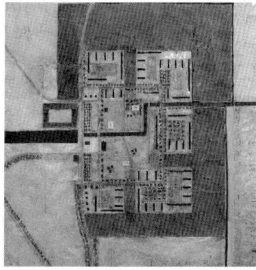

Nagele (sketch 1953)
p. 84

Hexagonal table
p. 83

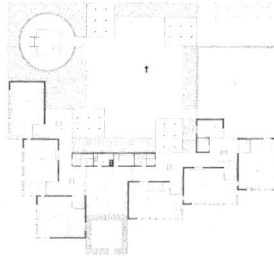

Schools, Nagele
p. 86

Orphanage, Amsterdam
p. 88

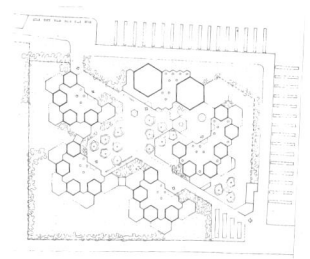

Open Air School, Amsterdam
p. 110

number' led to very rhythmical ground plans. The six classrooms were not divided into three groups of two with access via three small halls, but by two groups of three, with access via two small halls. This relationship, between indivisible numbers, sees to it that in spite of the repetition, the rooms do not appear additive. The two groups are linked by the playroom and the playground, by means of entrances matching those of the rooms. With a correction to its measurements, the last of each of the three offset rooms is turned through 90°. Just as the two groups are at 90° to each other. The imaginary extension of this rotation creates the outline of the playground, where the two canopies do take material form, but the two legs on the swastika-shaped open space formed in this way do not. The school's asymmetrical composition not only opens out to its surroundings, but also provides a specific response to the existing context. In connection with this there is a remarkably consistent continuation of spatial principles. Just as the **village of Nagele** (1948-58) formed a space in the open polder with its surrounding trees, the school does the same with its green edging in the open space at middle of the village. And just as the residential ring and the central open space, as well as the housing clusters with their central spaces, define each other reciprocally – the same thing happens between the school and the playground and between the classrooms and the small halls. In this context the swastika provides a connection between part and whole, throughout the range of scales. The classical method of composition using axes and mirror images – means that van Eyck was to revalue later in the Orphanage – makes way for a configurative design in which the possibilities of asymmetric shifts rotations and formal analogies are examined in order to control 'the greater number' in a rhythmical way.

In common with the schools in Nagele, in the **Orphanage** (1955-60) both a number of shifts and a rotation were applied in order to give the basic units their independence and to differentiate the areas of access into easily visible parts. The corridors became 'streets' that linked the pavilions like 'houses'. The roof also has a connective part to play and can be read as a collection of small domes. These square dishes contained in a grid of beams are a constant presence, both in the living quarters and in the streets, both close to and at a distance. The pavilions are individualised by their larger domes (the smaller the child the higher the dome!). These domes, four low and four high in two perpendicular rows, are diagonal to the elevated staff block, all of them above a sea of small domes. This produces a balance between an in-finite number of small domes, two finite groups of larger domes and one single large, long block, completely in line with the non-hierarchical composition of the complex.

The effect of the diagonality of the complex, related to its situation, extends into the interior streets and pavilions. Part and whole are repeatedly mutually linked, as also appears in the pavilion for children of 4 to 6 years, where a diagonal outwardly-directed focus of attention springs from the small play-house.

The diagonal perception intensifies the plasticity of the objects and gives more information about the spatial structure. What is striking here is that the diagonals are not made material, but are evoked by the shifts in orthogonal direction. The exception that confirms this rule appears at those places where the internal corners of the full-length windows intrude into the interior street. Cutting off this corner releases an ambiguous space between the diagonal window and the now free-standing corner column, without this column getting in the way.

By the use of clean but solid masonry, columns with gentle concrete vaults, full-length windows in either clear glass or glass blocks, the Orphanage breathes a similar atmosphere as Le Corbusier's 1935 holiday home in La Celle-Saint Cloud. In this

37

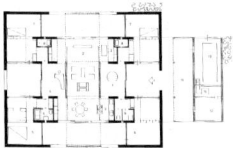

Four Tower House,
Baambrugge / **p. 111**

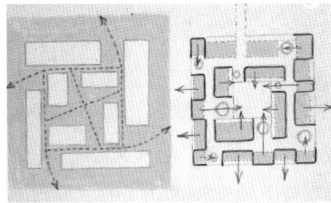

Congress Building, Jerusalem
p. 114

War Memorial,
The Hague / **p. 116**

Urban extension,
Buikslotermeer / **p. 117**

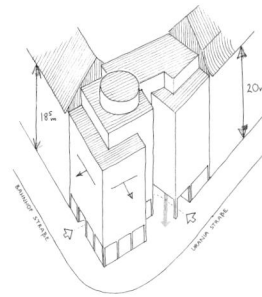

Modissa fashion shop,
Zurich / **p. 120**

house Le Corbusier reconsidered the position taken up in the villas in his 'white' period. We no longer see the box as the ideal outline, nor the functional separation of columns and internal walls. Walls and columns are given equal status. Together with the vaults they form an additive structure that defines a differentiated space, made qualitatively measurable by a freestanding element that includes a column. These events in the work of Le Corbusier, which go hand in hand with his reorientation of traditional architecture, seem to have had an influence on the design of the Orphanage.

Whereas in the Nagele schools van Eyck distanced himself from classical composition by way of the dynamics of 'the aesthetics of number', in the Orphanage it was precisely the basic values attached to the traditions of the classics, the moderns and spontaneous building that he tried to link together. He was later able to work these values, summarily defined as 'immutability and rest', 'change and movement' and 'the vernacular of the heart' into a 'manifesto' – the so-called 'Otterlo Circles' (for the CIAM congress in 1959) – and to provide it with an explanation: 'Each culture stresses specific aspects – fundamental solutions – which are universally relevant but which, for various reasons, particular and random, are emphasized whilst others are repressed. Ultimately man suffers

from these limitations, from what is overemphasized at the cost of what is omitted and often forgotten. Now, today, what is specific, what gives meaningful identity, should no longer depend on what is thus arbitrarily omitted or stressed, but on how these specific aspects are absorbed, adapted, and combined for the sake of more inclusive solutions which can respond to the nature of the human person as a whole instead of in part'.[4]

Although his work is restrained as far as the use of materials is concerned, van Eyck always had the need to enrich it in parts. The Orphanage, for example, has mirrors, coloured tiles and small sheets of glass at specific places to make the building sparkle. He saw all materials as equally noble,

Le Corbusier: weekend house near Paris, 1935

as was usual in Art Nouveau, from jewels to buildings. His passion for non-standard and independent use of materials can be seen in the different sorts of wood (purpleheart and greenheart) he used in his initial teak **hexagonal table** (1953 and 1989), but more especially in the moving combination of materials in the **War Memorial** (1959) for the Lower House in The Hague. The monument consists of a porous lava stone block on legs, from which a rectangular niche has been cut, lined with 24-carat gold sheet rubbed against the lava stone. This niche contains a pile of papers on which are written the names of the fallen, enclosed by indestructible gold and surrounded by the turbulent lava – everyday the bottom sheet is laid on top.

The Orphanage was followed by a number of projects ranging from a detached house to an urban extension, plans in which the configurative design was examined. As in the case of his own house, the **Four Tower House** in Baambrugge (1958), which is both one house and four houses; the **Congress Building** in Jerusalem (1958), which can be seen as a double reversal of the Orphanage; the **Modissa fashion shop** in Zurich (1963) which, as a plastic spatial system, contains the seeds of the later Hubertus House (1973-81) and the **Buikslotermeer urban extension** (1962-3), the first plans for which, from before his collaboration with Jaap

38

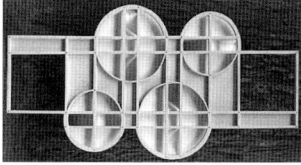

Protestant church,
Driebergen / **p. 122**

Roman Catholic church,
The Hague / **p. 127**

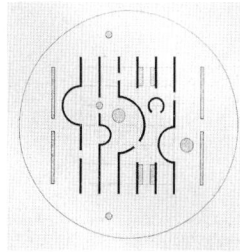

Sonsbeek pavilion,
Arnhem / **p. 134**

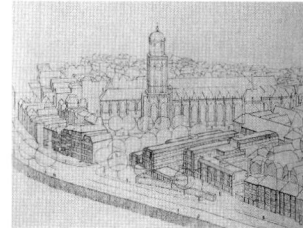

Town hall, Deventer
p. 145

Labyrinth, decor,
Amsterdam / **p. 144**

Bakema, were the most radical configurative designs in the series of proposals for this area. All these plans led to the article 'Steps Towards a Configurative Discipline', in which van Eyck made a plea for another approach to 'the greater number' in urban extensions.[5]

The **Protestant church** in Driebergen (1963) that followed this, the **Roman Catholic church** in The Hague (1964-9) and the **Sonsbeek pavilion** in Arnhem (1965-6) were all three single buildings in which van Eyck was able to devote himself entirely to spatial qualities, without being subject to problems such as 'the greater number' on a large scale. Like the Orphanage, these projects made the contrast between traditionalism and modernism meaningless. In the Roman Catholic church the playing with tradition is reminiscent of the process Magritte used in his drawing of the mermaid, which was composed of the lower body of the woman and the upper body of the fish or, in other words: from what was left over after the creation of the archetype. In van Eyck's design it seems as if the traditional church has been dismantled with the aim of bringing the still usable parts together in a new spatial relationship without a hierarchy. His comment on this building was just as humorous as the building itself, 'for once I have served the cross!'

The outside of the building displays a Loosian stillness. Despite this, the asymmetries and offsets in the interior have their effect on the exterior. The role of the high central volume of the nave, perpendicular to the length of the low building, is put into perspective by the high volume of the presbytery at the end. The two entrance areas, set opposite each other in the longitudinal façades, form a new centre between these two high volumes. They are flanked by a half-cylinder that projects from the façade, as part of the series of cylinders inside. The asymmetry and offsets in the interior also extend to the door. At the main entrance, where the approach by way of a number of steps downwards is parallel to the building, the door consists of two closed panels, of unequal size,

Le Corbusier: weekend house near Paris, 1935

which partially overlap each other with the in-between space facing the visitor. As if the doors were always ajar. The pieces of opal glass in the part connecting these two doors, provide spatial continuity between inside and outside – just as Mackintosh would have done it?

The **Sonsbeek pavilion** is one of van Eyck's purest buildings. Like the Neoplasticist, van Eyck saw the city as the landscape of the spirit, as the perfect place for art to thrive. This pavilion, located in an outside space with trees on three sides, is a city for sculptures and their admirers. Six parallel walls of equal height, under a light, translucent roof, form five streets just under 2.5 m. wide, which towards the inside are transformed into a swirl of convex and concave spaces. Since it approached perpendicularly to the parallel walls, it only shows its riches when one enters it. Inside, by means of openings in the walls, it opens up sideways to the adjacent streets and open spaces as well as to the exterior lawn space. Its surprising vistas repeatedly show new aspects of the sculptures and their mutual cohesion. People and sculpture physically shift and turn around each other, with a density and tension typical of the city. In this sense too the pavilion forms a counterpart to the sculpture pavilion built on this spot by Gerrit Rietveld. In his pavilion, Rietveld had aimed for gentle transitions between

39

Maas house, Vreeland
p. 142

Tajiri exhibition,
Amsterdam / **p. 148**

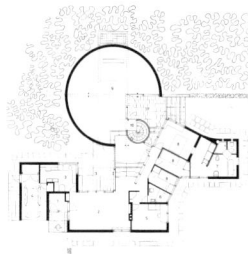

M. Visser house, Bergeyk
p. 150

Washing and toilet buildings,
Mijnden / **p. 153**

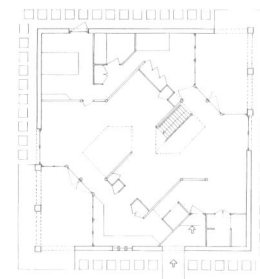

Verberk house, Venlo
/ **p. 160**

the spaces, between inside and outside and between art and nature. The two pavilions are to each other as Arcadia is to Urbania.

The difference in the conception of space is also shown up in the **Visser house** in Bergeyk (1967-9), which Rietveld built and van Eyck converted. The large drum, located in front of the glass wall looking out onto the garden of this hook-shaped house, as a second living and art room introduces new interior and exterior areas between the old and new parts. This not only made the vague angle in the garden window wall more definite, but also, and more especially, gave a greater intimacy to the old living room. The accompanying diminished view in the breadth was compensated by a varied liveliness in the depth. In this house Rietveld opted for a broad view and introduced the modern 'weak' dynamics: dynamics characterised by a gradual spatial broadening from inside to outside, without removing the difference between the various rooms. By contrast, van Eyck applied classical, 'strong' dynamics, whereby this broadening unfolds in steps, by way of contractions that again and again generate the spatial expansion ('strong' and 'weak' do not indicate a qualitative difference).

Rietveld intended the Visser house to be a country house with a great openness towards the exterior – so open that the interior became almost redun-

dant. Under van Eyck the house was given a spatial character suited to a house in a densely-packed urban setting. The house is not embedded in the city, however, but in itself. The aim is to direct attention inwards and then to lead it outside again, but now measured and focused. These are refinements that van Eyck identified in the interiors of town houses belonging to seventeenth-century Dutch painters: 'Pieter de Hoogh... shows us that the kind of openness which brings about the right sense of enclosure, does not depend on dematerialisation and a lot of glass...'[6]

The interiors of his homes internalise themselves. The accompanying top-light makes them more free in their exposure to the sun and creates the possibility of deep terraces within a rather closed periphery. These independent areas, intermediate between inside and outside, within the outline of the house, develop into a favourite theme in his work. This is certainly true of the entrances, where in the course of time they take not only other, but also more complex forms. Beginning as simple forecourts for the **Protestant church** in Driebergen (1963), the intermediate area was later worked into a domestic 'delayed entrance' in the **Maas house** in Vreeland (1966-7), where the entrance, as an interior glasshouse, forms a pair of opposites with an adjoining outside

glasshouse, on both sides of the façade. The same thing occurs in the rear façade of the **Bute house** in London (1969), except that here the pair are formed by a single continuous movement of the full-length windows. Next, the delayed entrance became a very generous hall in the two **washing and toilet buildings** in Mijnden (1967-9). Then on to spin out the ambiguity of the intermediate area in the entrance to the Hubertus House (1973-81) and let it expand into the motif of the design in the G.J. Visser house in Retie (1974-6).

But the **Four Tower House** in Baambrugge (1958), which van Eyck designed for himself – but which was never built – preceded these developments. The desire to emancipate the interior space created the necessity for linking the interior and exterior spaces as extremes, or in other words to draw inside the exterior by means of the loggias within the walls. At the same time the house became more autonomous, certainly in relation to the Damme house built before it, whose volume was articulated by bending to fit the situation. The outline of the façade was put in perspective by the loggias and that of the roof by the towers. The high gutter board where the façade and roof come together forms the reference for the recesses and bulges. There is a 'corner house' for each member of the family, made independent by the loggias,

40

Schmela house and gallery,
Düsseldorf / **p. 156**

House for Robert van Eyck,
St-Paul-de-Vence / **p. 164**

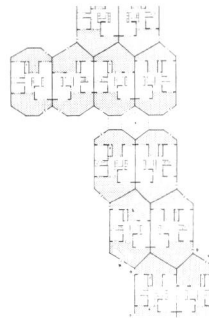

PREVI, housing,
Lima / **p. 168**

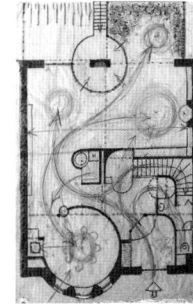

Bute house, London
p. 166

Joost van Roojen exhibition,
Eindhoven / **p. 174**

and with a tower and mezzanine floor reached by ladder. The mezzanine, which in spatial terms forms part of each house, opens inwards by means of windows – onto the common living room – and outwards to the morning sun (whereby the symmetrical order is broken). This gives the essentially centripetal tower-house a centrifugal aspect.

Van Eyck also produced an independent, closed inner world in the **Verberk house** in Venlo (1967-70), a tent on a box in the middle of a wood. This inner world makes best use of the outer world, modestly but with refinement. The spatial indifference of the wood is answered by the way the walls of the house form a square. But two loggias opposite each other, incised from the corner of the volume and oriented towards the morning and midday sun, introduce a diagonal direction. At the loggias, the planes of the façade continue as brick columns, like a wall. The floor of the terrace extends a few paces into this colonnade, to indicate the only relative importance of the boundary. Two mutually connected places (study and dining room), positioned diagonally within the outer walls, are oriented over the loggias towards the outside. The wooden walls underpin the independence of the inner world. The attic room, the children's domain, is connected to the living area by two voids. These voids, between which runs a

bridge that links the two children's rooms, protrude like vertical spaces through the roof, ending up as dormer windows on the flat roof. From the children's beds, on a small mezzanine directly under the ridge and above the door to the room, an interior window offers a view both of the playroom and, through the voids, of the crowns of the trees and the living area. At the head of each bed there is, moreover, a small window. Round on the inside and square on the outside, these windows are oriented in the same direction, despite the completely rotated symmetrical order. Put your head through the window and you see the morning sun or the stars! In common with the Four Tower House these *couchettes*, as places of the greatest intimacy, appear to be linked to the entire universe. It is one of the mysteries of the work of van Eyck that inside it is more spacious and kaleidoscopic than it appears from the outside.

It is the same thing at the **Schmela gallery** in Düsseldorf (1967-71). This is a building set in the street frontage, with a surprising outside space behind the brick façade. This vertical exterior void, a secret presence behind three different openings running diagonally over the façade, connects the gallery in the cellar with the dwelling on the second floor. In this area in which the street is continued, the exterior space becomes an intimate

'inner space' out of which opens the double-height gallery, with its lower floor, that much more acutely. Looking from the gallery to the street, the exterior space becomes a column of space standing on a concrete pole. As a figurative bearer of the building, the column is a reversal of the original Atlas – not one that bears up the firmament, but which lightly brings the sky inside. The Schmela gallery continues above and below the entrance to a planned multistorey car park within the street block, so that the ground floor is largely occupied by a tunnel opening in a closed street frontage. As a building in the old city, at least what remains of it at ground level, it adds something to the surroundings in a very special way.

As van Eyck became more convinced of the bankruptcy of modern urban planning, and as the flattening of the historical city centres rampaged on, he emphasised that much more the spatial significance of the inner city, without being sentimental about the past. His ideas led to articles like 'City Centre as Donor',[7] and in designs in which the urban context, with its 'mute demands' was included on a par with the demands of the programme. In so doing, he saw it not only as a question of retaining site-specific qualities and characteristics, but just as much of letting the new complement the existing, without losing any of its independence.

Nieuwmarkt area,
Amsterdam / **p. 176**

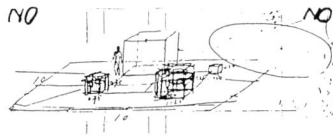

Cube project, Amsterdam
p. 179

Projects van Eyck & Bosch
p. 178

Hubertus House,
Amsterdam / **p. 184**

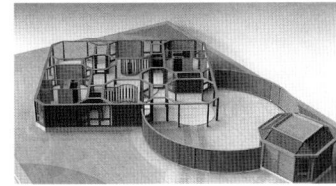

G.J. Visser house, Retie
p. 204

It was only in the seventies that van Eyck was able to further develop the contextual approach, as a consequence of the briefs that presented themselves at that time. First in the proposal for the restructuring of the **Nieuwmarkt area** (1970), then in the collaboration with his associate Theo Bosch on the **housing projects** in Amsterdam (1972-80), Zwolle (1971-5) and Dordrecht (1975-83). Also in the building for the Literature faculty in Amsterdam (1975-84), where it is only the original idea that stems from van Eyck. The shopping arcade in the substructure and the public roof terrace on the faculty accessible by glass lifts were stipulated in the assignment phase and are to be seen as the consequence of the principle, as apt as it is simple, that a new building should not take anything from the city without giving something back.

The winning design in the competition for the town hall in Deventer (1966), under the suitable motto of 'between the roofs', gave van Eyck his first chance to show how a new, large building can fit into the structure of an historical city centre. With its elongated, more or less continuous building sections, it complies with the existing large buildings, and with its regular transverse direction and variable height it connects up with the surrounding medieval houses. As well as this, the highest part of the complex does not extend higher than the old town hall and is only one storey higher than the highest adjacent house. Access is not via a new monumental entrance competing with the classical doorway of the old town hall, but by way of existing narrow streets that are incorporated into the plan. The building grafts itself onto the existing historical pattern of streets, which are thereby given a new significance, without losing any of their independence.

The playing with the architectural tradition, which is so characteristic of van Eyck's work, is expressed explicitly in the projects for urban renewal. From the time of the **Hubertus House** (1973-81) however, tradition was once implicitly incorporated into his work. In this period of renewed orientation towards the avant-garde, the configurative method, which in the urban renewal projects had receded into the background, appeared once more, reborn. This can be seen in the **G.J. Visser house** in Retie (1974-6), whose structure underpins the equality of the interior and exterior spaces. It consisted of a complex repetition of several identical pavilions – with or without walls, but all within a simple rectangular volume. The accompanying ambiguity of intermediate areas clarifies the difference in content between the spaces. This woodland house, located in the narrowing of an open space like a sea inlet, has a large, round enclosed forecourt on the entrance side, which increases the difference in tension between the spaces on the two sides of the house. The hall of the house forms the link between these two spaces and locks into them there by means of its two diagonal loggias. One as a delayed entrance, the other as an advance entrance, each loggia is directly linked to an octagonal space roofed with glass, one of which is outside and the other inside, while together they determine the spatial dynamism of the house. Also in figurative terms, the house is supported by the pillars of the pavilions. The open corners, which are formed by a duplication of the columns at the opposite corner, extend their effect into the diagonal openness of the house. The rectangular section of the columns is detailed in such a way that when it is combined with walls and areas of glass, it remains identical to the freestanding columns. The vertical strips of translucent glass between the window and door frames and the columns keeps both of them free and produces a gentle flow from wall to opening, which prevents glare at the edges. In the **De Jong house** in Bergen (1976) the columns are farther apart, while because of their space-defining effect they are also sturdier. Round rings of concrete are piled up on each other like cheeses and then filled

De Jong house, Bergen
p. 208

Padua psychiatric clinic, Boekel
p. 210

Wilhelmina Monument,
The Hague / **p. 216**

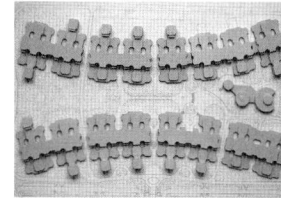

Siemens, Moorenbrunn
p. 218

In Association
Projects Hannie van Eyck
p. 180

in. Despite this they play a melody comparable to that of the slender wooden columns in Retie.

The four freestanding columns outside, which link the house and the shed to a square space, are repeated inside, in the middle of the house. There they form the central core which at the same time supports the void that links together the spaces from the ground floor up past the roof. (The staircase, which starts from two rooms on the ground floor by way of two short straight sections, and which continues as a single staircase, was later to be used as a mechanism for access in the house in Moscow, 1994). The house was given a large hipped roof, characteristic of traditional farmhouses in the region. This seems remarkable for a modern architect, but to van Eyck contemporary architecture meant more than the symbol of a white box with a flat roof.

The 'between the roofs' plan for the town hall in Deventer was, ten years after the domed Orphanage, the first project which, under the pressure of urban reconstruction, distanced itself from the flat roof. The bevels on the façades in the length, between the façade and the flat roof, are reminiscent of mansard roofs, but in essence they are planes that reflect deep into the building the light entering by a row of skylights on the flat roof behind them. It was only in the Schmela gallery

that 'real' frame roofs were introduced. The curious tent above the detached box in Venlo was soon to follow. At this stage the a priori flat roof seems to have vanished for good, unless it could be used by the occupants – as a symbol of modern architecture it always had been obsolete (Orphanage!). In the sketched proposal for the **house for Robert van Eyck** in St-Paul-de-Vence (1968), where the ridge is offset with regard to the break-line in the ground plan (the corridor and the exterior space within the periphery), the roof planes remain schematic. The project stopped at the sketch stage, which allows us to see quite well that, as a design problem, van Eyck kept the roof for later, until it became clear in what way the interior needed to be closed off. This is also what happened in the design for the Orphanage, where the introduction of the square domed roofs was only able to take place when the ground plans had more or less settled down. But only after the undifferentiated flat roof had been replaced by barrel vaults in various directions in order to avoid a single dominant direction. All this insight led, by way of a system of gently hipped roofs, to the final square grid that came to form the basis of the complex. Van Eyck's renewed orientation towards the moderns seemed to go hand in hand with a reassessment of the cross-section: in combination with the vertical definition and the

colours, the ceilings of the Padua psychiatric clinic, the Moluccan church and the ESTEC complex summon up spatial ambiguities which his roofs, as planes above the ground plans, had never before displayed. In the serene **Padua psychiatric clinic** in Boekel (1980-9), where, by means of short passages, the rooms are arranged in a square form round an inner court in order to avoid a number of cells in a row or along institutional corridors, the skylights added here and there to the flat roof play a not insignificant apart. The round cut-out in the sloping roof forms a salutary opening that draws the sky inside. The roof also sees to it that the corridor, loggia and patio altogether become one large space, without losing their independence. It is remarkable here that the vertical definition of these spaces – blind wall, full-length window (with narrow intercolumniation) and the slender colonnade (with broader intercolumniation) – develop in serial form towards a greater openness, which intensifies the spatial dynamics. Colour then gives a final twist to this ensemble. The pale sky blue on the two mirrored walls in the patio also falls onto the passage wall inside. In this shift from outside to inside, this blue reinforces the suggestion that inside and outside are one, despite their fundamental differences, especially in the case of a closed institution, like Padua.

43

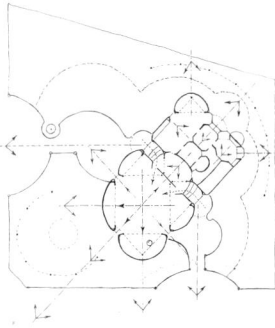

Moluccan church, Deventer
p. 220

Urban development, Giudecca,
Venice / **p. 226**

ESTEC complex, Noordwijk
p. 230

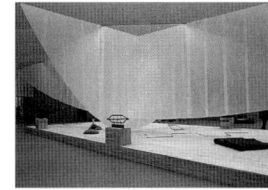

Visser exhibition, Otterlo
p. 250

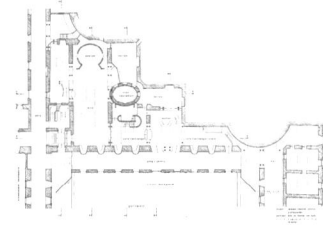

Sala de Notte, Catania
p. 247

44

The exterior of the **Moluccan church** in Deventer (1983-92), embedded in green surroundings, is veiled by roses, above which undulating wooden eaves float like arbours. Inside the church is like a canopy standing free in a luminous blue. The central area is defined by a gently vaulted cross-shaped roof with a rotated domed skylight at the top, all of which is supported by beams with double corner columns that form gates towards the top-lit entrances and exits. This arrangement is turned 45° inside a larger square of beams with corner columns, which is surrounded by higher, concave walls that curve towards the middle and have hidden light openings in their ceilings. The bevelling of one of the corners of the outermost square creates a new orientation – diagonal to that of the inscribed square and in equilibrium with it. Each of the two orientations makes reference to an area for liturgical functions (pulpit and Communion-table). The offset symmetry is combined with several sub-symmetries, both inside and outside. This keeps the spatial image in motion. This is also true of the blue on the top-lit concave walls, which fade upwards from dark to light blue and are crossed by lines of shells collected from Moluccan beaches, sailing through a relaxed space.

With briefs for several large buildings, his favourite theme – the rhythmic handling of 'the greater number' – turned up once more. His work became not only more exuberant, but also opened the door wider to a meta-stylistic space in which the architecture of every age and place could be united without any hint of eclecticism. Van Eyck had the capacity to combine his homogeneous architecture with a broad associative range. This is evident in the **ESTEC restaurant and conference centre** in Noordwijk (1984-9), an abundance of undulating roofs (in four different tints of iridescent grey neoprene, with copper edging), which, depending on the angle of view, appears either like a series of Bedouin tents or an organism, crystalline or scaled, that has crawled out of the huge piece of wooden furniture in the background (the new ESTEC offices). Reminiscent to whatever – not a sign of the fashionable repertory of pylons, cables, swivels, etc., but instead arabesques of columns and portals equally classical and curious.

In the initial plans the portals and columns were conceived in white-painted steel. The large number of them in the final plan led to their being coloured differently, so that in their movements and their significance in structuring the space they still remain readable. Just as in the Hubertus House, spectral colours are used in order to avoid a random range. The columns on the periphery are yellow, for its reflective and lively effect. The colour on each of the rib constructions appears in three tones, the strongest near the column and the softest in the portal section above the vertical elements on which the sloping, natural plywood ceilings rest. Colour is not restricted to the supporting structures, however, but is developed throughout the space. There is no symmetry that fixes the whole around one central point and axis in this building either. It is poly-axial as well as poly-centric. Architecture that is developed partly out of the cross-sections is not easy to read from the ground plans, however. That also applies to this complex, which does not leave the third dimension mouldering on the shelf.

The **ESTEC offices** (1984-9) is another building which, in both the plastic and spatial senses, transcends its ground plan which otherwise seems no more than a series of convex and concave towers. Local symmetries see to the independence of the parts and the liveliness of the spatial image of the building, which is symmetrical in plan but asymmetrical in cross-section. With its ascending and descending heights the offices make the link between the higher main building and the lower congress centre.

In order to protect its concrete skeleton, the building is clad in untreated iroko wood. This means the structure is concealed, at least on the

Arts centre, Middelburg
p. 252

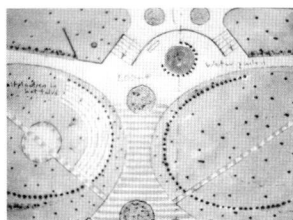

Apollolaan, Amsterdam
p. 262

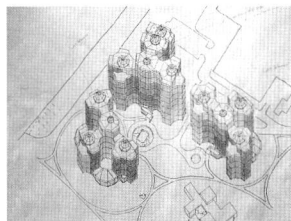

Tripolis office complex,
Amsterdam / **p. 258**

Court of Audit,
The Hague / **p. 264**

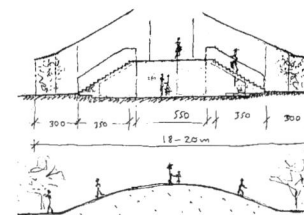

The Moscow house
p. 282

outside. The vertical grooves in the façade, containing half-open copper drainpipes, are no more than an indication of the columns. These grooves, next to the corners, shift the attention from the ribs, like syncopation. This leads to a tension between the two, which in each case comes to rest in the middle of the convex towers, where ribs and grooves coincide. At right angles to this rhythmic, horizontal movement are the cantilevers in the façade (two per storey), as well as the tapering of the window jambs which, coupled with the height of the breastwork (which increases on each storey) breaks the monotonous stacking of storeys. The coloured anodised weathering on the cantilevers makes the windows twinkle like eyes. Under the influence of sun and wind, sand, salt and rain are given the chance to show their effect on the skin of the building. This play of alternating irregular dark-brown and silver-grey patterns on the regularly undulating wooden façades creates a connection between the building and the coastal landscape. It may have been hard for an architect with his roots in the 'Nieuwe Bouwen' – which was so fascinated by the purity of skeletons – to accept the cladding of a structure, but the independence of the skin put van Eyck on a new track. The wooden cladding underpins the significance of the building in its context. This area of visual relations between

a building and its surroundings was to be explored further in the building for the Court of Audit. Between these two, van Eyck also designed the **Tripolis office complex** in Amsterdam (1990-4), which, although it is not a clone of the ESTEC offices, is the exception that confirms the rule that his buildings do not resemble each other.

Once Berlage remarked to Rietveld: 'You break down what I build up!' Rietveld passed this on to van Eyck, but in reverse: 'You build up what I broke down',[8] with reference to the heaviness he experienced in the brick and concrete of the Orphanage. In the Tripolis building however, van Eyck built on Rietveld's work: the easy details of the façades with broad planks of untreated hardwood might, in its directness and openness, have come straight from Rietveld's carpentry box. This skin defies the image of trendy offices as palaces of smoked glass or marble bunkers.

The old and new buildings for the **Court of Audit** (1992-7) in The Hague – evenly matched and also equal to the old city – stand as objects directly facing each other, though as spaces they are interwoven. Between the two parts there is a central hall, with an open staircase that serves both parts, which also links together two new alleys, outside. The heart of the new part consists of a library on two storeys, with a roof terrace above. The three

office cores around it, with round stairwells that form part of a system of access which, as in the ESTEC offices, treats horizontal and vertical circulation equally, make this building poly-centric too. Vertically, the interior tapers in steps, becoming lighter towards the top and offering an increasingly broader view of the old city. Each storey assumes a specific character. Horizontally, the building fans out asymmetrically from its three symmetrical cores. In this way every room is given its own orientation, depth and degree of broadening towards the façade.

These two shifts are directly linked to the situation to which the building reacts by means of its 'contour'. This leads to the formation of a number of urban spaces and a complex volume comes into being, which is made readable with façade surfaces framed by corner columns. These planes, of equal breadth but at varying angles to each other, are interrupted by a number of smaller planes. And this occurs precisely in those places where, as one approaches the building, an acute projecting corner would emerge in the direction attention is focused. These narrower planes are answered by three narrow planes at recessed corners; all the planes tune the dimensions of the façade to the location, and in such a way that the difference in measure between the façade surfaces becomes

45

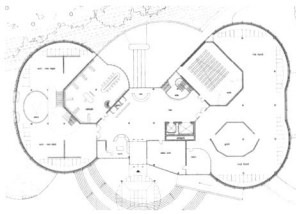

Museum, Nijmegen
p. 278

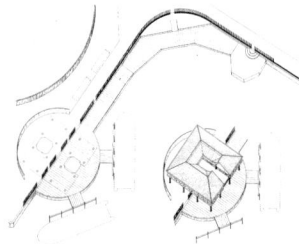

Jetty, Thessaloniki
p. 285

Exhibitions of own works
and ideas / **p. 289**

There is a major formal difference between the Orphanage and the Court of Audit. But intrinsically they lie on the same line. It is typical of van Eyck that he continued to investigate the configurative method for its possible combinations. It is expressed in every work, composed as they are by balances of polarities. In each project these balances are related to the use and the context, within a specific and coherent architectonic order. In this way the configurative process remains 'open' and his architecture free of any *a priori* formal language. 'Reciprocity is my credo' – an attitude that gave a specific character to every piece of work – as a 'matter of course': Aldo van Eyck.

Note: the years listed with the projects indicate the period between the beginning of a design and the final delivery of the structure involved.

active. In van Eyck's work differences are not smoothed over but are put on display!

The blue exterior – in ceramic tiles – is answered by a blue interior. Its blue walls veined with tiles are set against veined, natural, untreated Oregon pine on the ceilings, windows and doors, whose detailing is taut but has plasticity; the parts are linked by seams. On the outside sixteen seemingly casually strewn spectral colours give relief and sparkle to the blue-grey façade, which are however underlain by full-length circular orders designed by the painter Jaap Hillenius.

The Court of Audit leaves behind it the ideal of the Moderns of making the inside and outside of buildings as a single thing. As a sequel to the ESTEC and Tripolis office buildings, the skeleton here is covered. But the abandonment of a homogeneous structure is compensated – inside and outside are reduced to the same denominator: blue forms the horizon for both.

The structural discontinuity can also be read in the columns. Whereas in the earlier configurative designs – such as the Orphanage, the Hubertus House and the house in Retie – the column had a constant diameter, independent of its position and the load to be absorbed, the columns in the Court of Audit are by contrast constantly differentiated in relation to their context.

Remarkable are the façade columns. On the inside (unclad) they appear as narrow areas of wall. But from the outside (clad) they seem to shy from their role as columns. In their decrease in width the higher they go they show a preference for making the windows wider on each successive storey while helping the rainwater to fall, rather than become involved in questions of gravity. Like caryatids they sublimate themselves as columns. Their cladding is like the drapery of a caryatid, concealing the structure. Together with the colour, which moves independently over the structural elements of the building both on the inside and outside, the picture becomes atectonic.

Whereas the ground plans of the earlier configurative designs can be read as compositions whose repetition of a basic element suggests infinitude, while retaining their relative finiteness at every stage of multiplication – and thereby being able to relate to variables that occur beyond this multiplication[9] – in the Court of Audit[10] the vertical elevations play their part in this. The 'contour' not only determines the formation of the interior and exterior spaces, but also takes on an independent role as the façade (without any sign of a front, side or back), with columns and windows. As a façade it mediates in the spatial transition between inside and outside, between the building and the city.

Notes

1. Aldo van Eyck, 'Ex Turico Aliquid Novum', *Archithese* (1981, no. 5), 35-8.
2. Aldo van Eyck, idem.
3. Aldo van Eyck (ed.), *Niet om het even, wel evenwaardig, van en over Aldo van Eyck* (Amsterdam, 1982), 28.
4. Aldo van Eyck, 'Is architecture going to reconcile basic values', in O. Newman, *CIAM 59 in Otterlo* (Stuttgart, 1961), 26.
5. Aldo van Eyck, 'Steps towards a configurative discipline', *Forum* (1962, no. 3), 81-94.
6. H. Hertzberger, A. van Roijen-Wortmann, F. Strauven, *Aldo van Eyck* (Amsterdam, 1982), 83.
7. Aldo van Eyck, 'Stadskern als donor', *TABK* (1971, no. 22), 556-60.
8. Aldo van Eyck (ed.), *Niet om het even, wel evenwaardig, van en over Aldo van Eyck*, op. cit., 74.
9. See also: Johan van de Beek, 'Een ingezonden brief naar aanleiding van het centrumloze labyrint; Gerrit Rietveld en de Stedebouw', *Oase* (1989, no. 25), 22-3.
10. In the Court of Audit, the freely divisible zone between the core (stairwell) and the façade was used as the unit for multiplication.

46

There is a kind of spatial
appreciation which makes us envy birds in flight;
there is also a kind which makes us recall the sheltered
enclosure of our origin. Architecture will fail if it
neglects either the one or the other.

tree is
leaf and leaf
is tree - house is
city and city is house
- a tree is a tree but it
is also a huge leaf - a
leaf is a leaf, but it is
also a tiny tree - a city
is not a city unless it
is also a huge house -
a house is a house
only if it is also
a tiny city

Projects 1944-99

Tower Room Conversion for Prof. Loeffler, Zurich, 1944

An old room was transformed into a studio for a lover of modern art – for his art books and small collection of works by among others Klee, Miró and Ernst. Thus an appropriately different place was installed within the existing shell and set at a slight angle to it. What was already there – everything – remained physically untouched. Two vertical screens for the paintings, a horizontal one over the sitting area to reduce the height locally, and a large bookcase were 'positioned' in space, all three suspended from the rafters of the roof construction and which, due to their mass, inclination and the equal interval between the suspension wires fixed to each of them, became an integral formal ingredient from another world. All these components were white; the existing walls pale grey, the curtain midnight blue. Although no fireplace was required, the one already there was not removed.

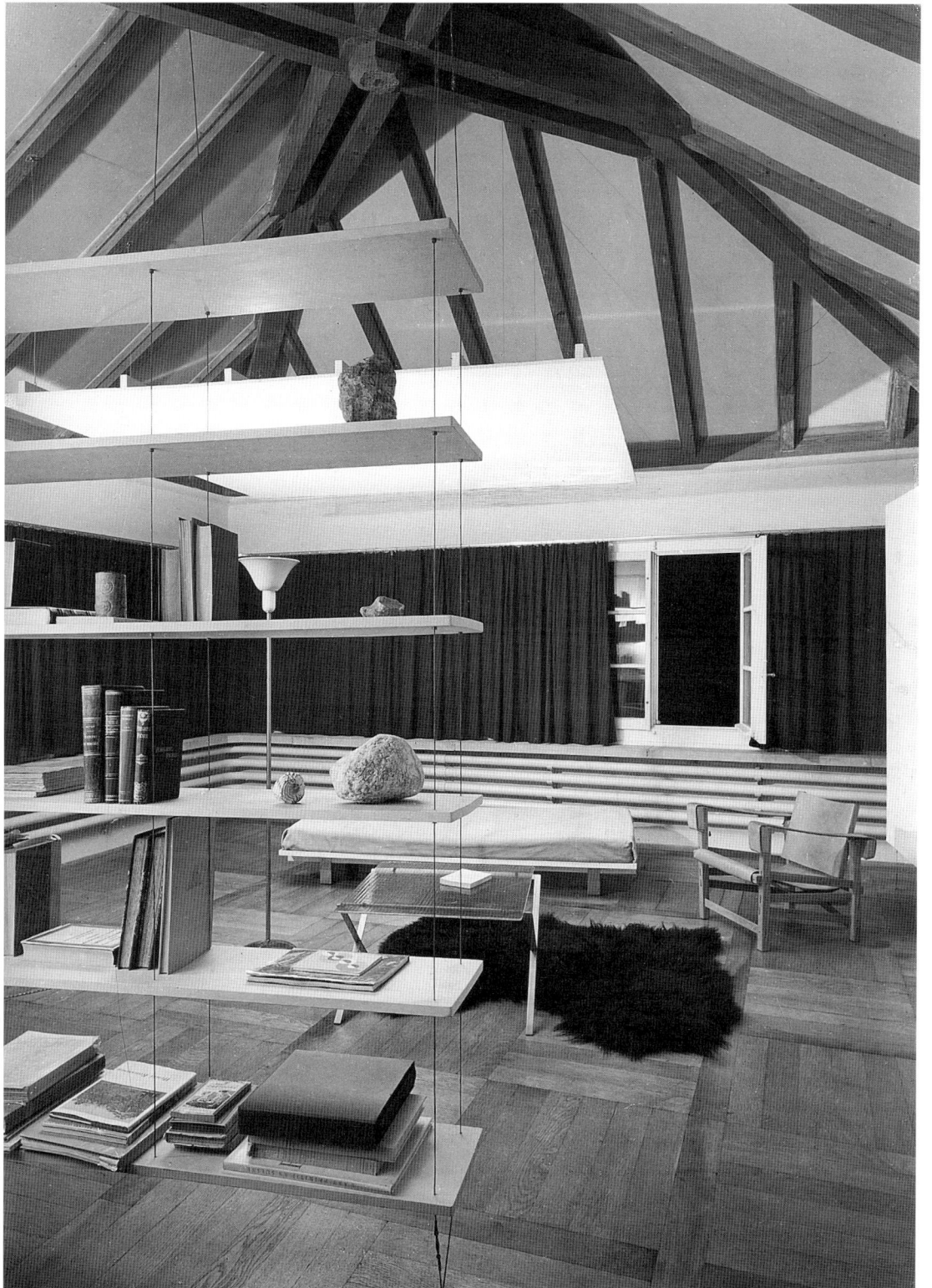

1 bookcase
2 screen
3 seat
4 bar

Architect's Apartment, Amsterdam, 1948

The tower room in Zurich was 'empty' to begin with, so it was 'filled' ever so slightly. A short time later in Amsterdam, however, nothing so gratifyingly empty was available. On the contrary, the small 4th-floor flat with a magnificent view over the old city had to be cleared almost entirely – emptied – before a start could be made turning it into a habitable place. Once again just a minimum of new elements proved sufficient: a single bookcase from floor to ceiling; two parallel curtains across from wall to wall (the one dark grey and the other translucent) and a steel ring round the stove with a plank across it to sit on. Since there were quite a few built-in cupboards, that was all. Yes, and paint, of course – white and metallic grey; metallic to give the grey more substance next to the floating white. The floor boards were yet stained black. As for the steel ring, it was my very first circle in space with the quality of place – what with the seat, warmth from the stove –

and the little mystery that circles do occasionally provide. Actually this is where it all started, because it was on that very plank that Frans van Meurs sat as he explained what it was he wanted me to build for 'his children'. Himself an orphan, he was head of the Municipal Orphanage.

More circles were to follow, which for me represent what is there on all sides – *the imagined horizon*. It's the ring and the disc I'm particularly attracted to – not radials, which is why I draw circles round odd tins, saucers and plates instead of using a compass (the ancient Peruvians worshipped both the sun and moon, were incomparable highway builders, yet managed without wheels – and that makes sense!). Eventually the place became our home and a meeting place for Cobra. It was there too that hundreds of playgrounds for Amsterdam were designed over the years.

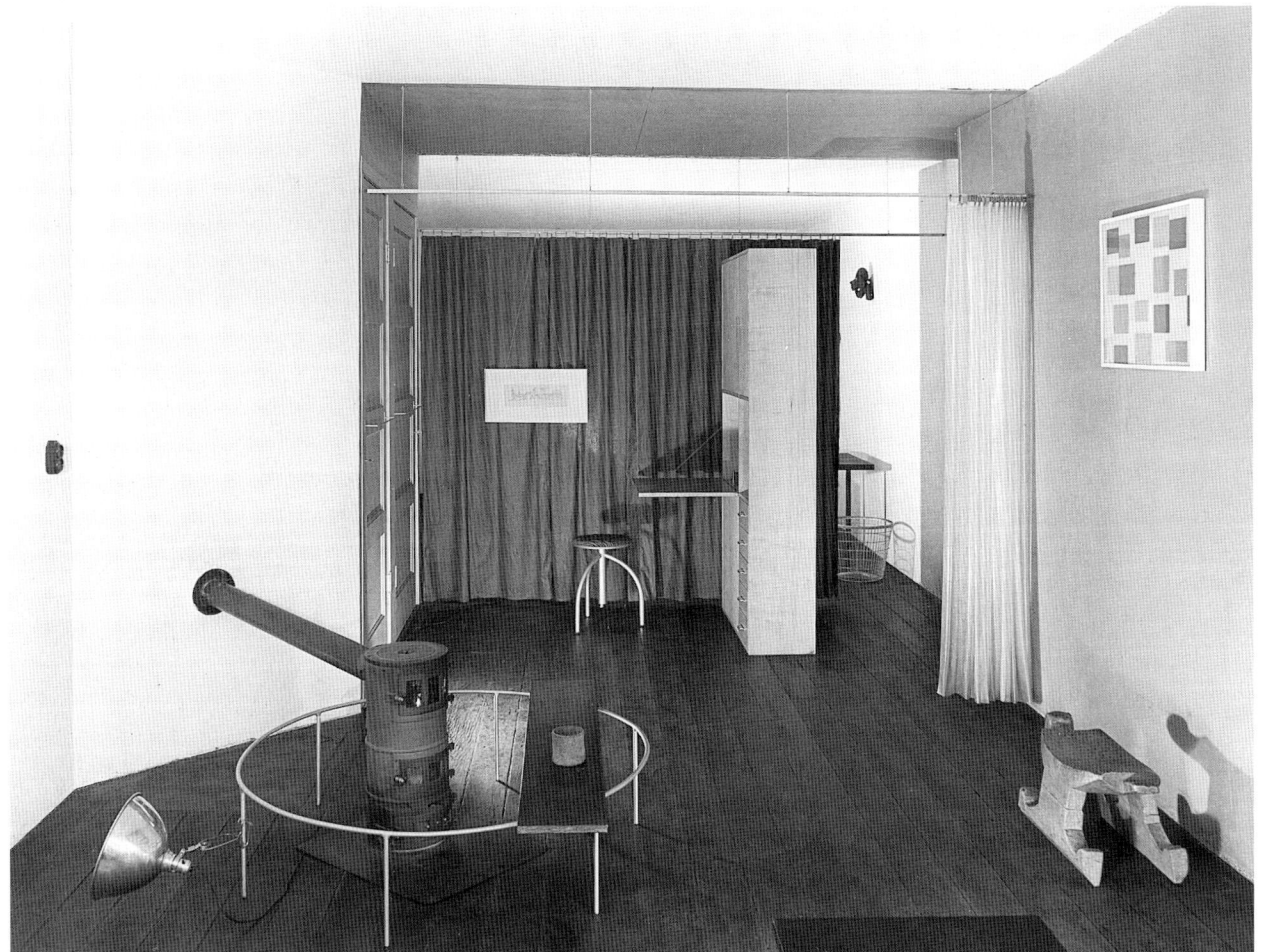

54

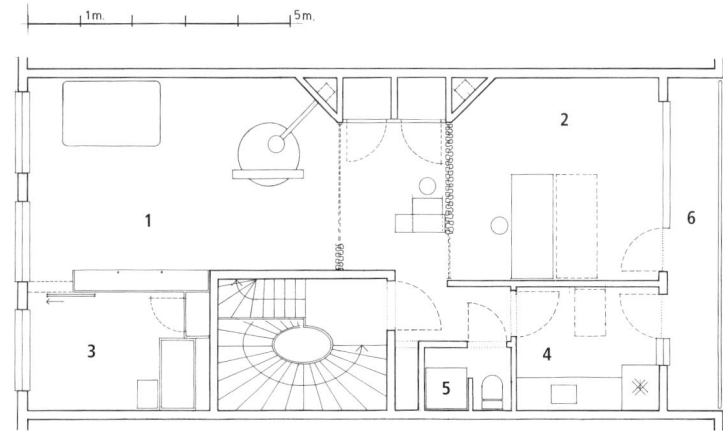

55

1 living room – bedroom
2 study
3 children's room
4 kitchen
5 toilet – shower
6 balcony

Outside: the city skyline; inside: pictures by Mondrian, van Doesburg, Miró, Klee and Ernst extended the 'interior horizon' in every direction.

Karel Appel painted special pictures for the children of his close friends, from which each could choose one.

Bank Directors' Rooms, Heldring & Pierson, The Hague, 1948

The brief was to transpose two rooms facing each other and the hall between them into three separate rooms: one small meeting room with adjacent cloakroom and toilets, one larger meeting room and a central space for the three directors who wished to share a single space openly connected with the large central office space, in order to assure immediate contact with each other and their employees. The visual openness this suggested was exploited in the design as a positive asset in that it motivated the kind of spatial continuity which ample use of glass can bring about. Although the openness and spatial continuity achieved was appreciated by my '8 en Opbouw' (CIAM) colleagues, the use of luxurious mahogany for both vertical partitions and the horizontal ceiling was not. This was regarded as quite wrong. Only Oud had no difficulty with this transgression (nor would Bijvoet have, but he, alas, never saw it!). The door frames and loose furniture were also of mahogany. Removing the load-bearing wall between two of the principal spaces certainly enhanced the desired spatial continuity but was in hindsight a rather drastic and inconvenient measure.

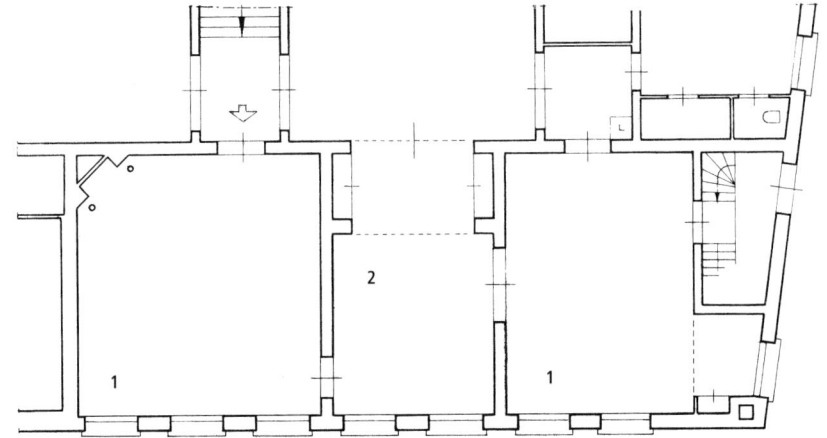

1 director's rooms
2 waiting room

Where glass planes meet

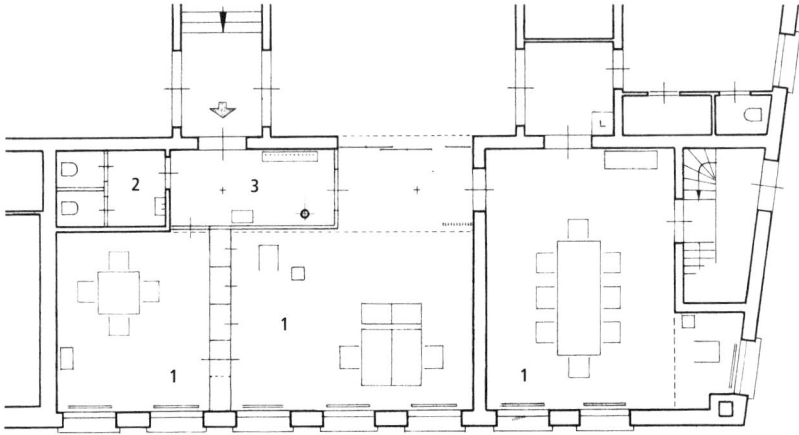

1 director's room
2 lavatories
3 entrance/cloakroom

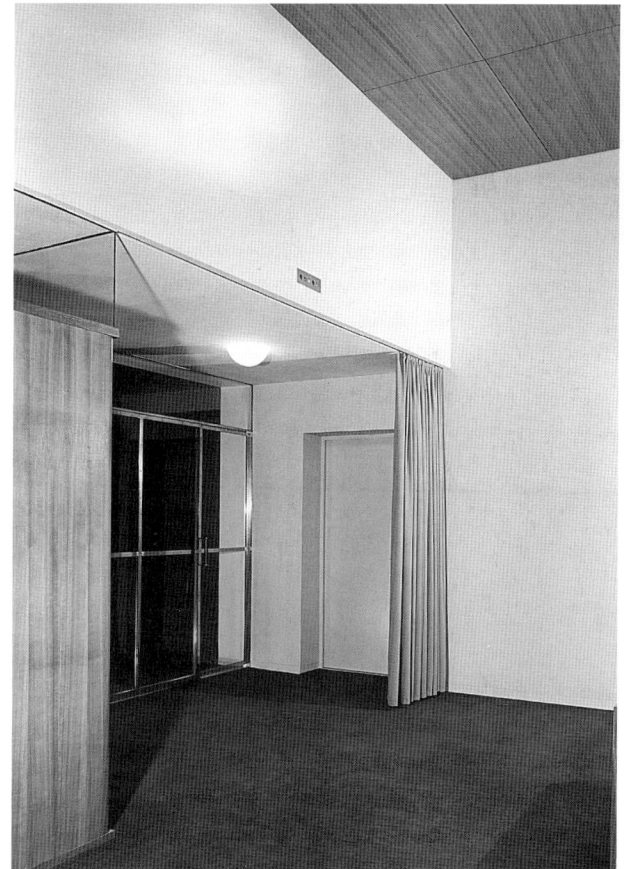

Entrance Sign for the National Maritime Exhibition, Ahoy', Rotterdam, 1950

The event to celebrate the reconstruction of Rotterdam's centre, which had been destroyed in World War II, took shape under the general supervision of van den Broek and Bakema. The latter, impressed by what he saw at the Cobra exhibition in Amsterdam's Stedelijk Museum, asked me to design an entrance sign to mark the place where the exhibition area is approached from the city, thereby bridging a considerable gap, and Karel Appel to produce another in the main hall. Appel, who collaborated with Bakema on a number of occasions over the years, 'nailed' together an enormous brightly coloured 'tree of life'.

At first the nature of the sign moved between a constructional form and a non-constructional, more sculptural one, ending up closer to the latter than the former, since the formal – not the constructional – logic prevailed in this case pointing towards its intrinsic instability. Hence the eerie tension between the two horizontal portals crossing overhead at right angles and the tall portal balancing with a leg on each. And of course the unavoidable cables holding it stable like a mast and lastly the little flags – white and green for Rotterdam – suspended along them. The point 2.35 m below the top where the girders turn 90°, shifting 30 cm along each other, was the appropriate one to fix the cables. Structurally it is a kind of zero point where the two component elements meet, the one as it were ascending and the other descending, making the sign a two-part as well as a three-part entity.

Related to its ambiguous character, somewhere between architecture and sculpture (i.e. between different kinds of logic) was the question whether its shape should derive from site characteristics or maintain a certain independence, which is what was actually done.

58

The tension at the junction of the two horizontal portals

DIN I 30

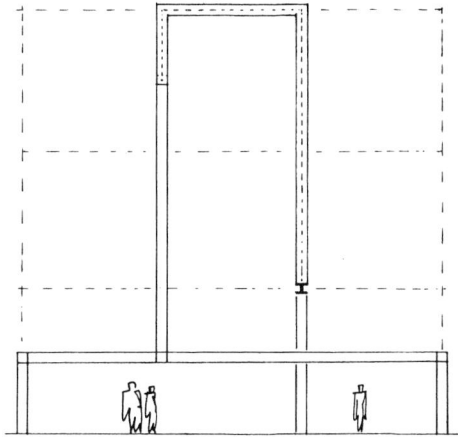

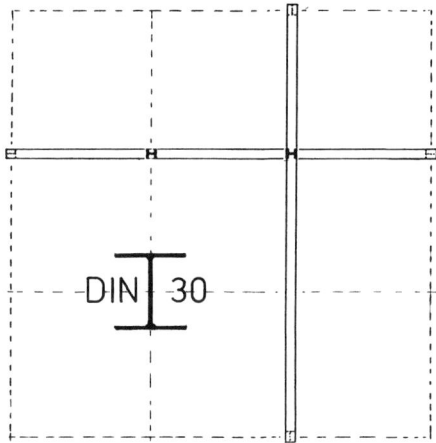

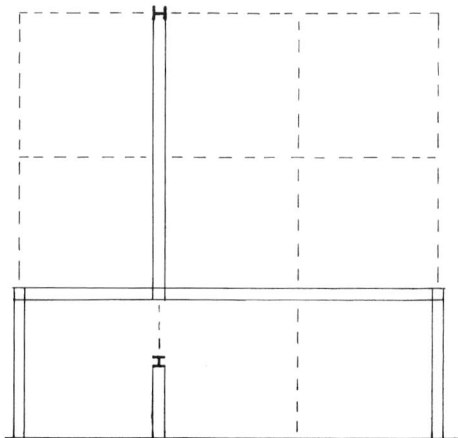

View with the exhibition in the background

Cobra Exhibition, Amsterdam, 1949 / Liège, 1951

Cobra swept over the art world like a storm as if from nowhere, shook it thoroughly, shifted to Paris and, not long afterwards, disappeared, but not without leaving it a different place. It was clear from the start that both events were going to be exceptional – requiring a fitting, 'exceptional' presentation. Not merely because it concerned a group of exceptionally gifted but still barely known young artists from several countries, but because they wished to put across a joint credo – one not confined to art alone. That Cobra would soon acquire worldwide recognition was already in the air. In that sense both events were triumphs in advance. The art works were there all right but not the 'exceptional' presentations! How to go about it was a problem that loomed ahead. Not only that, but it so happened that Amsterdam's 'heroic' Stedelijk Museum charged the penniless Cobra for literally everything – for each brush stroke, each nail or hook; each floor swept: in fact for whatever we did not find discarded in the museum's vaults. Beyond that were the available Cobra art works – their size and quantity seemed negligible in comparison to that of the available space. How to achieve the desired joint impact was one thing but how to avoid the menace of emptiness was another. Especially in Liège. When I first saw those huge barren outsized halls and all those endless walls behind soiled, time-browned burlap – all of it oddly Belgian – I was at a loss. Then, to make it worse, I beheld the crates containing the artworks still closed. Unpacked and spread out provisionally around the spaces, I told Pierre Alechinsky in despair that just two of those vast spaces would surely be enough, to which he replied with a grin: 'Mais non, mon chèr, ca deviendra une veritable événement avec des gens de partout'. D'accord, but how and with what.

It was brought home to me there and then that presenting any number of art works at the same time in the same spaces – organizing a joint performance – while perhaps legitimate and desirable, is still something done in retrospect – an artificial undertaking – and, like art, is wilful, requiring artistry in order to bring it off. The works assembled were after all made separately; each one basically a self-sufficient entity which does not necessarily require the presence of other works next to it to accompany or support it.

A work of art – each one – effectuates its own 'space' through its pictorial potential if it is given the chance to do so and is not hindered as is so often the case owing to faulty presentation. The worst possible thing that can happen, to paintings in particular, especially when they are as divergent and inventive as those of Cobra (or the entire Avant-Garde for that matter), is to encounter them fixed to the walls all round a space at eye level and – equally disastrous – with a more or less equal distance between them, thus

60

COBRA

AMSTERDAM

EXPERIMENTELE KUNST

imposing a false horizon from which there is no escape. Maltreating the perimeter of a museum space renders it empty – and emptiness is hostile to art – to painting and sculpture and architecture alike, which inevitably implies hostile to PEOPLE as well, who, with a variable height above the floor, variable interval and variable size, will at least no longer have to crabwalk from one painting to the next along the perimeter of one space after the other, but instead will soon be moving naturally through the entire space, changing their position from painting to painting (eye-level is appropriate when close scrutiny is required, otherwise either below or above is preferable – the way artists lean paintings against the walls of their studio to view them, or up high, safely out of reach to dry).

It is in short the only way (if you know how) to separate as well as to bring together works of art in a single space.

If effectively positioned, the combined pictorial potential of works shown together in a single space will of itself establish the architectural space they are to share – *share also with whoever is in the space with them.*

To exhibit implies bringing together, which in turn implies composing – there is no escaping the question: What is to be shown together and why? If that makes good sense then the question as to how it is to be done is still an open question – each and every time!

Appel's paintings in particular are entitled to the entire wall from top to bottom: birds flying way up; heavy quadrupeds plodding along the plinth and the rest of his menagerie anywhere in between.

STEDELIJK MUSEUM

1948

In Liège, there was much more space, whilst at the same time there were fewer platforms available. Instead I used a layer of anthracite, of which there was of course plenty, spread out within a timber frame, creating a vast glimmering base for the sculptures.

Sculptures: Henry Heerup

COBRA

LIÈGE 1951

We put an end to the absurd prevailing division between painting and sculpture – small and large – small paintings together in a small room and large ones together in large rooms. We also put an end to the inexplicable division between the various techniques such as etching, lithography, watercolour, gouache and (oil) painting – no longer presented separately as usual but together, where appropriate. The Avant-Garde, after all, broke through all categories and even created new ones. The same applied to Cobra and this was the moment to find a different solution.

I used some low platforms which I found lying around in the vaults of the museum, sometimes joining these together into a single large platform on which I placed not only sculptures, but also other work, such as lithographs, collages, etc., which lent themselves particularly well to being presented on the horizontal plane, as they were created horizontally and therefore not that dependent on being seen the right way up, unlike paintings which, on the whole, are created in a vertical position. Thus I avoided the problem of seeing the image back to front or upside down, whilst giving top and bottom a relative meaning.

63

Sculptures: Shinkichi Tajiri   In Liège, two Giacomettis, among other works, were generously given what they were asking for.   Paintings: Pierre Alechinsky

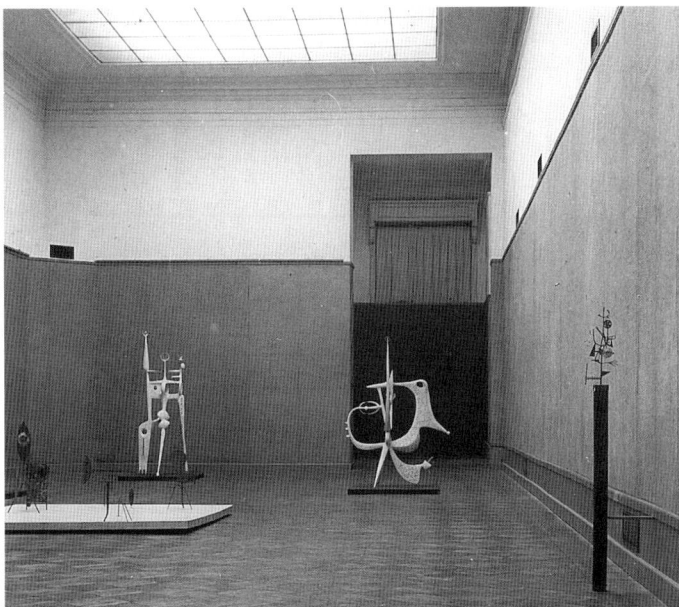

Damme House, Amsterdam, 1951-4 with Jan Rietveld

At the time of building approximately half the planned detached houses had living rooms facing south-west and south, but alas so did the street and the neighbouring garage wall! Those houses which were still to come followed suite so that finally only this house has the living room facing north-west, with a wide view over the water in both directions and ample sunshine entering from above through the double floor-height staircase fenestration on the street side. The garden door in the north-west elevation is without glass so as to draw attention, when entering the living room, towards both the open corners and the view over the water in both directions beyond. Thus when the door is

finally opened and light enters spring will have come.

In order to provide direct access to the exterior and garden from the bedroom floor the staircase landing opens onto a roof terrace over the entrance lobby which has a staircase down to the garden.

The original dark brown manganese brick walls as well as the light blue frames were later both painted white causing the latter to appear harshly cut out, which when still dark-in-dark was not the case. (If repainting one's house just meant a change of colour that would be all right.)

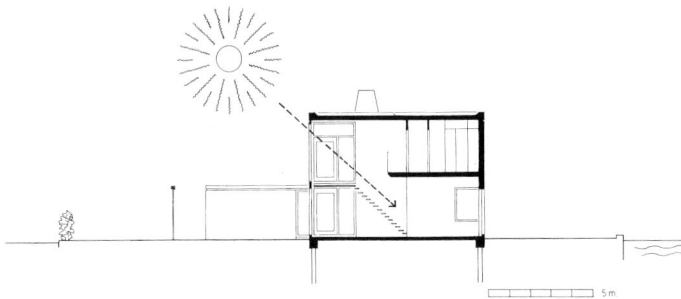

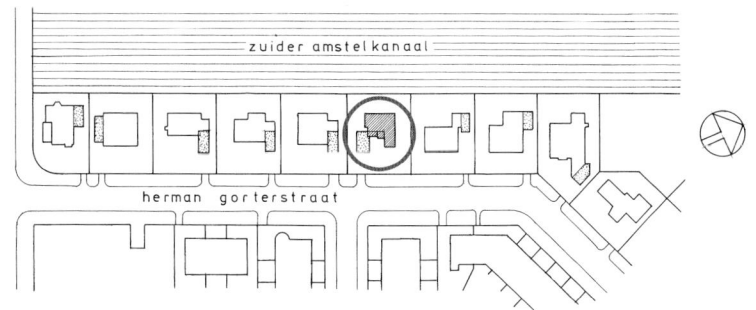

zuider amstelkanaal

herman gorterstraat

64

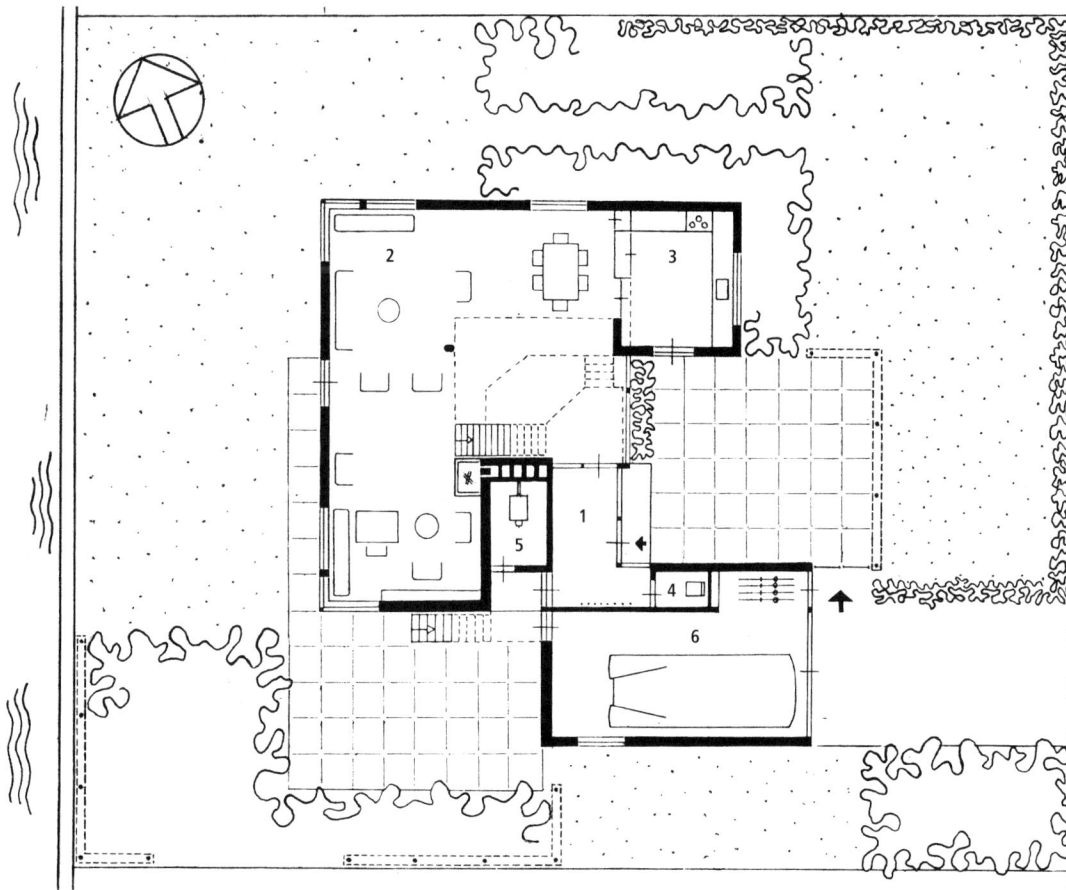

1 entrance   6 garage
2 living room 7 bedroom
3 kitchen   8 bathroom
4 toilet   9 void
5 heating   10 roof-terrace

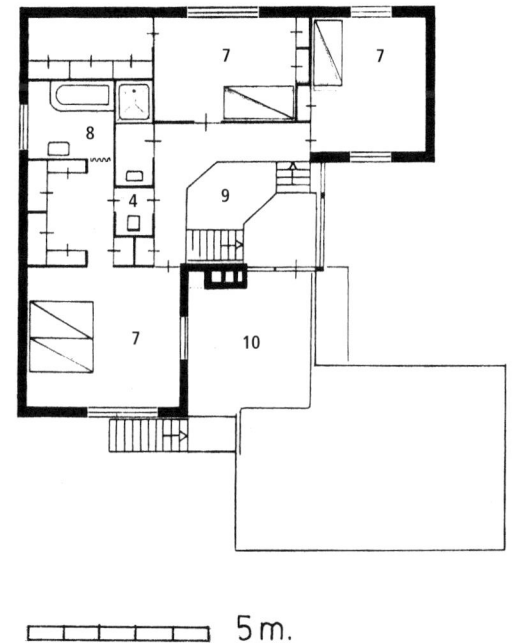

5 m.

Houses for the Elderly, Slotermeer, Amsterdam, 1951-4

with Jan Rietveld

Since openness and enclosure are qualities which apply to both the individual and collective spheres, we sought to find the right balance between them inside the dwelling as well as outside: to extend the exterior world into the interior and *vice versa*, but also to separate them. This implies considerable re-thinking as to what architecture and town planning are all about – and to what extent they overlap – or even coincide! The dwellings are situated between the built up area to the north of the Burgemeester de Vlugtlaan and the green zone which wraps round it to form two interlocking urban spaces. The southern one is a field and as such a continuation of the green zone, whereas the northern one is a continuation of the paved world.

The town-planning authorities presented a miniature scale (see drawing) arrangement with short, mostly single-storey rows with little space between them. Since we were asked to build for old people but not for dwarfs, our idea went in the opposite direction by counteracting the given negligible building height by increasing instead of diminishing the space between the rows, thus maintaining the *same scale* as the other housing nearby. In order to achieve basic simplicity we came up with a single plan for both a north-south and an east-west orientation, adapted to the advanced age of the residents, which is also why we rejected the proposed double floor unit with risky external stairs.

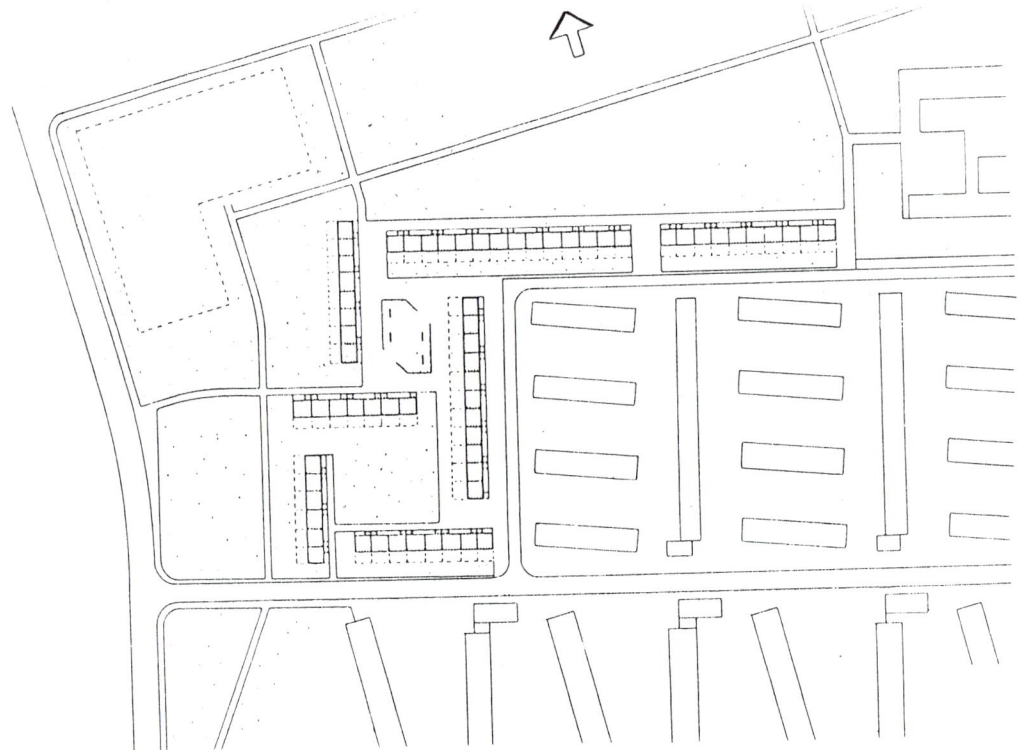

66

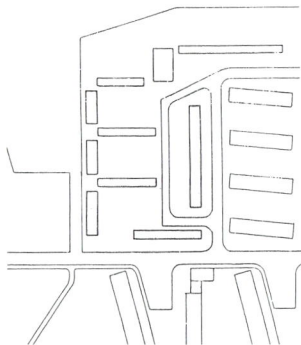

City council plan

Railing on the doorstep

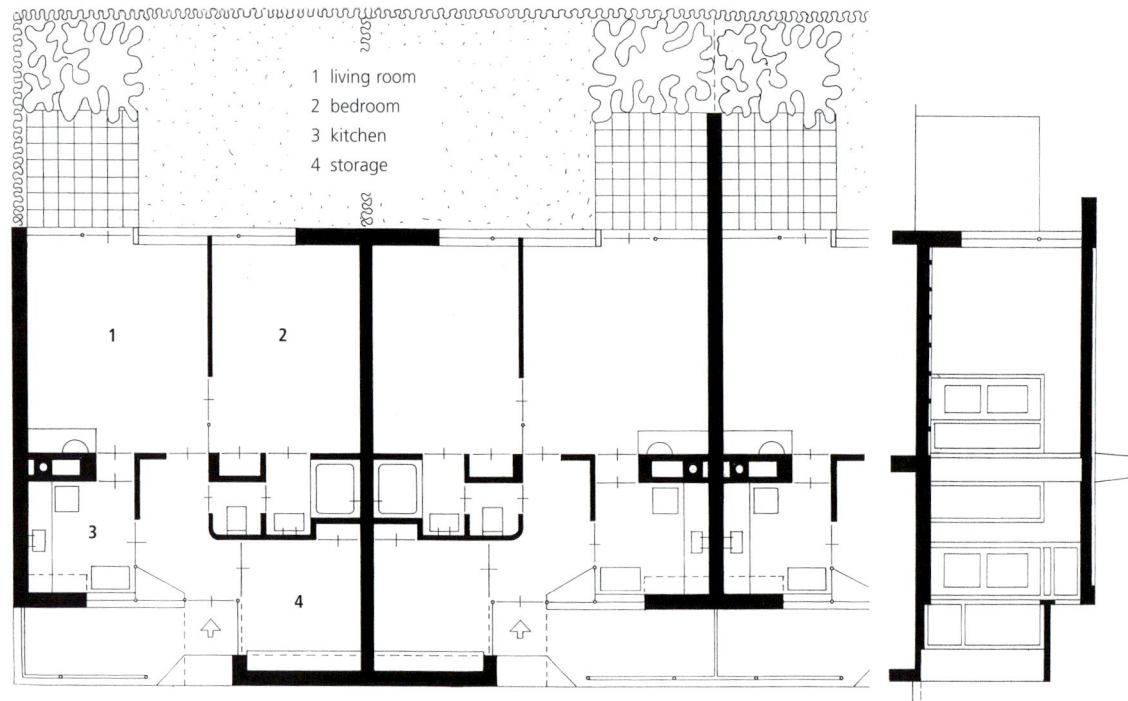

1 living room
2 bedroom
3 kitchen
4 storage

The Amsterdam Playgrounds, 1947-78

A city without the child's particular motion is a malignant paradox. The child is left to discover its potential against all odds, damaged and damaging, in perpetual danger and incidental sunshine. Edged towards the periphery of urban attention, the child survives, an emotional and unproductive quantum. Then, behold, when snow falls on cities, the child takes over, Lord of a transformed realm. All at once, with miraculous assistance, the child is everywhere, rediscovering the city whilst the city in turn rediscovers its children, if only for a while. A gratifying visual simplification takes place but it is also a revealing one, because, as everything merges and differences are rendered invisible it becomes apparent that something more permanent than snow, if less abundant, is missing, something which can still be provided as a modest correction where there is room – as an afterthought long overdue. Something, quite unlike snow, the city can readily absorb, and not altogether unlike the countless incidental things already there which the child adapts to its own needs and imagination anyhow, at its own risk.

Since 1947 approximately 700 open places adapted specifically for children were executed according to my designs and specifications on spare sites, overlooked spaces and insignificant dusty patches of greenery. But also on empty lots where houses belonging to people deported during the Second World War were demolished to provide fuel.

The ultimate advantages have proved to outweigh the obvious disadvantages such as danger and pollution! The children are no longer apparently nowhere yet unpredictably everywhere. They are now, at any rate, more visibly located – clearly there or on their way. Beyond that the playgrounds together form a network of focal points spread all over the city: an additional urban fabric of public places where not only children gather but parents and the elderly too.

when snow falls on cities

The sad side of the story

There is indeed a sad side to the Amsterdam playground achievement. What was thought to be 'more permanent than snow' has since proved not to be permanent enough. It has at any rate become clear that an urban ingredient, as vulnerable as the playground fabric is, cannot survive without permanent attention and special care. The mood has changed since the '50s. As the playgrounds receded from the forefront of municipal attention the care they constantly require slackened. What was once an homogenous fabric all too soon began to fall apart. One by one the playgrounds were disfigured as a result of only casual maintenance. Faulty repairs, loss of equipment or, worse still, when they had to make way for something else. One still comes across bits and pieces. Here and there an old playground has survived, but the gratifying impact of countless children playing in so many places, made especially for them all over the city, has gone AS IF THE CHILDREN TOO HAVE GONE.

69

If childhood is a journey, let us see to it that the child does not travel by night.

What the snow image suggests in terms of the city is a careful adjustment, adaptation, modification and addition. Cities are chaotic and necessarily so. They are also kaleidoscopic. This should be accepted as a positive credo before it is too late. Order has no function, on this side of evil, other than to make what is essentially chaotic work. Add to this the notion that no abstract norm imposed from above or any other motive, sanitary or speculative, can further justify the wanton destruction of existing buildings or street patterns, nor that which invariably accompanies the demolition of old 'sub-standard' or 'obsolete' housing: the involuntary removal of people from their domicile, be it house, street or neighbourhood. Ultimately, the world today can no longer afford such waste, nor can it afford to overlook the right of people to maintain both the built form and the social fabric of their domicile if that is their choice. Anything else is sociocide – with the people left alive.

Nieuwmarkt, 1968

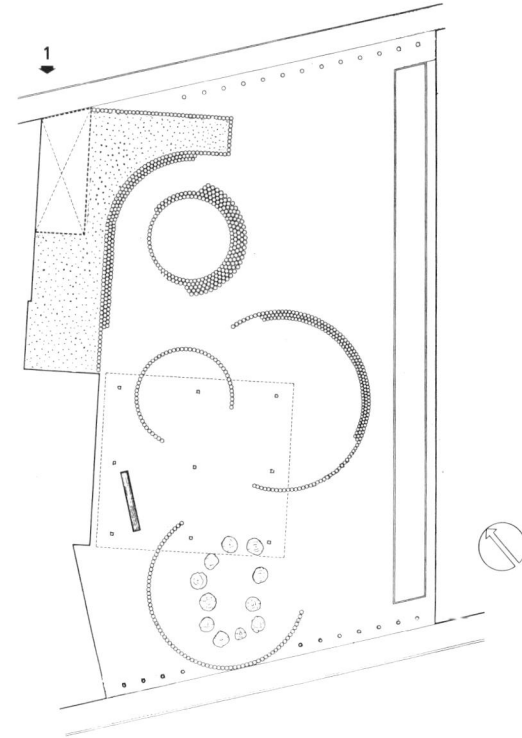

In the historic inner city, especially where practically no fully suitable space is available, it was decided to use old left-over spaces and lots left empty when houses belonging to people deported during World War Two were demolished.

Playgrounds in Nieuwmarkt area

Koningsstraat, 1955

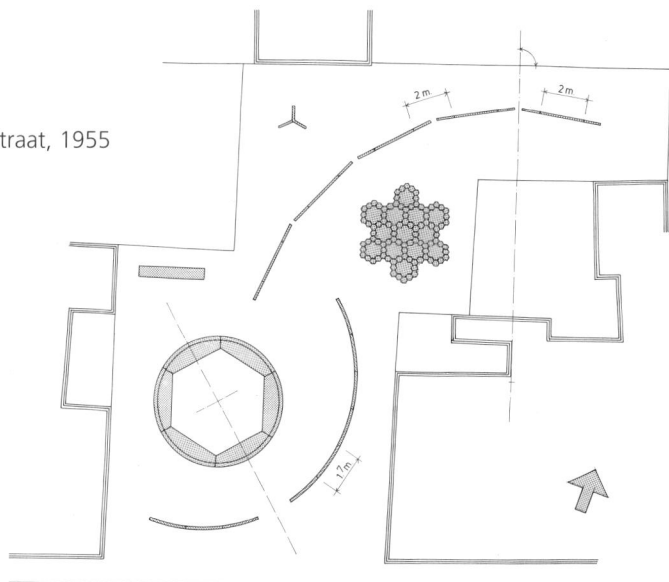

3

71

Dijkstraat, 1954

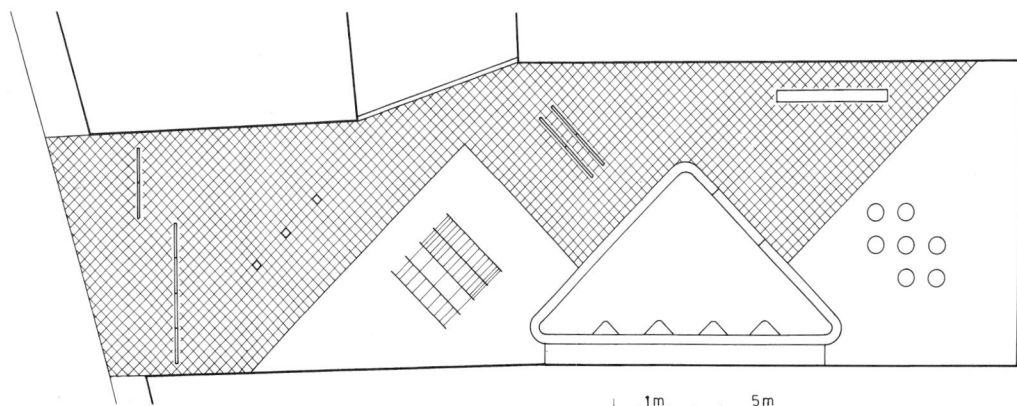

2

1m   5m

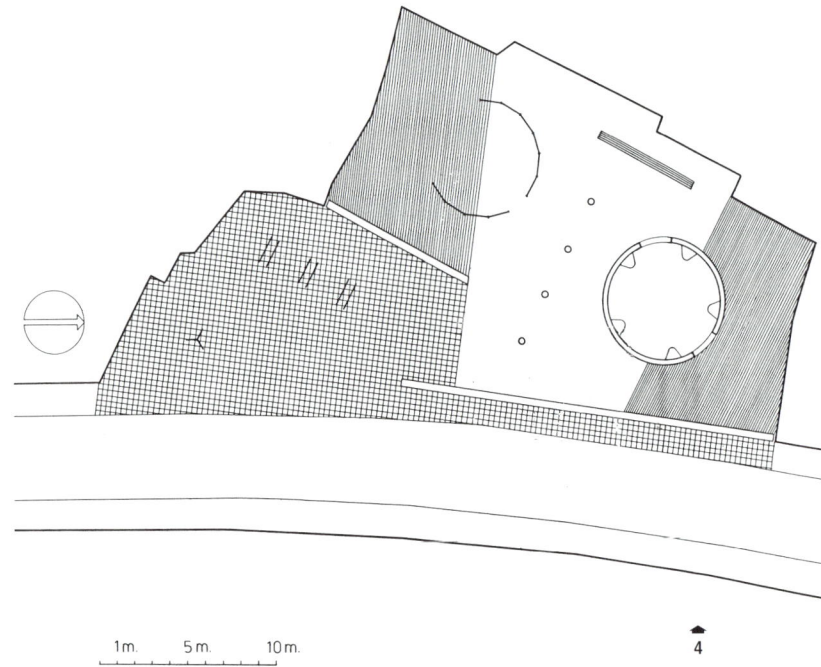

Zeedijk playground, with painting by Joost van Roojen, 1955

When designing the many playgrounds in Amsterdam it was always possible to reach a solution using architectural means. It was not possible at Zeedijk. The architect's specific capabilities did not include control over this exceptional circumstance. Other capabilities and other visual means were essential. Yet there 'arose' a space organised purely by means of colour.

Standing in front of or in the playground, Zeedijk no longer exists as a street space – but the space defined for the child by the totality of the colour-form-panorama does. What is therefore significant is the way the scheme gradually becomes more active towards the middle. One would almost nevermore want to miss the fitful world of the inner area which here suddenly appears over the colour explosion of the painting. It allows one to see once more!

Joost van Roojen restored the whole thing after a few years but after that it fell into decay and vanished.

A stone-carver was brought in to create an attractive connection between the concrete tiles and the circles of clinkers. But not a second time for the repaving – so the circles had to go!

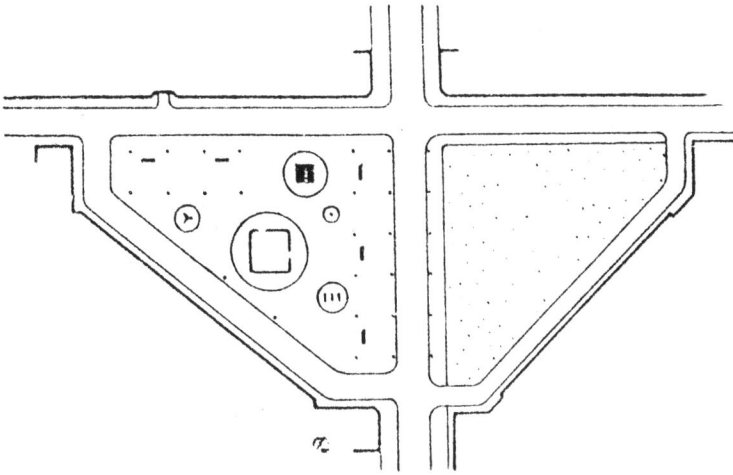

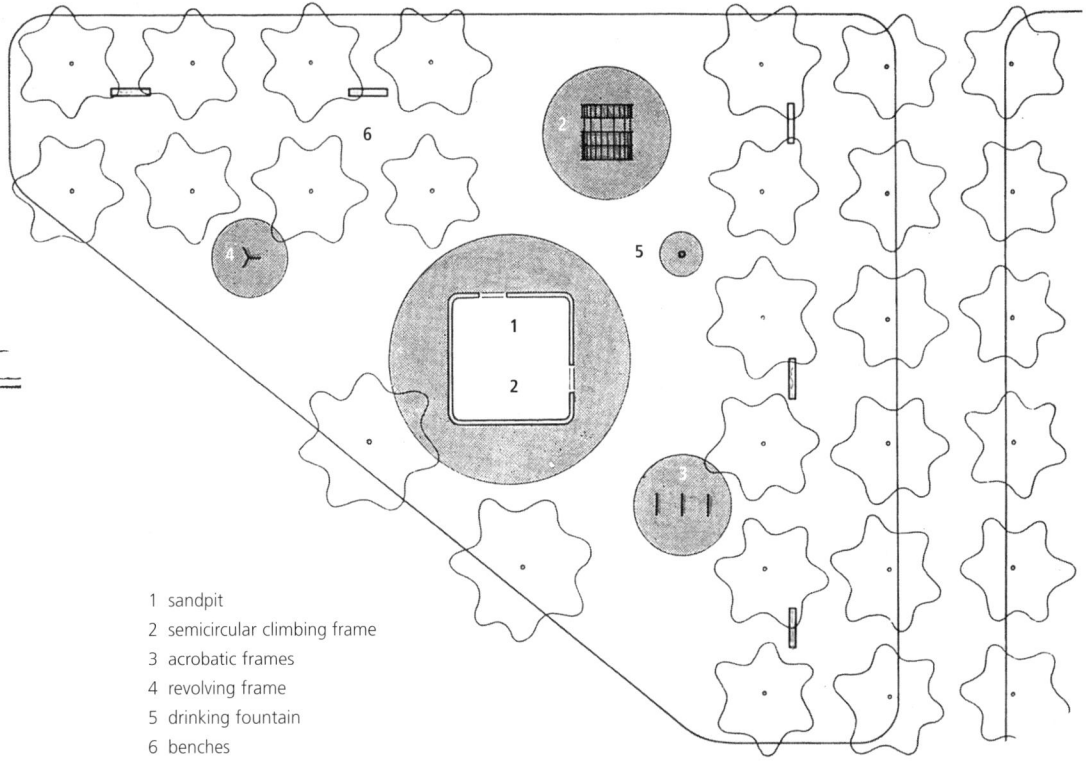

1 sandpit
2 semicircular climbing frame
3 acrobatic frames
4 revolving frame
5 drinking fountain
6 benches

Jacob Thijsseplein, 1949

73

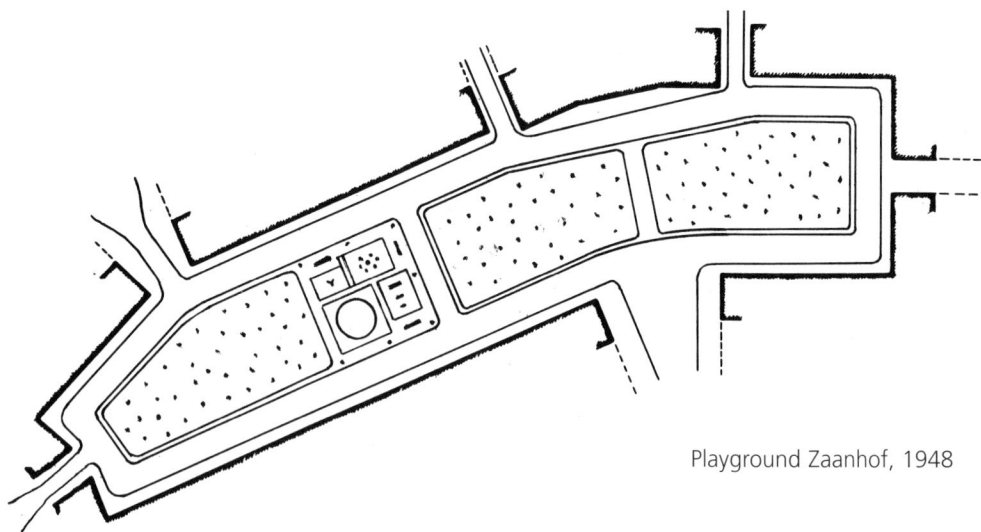

Playground Zaanhof, 1948

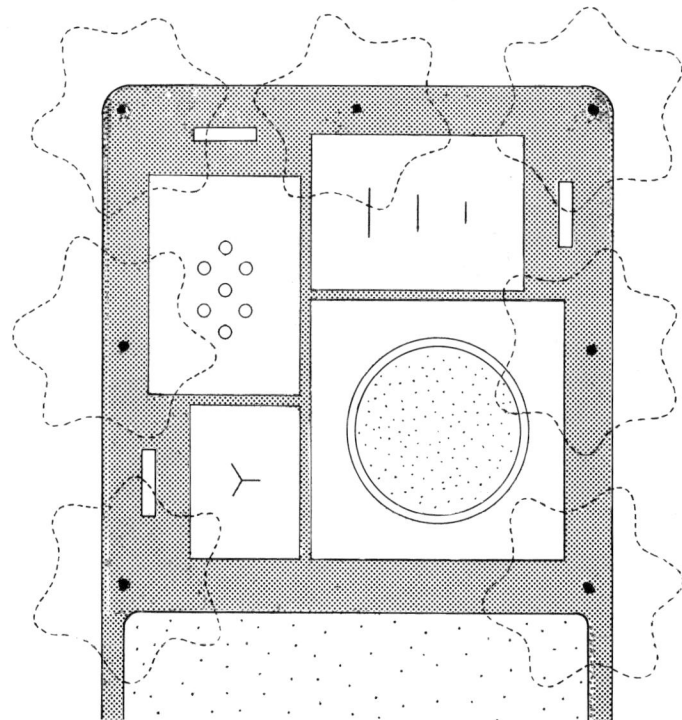

74

Stepping stones – here the same height – elsewhere different heights.

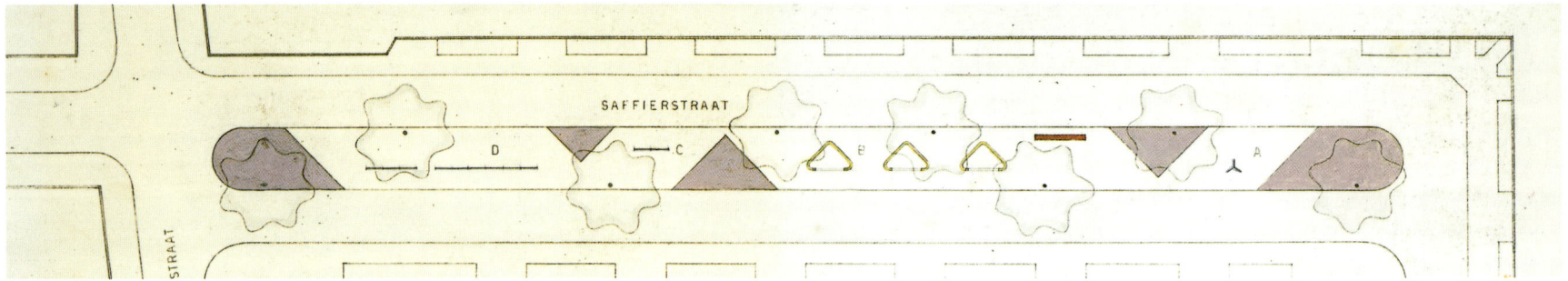

Saffierstraat, 1950

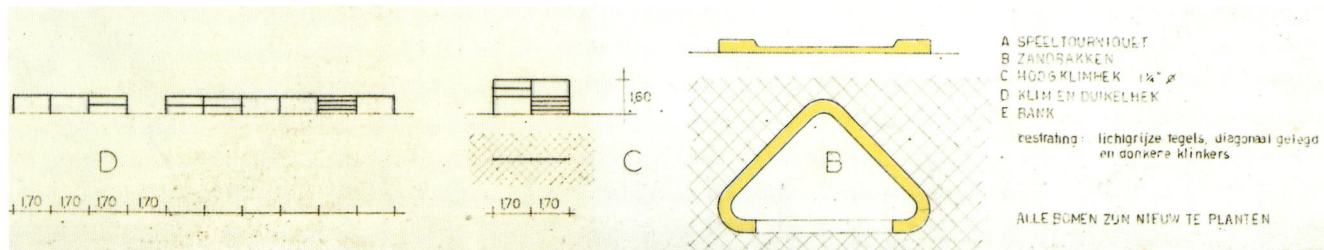

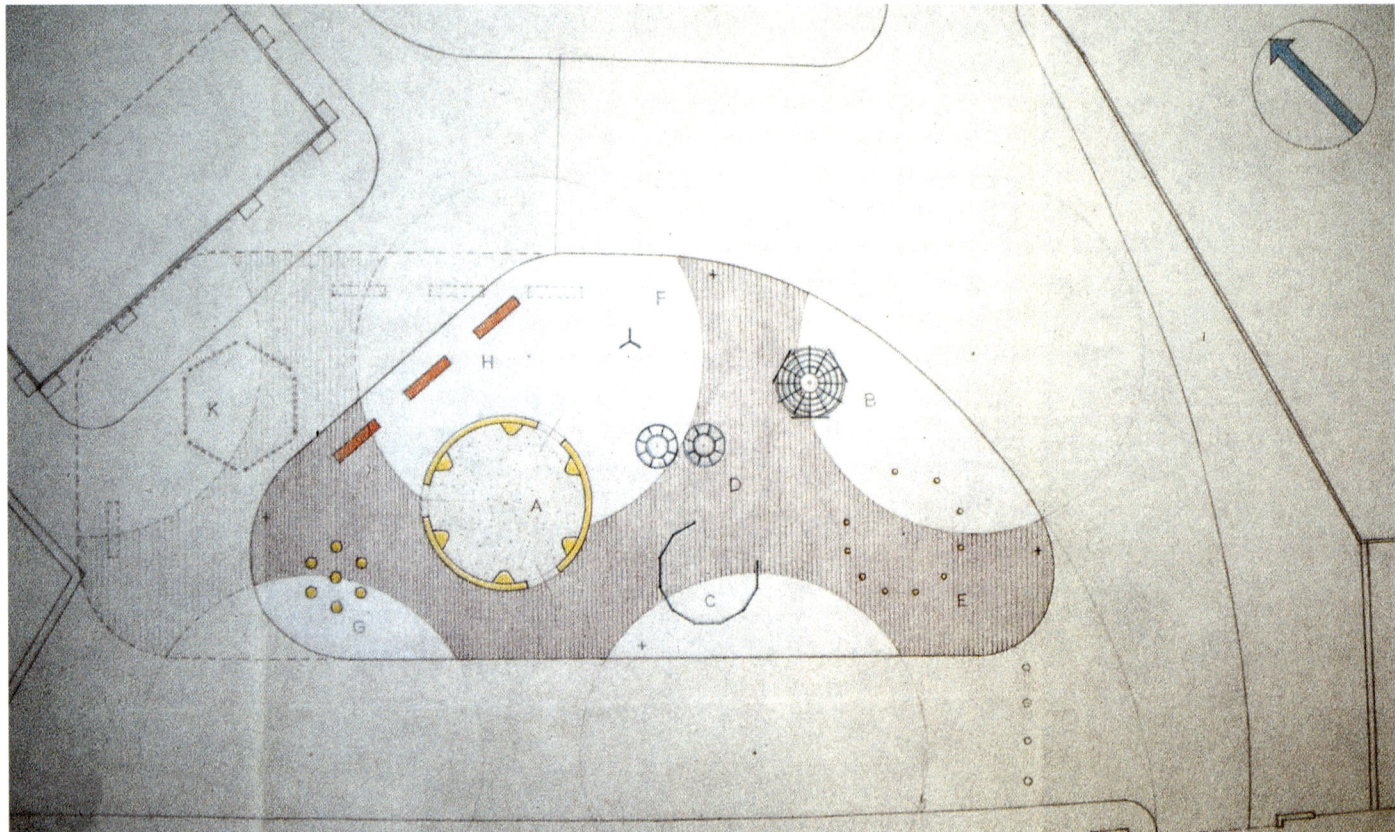

A SPEELTOURNIQUET
B ZANDBAKKEN
C HOOGKLIMHEK 1¾" ∅
D KLIM EN DUIKELHEK
E BANK

bestrating: lichtgrijze tegels, diagonaal gelegd
en donkere klinkers

ALLE BOMEN ZIJN NIEUW TE PLANTEN

Bickersplein, 1957

Saffierstraat, 1950

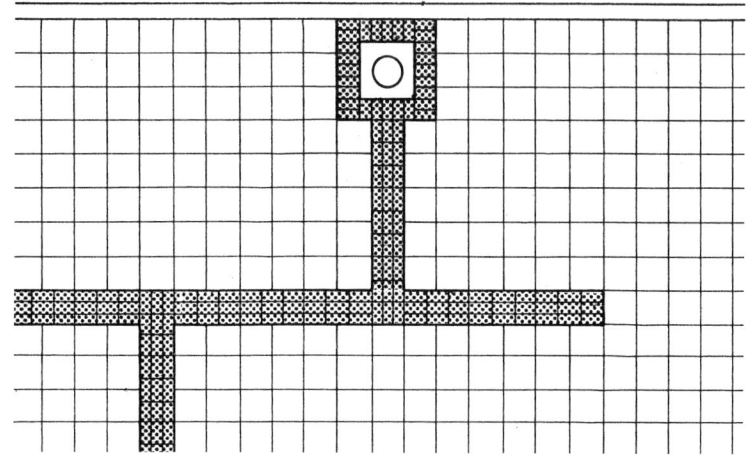

Diverse objects, including two groups of five trees, a bench, a sandpit and a row of acrobatic frames have been brought together by the clinker path.

Woestduinstraat, 1949

1 acrobatics frames
2 sandpit
3 bench

10 m.

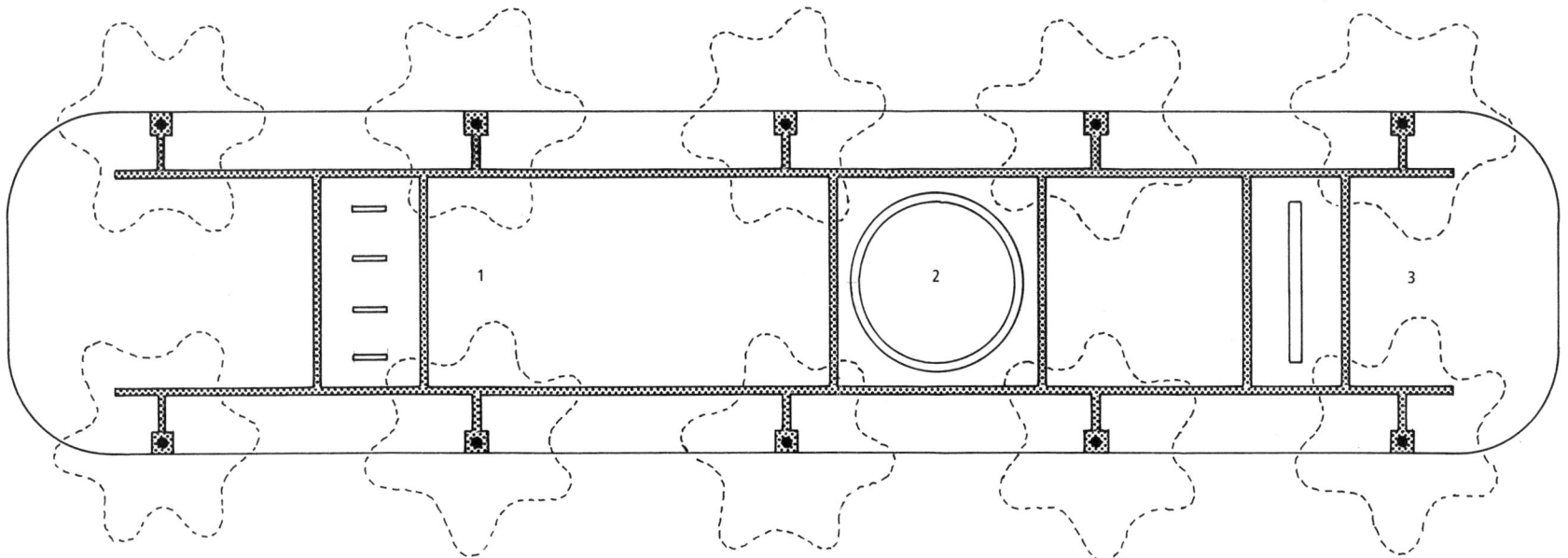

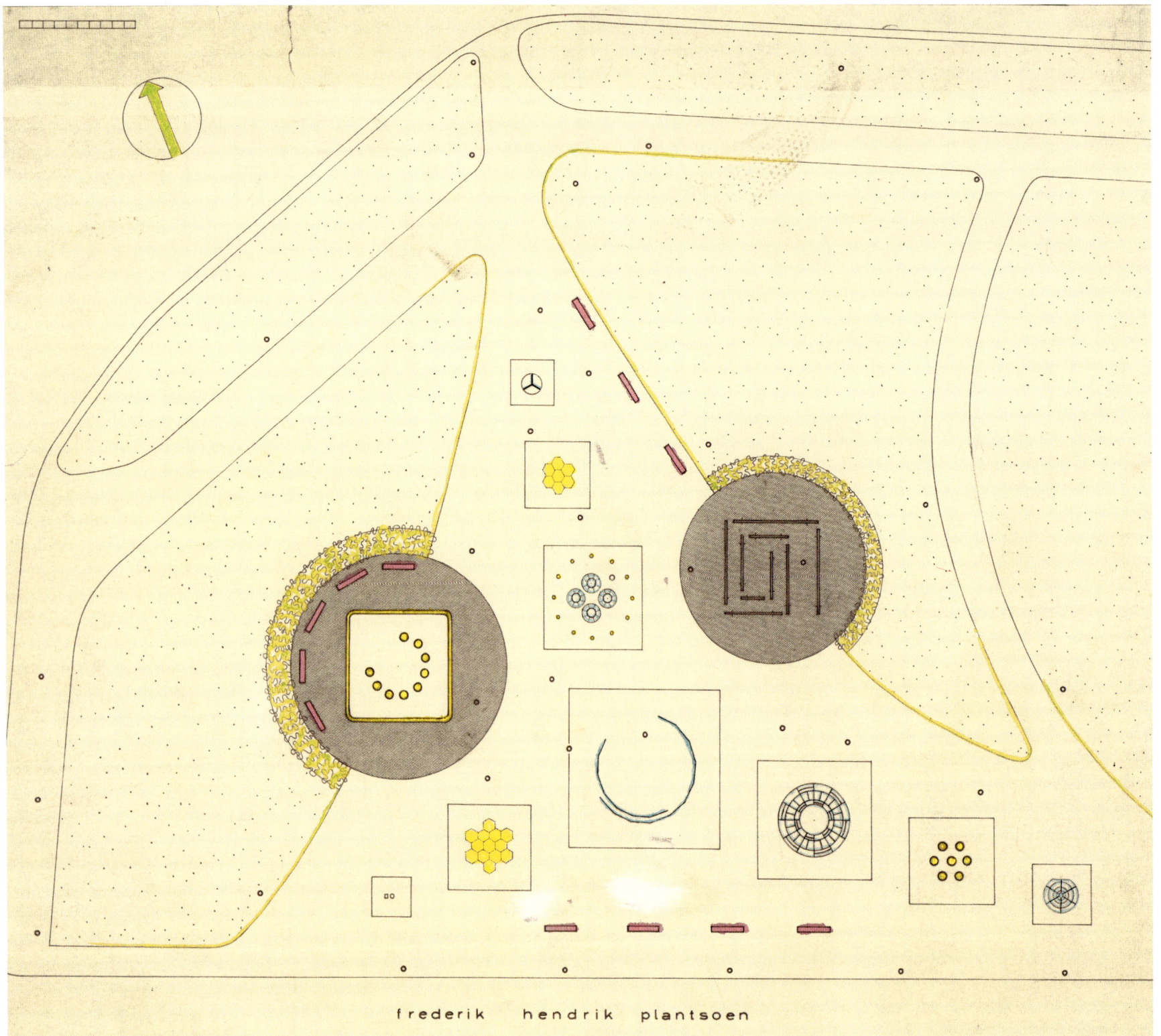

78

frederik hendrik plantsoen

1949

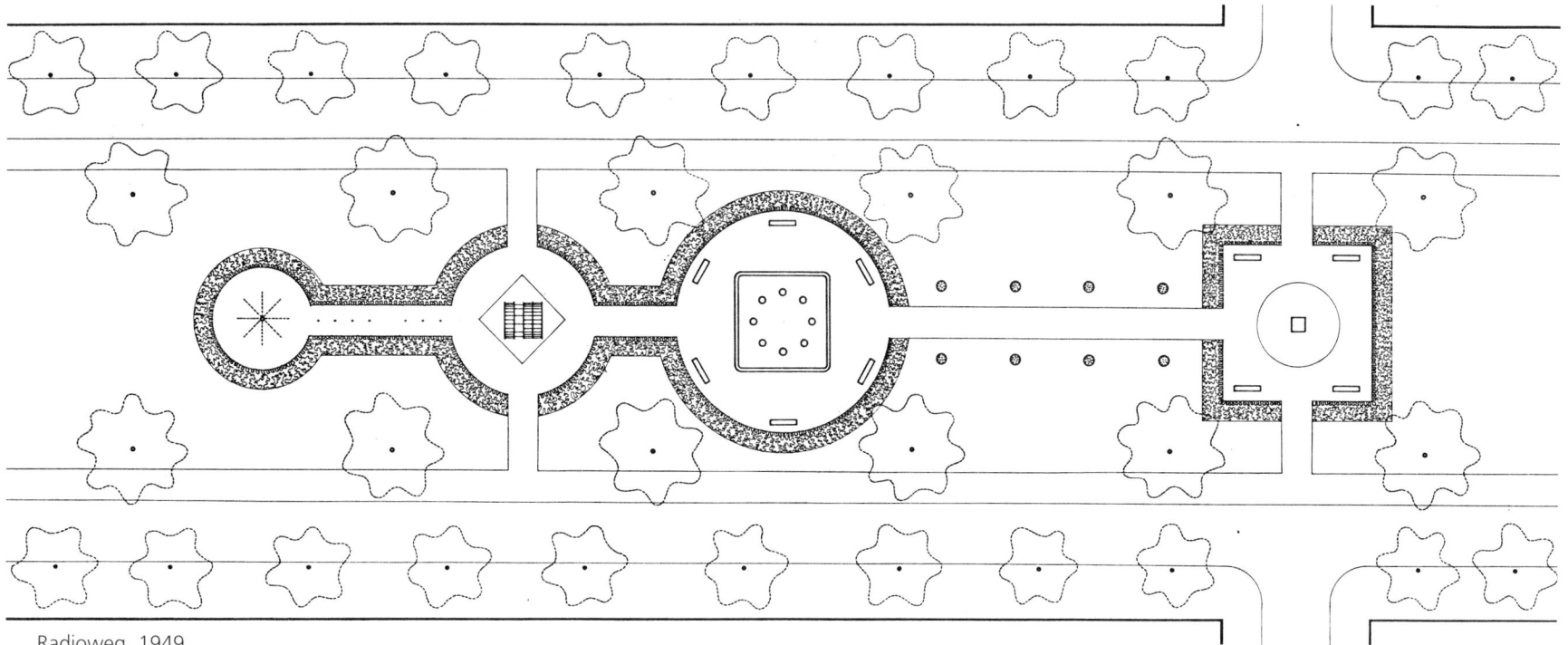

Radioweg, 1949

Along the axis, the spatial aspect is dynamic; off the axis – so along the playgrounds – the spatial aspect is also dynamic but in a different way, because the high plants alternately come closer and move away, which means the space narrows and broadens. Where there are no plants, the other side suddenly becomes visible.

Dulongstraat, 1954

79

Mendes da Costahof, 1957

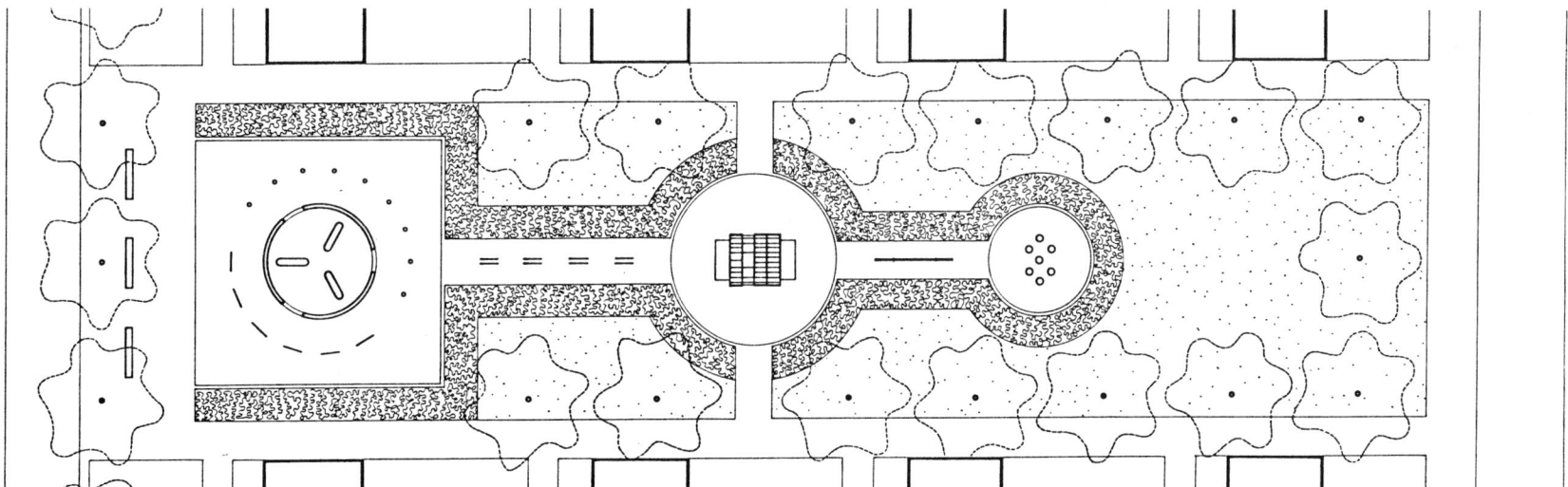

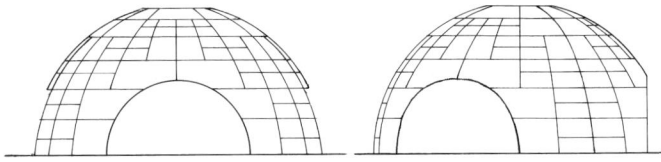

Hardly had these arches been introduced in Amsterdam before they appeared across the globe – 'we want one or two of those' was the cry.

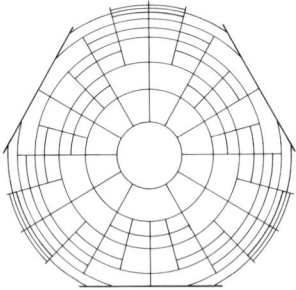

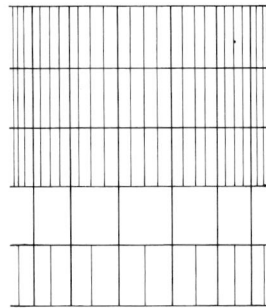

3 m.

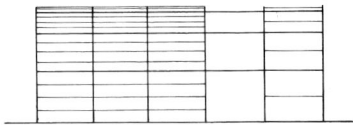

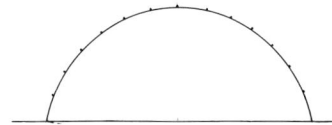

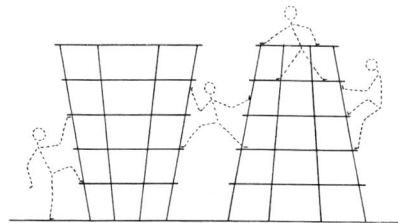

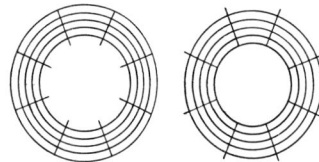

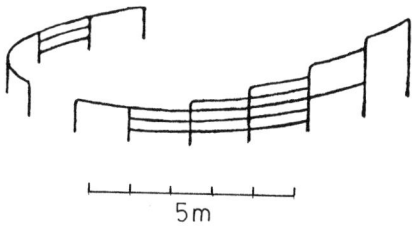

5 m

The play equipment for the playgrounds was designed bit by bit over the years and subsequently continually amplified, modified and adjusted. Together the items constitute 'families' of elementary abstract forms according to the material used: aluminium, steel, wood or concrete, all of which respond to the basic urge to jump, climb, swing, creep, crawl, hop, stretch, hang, balance and somersault. Mobile equipment like swings, seesaws and large roundabouts were avoided on all the smaller unattended playgrounds. Gaudy vehicular and animalesque gadgets available on the market were added willy-nilly spoiling the visual homogeneity whilst contributing nothing to the child's basic repertoire of movements.

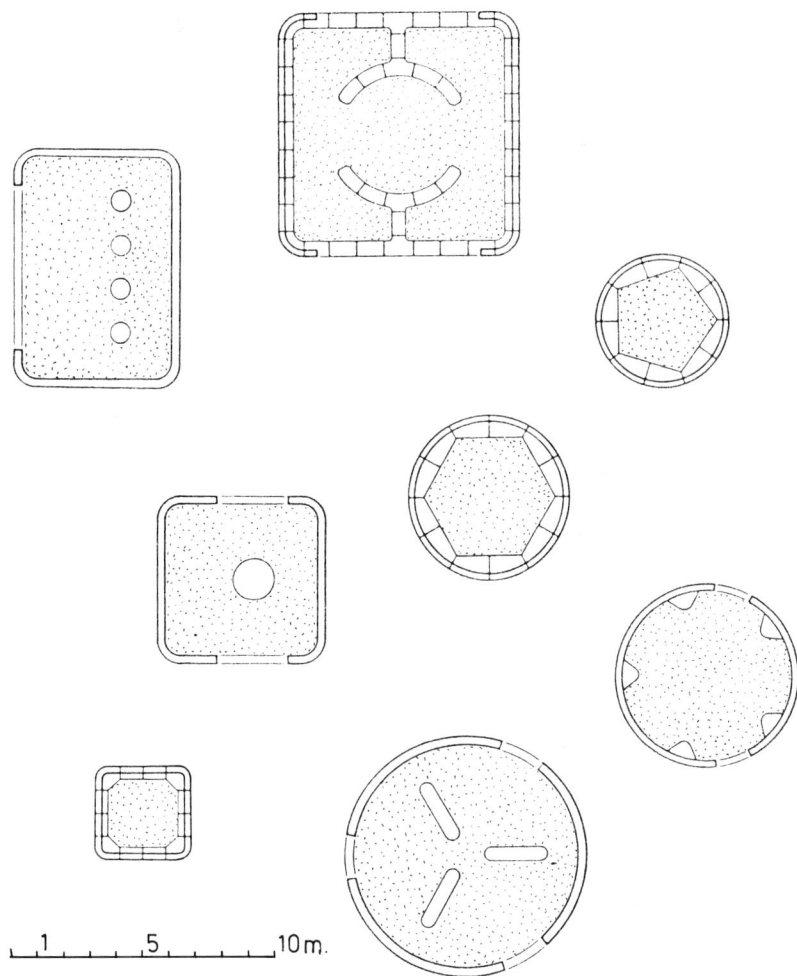

5 m.

1 5 10 m.

Some of the many concrete sandpits used in Amsterdam. Screen is clinker paving, the rest basaltine paving.

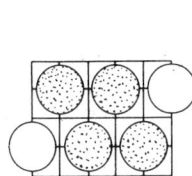

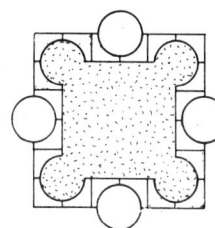

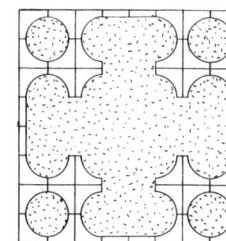

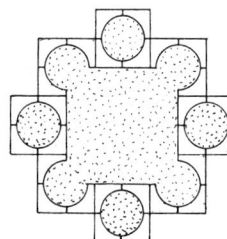

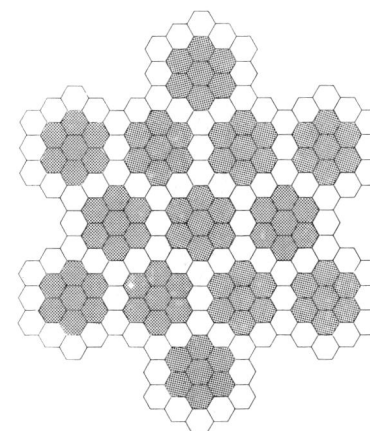

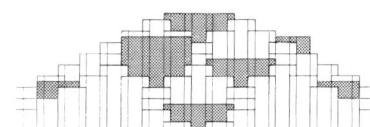

The Blue-Purple Room, Stedelijk Museum, Amsterdam, 1952

The People and Home (Mens en Huis) exhibition, an event initiated by the 'Good Living' Institute, conveyed moralising messages like 'pour milk from the bottle like wine, but never from a jug' (as if milk in a half-full bottle looks appetizing) and 'never eat from decorated plates', etc. I did not appreciate it.

The Blue-Purple room was meant as a critical aside, what with the assertive colours, the 1000 watt bulb and the motto on the wall *everybody's right to bad taste*, which I replaced later by Lucebert's verse so as to divert attention in the first place towards the painting and theme of 'spatial colourism'.

To this end an accessible half-cube was installed at a slight angle in one of the museum's spaces, around an existing square painting by the Cobra artist Constant, which I asked him to enlarge for the occasion to wall height, 3.65 m.

For the interior I chose two adjacent, equally active colours – blue and purple – one for each half, in such a way that there would be no light-dark contrast. The two halves merged into the flat surface of the painting resulting in the apparent dissolution of the accepted notion of articulated space, thus acquiring a new content through which space and colour became reciprocally dependent, in the sense that, to quote Constant: 'shape is the shape of the colour and colour the colour of the shape'.

This, we maintained, opened the way for *spatial colourism*. The experiment opposed the passive role hitherto allotted to colour in contemporary architecture. The fact that the accent came to lie on the pictorial – painterly – aspect of the space, giving the result a certain expressionistic, non-architectural quality, is due to this, and also explains the heavy wooden frame round Constant's wall-height painting saying: here's a *painting* not a mural commissioned according to the generally accepted X m at Y% of the building cost, an accepted practice which makes a farce of both architecture and painting.

the dragonflies caught in iron lungs
have of stone wristwatches
the strength and speed

Lucebert

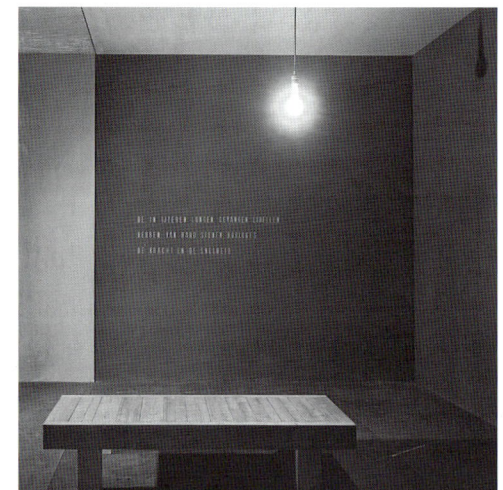

82

Hexagonal Table, 1953 and 1989

This table assumes a particular place in my mind among the other – larger – works i.e. the buildings! I see it as large-scale miniature architecture in which practical considerations, formal aspirations and personal associations are assembled and resolved in a way I would like them to be in buildings too – but this is simply too damned hard to bring about: the sheer complexity of the design-building process has become so dense as to be no longer completely penetrable. What may still occur in the other arts – in painting, sculpture, poetry, music and artfully conceived smaller objects, eludes the accumulative amalgam of data confronting the unfortunate architect today. Buildings which appear to have it all do exist. We all have our own in mind.

A table with a surface as ample as this one and as low, needs to be at least partially transparent, but never wholly so, i.e. not glass-topped from edge to edge and angular (such a table is a dangerous folly). Here the transparent centre is too far away to put one's glass on, with that nasty sound, whilst there is enough robust material around it for the table to be a clearly visible point of focus in any fairly large room. About the shape: there is enough openness for transparency and enough flat surface for linear configuration, and to put glasses on and goodies and all the rest!

Although not circular, it has the articulated rotundity I would like even angular – orthogonal – buildings to have – at least my own.

There is, besides overall centrality, also local centrality and shifted symmetry. It is both one piece and many pieces. It is, in fact, what the material has made of it.

The fact that the diameter of the cylindrical legs as it appears on the surface of the table top is smaller than it is further down was an unfortunate imperfection resulting from the way the one rests on the other. So when, years later, the opportunity came to have a few more tables made I let the legs pass straight through the table top, which now rests on pegs projecting from them. Greenheart, used here in combination with purpleheart for the legs and pegs, is so heavy that its mere weight ensures the table's stability. Both woods are from magical Surinam where my mother grew up!

83

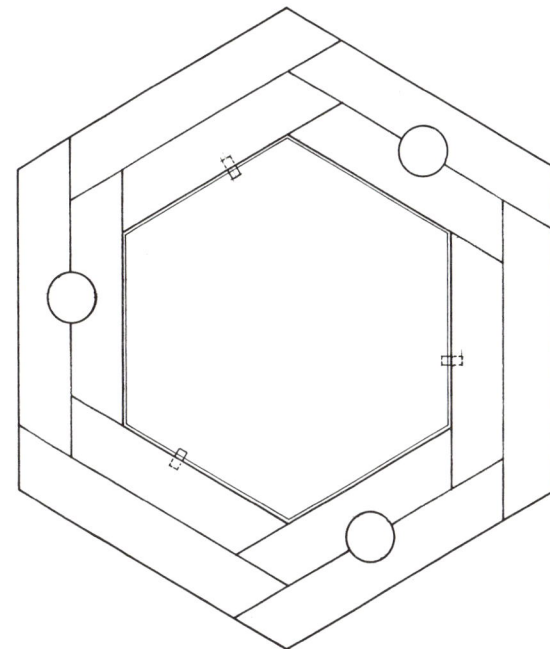

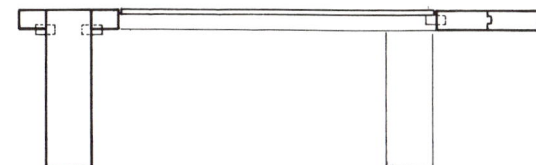

Left: Table in greenheart and purpleheart (1989)
Right: Table in teak (1953)

Nagele, Plan for a Rural Village on Reclaimed Land, Noordoostpolder, 1948-58
Contribution to the group design process with members of 'de 8 en Opbouw' (Dutch CIAM group)

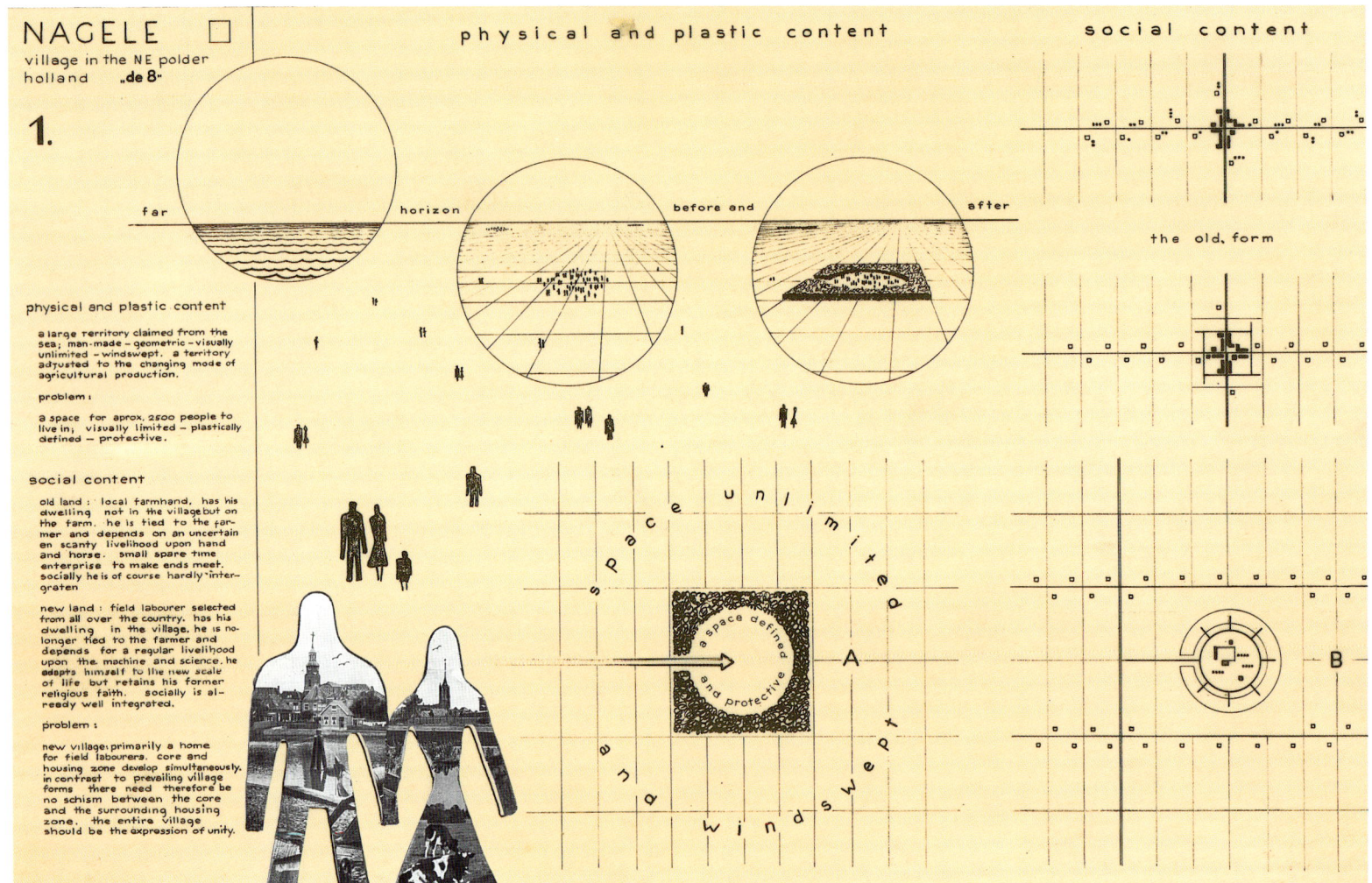

The first of the four drawings presented at CIAM Dubrovnic in 1956

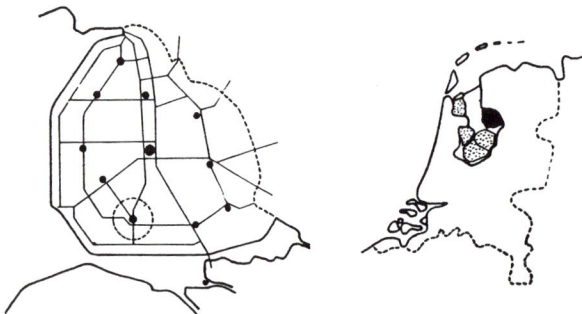

With M. Kamerling and W. van Bodegraven, 1948

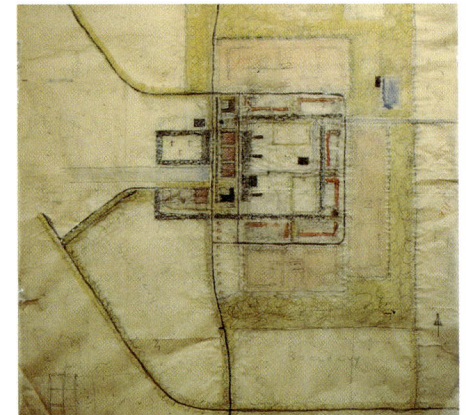

June 1953

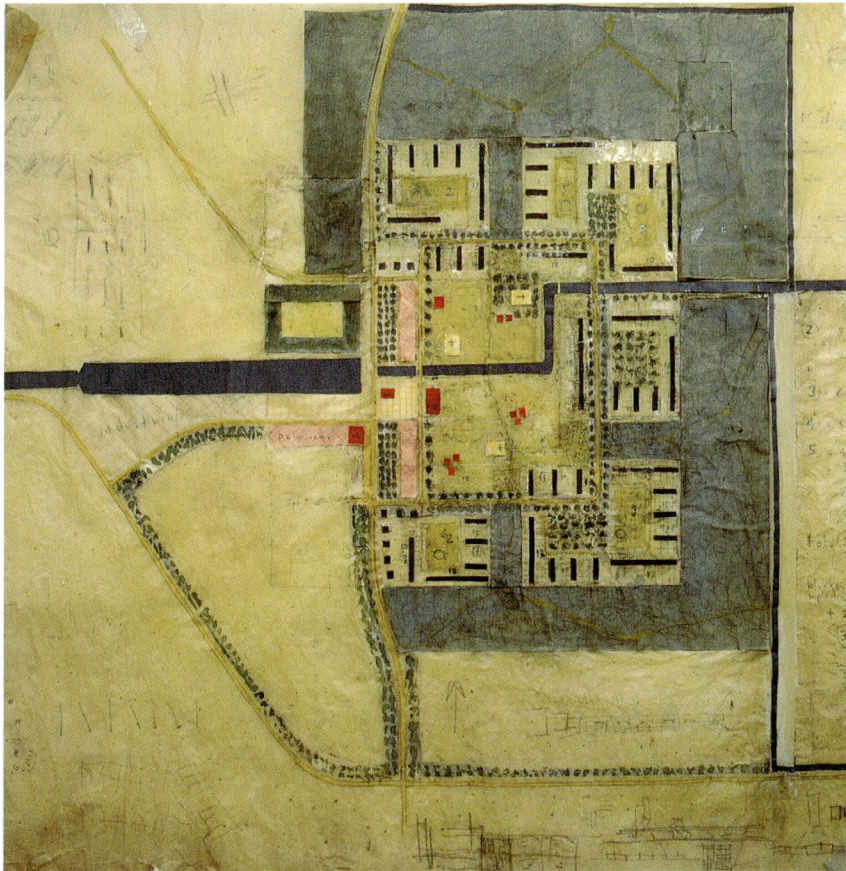

October 1953

D Relation between dwelling and core district.
Some places of contact with people from outside the village.
E Relation between the dwelling, dwelling group, central green and polder.
Aspect of ascending dimensions.
F Relation between dwelling group, grove, dwelling group, central green, grove, wood and polder.
The groves where children play and parents meet lead to the wood.
G A large central green, groves, woods and places for fun, rest and seclusion:
Instead of the rigidity of the vast polder or the 'streets' of the usual village form.

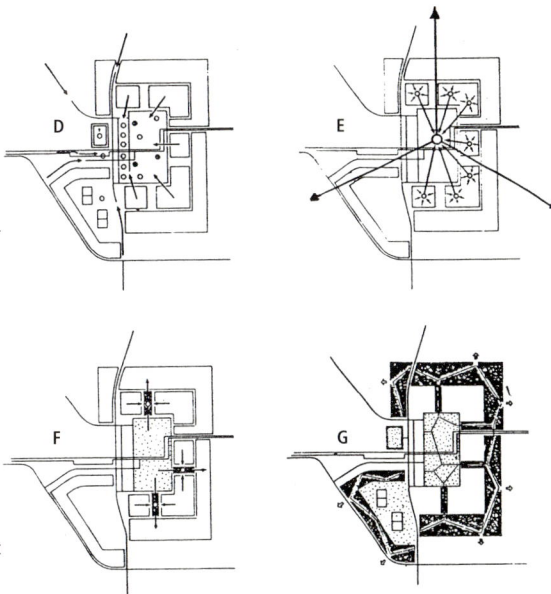

Nagele is one of the ten villages built shortly after the Second World War on reclaimed land in the North-east polder. Asked to draw up plans for the village and eventually build it as well, the Dutch CIAM group – which was already on the decline – cherished team work and anonymity as ideals and wished, above all else, to try them out on Nagele.

All sorts of alternative schemes were put forward by individual team members before it was decided, though reluctantly, to continue at least in principle along the lines set out independently by Mart Kamerling and myself during the first meeting. On this occasion Rietveld showed refreshingly inventive drawings – all of them different and equally Rietveldian – but unfortunately too far out to be taken seriously by the majority present. Understandably he withdrew from the team soon after.

The sketches and diagrams I presented at the first team session took account of what I regarded as the central twin-issues: the spatial one with regard to the new environment, and the social one regarding the specific nature of the immigrant population. With regard to the former, I wished to provide a marked and contrasting transition, not the usual one from unlimited exterior space and a distant horizon to small scale village streets with small communal buildings along them, but instead to a large well-defined inner space – a communal enclosure – which was to be cut out of a mass of tall trees serving as windscreen. This idea was to coincide with the social issue, i.e. besides catering for the surrounding farmland as of old, Nagele was from the start to accommodate peasant working class immigrants – a socially accepted category by now – and to do so in such a way that avoided the hitherto inevitable dualism – visual conflict – between the centre of the community on the one hand, and the houses built around it afterwards on the other. My proposal was to build a housing zone round an open central space with communal buildings in and along it. For once no village 'centre' with housing around and beyond it, but the entire village a centre without the usual unfortunate dichotomy.

Not being on CIAM's urbanistic wavelength, I made it my job henceforth to prevent the central space – or communal interior – I had proposed from becoming too large, too open and spatially too loose. Attempts to articulate and reduce the size of the central space succeeded only partially. One way, shown here, was to build terraced houses on the inside of the ring road. That would also have differentiated the central green space from the ones within the four housing groups, instead of simply pooling them, which is what finally happened. Beyond this, terser landscaping would have helped. Thus my proposal to 'line' the communal interior space with red leaved trees was met with dismay by the team. Nor was the proposed double row of trees along the ring road ever planted. Such a tree bordered 'lane' would have become a unifying intermediary.

Although individual team members designed the actual buildings, the village as such falls short of what it could have become. Beyond the basic concept it is still far too random. Now that Nagele is listed – what irony – whatever is built there must be 'modern' and have a flat roof which I, of course (the only member of the team still around) have always opposed on the grounds that an inaccessible flat roof in Holland is simply a bad one. As to the housing, no attempt was made to transcend the habitual suburban types, as though Nagele was not to become a rural place for rural people.

85

Three Primary Schools at Nagele, Noordoostpolder, 1954-6

with H.P.D. van Ginkel

In the plan, the three schools, a Protestant-Christian, a Roman Catholic and a larger state school (pictured here) were located (originally) along one single school street.

There are rooms for the 'lessons', and a stone area for the 'play area', a room for teaching resources and one for the head – sun and light have not been forgotten! What is more, there is a view of the toilets from each teacher's desk in every classroom, through an extra display case for creative work built into the wall!

The schools were built, and even satisfy the demands of education! However, for us, who are very much concerned with the children, but little with that sort of 'education', they are there for the introduced contraband, for precisely what slipped through the index finger there, but since the appearance of the 'new perceptions' has become a precept.

The corridor between the classroom and the entrance has become more than just a space to move about in, it is also an intermediate area, which is extended as a cloakroom and entrance to the classrooms in the high volumes of these rooms.

The classrooms, which according to regulations must not have doors to the outside, are surreptitiously given windows that are doors nevertheless! The large concrete windows extend the peripherally enclosing effect of the walls. In addition to this an extra corner for the imagination has been added to each classroom.

86

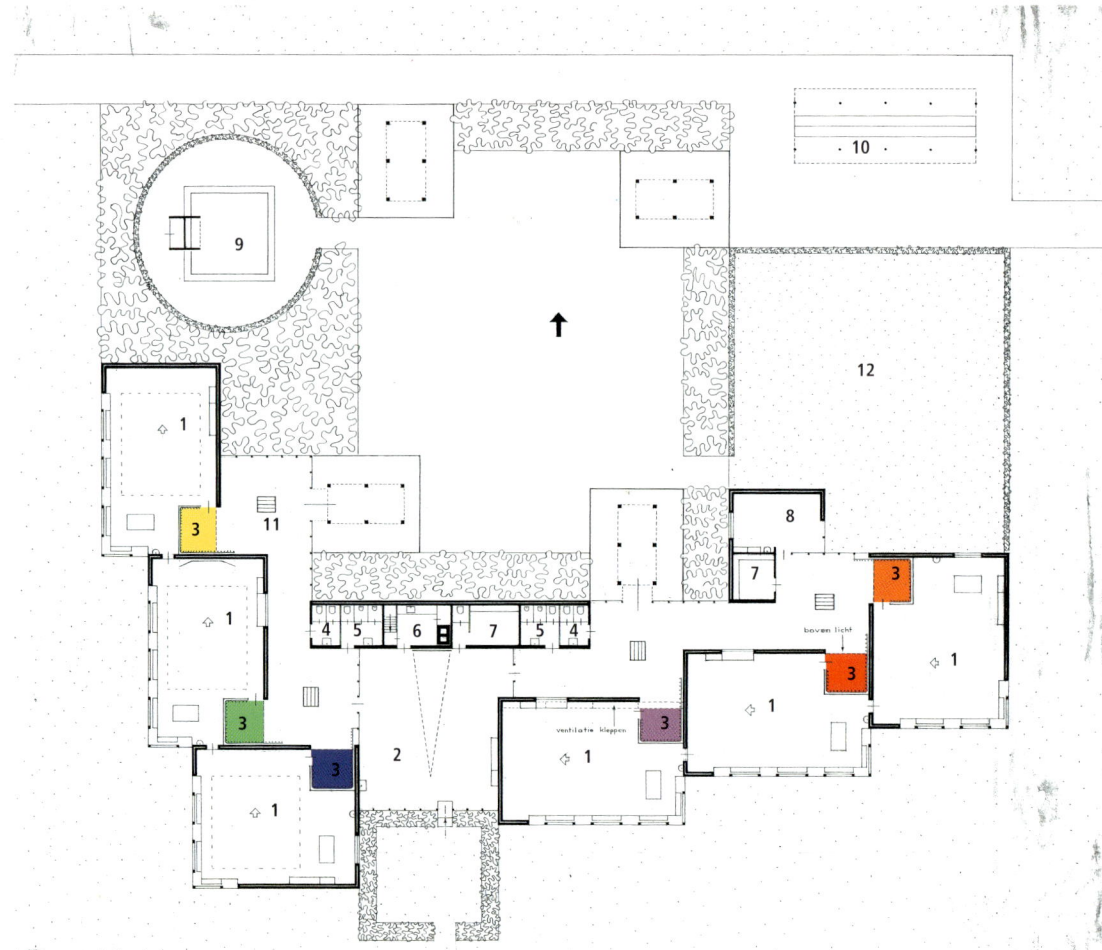

1 class-room with corner for study	5 boys' toilet	9 sandpit with storage
2 play-room	6 kitchen	10 bicycles
3 wardrobe with toplight	7 educational appliances	11 benches
4 girls' toilet	8 head	12 school-gardens

The original idea was for four rather than two of these entrance porches. In this way, the playground would, with an entrance in each corner, have become a clearly defined exterior space with the actual school entrances at the heart of the whole area. Those that were built were financed by the architects.

Each of the six high entrance fronts to the classrooms was painted in one of the six colours of the spectrum and in the order of the spectrum: red/orange/yellow/green/blue/violet.

Windows that are in fact doors on the sly!

The schools have been badly maintained and altered and are now as unsightly as the rest.

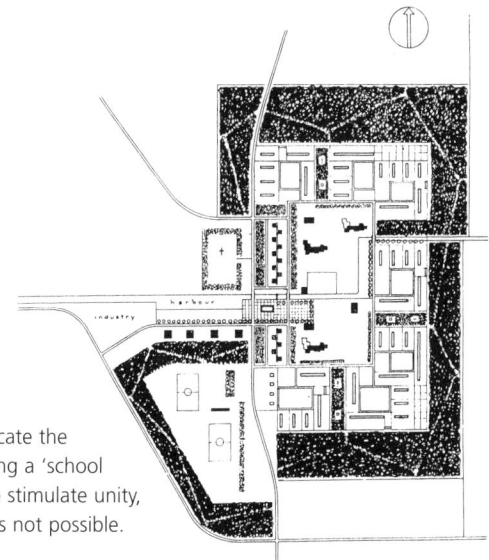
We wanted to locate the three schools along a 'school street' in order to stimulate unity, but even that was not possible.

Orphanage, Amstelveenseweg, Amsterdam, 1955-60

The Medicine of Reciprocity Tentatively Illustrated

This building is a house, a particular house, as all houses should be, within the framework of a certain generality. Peopled, it provides a home for approx. 125 children of all ages, between a few months and 20 years, who have no other home, i.e. nobody willing or able to take care of them properly. Poverty, illness, imprisonment, death of parents or foster parents, neglect and irresponsible treatment are the most frequent causes for a child's stay. This is therefore a house for the unprotected child, and has a short and a long term function: as a home for those temporarily unprotected – often for only a few weeks – as well as for those who would otherwise be permanently unprotected and are often in a sorry state, requiring a lot of care. Still, the children are not cut off from society: they go to the same kindergartens and schools in the city as other children do, have the same jobs, follow the same courses, or go to the same clubs. There are between 30 and 40 on the staff; 12 live on the premises. Since the plan of the house derives from, and sustains, a particular daily life pattern evolved for its inmates, it follows that its flexibility or adaptability, whilst permitting development of this pattern, cannot adequately sustain a daily life pattern or group structure that varies fundamentally from the one the house is based on. Extreme flexibility of this kind would have led to false neutrality, like a glove that suits no hand because it fits all. This is a worrying reality that many flexophiles will prefer to disagree with! But a troublesome one none the less. The plan attempts to reconcile the positive qualities of a centralized scheme with those of a decentralized one, while avoiding the obvious pitfalls that cling to both: the concentrated institutional building that says: 'get into my bulk up those steps and through that big door there', with children heaped up close around a well-oiled service machinery, as opposed to the loosely knit additive sprawl of the false alternative to which contemporary planning still sentimentally adheres (a number of small scale units for individual groups strung along traffic spaces of an even smaller scale, connecting them with some marked larger-scale communal elements). The plan attempts to provide a built framework – to set the stage – for the dual phenomenon* of the individual and the collective without resorting to arbitrary accentuation of either one at the expense of the other, i.e. without warping the meaning of either, since no basic twin phenomenon can be split into incompatible polarities without the halves forfeiting whatever they stand for. This indicated the necessity of reconciling the idea of unity with the idea of diversity in architectural terms or, more precisely, of achieving the one by means of the other. As work progressed, what took shape began to verify the old forgotten truth: that diversity is only attainable through unity; unity through diversity. There are, of course, many ways of approaching this objective. The one chosen here was, first, to allow the various units to

* To avoid any suggestion of dualism, twin phenomenon was subsequently used instead of dual phenomenon.

form a dispersed complex pattern. Then, to draw them together again by imposing a single structural and constructional idiom throughout and introducing a device with an unquestionable human content – the internal street. Although all the spaces, irrespective of their function and span, were subjected to a single principle, their place, sequence and subtreatment; their relation to each other, the whole and the site-content, give each the specific meaning it demands within the total context, the general pattern of the plan and the constructional idiom. I hope that in its final form the architectural reciprocity of unity-diversity and part-whole (closely linked twin phenomena) will to some extent cover the reciprocity of individual-collective. There are two more twin phenomena closely linked to those just mentioned which still elude adequate translation into planning – a twin set: large-small and many-few. The irreconcilable polarities – false alternatives – into which they are split cut no less brutally across the gaunt panorama of urbanism today. Failure to deal with multiplicity creatively and to humanize number by means of articulation and configuration has come to be the curse of most new towns. The mere fact that habitat planning is arbitrarily split into two disciplines – architecture and urbanism – demonstrates that the principle of reciprocity has not yet opened up the still deterministic mind to the necessity of transforming the mechanism of the design process. As it is, architecture and urbanism have failed to come to terms with the essence of contemporary thinking. Inseparably linked as all basic twin phenomena are, a few were extracted from the rest and split apart: those already mentioned (part-whole, unity-diversity, large-small, many-few) as well as others equally significant (inside-outside, open-closed, mass-space, change-constancy, motion-rest, individual-collective, etc.). Disregarding the inherent ambivalence in each one of them, the conflicting halves were twisted into meaningless absolutes ending up... as a 'new town'.

The time has come to conceive of architecture urbanistically and of urbanism architecturally (this makes sensible nonsense of both terms), i.e. to arrive at the singular through plurality, and vice versa. As for this home for children, the idea was to persuade it to become both 'house' and 'city'; a city-like house, and a house-like city. I came to the conclusion that *whatever space and time mean, place and occasion mean more, for space in the image of man is place, and time in the image of man is occasion.* Split apart by the schizophrenic mechanism of deterministic thinking, time and space remain frozen abstractions. Place and occasion constitute each other's realization in human terms. Since man is both the subject and object of architecture, it follows that its primary job is to provide the former for the sake of the latter. Furthermore, since place and occasion imply participation in what exists, lack of place – and thus of occasion – will cause loss of identity, isolation and frustration. A house should therefore be a cluster of places, and the same applies no less to a city. Make a configuration of places at each stage of multiplication, i.e. provide the right kind of places at each configurative stage, and urban environment will again become liveable. Cities should become the counterform to man's reciprocally individual and collective reality. It is because

we have lost touch with this reality – the form – that we cannot come to grips with its counterform. Still, it is better to acknowledge the sameness of architecture and urbanism – of house and city – than to continue defining their arbitrary difference, since this leads us nowhere – i.e. to the new town of today! Whilst constituent contemporary art, science and philosophy etc. have joined hands wonderfully for half a century, reconciling split polarities through reciprocal thinking – tearing down the stifling barriers between them – architecture, and urbanism especially, has drifted away, indulging paradoxically in the arbitrary application of what, after all, is essentially based on relativity and is thus misunderstood. In the light of what the other creative fields have managed to evolve – a relaxed relative concept of reality – what architects and urbanists have failed to do amounts to treason. All the more so since what is done is done and cannot be torn down again (nobody is forced to look at a bad painting, read a bad poem, or listen to bad music).

To return to this house and how it was saved from becoming a bad house. It seemed best to anchor the children's large house – little city – to the street, i.e. to the public sphere, there where they enter and leave it, by introducing a large open square as a transition between the reality outside and that inside. It is an in-between domain leading the trail gradually, in stages, helping to mitigate the anxiety that abrupt transition causes, especially in these children. Leaving home and going home are often difficult matters; to go in or out, to enter, leave or stay, are sometimes painful alternatives. Though architecture cannot do away with this truth it can still counteract it by mitigating instead of aggravating its effects. It is human to tarry. Architecture should, I think, take more account of this. The job of the planner is to provide a built homecoming for all, to sustain a feeling of belonging – hence, to evolve an architecture of place – a setting for each subsequent occasion, determined or spontaneous. There are eight departments, each marked by one of the large cupolas in which the children live in age groups – children leave and new ones arrive too often to allow all ages to be combined within one group. Yet this grouping is by no means a restrictive hierarchy, for all departments, service spaces and rooms for special activities give onto a larger interior street in such a way as to invite the children to mix and move from one department to another, visiting each other. This interior street is yet another intermediary – there are many more, *in fact the building was conceived as a configuration of intermediary places clearly defined*. This does not imply continual transition or endless postponement with respect to place and occasion. On the contrary, it implies breaking away from the contemporary concept (call it sickness) of spatial continuity and the tendency to erase every articulation between spaces, i.e. between outside and inside, between one space and another. Instead, I tried to articulate the transition by means of defined in-between places which induce

simultaneous awareness of what is significant on either side. An in-between place in this sense provides the common ground where conflicting polarities are reconciled and again become twin phenomena. For thirty years architecture – not to mention urbanism – has been providing an outside for man even on the inside (aggravating the conflict by attempting to eliminate the essential difference). *Architecture (sic urbanism) implies the creation of an interior, both outside and inside. For an exterior is that which precedes the man-made environment; that which is counteracted by it; that which is persuaded to become commensurate by being interiorized.* Since the interior street is an intermediary place, I wanted the child's behaviour and movement in it to remain as vigorous as they are outside. No sudden curbing of spontaneity this side of a narrow doorstep; no living-room manners here. So, the materials used in this interior street differ in no way from those used outside. Inside the child is like the child outside – the same child – with a roof over its head instead of the sky. What is more, the electric lighting is like street-lighting in the sense that the child moves from one illuminated place to the next through comparative darkness. No lux meter was allowed to prove the advantages of an even distribution of light. Darkness outside demands a reduction of the space dimension inside. Then there are the courtyards – patios; all of them different exterior rooms strung along the interior street and accessible from it as well as from the departments between which they lie. They also form intermediaries – reconciling the movement of the traffic rushing by outside to the child inside. I think it is wrong to see these as incompatible realities. All external and internal walls, as well as all the major built elements they enclose terminate at column height. The space between here and the roof is either occupied by horizontal precast reinforced concrete architraves – intermediary elements that bind and enclose, form an upward extension of the walls, a downward extension of the roof – or is filled in with glass. Sometimes it is left open. The walls envelop, interlock and open up consecutively. Within the actual departments of the groups the walls are plastered and there is more active colour (patches of red and violet here and there throughout) as well as a gamut of smaller elements built within the main structure. But the architraves and cupolas continue. In the interior street, the walls are like those outside – rough, brown and powerful, like a outside of a coconut; whilst in the departments they are white, smooth and softer, like the milky inside of the same coconut. Two kinds of protection: a winter coat with a soft silky lining on the inside close to the body, heavy rough tweed on the outside where it touches the world – the elements and other people. Since concrete, brick and white surfaces do not sparkle – and something always should – there are, here and there, tiny mirrors embedded in concrete slabs and some large ones in the street floor that distort. All of them jewels, and cheap at that.

THE MEDICINE OF RECIPROCITY TENTATIVELY ILLUSTRATED

90

Open space requirements pointed towards a site just outside the city's abrupt S.W. periphery. The orphanage lies a
few hundred yards south of an enormous stadium along
the highway from Amsterdam to the national airport at
Schiphol and the city's only real recreation area a mile to
the south. The content of the site is simple and emphatic;
exciting in that it includes many of the great motions that
belong to the metropolis of today. Places near and far are
present here, for there is always traffic moving north-
south on the main road and diagonally overhead in the
air. From time to time, thousands from all over the country
gather in the stadium for international matches. And when
the weather is good thousands more pass by on foot or on
bicycles on their way to the recreation area. Fifty thousand
packed together in a huge oval cheering, and, quite close,
lots of little domes with children underneath, protected,
chatting, laughing. People flying overhead in planes watch
both pass below – lots of domes in a multiple pattern, and
a single oval.

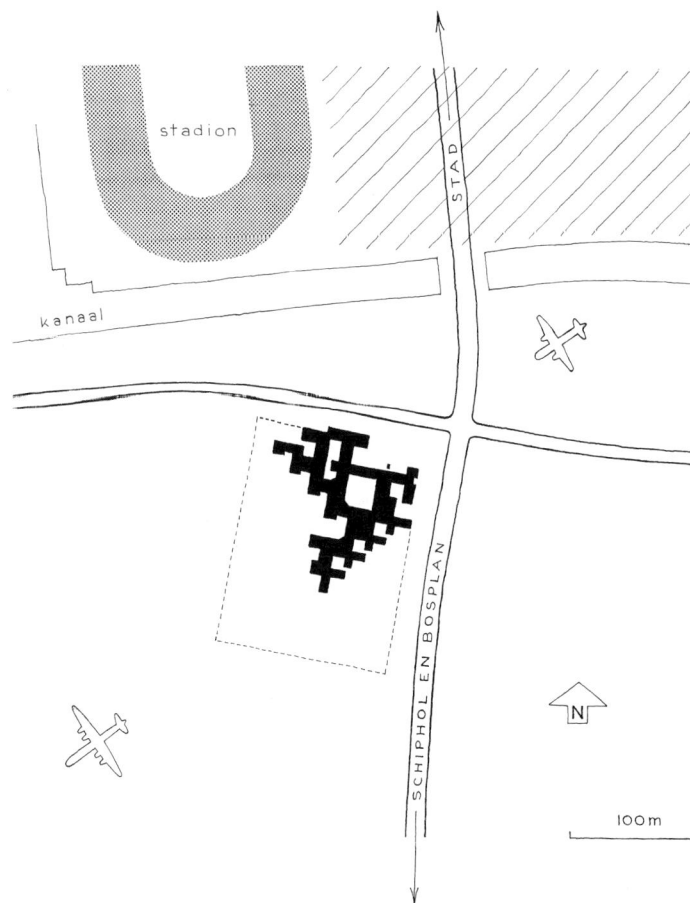

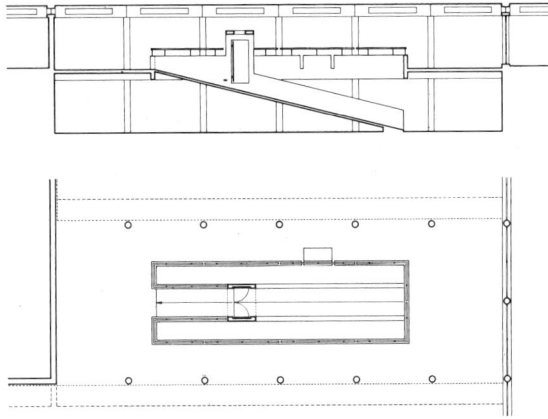

Ramp to bicycle cellar

92

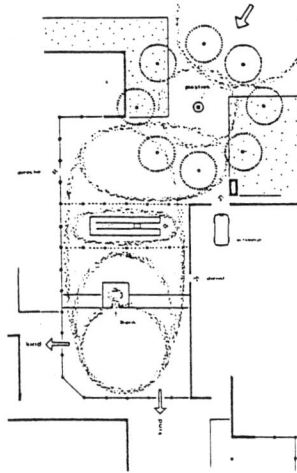

Scheme to illustrate the sequence of interlocking spaces and places between entry and exit: score for coming and going. Place for Carel Visser's sculpture.

The indoor street is alternately two steps higher or lower where it broadens into an indoor square. These minor differences in level are artificial because the site was made *completely* flat. (Even though this is neither necessary nor desirable, it is often the reality in the Netherlands). Up a bit, down a bit – a game of levels, creating a variable distance to the ceiling.

93

One of the three chamfered corners next to the detached column.

Concrete wall lighting along the entire indoor street. The lighting here was made like street lighting. The child walks from one lit area to the next, from light to shadow to light.

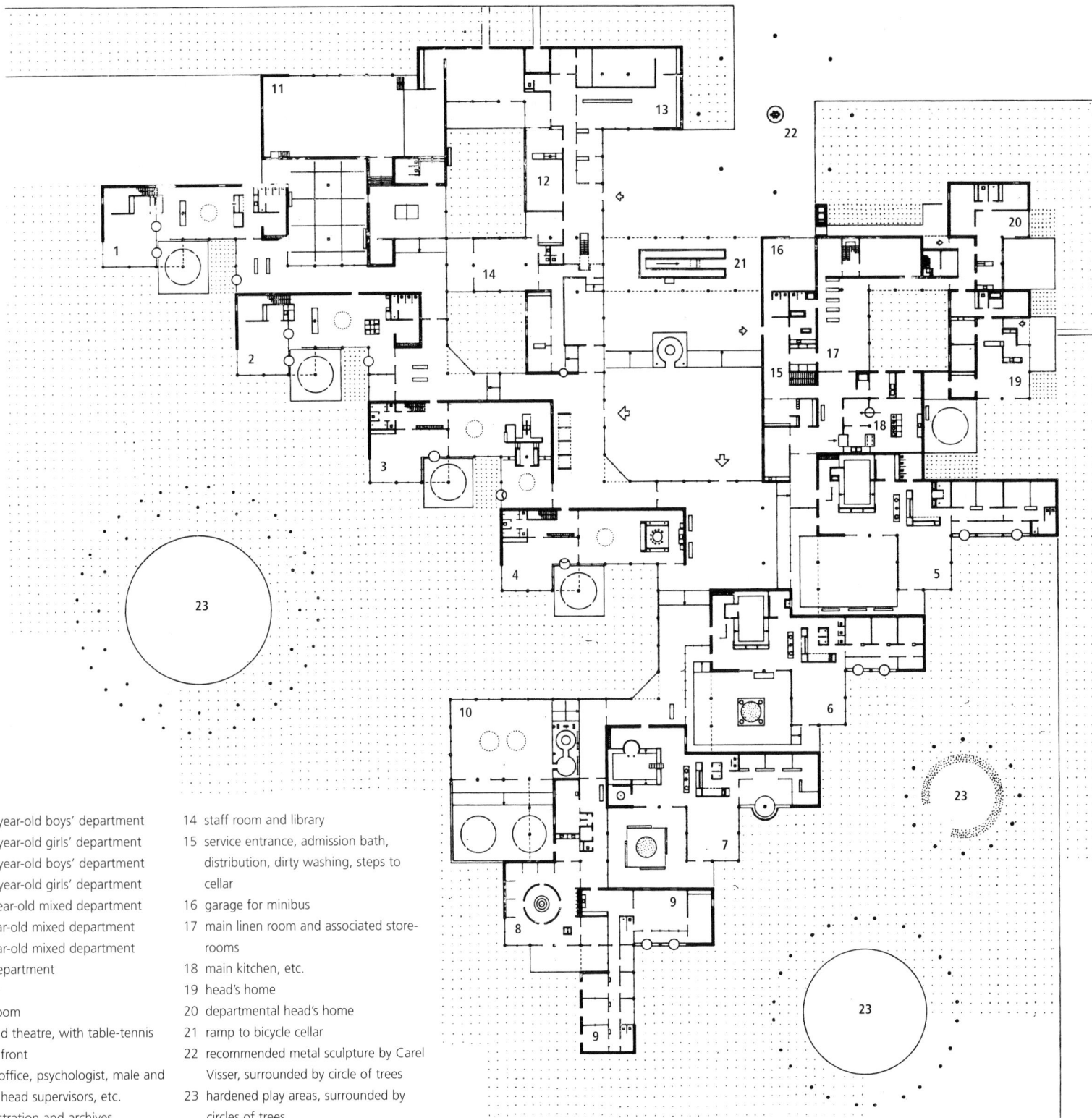

1 14–20-year-old boys' department
2 14–20-year-old girls' department
3 10–14-year-old boys' department
4 10–14-year-old girls' department
5 6–10-year-old mixed department
6 4–6-year-old mixed department
7 2–4-year-old mixed department
8 baby department
9 sickbay
10 party room
11 gym and theatre, with table-tennis
   area in front
12 head's office, psychologist, male and
   female head supervisors, etc.
13 administration and archives

14 staff room and library
15 service entrance, admission bath,
   distribution, dirty washing, steps to
   cellar
16 garage for minibus
17 main linen room and associated store-
   rooms
18 main kitchen, etc.
19 head's home
20 departmental head's home
21 ramp to bicycle cellar
22 recommended metal sculpture by Carel
   Visser, surrounded by circle of trees
23 hardened play areas, surrounded by
   circles of trees

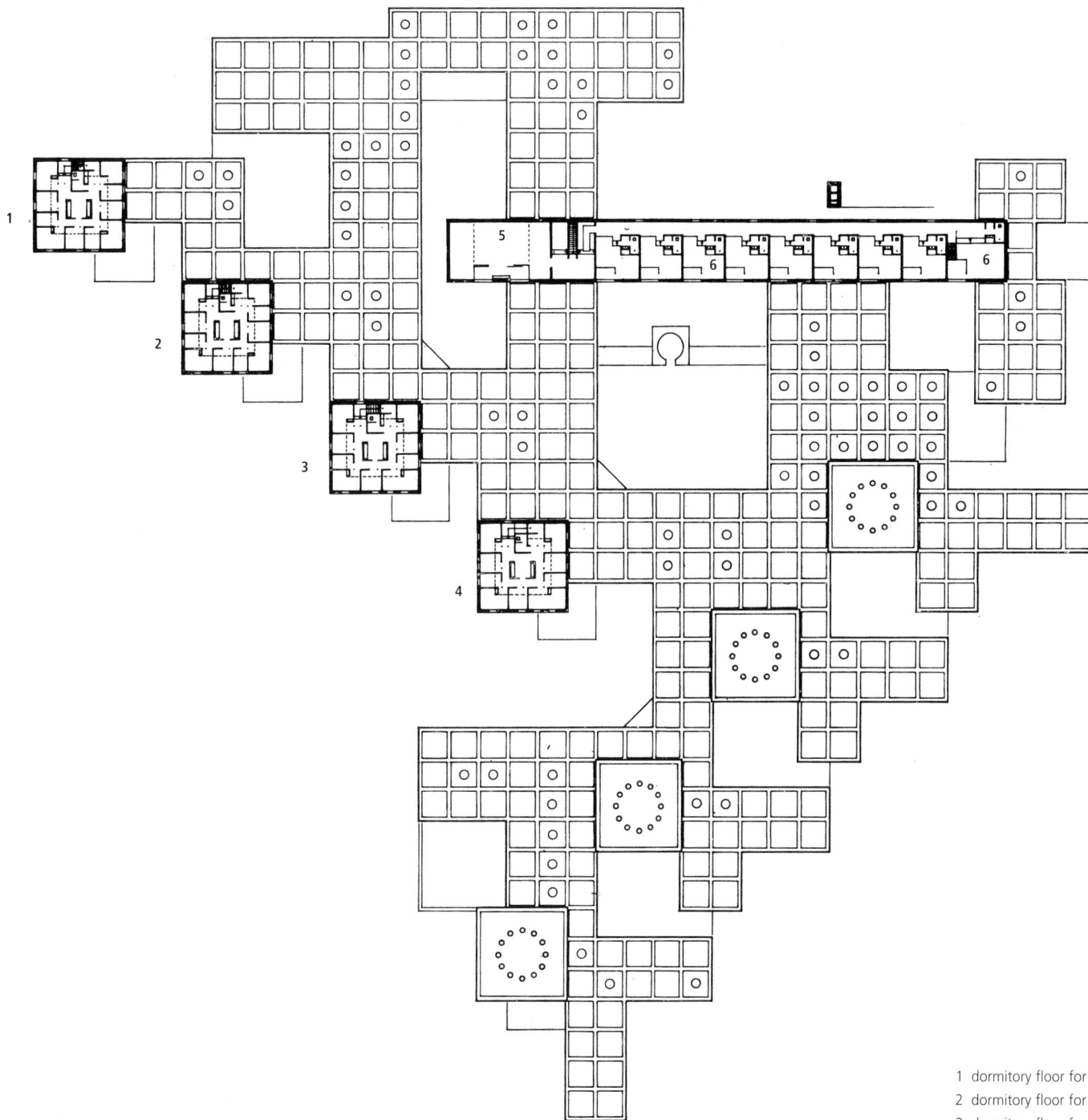

95

1 dormitory floor for 14–20-year-old boys
2 dormitory floor for 14–20-year-old girls
3 dormitory floor for 10–14-year-old boys
4 dormitory floor for 10–14-year-old girls
5 meeting room
6 homes for resident staff

The road seen from a patio

A patio seen from the road

Rietveld architect

Utrecht 27-11-'60

beste van Eyck, dank
voor de foto's, die ik hierbij terug
stuur ; van een wilde ik snel
een lantaarn plaatje laten maken
  en stuur de foto's dan direct na.
          ik moet n.l. in een
rij voordracht over de laatste 40
jaar architectuur, als laatste
wat zeggen op het kunst historisch
instituut in Utrecht.
          Ik vind de plattegrond
van j. gebouw a/d amstelv. weg
Meesterlijk. die wordt ook binnen
als buiten beleefd.
          Ik herinner me een gesprek
met Berlage tijdens de opr. vh. congres in
La Sarraz - hij zei : jij maakt kapot wat ik
opbouw. (hij deed ook niet mee met ons)
     Ik heb de neiging om te zeggen tegen jou :
Jij bouwt op wat ik kapot maakte, zo
Berlagiaans doet me de zware balkons aan
en de beton balcies. Ik hoop, dat je enthousiasme
het verburgerlijken van het z.g. functionalisme
zal tegenhouden.
     hartelijke groet van Rietveld

Oudegracht 55, Utrecht · Tel. 17038 · Giro 164496

Small circular dips become reflecting pools after every shower

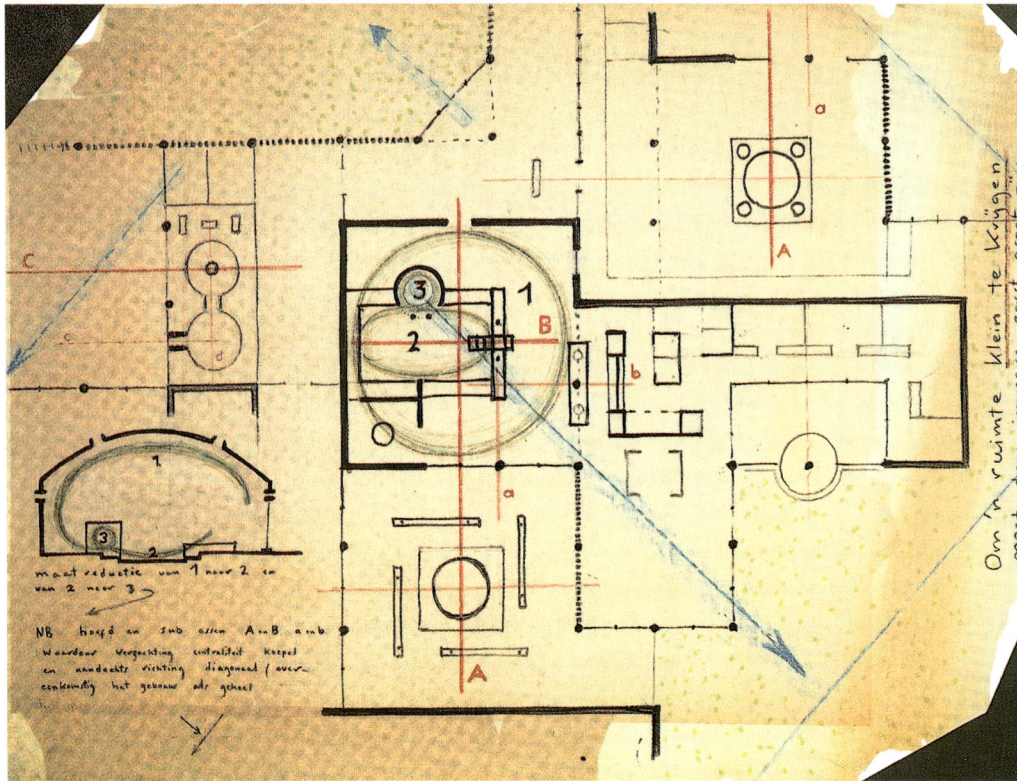

shifted centre – shifted symmetry – diagonal attention – twofold dimensional reduction

A few remarks about the playing spaces for infants of which this is one. So as to mitigate the cupola's emphatic central point and the quite considerable dimensions of the space, a sunken floor with steps and seats all round, as well as a tiny circular 'house' are given a double eccentric shift, providing a twofold dimensional reduction. The dimensions are still big, but no longer only big; the space still central, but not only central. Besides the main axes A and B, note the shifted sub-axes a and b (one through the middle of the open kitchen – composed symmetrically as a family of associated forms – and the other through the middle of the door opening onto the play-court).

The result of all this is that visual attention is drawn diagonally outwards from the depth of the interior towards the garden beyond, with the little house as pivot.

Ordinary building material does not glitter, so here there are small mirrors.

Boiling kettle

well protected

100

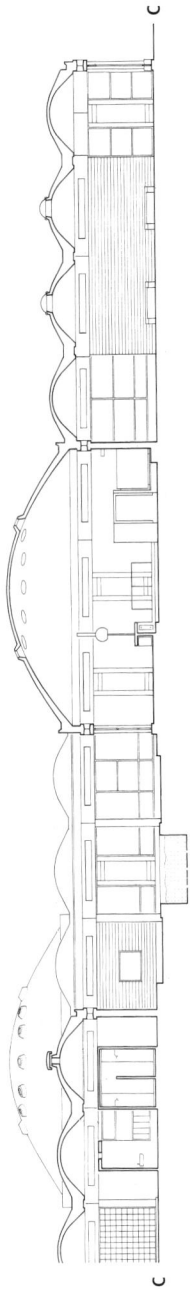

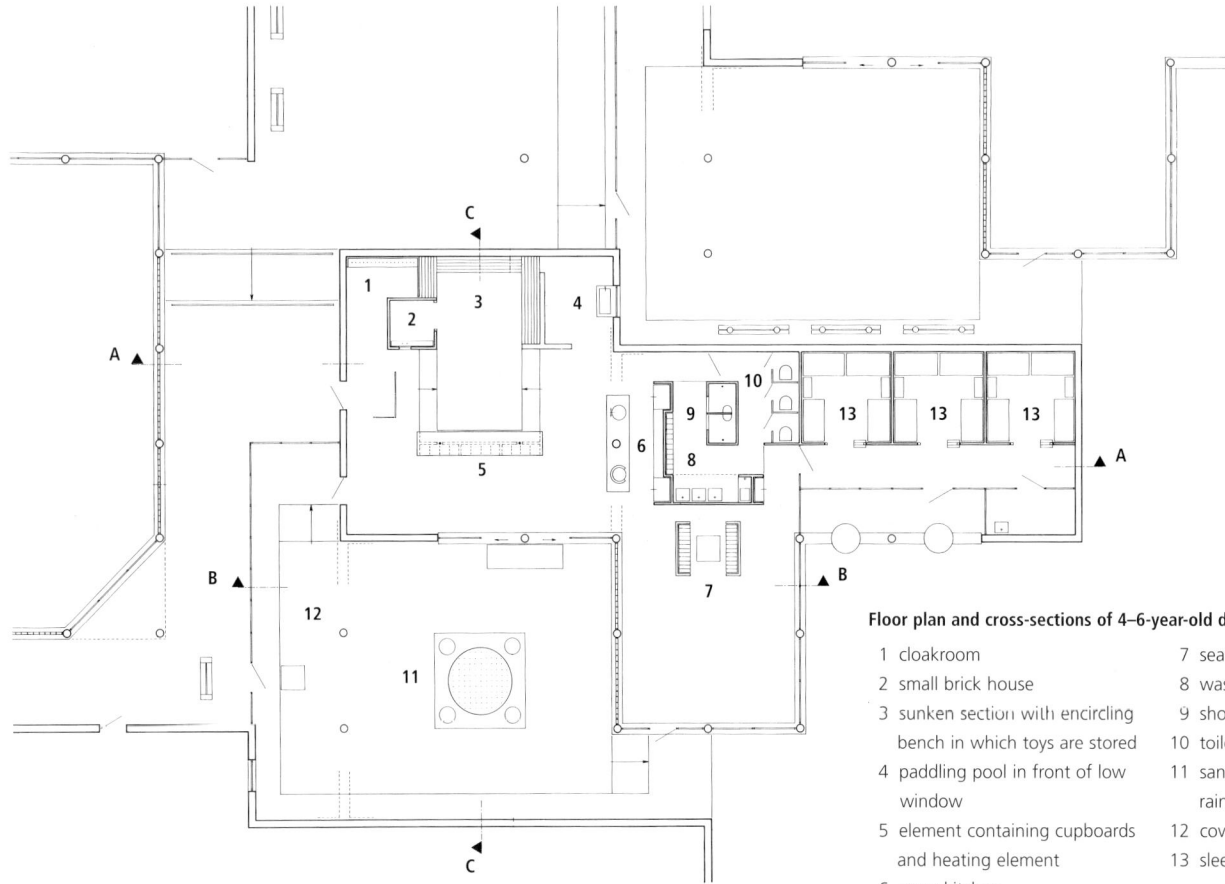

Floor plan and cross-sections of 4–6-year-old department

1 cloakroom
2 small brick house
3 sunken section with encircling bench in which toys are stored
4 paddling pool in front of low window
5 element containing cupboards and heating element
6 open kitchen
7 seat
8 washing room
9 showers
10 toilets
11 sandpit with hollows for rainwater
12 covered playroom
13 sleeping compartments

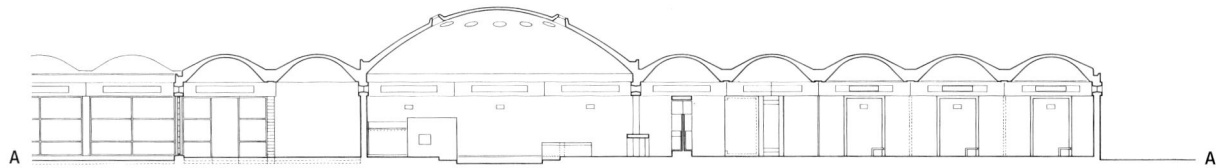

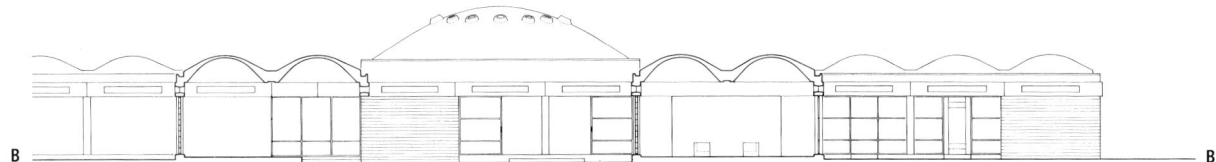

Antique tiles from the

country of St Nicholas

101

Violet for all niches throughout the building

Red inside for the

miniature houses

right size   right-size   rightsize

The birth of a new word!

Play-pool alias seat

Pink glass in the grooves

Party room

Children's gateway in light pink glass

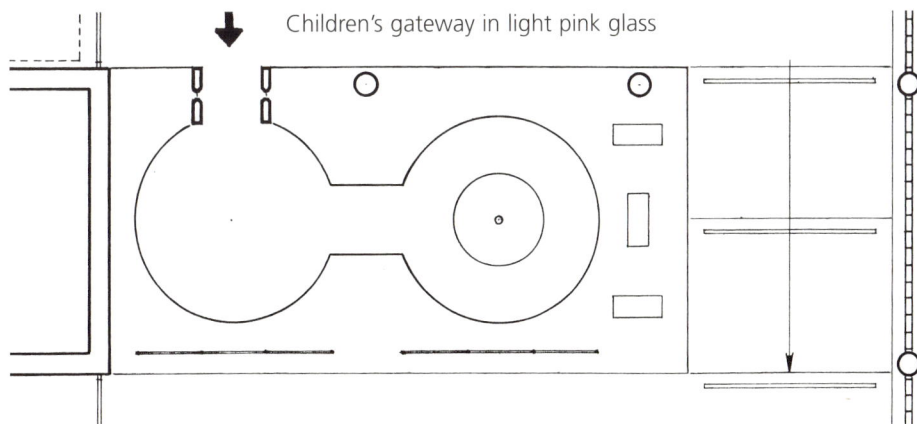

The children very
much appreciated
the distorting mirrors
– they saw all sorts
of things in them –
which is why they
were removed!

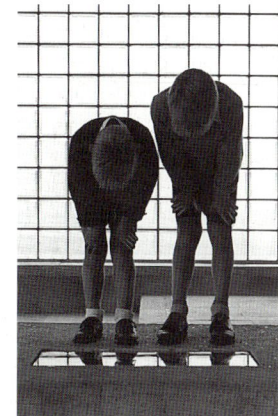

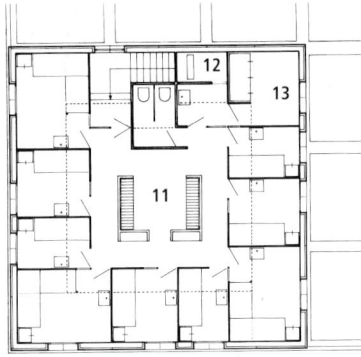

1 living room
2 tea-kitchen
3 study
4 reading corner
5 cupboard
6 wardrobe
7 toilet
8 shower
9 steel ring with lamps
10 double bench
11 bench
12 bathroom
13 linen-room

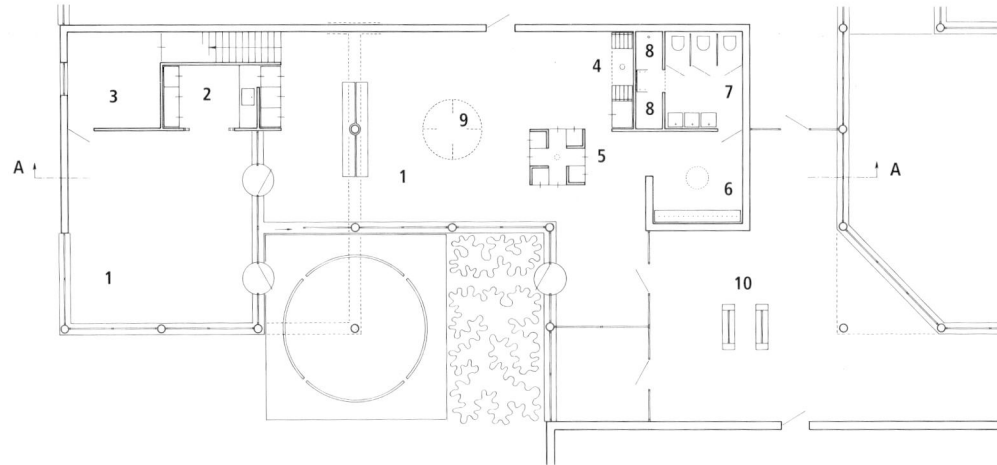

One of the 14–20-year-old departments

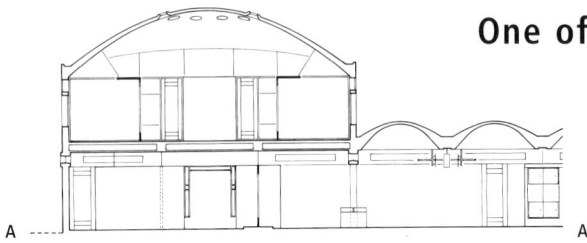

106

In the 10–14-year-old departments

Puppet show for the boys, who invite the girls

1 reading corner
2 puppet theatre
3 scullery

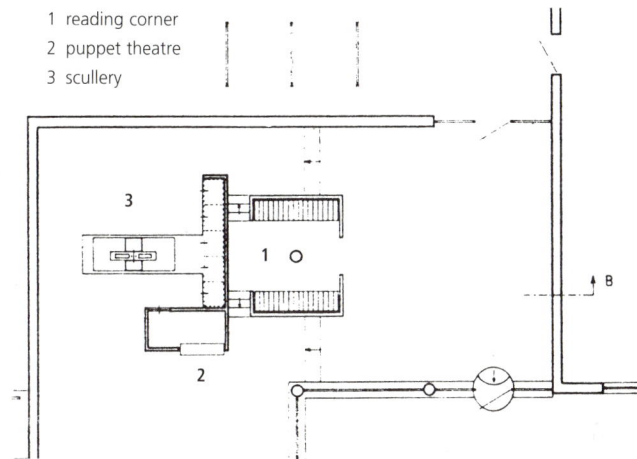

Cooking for the girls, who invite the boys

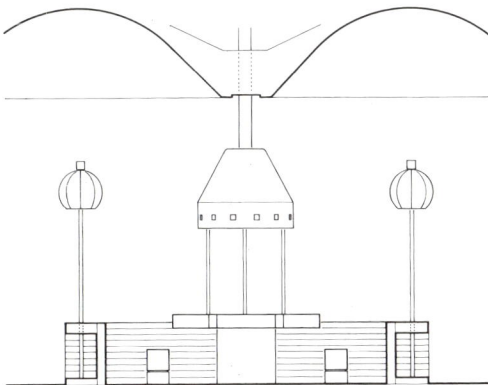

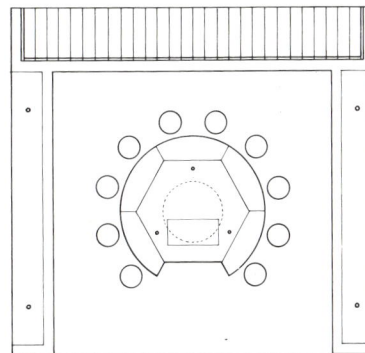

The same 'order' prevails throughout both for the main and connecting spaces. Where there is an upper floor the diameter of the columns is not increased – only the reinforcement – so as not to disturb the order's lateral continuity (stressing muscular effort is offensive – also in architecture!).

108

Uno degli palazzi per bambini – I wanted them to look the way it sounds.

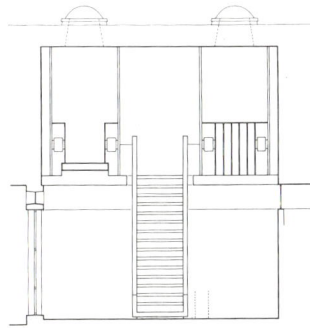

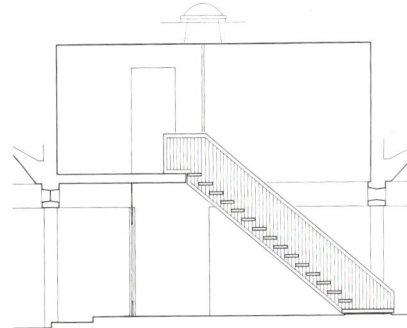

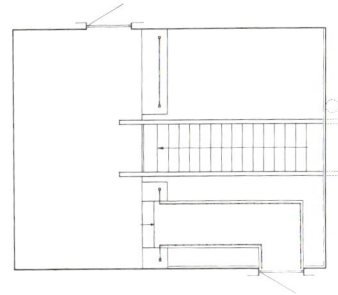

Staircase to staff-flats and meeting room
Extended banisters at the bottom and top of the stairs

Staff flat, window with loggia

Open-Air School, Amsterdam, 1955

Imagine a six classroom school with each classroom space a different shape, different height, different orientation – not just 'different' but essentially so! There are of course so many solutions that I never got down to actually drawing one! The idea was there but it never took shape – perhaps because there would have been so many to think of, all the different kinds of differences, since six classrooms or six dissimilar ones (6 times dissimilar) make a world of difference. I leave it to others now, just say to yourself: all of them different would make all the difference.

Use of hexagon for flowing continuity. Acute angles were avoided.

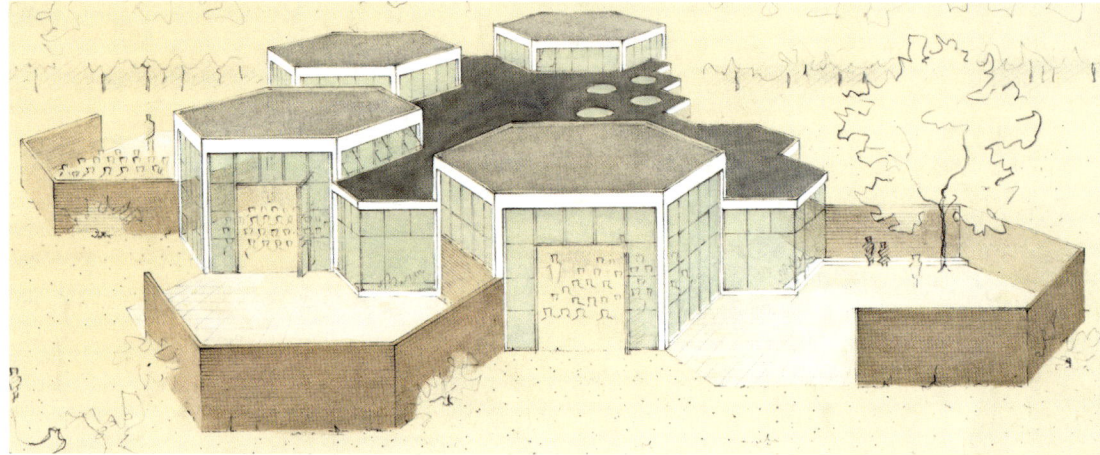

Pavilions

1 indoor classroom with lower part	6 gate
2 outside classroom	7 playground
3 cloakroom	8 grounds
4 wash and toilet area	9 gardening tools
5 entrance	10 teaching material

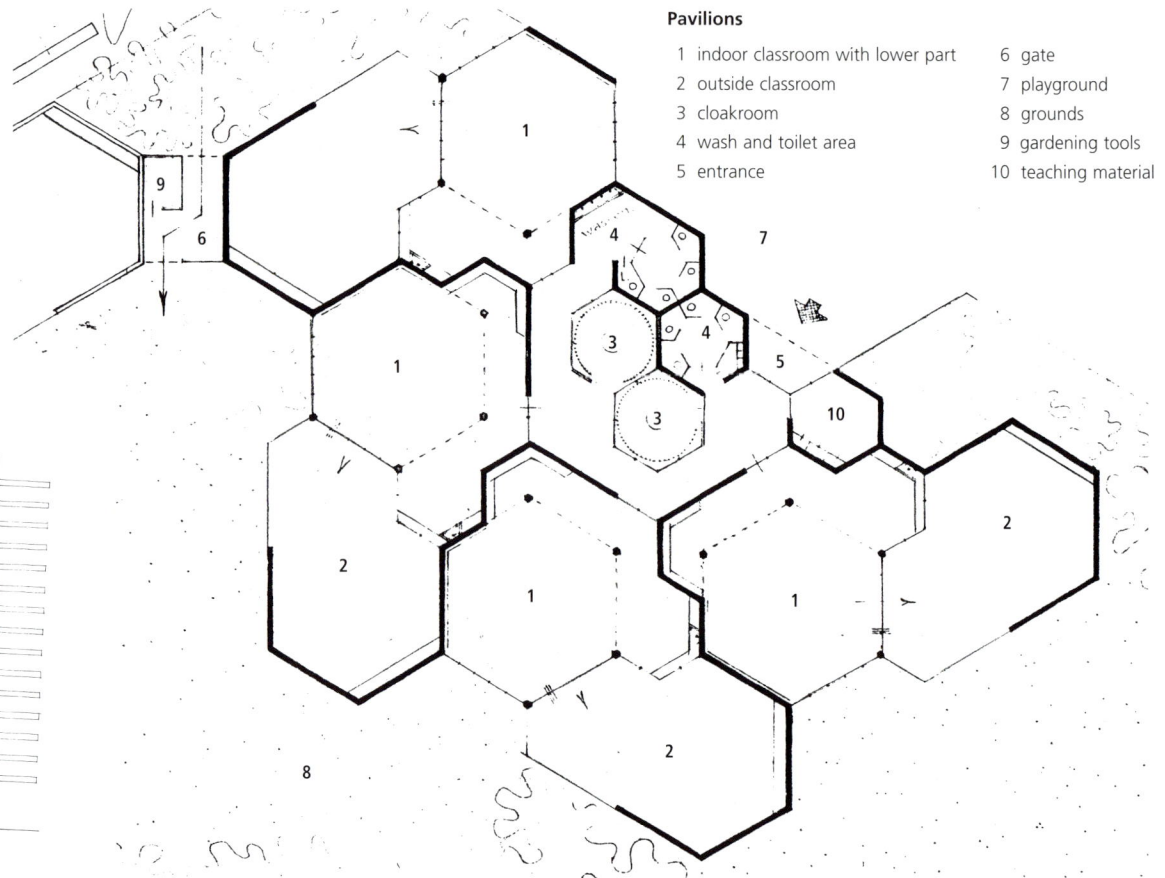

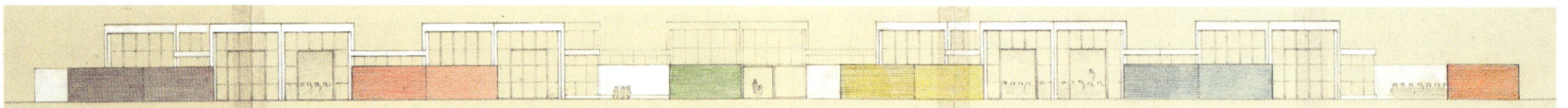

Site plan

1 pavilion with 4 classrooms	5 schoolpath
2 pavilion with 6 classrooms	6 bicycle shed
3 main building with gym and playroom	7 caretaker's home
4 playground	8 grounds

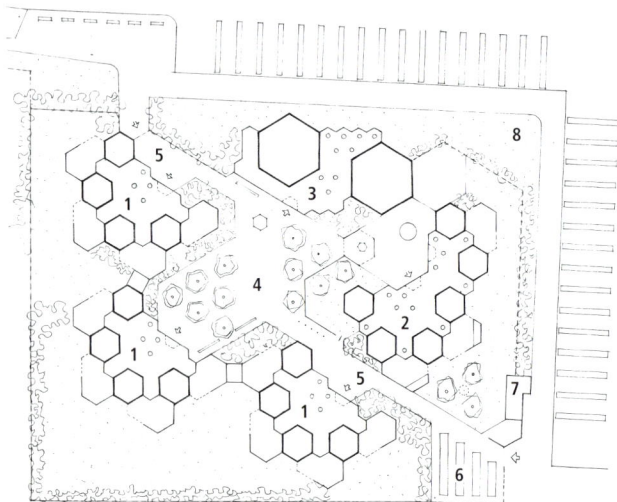

The Four Tower House, Baambrugge, 1958

It would, I'm sure, have looked the way it was made and worked the way it looked! A singular rectangular volume with four covered exterior spaces contained within its perimeter and in each corner a miniature unit – one for each family member. All four are accessible from the inside via a two-storey tower leading from the central space, as well as directly from the outside, unnoticed, so each can come and go freely.

Looking outwards in whatever direction, part of the house is always incorporated in the view; and, after sunset, light may be on in the room opposite, a sign that somebody is there – city-like. To be able to say this is where we live – *but over there too*, calls for interiorization of the exterior; drawing into the house what belongs to it outside. Enclosure through transparency – no paradox – is extended outwards but the house remains a contained – introvert – place.

Each of the towers has a window looking inwards so, with lights on, the living room will never be completely dark.

A light steel framework with a glass brick screen on all four sides – two inside and two outside – and lamps between them – passes right across the house 'through' sliding doors from loggia to loggia, articulating it in depth 5 times. The wooden cylinder on the roof – reached by a ladder up the chimney – conceals a sunbath. We – the whole family – virtually lived in it, but build it we never did.

It was a theory extracted from experience, one which I hope was subsequently brought to life, if only partially, in other works.

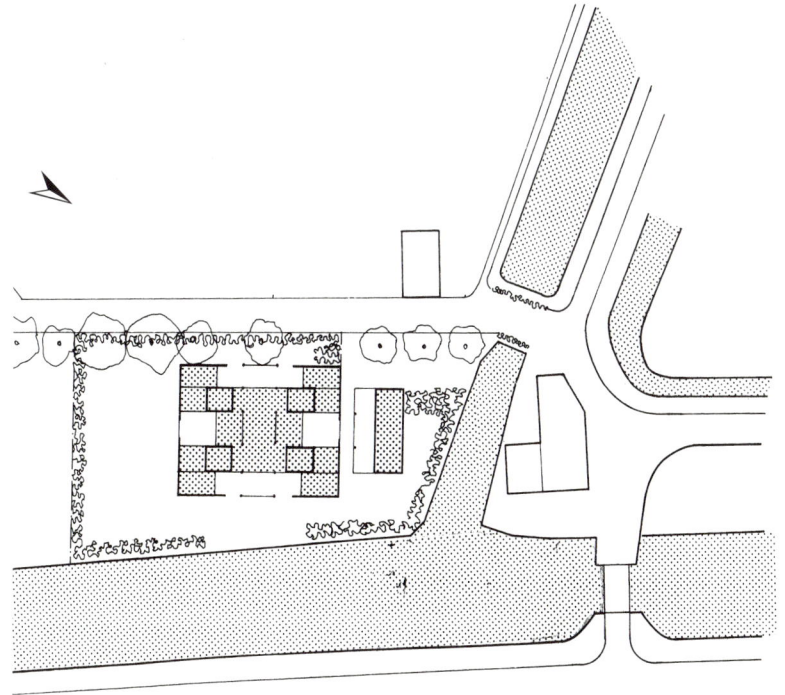

Preliminary study

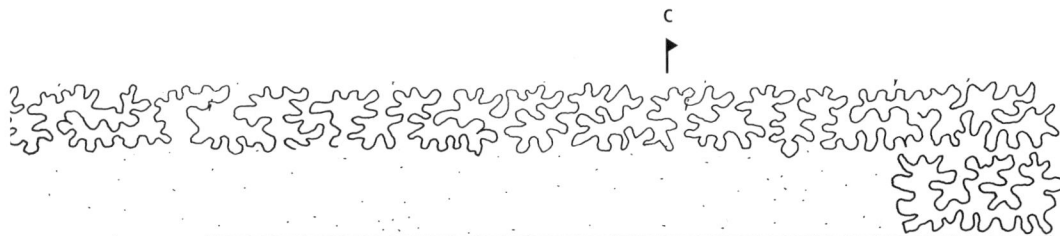

1 hall, cloakroom
2 living room – dining room
3 kitchen
4 music room
5 bedroom
6 study
7 children's restroom
8 shower

9 laundry
10 garage
11 central heating
12 bicycles, tools etc.
13 covered outdoor space
14 bedroom loft
15 screen for sunbathing

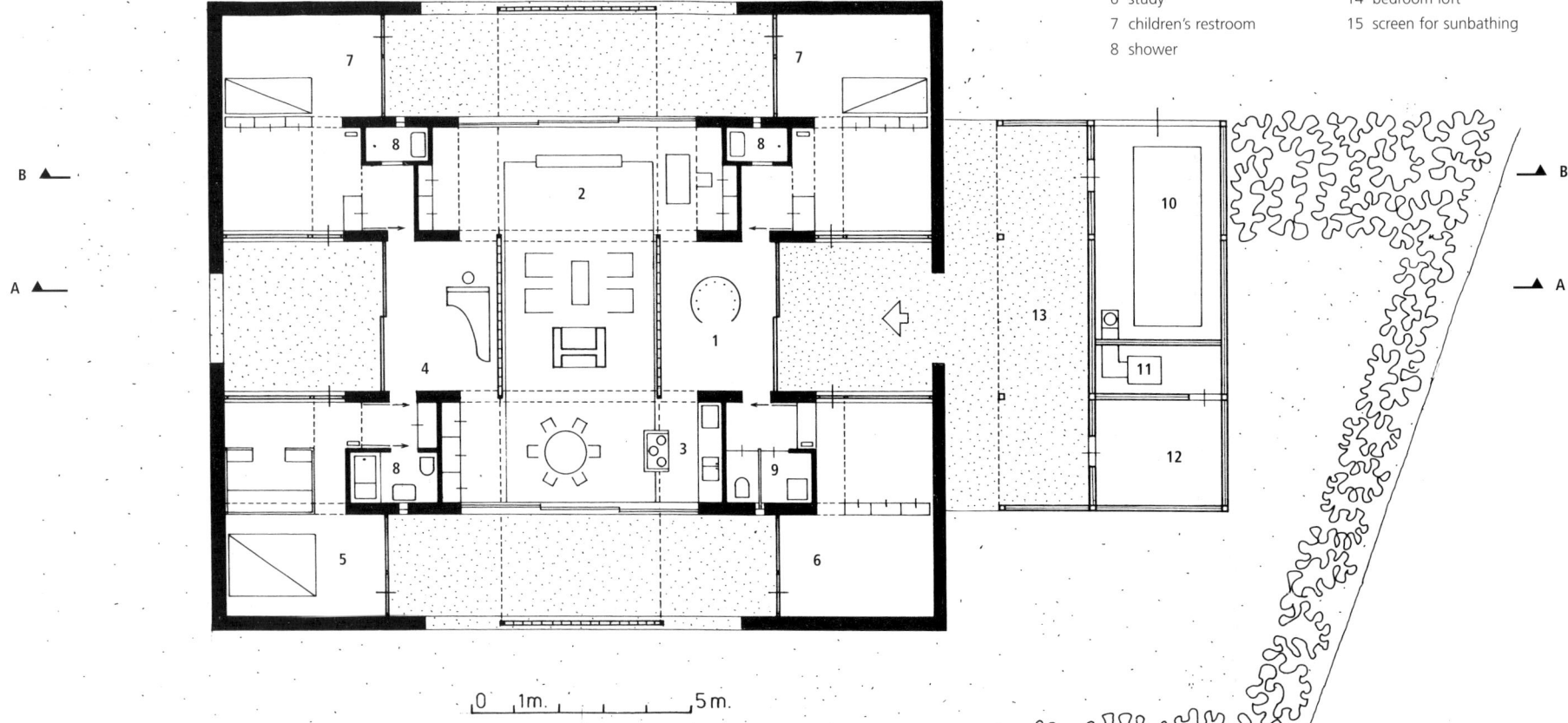

0   1m.   5m.

112

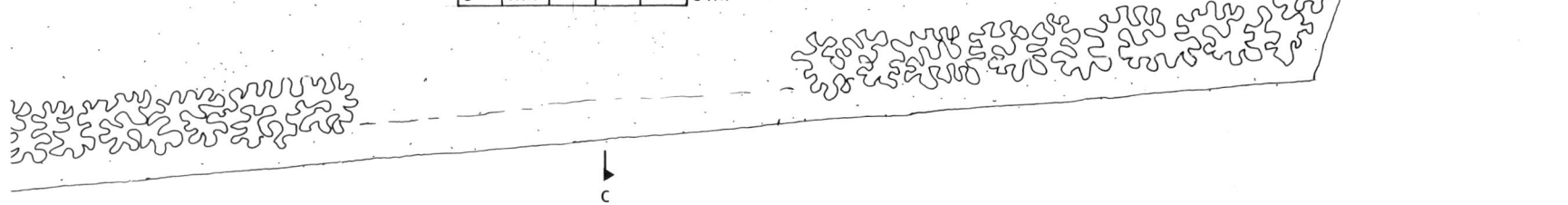

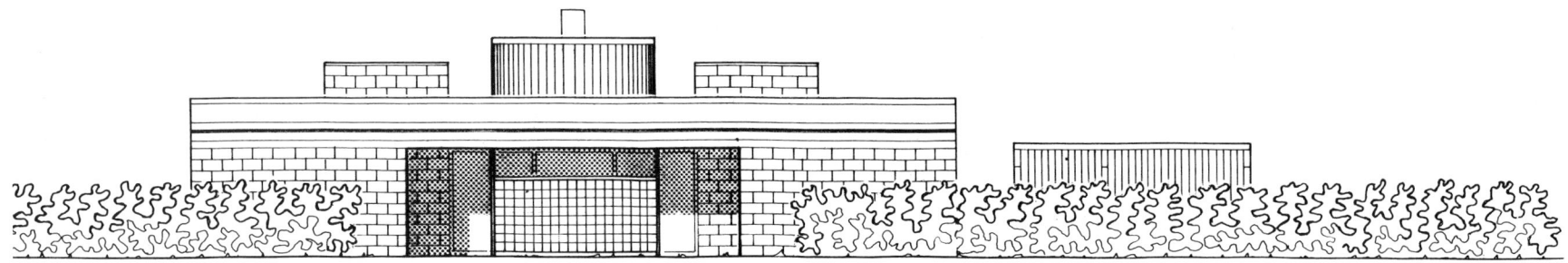

Section A–A

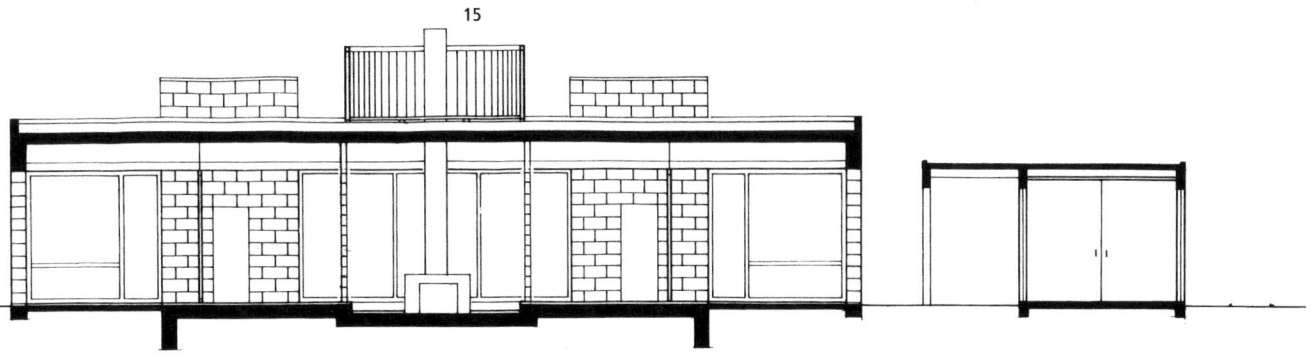

15

Section B–B

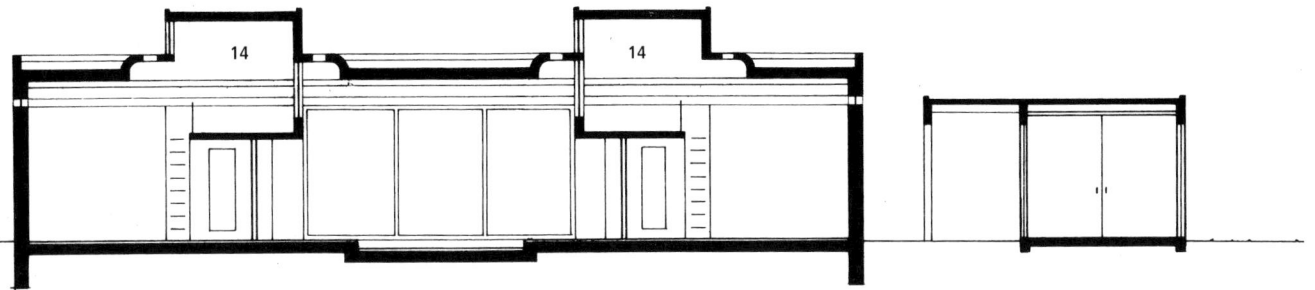

14   14

113

240 +

Section C–C

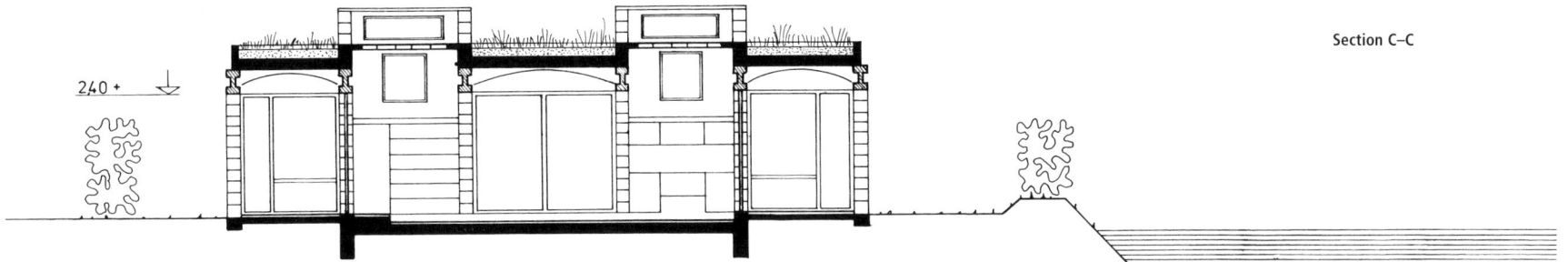

15

Southeast elevation

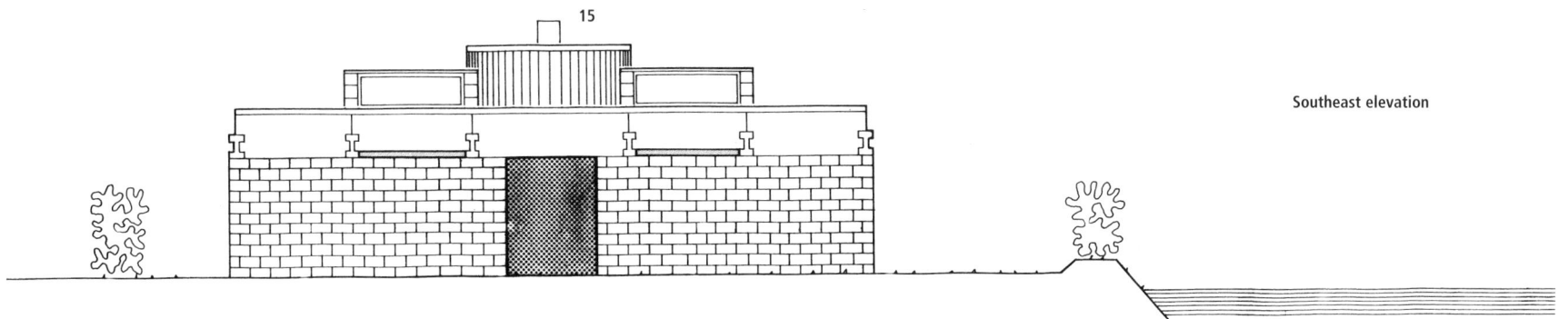

Congress Building, Jerusalem, 1958

In the Congress Building for Jerusalem I ran up against many of the same problems as in the Orphanage, though I reversed the point of departure for reasons relevant to the building's purpose. In the children's home a multiplicity of elements forming a very irregular and dispersed pattern was transformed to become a single thing. In the Congress Building, a single thing (I refer to the academy part), forming a very regular concentrated pattern, was transformed to become a multiplicity of things. On the one hand the singular embraced the plural; on the other the plural contained the singular. The one expands and then contracts, the other contracts and then expands (you can start the breathing both ways; you simply choose to effect the best start).

The academy consists of two separate buildings; one within the other with an ambulatory that runs all the way round between the two. Besides containing all the required interior spaces, in each one there are also exterior spaces at each corner, also square, where groups can sit outside at any time of the day, season or year. It is these that give the plan its special quality – seeing to it that the otherwise hermetical square breathes.

Walking along the ambulatory you can look – and go – outwards, inwards, and across. You can also choose a study room in the outer element that looks inwards towards the central lawn or one in the inner element that looks outwards towards the magnificent surroundings.

If you're not so reciprocally-minded you can also choose a study room in the outer element that looks outwards or one in the inner element looking inwards. There are enough rooms, so that each participant can change rooms according to mood, weather or time of day – like changing clothes to suit the occasion.

The large meeting hall is glazed on all four sides and opens onto a terrace covered by the upper floor which runs all round the hall and is partially closed by L shaped walls at the four corners. Note what you see: through the openings between the wall ends – rock, heat glare, and distant mountains; in the enclosing corners between the glass hall and the L-shaped terrace walls – perpetual shade, half light, breeze, and the hall's interior.

(from CIAM text, Otterlo 1959)

Ground floor

1 main entrance	7 library
2 main hall	8 conference-room
3 covered terrace	9 study
4 cafeteria	10 academy sitting-room
5 pantry	11 administration
6 lawn	12 editing

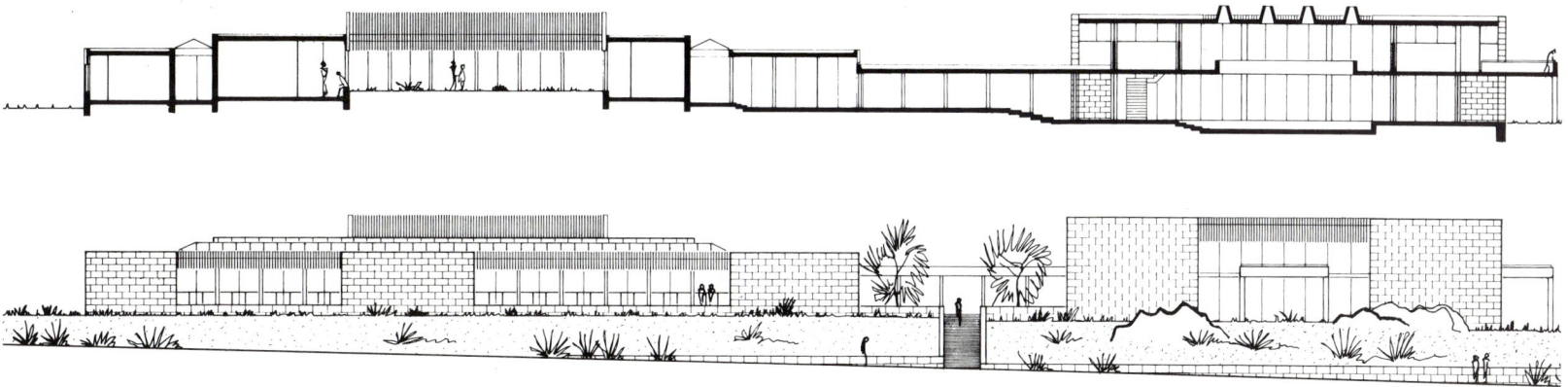

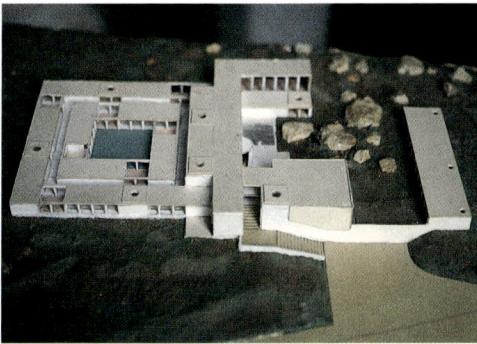

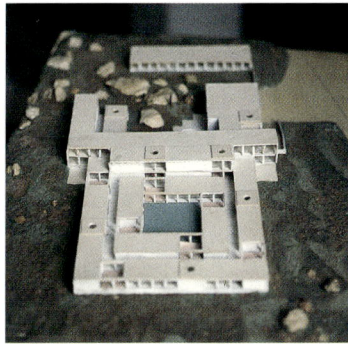

Model of preliminary design

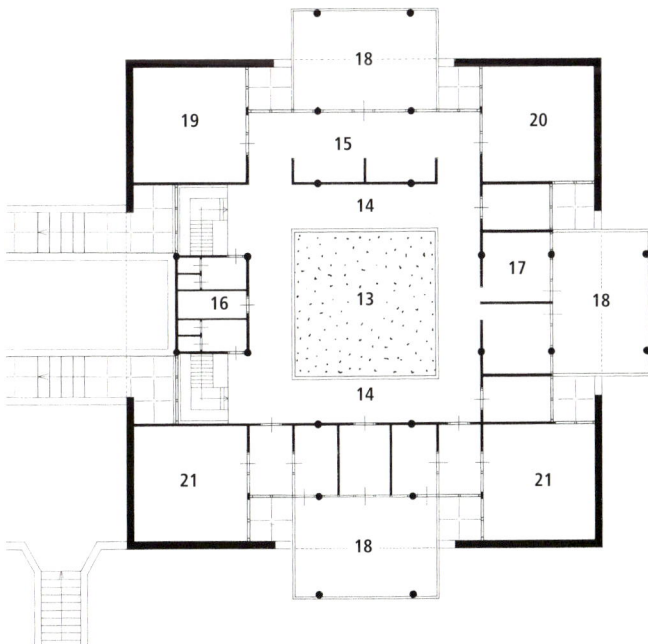

First floor

13 void main hall
14 gallery
15 lounge
16 toilets
17 study
18 covered terrace
19 club dining-room
20 library
21 meeting-room

A SQUARE···
THAT BREATHES

War Memorial in the Lower House, The Hague, 1959

What was initially required was a stand to carry what was to become a huge book with the names of civilian casualties of World War Two handwritten on each page. The stand was to be placed in the entrance lobby of the parliament building in The Hague where a page is to be turned every morning and those concerned come to pay their respects. Wishing to avoid caging all those names in an unwieldy leather-bound book, I suggested leaving them as they were: loose sheets, like wings, with a crease down the middle. This was to begin with and at any rate not a book! Instead the sheets were to be laid in a hollow of 12-14 cm deep, cut into the surface of a single piece of volcanic lava-like rock lined with pure 24 carat gold. There was to be nothing else – no intrusions, just four materials brought together: white paper, black ink and pure gold in volcanic rock. Beyond gold's worth lies its ultimate simplicity and immutability. That and the turbulent history of volcanic rock was the idea. But it was not to be, for, as in ancient Egypt, where the tombs of the pharaohs were almost immediately robbed, the possibility that the sheets bearing the cherished names could be rudely soiled whilst someone snatched the gold was real enough. And so, in order to safeguard what was intended to be an open grave – just names in a nest – a plexiglass hood was added as well as alarm gadgetry. Pollution for certain, but also purposeful. And so once again, it was brought home to me that use and misuse form an unavoidable twin reality the architect is alas destined to deal with.

116

Urban Design for Buikslotermeer, Amsterdam, 1962
with Jaap Bakema

Fragments from the Team 10 discussion with Jaap Bakema, Georges Candilis, Peter and Alison Smithson, Rotterdam, April 9th, 1974

Bakema: Aldo, I brought two things; work we did together. We did this I think, a long time ago, Stokla and me, and you said: 'It seems to me there is something missing', and you made this. Do you remember?

Van Eyck: It's very nice that Jaap brings up this thing, because I had forgotten it. We discussed the whole evolution of this idea of Jaap's quite often. He was actually providing the ingredients of the housing types and I started to spend weeks getting around it. I didn't see it for years. In the first place, there are all kinds of things. There is firstly, of course, a different concept of addition. You can see there is one form here and another form here, and there are some intermediate spaces, and here is a variation. And the relationship between the density and the extent of this sort of low flat and the way it grows up to the high ones.

This thing should feel that you are in a system, that you should be able to work through it, and the attention the space elicits is – I think – in principle diagonal. You see, all the additions, you can't count in the same way anymore – it's triple, it's double, it's quarto, and it's single. It's difficult to say what it is.

Nevertheless, what I did isn't a sort of initial urbanism done with cubes on plans. Every one of these corners and the way the people live in these corners – I had detailed drawings of every type of house.

The way of this little street – around through here and out on the other side – has all been very well designed. So I took Jaap's whole vocabulary, except a few types I didn't like so much so I eliminated them. But the other types, and why you live on that side of the window, that has been Jaap's concern all his life; so I took that whole vocabulary, because I thought it was very effective.

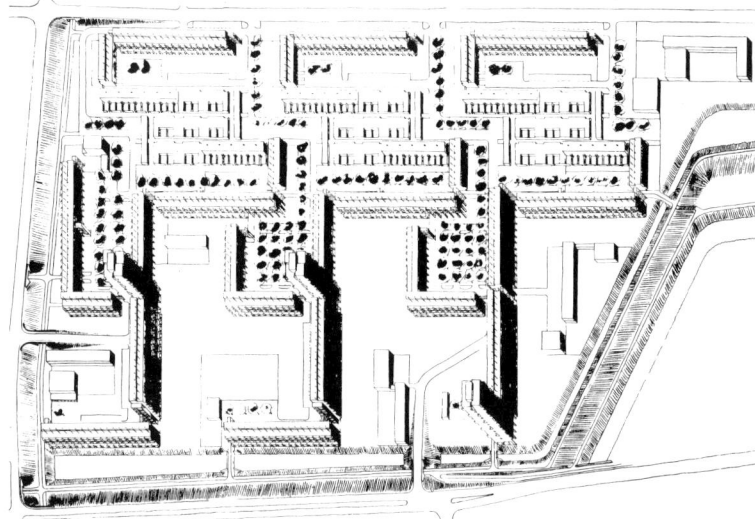

Jaap Bakema, urban design for Buikslotermeer, 1962

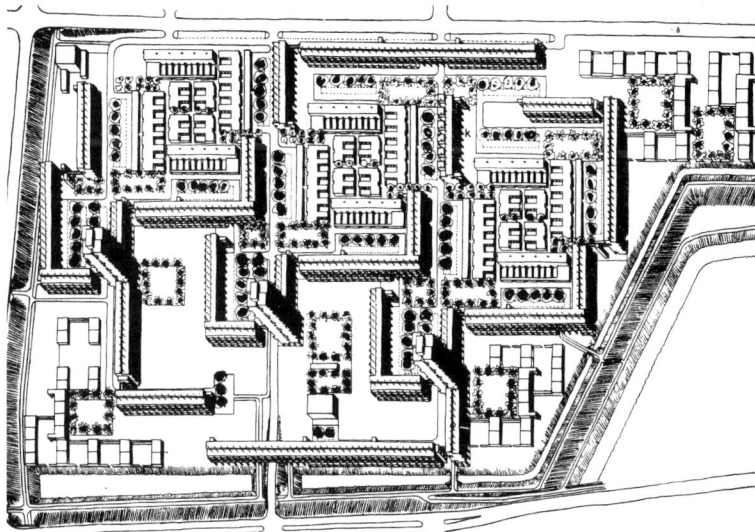

Aldo van Eyck, urban design for Buikslotermeer, 1962, based on houses by Jaap Bakema

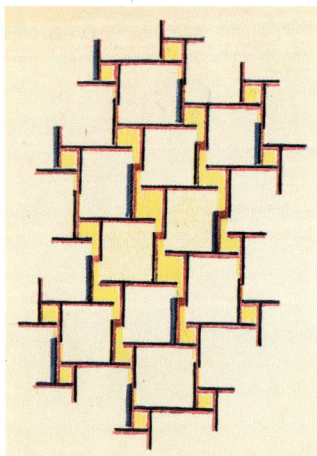

Preliminary studies for an urban structure, Buikslotermeer, Amsterdam, 1962

118

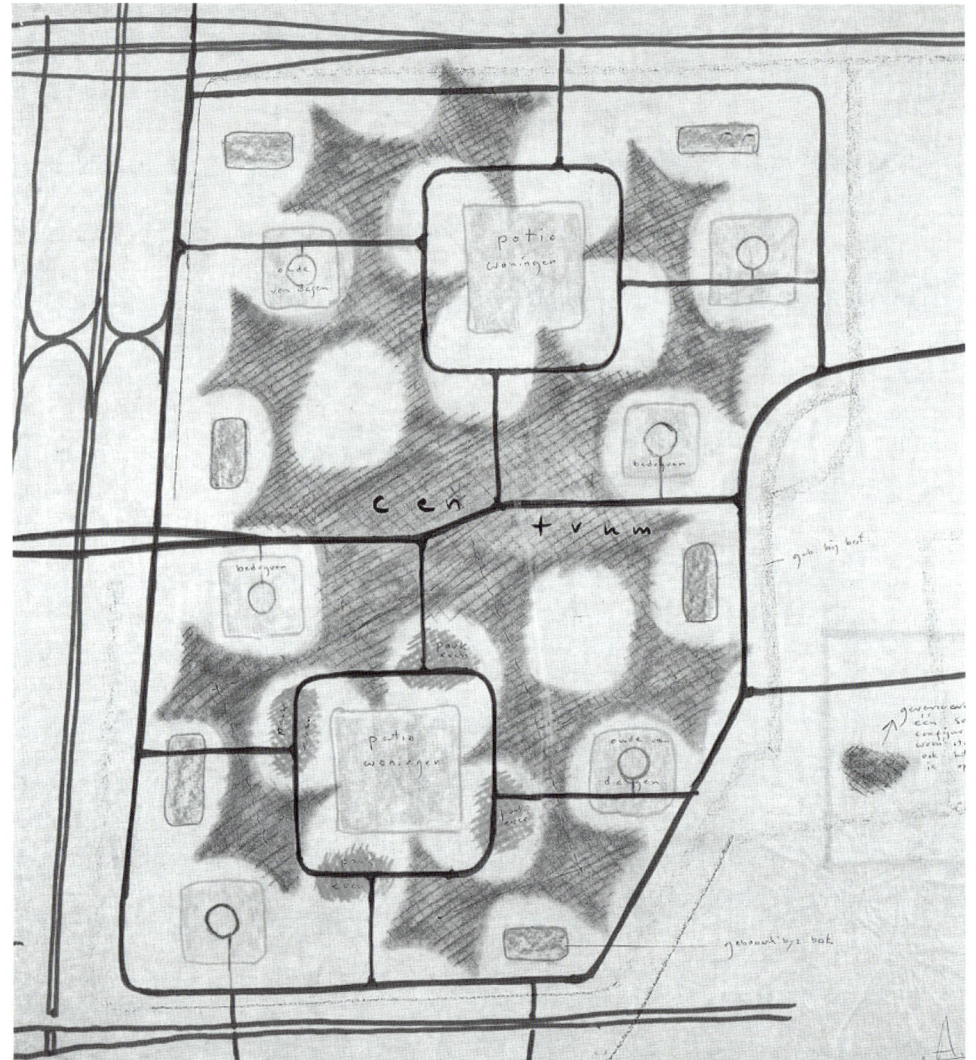

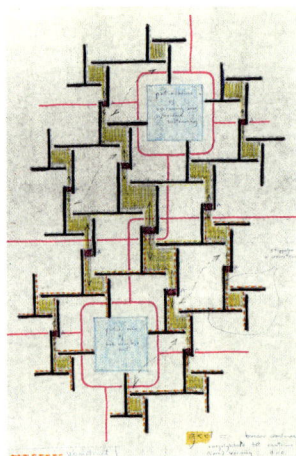

Dotted line = residential street

Yellow = broadening
possibility of
forming a central
point

Red (in A) = crossing points with
towers over them
(the highest in the
middle) and other
communal activities

Blue = houses round patio,
or buildings for
special purposes

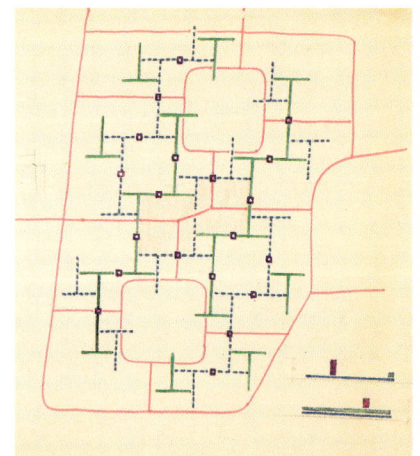

Varied building, a single coherent
configuration, including both
residential streets and the centre

119

Fashion Shop, Zurich, 1963

(competition)

The site is on one of the corners where the Bahnhofstrasse opens sideways into the emptiness of the Uraniastrasse, interrupting the course of Zurich's famous thoroughfare. Had both streets been equally attractive, with a continuous shop front, the corner building could have followed the curve of the building line round the corner – which is how it was eventually built. However, since this is not the case, this project takes a different position in that it attempts to reduce the unfavourable impact of the interruption by cutting the volume of the building back all the way up from street level, so that the course of the Bahnhofstrasse prevails as much as possible. Even the large display window along the Uraniastrasse faces the latter. I believe an indentation of this kind has general relevance whenever, where streets cross, one is the most attractive and prevalent, whilst the other merely interrupts.

The shop entrance is set far back from the building line, providing a large covered shop window area. Once inside, the staircase is the main spatial feature: winding upwards round a drum in which there is a circular space on every split-level floor facing in the opposite direction to the one above and below, thereby providing vertical visual continuity. The stairs continue downwards into the lingerie department below street level, not round the drum, but within it.

The nature of the design is such that it would not be suitable for the sale of a very large variety of clothes. It is, in fact, an ambiance for more or less sophisticated fashion. Shows would benefit from the vertical arrangement of circular split-level spaces in and around the staircase and in this way acquire a certain specific quality.

120

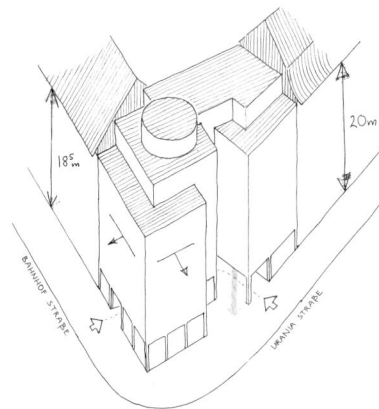

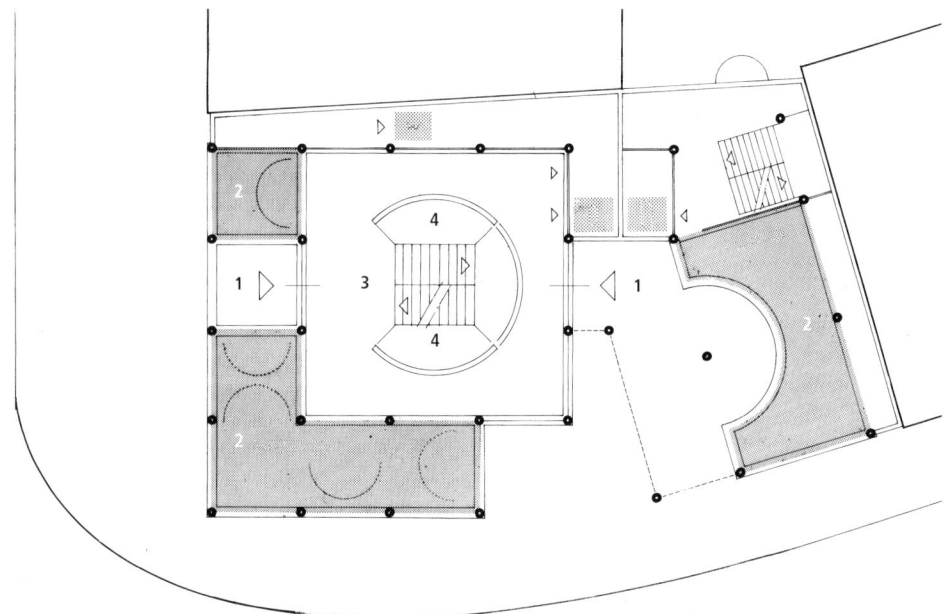

1 covered entrance
2 shop-window
3 entrance room
4 void
5 sale
6 changing-room
7 clothes

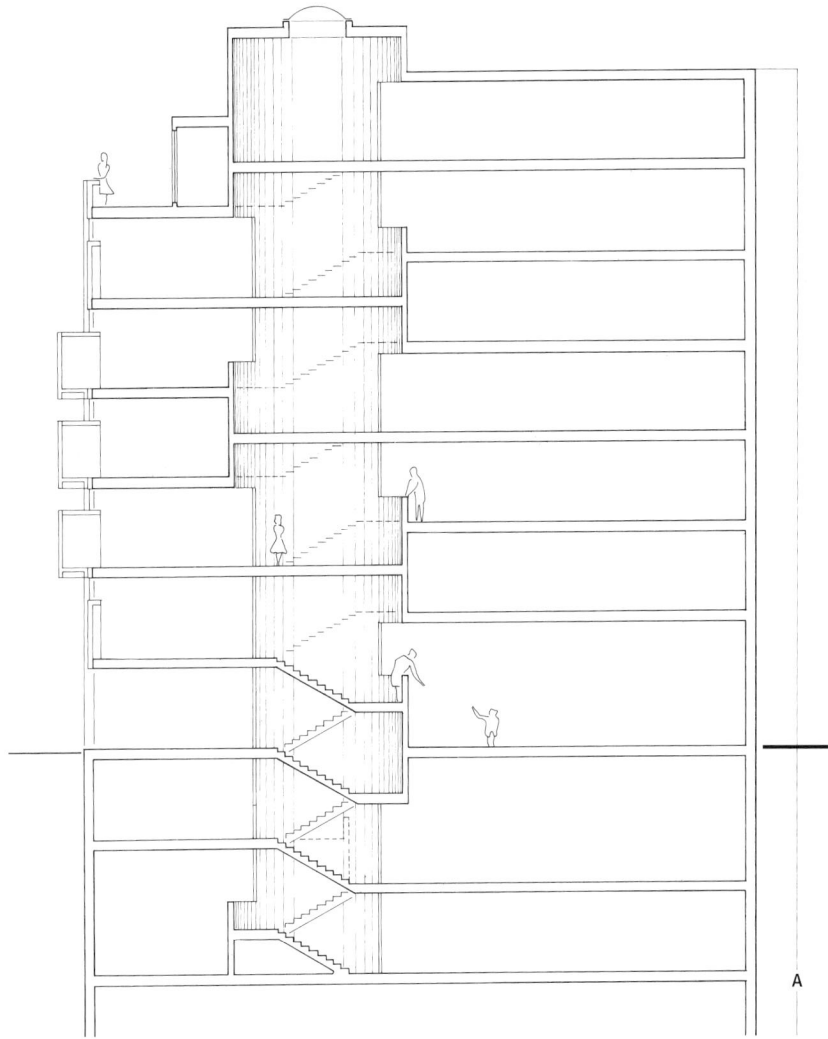

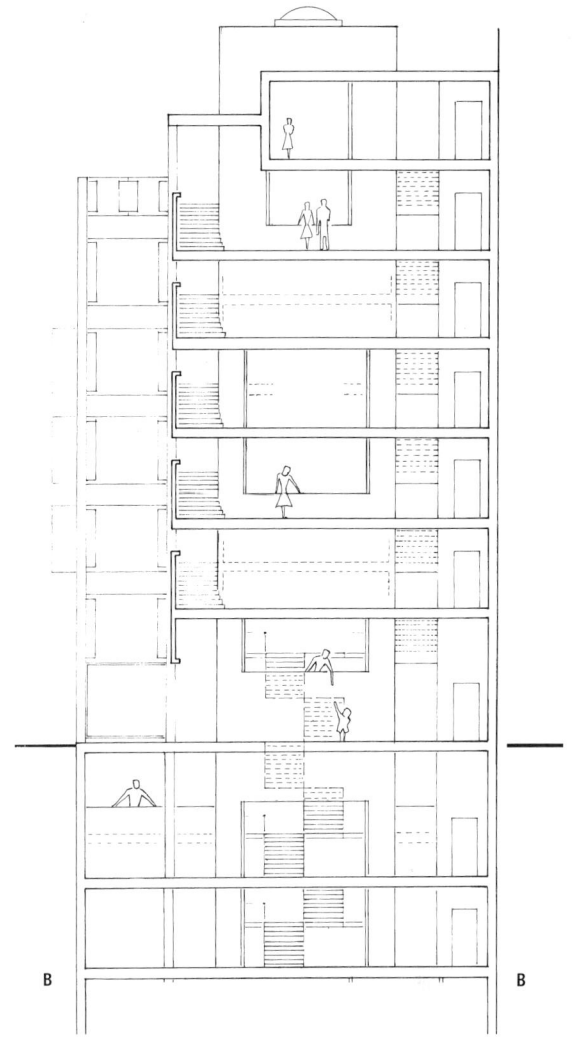

special shop

self-service

A ▲   A ▲

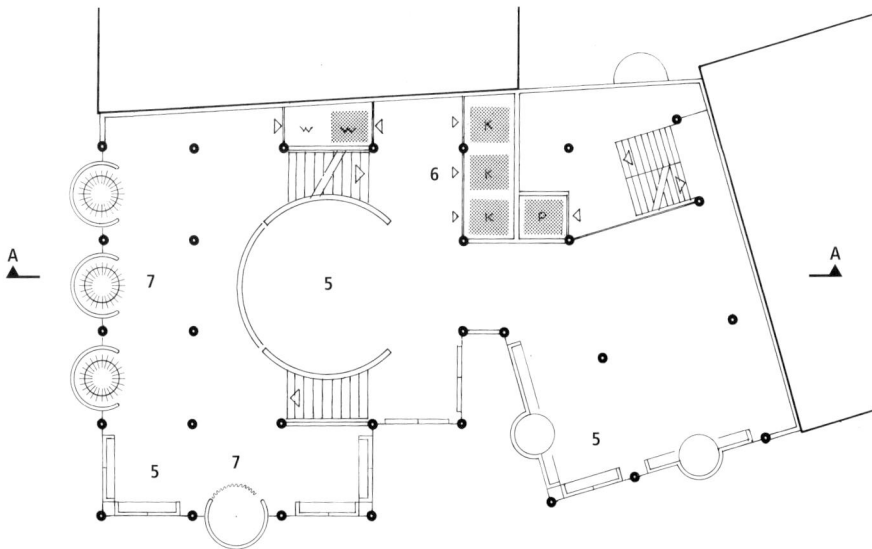

6

7   5

5   7

B ◀   B

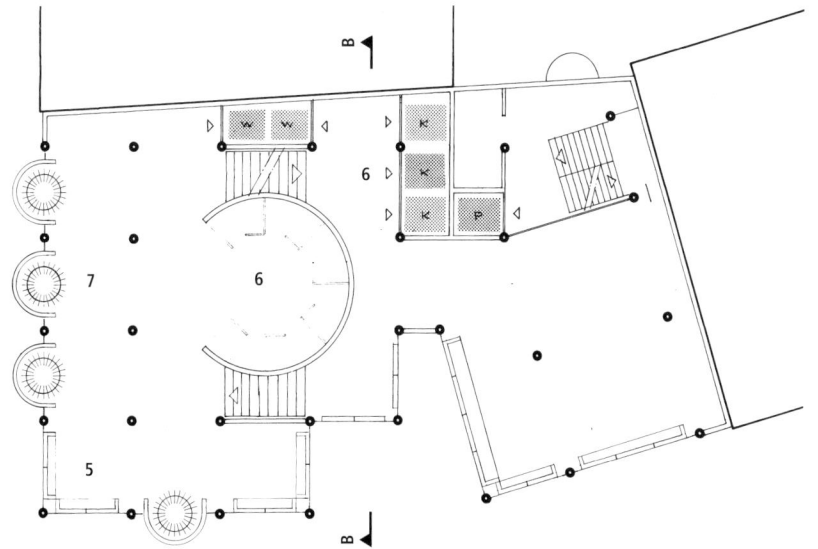

6

7   6

5

'The Wheels of Heaven',
Protestant Church, Driebergen, 1963
(prizewinning design)

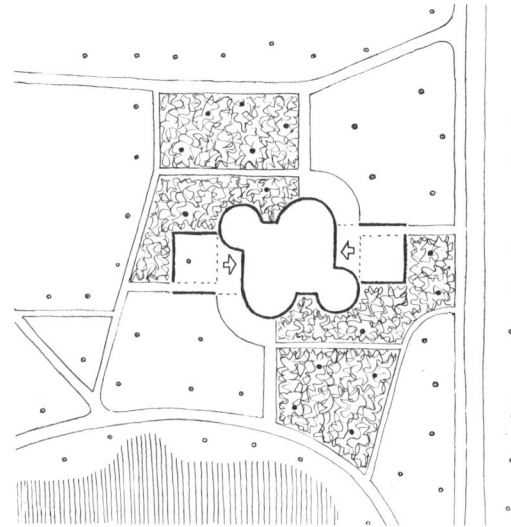

Between tall trees cylindrical concrete columns; between these, screenlike walls and, low over column and wall, a framework of concrete beams spanning horizontally and carrying four circular skylight structures, the configuration of which, seen from below, I named 'The Wheels of Heaven'.

The four circles together have two points of focus. They are situated in the 'path' which passes through the entire building from door to door and beyond through the courts into the park. One 'encounters' two essentially ambivalent places: one for the sacrament of the Lord's Supper, the other for the spoken word.

As to the complex diagonality, I think it assists the idea of multi-centrality. The seating arrangement (only a suggestion) exploits the various implicit directions so that each person may experience the same space in a different way according to which group he chooses – proximity, too, according to individual inclination. Where the diagonals cross there is, for once, just space!

One of the circles is amphitheatrical; it can be used for small gatherings during week days, baptizing, marriages or choir. The other three circumscribe mildly without asserting their centres. (All three groups are shown facing the pulpit here.)

The chapel opens upwards suddenly in different directions taking in the treetops, but also downwards here and there towards the soil. In-between it tends inwards – churchwards – and is translucent rather than transparent.

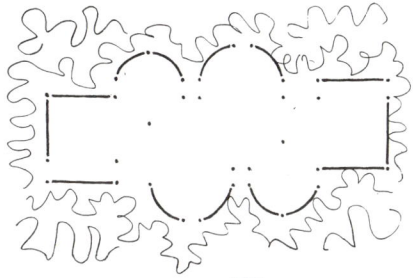

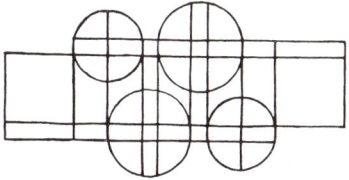

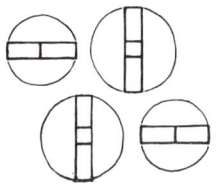

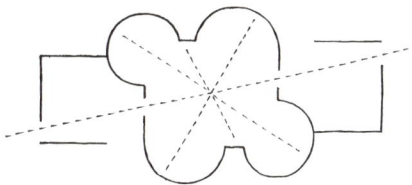

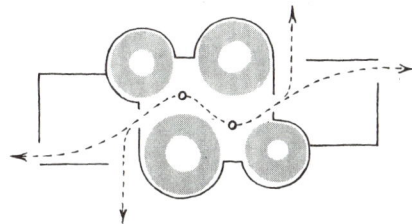

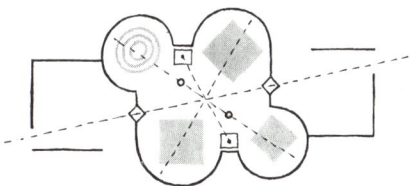

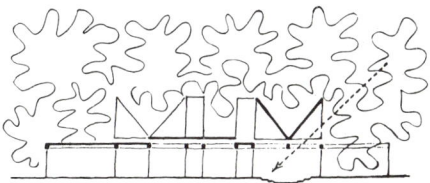

123

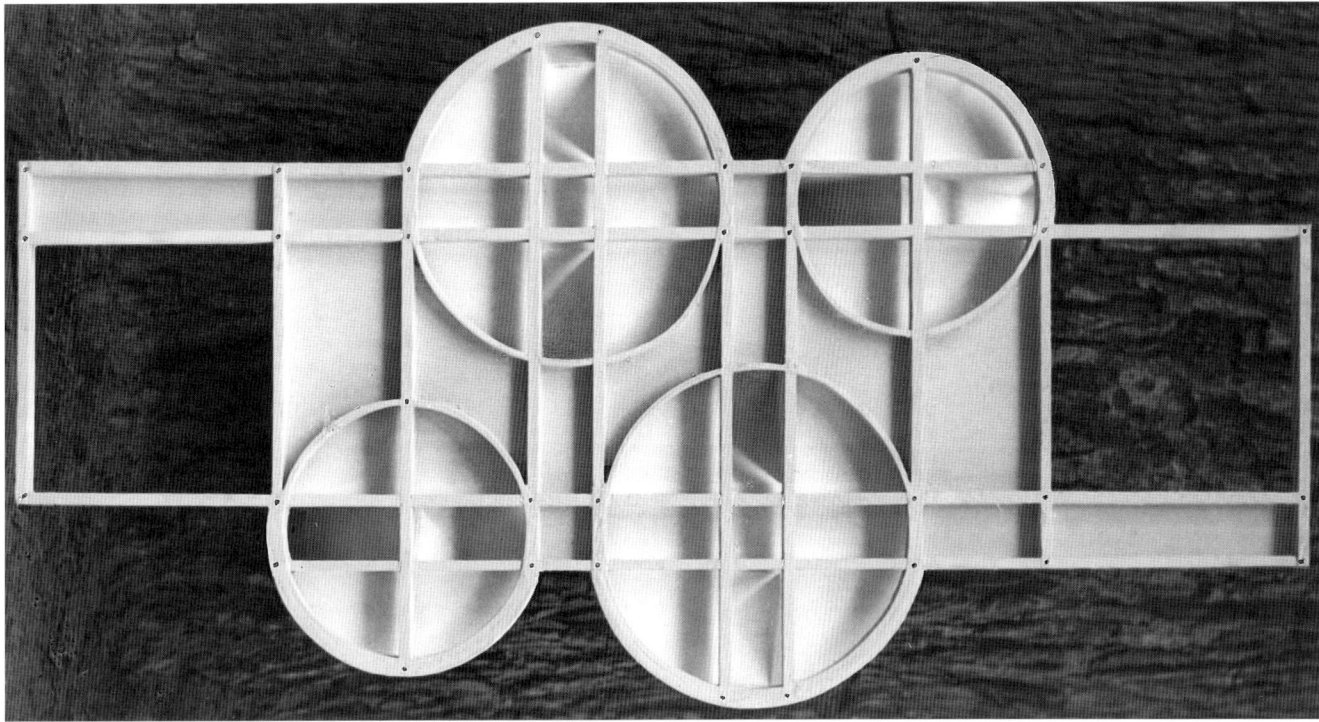

Protestant Church, 'The Wheels of Heaven'

To be thoughtful in a space, one's thoughts must be able to wander – one even needs to be without them – certainly in a church!

The attention of ALL should not be 'summoned' peremptorily by a single central place and what occurs just there. Instead the attention of EACH should be 'granted' liberally to a number of places.

From the very start, I wanted the church to be *multi-centred, but not a-central*. I wanted a single space clearly articulated (the singular embracing the plural; the plural contained in the singular).

The centres or articulated places which resulted are not the same, though they are equally valid. In fact there is no fixed place-hierarchy – the quadripartite articulation (3+1) takes care of that. Whilst the different 'centres' are precisely determined, their use is not. I hope they are also multi-suggestive – that they possess the right scope, for this is what, among other things, multi-centrality can effect (through articulation but not through lack of it).

The four circles together have two points of focus, oval-like. They are situated on the 'path' which passes through the entire building from door to door and beyond through the courts into the park. One 'encounters' these two essentially ambivalent places – one for the sacrament of the Lord's Supper, the other for the spoken word, the sermon.

As to the space's 'diagonality', I think the diagonal attention it promotes supports the idea of multicentrality. The seating arrangement (one suggestion) exploits the various implicit directions so that each person may experience the same space in a different way according to which set of benches he chooses – proximity too according to individual inclination. Where the diagonals cross there is, for once, just space!

One of the circles is amphitheatrical; it can be used for small gatherings during week days, baptisms, marriages or the choir. The other three circumscribe mildly without asserting their centres.

Finally a few remarks about the roof, the configuration of which, as seen from below, I named 'the wheels of heaven'. Between tall trees round circular concrete columns; between these screen-like walls and, low over column and wall, a framework of concrete beams spanning horizontally and carrying four circular skylight structures.

The chapel suddenly opens upwards in different directions taking in the tree tops, but here and there downwards too, towards the soil. In between it tends inwards – churchwards – and is translucent rather than transparent.

The spaces between the framework of beams and the skylight structures are, I believe, quite enigmatic.

They are intermediaries, an in-between world; which hold and transmit that which is outside and above the roof to those inside: sky with passing clouds, trees, birds – from season to season – and light which passes through the 'wheels' into the space below and falls on the people, as it should.

The chapel is only four metres high. It may, if I am lucky, acquire something of the altitude of light itself. I leave that to the wheels.

The Horizon and the Shifting Centre

People seated concentrically in a hollow, gazing inwards towards the centre; and people seated concentrically on a hill, gazing outwards towards the horizon. Two kinds of centrality. Two ways of being together – or alone. The images, of course, have ambivalent meanings – though the hill reveals what the hollow may conceal: that man is both centre-bound and horizon-bound (the horizon and the shifting centre, the centre and the shifting horizon). Both hill and hollow, horizon and centre, are shared by all seated concentrically either way; both link and both lure.

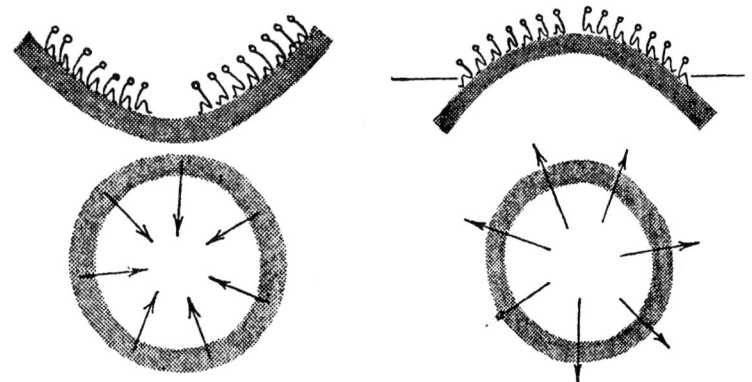

Roman Catholic Church, The Hague, 1964-9

Although neither Catholic nor anything else, I have over the years been familiar with innumerable churches and sacred places of all sorts; entering them, staying for a while, then leaving again (as an architect-tourist, for the sake of the architecture) whilst noticing with detachment what takes place there.

It is from this accumulated secular experience that I started on both the present and the previous church ('The Wheels of Heaven'), confident that specific paradoxes appertaining to the subject could still be translated into architecture.

Far from wishing to secularize (i.e. neutralize or banalize) what for others is sacred, I have in both cases tried, as an outsider, to mitigate the outworn hierarchy's irreversibility; persuading it to become hence more reversible – relative. Only the mild gears of reciprocity I thought could help me here.

The available rectangular site was prohibitively small, so I decided to limit the overall plan of the church to a single rectangle, thus giving up the idea of gradual entry that a complex periphery allows. This time entry is so sudden that only the church doors become the sole representation of that idea. Having *descended* towards the entry from street level, one slips in from the side one by one through the narrow door which opens inwards and leaves with others after mass through the wide one which opens outwards. Light enters sideways through tiny square panes where the two doors overlap. 'Entry' starts, as it were, once one is inside! An unavoidable limitation but at any rate architecturally resolved in the details of the doors.

As to the interior of the church, I wished to combine the quality of a low crypt-like space with that of a tall gothic-like one. Low when seated during mass; tall when walking (after entry and before leaving). Because it was so narrow – only 3.40 m between the columns – 11 m seemed high enough for the tall space, and 2.50 to 3.50 not too low for the low one, if sufficiently articulated horizontally, and – this in particular – also vertically; for, generally speaking, the articulation of height is still a neglected facet of contemporary architecture. There has been little sense of right-height in today's buildings since the minds of 20th-century architects began to function only laterally! What my wife once called the interior horizon of space is nowadays sadly missing.

The tall space – neither narthex nor nave, but something of both – became a kind of interior street with the divers sacred places strung along it. People filter out of and into it from end to end between the semicircular chapels, piers and outer walls. All three spaces open upwards into spacious circular drums above, through which light falls onto altar and people alike. In front, the church is situated 1 m below

the original street level, thus reducing its bulk as well as the depth of the canal. This artificial difference in level between the entries on either side made it possible to incline the floor of all three church spaces at a right angle to the axis of the altar. Thus the tilt, for once, became a counter tilt!

There are three levels for the low part and five for the tall part, between the two entries. So one either ascends or descends, depending on which entry is used. The altar stands halfway down the middle level. For those passing it in either direction up or down the 'sacred way' it is a mild and relative place, I thought. However for those seated in the low crypt-like space during mass, no arbitrary tampering with the altar's place on the lateral axis – as so often occurs today – is allowed to disturb the significant equipoise that the traditional place ensures. Except for the altar, which I designed, all the ecclesiastical objects were introduced by those who believe in them. I just provided the places to receive them. There are also no built-in sacred signs or symbols of any kind anywhere, nor any church bells to alarm people still asleep.

If the space is experienced by many as a sacred one after all, that may, I hope, be due to the way matters not specifically sacred were handled architecturally. Reima Pietilä's observation in this respect is intriguing.

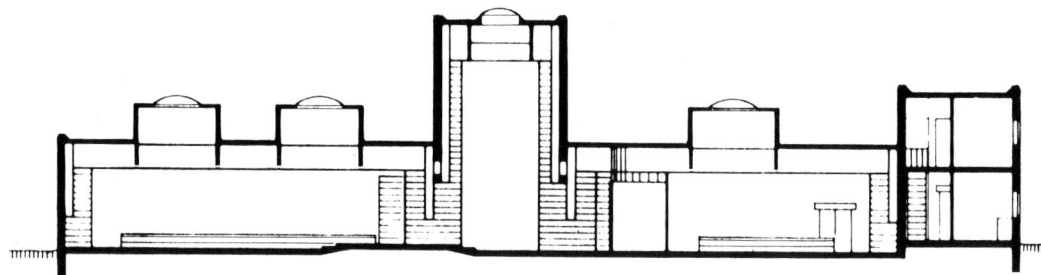

Section A-A

1 congregation space
2 extension and space of general use
3 altar
4 chapel
5 font
6 confessionals
7 kitchen
8 sacristy
9 toilets
10 meeting room
11 office
12 bicycles
13 heating

Post religious space

In the tall space there is a definite Catholic air, whilst in the low one, where people are seated, there is another feeling – another reality from that which belongs to the western concept of religious experience. As daylight cascades from above through huge drums there is a direct presence of the external cosmos.

These skylights materialize daylight in a way that keeps people in union with their own real world. As the Christian ceremony proceeds they remain in their normal reality aware that what takes place before their eyes is an event of the past. Is my impression of atmospheric duality in Aldo's church a subjective one or is this church a post-religious work of architecture? The interior of a church expressing the basic oneness of cults now belongs to the history of mankind. Religion can no longer influence people's minds without restricting. So the architect installs countermeasures and designs a building for the era of post-religious culture.

Pietilä

If Pietilä is correct and I actually did come up with a post-'Christian' space, which is nonetheless experienced 'as sacred', that is all right with me, inclined as I am to situate the transcendental on this side of the beyond as soon as 'gods' are left behind and the mild gears of reciprocity take over.

Apparently, as a tourist-architect, I seem to have made a contribution to church architecture when it was no longer required!

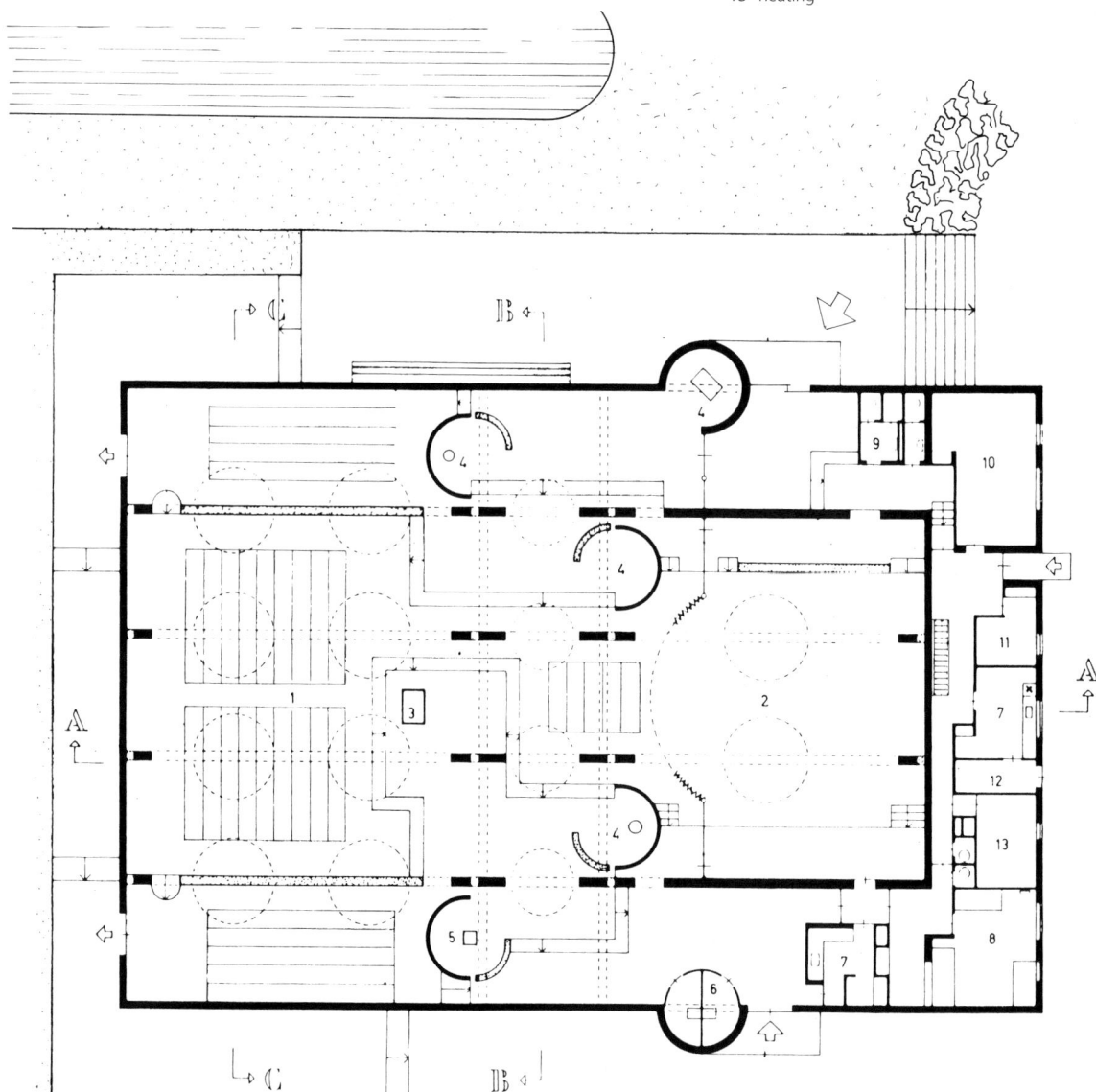

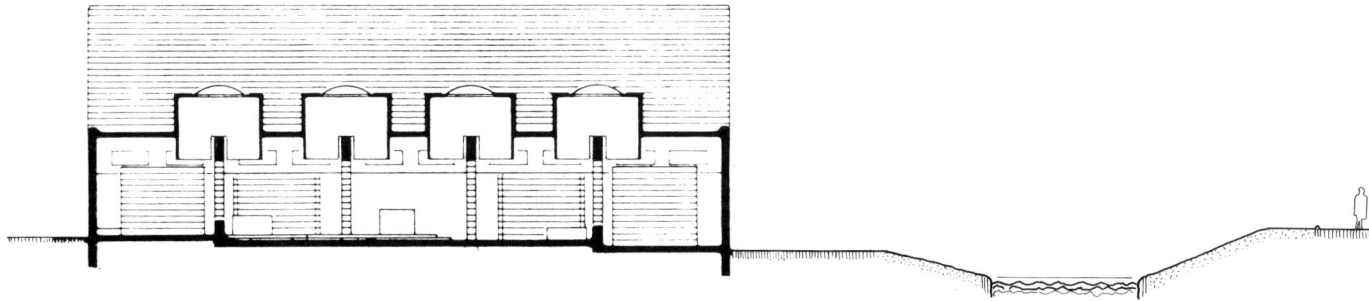

Section C-C

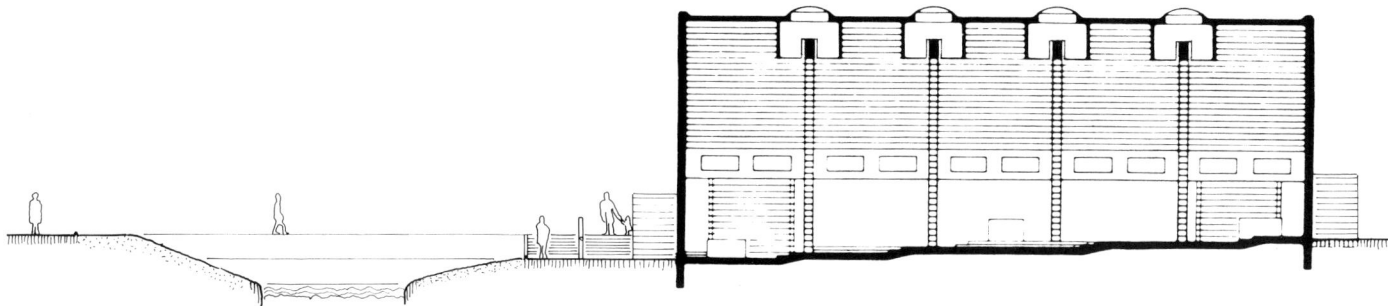

Section B-B

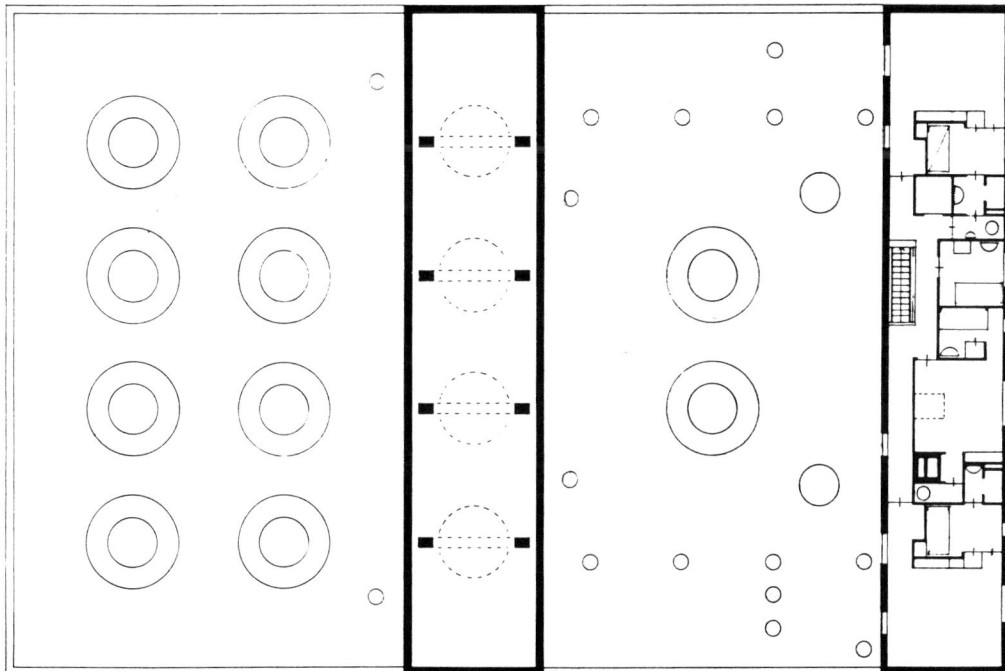

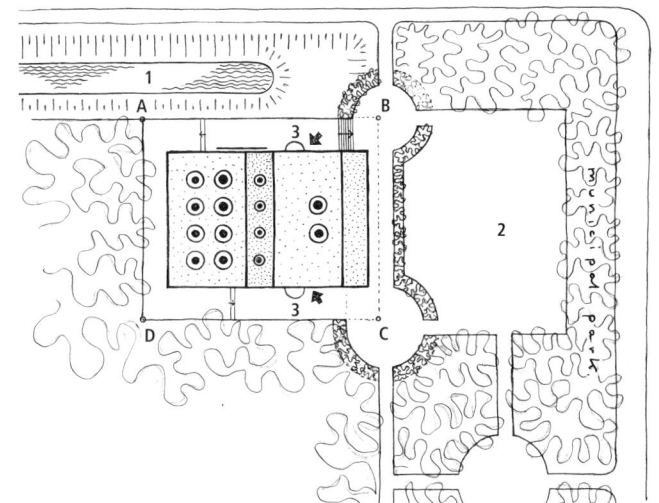

Available plot ABCD, 40 × 48 m
1 canal
2 playground
3 entrance

Entrance

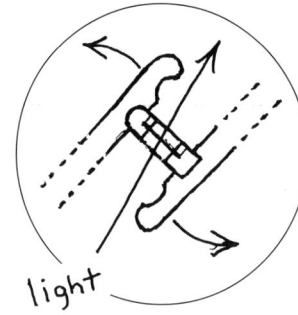

Small glass panels in the overlap
of the two door sections

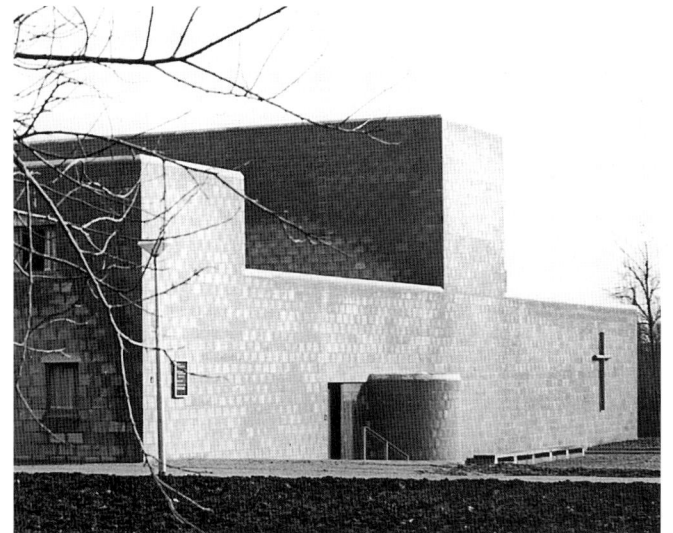

light

Walk from the alter to the baptistry. The intimate
ceremony takes place away from the community.

3 altar
4 chapel
5 font

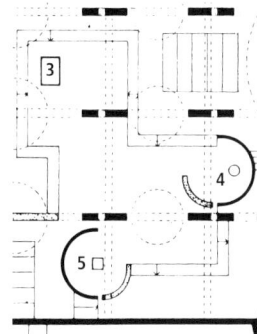

Sculpture Pavilion, Sonsbeek Exhibition, Arnhem, 1965-6

Rietveld, who made the previous pavilion on the same spot, must have approached the problem quite differently, judging from the structure which stood there – frail and weightless – twelve years ago. It was a beautiful thing in an uncontroversial way and widely appreciated for it; a fairy tale that cannot be retold – though it was rebuilt on another site as a tribute to the architect.

An extraordinary sense of continuity prevailed – the trees had their way. Nothing was essentially interrupted, though much was quietly articulated. Park and pavilion were in accord and so, it seemed, were the people. Nor did the exhibited sculpture challenge this unity – such was the nature of the choice made. Rietveld's disarming mischievousness – no work of his is without it – made it easier to accept such equipoise on a summer's day in the park.

Although the immediate requirements were the same this time – to accommodate those objects which because of small size, material, fragility or value could not be exhibited along the lanes in the parks – I thought the time had come to reconsider the whole question of contemplating sculpture out of doors, since this still presupposes fields and trees and sunshine, a very obstinate misunderstanding – as though art has more to say (or says it more gently) when mother nature is around (here in the guise of a Victorian park). But Caros, Kings and Turnbulls do very well without her special grace, for art today is singularly autonomous. It is, moreover, distinctly urban in spirit – often perplexing and provocative. If it relates to the physical world of nature at all it is through metamorphosis, but primarily it relates to itself. The 'landscapes' that are disclosed are those of the mind. And like the mind, the dream and the city, they are kaleidoscopic and labyrinthine.

I therefore decided that the new pavilion should possess something of the closeness, density and intricacy of things urban – that it should in fact be city-like, in the sense that people and artifacts meet, converge and clash there *inevitably*.

Central to my idea was that the structure should not reveal what happens inside until one gets quite close, approaching it from the ends. Seen from the sides, it appears closed and massive – guarding secrets. The four doorways (one has a seat) open the walls sideways and diagonally, but only at close range. A huge black circle encompasses the pavilion. Its counterform – the square round it – was, like the walls, meant to be painted dull aluminium to give the place a more autonomous quality – disconnect it from the trees – but this was never carried out.

Distance and a slow impression-sequence in the park; proximity and a rapid impression-sequence in and around the pavilion. Affected harmony – lawns, trees and sky; next to intrinsic controversy – a stony place, thick walls and a translucent roof.

Bump! – sorry. What's this? Oh hello!

134

About light: I wanted it to be diffused, falling on the sculpture equally from all sides rather than striking it from one side. Furthermore, I find that the reduction of light intensifies tactile values and increases an object's presence. Seen in twilight especially, hollows remain hollows and sculpture in general invites the touch. Hence the translucent roof (flexible nylon stretched over steel tubes).

The circular slabs and low walls were for people as well as sculpture; the smaller cylinders just for people.

Arp, Brancusi, Pevsner, Gaudier Brzeska, Gonzáles, Hepworth, Giacometti, Richier, Ernst, Matta, Noguchi, Tajiri, Caro, Turnbull, Constant, Wouters, Pomodoro, Paolozzi – small, large, thin, squat, wood, stone, metal, dark, light, heavy, wiry, solid, polished, precise, rough – all within a single structure. And people – many, too many or hardly any – passing in and out, round, between and through the walls (running if they happened to be children).

As rain poured down from day to day, some of the things I wanted were curiously emphasized.

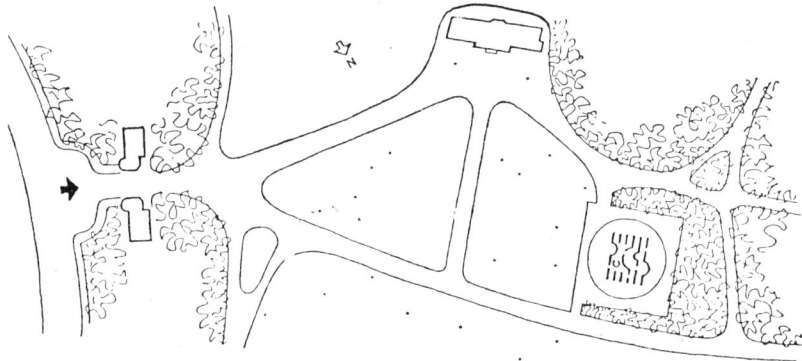

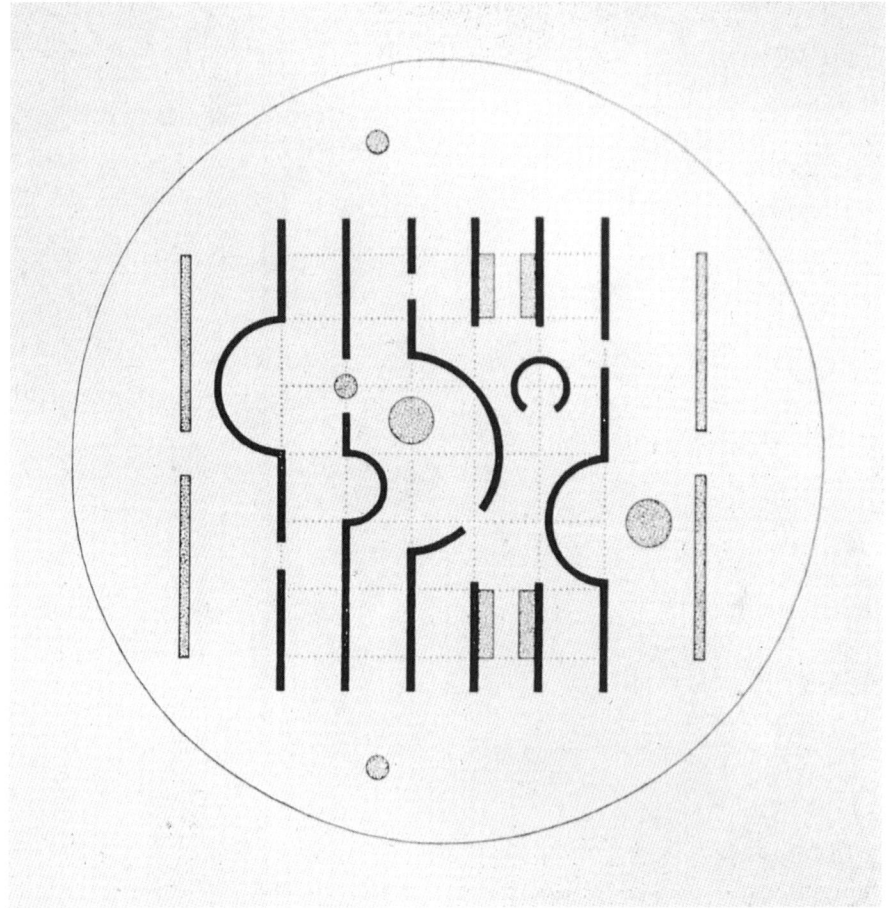

135

Sculpture in twilight
Hollows remain hollows

136

Constantin Brancusi
La Muse Endormie

This mark appears on the side of the cylinder seat, and is based on a Zuni Indian rain amulet – with a middle-line that was originally about 3 cm!
(Eyes and mouth in jet. Mountain range through the face in mother-of-pearl. Here in stone and aluminium respectively.)

Hans Arp, Rik Wouters, Constantin Brancusi, Pomodoro

Fontana, Zuni, Gonzáles

In some places there is no sculpture

139

140

Preliminary studies for the Roman Catholic Church in The Hague

as it was on the exhibition of his own wo

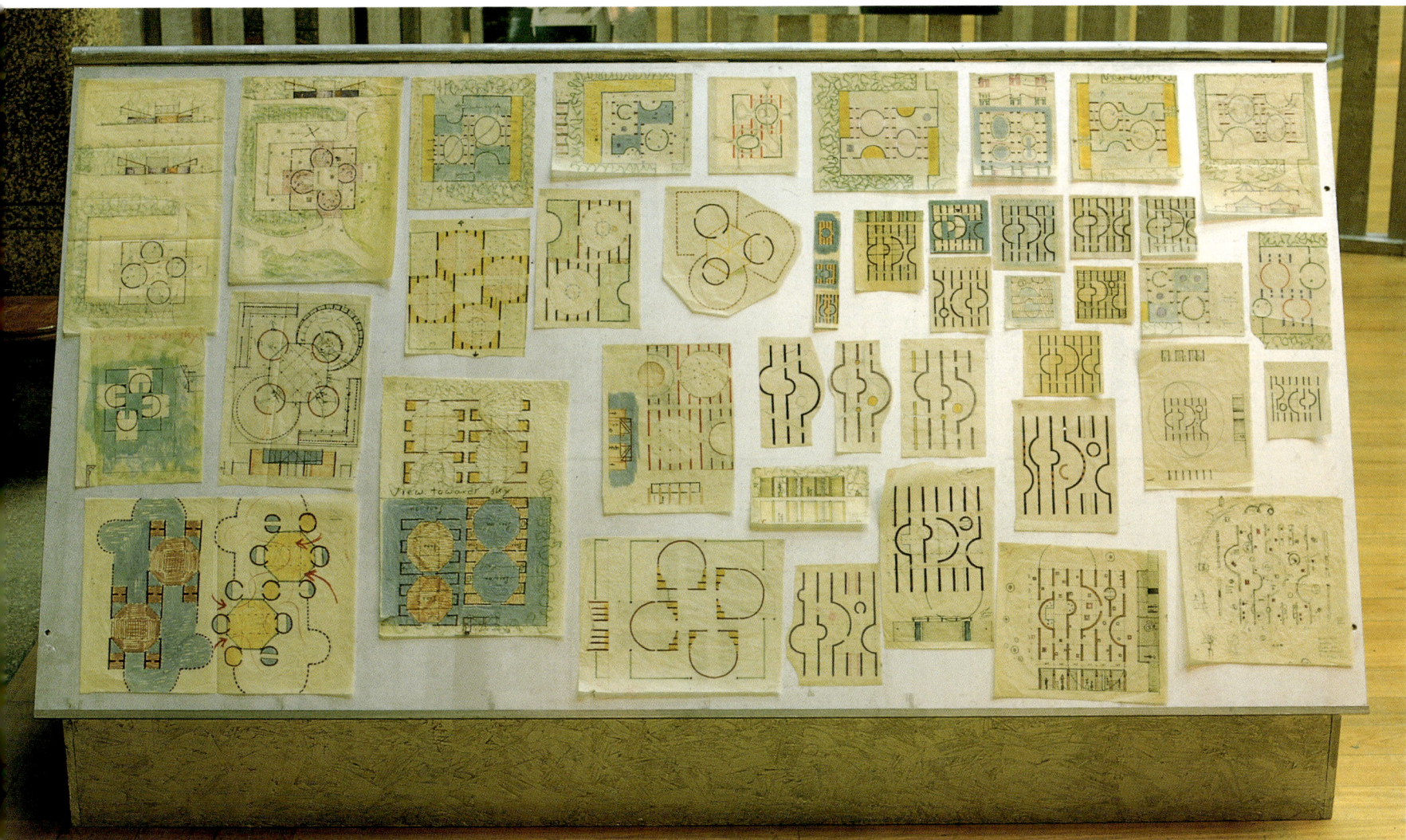

Sculpture Pavilion in Arnhem,

...age's Stock Exchange, Amsterdam, 1989

Maas House, Vreeland, 1966-7 (conversion)

By adding a new opening in the exterior wall next to the one left by removing the existing front door and cutting back the winter-garden diagonally, a broad intermediary exterior space within the perimeter was created. Thus the interior is exteriorized by bringing the entrance, two actually, into the interior of the house. The desired enclosure is brought about by opening what was closed.

142

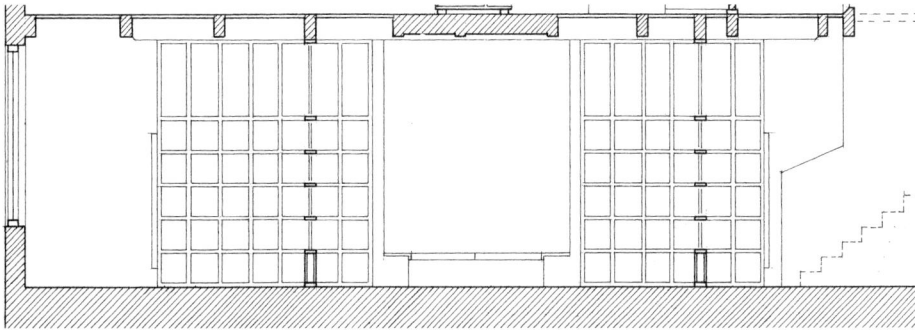

Elevation indoor/outdoor area

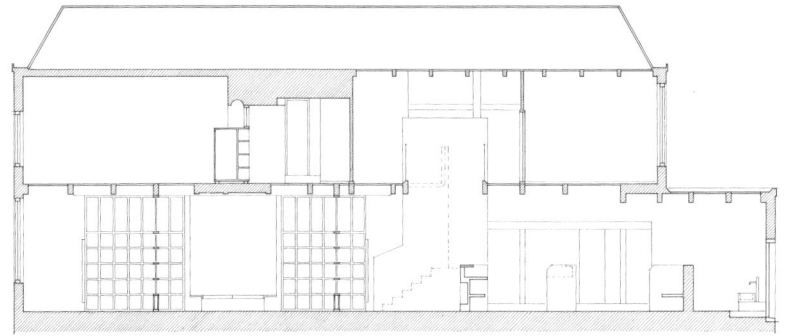

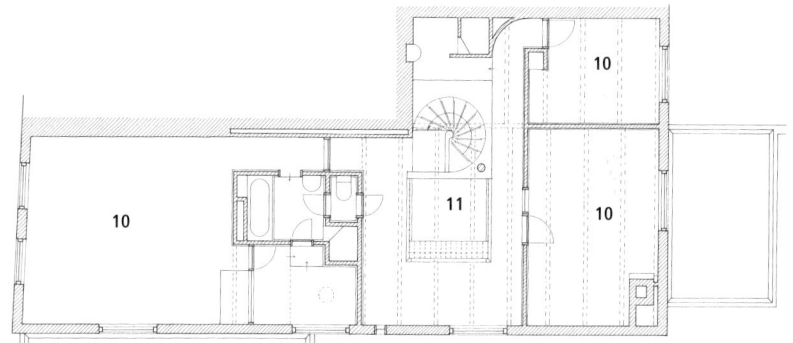

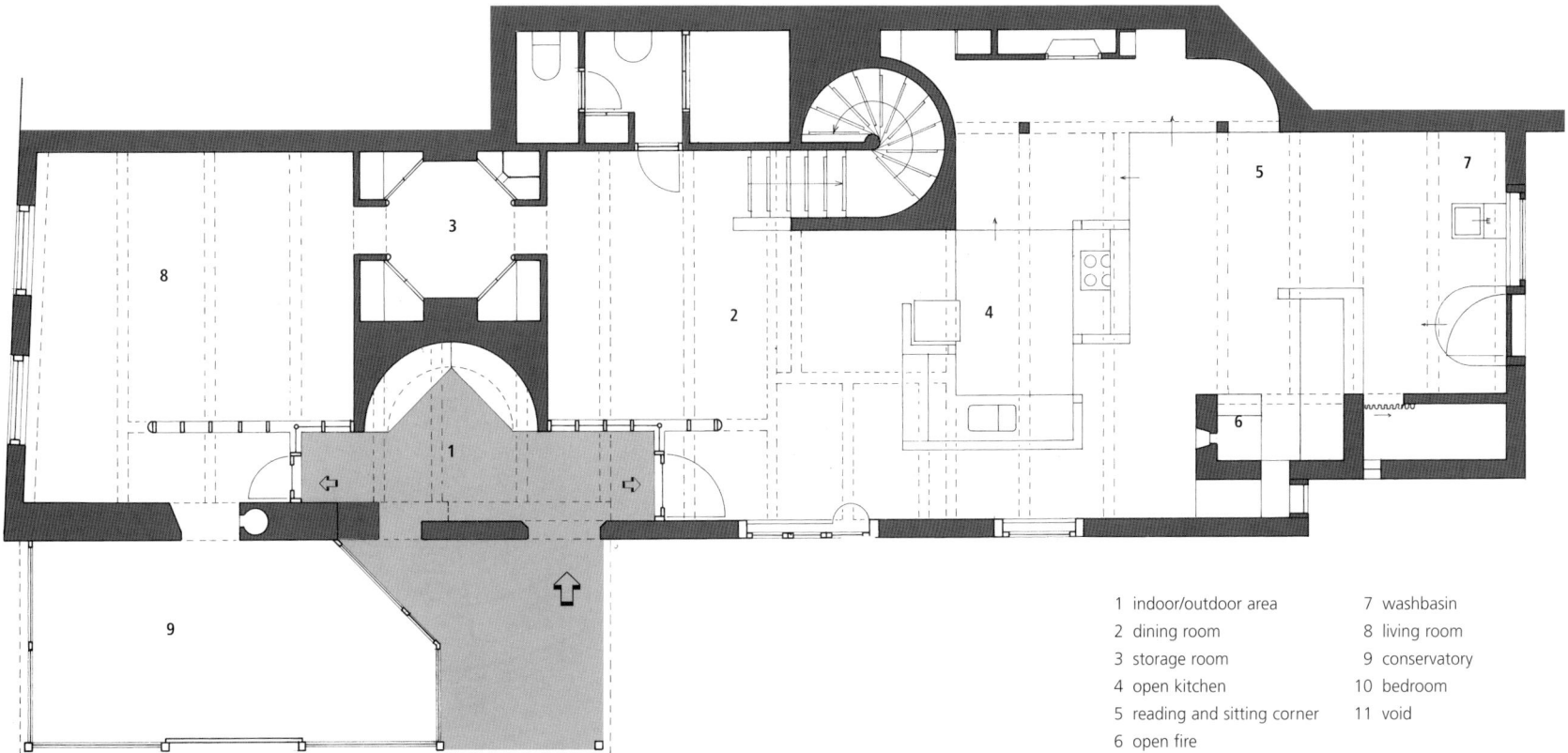

143

1 indoor/outdoor area   7 washbasin
2 dining room   8 living room
3 storage room   9 conservatory
4 open kitchen   10 bedroom
5 reading and sitting corner   11 void
6 open fire

Scenery for 'Labyrinth' Multi-Media Event

The 'Total Theatre' concept implied the experiential inclusion of music, theatre, ballet, film and stage design combined and interacting in a single performance. My job was to propose the overall setting in the given space – an enormous amphitheatre playhouse with a huge stage.

Peter Schat's orchestral score, Bruno Maderna's conducting, as well as Kurt and Ellen Edinof Stuyf's Contemporary Dance group were excellent and fully up to the total theatre challenge. Not so the theatre people with their rather stale theatre school background. Particularly unfortunate was their refusal to perform whilst the platforms were being either turned or shifted, which was a deplorable limitation since the crucial idea was that the actors would perform on the platforms whilst the dancers below were moving them 'choreographically' with great precision, which was a delight to watch. One of them held a leg firmly, the others swivelled the platform round it in either direction, followed by the next. In this way the platforms 'walked' to their next position in 15 to 25 seconds.

The full orchestra was seated on a multi-level platform to the left of the stage, as well as in odd places opposite the spectators. The dancers would be almost anywhere in the entire theatre space, even in mid-air with the help of ropes. Film was projected on screens in space whilst the others were performing.

144

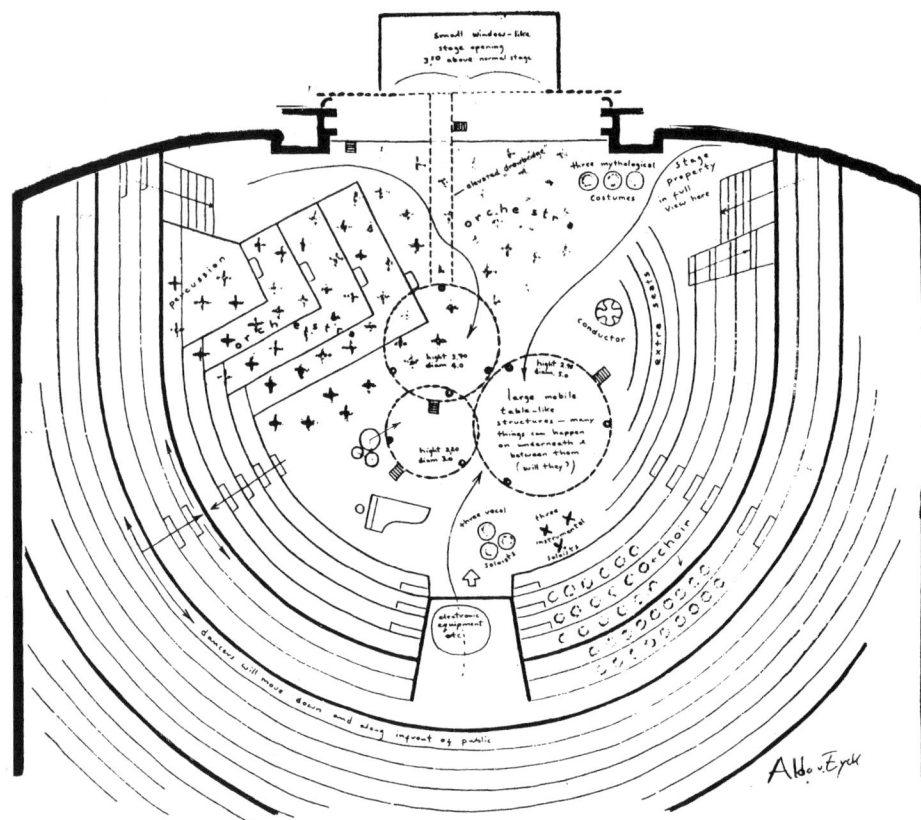

Town Hall, Deventer, 1966
(winning competition design)

What I saw from the fields across the river on my first site visit was the city's almost unspoiled skyline – an irregular assembly of pitched roofs with those of the great church and the old town hall rising above them. Something one could clearly not disturb, let alone contemplate the imposition of a large new town hall in the midst of it all. This seemed ludicrous before I made up my mind what I should avoid doing at all costs.

Building a new town hall, especially when the town is a small or medium-sized one, more often than not lures architects into the monumental trap. If we are lucky something explicitly worthy, dignified and lofty will be the result – representative; or, if we are not: something expressing authority or even power.

In Holland, in spite of an Erasmian sense of moderation, results have failed to strike an acceptable chord. Dudok managed in a decorative way in Hilversum, so did Peutz in Haarlem, a superbly idiosyncratic building.

Deventer is lucky in that it already has a beautiful grey stone renaissance town hall next to the site waiting for the new one – not to replace it but to augment it. Built when they still knew how to erect buildings that stand for something, there was no need to compete with it on that score since it would harbour all representative functions. Hence, I thought, no impressive domi-nance here, or grand entry. Let the building settle in as modestly as possible, notwithstanding its very considerable size, between the old roofs without altering or enlarging the existing urban space.

Assuming that my competition competitors might well do just that in several ways I decided to let myself be guided as a first principal by what NOT to do at each stage (I actually formulated what that was in writing on the plans so it couldn't be overlooked) and choosing as the motto for my entry: 'Between the Roofs'.

Thus, to start with, the perimeter of the old triangular urban space is neither enlarged nor altered, nor is there a second, new grand town hall entrance competing with the beautiful ancient one next door. Instead the existing street morphology forms the prelude to entry from both city and riverside.

Linking both entrances is the top-lit central public space – an interior urban transit space as it were. Instead of ascending towards the town hall entrance – the usual gesture – one now descends towards it, sideways from the Polstraat, down some steps from *riverside level*.

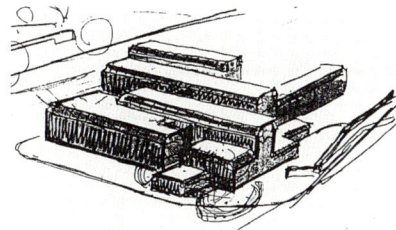

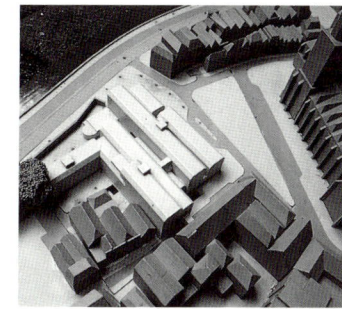

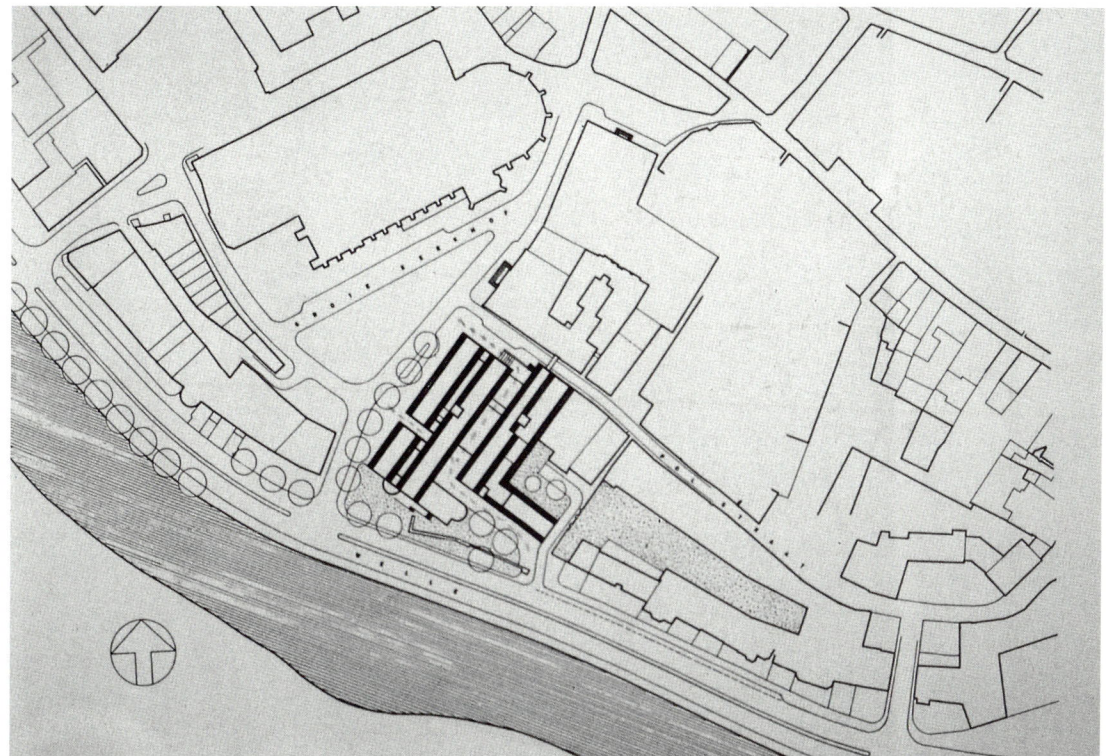

145

146

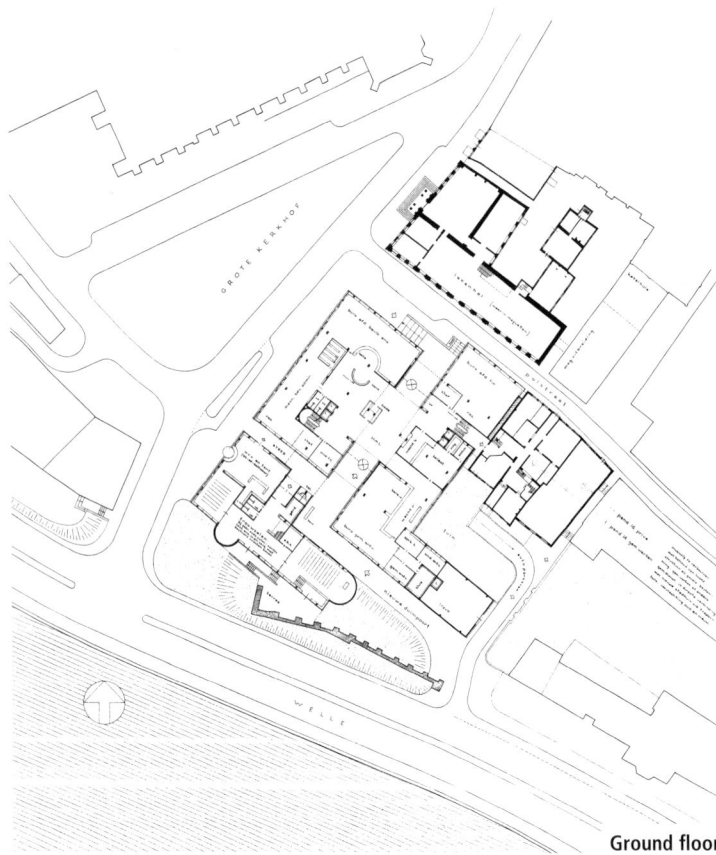

Ground floor

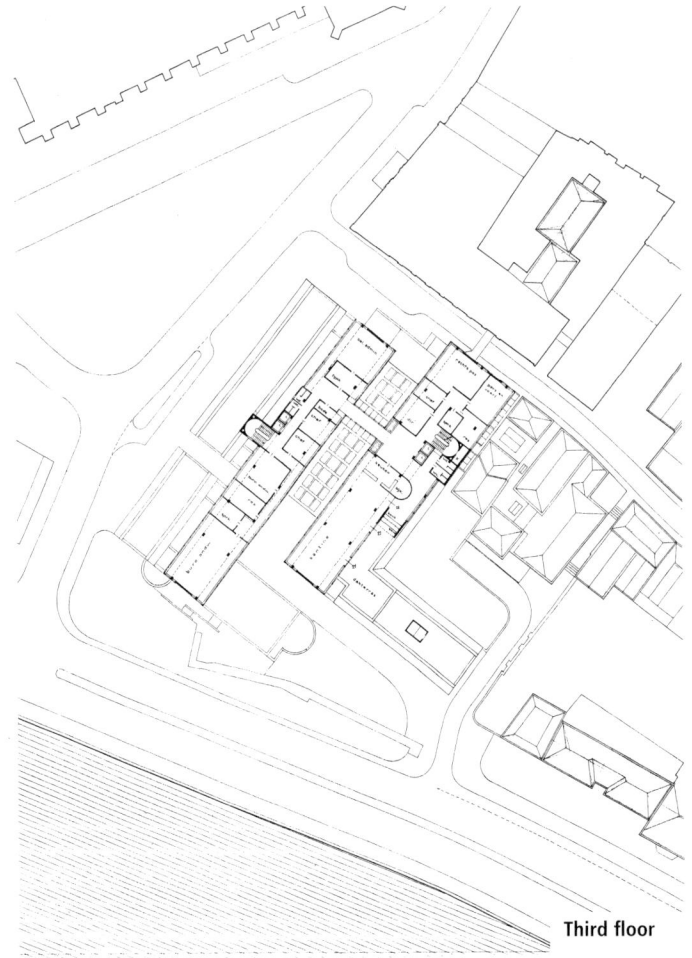

Third floor

'Between the Roofs'

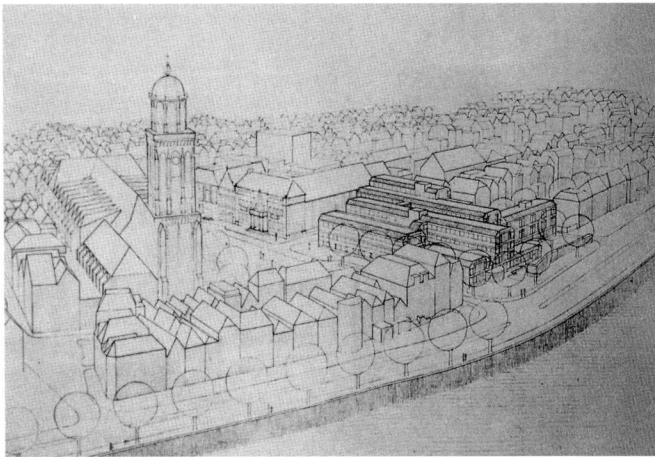

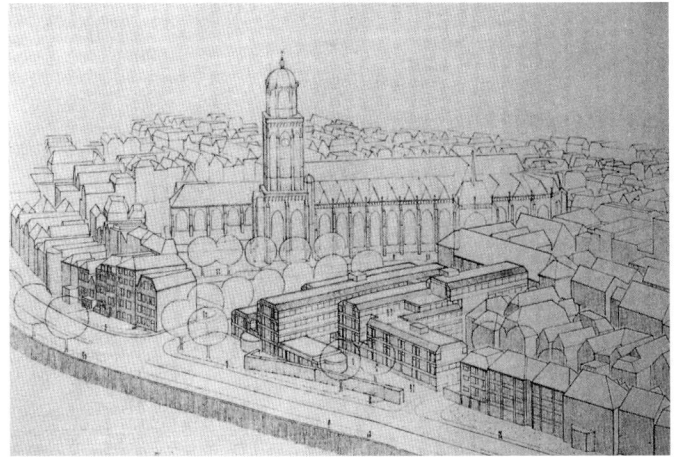

Northwest façade

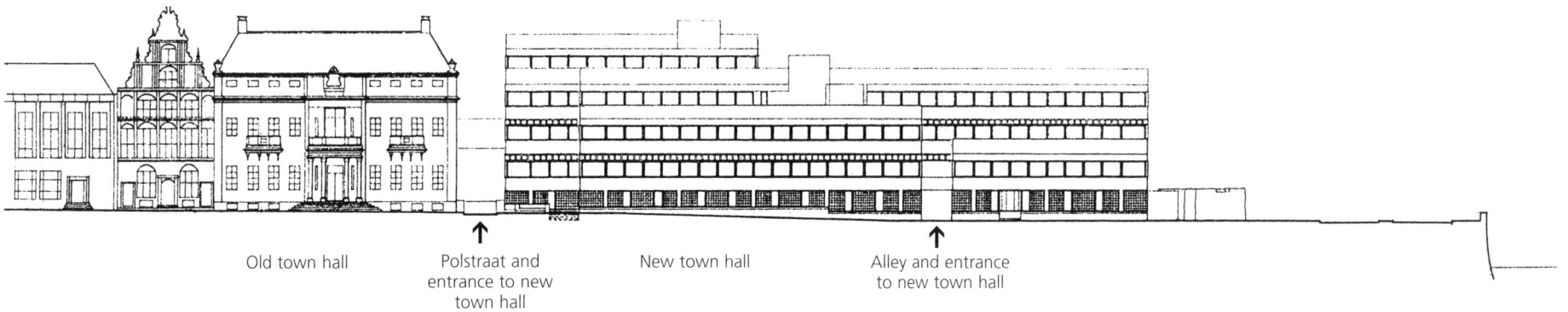

Old town hall   Polstraat and   New town hall   Alley and entrance
entrance to new   to new town hall
town hall

The building is oriented in all directions. Thus whenever you happen to be inside it or moving through it, the city is there continually – the river, the great church and the roofs all round. The interior tells you where you are in the building by the changing view of the city i.e. THE BUILDING IS THE CITY, not merely somewhere in the city. The first design of many, accommodating buildings within the close and intricate fabric of historic city-centres, without destroying them by opening them up. The perimeter of the church space has not been altered. There is no second, monumental, town hall entrance to compete with the magnificent ancient one next door. Instead, two existing streets (one passing under the building) are connected by a glass-roofed arcade which serves both as a pedestrian transit and central town hall lobby.

The building is very compact in order to save some 17th-century houses awaiting demolition on the proposed site. A lesson more frequently understood since.

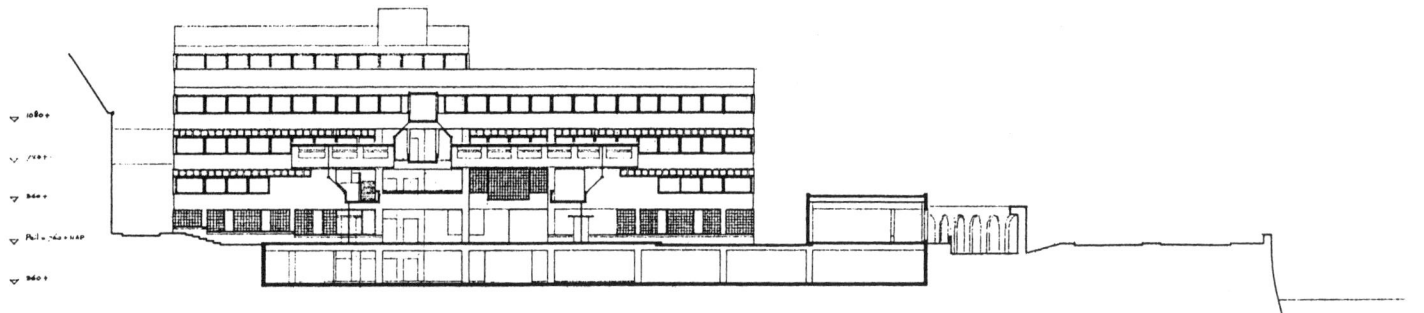

Longitudinal section through Polstraat, entrance and main hall

147

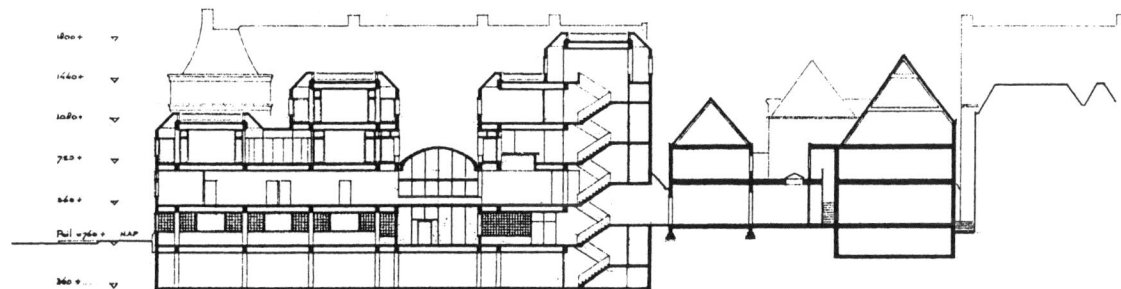

Cross-section with main hall and existing houses

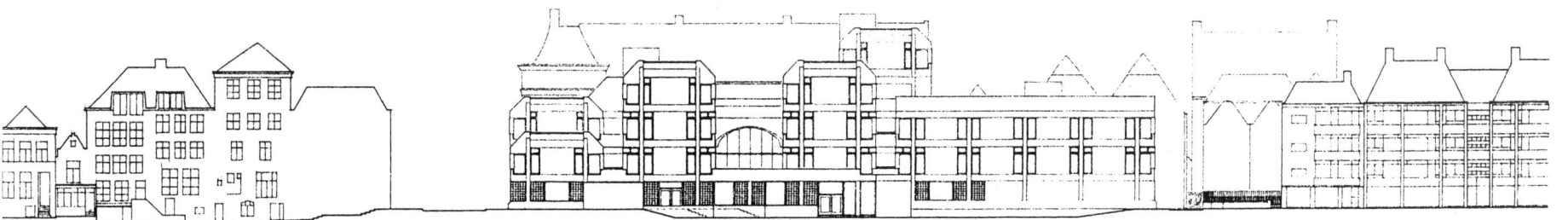

Cross-section with entrance and main hall through new and existing streets

Tajiri Exhibition, Stedelijk Museum, Amsterdam, 1967

An existing place 'filled' with new ones. Two translucent cylindrical spaces (diameter 11 m) appeared there within hours, rustling as you passed! Sheets of thin tracing paper suspended from the ceiling and glued together vertically. Inside the drums some artificial light. Thus as natural light diminishes towards evening the light inside the drums takes over, slowly turning them into huge lamps.

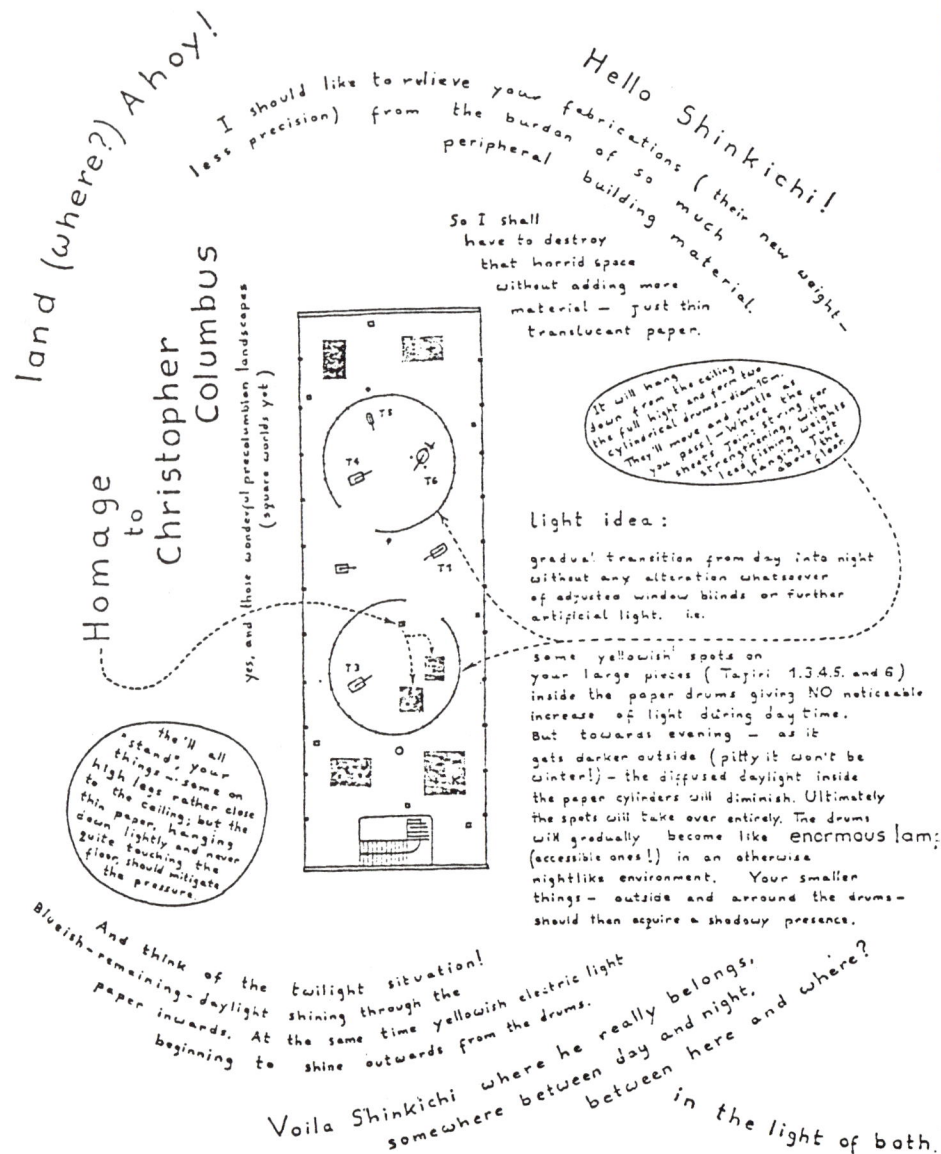

land (where?) Ahoy!

Hello Shinkichi!

I should like to relieve your fabrications (their new weight, less precision) from the burden of so much peripheral building material.

So I shall have to destroy that horrid space without adding more material — just thin translucent paper.

It will hang down 2 cm from the ceiling and form two cylindrical drums — diam. 10 m. They'll move and rustle as you pass! Where the paper joins it will need fixing for strengthening. Weighted hanging just above floor.

Homage to Christopher Columbus

yes, and those wonderful precolumbian landscapes (square worlds yet)

light idea:

gradual transition from day into night without any alteration whatsoever of adjusted window blinds or further artificial light. i.e.

some 'yellowish' spots on your large pieces (Tajiri 1.3.4.5. and 6) inside the paper drums giving NO noticeable increase of light during day time. But towards evening — as it gets darker outside (pitty it won't be winter!) — the diffused daylight inside the paper cylinders will diminish. Ultimately the spots will take over entirely. The drums will gradually become like **enormous lamp** (accessible ones!) in an otherwise nightlike environment. Your smaller things — outside and arround the drums — should then acquire a shadowy presence.

they'll all 'stand': your things — some on high feet rather close to the ceiling; but the thin paper, hanging down lightly and never quite touching the floor should mitigate the pressure.

And think of the twilight situation! Blueish—remaining—daylight shining through the paper inwards. At the same time yellowish electric light beginning to shine outwards from the drums.

Voila Shinkichi where he really belongs; somewhere between day and night, between here and where? in the light of both.

Tajiri tearing down the paper on closing day:
fragmentation

and the 'opening' of space through aggression

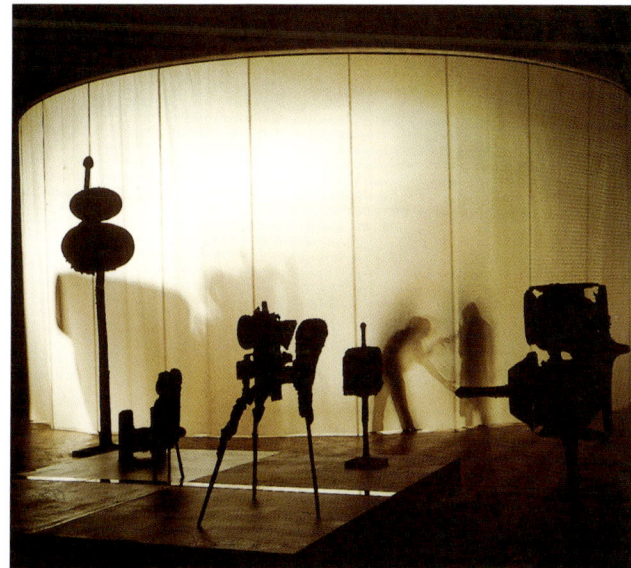

149

M. Visser House, Bergeyk, 1967-9 (extension of a Rietveld house)

Avid collectors of contemporary art begged me to refashion the house G. Rietveld had built for them twelve years earlier. The chief dilemma was that there was far too little wall surface left for their paintings and art objects between all the glass. Beyond that, going to bed and getting up had too long been a spartan undertaking for more or less the same reason. So something had to be done. Although for once a rather inappropriate house, it was after all still a Rietveld house.

Altering it for sound reasons was disturbing because the required changes called for radical, not minor interventions. I did, however, try to bring about what was necessary whilst leaving the architectural structure and fabric of Rietveld's original house practically untouched – still there, I feel, in a phantomlike way.

A large $^3/_4$ cylindrical space providing 25 m of uninterrupted wall surface was built opposite the existing living room on the south side, at some distance and accessible from it, precisely where garden doors once were. The connection between old and new – where they meet – is thus minimal. The floor level was sunk below the existing one so that, besides reducing its considerable bulk, the extension could be inserted under Rietveld's projecting roof leaving room for the same horizontal window strip he employed for the existing kitchen-garage annex.

The narrow passageway along the bedrooms, originally glazed from floor to ceiling – brrrrr – now runs through the interior at an oblique angle, with a handrail along the original posts replacing the former fenestration.

The bathroom extension I proposed later on was a well-deserved extra!

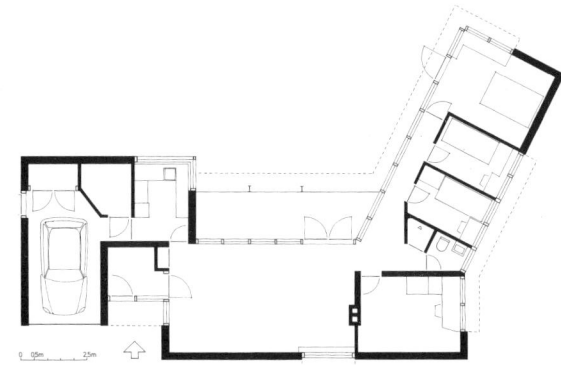

150

The original house designed by Gerrit Rietveld

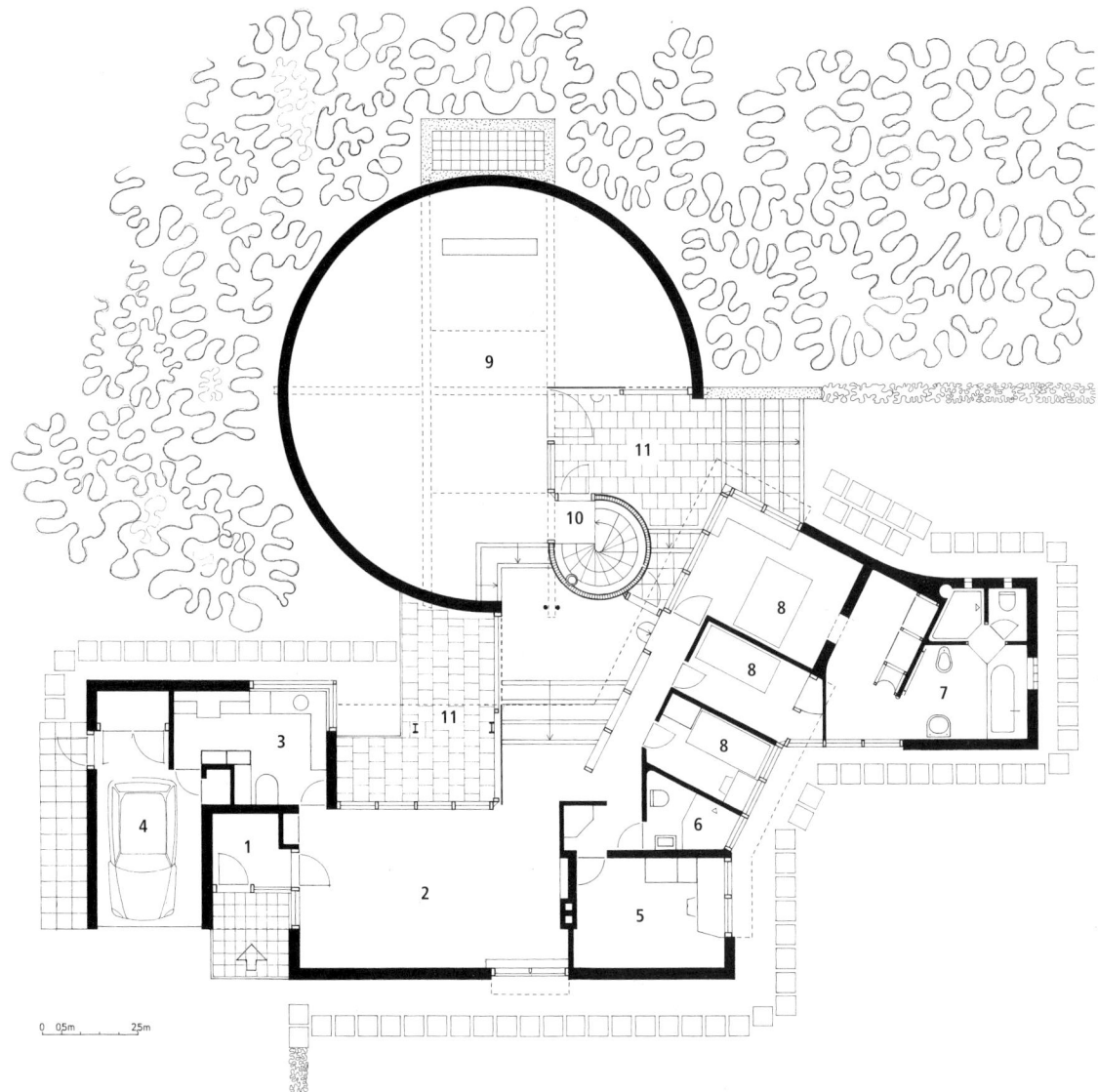

1 entrance	7 bathroom
2 dining room	8 bedroom
3 kitchen	9 living room
4 garage	10 steps to cellar
5 study	11 terrace
6 toilet and shower room	

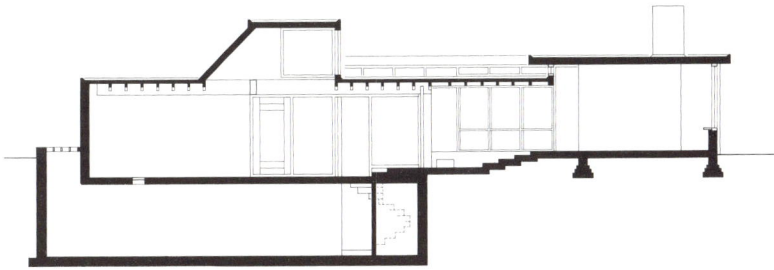

Cross-section of old and new building

Where old and new meet

Sanitary Facilities and Camping Site, Mijnden, 1967-9

Instead of 5 small units with separate entries for men and women, as commissioned, just 2 large ones which can be entered generously without first separation by gender. However, to ensure the requested intimacy after entry, access to each half is postponed spatially as far back into the building as possible – out and away from the entry. Hence the triangular washrooms and diagonal skylights. Since timber is not regarded as 'hygienic', the entire camping is listed as 3-star instead of 4-star... Only in paradise are architects granted an extra star for extra qualities.

The notion that a child should be able to move about freely, without having to cross a road with car traffic to and from the plots, brought about the alteration of the general plan that was provided. This, and the reduction from 5 to 2 of the number of buildings prescribed, each with joint entry for both sexes, was an accepted reality. Luckily a considerable reduction in roads and canals was seen as real advantage!

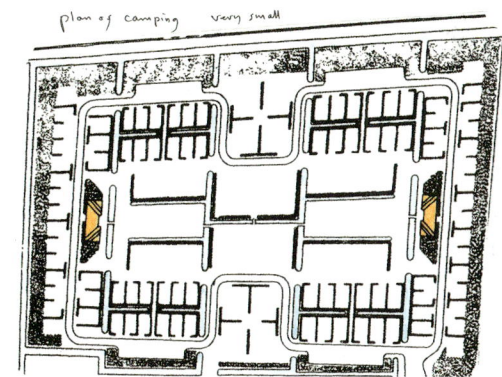

plan of camping   very small

153

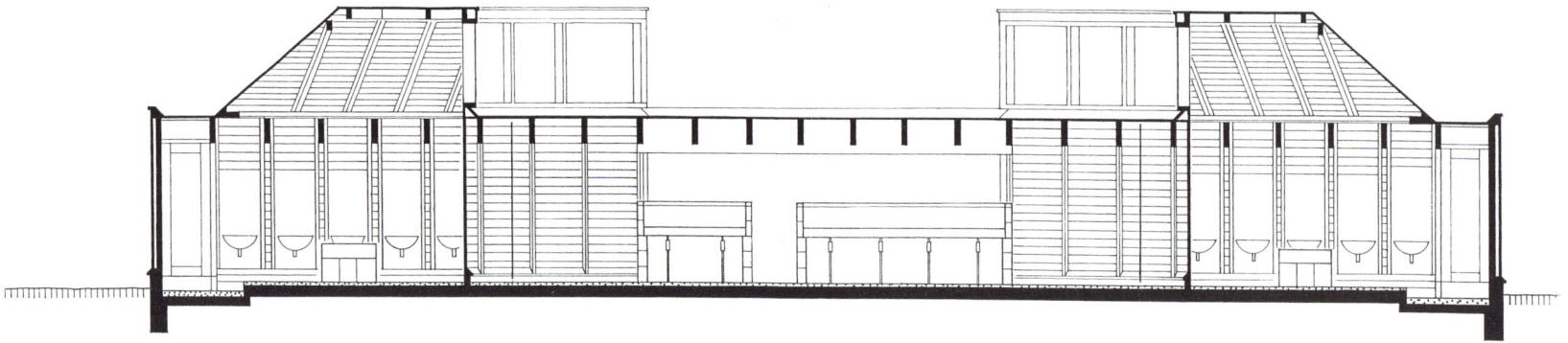

1 vegetable rinsing area   4 showers

2 men's washroom   5 toilets

3 women's washroom   6 rubbish area

Schmela House and Gallery, Düsseldorf, 1967-71

Built on a narrow site in the densest part of the city centre. A parking garage which will flank it on one side required 6 of its total width of 10 metres for a car exit, leaving only 4 metres at ground level for the gallery. What is left is used as a kind of spatial mediator between the street and the exhibition spaces above and below it.

Through an opening in the front exterior wall the public domain extends inwards, where it rests – as a glass drum – on a single column in the midst of the private domain of the gallery. This cylindrical interior outdoor void was de-signed to continue all the way up, so that a bird flying in through the entrance opening could fly out again just below the top floor. This was until, prior to completion, the client had it filled in on the 2nd floor in order to gain a few square metres of extra space. A great pity because the desired exterior-interior ambiguity is now far less evoca-tive as is, consequently, the merging of the private and public domains – their overlap having been intended as the building's architectural message beyond what it pri-marily provided for: an art gallery.

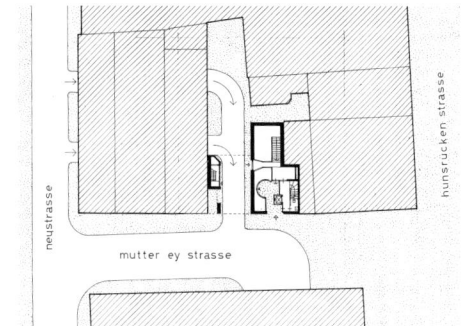

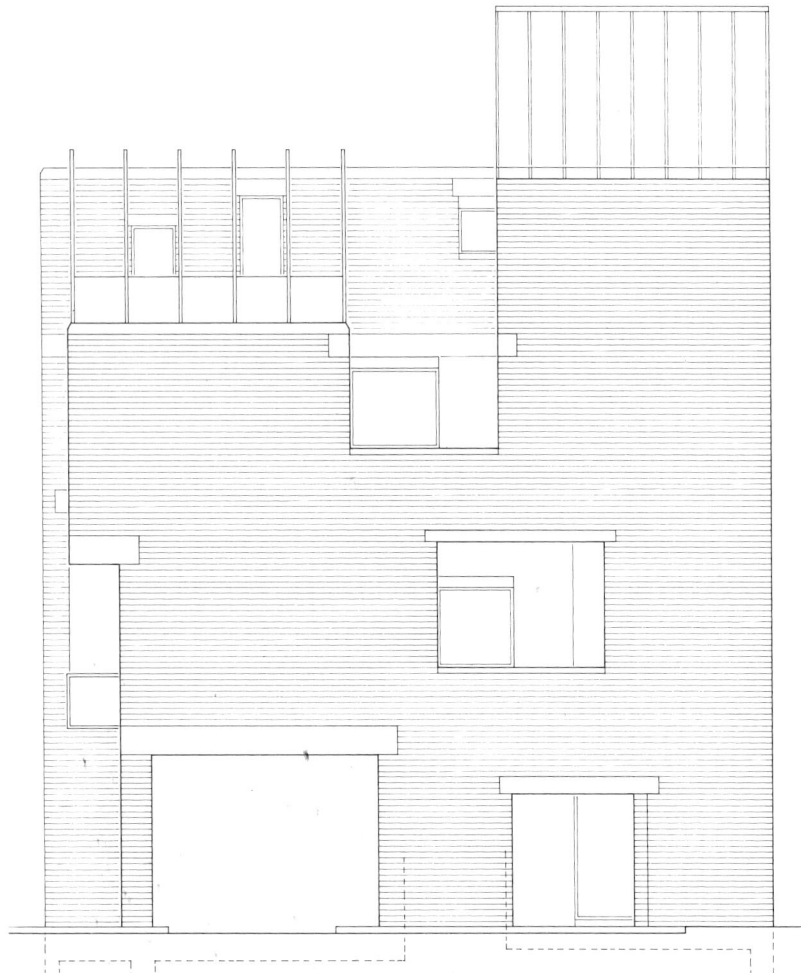

Front elevation

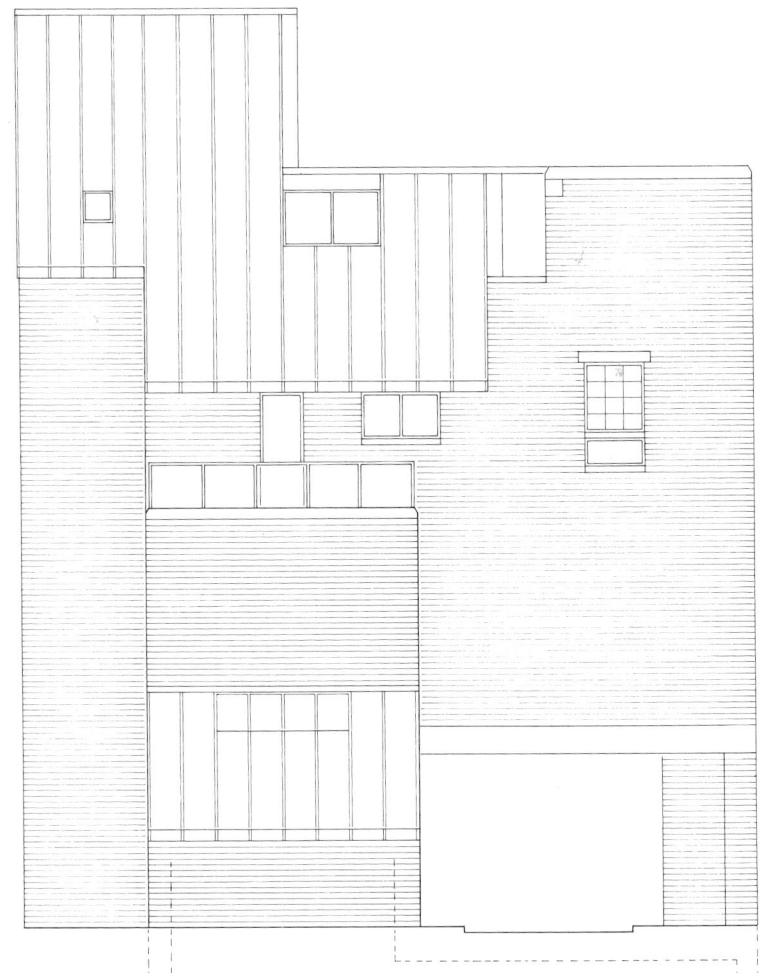

Rear elevation

Public space resting on a pillar in a private domain

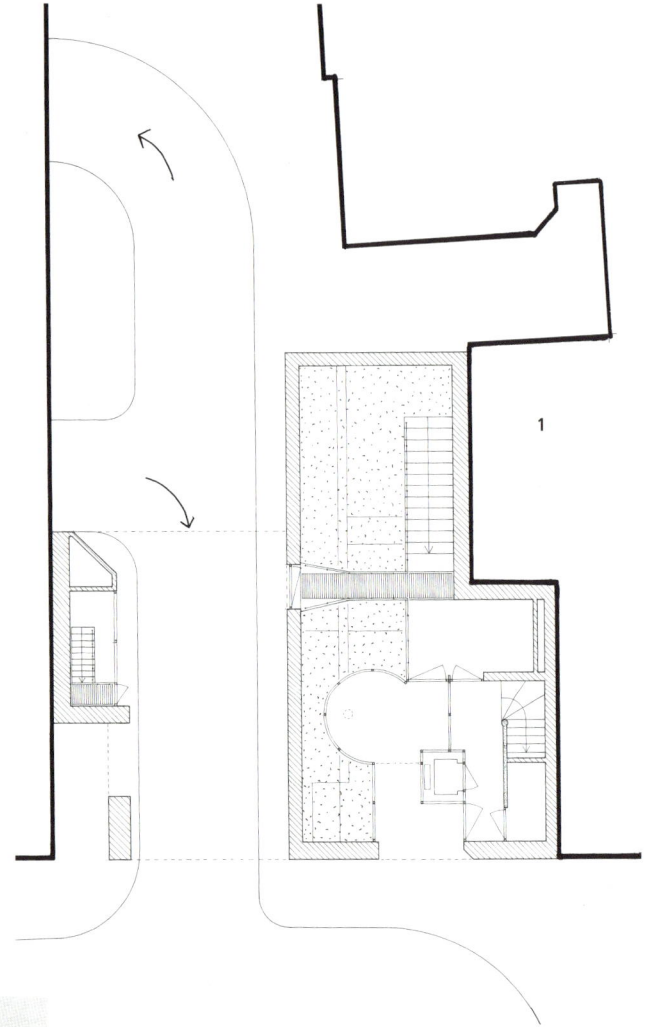

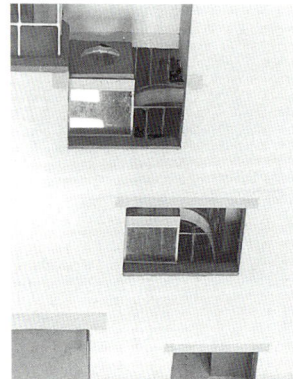

Model showing original void reaching up to the terrace of the second floor

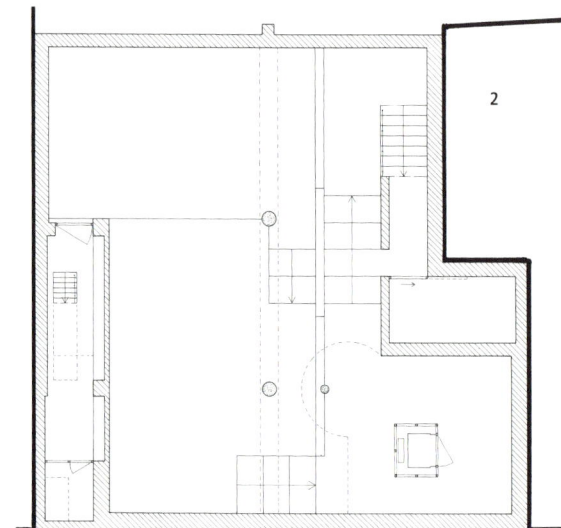

1

2

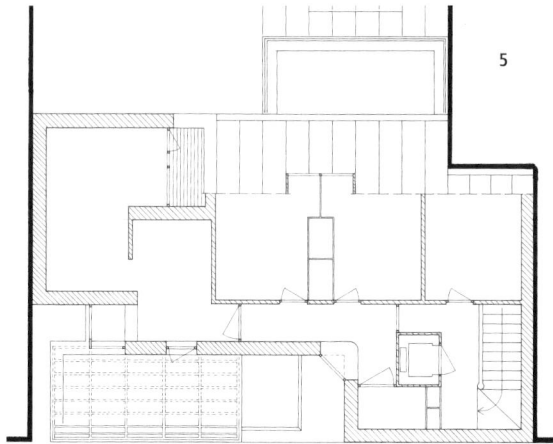

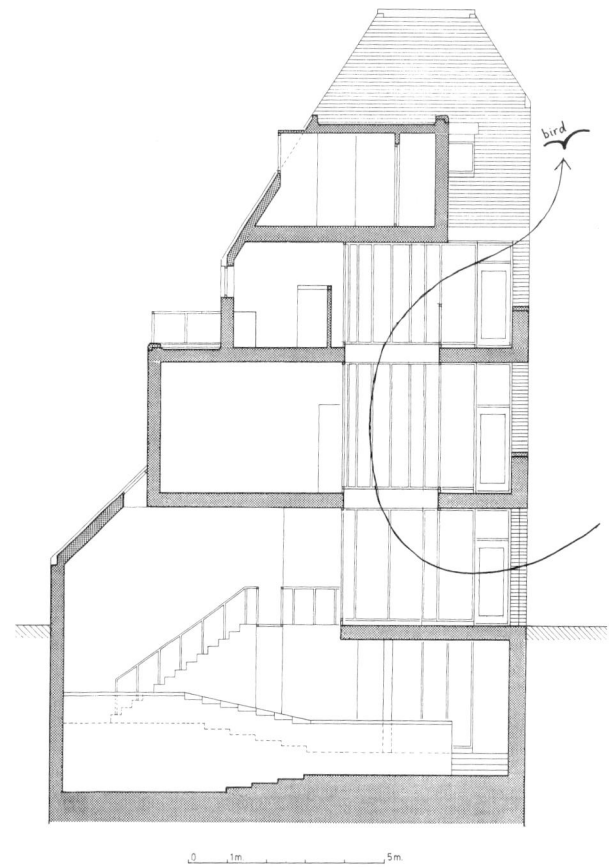

1 location and ground floor gallery
2 basement – gallery
3 first floor – gallery
4 second floor living area
5 third floor bedrooms

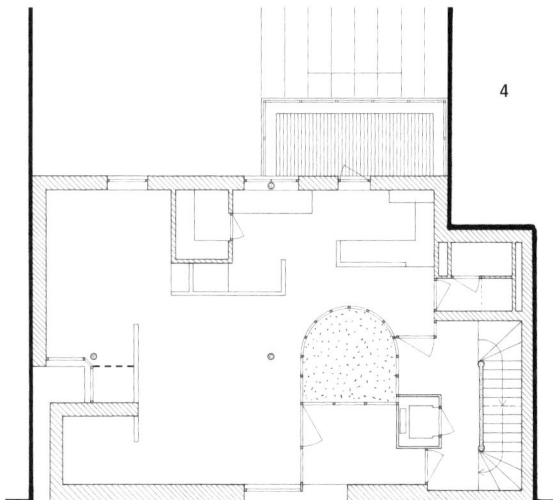

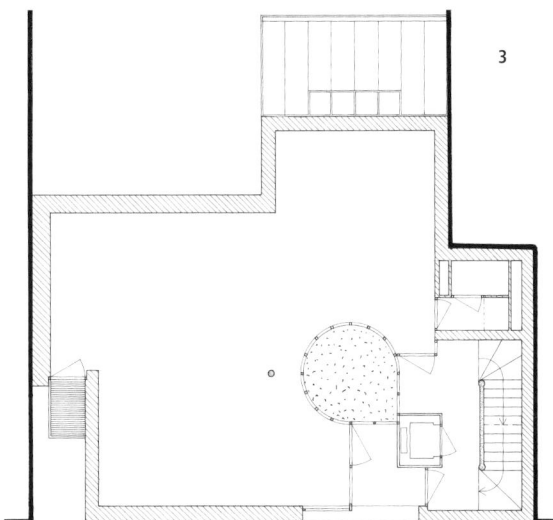

159

Cross-section with void connecting gallery with living area

Living area

Verberk House, Venlo, 1967-70

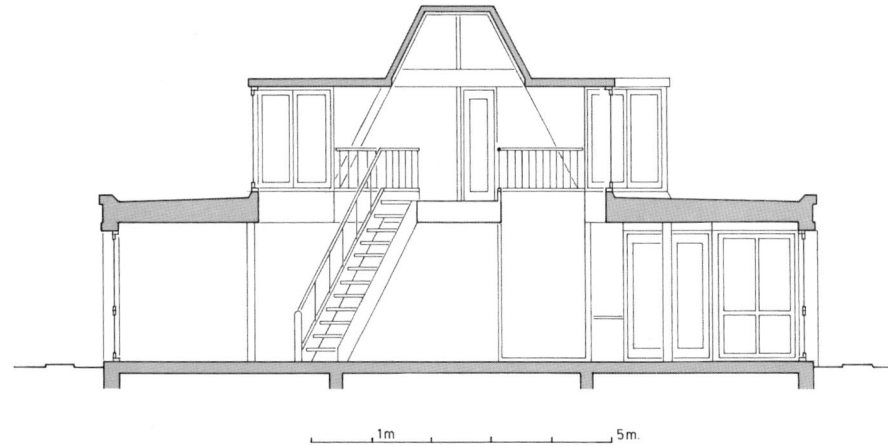

The first owner, who had the house built, cherished distinct notions as to the way the family (parents and two adolescent daughters) was to live in it – each space for more than one person. Most specific was the division between the social and convivial side of the living space: meals, watching television, conversation and games, and the serious cultural side: study, reading, listening to classical music and, after the children's bedtime, discussion.

Spatially the plan developed in depth equally in all directions. Within the exterior perimeter wall and columns – both in masonry – a system of timber framed partitions was devised. The introduction of lighter material for these and their placement at a different angle was meant to underline the specificity of the arrangement but not the permanence (the very next owner immediately altered everything – a pity nonetheless!). The pitched roof, or upward protuberance, was for the girls and included a two-floor unit, attic-like, with room for a guest in each and connected across the centre of the house by a bridge with stairs and, on both sides, windows around ample voids allowing light to enter the living spaces below.

1 family room
2 living room
3 library
4 dining section
5 workroom/bedroom
6 bedroom
7 bathroom
8 kitchen
9 covered terrace
10 bedroom with mezzanine
11 children's area
12 bathroom
13 void
14 stove

160

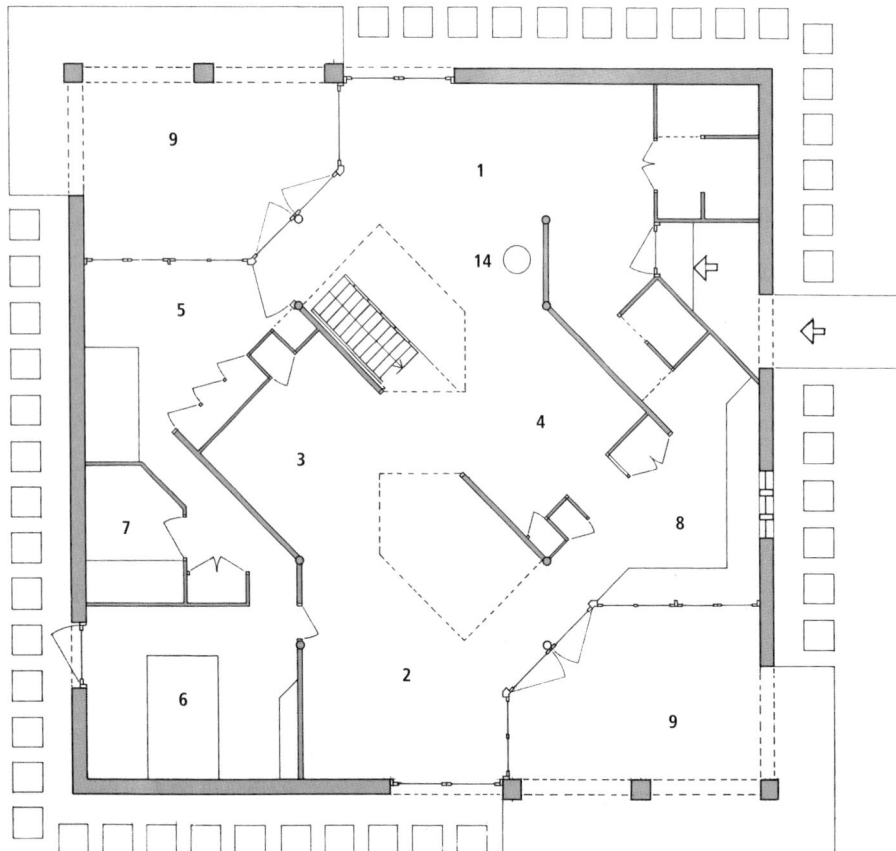

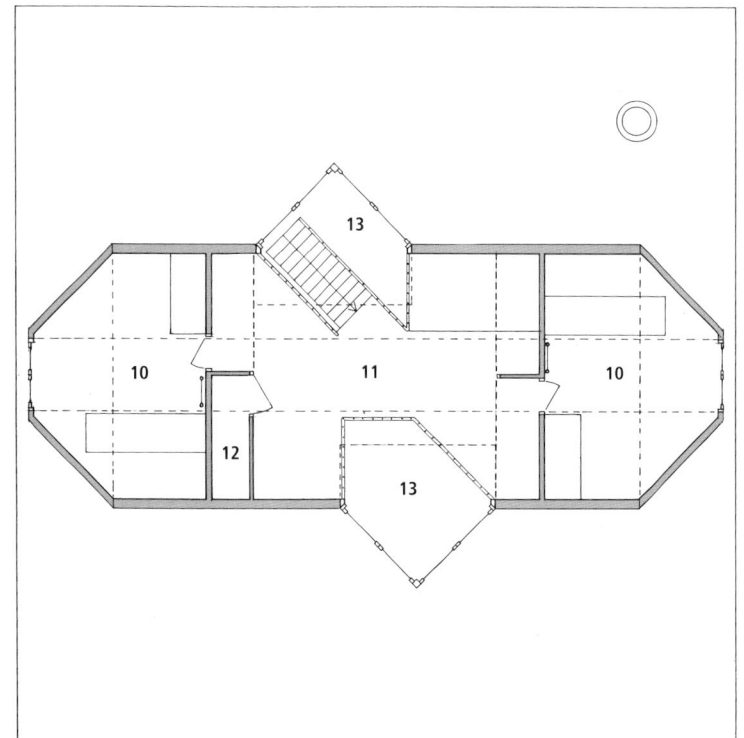

View from mezzanine

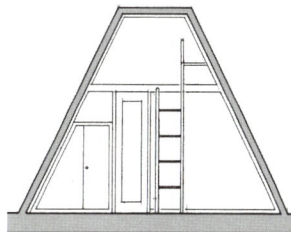

Bedroom with mezzanine

The 15th Triennial Milan, 1968
'il grande numero'

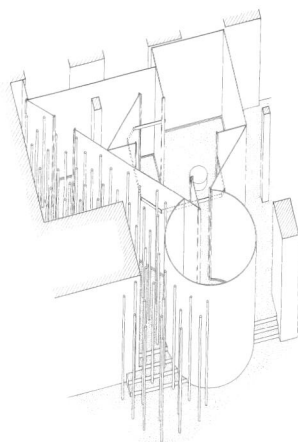

Invited by Giancarlo de Carlo, along with, among others, Arata Isozaki, Peter and Alison Smithson and Shadrach Woods to contribute a personal statement on the main theme of the Triennial: The Greater Number.

Huge halls built by order of Mussolini were subsequently painted a sickly brown in their entirety so that all the contributions would stand out in hopeful contrast to them, radiating technological progress and optimism.

However, since the general subject of the Triennial was to be: The Greater Number, all the walls of my contribution (rough unplaned horizontal planks five metres high from floor to ceiling) were appropriately painted in the same sickly brown as the rest, there being nothing to boast about. The structure, like a set of outsized crates and containing uncomfortable items, was appropriately painted the same sickly brown and rendered scarcely accessible through a forest of slender tree trunks reaching, like the walls, from floor to ceiling. In the triangular space entered next, mirrors glued onto rubber and then broken covered all three walls and produced a disquietingly fragmented and distorted image of yourself and others in all directions, whilst all sorts of laughter resounded in the distance.

In the next – and largest space – two enormous wall-size photographs of the jungle and a destroyed village, as well as handwritten inscription on the wall: *Rimpiangi anche tutti le farfalle* (Mourn also for all butterflies).

In the final cylindrical space Joost van Roojen's beautiful multicoloured banners made it clear that vast multiplication need not imply disaster.

Ironically the entire Triennial was occupied by dissatisfied artists immediately after the official opening and thus remained closed – literally inaccessible – to the end.

mourn also
for all
butterflies

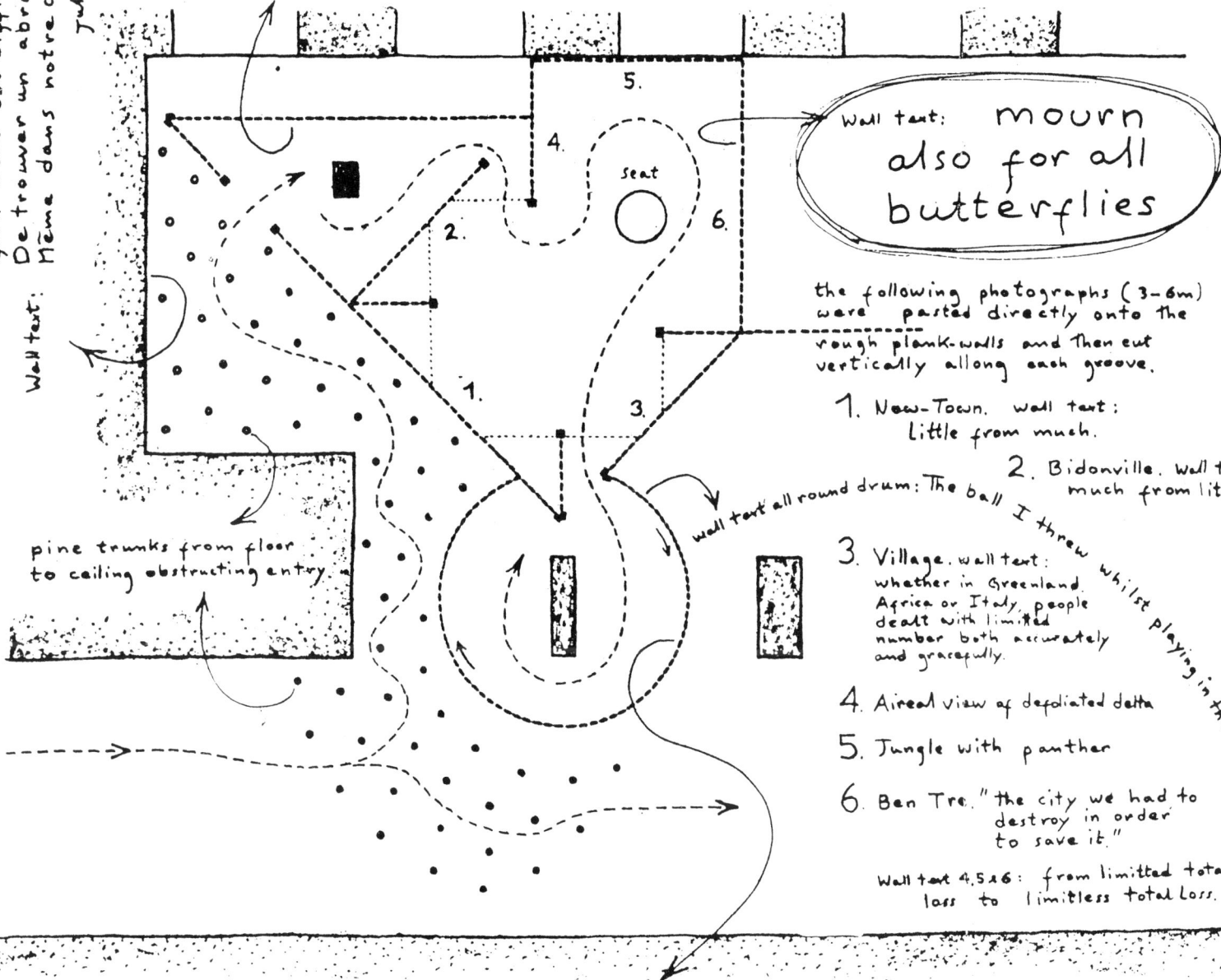

many kinds of laughter from different loudspeakers; the 'sound' slowly & continuously increasing and decreasing from place to place

mirrors from corner to corner on all sides of ▽
glued onto rubber and then broken:
one's self in space, multiplied, fragmented, distorted.

Qu'il nous est difficile
De trouver un abri
Même dans notre cœur

Jules Supervielle

Wall text:

5.

4.

seat

6.

Wall text: mourn also for all butterflies

the following photographs (3-6m) were pasted directly onto the rough plank-walls and then cut vertically along each groove.

1. New-Town. Wall text:
   Little from much.

2. Bidonville. Wall text:
   much from little.

pine trunks from floor to ceiling obstructing entry

2.

1.

3.

wall text all round drum: The ball I threw whilst playing in the park has not yet reached the ground.

3. Village. wall text:
   whether in Greenland,
   Africa or Italy, people
   dealt with limited
   number both accurately
   and gracefully.

4. Aireal view of defoliated delta

5. Jungle with panther

6. Ben Tre. "the city we had to destroy in order to save it."

Wall text 4,5 & 6: from limitted total loss to limitless total loss.

general wall text: Disturb the delicate intricacies of the limitless microcosm. Trespass into the limitless macrocosm. Frighten the angels. Inbetween, mess up the Mississippi and the Mekong. If that is the choice, it will soon be here, for there's a limit even to limitless: man falling in line with entropy after all!

cloth streamers by Joost van Roojen; their length as well as their complexity and intensity increasing as the intervals between them decrease. Wall text: that more does not have to mean less.

Dylan Thomas

163

Villa Robert van Eyck, St-Paul-de-Vence, 1968

This was to be a large house on a heavily wooded site with a magnificent view of the Mediterranean in the distance. The idea was to split the plan open, so as to draw the view beyond into the depth of the interior through the two covered terraces, facing each other on different levels as well as through the gap between them. The site is a large one, so the drive to the house past an ancient orchard is quite impressive in itself. Once there, the front door, the interior courtyard and the covered terraces beyond are reached successively from below by steps cut between huge rocks. Thus the house wraps round the landscape in which it is set. From across the interior courtyard, around which all the spaces are strung, the covered terraces appear as part of the panorama.

Distance is captured – the exterior is interiorized, whilst proximity is extended.

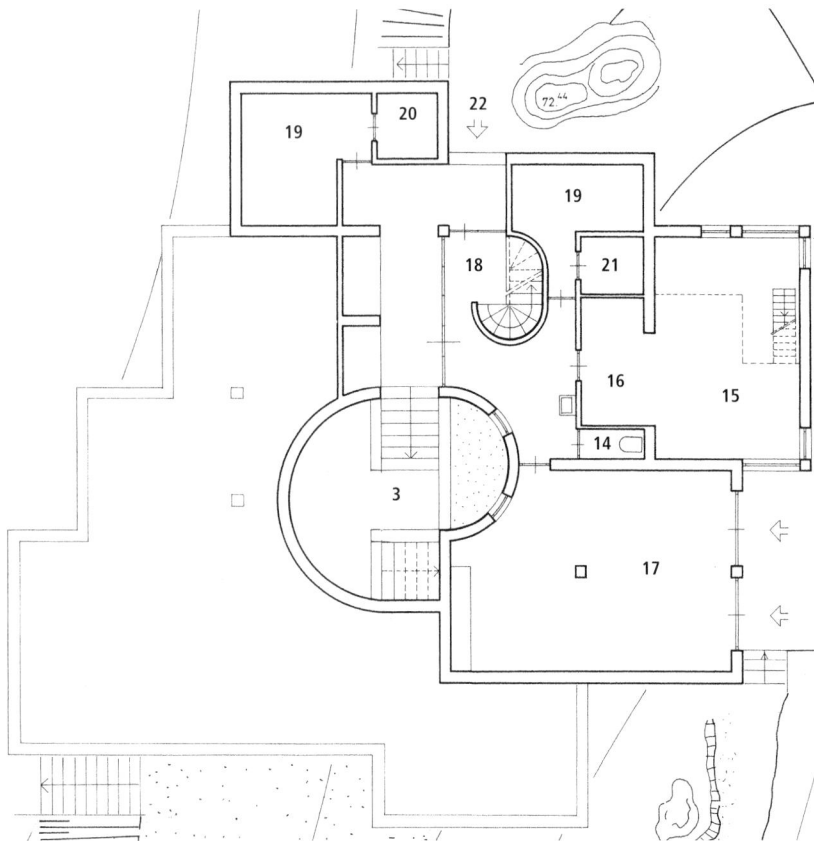

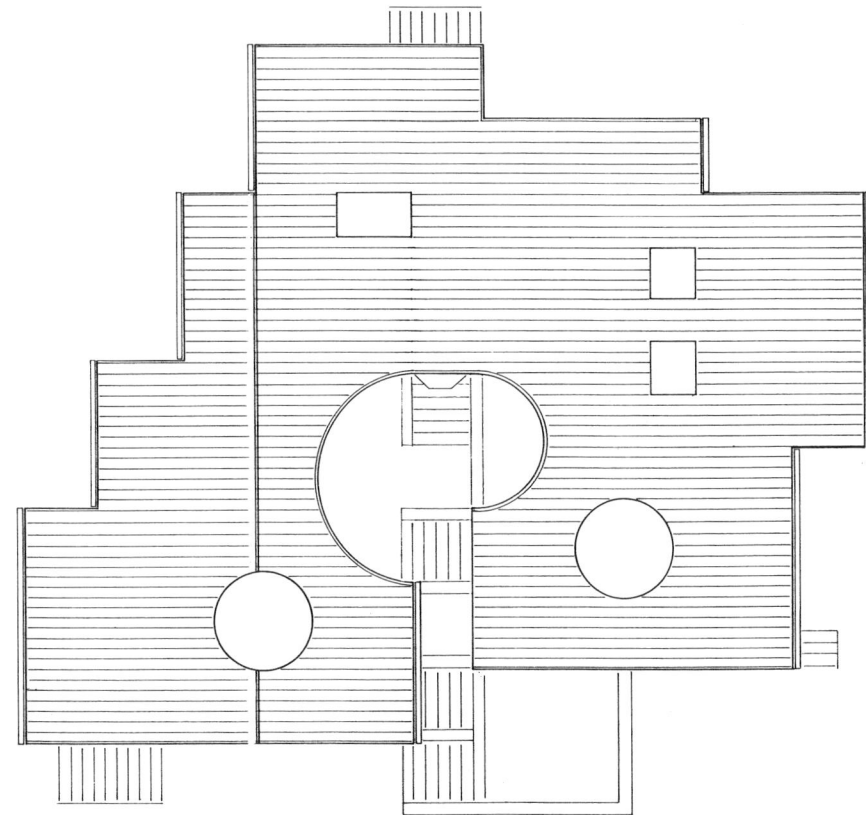

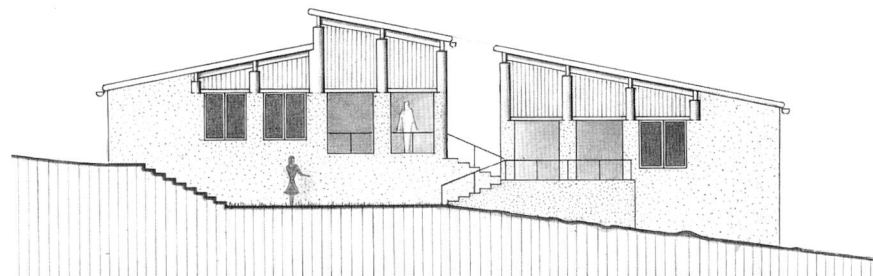

1 loggia
2 pool
3 court
4 living room
5 kitchen
6 dining
7 bedroom
8 guestroom
9 mezzanine in studio
10 void
11 bedroom
12 bathroom
13 garderobe
14 toilet
15 studio
16 storage paintings
17 garage
18 lobby
19 storage
20 wine
21 boiler
22 entrance

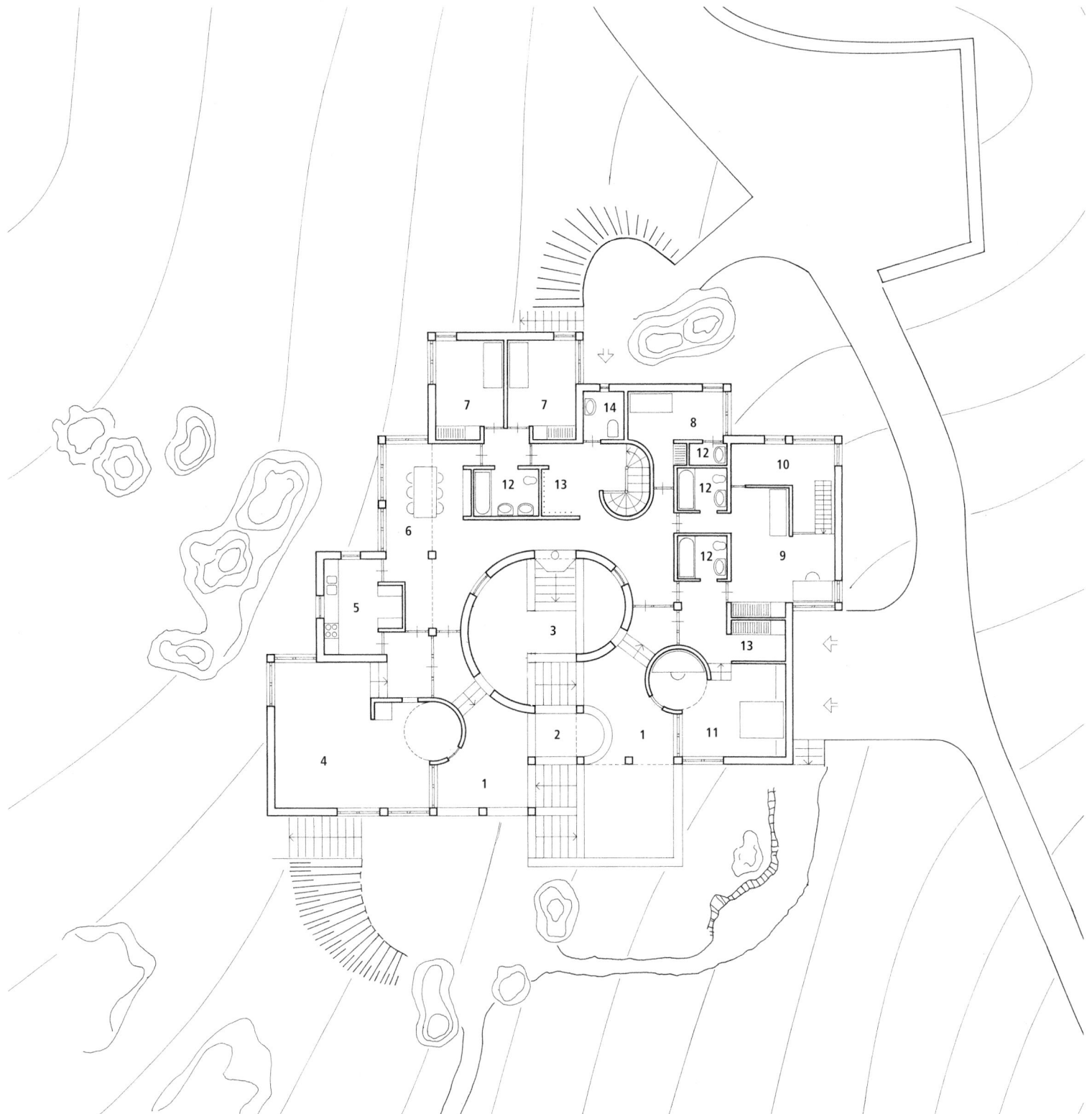

Town Residence Marquis of Bute, London, 1969
(conversion)

This was to become the London residence for a family used to lots of space and air. The orientation of the existing Victorian house was to the north. This and the overall clutter of boxy spaces called for some rather marked alterations.

In order to bring at least some sunshine into the main living room it was given the full width of the house. Beyond that the massive protrusion on the north, garden side was replaced by another, extending outwards and made entirely of steel and glass. Entering the living room diagonally from the opposite corner, it should be a welcome surprise to discover sunlight on lots of indoor foliage if only in the morning and late afternoon. The desired serpentine movement through the ground floor spaces, which contributes towards the 'width-towards-light' idea, starts at the front door, placed inwards at a slight angle.

On the first floor the main bedroom shares some of the same features as the living room below. The balcony round the new bay has a glass roof. All existing openings in exterior walls, however, are maintained throughout (quite a few became recessed balconies).

The main staircase changes shape, construction or position twice on its way up to the children's play loft; the idea being to bring some extra light down into the house from above.

Sunlight in spite of north oriented living room

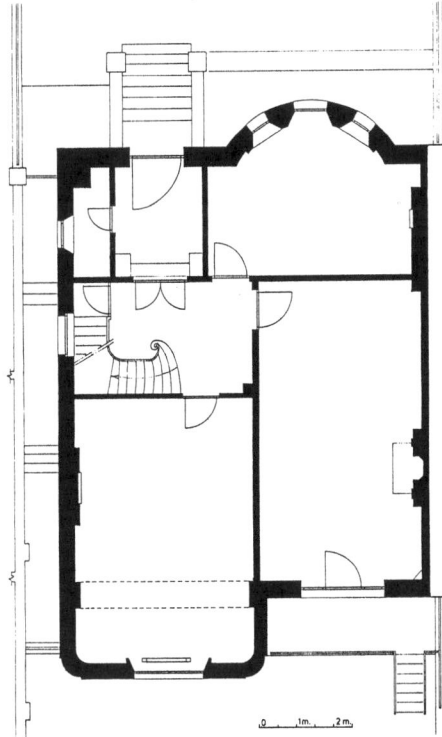

Basement
1 living room   4 lift
2 bedroom   5 lobby
3 kitchen

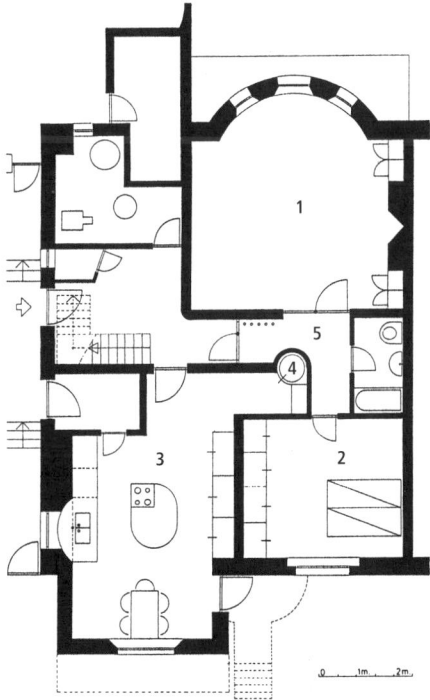

Ground floor
1 hall   4 lift
2 dining room 5 living room
3 pantry   6 loggia
             7 terrace

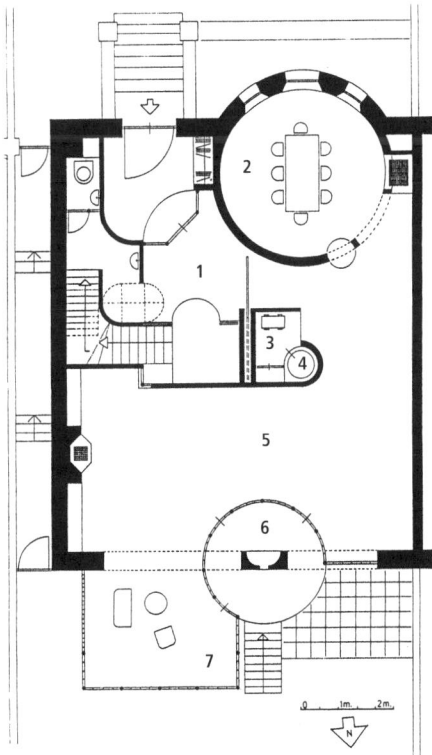

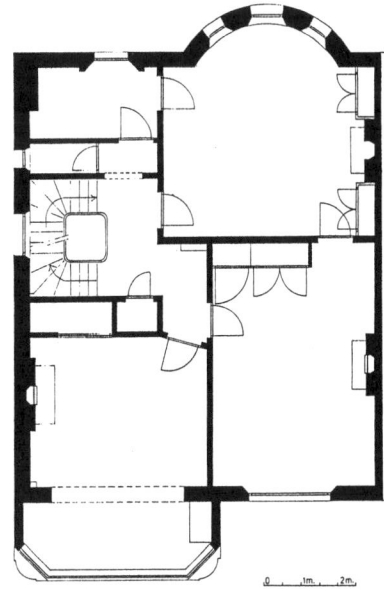

First floor
1 bedroom lord Bute 4 lift
2 bedroom lady Bute 5 loggia
3 bathroom   6 balcony

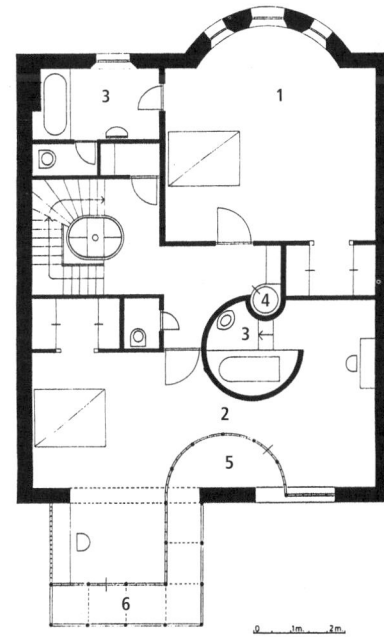

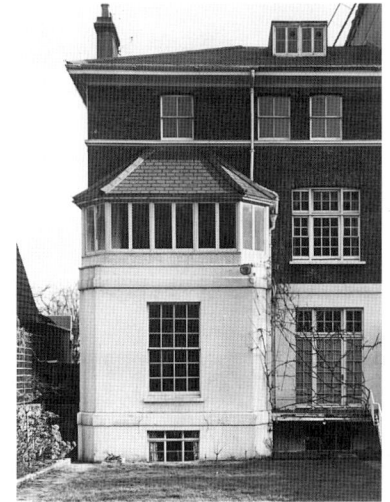

Second floor
1 bedroom
2 bathroom
3 loggia

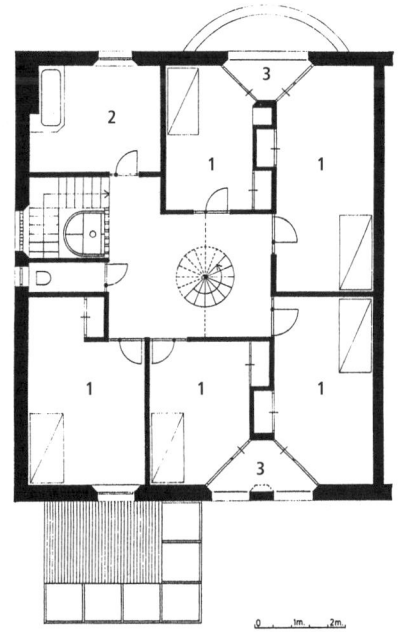

167

PREVI, Housing Development, Lima, 1969-76
with Sean Wellesley Miller (competition)

The notion that future free development should not work against the best interests of the occupant is still insufficiently realised when designing expandable dwellings!

Like the typical Barriada house, this one can in the course of time be expanded by self-help, horizontally and vertically, from one to eight rooms, and according to a family's requirements and resources. No minimal existence solution for the poor à la CIAM here! The saw-tooth, non-loadbearing yard walls discourage expansion outside the house's maximum orthogonal perimeter, i.e. into the yards.

Small patios so often provide 4 walls for a subsequent roof, resulting in the loss of outdoor space, of direct access to all rooms, and a serious reduction of light and air in the surrounding rooms – even complete loss of both when lots adjoin along two or three sides, which is so often the case. So instead, each house has an enclosed front and back yard (or garden) connected by a central space which can be partially or entirely opened onto either one or both for ventilation and free movement.

The central, multi-interpretable outdoor-indoor space, which runs somewhat diagonally through the middle of the lot from end to end, contains the kitchen and gives access to all the rooms and roof terraces. The prevailing wind direction (SSW) called for approximately east to west placing of rows; 90% humidity all year round called for a fairly loose open structure. The deep access paths to the dwellings allow breezes to penetrate far into the clustering bands. The lots are offset laterally, facilitating the penetration of air through the houses.

Although not mandatory, the competition programme stimulated the development of new prefabrication or industrialized building methods. For obvious reasons however we declined the use of materials or constructions not currently available or used by people with little building experience and equipment. Painting the houses should have been left to the people. Literally dipped in white it looked like a postwar Weissenhof Siedlung. When people eventually added colour, no walls remained looking like the original material (brick or concrete block), which is customary in Peru and very effective.

168

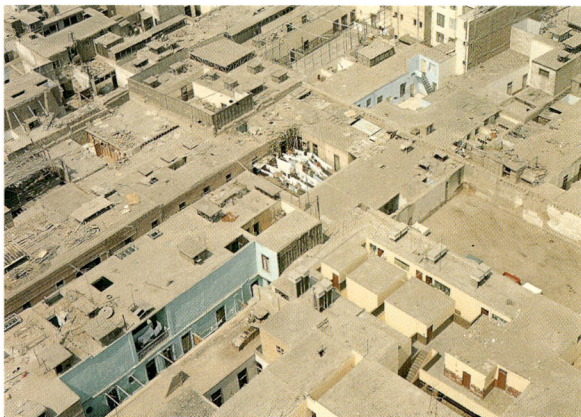

Barriada Pampa de Comas, near Lima (1962)

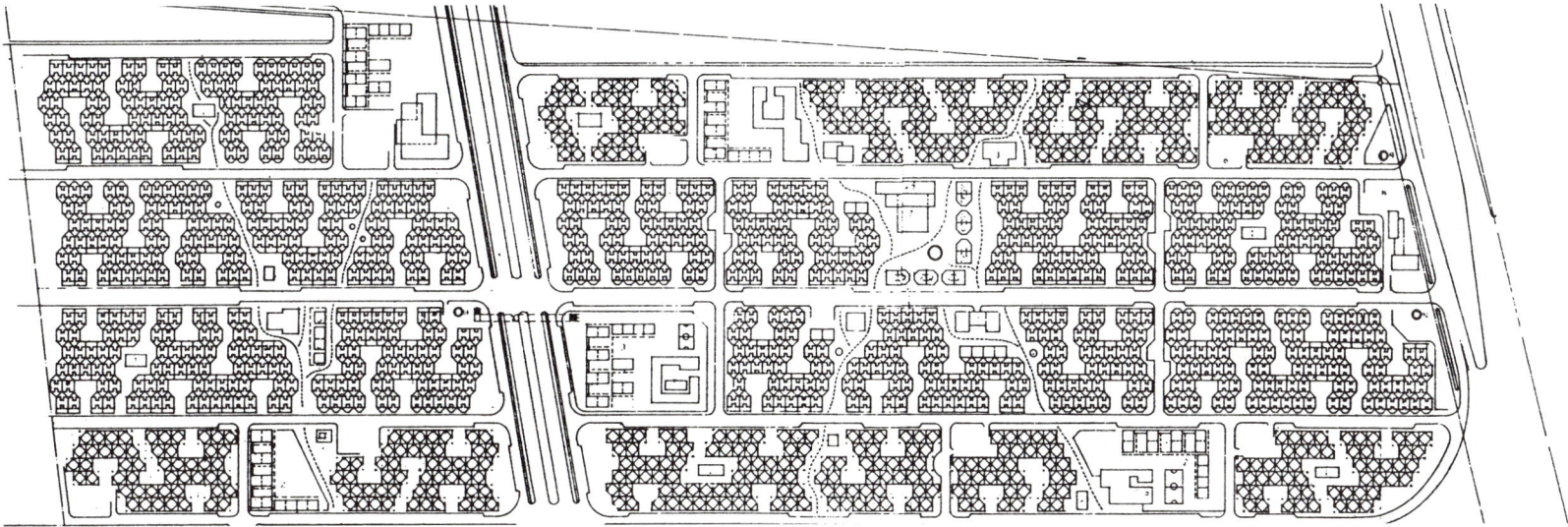

No Misplaced Suburbia

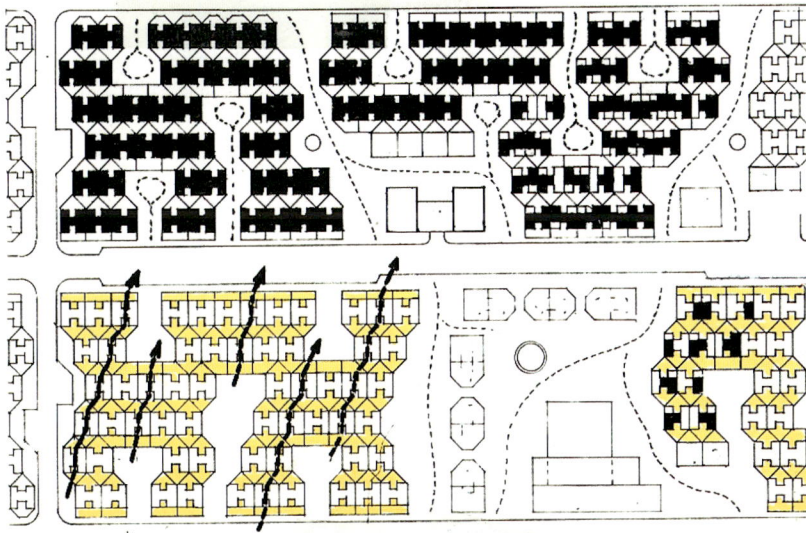

In 1968 a competition was organised which was open to all Peruvian architects and to thirteen invited foreign teams. The competition was for the design and construction of a community of low-cost dwellings for 1500 families on a 40 ha site located 8 km north of central Lima. The brief included very precise requirements as to layout and dwelling types. It was decided to build a sample of all the principle types (approx. 25 units) entered by the various competitors including Charles Correa, Christopher Alexander, Atelier 5, Kisho Kurakawa, Fumihiko Maki, Candilis-Josic-Woods, James Stirling and Aldo van Eyck.

169

The general settlement layout is dealt with in some detail because the 25-odd dwellings which were finally built do not demonstrate the full potential of the originally proposed clustering system. The urban structure for the entire site submitted for the competition is based on a clustering principle which is independent of either dwelling type or shape of lot. It thus possesses a general relevance beyond the given context and underlines the notion that rather than introducing endless variations on a single dwelling type, several completely different types can go together within a single configurative urban fabric. The rows of clusters are six lots deep, thus greatly reducing the number of parallel streets. Placed well apart, these streets – busy *avenidas* – serve both pedestrian and vehicular traffic, which may well offend established planning ethics! However, in view of Peruvian urban reality, such a combined use of straight avenues (one km. long with a view of distant hills in both directions) need and should not be avoided. Whilst local traffic flow will be modest, its social and economic significance is considerable (e.g. 'collectivo' taxis). In contrast to the East-West, North-South traffic net, de pedestrian paths – *paseos* – run diagonally towards the wide middle avenue in the direction of the central plaza. All schools are accessible along these *paseos*. Access paths penetrate into the housing bands. They are wide enough to permit car entry for bringing building material to each dwelling when needed. Children's play areas, trees for shade and fountains are situated at the ends of these paths, whilst kindergartens are placed in the centre of the rows of clusters. It is expected that small shops will develop spontaneously along the principle *avenida*.

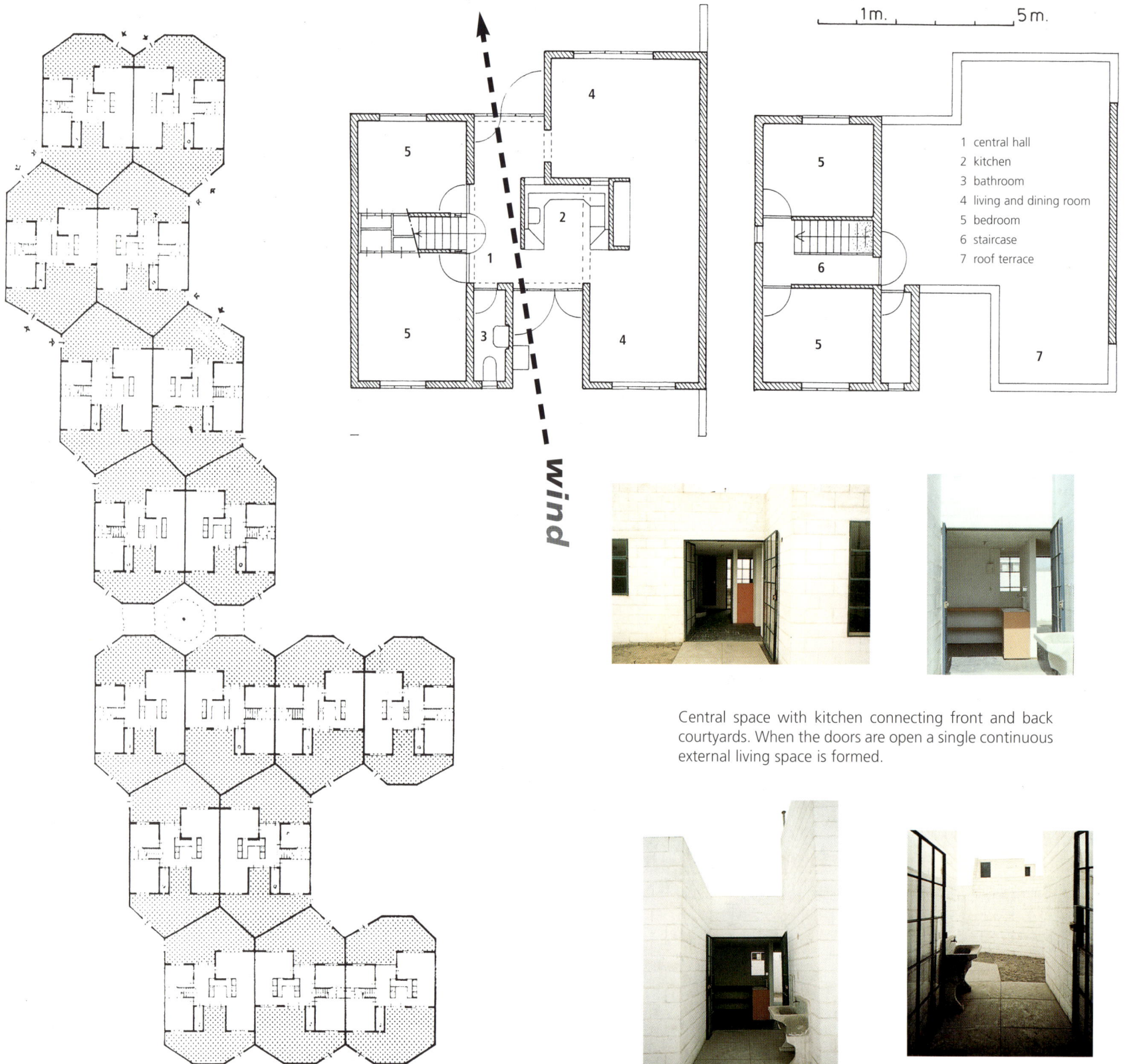

1m.   5m.

wind

1 central hall
2 kitchen
3 bathroom
4 living and dining room
5 bedroom
6 staircase
7 roof terrace

Central space with kitchen connecting front and back courtyards. When the doors are open a single continuous external living space is formed.

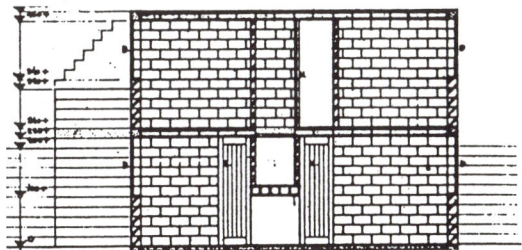

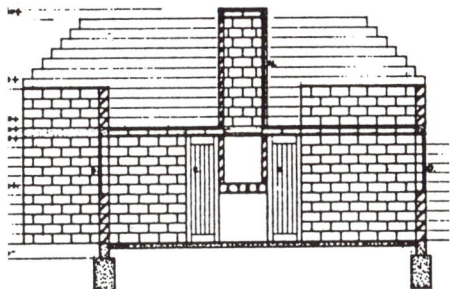

172

The walled gardens shortly af

completion and some years later

Joost van Roojen Exhibition, Van Abbemuseum, Eindhoven, 1969

 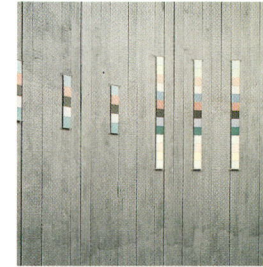 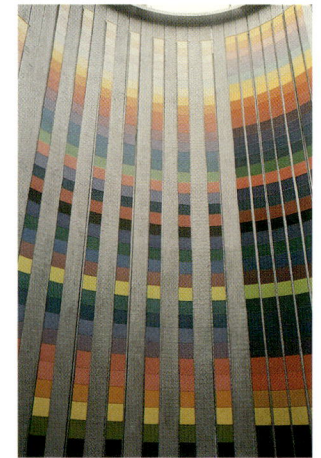

The exhibition rooms were once again 'filled' and 'broken' as they were by Tajiri and again 15 years later in Athens. In Eindhoven it was done by putting blind panels and corner mirrors directly opposite transparent areas of glass. This led to a strange confusion between what is reflected and what is directly visible.

What is more, I was able, where it was meaningful, to have works that hung opposite each other suddenly appear in the same image, which reinforced the repeatedly surprising elements within the overall unity of the work.

Strips of coloured fabric on aluminized screens

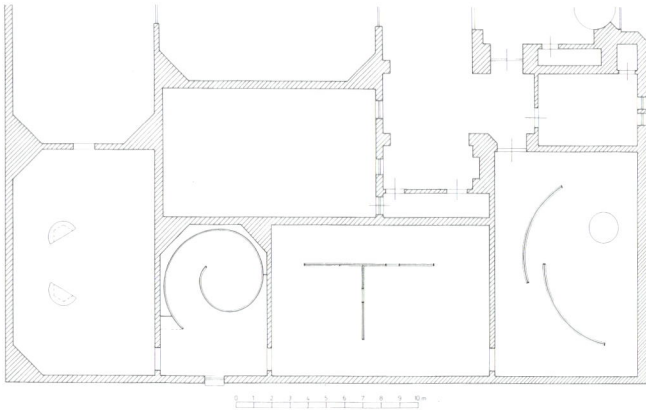

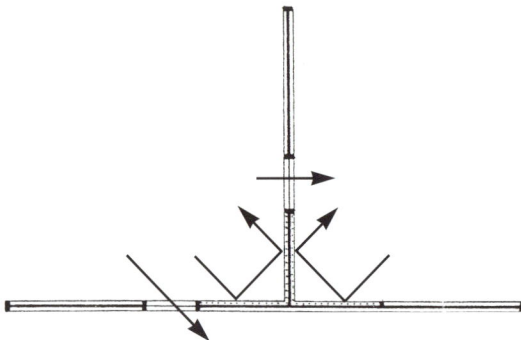

City Centre as Donor

There are a number of general concepts at the basis of our plan for the Nieuwmarkt neighbourhood. These ideas apply to Amsterdam in particular, but they are also relevant to other old, spatially homogenous urban cores, large and small, in Holland and elsewhere.

To regard a city centre as the place where social, cultural as well as economic activities are largely concentrated, produced and distributed, is an obsolete nineteenth-century notion.

Today's means of communication render this superfluous, while the increasing size of the economic establishment and all the concomitant accretions render their combination impossible.

We believe that today old city centres – both their spatial reality and their content – are psychologically indispensable for their own sake, simply because they exist in all their multicoloured intensity and enclosure, and because so far no newly-built districts possess these essential qualities in the least, not even in a contemporary version. They are rigid, empty and sterile and are therefore inadequate as places to live. As long as they remain this way, the city centre will continue to function as a donor. Nowadays, however, its donor task is too great for its size. It is therefore absolutely essential not only to keep its size as large as possible, but to ensure that the addition of certain quanta does not have the effect of losing precisely those qualities that, owing to the sterility of the suburbs, make it into a donor.

Breaking open the old city centres to make them more easily accessible to traffic for the convenience of those people who have no choice but to travel there every day, results in the creation of a space where those very concentrations can and probably will occur which, because of their function, are alienated from the existing structure, which have no obvious and direct human relevance and which are therefore emotionally inaccessible.

The mutations which take place constantly in every city and which are truly necessitated by changed circumstances will have to be shaped with more imagination, more subtly, more circumspectly, and more organically. The results of this continuous process must always be a reflection of collective behavioural patterns. If society is to safeguard its own identity, everyone alike will have to contribute to the continual changes in the urban environment. This will not be made any easier by the far-reaching changes that are wrought for the benefit of the community, but nor will it be rendered impossible.

A city which dismisses the creative potential and spontaneous initiatives of its inhabitants, which reflects only what people do there and not what they are always doing to it: adding to it and changing it, will end up dismissing its own self – it will die.

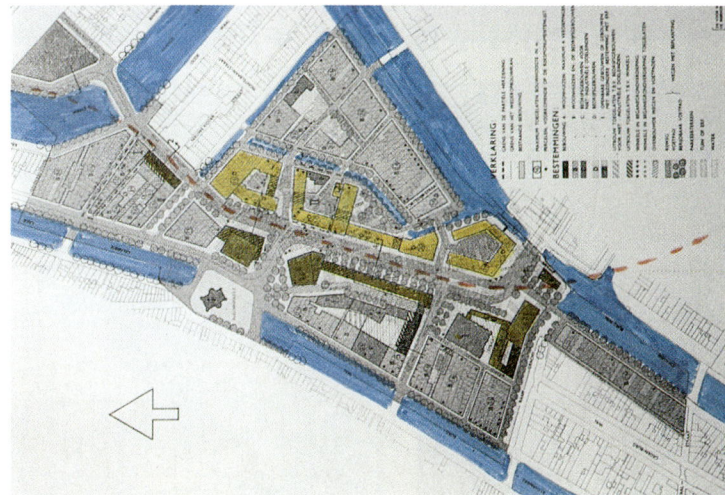

The current city council plan for Nieuwmarkt area

Urban Reconstruction, Nieuwmarkt Area, Amsterdam, 1970
with Theo Bosch, Guus Knemeijer, Paul De Ley and Dik Tuinman

In the framework of the way it was formulated, we could only interpret the brief for proposals for the reassessment of the reconstruction plan for Nieuwmarkt in one way, which was to make a suggestion involving the existing structure. The inner city memorandum protected the Nieuwmarkt area as a whole as a residential district, a paradoxical decision when one considers that an underground railway station, a good access road and plenty of parking make an area exceptionally attractive to business. We intend the road and the underground exclusively for use by those who wish to move in or through the inner city and not as access to this part of the city for the benefit of business premises.

Nieuwmarkt area – neighbourhood or urban district?
The Nieuwmarkt area has, since time immemorial, been densely inhabited and lay between the city and the port. But the neighbourhood had sufficient function of its own to hold its own as an urban district when the port activities shifted to the west.

It was mainly oriented to the east, where many Jewish refugees from Eastern Europe settled on the Uilenburg, Valkenburg and Rapenburg islands.

After 1945 these places were empty, and large gaps between buildings provided evidence of the war. The Nieuwmarkt area had become the edge of the inner city, not undamaged but certainly not destroyed. But vulnerable. Amsterdam city council left these areas for what they were, with the plans for the city of Amsterdam, the IJ tunnel and a North-South connection at the back of their minds. The uncertainty that arose from the continuing lack of a clear zoning plan kept new establishments away. House owners refused to carry out essential repair work; it was preferred to demolish than to finance expensive facilities.

Dilapidation increased rapidly, also as a result of part of the population being cleared away. Those who stayed, of necessity or choice, lived in total uncertainty, and allowed their houses to deteriorate, since the demolition men might arrive tomorrow. A horrible situation that has now been going on for 25 years.

One would not heal the area as a neighbourhood only by

Nieuwmarkt area after the demolition for the underground railway

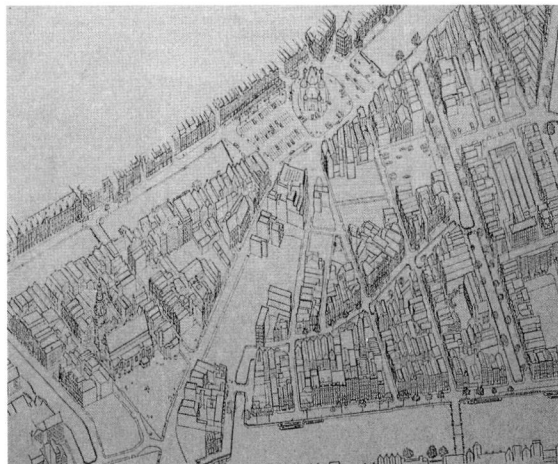

Plan of the buildings

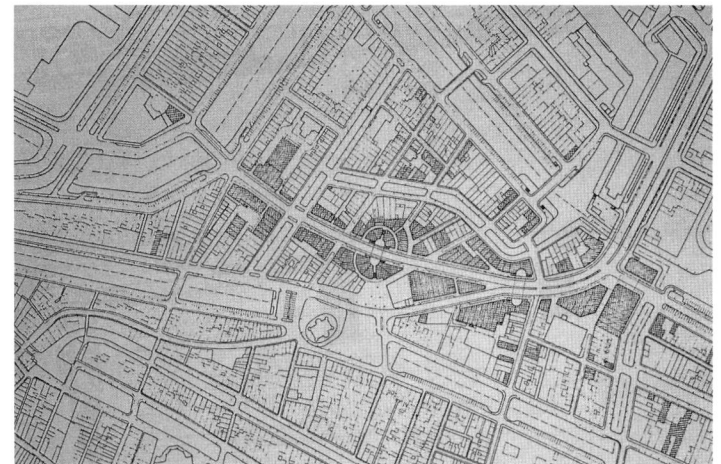

rebuilding the vanished houses, improving those still there and cleaning up the streets and inner spaces. To do this one needs initiative and imagination, and people who understand that an inner city is indispensable for our present-day existence; that its enclosedness is essential for those forced to live in unendurable outer districts. Those who want to must now be given the chance to make the neighbourhood their own once again, together with anyone who wishes to use the inner city in a meaningful way. This plan very strongly suggests this possibility. The present buildings have not been pushed back any further than was absolutely necessary for the underground railway tunnel. Existing gaps in street blocks have been filled in and the new buildings are adjusted to fit the scale of the rest.

By only allowing small establishments attracting a limited amount of traffic in the ground floors, and reserving the floors above for housing, the new street become a residential one.

Description of the plan

In order to guarantee the inner city to the furthest possible limit in the light of the significance that we ascribe to it as a donor, the existing island structure west of Valkenburgerstraat must remain untouched regardless of the activities that will develop between that street and Oude Schans.

The outer limits of the inner city are defined by the route of the IJ tunnel, which is a fait accompli; the broadened Weesperstraat and the way, without reference to scale, the two together make themselves felt as a no man's land deep into the formerly closed urban structure. These brutal and barely comprehensible rifts are not only unnecessary but also completely impermissible. The proposals contained in our plan in the vicinity of the Zuiderkerk are essential in connection with the above. The opening caused by the penetration on this spot of the dual carriageway heading into the city, which has already been built, must not be wider than is absolutely necessary.

Since it is precisely at this point that the route of the underground railway turns away from that of the road, we consider it necessary to erect part of the new buildings immediately south of the Zuiderkerk over the route of the underground. We also consider it an error to expose the Zuiderkerk.

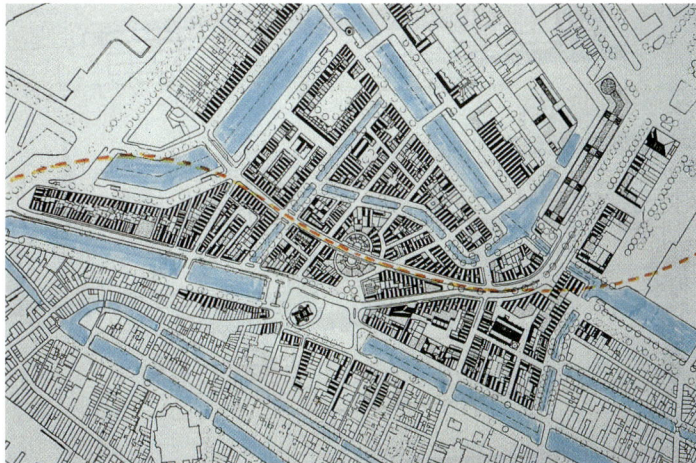

Roof plan

Proposal for traffic to run through the Zuiderkerk – the shortest route to the Dam? The unpleasant thing about the joke is that you know they will not do it!

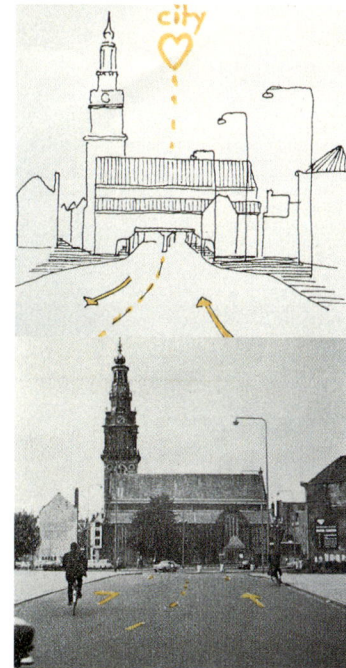

Bureau Van Eyck & Bosch, 1971-82

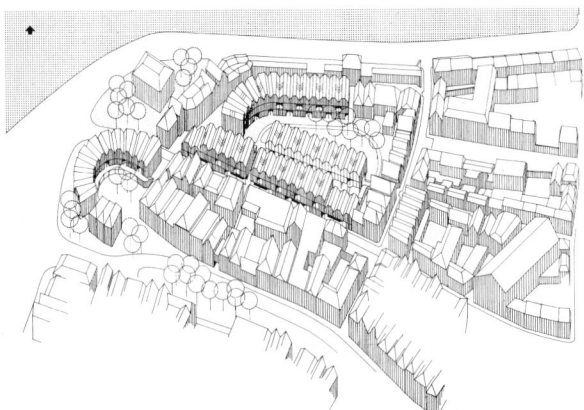

Rode Torenplein, Zwolle, 1971

De Boogjes, Dordrecht, 1975

Faculty of Literature, Amsterdam, 1975

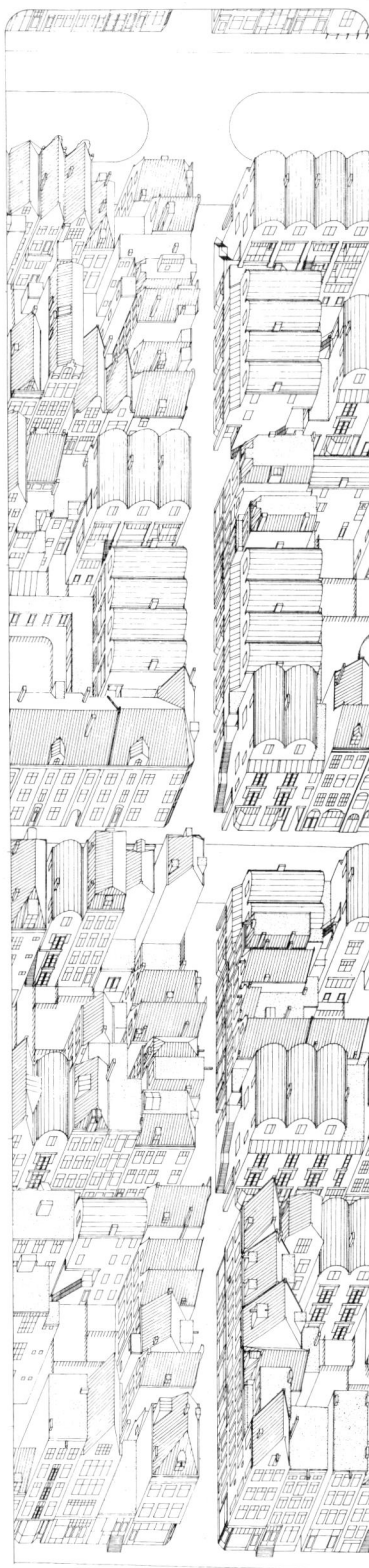

Palmdwarsstraat, Amsterdam, 1972

The Cube Project, Stedelijk Museum, Amsterdam, 1971
with Carel Visser and Ton Bruynèl

The visual aspect: the project is designed for a room of about 10 metres square. The floor is covered with a layer of sand. The walls are completely blind (apart from the entrance and exit) and covered with steel sheeting. The sheet-steel walls do not meet completely in the corners. Through the narrow slit this leaves falls indirect light, which is the room's only lighting. The ceiling is black. The room contains four sheet-steel cubes with edges of 50 cm, 75 cm, 125 cm and 200 cm respectively. The two largest and the two smallest stand diagonally opposite each other. Only the underside of the cubes is open. They rest on rubber feet.

The auditive aspect: sound is produced by mechanically imparting vibration to the cubes by drive units. The tone of the sound is determined by the sum of the frequencies in which the drive unit sets the cube in motion. The drive unit itself receives sound structures electrically from a tape. These sound structures derive from the cubes themselves. The method by which the structures were reached is as follows: the cubes were made to vibrate continuously by conveying noise electronically to the drive units. The sound the cubes produced was recorded on tape by means of contact microphones.

The material so created was then processed in various ways (added together, subtracted, multiplied) but without adding sound from other sources and without using crescendo or diminuendo. The sound starts and finishes abruptly. The criteria for the treatment were provided by the characteristic acoustic properties of the cubes. In this way at least 100 distinct sound structures were formed, distributed over two 80-track recorders. One recorder is connected to the two larger cubes, the other to the smallest. The two recorders are arranged so that the public can operate them and thereby choose a combination itself. So the system works without loudspeakers. The sound derives from material and form and after it has taken the electronic path described is transformed back into sound by the cubes.

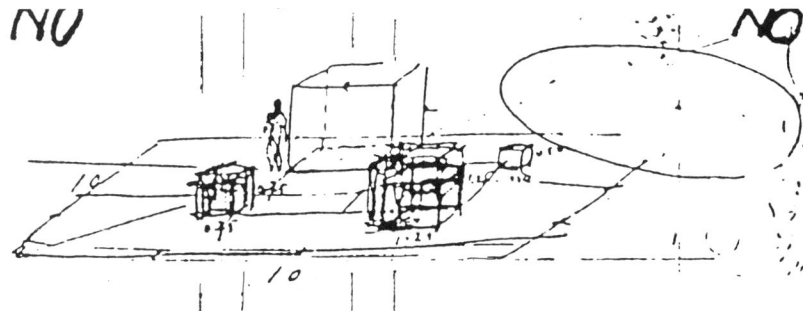

179

Hannie van Eyck, Florist's in Existing Shopping Centre, Utrecht, 1969

A tall space with light entering from both sides. One enters through a door set back in the centre, under a canopy of dried flowers. Fenestration, shelves, display window equipment and perforated screens are all in steel with a transparent coating. Interior walls: B2 concrete blocks painted matt grey in several gradations, as far up as the canopy. Floor tiles inside and outside: concrete.

180

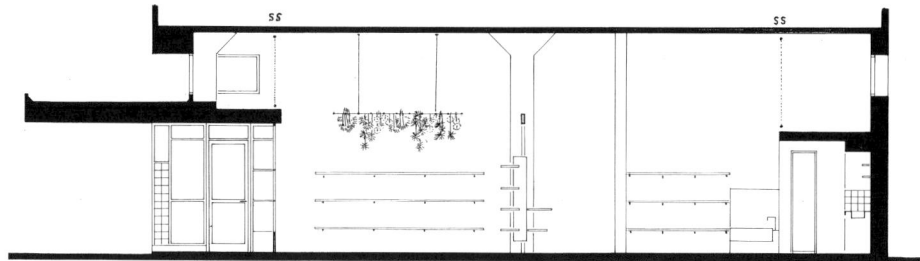

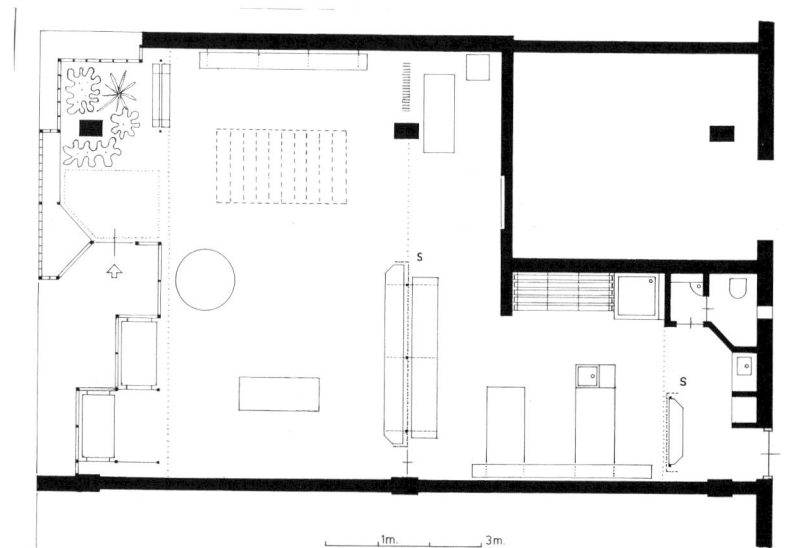

1 living
2 library
3 kitchen

Hannie van Eyck, Renovation of an 18th-Century House along an Amsterdam Canal, 1971

A single large space from front to back after random interior walls had been cleared. Characteristic are the timber posts set into both side walls at regular intervals from front to back, articulating them in their depth. In order not to interrupt their sequence, the required study with library was designed as an island between walls terminating 2.10 m above the floor – a secluded enclosure within a very large living space which has ample light entering equally at both ends. A radiant spaciousness was attained through the use of white gloss paint for the posts, beams and windows, matt for all the walls. Beyond that, generally speaking, no more was done than strictly required, so for instance the lighting was fitted flush into the interior walls round the island to avoid small scale additions. The mantelpiece, an essential factor in these canal houses, was however remodelled. The floor was stained very dark brown.

Hannie van Eyck, Gallery,
Amsterdam, 1976

A gallery looking out onto the street through an already
existing shop window covering the entire width and
height. No display window was arranged for the street
and the gallery was conceived as a small square alongside
the street, with an item of urban furniture in the middle: a
two-part round construction with its own interior where
the smaller items were displayed in showcases.

182

1 bench
2 low platform
3 administrative department
4 depot

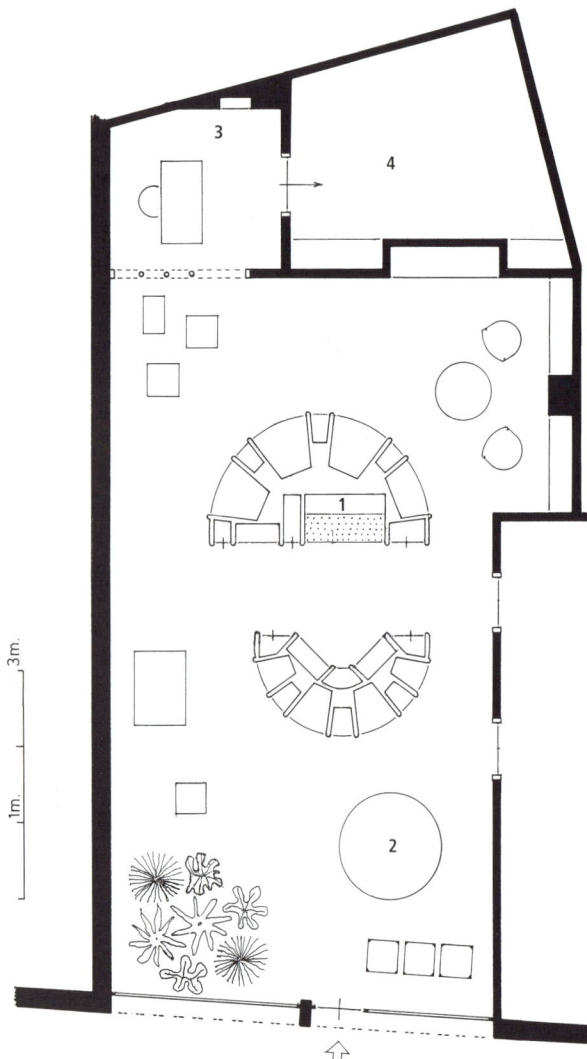

Hannie van Eyck, Gallery, Amsterdam, 1977

The gallery is on the first floor and is introduced by a series of recesses alongside the stairs. The gallery space, which at the rear captures light by way of projecting display windows – looking out on a small inner court – is divided into two zones by three revolving cylindrical display cases. The sides and inside of the display cases are in matt light grey, and the rest of the paintwork is in glossy white. A large pink surface activates the long light-grey side wall.

1 entrance downstairs
  with display case and
  cloakroom
2 lounge
3 court
4 kitchen

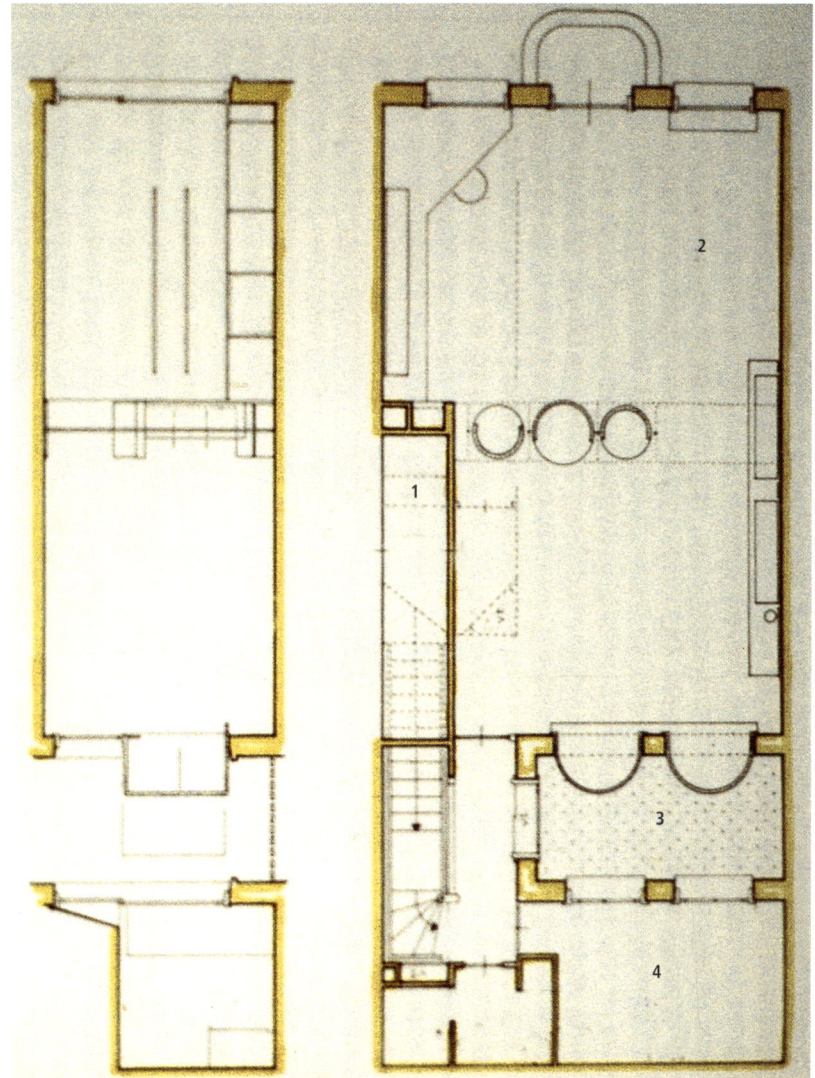

Hubertus House, Home for Single Parents and their Children Plantage Middenlaan, Amsterdam, 1973-81

Interior with Hannie van Eyck

Another building in whose design process the requirements regarding what already exists on and around the site – the mute kind – are no less significant than the verbalized ones the new building must fulfil. I believe that buildings which misbehave towards what exists outside them will also tend to misbehave towards what is inside them – towards what they were meant to fulfil. Thus the right relationship between inside and outside is not only a spatial one but also a temporal one. A building as a neutral alien object in time and space is just another modern invention.

Here extension and conversion form a combined process. Entry is provided for where old and new meet. The vestibule of the old house becomes an external portico. Accessible from the new by way of some steps, it in turn gives access to the new through the old. Conflict between the existing home and its new extension is resolved at the entrance – an in-between realm, also in an associative temporal sense.

The irregular floor levels of the old building are extended into that part of the new one immediately adjacent to it, so that the 'split' with the new levels is shifted away from the party walls between the two: like the portico, this is another unifying device, since this is where stairs connecting the floor levels of both buildings occur.

By reducing the floor area upwards from floor to floor, i.e. stepping back the volume from floor to floor, sun and air penetrate deep into the building, by way of loggias and roof-terraces. Buildings in general (and certainly those along an urban street) should be populated externally, so that nobody feels tucked away behind walls and windows cut off from the world outside. Especially in a home like this, something more generous than balconies is required. A glass-roofed 'passageway' feeds the five children's departments from above, bringing light into the interior. After dark, parents looking from above will see movement along it... and vice versa.

184

185

Whether its conspicuous appearance stigmatizes the residents of 'Hubertus' is a question repeatedly asked. Addie van Roijen, directress of Hubertus House, replies, not without indignation: 'If a building such as this is good for people in general – and I believe that is the case – then to have consciously withheld from those it accommodates the characteristics that made it look the way it does would have meant discrimination.'

186

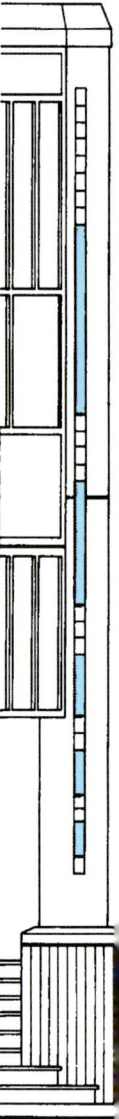

Coloured tiles in spectral sequence – down – from violet to red

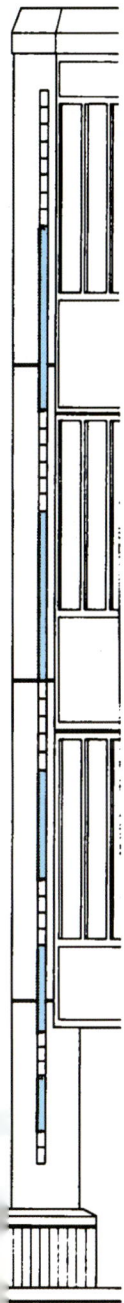

Coloured tiles in spectral sequence – up – from dark blue to red

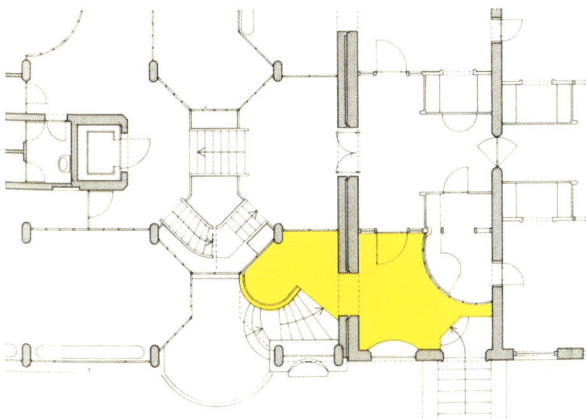

beyond the front door

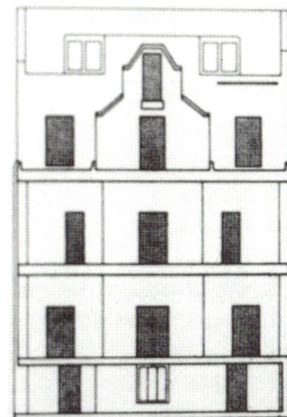

HUBERTUS   1 Sept 78

**twelve doorways
between
old and new**

Building a House

'An open house is what we want'. That is what I kept hearing. Which, of course, can mean all sort of things – indeed anything from a great deal to almost nothing. But Addie van Roijen knew what was implied and what was not! The Hubertus 'style' above all else breathes equality. Open – yes, but in no way vague or fluctuating. In fact, *open and protective at the same time*. The limitations of the existing accommodation sustained but also hampered the unfolding of this style – this distinctive way of doing things. The twofold assignment – conversion as well as building – pointed the way: reinforcing the favourable factors whilst eliminating the detrimental ones. Particularly gratifying – and certainly exceptional – was that the notion of *art* (here architecture!) was looked upon as something useful instead of as a superfluous extra. A pleasant appearance (beauty even!) constituted something concrete, tangible, and obviously necessary and was therefore also explicitly requested. Though hard to believe, this too can come to pass – can befall an architect!

The irony is that the latest tendency appears to be to shift the endangered mothers away from the wicked city.

By the time van Eesteren, not long after the war, introduced me to *De 8 en Opbouw* group, what in Holland is called *New Building* (Nieuwe Bouwen) was already slipping away into millions of square feet of wall, glass and floor surface in countless 'modern' buildings.

What is characteristic of most second-generation 'modern' buildings of that period and later, is that the meaning of twin aspects like inside/outside, open/closed, small/large, many/few and far/near had become thoroughly exhausted, neutralized by poor and hesitant aesthetics. The exterior tended to trespass into the interior, which was then allowed to ebb away into what was called *'spatial continuity'*, but all too often amounted to the annihilation of space. Glass from wall to wall; doors and windows preferably in the corners of rooms. Walls, ceilings, roofs all flatter than flat. This has led to those stark, box-like buildings and new towns fit for population but not for people.[1]

'For thirty years now architects have been providing outside instead of inside, but that is not their job at all; their job is to provide inside even if it happens to be outside.' That is how I put it twenty years ago. For exterior is what precedes what is locally counteracted by it. In this sense architecture – building activity at whatever dimensional level – should be seen as counter-play.

Away with enclosure; away with 'closed' rooms, away with streets and urban spaces. Open up those tight ancient city centres. This is the kind of mania which afflicts every 'respectable' urbanist! And so began the wanton demolition of the very centres they thereby hoped to reach more easily. Of all the irreversible things people ever chose to do in their long history this is surely one of the most absurd.

Countless urban centres, large and small, were thus severely damaged or lost at the hands of the professional fools of the day. Had it not been for the few architects who raised their voices, most old Dutch towns would by now look as neat and empty as the new ones around them, with here and there a few protected canals and other historical items retained to remind people of bygone glory. Local authorities backed by a host of 'experts' (architects, planners, traffic engineers, and socio-.... this or that) certainly went to work like halfwits with ten thumbs.

Still the gentle gears Space presupposes light (but is fortunately still here in darkness); light presupposes visibility and visibility... presupposes the presence of colour. This is not the only sequence, however – not since Seurat, not since the mild gears of reciprocity began to lift the burden of causality (that at least is what I shall continue to believe). Complementary or opposing aspects, qualities or notions (twin phenomena I have called them, two by two), such as open-closed, inside-outside, old-new, often brought up here with others like large-small, many-few, far-near, light-dark, unity-diversity, single-plural, part-whole, similar-dissimilar, rest-movement, order-chaos, space-matter, individual-collective, form a vast network of meaning from which nothing can be lifted – no twin phenomenon (or twin phenomenon-split-in-two) extracted – without impoverishment or becoming altogether meaningless – mind-splitting.

All twin phenomena together form the changing fabric of this network – and the constituent ingredients of architecture. Though each of them is different, they are at the same time – this is the point – also reciprocally open to each other. Far from being mutually exclusive or independent, they merge, lean on each other. Equality is their cardinal common denominator. Their very essence is, in fact, complementary, not contradictory. Along the dead-end track of contradiction (unlike significant paradox[2]) whatever goes into the making of a good building is lost in the resulting wilfully cultivated conflict.

A good building, *one that has what it should have and hasn't got what it needn't have*, will result when the multiple meaning (intrinsic ambiguity) of every twin phenomenon begins to replace the single one-sided false meanings of the separated halves. Meaning continually embraces further meaning. Since the meaning of one component carries that of its complement within it (forms its reciprocal extension) leading to the meaning of the other, this dialectic relies on a fast *both-and* instead of a faltering *either-or*. It depends on a more inclusive kind of thinking: what, when I was working on the Orphanage, I called the *mild gears of reciprocity* or the medicine of relativity.[3]

Twin phenomena cannot be split into false alternatives with impunity ('false' because of the false choice they provoke) nor extracted from the fabric of meanings to which they belong, isolated from other twin phenomena. In the constantly kaleidoscopic network in which schizoid situations find no nourishment, twin phenomena get along with each other admirably!

A dialectic based on reciprocity and equality is a nimble and penetrating one – because it makes cross-alliances between diverse twin phenomena possible, which affects (alters without distortion) their assumed meanings, imparting an added – often unexpected – dimension. Only in each other's light are binary aspects rendered tangible, and can be assessed and the meaning within each dichotomy clarified.

A wealth of such cross-alliances comes into play when making a building. To name some obvious ones: open-outside, closed-inside, closed-outside (i.e. open, closed, small, large, many, few, outside, inside, in any combination).

The spectral colours, in spectral sequence, form a single phenomenon, a multiple unity but not a twin phenomenon. Feeding them into the thought process, the dialectic just described, was very hard at first but then after a while they started to oil the works, increasing the intricacy and lustre of the binary fabric upon which all equipoise depends.

33 Plantage Middenlaan 33-35 Plantage Middenlaan: two nineteenth-century houses planned as is usual from front to back, from street to yard and garden. Next door, the new building does the same, though more emphatically forming a visual bridge between the two worlds. The three buildings together were designed to form a single home by linking them along a new transverse axis parallel to Plantage Middenlaan. There are twelve openings in the five-storey wall between the new house and the adjacent old one, and eight in the one between the two old ones. These twelve openings, arranged symmetrically around the central axis, ensure that what was previously a divider is now a unifying device. The embellishments around the main openings stress the meaning of this multi-storey interior doorway-wall, linking two epochs. For a while I considered the possibility of a colour composition all the way up this wall, on both sides. It would have become a striking interior façade between *two and the same worlds!* However, if walls or doorways are to be links then surely it is in the first place those between the world inside and the world outside, i.e. between house and street, which require extra attention. And so the colours ended up playing a different role elsewhere.

I wish – still wish – to identify a building with that same building entered, and space with the appreciation of it. In fact, I spent half a lifetime waiting for the chance to make an entrance like the one for Hubertus. Meanwhile I did make 'preparations' so as to be able to deal with the question of entry and departure in architecture, should the time come.

By shifting the front door 12 feet inward and back from the existing nineteenth-century façade, an open porch resulted behind the building line, accessible from the street through the original front door opening, and from the side through a new opening in the wall between old and new. This covered external space between the pavement and the new front door is extended laterally along the ground floor of the new building via the opening in the wall just mentioned. Thus the world outside is drawn inward beyond the building line, partly at street level but mainly six steps up – like a brace in space and time, spanning old and new. Although the hall (with the main staircase) is situated in the new part, access to it is from the side via the old part through a central opening on the longitudinal axis. Old and new are, as it were, strung by means of a loop to the main road, thus avoiding all conflict as to the place of entry.

Standing in front of the building, certain essentials can be read off straight away. For example, that the tall rooms in the old part continue sideways at and equal height into the new in the form of bay-window rooms set at right angles to the street, though accessible only from the old part. Also, that only the first floor continues on the same level right across both old and new, whilst the remaining floors are connected in a split-level on the longitudinal axis by a short flight of stairs.

188

1 Only the RPP could 'improve' upon this! – see *Forum* No. 3, 1980/81; *Lotus* No. 28, 1981; *AD News*, supplement to *AD* No. 7, 1981

2 Robert Venturi, *Complexity and Contradiction in Architecture*, New York, 1966
3 *Forum* No. 6/7, 1960/61)

The curved main staircases – all different – are situated in front, with a direct view of the street, as far as the first floor. From there upward, they are at the back, with a full view of the courtyard and the children's world, and in the distance cranes and masts of ships.

Beyond the front door The columns, it will be noticed, were made to stand on a firm plinth. They do not, as all too often today, simply start at street level. The superstructure of glass and steel rests on a massive substructure. The desired massiveness is then partially relieved again by coloured tile areas with mirror surrounds. The mirrors see to it that the other side of the road (and the morning sun) appear quite unexpectedly on this side whilst the tram passes by on both sides. What mirrors can do!

A little tight-rope dance along the building line, which is thus momentarily granted an extra dimension.

The reduced space between the yellow tram, each time one stops, and the front door, set far back behind the façade under a radiant yellow ceiling, strikes me every time.

Those building lines! Either straight ahead to the very end and straight up as far as the roof or else they are abandoned altogether, these relentless lines – and with them whatever resembles a proper street. And that in the flat open country around every village, town or city! Few professional misjudgments were ever devastating.

Tight-rope dancing along building lines the way Duiker could (Cineac and Gooiland), is alas rarely performed. Yet to permit any kind of life along those taut lines, something must be done to them (other than rejecting or accepting them wholesale) so as not to end up trapped in a vast CIAM-RPP new town mélange the size of Holland!

'When are you going to stop building bay-windows and semi-circular balconies?' architects keep asking us. Stop? Isn't it time to start making them instead of asking foolish questions? As long as people live behind building lines or wish to do so again (?) – even in narrow streets – the best window is still a bay-window. Who does not prefer to look right down a street (perhaps to see if someone is coming) than straight across at the windows opposite. Besides, bay-windows still catch the sun obliquely. Imagine streets filled with people inside their houses watching (say on Guy Fawkes Day) those outside – both on the *same* side of the building line!

Hubertus has bay-windows of a rather special kind because they are at right angles to the street and thus face both inwards and outwards. But there is more, for by cutting back the building volume towards the top and hollowing it out, light, sun and air are drawn in from all sides – but also exterior space and a simultaneous view of the world outside and inside. Roof-gardens, furthermore (four of them covered) came about quite naturally; most of them immediately accessible from adjacent rooms.

Thus living along even a fairly narrow street behind the building line would still be acceptable. If this sounds new it is only because it has been forgotten. Or is it that town planners simply didn't care to either know or think – their patent hallmark? Renewal often depends on just jogging one's memory. *What architects know already still surprises them!*

Where the main elements should go was settled in principle before

there was even a design sketch. It so happened that approximately half the ultimately built volume (the two old houses) existed and had been in use by the Hubertus Association for the same purpose for decades. So the issue of what could best go in the old and what in the new was a reliable point of departure.

My first thought was to have sixteen private rooms for resident parents on the top floor of the outermost house and in the attics of both where rooms would be naturally varied and never look like cells. It would be pleasant to nestle there, tucked away behind and above the living-rooms, between irregular roof beams and sloping surfaces, with dormer windows and skylights.

Following from this, the parents' living quarters were given a place in the already familiar middle house, directly under or next to their private rooms. Situated high above the street over the full width and depth of the building, they form a link between the world of the city in front and the world of the babies and children at the back. The babies are on the top two floors of the tall new building, each room with its own covered loggia and fully up-to-date equipment, whilst the children – 1-6 years old – are in the low wing on the ground floor next to the playground at the back. The canteen is where it belongs, in front on the mezzanine ('piano nobile') of the new building, overlooking Plantage Middenlaan rather grandly from above!

All offices, work, staff and group rooms are located in the tall new house and the two converted old ones. As the main link between old and new, front and back, top and bottom there is the tall – vertical – central hall with the lift and seven flights of stairs – each one different: a link between the ground floor (children's departments and playground at the bottom) and the narrow bridge connecting old and new (babies and parents) right at the top.

Nurseries The nurseries are situated one above the other – where it is quiet – and serve a double purpose: as places where babies are put to bed, play and are washed, etc., and as day-rooms where mothers gather and tend their babies. Both arms of these L-shaped rooms open onto large covered terraces. Between the two, there is a quarter-segment void, which allows the morning sun to penetrate the space below, and also makes direct vertical contact possible. Special cradles can be clamped to the balustrade around this opening, so that babies can rest outside even during bad weather.

The double doors of the upper nursery are like those below in spite of the void just mentioned, except that the inner door of each pair now opens on to a 'French balcony'! Finding this kind of solution is always pleasant, because without it something worthwhile would be lost. Here, for instance, shifting the double doors or accepting just single ones because of the void, would in both cases have resulted in limited vertical contact or else restricted openings.

Parent's quarters Situated high above the street on the second floor of the middle house, they are generously oriented in all directions. This is due to two ample roof-terraces at the front and back as well as the chosen pivotal place between, on one side, the central hall with the babies beyond and on the other the private rooms.

So there you are with the city at your feet after all! Though structurally part of the new building, the two roof-gardens – the front one

glass-covered – are only accessible from the parents' living-rooms in the old part. What is true of the bay-window rooms below and the entrance on the first floor, is also true here: access to the new via the old – little detours which make for seclusion and protection.

The link (and escape route) between the central hall on one side and the parents' bedrooms on the other, lies on the lateral axis halfway between the front and rear living-rooms. Here, where it is of particular significance, the three buildings were interwoven spatially by shifting the two main access doors inward on either side.

When the large sliding doors are open, visual attention is drawn diagonally in both directions. This is not so when they are closed, because the doors are less transparent (for rigidity) than the wholly glazed partitions in front of which they slide. The rounded bars, three to each door and three to each glazed partition, are painted in spectral sequence. As the doors are moved the colours are seen passing each other!

Children's quarters What would the actual depth of the children's quarters be? 30 feet? And the width of the playgrounds across the front – 18 feet? Certainly, but the same measurements apply in reverse, i.e. 18 feet for the depth inside and 30 feet for the width outside. This is because the doors between the living-rooms inside and the playground outside are set far back in the interior of the former, resulting in deep covered alleys which together form a continuous 12-foot intermediary zone. Thus, alternating, the interior depth and exterior width are experienced as more or less equal.

The glazed roof beyond the line of columns in front covers all the conservatories and alleys, reinforcing the variable impression of the depth inside and the width outside. Moreover, the low L-shaped play tables shift one's attention obliquely to the left, along the play street, instead of straight across to the high wall of the adjacent property opposite.

The doors at the top of the stairs, in the full light of the glass-covered interior passage, look as though they were 'front' doors giving access to exterior space, whilst those below, set deep in the shade of the interior, have a more interior look although they actually give access to exterior space (alleys and playground).

This ambiguity is intended; in the first case the child 'leaves' the 'house' in which it lives. In the second it 'enters' the exterior alley which is still part of that house's interior.

Since the five children's quarters, the connecting passage above and the playground outside are all fairly well enclosed between walls, the degree of openness there is mainly determined by the different intensities of light from one place to the next (when it is dark outside this is no longer so – nor should it be!). It follows that to reflect on enclosure as if it depended mainly on peripheral containment (in this case closed walls) is both too literal and too limited. It explains why so many contemporary buildings are either too open or too closed, which simply means either one or the other in the wrong direction. It also explains why at this point I am placing special emphasis on the importance of light and light gradation and thus, once more, on transparency, so as to get closer to the meaning of enclosure by reassessing that of openness.

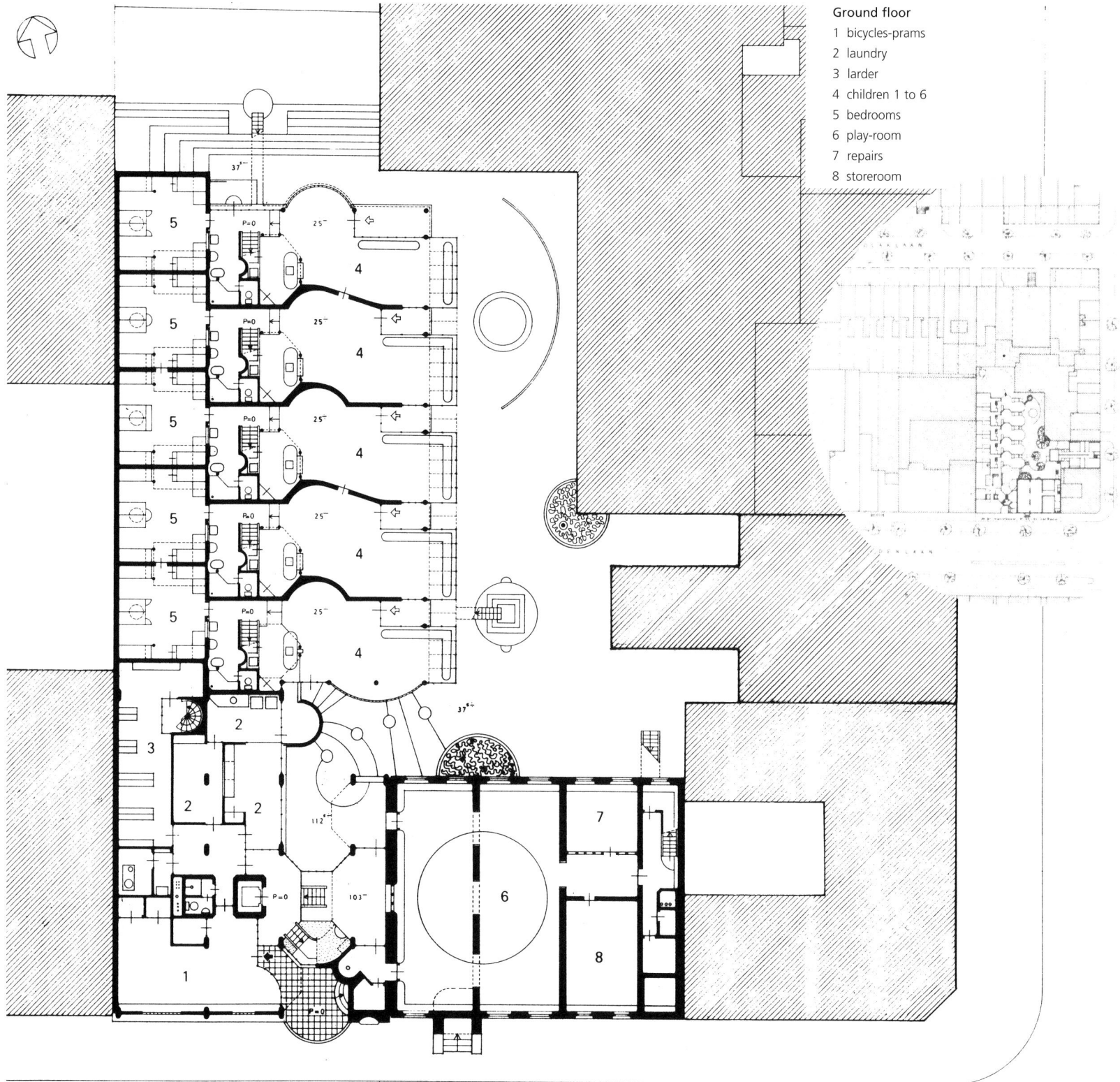

Ground floor
1 bicycles-prams
2 laundry
3 larder
4 children 1 to 6
5 bedrooms
6 play-room
7 repairs
8 storeroom

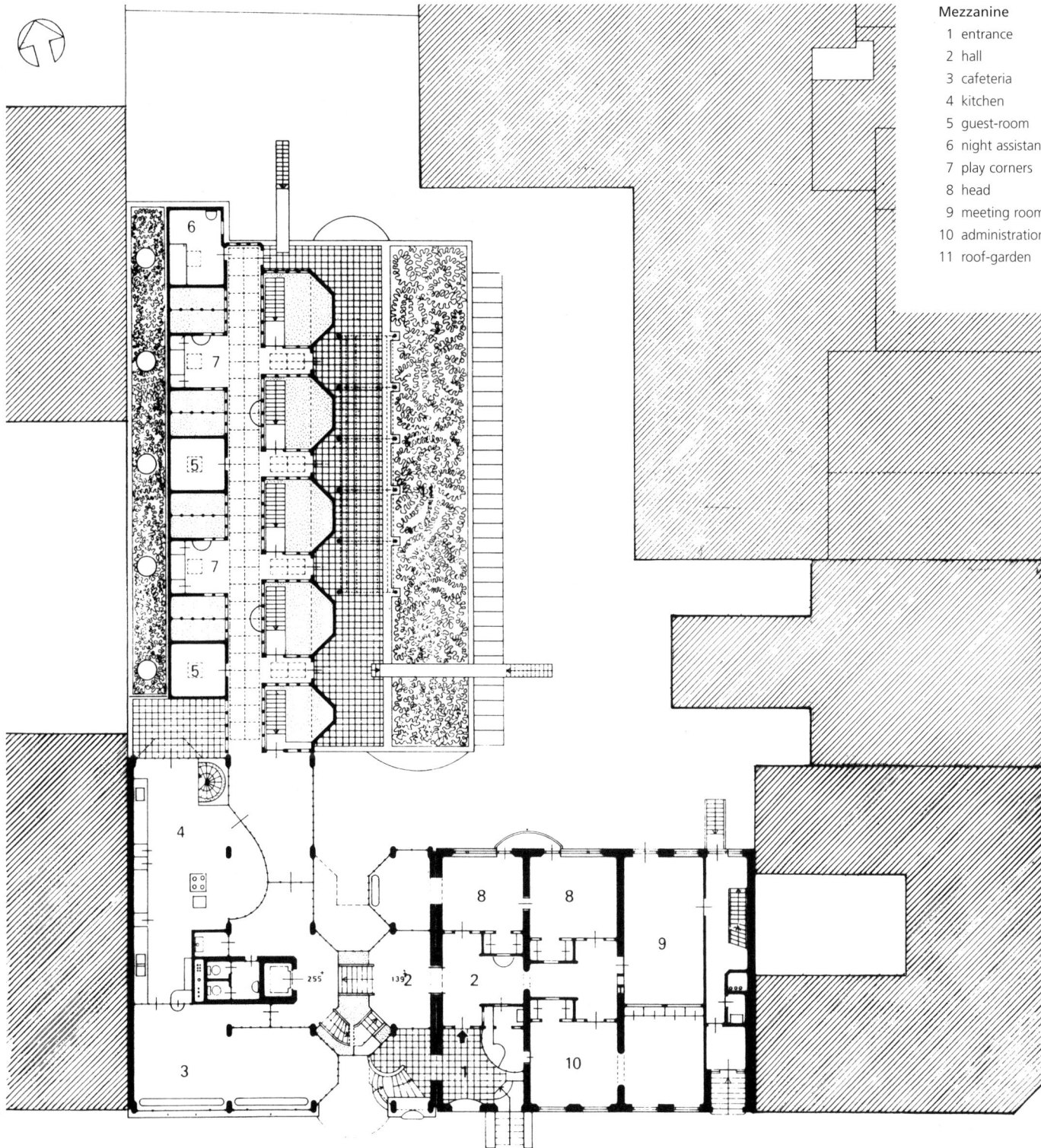

Mezzanine

1 entrance
2 hall
3 cafeteria
4 kitchen
5 guest-room
6 night assistant
7 play corners
8 head
9 meeting room
10 administration
11 roof-garden

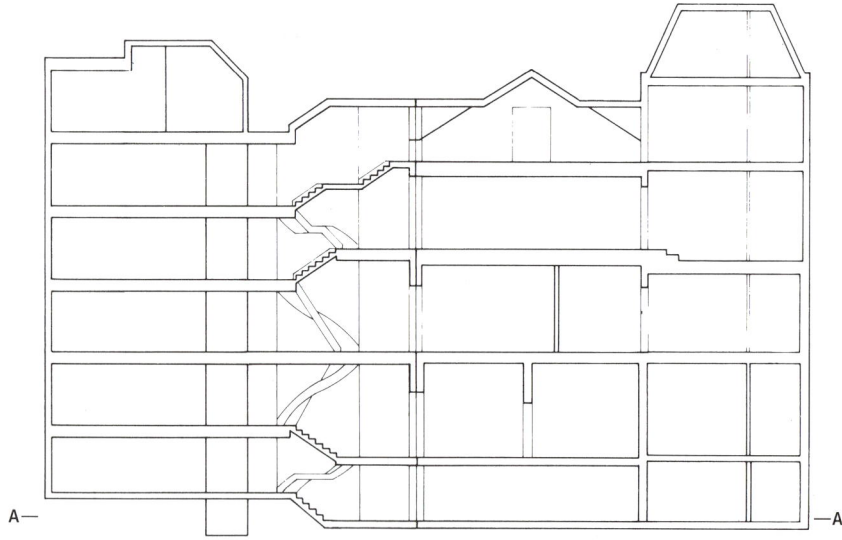

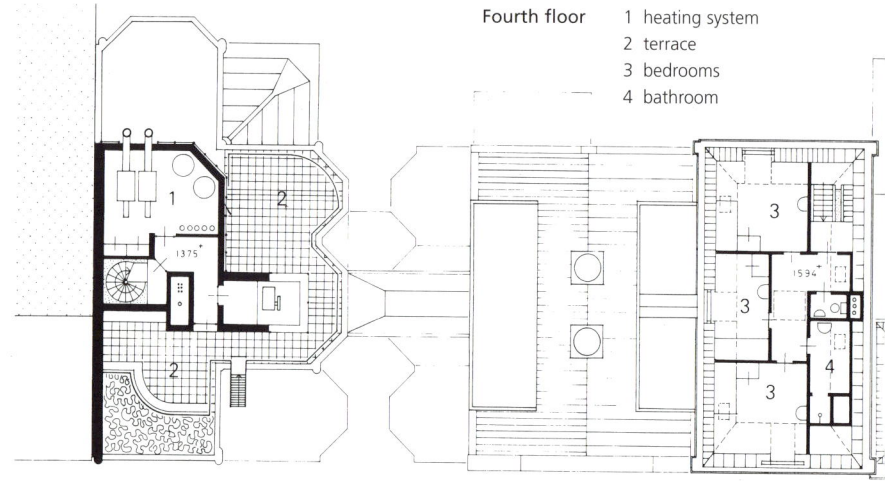

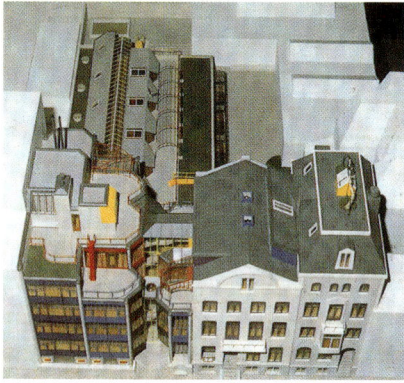

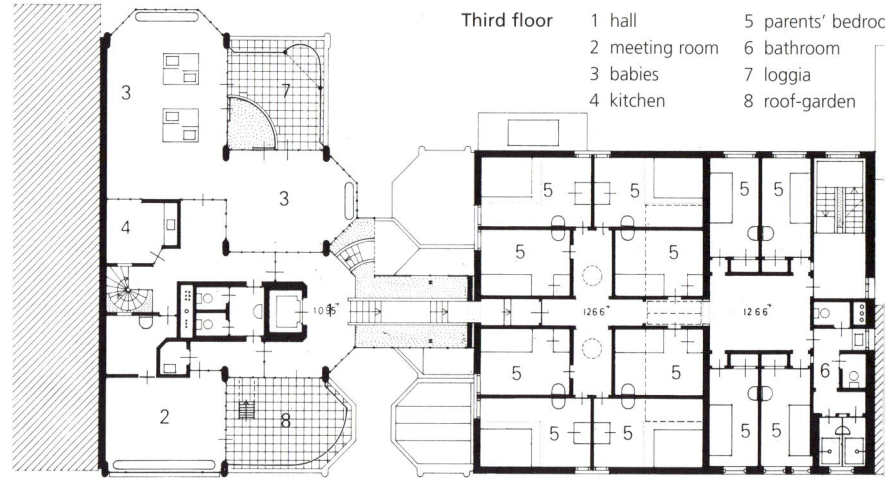

Fourth floor
1 heating system
2 terrace
3 bedrooms
4 bathroom

Third floor
1 hall
2 meeting room
3 babies
4 kitchen
5 parents' bedroom
6 bathroom
7 loggia
8 roof-garden

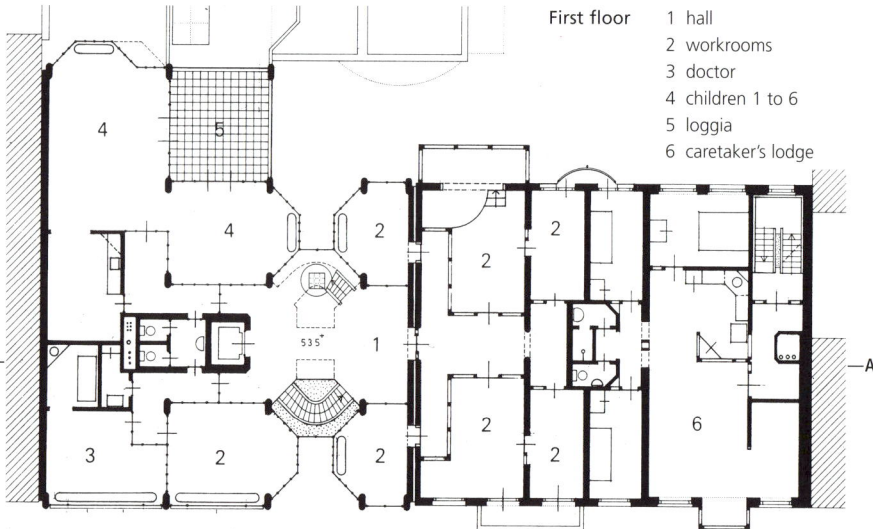

First floor
1 hall
2 workrooms
3 doctor
4 children 1 to 6
5 loggia
6 caretaker's lodge

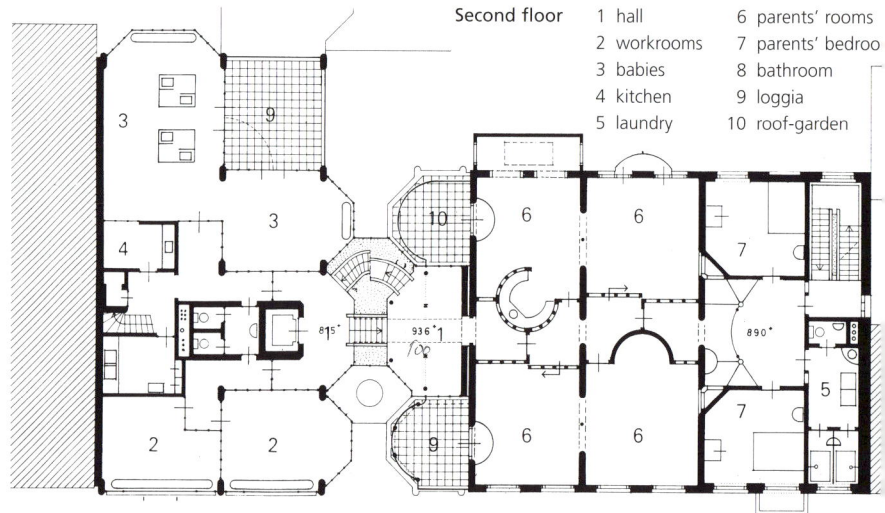

Second floor
1 hall
2 workrooms
3 babies
4 kitchen
5 laundry
6 parents' rooms
7 parents' bedroom
8 bathroom
9 loggia
10 roof-garden

The violet which 'closes' the spectral sequence here between the red high up and the blue of the façade in front.

193

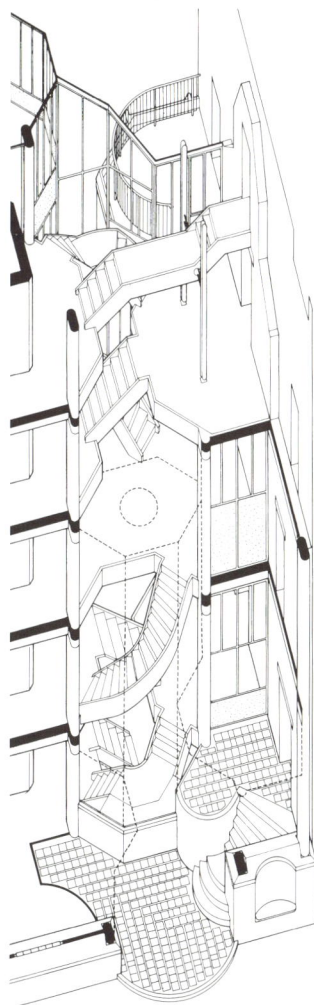

From the basement to the first floor the stairs are on the street side… from there on to the top as far as the bridge between old and new the stairs are at the back overlooking the children's quarters.

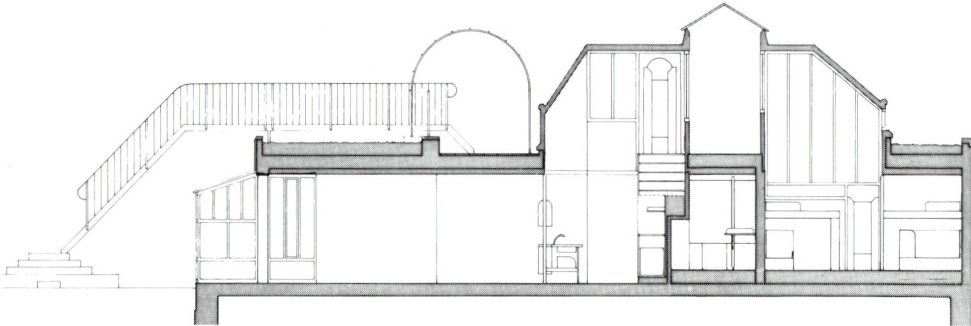

30 ft inside – 30 ft outside! In between is a shared 12 ft inside-outside zone with alley and glass-covered play corner.

197

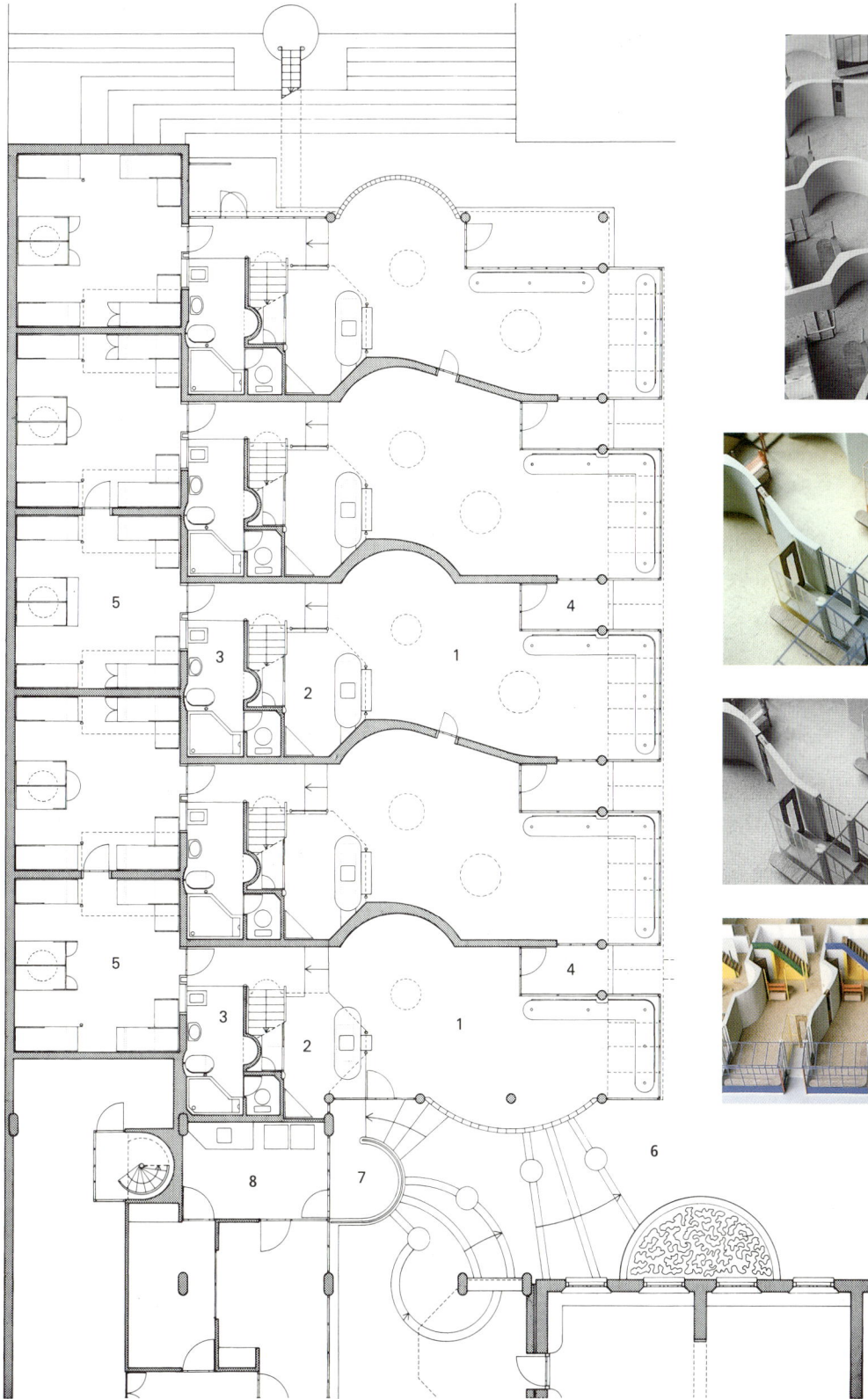

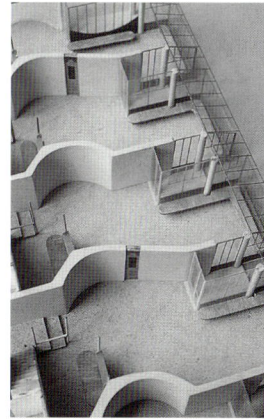

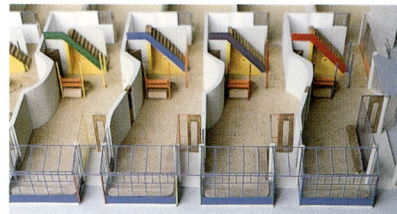

Children's quarters

Ground floor

1 living & dining rooms
2 kitchen
3 bathroom & wc
4 alley
5 bedroom
6 play courts
7 staff balcony
8 laundry

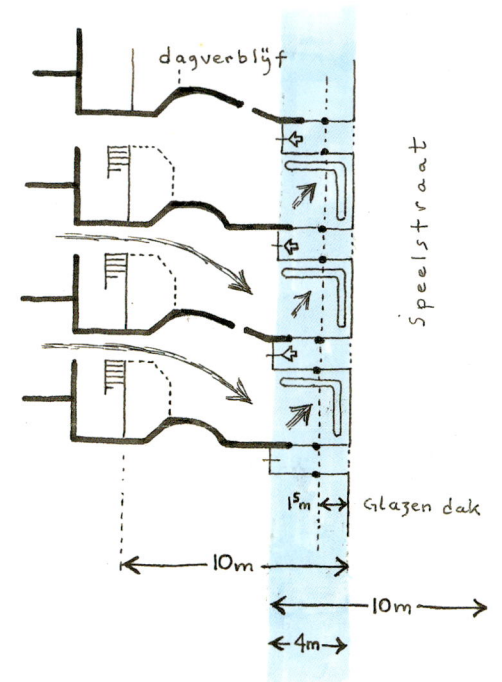

Again the Prisms of my Childhood

When I was fifteen or so, I had a set of prisms I kept in a box which I had made specially for them. They fitted exactly between velvet strips together with various lenses and didn't rattle when the lid was closed. My first Prism House! In a dark room I would pass bright light through a narrow slit. As the ray was refracted through the prisms at a certain angle, gorgeous spectra would fan out over the sheet of white cardboard on which I had placed them.

The phenomenon to me then, I remember, seemed both wonderfully clear and mysteriously elusive – somehow, as complete as can be. That is how it was, nor has it changed. On the one hand, it is linear: infinite beyond red and violet; on the other, contained within itself; circular and finite – because red and violet are not only adjacent colours but also the two outermost, with the other four in between. Unexpectedly, that dull number six yields utmost diversity and complete unity (so why keep turning towards trinity when looking for light?) After all, beyond infra-red and ultra-violet so much is still unknown! In a little book I bought in Paris once I discovered written in Robert Delaunay's own hand: 'dans l'ombre des ultra-violets...'. That shadow and that plural!

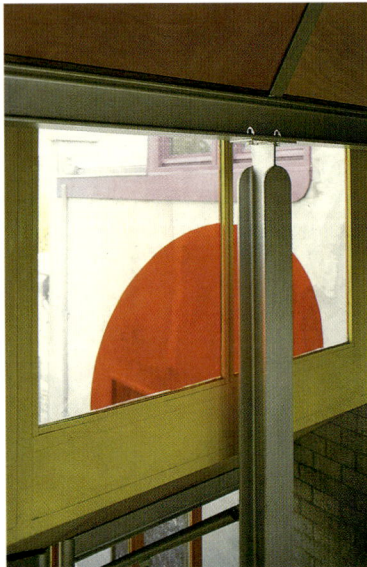

198

only Alice after all

The partially spectral tile tableaux (red-orange-green-yellow-blue) with mirrors all around, set in the four concrete panels along the street, are repeated in the toilets without any change in height ($5 \times 15 = 75$ cm), but merely a reduction in width, forming 4-cm narrow vertical strips. Thus, between the main road and the WC, the *intensity changes but not the scale*, which is one of many devices to keep it in hand, or constant, by careful local adjustment. Only Alice, after all, grows bigger and smaller in turn. The rest of us on earth are left to witness how, albeit through our own doing, everything around us is continually expanding and contracting with nerve-racking abruptness – perpetually too large or too small, in short, always the wrong size – always outsize. A characteristic of any good building is that it possesses what I call: *right-size*.

The exterior steel transoms over the large middle windows in the canteen and the common rooms on the first and third floors are curved. Now whoever looks out, whether child or adult, sitting or standing, can do so nobly without any horizontal obstruction. Something odd – even a little embarrassing – takes place every time somebody's hair, head or bit of upper body is seen passing along a narrow passage behind a glazed wall because of the 'wrong height' of the unglazed part.

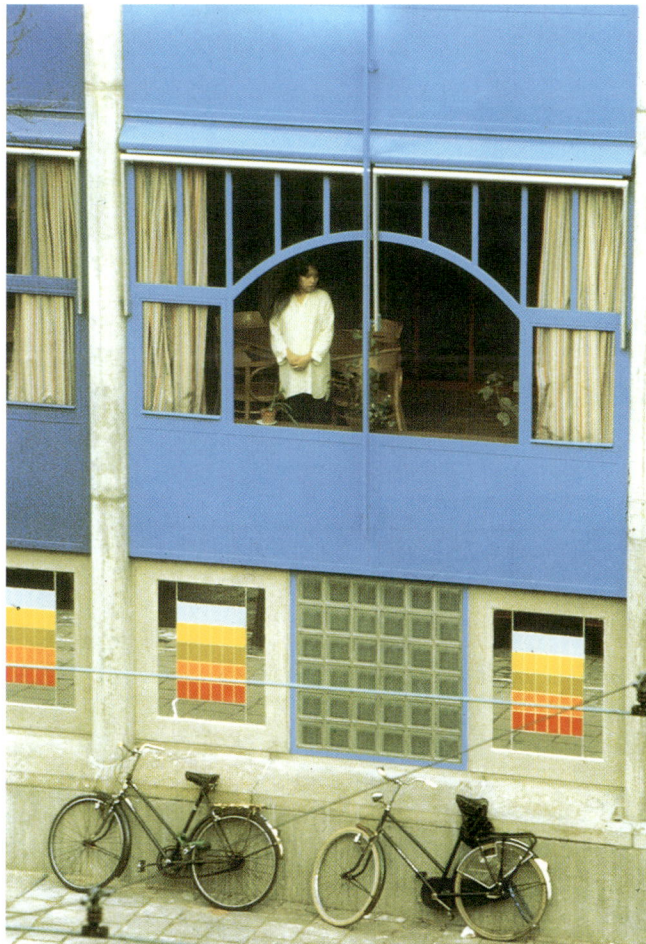

Which is why it is impossible to choose the right height at which to start glazing. So the curved line was applied once more, this time downward. In both cases lines 'bow' to the present and not nostalgically to the past, as if time were still ticking or ever did run backwards. Eclecticism? Balderdash!

200

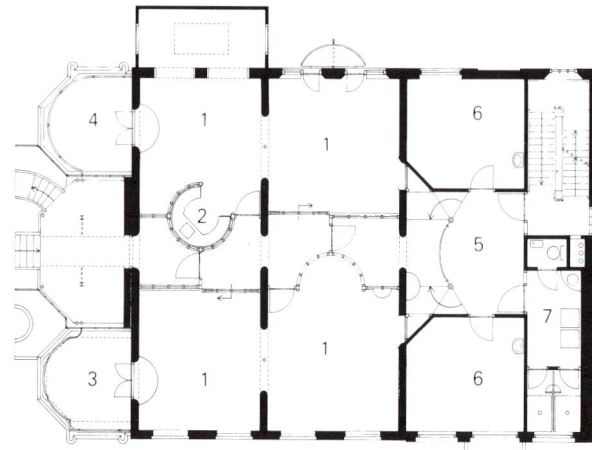

Parent's quarters
Second floor

1 living and dining-rooms
2 kitchen
3 loggia
4 roof-garden
5 hall
6 bedrooms
7 bathroom & wc

Transparency

Reduction of the building's volume towards the top whilst hollowing it out at the base has produced a rather complex outline, which allows the world outside to penetrate the interior in a different way from floor to floor. *The building is thus always present as part of the view and continues to be part of it as one moves about from place to place.* It seems to me that the continued presence of one's own home within the larger view of the city outside could well help to sustain a feeling of security and involvement.

In some places, when looking out from one part of the building (e.g. the bay-windows facing each other in front) another part of it – almost within reach (with people inside) is all at once there, outside, incorporated in the overall view of roofs, trees, masts, antennae, birds and sky – and movement in the street. Then there is the more limited view inward from a particular room, roof-garden or loggia, looking across a small slice of outside world. The sense of security stimulated by awareness of one's own interior domain and that around it outside (locating oneself from within with regard to one's surroundings as one moves from place to place) also leads to the desired sense of enclosure. Not so much in spite of openness but because of it, as a reward for it. Protected yet involved – at home in the city after all! All this with the help of transparency – a paradox which no longer needs to be one. Looking through a wall, a room, or a building – even all at once – is possible but the question is: which is it to be? When the one, when the other, how, and to what extent? Such questions have been insufficiently considered since the early days of the modern movement, so that qualities like transparency and continuity have become detached, isolated from the meaning of space and enclosure. What has been offered instead is a view straight through, just like that – with emptiness on either side – outside and inside!

What was to be made visible by dematerialisation and why, didn't seem to matter – nor what transparency and continuity as such could bring about in human terms. That got lost in the trend – in that style without a style. When space vanishes emptiness is all that we are left with.

There can be no question of interior quality, nor of enclosure, since there is nothing there – nothing left to 'open'. Can a building be opened towards what is outside, if there is no space to speak of on either side? No inside, no interior and thus no enclosure? In the case of Hubertus this openness also opens inward, disclosing the interior along with the exterior within.

I remember saying once: 'It is not space that counts ultimately, but the interior of space and, above all, the inner horizon[1] of that interior – whether it be inside or outside. See to it, therefore, that this interior horizon is never missing but is always present as one moves through a building (or city), stands or sits, looks up or down – for the gratifying sense of reference it can offer.'

Nor is the horizon outside ever fixed – it shifts up and down as one ascends or descends. The same applies inside a building provided it has an interior horizon. But this, unfortunately, is precisely what is generally lacking – lost at all levels of magnitude from house to city.

Obsessed by movement and hence all too busy with horizontal continuity, the attention of architects has been diverted away from vertical articulation far too long (people after all do close their eyes when asleep!). It is quite pointless to come up with the wrong sort of enclosure (void) as a remedy for the wrong sort of openness (also void). Trying one poison against another as alternating antidotes is certainly not going to save architecture. Vast suburbs and new towns, built here and elsewhere since the last world war, bear ample witness. I wish to skip the loathsome – backlash – monstrosities drawn and published the world over, and now, sadly, also being built. What the Rats, Posts and other Pests are perpetrating is discussed elsewhere.[2]

Open what would otherwise close What is at stake, what is really needed and must still be sorted out (if what is still to be built is to become more accessible and emotionally able to respond) is a kind of openness in which enclosure is, as it were, innate – included *a priori*. For why should the one exclude the other? Openness, after all, does not necessarily exclude – annihilate – space; though one might have reason to think so! Space can even rest enclosed within it. Both Zonnestraal and van Nelle have shown that, and not so long ago. The time has come to follow that lead – proceed along it patiently.

The meaning of space – that little word with a big meaning – is in the process of being hollowed out, whilst the spaces themselves currently contrived by architects and town planners – (still around?) – are becoming emptier and emptier (or more and more solid!). Space is now just another magic word without effect! That is why I tried to avoid using it for some years (though surreptitiously busy with it all the time). 'Stop talking about space, provide that place', I protested – taking the edge off it by adding 'start with this for the present'.

Lo and behold, places for this, that and the other came crowding in by the million like a new curse, as void as spaces had become before. That new word (like 'space' before, though there is nothing wrong with either) has dribbled from almost every architect's mouth since. Besides, I failed to foresee that these places would – in Holland – turn out to be quite so cosy. It didn't have to be that way – straight from cold and meagre to snug! But it did show how 'place' too became a magic word without content – and how, without receiving much in return, words are wasted on architects ('language' doesn't really rub off on them). Place, like space, is elusive, cannot thus be 'provided for', or so it appears. All the same, we cannot do without either the one or the other. Now, twenty years later, when I say provide the openness which is being closed so rudely (for the sake of enclosure which was as rudely broken open before) I no longer wish to add 'start with this for the present!' If places cannot be 'provided', who then is going to provide spaces with the kind of openness that makes enclosure possible if even architects are no longer willing or able to do so? That comes close to being a paradox without actually becoming one because, sooner or later, architects will stop playing the fool (or foul like the RPP) and start playing the game as before, seeing to it – stage by stage and assiduously – that this time the meaning of openness embraces the meaning of enclosure, instead of negating it. Includes what it cannot exclude without impunity.

'Open what is closed and allow space to enter' therefore refers above all to the mental equipment which alone can bring it about.

To this I should add that I am not disposed to neutralize the significance of openness which makes enclosure possible by adding, and vice versa. The reciprocity such a reversal suggests could easily lead to a misunderstanding in spite of the fact that spaces, like people, breathe both in and out – or not at all, in which case they are not spaces in any architectural sense. Openness precedes every space-articulating activity; exists *a priori* and is 'interiorized' by it. Thus openness is rendered measurable once it is properly reconstituted by means of architecture.

However, what people are always so diligently subtracting from virgin – open – exterior space with the help of material and construction, all too often closes in the process. Instead of being 'interiorized', it is rendered empty, and emptiness precludes accessibility. That is why the recent trend towards emptiness (the perforated solid) is so very malicious. It is precisely because constructing in exterior space inevitably entails demarcation, enclosure, separation, and size reduction that I now wish to place special emphasis on the quality which does not without conscious effort survive all this limiting activity: openness. This quality, therefore, demands all the more attention. It is in fact the very thing architects in particular are required to maintain: to reconstitute by means of construction, thus keeping open what (without their special care and competence) would otherwise close.

So open – keep opening – that which, if you fail to do so, would sooner or later cease to be space altogether. In the face of such a ghastly prospect, never forget that space can still bring light, and light reveal enclosure.

Whilst constituting light itself (which is filled with it) the spectrum usually manifests itself all round us, only partially – fragmented, through one or more of its colour components at a time. As a composite unity, however, the spectral colours, together and in sequence, form a world within themselves, almost a world apart – both endless and finite. No greater cohesion is imaginable. Painters are its primary interpreters and explorers, meriting our boundless gratitude. They are therefore an indispensable and irreplaceable necessity. Still, now and then, just for a while, the six great colours appear in unison across the sky to confirm the simultaneous presence of sun and rain – fire and water. It is then that we know again that *all things are two*.

---

1 As my wife put it after visiting Frank Lloyd Wright's Imperial Hotel in Tokyo – now gone.

2 *Forum* No. 3, 1980/81; *Lotus* No. 28, 1981; *AD News*, supplement to *AD* No. 7, 1981

Pieter de Hoogh

Varying spatial depth and perceptible distance through transparency

Beyond a space limit close by, one or several further away

On this side of a space limit which is further away one or several closer by

Modulation of spatial depth and perceptible distance from place to place as well as from one place, i.e. both consecutive and simultaneous

Pieter de Hoogh shows us beautifully what enclosure through openness and transparency can bring about, when he paints an open door or window and a doorway, passage or alley on a single line of view, thus allowing one to see right through several interior and exterior spaces – sometimes even as far as the house gables across the street or canal – and always there are some people articulating the entire depth once more, though in other places. This shows that the kind of openness which brings about the right sense of enclosure, does not depend on dematerialization and a lot of glass. Similar to the Sonsbeek sculpture pavilion, where a few openings in the walls were enough to ensure considerable lateral openness that modulated perceptible distance, those in the load-bearing walls running parallel from front to back in the two converted Hubertus houses also provide transverse views.

The Gift of Colour

When the scaffolding was finally removed, the steel frames were still under grey primer and the glass, which always established a certain degree of containment through reflection, had not yet been fitted. At this point it became quite clear that active colours alone could give the slender steel the visual presence necessary to establish the sense of enclosure the desired openness called for.

Without colour differentiation, moreover, the dematerialized partitions in particular would remain too undefined, hence also the spaces on either side. I considered that their relative position and the distance between them when viewed one behind the other would have to be made clearly discernible. For here again vagueness through visual confusion (lack of colour differentiation) counters what was intended. But – having once decided on this course and opted for active colours, how was one to proceed in a built environment, which, though intentionally transparent, was still undefined and amorphous? That was a question crying out for an answer.

Although active colours are a major ingredient within the reality of the senses, they are still hardly recognized for what they are worth in architecture. As a consequence, they remain, each one and together, intractable and illusive spatial media. That colours were going to play a significant role this time was certain. Whether this meant that the building was to be a coloured one, or that I was actually going to colour it, I didn't yet know, for there is more to it than just two ways of saying the same thing. In the everyday urban scene active colours still play an insubstantial part, appearing incoherently on signs, advertisements, vehicles, clothing, packaging – on whatever is mobile, loose or temporary. In a spatial sense they unfortunately contribute next to nothing. So I realized that I was in for a solitary search, without knowing just where it would lead me. But I did know why and, moreover, felt supported by what I knew through long and close contact with painters, for whom colour is never either peripheral or merely incidental, but always central in their search, just as space constructed for people is – or should be – central in the world of architecture.

Only by actually colouring the entirely grey and amorphous framework was I able to see, step by step, what should be actively coloured and in which colour so as to give the building's complex outline and internal partitions the spatial articulation and differentiation in-depth without which the openness I was looking for would not have been brought about.

Steel is protected against the elements by means of painting, and in that process is quite magically transformed. Ships, trains, motor cars (vehicles in general), steel bridges and railings: they are all, of necessity, painted and constantly repainted, according to tradition, custom, trend, and, of course, ad hoc.

Steel and paint have thus become close allies – inseparably associated. However, like so much else in architecture, the significance of this is hardly acknowledged. Paint for protection may well be unavoidable but it is still dealt with as an extra; as something secondary, added, hence also the colours applied with the paint onto whatever is painted. When an object is painted a given colour, that colour takes on the shape of the object – that's an easy one to follow, but what about the consequences? It is alas true that things all too often turn out the way they are painted, instead of being painted the way one wishes them to turn out! In a hundred years' time Amsterdam will have become a 'coloured' place – or it will have disappeared!

When I think of colour – especially active colours – in cities, what I see scattered around in a world of flat tones, are hard, random patches associated chiefly with traffic, advertising and consumption – with what is bought, sold, packaged, transported or thrown away. All of this attracts colour, is artlessly wrapped in it and thus rendered conspicuous. Not the way poppies are along a bank, or in a roadside flower-stall, although these are how it should be, and also why the bouquet I gave Hubertus was such a big one – why it was persuaded to become a building!

For the rest – elsewhere – colours end up in dustbins or on rubbish heaps. The urban scene pales when hit by so many little random bits of active colour-without-colour. To be sure, the impact of active pigment is there all right in the urban scene, but never that of any conscious spatial use of the colours which emerge. So there is little that is coloured in the urban scene worth looking at – not in the way we look at even a modest painting, a beautiful bunch of flowers now and then, someone passing by with a really good sense of colour or when sunshine passes through raindrops. The use of colour in cities has indeed sunk to the level of misuse, of something precious spilt, though it's true that now and then a not unpleasant effect is achieved – and that is already something! For example, those pipes and ducts running up and down the Centre Pompidou in Paris. They are certainly amusing, but where there are no pipes the effect is at once less amusing!

Of course, there are still buildings, streets, villages and neighbourhoods that are actively coloured: Casa Batlló in Barcelona, that palace in Mexico City, blue-tiled all over, Elklutna Indian churchyard near Anchorage, the Watts Towers in Los Angeles, La Bocca Italian neighbourhood in Buenos Aires and mosques all over Persia. There are villages in India which are at once blue and green; others – delicately multi-hued, in Ireland. In Burano, on the Venice lagoon, each house has its own strong colour. On volcanic Santorini in the Aegean the villages are snow-white, and pink at sunset. The urban scene was more colourful in the past, especially during ceremonies and celebrations; in fact it still is that way today in a large part of the world.

In the case of Hubertus, I realized that the moment would arrive when, once again, a building, mostly of steel, would have to be painted in the absence of any tradition or local usage, which, like the white bridge railings across the canals in Delft or the dark green ones in Amsterdam, can be admirable. But also without recourse to knowledge, experience or precedents to indicate what the meaning of active colours as an ingredient of architecture in particular and environment in general could be. In our field there is so much that is still *terra incognito*, forgotten or simply left unnoticed – areas that were bypassed. Mies van der Rohe's steel tends towards black but my steel is not Miesian, and my spaces anything but. So when the Hubertus house was still grey all over, the question as to what to do next was certainly a tough one!

When I think of paint and colours, I immediately think of painters, and when I think of painters it is, of course, their paintings I recall (and what they had in mind). For there, on those flat surfaces, colour and space – two-dimensional pictorial space – come into being by means of pigment and paint. But not just like that, for in every good painting, as in every craft, thought, insight, craftsmanship, knowledge, tradition, experience, discovery, etc., blend – fall in line. Could it be that painters and their like think better than architects do! I think they do – but then I am not a painter! With the building in grey waiting in front of me, and following the path of a rather different logic and rules still more or less unknown, I set about giving the building a two-dimensional quality by means of active colour, as though it were a painting. I was aware of the fact that, once coloured, it would no longer be in front of me, but wrapped around me, that I would in fact be 'immersed in it' (to borrow Cézanne's marvelous term regarding nature and use it for architecture just this once). In other words, the three-dimensionality of the exterior was reduced – counteracted as it were – by the fragmentation of building components distinguishable as volumes, through colour. Something in the nature of a (pseudo) two-dimensional configuration resulted. For, seen from some distance, the different colours appear simultaneously as if, indeed, composed on a flat surface.

Volume components were thus not accentuated as such by painting each one differently. Instead I did the reverse, ending up with *planes of colour in space*, which shift in relation to each other, appear and disappear as one's viewpoint changes. To put it another way: strengthening the two-dimensionality by subduing the tangible three-dimensional (beware!) impact – volumetric plasticity – also strengthened the spatial quality or, rather, the *changing* appearance in space (four-dimensionality one could say!)

This dissolution of volumes into separate colour planes assisted the intended dematerialization (through fragmentation) – a result which glass (transparent and reflective at the same time) and slender steel could not have effected on their own, other than adversely, due to the scarcely delimiting capacity of glass and steel if painted in one passive overall colour.

It was this lack of spatial definition, which unfortunately often accompanies dimensional dematerialization and the use of a lot of glass, which I wanted the active colours to counteract. Yet it was still transparency I wanted to achieve – a transparency which, none the less, also delimits space and articulates depth.

Compared with the time spent on the structure itself, that spent on colouring it may seem disproportionate. There was no short-cut. Still, probing, experimenting, trying again and again I do think I made some headway and managed to get beyond the first stage.

The Rainbow is my Favourite Colour

Yes, the rainbow set me off! To begin with, the particular beauty of two adjacent colours has always lured me, as earlier work shows. Apart from that it was not really a question of making a colour choice. Nor do I choose colours the way painters do. The spectrum in any case permitted me to skip that choice, but not the one still to be made in order to translate the spectrum into the right sequence of paints for this particular building.

That was by no means a simple matter, for rainbows cannot be trapped, stuffed into paint pots (during 'events' in Delft around 1968, I remembered telling rebelling students again and again: 'Don't ask for a rainbow – fetch it!'). Which active colour was to go where? How much of each? How soft, how bright? What would a yellow ceiling be like or a yellow wall, a yellow iron railing – yellow iron? What colour should this door panel be if that one is violet? All this, in changing light, inside and outside – whilst all the time the estimate specified 'standard' paintwork and colours at the architect's discretion! The extra time spent by Sikkens – manufacturers of paint – to this end was kindly donated to Hubertus by the company, as it had been to the Orphanage twenty years earlier, when true violet appeared on no colour-card, and could not be successfully made without using artist's pigments!

I did not use any colours other than the six main spectral ones (those whose images are immediately evoked). To ensure that the colour intervals between red and violet through the other four would be neither too gradual nor too abrupt, the full colour range was divided into twelve: two violets, three blues, two greens, two yellows, one orange and two reds. The inherent light-dark distinction between e.g. blue and yellow remained, of course, despite the more or less even colour intervals desired. In the urban scene primary colours appear as harsh random scraps, isolated from each other. What I wanted was something quite different, vivid, yes – but even so more gentle, clear, luminous and above all – together – lyrical! But I shall do so all the same!

Facing the building, from the pavement opposite, I tried to 'read' the elevation from left to right (notwithstanding those yellow trams stopping every few minutes!), but also outwards from the eccentric middle in both directions, and back again. Walking fifty yards back and forth also allowed me to read the façade, as it were, in depth.

Starting off on the left and right with blues and following the spectrum via the greens of the bay-windows resulted in yellows for the high main hall – the lightest, most luminous and transparent colour. Had I begun with reds instead of blues – with orange for the bay-windows – this recessed vertical part of the façade would also have become yellow (which seemed right in any case) but the remaining spectral colour

sequence would have brought the greens and blues inside – into the interior – leaving the exterior limited to the three warm colours, red-orange-yellow, and thus only partially spectral! Also, this would have appeared as a 'chosen' colour range after all, instead of the radiant – given – phenomenon of the spectrum, which only began to manifest itself more fully as the colours – following the hollowing-out of the façade, inward and back again in the right sequence – took their place next to each other one by one. Beginning with blues for the three elevation bays along the road in front, then, moving inwards, greens for the bay-windows (different shades so as to relax the narrow space between), and next, yellows in the hollow, distant back, right up to the top, where orange and reds take over while violet closes the colour circuit, joining the blue in front at right angles. Red and orange, used mainly on partitions inside the building, appear on the outside quite naturally where the façade is set back, at both the top and at entrance level. As for the rear façade, the procedure there is essentially the same, although, since the 'modelling' is rather different, it follows that the colour sequence corresponding to it is also different. The terrace balustrades at the various levels add to the spectral impact of the whole on both sides through transference of colour – colour elaboration.

What the tall building required was certainly not what the low wing at the back required. An altogether different story this, since the five children's quarters, held as they are firmly between walls, as well as the glass-roofed passage crossing overhead, are spatially already clearly contained. So they did not require active colours – not on that score at least (any more than the two renovated nineteenth-century houses did). But there were other no less valid reasons (there are so many!) which called for the use of active colours, though, as I have said, in quite a different way. The high new building in front displays its colours more or less simultaneously; the low one at the rear sequentially, except along the connecting passage. Colours here join in for their own sake and the cheerfulness they bring (not just because of the children) but to distinguish between the five departments.

At first this struck me as a lighter and less demanding exercise – a more decorative one, if you like, though no less difficult for all that, since I wanted each of them to be equally cheerful, equally different, and equally attractive. Each colour 'score' is based on a semi-spectral sequence of three colours from front to back: blue-green-yellow; green-yellow-orange; yellow-orange-red; orange-red-violet; and red-violet-blue. One of the three colours in each case is that quarter's own 'clan' colour. Two colours remain constant throughout – yellow inside and blue outside.

In the old buildings, with their high, clearly contained rooms, white and grey predominate throughout.

To provide an element of colour as a decorative note (for the fun of it and a little extra elegance), as well as to link the old premises to the new, more or less the same colours were used – though sparingly this time, except for the ceilings, many of which are in radiant yellows and, here and there, a lush green.

All had to be seen *in situ* to be believed – and sometimes altered – before the spectral colour sequence was persuaded as it were to return within itself in space, thus reaching its full effulgence for the sake of the unity, completeness and sense of enclosure through which I imagined the building would finally unfold. As the spectrum 'closed' in space, the building opened up. That at least was my intention. And, believe it or not, I saw it happen!

After all, it does turn out the way you make it! It's all a matter of the missing lost craft; the extra supplementary design technique necessary to make good buildings (assuming that to be a sane (RPP!) archi-

tect's intention), and good buildings are not only useful buildings, but cheerful ones as well. It seems to me justifiable to consider cheerfulness (that which neither depresses or oppresses), regardless of mood or state of mind, as a characteristic of any good building, and I therefore wish to recommend it as a valid objective for architecture. A serious matter if ever there was one.

In view of this I hope this building will help to stimulate the development of what I have just called 'that supplementary design technique'. Supplementary, because, whilst it seems as though, step by step, as much has been forgotten as was ever known (forgotten or just pushed aside, one may well ask those currently painting in the silliest trends). The fact remains that architects like Rietveld, Duiker, van Loghem and van der Vlugt, to name a few enlightened Dutchmen, had in their time already advanced towards it. How admirably they did so is still insufficiently appreciated. Their hope (faith in the future) shines from what they made – Zonnestraal.[1]

Be that as it may, hope or no hope, faith or no faith, that is how it must be. The question therefore is: how did they do what they did, and what is the secret (if secret it is). Well, that can be established, analysed, read from what they made: how they put those radiant, cheerful buildings together. From them it can be gauged... how it was actually done. Not everything, after all, is inimitable. (Or is there nothing useful left that's worth learning in this trade except from Las Vegas?)

To discover that it can still be done, step by step, in and for our time, and how to do so, can yet counter the shrinking scope of architecture. For what began with such élan has since remained practically untouched, forsaken. Continuation has faltered because no clear sequel was forthcoming. *What is needed in the first place, is that very sequel*, that supplementary design technique – stage by stage and without haste. For even without faith in the future – if such faith is absent – buildings can still become good buildings if they possess qualities that assist and in no way arrest well-being: fundamental usefulness, right-size and, finally, a certain intrinsic cheerfulness. That is how it is; that is how they are to be made – not otherwise. The conscientious architect is freer than the fool who does whatever he likes or whatever enters his head.

To argue on this score is simply hiding from facts. Must there always be a question mark after every reasonable answer? It isn't really all that difficult. If Hubertus has become a cheerful building, that is indeed gratifying, for the intention was not otherwise. However, to avoid misunderstanding, if it did turn out the way it was *meant* to – it is because it was *made* that way. But I do not wish to suggest for a moment that it is therefore also an 'expression' of cheerfulness, or the result of a passing mood or state of mind, for that is *not* the purpose of architecture. The building became what the Hubertus people, and Addie van Roijen in particular, wished it to become.

Now that there are so many disenchanted spoilsports in our field (these bleak times!) it seems right also to consider what one should consciously abstain from doing if one does *not* wish to prevent buildings from becoming good and useful ones – or even does *not* wish them to obstruct well-being! What is it then that must be done to ensure that buildings do assist well-being? Well... lots of things, like seeing that they belong where they are built and that one can truly say of them: they haven't got what they needn't have (but do have what they need). In both cases this is a lot – it covers all sorts of things.

1 Duiker's magnificent, now sadly disintegrating Sanatorium Zonnestraal in Hilversum

G.J. Visser House, Retie, 1974-6

This timber house combines several old preoccupations: entry extended far inwards; large covered outdoor spaces within the perimeter of a single form; light from above. Two octagonal glass roofs, one covering indoor space, give access to the core of the house from both sides.

It was decided to opt for timber in order to structurally equate the outdoor and indoor spaces under the overall perimeter of the rectangular roof. All the corners inside and outside could thus be articulated by the same vertical posts. Furthermore, by truncating these corners, 4 posts are juxtaposed instead of 2 where indoor and outdoor space come together. By thus reducing the formal difference between the two sorts of space the resulting ambiguity will, I believe, underline their intrinsic difference.

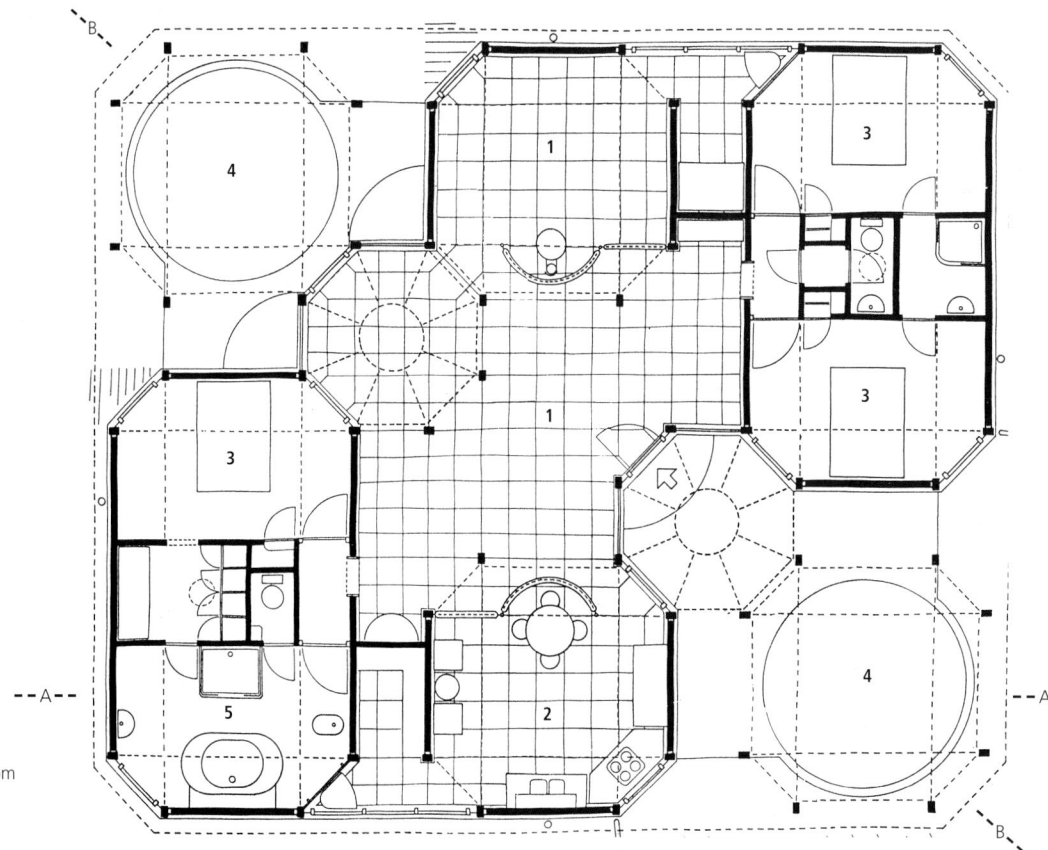

204

1 living room
2 kitchen
3 bedroom
4 terrace
5 bathroom

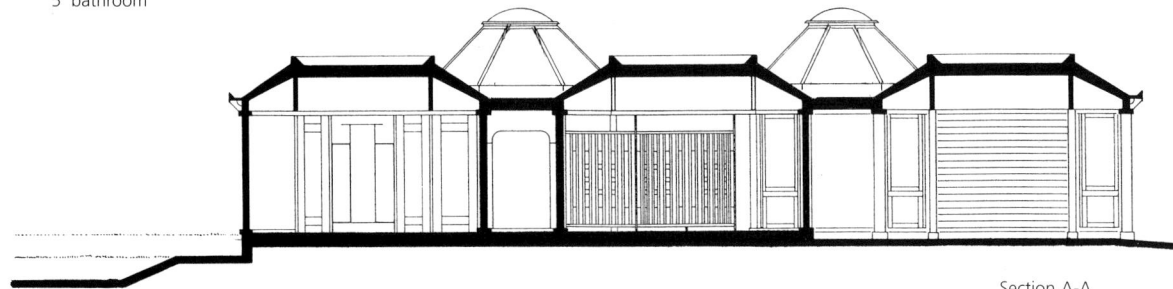

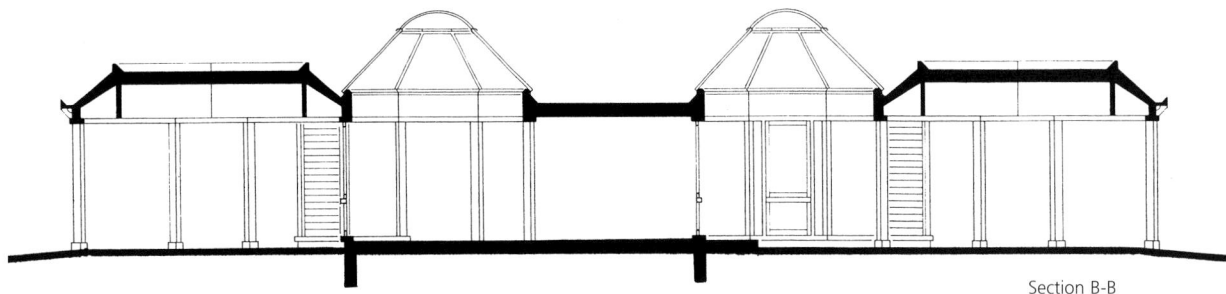

Section A-A

Section B-B

Roof seen from below

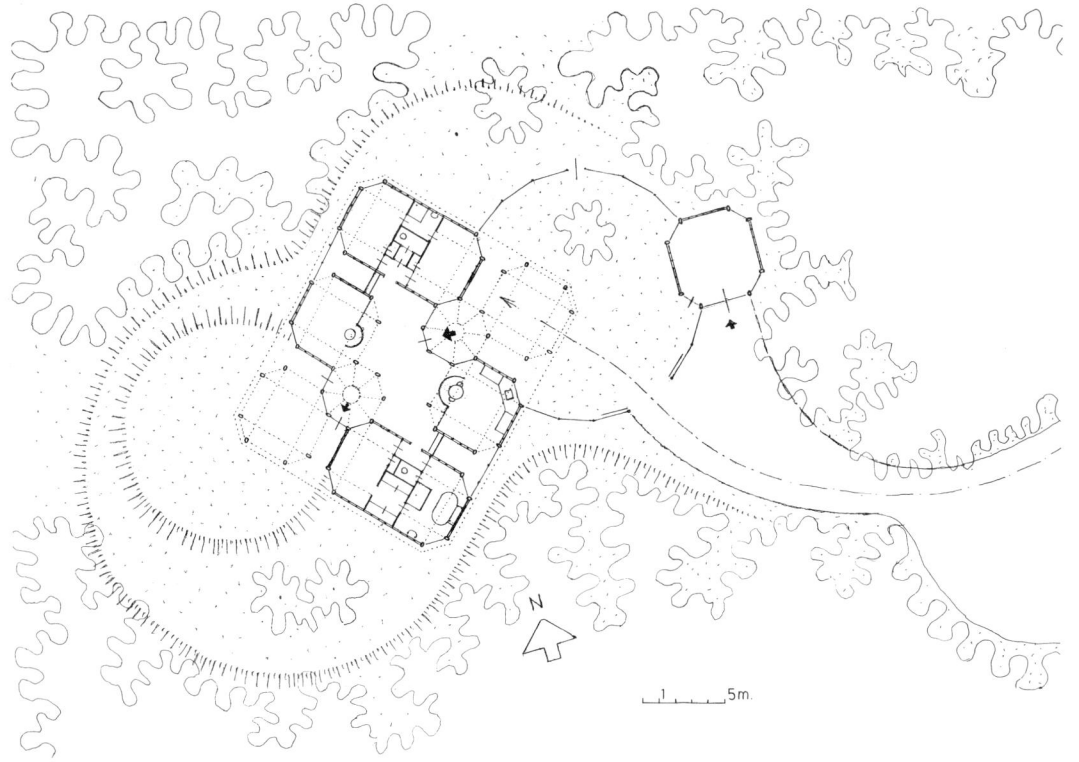

As a result of the detailing of the essential corner legs, both encircling the outside and the inside, it had to be a 'completely wooden house'.

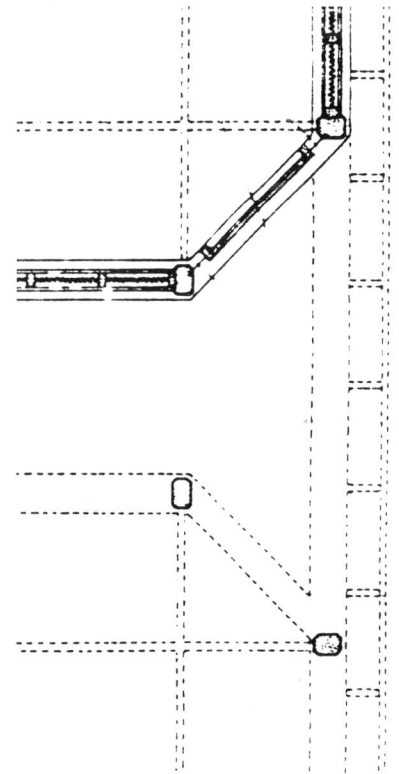

Horizontally striped roller blinds
Designed by Daniel Buren

De Jong House, Bergen, 1976

The house stands halfway down a deep narrow plot with lots of trees. A circular entrance court serves as an intermediary between the garden in front and that beyond. The four structural columns standing in it in a square anticipate four similar ones within the house. The client wished to enter his domain on horseback so an enclosure for horses near the front door seemed appropriate!

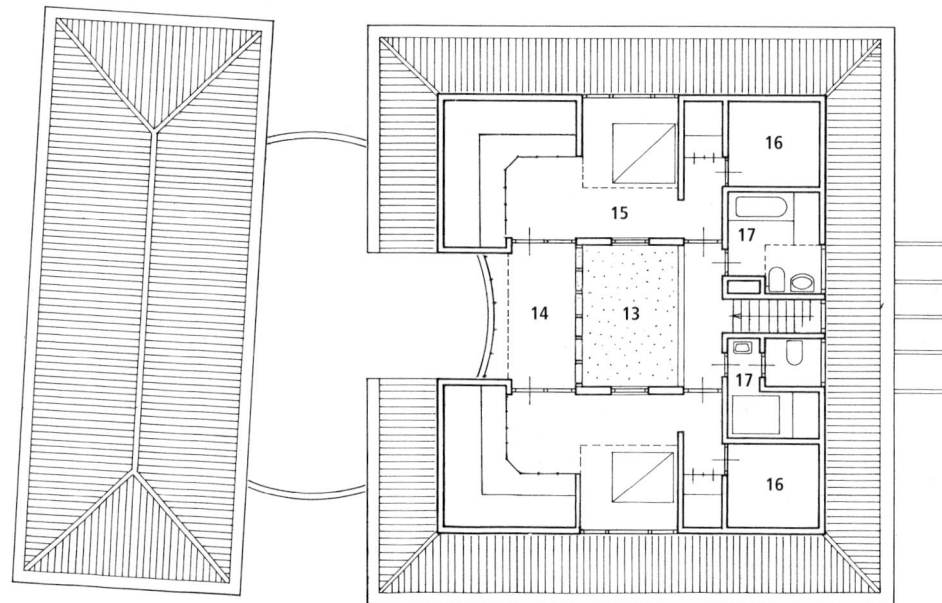

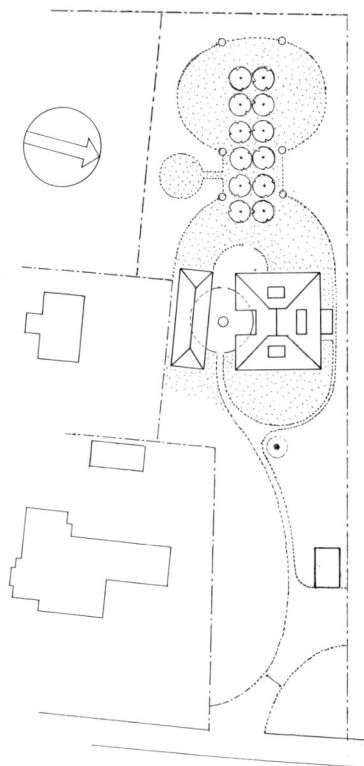

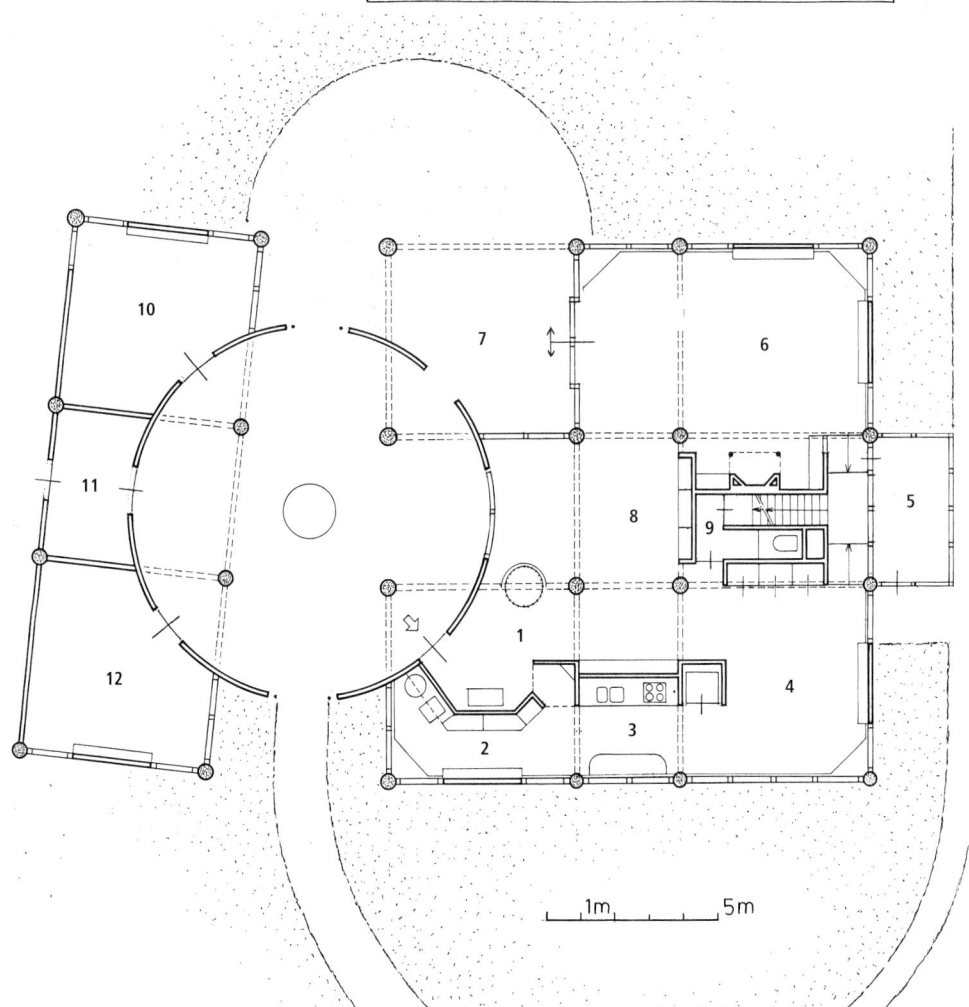

1 lobby	10 hobby room
2 pantry	11 logs and bicycles
3 kitchen	12 shed
4 dining room	13 void
5 hothouse	14 balcony
6 living room	15 bedroom
7 loggia	16 storage
8 hall	17 bathroom
9 toilet	

1m 5m

The pyramidal roof is not unlike those of old barns in that part of Holland, with four tall timber posts in a square in the middle. In the case of this house the columns are squat and consist of cylindrical concrete blocks. (NB: The fact that the roof form is a local one is an extra, though in no way a primary motivation: sensitivity to region doesn't make me a regionalist, Charlie J.!)

So as to avoid soaring verticality I resisted extending the four central columns upwards into the roof. Though the space is tall, the columns remain squat – close to the floor. Note the covered terrace: although an exterior space, it is also one of the house's four structurally equal quadrants and is entered through a door from the circular court. Just as the house is. The staircase, rising from a passage which passes a greenhouse, leads back into the house, i.e. into the hall on the upper floor. There are thus two ways *through the house* to and from the stairs. This is the main gist of the interior.

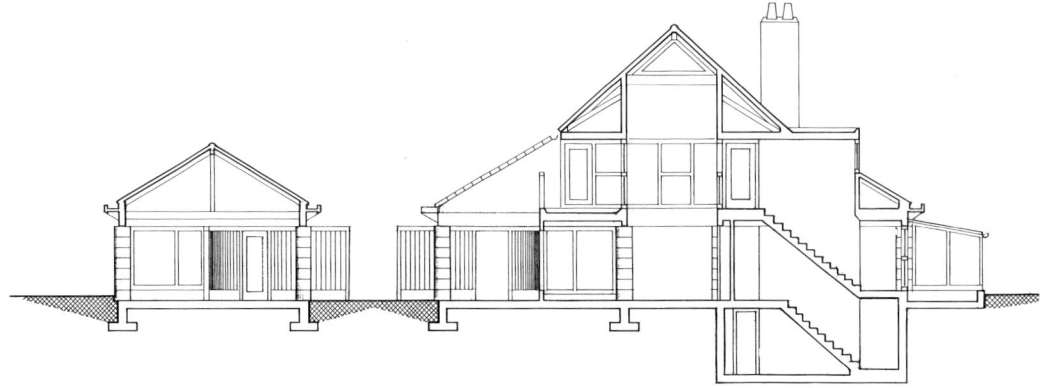

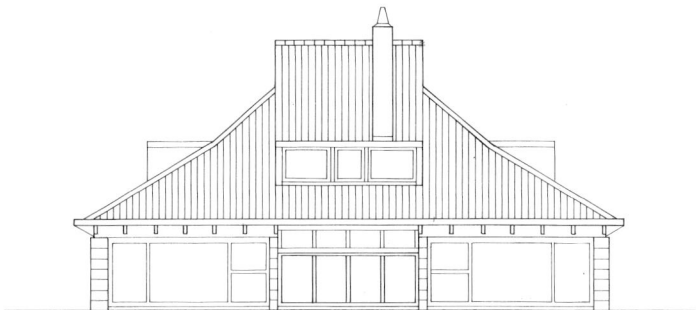

209

Padua Psychiatric Clinic, Boekel, 1980-9 with Hannie van Eyck

For those who are to live more or less permanently in the largest building, the domain accessible to them does not reach beyond the confines of a small exterior garden allotted to each of the four groups it accommodates.

The fact that the interior organisation of each separate department within the building is to be a closed circuit for all but staff and visitors, posed questions for which, so it seemed at first, architecture has no acceptable answer. A building one cannot even leave or enter is a cruel paradox (certainly if one wishes 'to identify each building with that building entered'). However, quite soon, accessibility as a notion not entirely dependent upon 'doors' provided a lead out of the problem. The two other buildings do not require complete confinement, hence their open L shape.

Since entry and departure are to play an unfortunate secondary role this time, the nature and sequence of the interior spaces and, in particular, the way exterior ones within its perimeter would be dealt with, required all the more attention: also window-openings between inside and outside (what are they to look like if one is to look alright looking through them?).

A few remarks regarding the above

The living room/dining room quarters and the walkways round the four interior courtyards are entirely of wood. They have pitched roofs and are also taller than the rest of the building, which has a flat roof and is in brick and concrete. By means of this formal device the living room/dining room quarters form a clear link between outdoor spaces within the building (courtyards) and those outside (closed gardens). It is hoped that the resulting exterior-interior-exterior continuity will help to mitigate the negative impact of complete enclosure.

As to the shape of the patients' 'own' rooms, these are based on an 'incomplete' rectangle. The 'missing' quadrant, though in fact outside, is visibly on the room-side as well, owing also to the arched arbours – screens providing enclosure, shade and even sunshine from the opposite side. Thus, a little exterior space completing the room's shape is held within it (density of foliage according to individual choice).

Since the size of the rooms is strictly prescribed, and minimal, a cell-stigma is hard to avoid. Nonetheless the room's 'missing' bit (actually an inverted bay window), subtracted from the theoretical plan-rectangle, actually allows for extra width and depth in the room, hence also extra wall length in relation to room height.

Note the vertical ventilation panels which open over the full height but are sufficiently narrow to prevent escaping through them. Windows set in walls are made to 'frame' the view seen from within, but will also 'frame' those watching the view.

About building clinics in Holland: the entire briefing, design and construction process is government-controlled and subject to endless constraints, leaving little scope for the specific wishes and approaches of individual institutes, and none at all for an architect's interpretation and ideas concerning the brief.

Because of this prohibitive procedure no really substantial advance has been made in medical building in Holland over the years. As it is, architects involved are checked at every step by officials who do no more than count and alter for the worse, while the first, already minimal, building budget is reduced again and again – even during the endlessly protracted drafting process.

Unless half hero and half fool (and who wants to be either?) an architect is not likely to end up with anything worth building; not in this field at any rate. It is still as it was in the case of schools 30 years ago, when those in Nagele were built.

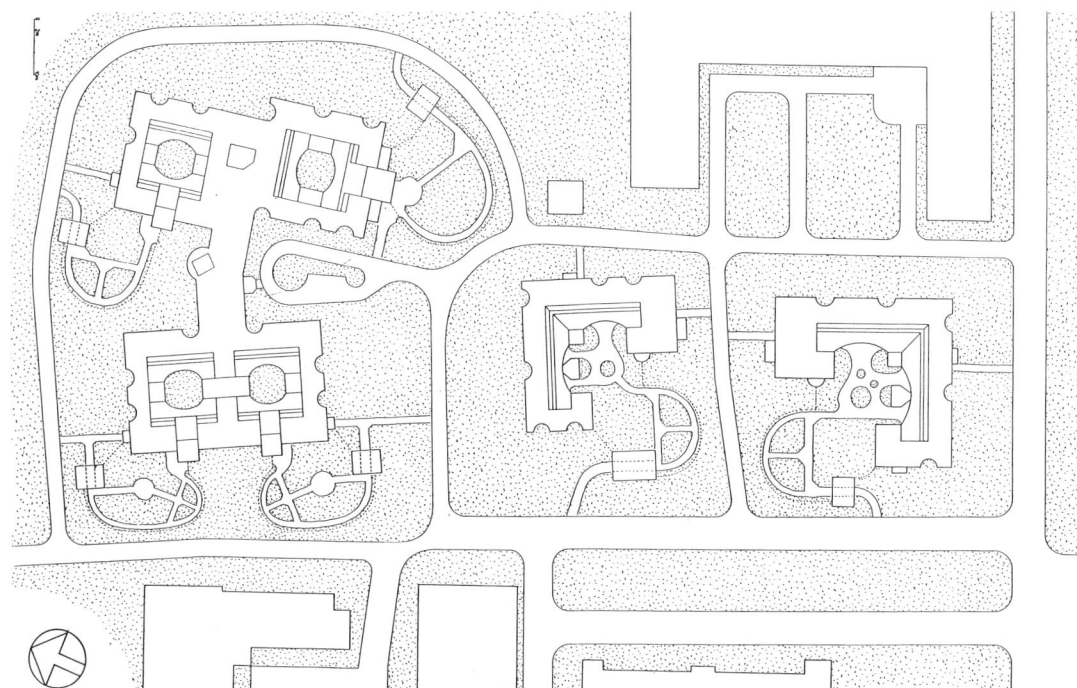

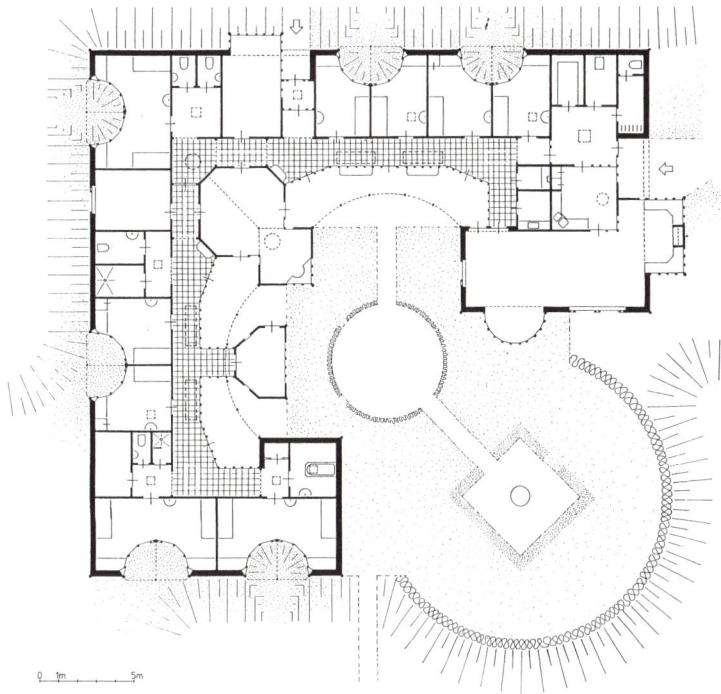

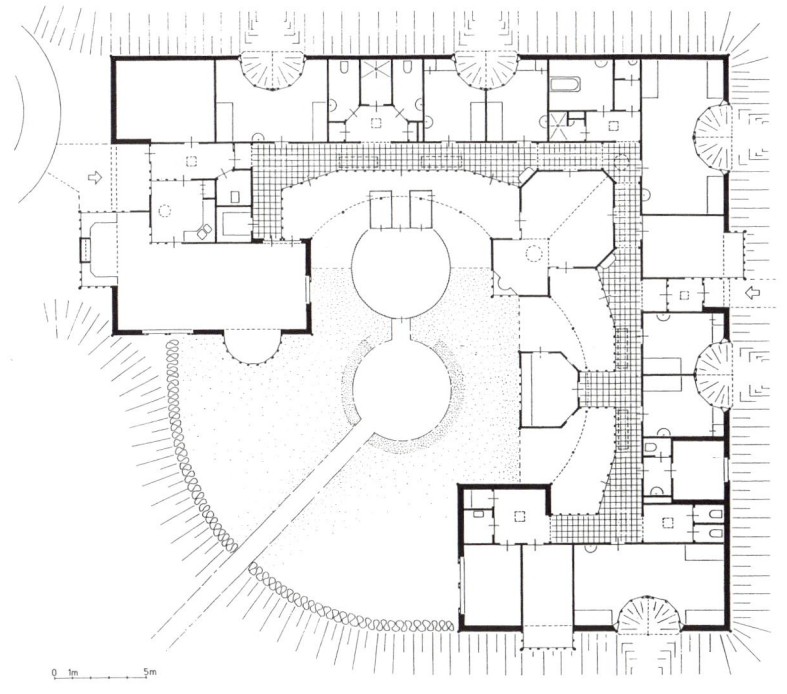

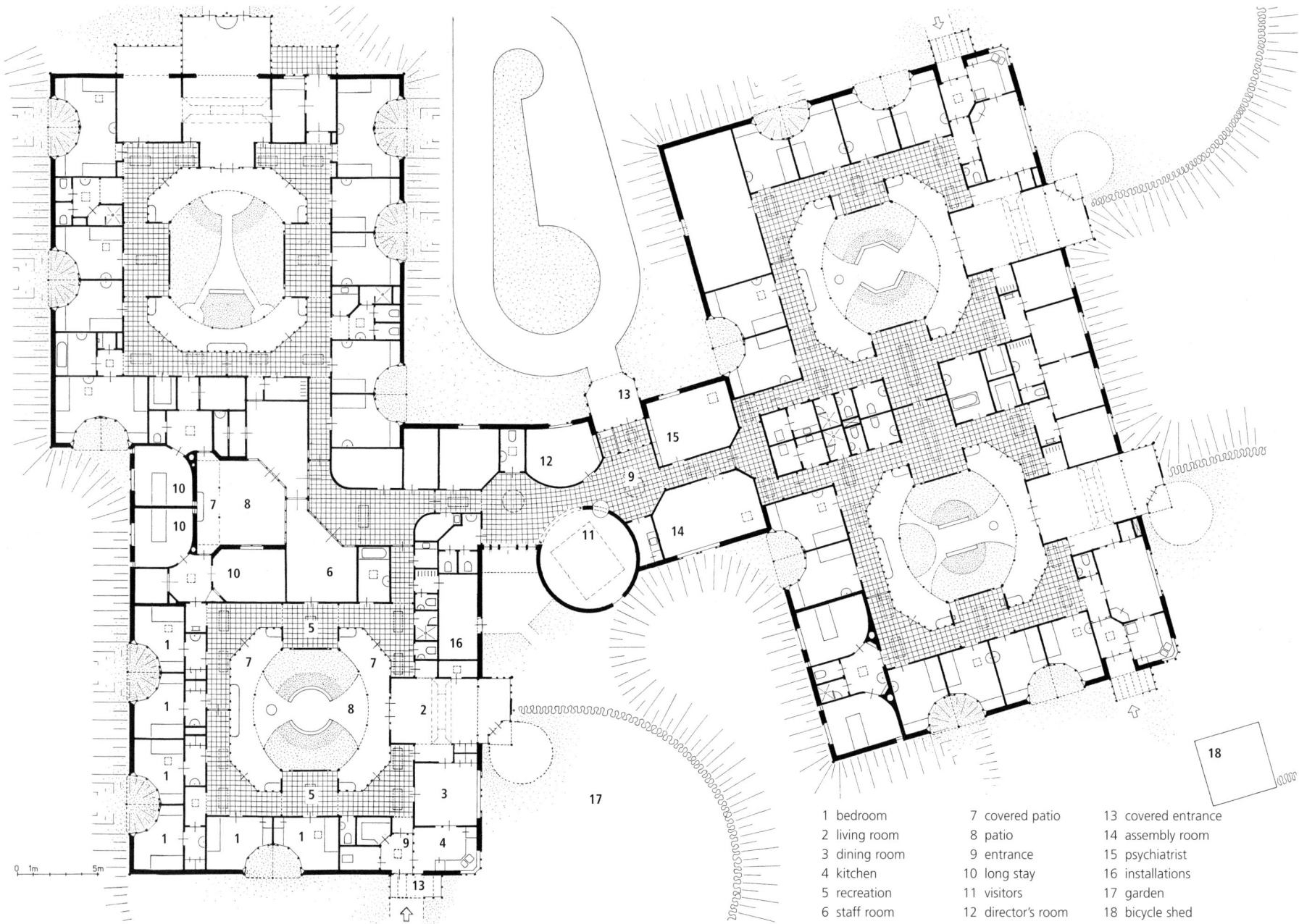

212

0 1m   5m

1 bedroom	7 covered patio	13 covered entrance
2 living room	8 patio	14 assembly room
3 dining room	9 entrance	15 psychiatrist
4 kitchen	10 long stay	16 installations
5 recreation	11 visitors	17 garden
6 staff room	12 director's room	18 bicycle shed

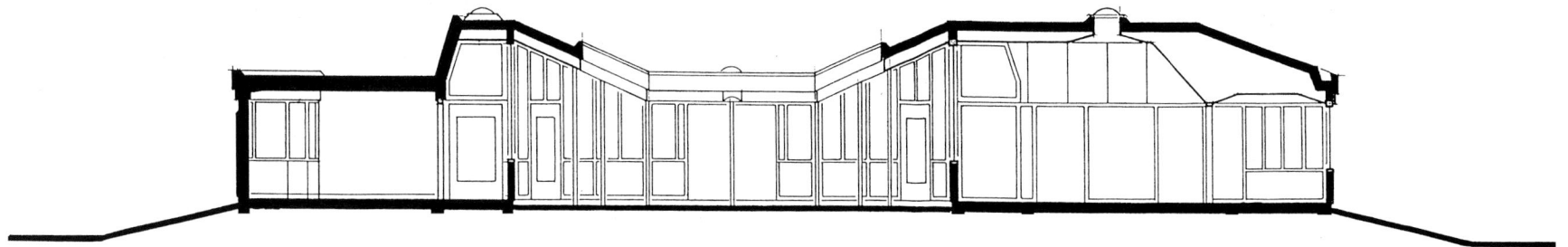

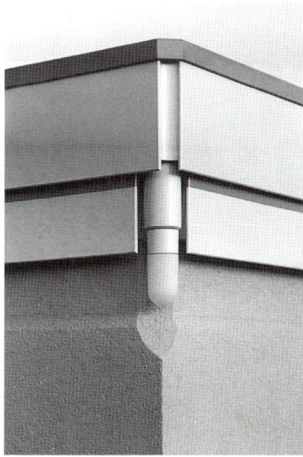

Steel arbours frame the recessed bay providing enclosure, shade and intimate outlook to the rooms. Foliage density will be trimmed or allowed to grow as each inmate prefers.

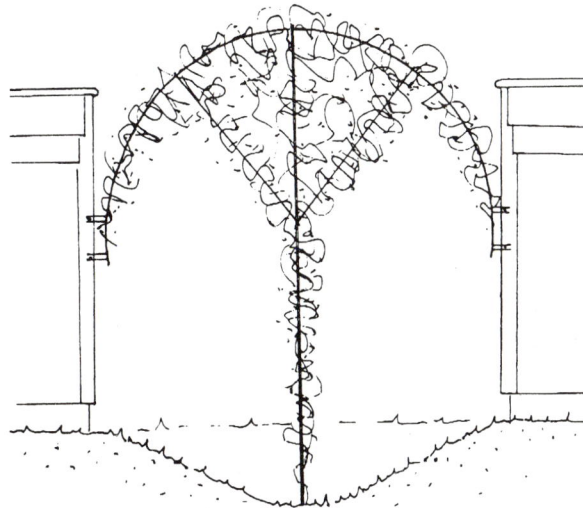

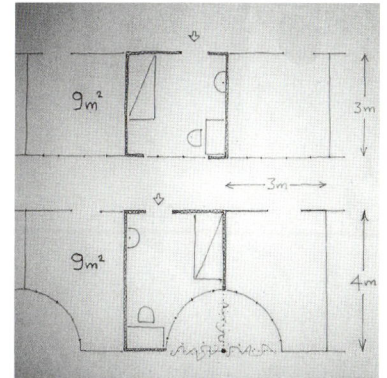

214

The living room/dining room quarters form a clear link between outdoor spaces within the building (courtyards) and those outside (closed gardens).

View from living room towards patio

Entrance area

Monument for Queen Wilhelmina, The Hague, 1982

The National Monument for Queen Wilhelmina, who died in 1962, met with many an obstacle. Politicians of the usual kind and far too many people who wanted a 'worthy', straightforward statue stood in the way.

The site in the historical centre – though attractive – certainly has its drawbacks. There are many protected trees and lots of activities (book and antique market, races, etc.) which take place between them all year round leaving little or no room for anything as substantial as a monument.

So I designed a dome-like steel construction to hold approximately 20 translucent images (black and white photographs) to be raised 10 ft from the ground and to be viewed from the inside: a multifaceted portrait of the Queen in her time or, to put it another way, an accessible three-dimensional picture frame through which people may pass freely.

All the steel is to be painted white like a ship (the Queen's funeral was in white, so it seems appropriate to 'set' her portrait in white also).

Many people think steel is utterly unsuitable for a monument and photographs undignified, but the Queen's own daughter and granddaughter – themselves queens at a later date – appreciated the project because of its directness and absence of symbolism.

In line with the middle row of trees only three, sick, trees had to go, so, being raised off the ground, the construction would not have obstructed any activity.

There were complaints, of course: steel? an abstract construction? Yes, I would reply, like a frame for photographs on people's mantelpieces – what could be more recognisable a national trait?

216

just an open space 'between' the trees.
this has created a new place in the city!
inside the old one

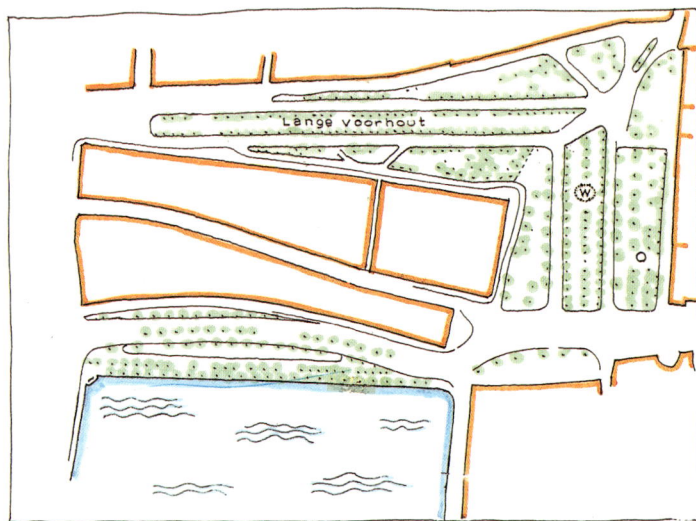

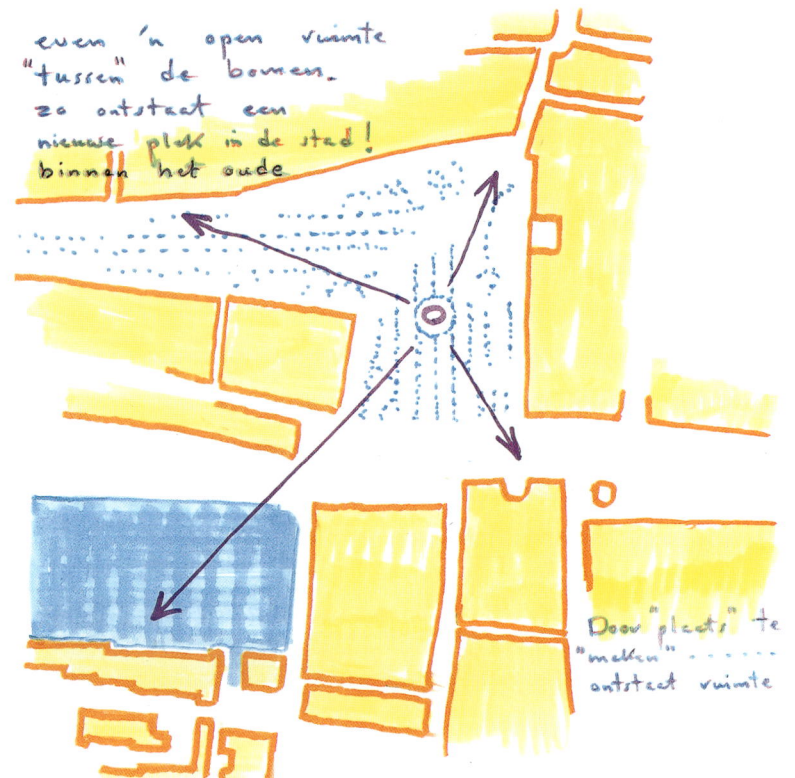

'making room'......
has created space

upper ring: photografic
transparancies of the
period.

lower segments: photografic
transparancies of the
person.

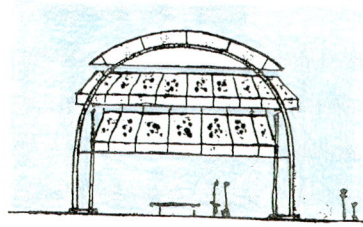

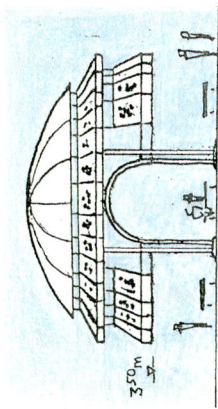

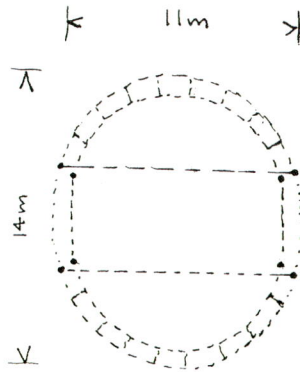

11m

14m

the entire construction to be
painted white.

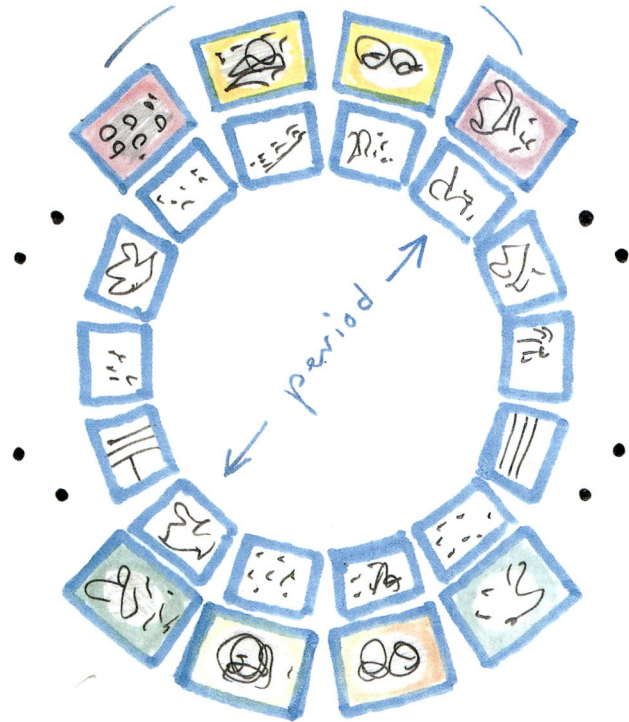

period

General Scheme for Siemens AG, Moorenbrunn, 1982 with Hannie van Eyck

A 'large' number of smaller building elements or a small number of 'large' ones? In both these extreme cases (or somewhere in-between) it involved the accommodation of a large number of people, and that is no small thing! This meant looking for a meaningful scanning of the set quanta; flexible and expandable – everything in the light of the given location – and which cannot be called either truly urban or truly rural. However, we did not just position ourselves somewhere 'in-between', but opted for the 'large form' containing a large internal landscape – more formal, paved and square as in the narrower middle – then broadening out, more free – almost wild – with lots of trees. Instead of a fragmented external area like public gardens round an abundance of angular office buildings, here we have two curved series of building elements which, although together they are 'big' in the sense of wide, start off with a salutary lowness to then rise from two to three storeys in the middle. One layer on the ground, one under the roof and one in between, with voids to promote contact in both directions, and through all three daylight from above by means of voids. Seen this way it is the ideal height for offices.

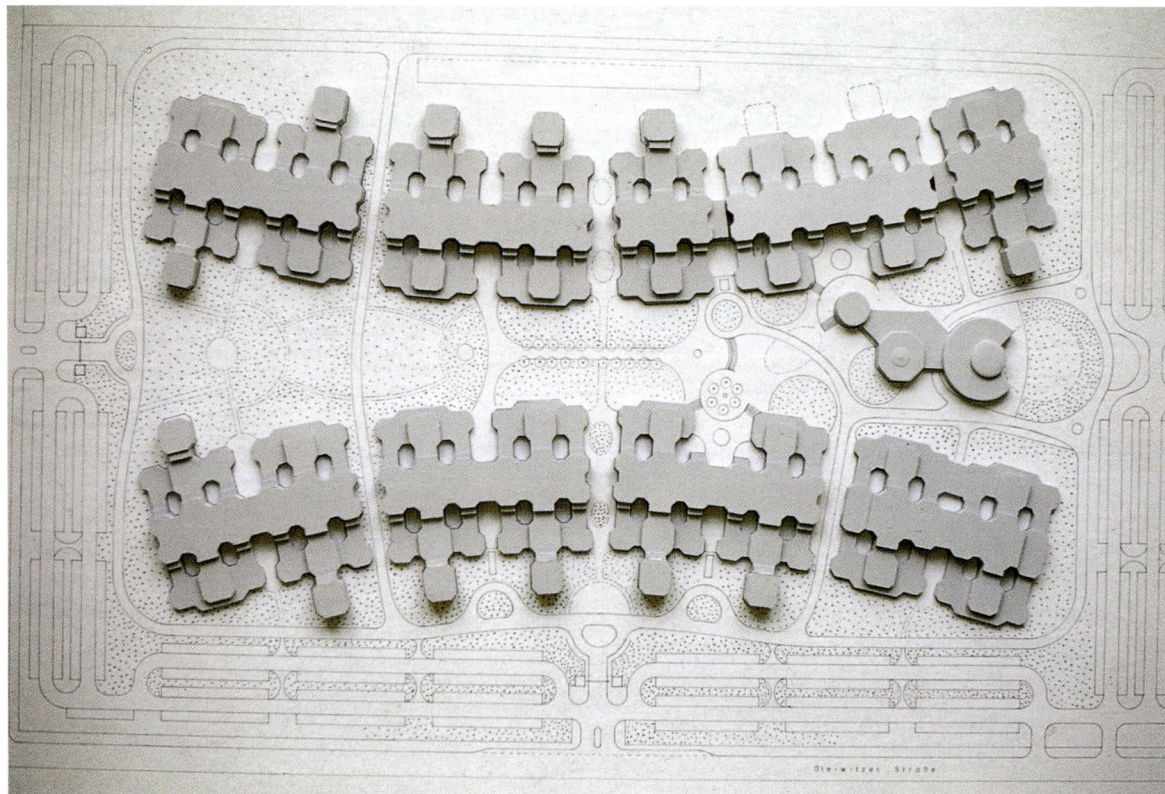

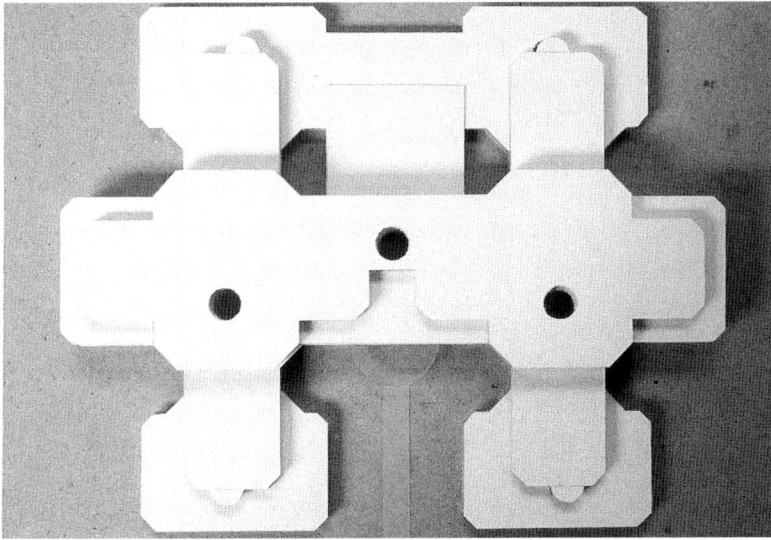

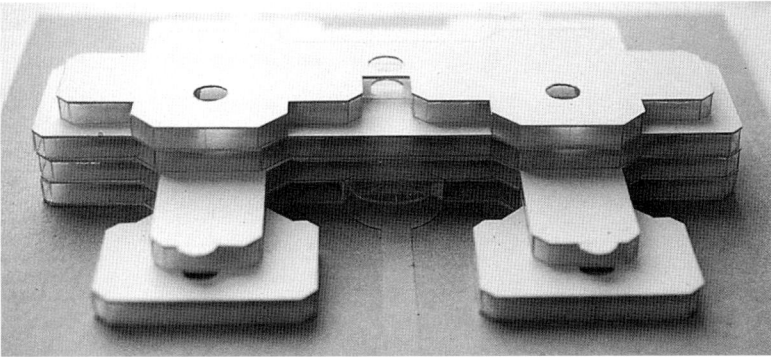

Protestant Church for the Moluccan Community, Deventer, 1983-92 with Hannie van Eyck

The site is the usual kind of non-space residue planners are in the habit of leaving between terraced suburban houses. Since one can't really build in (add anything to) non-space (or next to the kind of architecture that generally goes with it), I imagined this unfortunate space-residue solidified, with the church required to be scooped out of the mass. But alas, Holland is not Ethiopia! As to what building materials to use? A problem indeed, because the character of all that is readily available and affordable has already been squandered by random application all round the site. Besides, anything too different or conspicuous would isolate itself and thus work against the unity the Moluccans

envisage between their homes and their place of worship. Since the traditional church-going ceremony begins at home as an intimate family affair some time before the actual service, getting to the church – the way there – is regarded as a formal prelude to the service itself (extended entry). With this negative – or inverted – spatial notion in mind, I did away with all the exterior 'walls' by having roses grow up thin trellis screens right round the church (and looping out and over the entrance porches) – 30 cm away from the walls. Roses with a similar colour (white) will also feature in the surrounding garden linking it to the building. The belfry will be enclosed by the same trellis screen for roses.

220

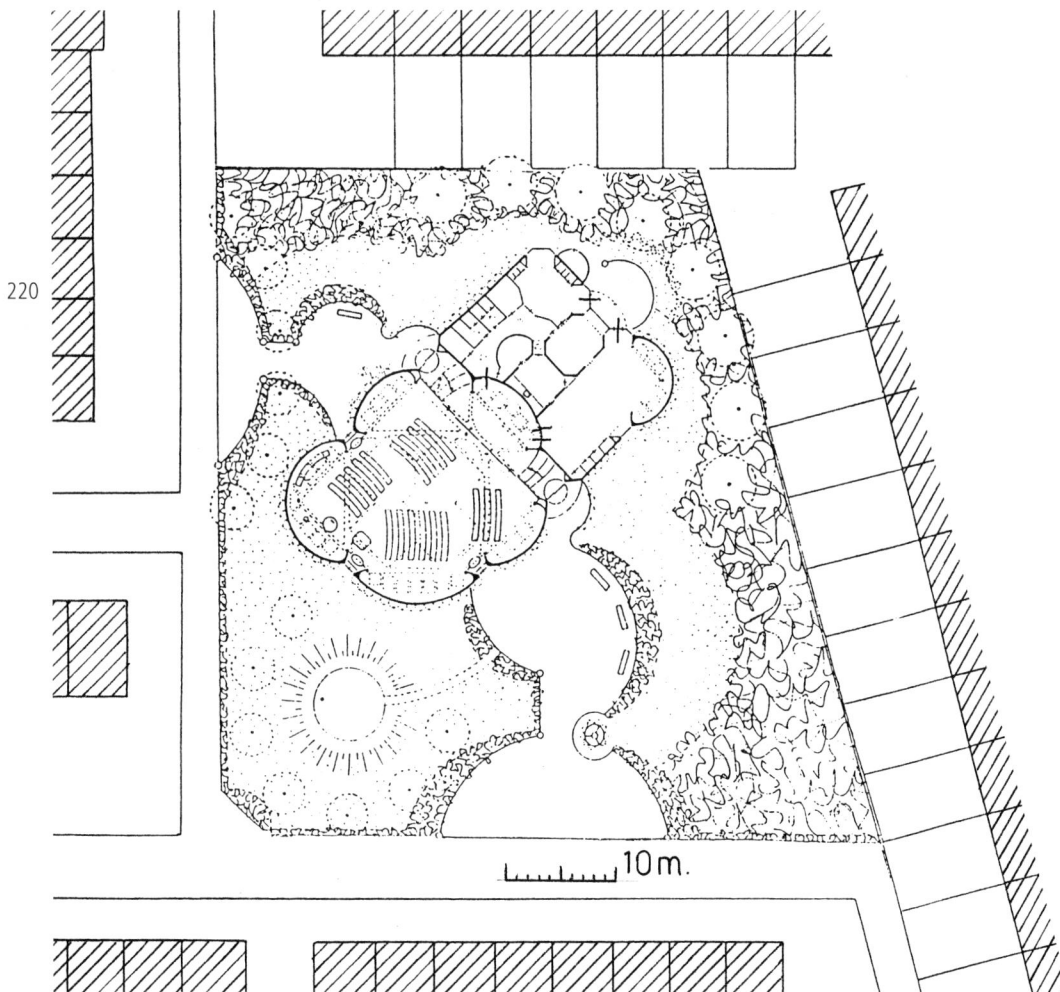

10 m.

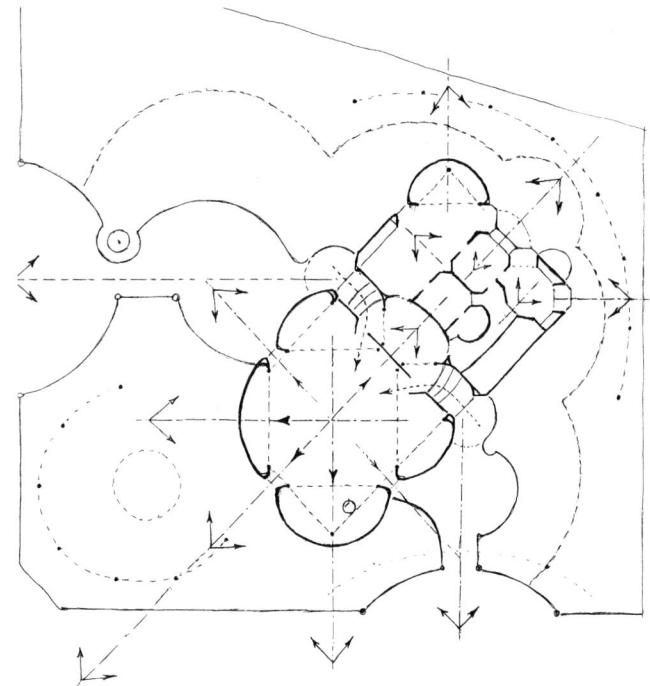

As far as the interior is concerned: I did not want one single point of focus (the pulpit) to hold people's attention involuntarily, but instead preferred to allow it to shift – wander – away and back again. Hence multidirectional axiality and multiple symmetry rather than asymmetry.

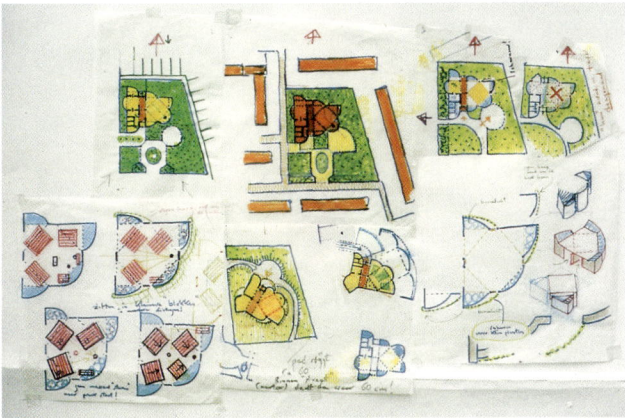

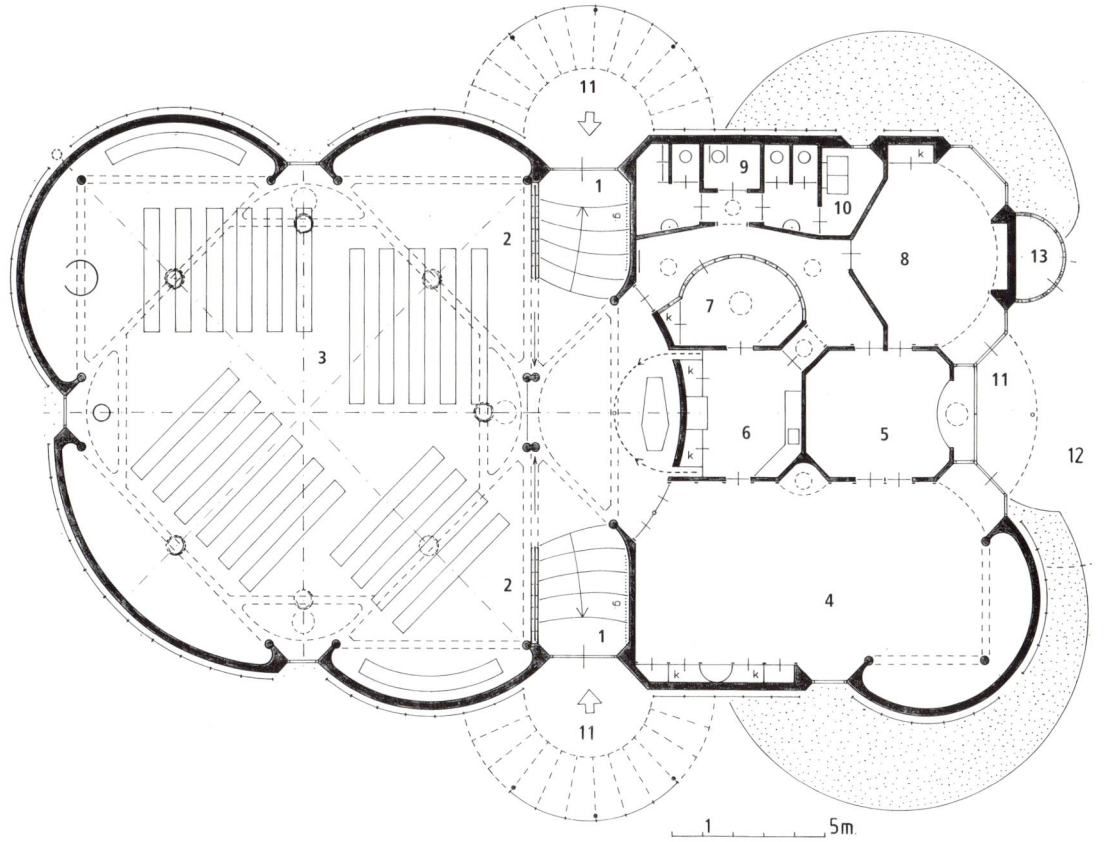

221

1 5m.

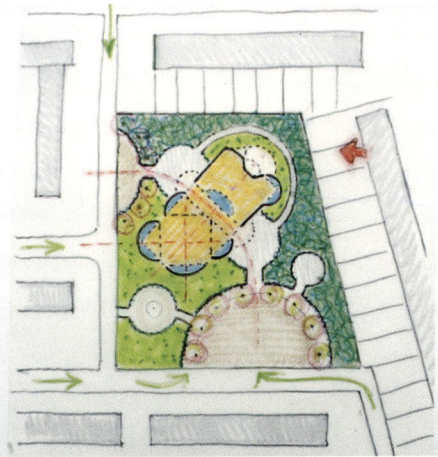

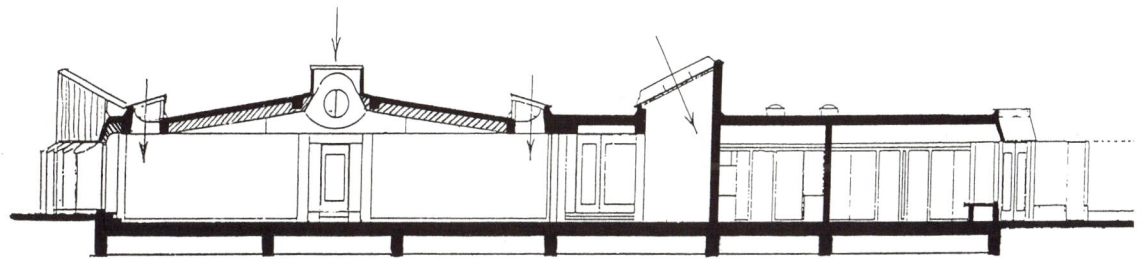

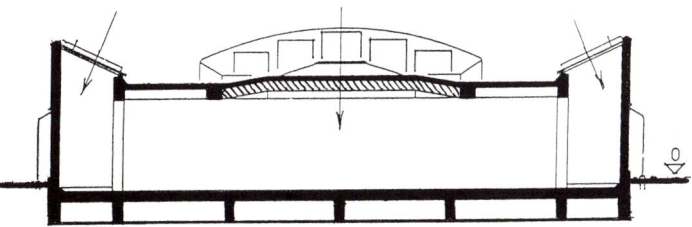

4500⁺

2600⁺

300⁻

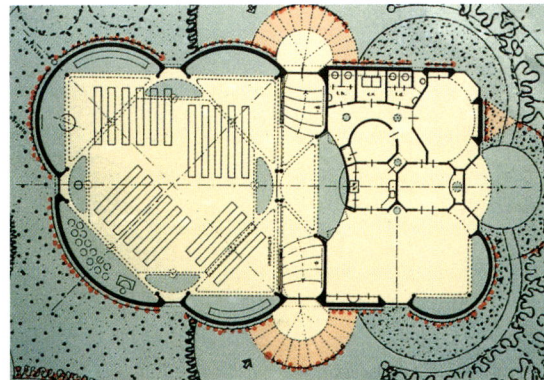

1 entrance
2 sliding door
3 worship space
4 large meeting room
5 office
6 kitchen
7 store room
8 vestry
9 toilets
10 boiler room
11 canopy
12 terrace
13 store room for gardening tools

222

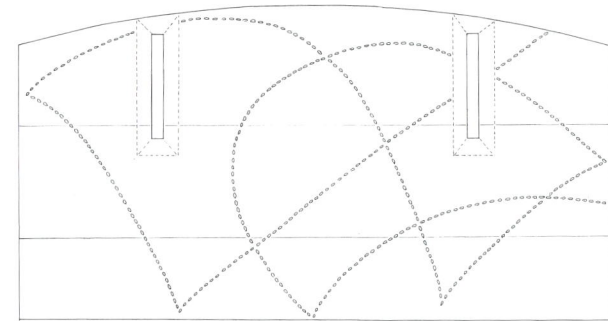

Iene Ambar drew her 'flying lines' on each of the six curved interior walls – each differently. The mother of pearl sea shells she pressed into the wet plaster one by one were sent especially from the Moluccan islands.

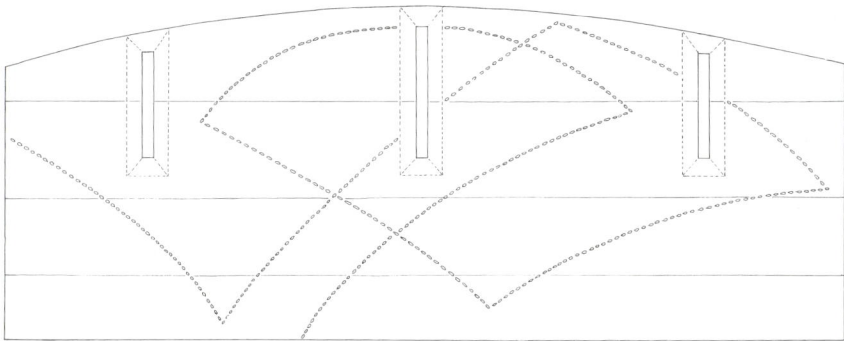

224

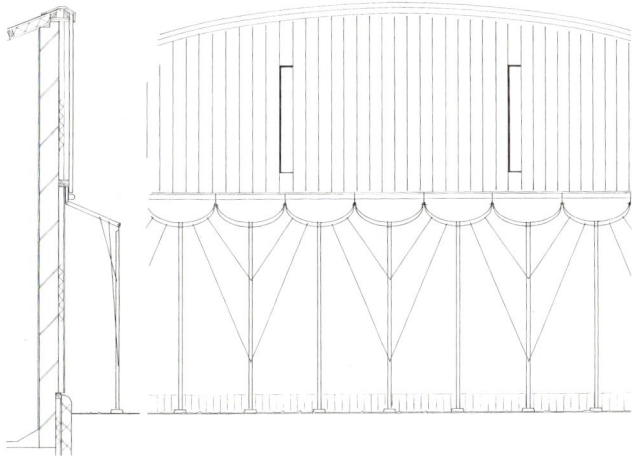

Urban Development of Campo di Marte, La Giudecca, Venice, 1984 competition entry with Hannie van Eyck and Julyan and Tess Wickham

Apart from the grander scale of the Spinalonga, the general 'feel' of the Giudecca, with the short distance between the open water on both sides, can be compared with Burano, where the housing configuration along and between the curved canals provided the image that pointed the way. There is the changing direction of visual attention as one goes from one urban space to the next, along with the changing orientation of the dwellings themselves; the agreeable transition from fully public spaces to more intimate ones between the dwelling blocks, which face in various directions and are both straight, curved and staggered: all these devices were regarded as appropriate in principle for the Giudecca, if carefully transposed to fit the different social situation.

The present social and urbanistic situation of the larger part of the Giudecca is a sad one – even shameful, judged in the light of Venice's vast reputation as a place of culture – and unique urban beauty – and taking into account that real slums in northern Italy are assumed to belong to the past. As to the Campo di Marte in its dismal setting: continuous access is blocked in every direction by harsh and clearly obsolete walls; barbed wire between different classes of people and various penal institutions stigmatises them. Nor is there any access to the lagoon. The present housing on the Campo di Marte remains all but walled in like a ghetto. It seems hardly acceptable to merely make replacements without breaking out of this confinement in every direction! But apparently it was.

226

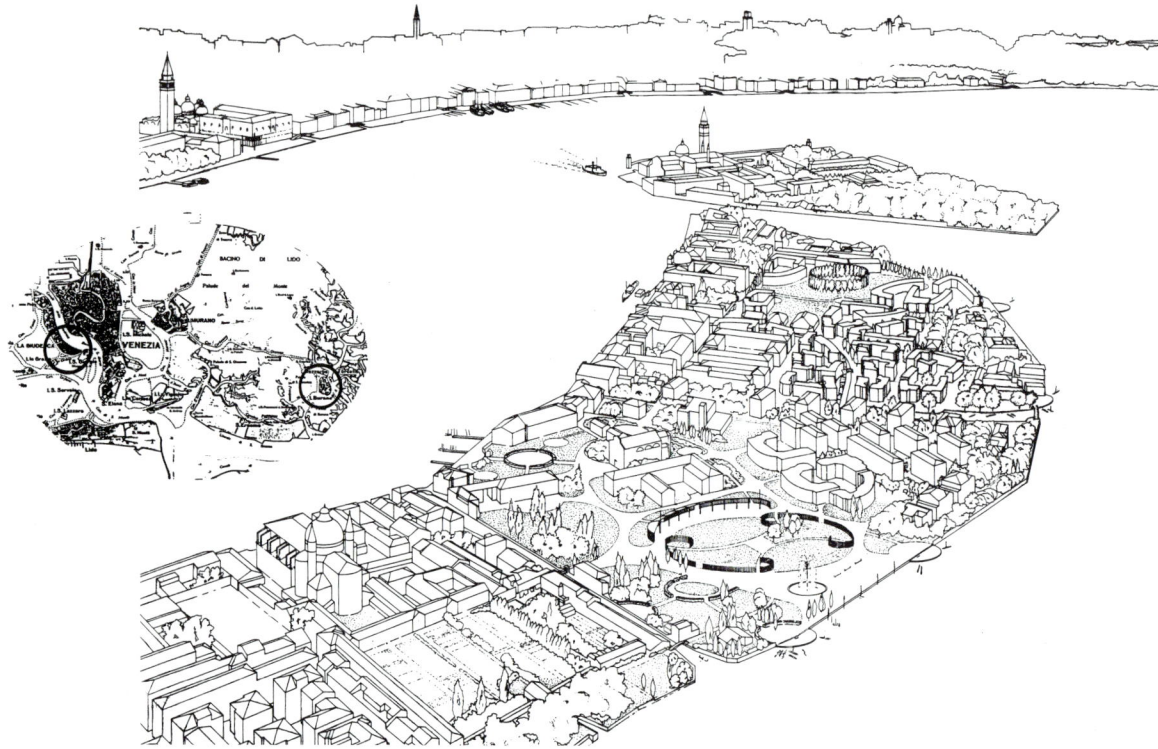

BETWEEN THESE TWO MIRACULOUS CHURCHES,
BEHIND THE STATELY SPINALONGA
FACING THE CITY OPPOSITE
WHATEVER WAS NOT DESIRED THERE OR FOR WHICH
THERE WAS NO ROOM
LIES SADLY HIDDEN

In between
new
Campo di Marte

Along
"Canal Piccolo"
to the Lagoon beyond

Through
the city park
to the Lagoon beyond

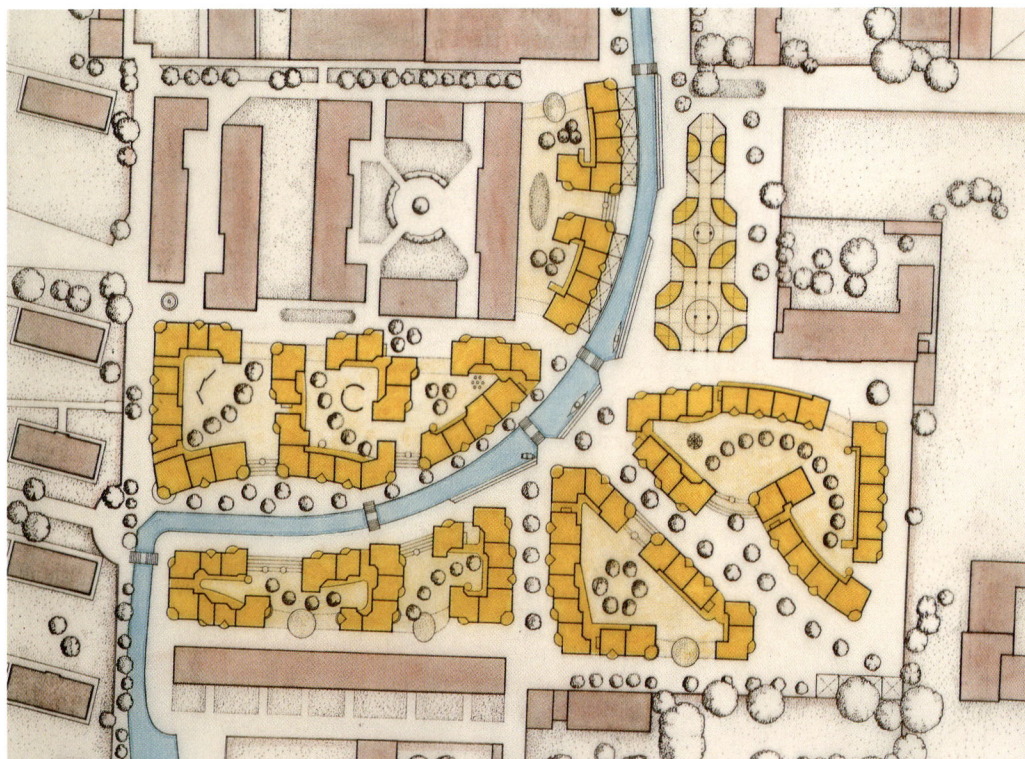

'Canal Piccolo'

'Venice' never really penetrated this part of the Spina-longa – not with a canal anyway. *A propos canals*: 'WE WOULD PROBABLY HAVE PROPOSED ONE EVEN IF VENICE HAD NEVER HAD ANY. BUT VENICE HAPPENS TO HAVE MANY (AND THAT DID MAKE OUR DECISION TO INCLUDE ONE EASIER!).'

Digging a new canal – instead of filling in yet another as in Amsterdam – would provide the site with the most effective communication artery and social identification device.

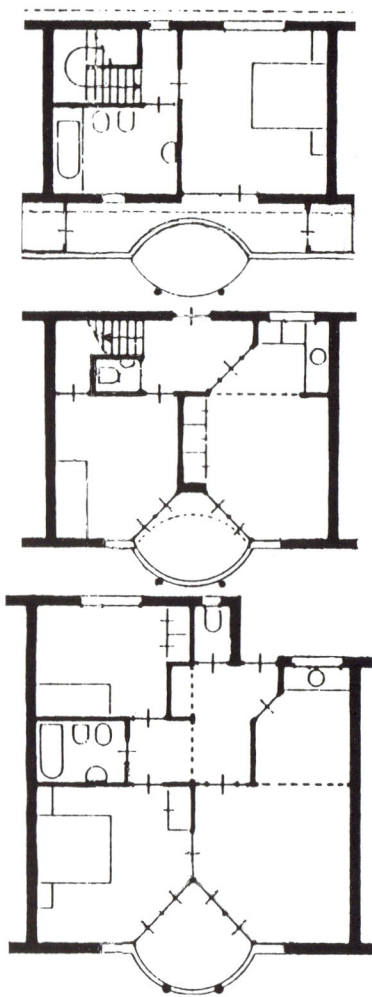

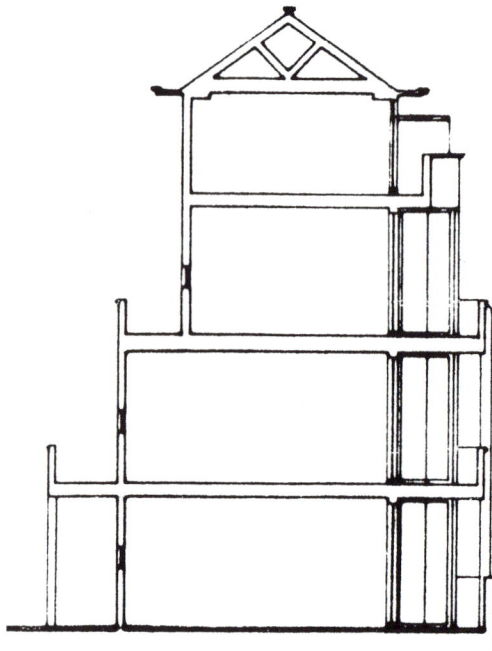

Outside, on the living room side, two design ideas define the appearance of the public space: the window-balcony formation, which might be able to ensure that the street is 'populated' in the third dimension too (while the height of the façade is thereby meaningfully segmented), and the wall surfaces between them with mosaics as a decorative accompaniment to the access to the outside. After all, no one can fool us into believing that at home he only wants to spend his time behind walls and windows when there are other possibilities, although that's the nonsense we always get to hear.

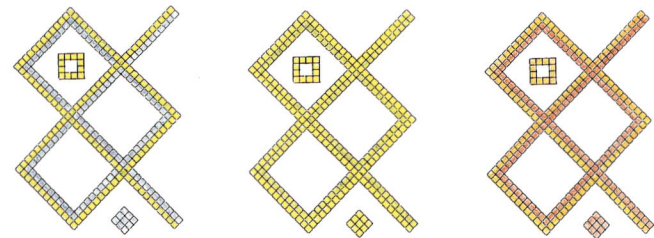

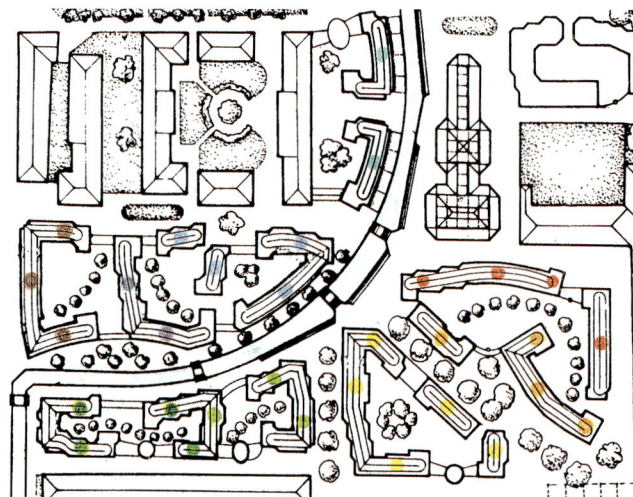

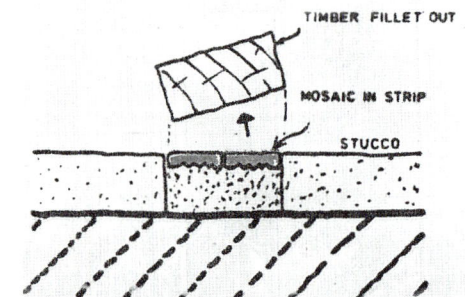

228

The intention was to apply patterns in mosaics to the wall surfaces between the balconies, as on the façades of the Palace of the Doges (something regal for every Giudecca resident, as an exterior sign that on the inside it is at last reasonable). Narrow strips of mosaic 4 cm wide in spectral colours, tapering and also in order of the spectrum. Thereby an essential change occurs, from court to court or along the canal.

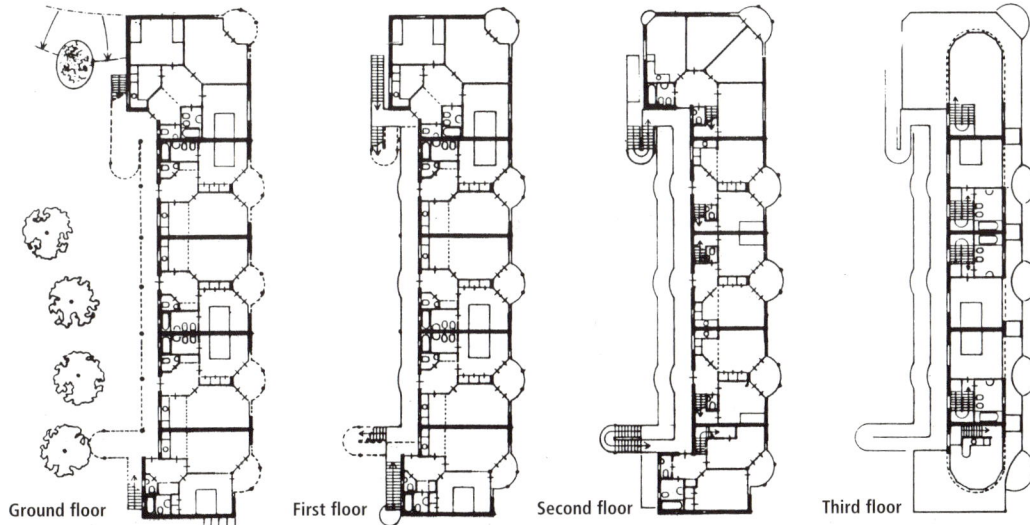

Ground floor   First floor   Second floor   Third floor

Access is by way of inner courts raised by 50 cm (partly with an eye to flooding) and short walkways (no more than two above each other) which at no point pass bedrooms. Apart from that it's the Dutch fire regulations – otherwise they will not manage if fire does ever break out there.

Regarding the houses: we have complied with the requirements with respect to housing density, although this is much too high for the confined Campo di Marte – we put this forward very explicitly. The term used there, 'housing for the homeless', is objectionable. After all, this category no longer exists as soon as these homes are available, and it is therefore an excuse for building more minimal homes (pseudo-slums). The jury, the authorities and the other competitors alike took no notice of the planning part of the competition brief, which is revealing in that it sheds light on a period when typophilia was rife and human and social issues were put aside for the sake of 'pure' architecture (the prizewinners even proposed rows of houses 3-4 metres apart, thus replacing the existing ghetto by another).

Beside the proposed canal running through the neighbourhood there will be two parks, a large one along the Rio della Croce serving Venice as a whole and a small one along the Cipriani Hotel wall for local use. All three elements will bring the lagoon closer to Venice's citizens.

There will be an oval lawn in the park with two small hills (ascend 2 m and behold the horizon rising!). It opens southward onto the lagoon and northward onto a covered shelter with benches in it. The two screens which partially enclose the oval are curved, free-standing, smooth concrete posts (height 3 m; diameter 22 cm; interval 12 cm). The horizon will be seen to continue through the screens whilst the lagoon will appear 'held' in the 35 m opening between them. There will be semi-circular hardwood landing jetties all along the lagoon.

The ESTEC Complex, Noordwijk, 1984-9 with Hannie van Eyck

First proposal

Since the existing building complex had no recognisable 'core' or centre of gravity, the idea of locating the new facilities halfway along the main internal traffic artery on the ground floor proved to be appropriate. The curvilinear interior and exterior walls made a compact linear organisation possible, whilst sustaining a fluent spatial development and easy movement from place to place along the entire length and width of the new premises. The formal contrast with the existing structure is intentional, i.e. the rectilinear angularity of the existing buildings is discontinued.

The ultimate buildings

The fluent character of the masses and spaces responds to the gentle contours of the exterior setting. The dunes were thereby 'extended' all round the building as it were.

As to the construction and materials, only the conference/meeting rooms are of reinforced concrete. The roof is the new building's most exposed feature. It holds the sequence of spaces together; transmits light from above; collects and channels rainwater; and, seen from the upper floors of the new office building, it represents from the outside what occurs below it inside. In general, representational extravagance has been avoided.

It is the construction, the proportions and the straightforward unadorned use of a small number of sound materials that convey what we believe to be the right atmosphere. Elegance and ease without ostentatious luxury. This, together with generous dimensioning, is expected to stimulate a rich variety of use in the future.

The greater part of the building, i.e. restaurant, kitchen, library, etc., is made of steel painted in the six spectral colours (in spectral sequence) so as to provide the required visual articulation in depth as well as a change of colour scheme between different parts of the building; e.g. blue and green where one enters (coffee corner and library) and orange and red for the far end of the restaurant.

The restaurant provides a considerable variety of places from which to choose. Some are orientated towards the outside while others are more introvert. Curved screens articulate the considerable size and length of the restaurant.

230

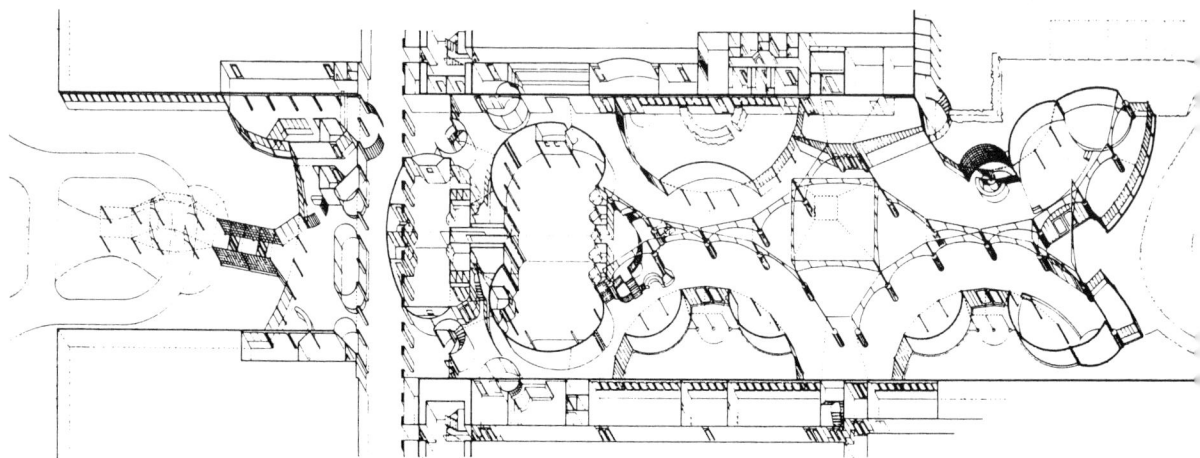

First proposal
Restaurant and conference facilities in a courtyard of the existing structure

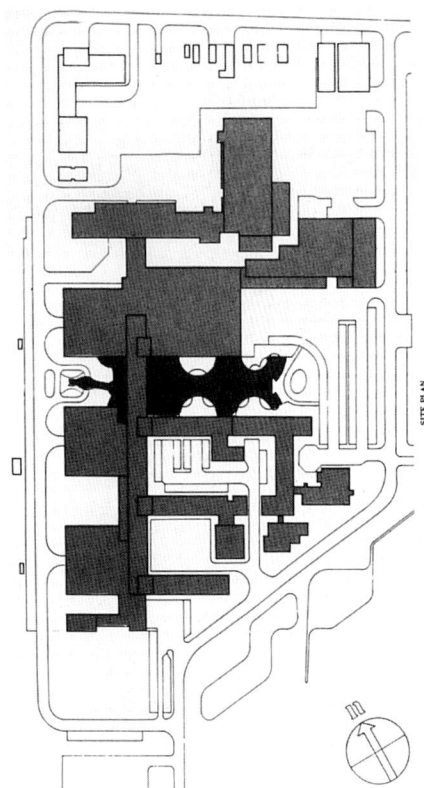

SITE PLAN

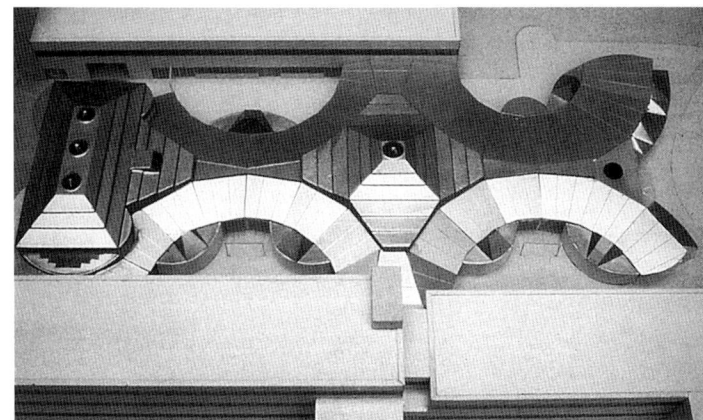

The ultimate buildings
An expanded program with restaurant, library
and conference facilities, and offices

Landscaping
The terrain round the building as well as between the entrance drive
and the parking areas extends the dunelandscape as it were. The
sequence of hillocks shields the interior from the traffic on all sides.

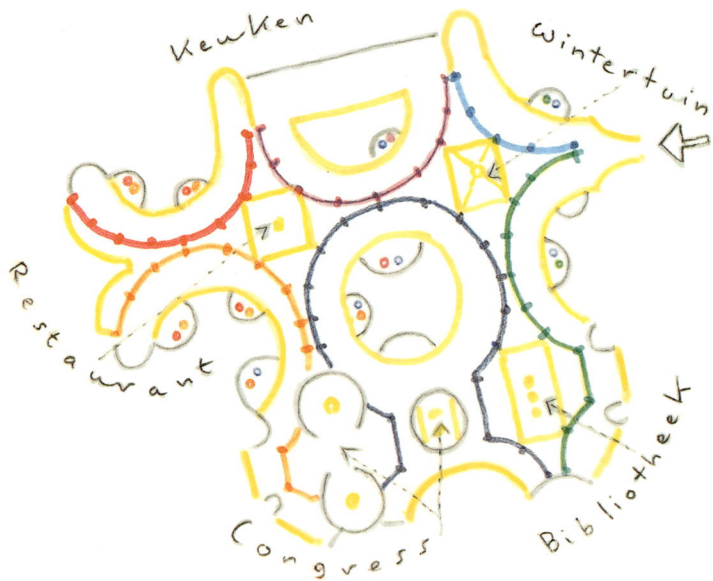

Keuken

Wintertuin

Restaurant

Congress

Bibliotheek

In order to bring about an effective articulation in depth and also differentiate the colour scheme locally, the main steel columns and trusses are coloured differently – per curved chain and in spectral sequence, albeit without yellow, which, together with light from outside, accompanies the active perimeter.

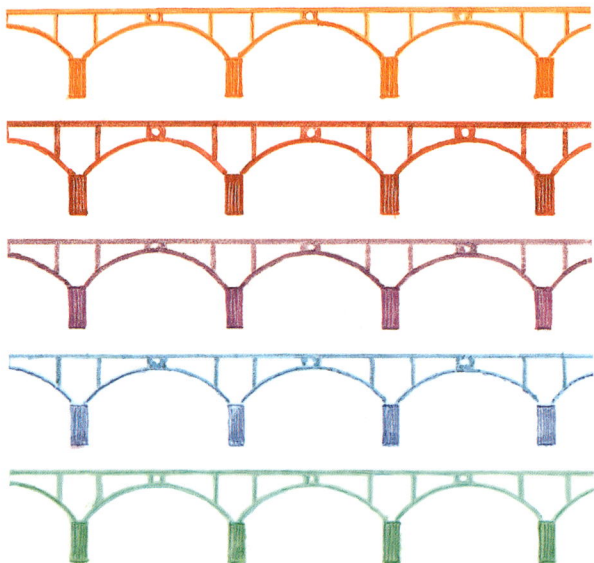

Restaurant and conference complex

1 restaurant	9 storage	17 stairs to translator booths
2 coffee corner	10 office	18 projection
3 coffee bar	11 cloakroom	19 storage
4 winter garden	12 pantry	20 audio visual room
5 dining room	13 linen	21 library
6 kitchen	14 toilets in basement	22 covered terrace
7 dishwashing	15 conference room	23 heating plant etc.
8 fridge	16 coordinator	24 terrace

0 2m   10m

Whether they carry a large or a small load, are thick or thin, low or tall, all the steel columns are made up of the same 8 cm tubes – from 1 to 11 to them. Thus one dimension, i.e. the diameter of the basic component, remains the same all the way through. The size of each column can thus be counted instead of measured.

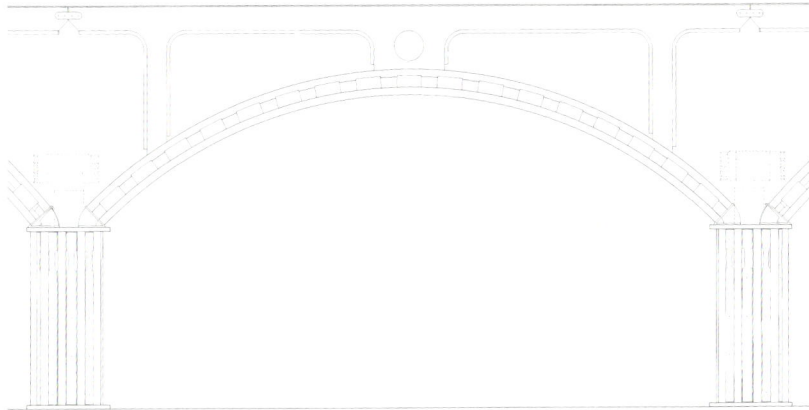

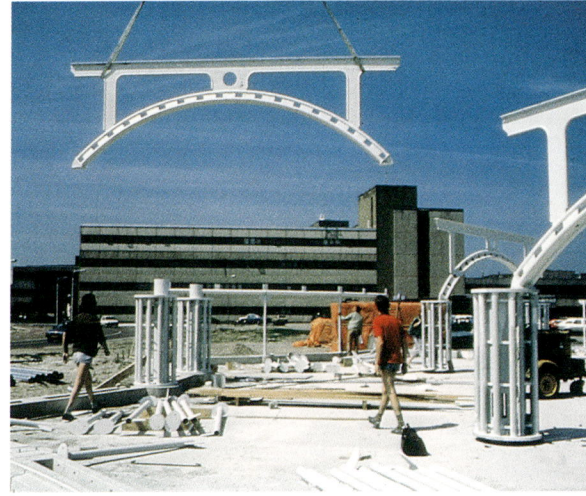

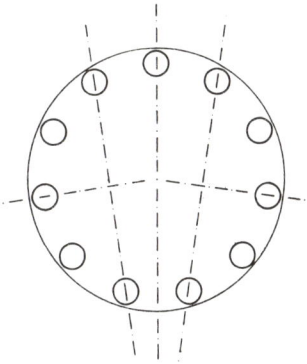

The hendecagonic column

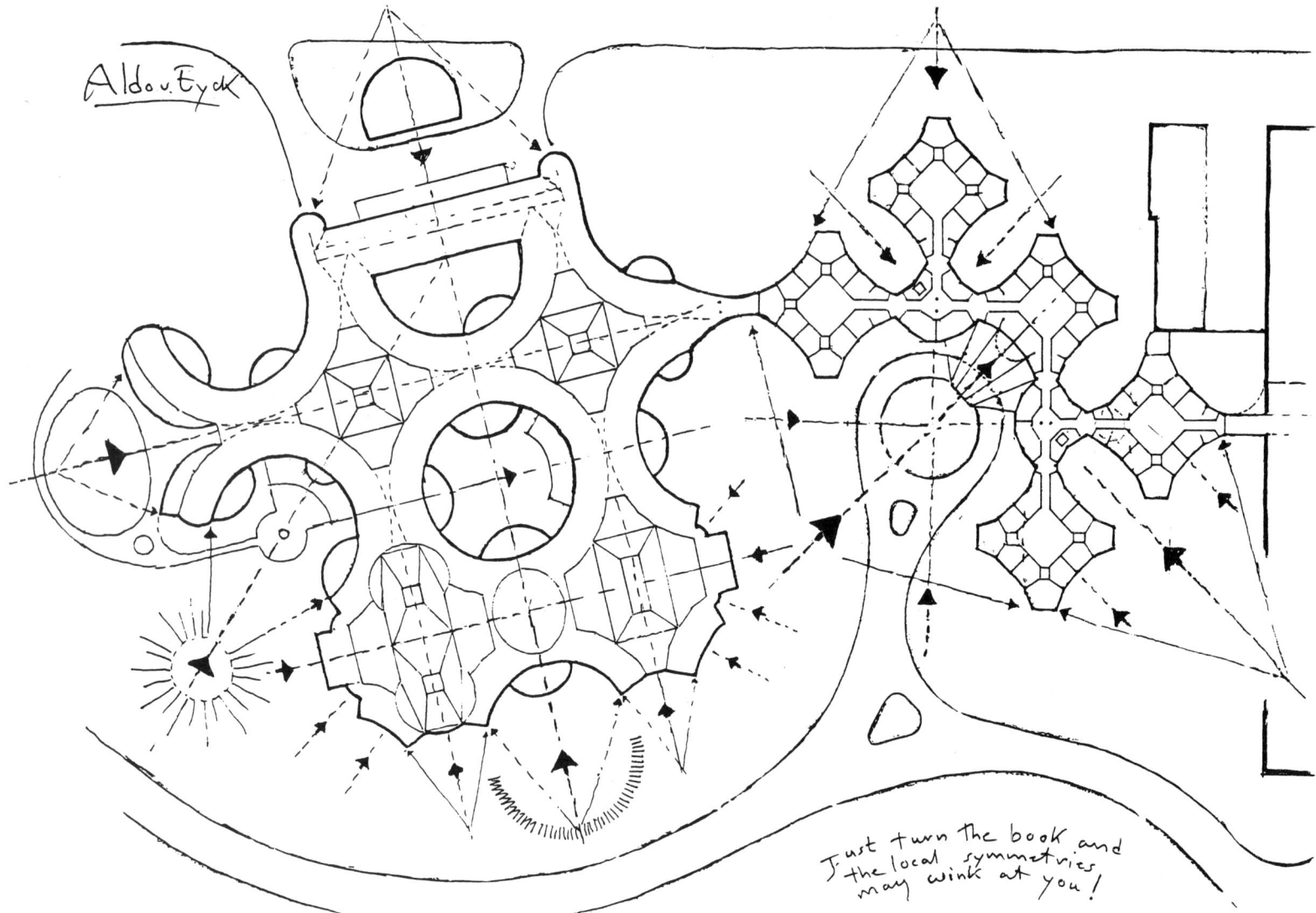

Aldo v. Eyck

234

Just turn the book and the local symmetries may wink at you!

Local Symmetry Winking

Il Redentore, on the water front in La Giudecca in Venice, is seen from across the canal as you walk along the quay side. It used to be approached on particular occasions over a temporary pontoon. The façade which faces out across the canal's considerable width is miraculously articulated and dense. The bold red-brick side elevations with, far back, their rounded forms that are conspicuous from afar, are only hidden from view at the *moment* you pass exactly in front of the church – when the pediment is precisely dome-capped. The way the building winks at you just then simply sticks in the mind.

Here at ESTEC there is, like Palladio's masterpiece, no exterior horizontal axiality, but there is, nonetheless, lots of symmetry. Symmetrical and partly symmetrical local façades wink at you one after the other at the *moment* you pass them frontally. So buildings facing in all directions can even accompany you as you go by.

About the curves: they did not arise freely or at random, but are the result of a strictly geometric order. Because of repetition of similar components throughout, the new ESTEC premises are curvilinear system buildings!

235

236

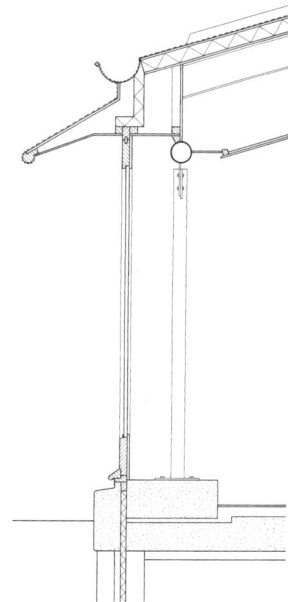

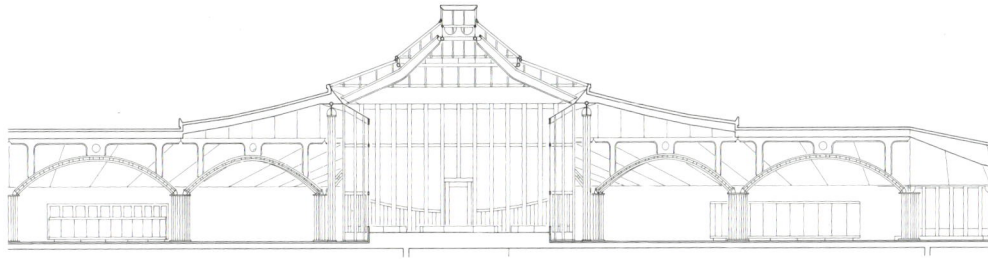

Section winter garden

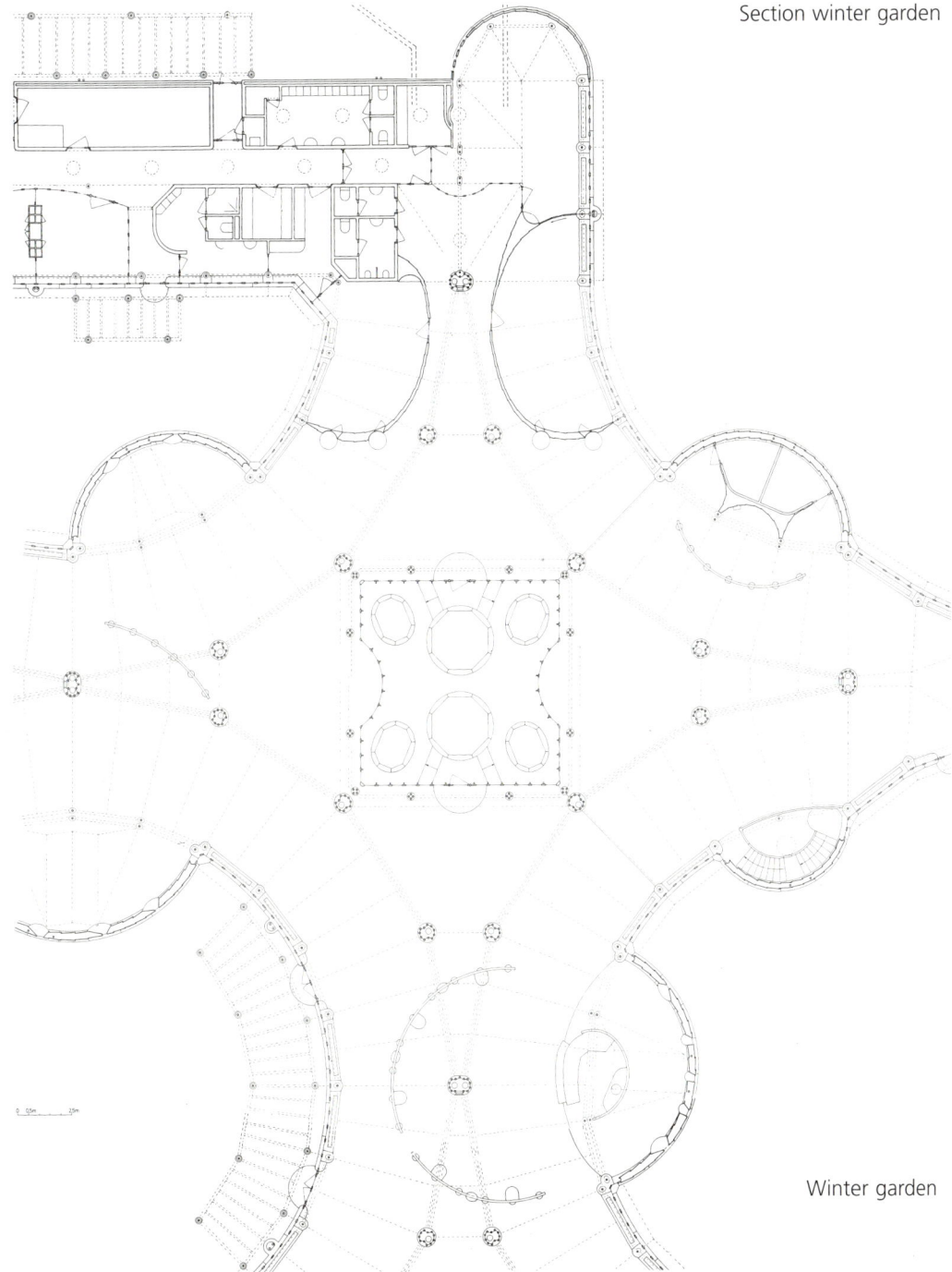

239

Winter garden

240

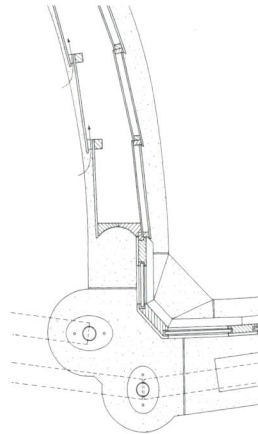

Air is drawn inside where the Oregon walls
overlap in the low semicircular drums.

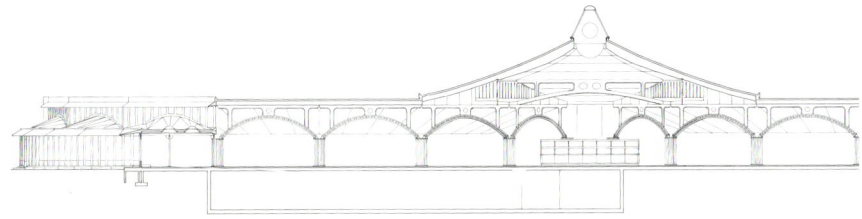
Section restaurant

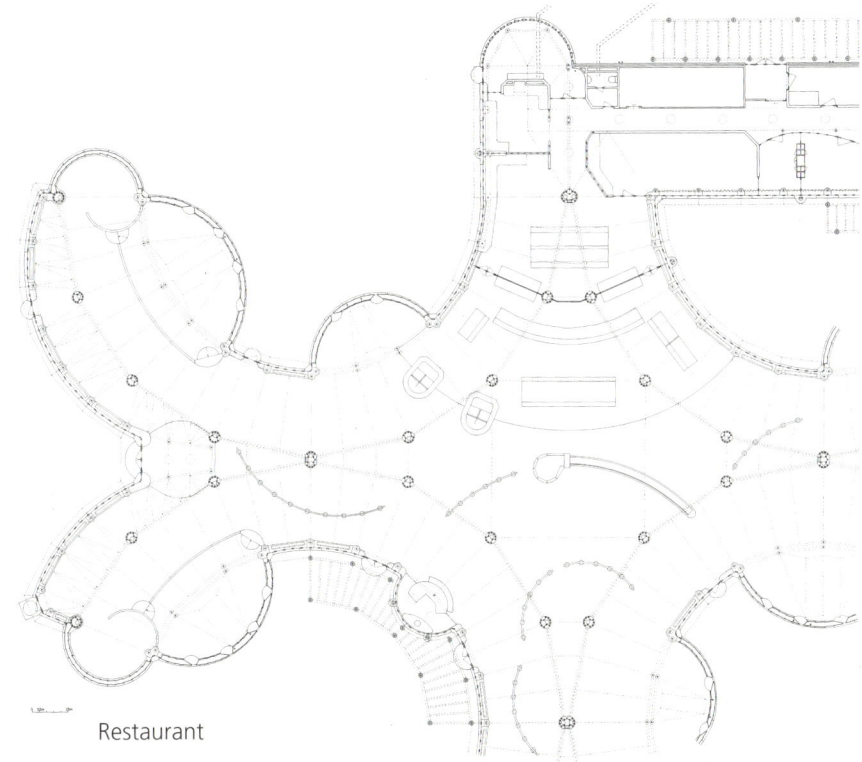
Restaurant

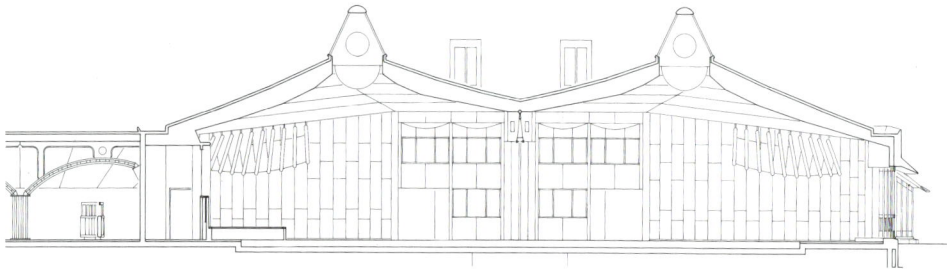
Section large conference room

242

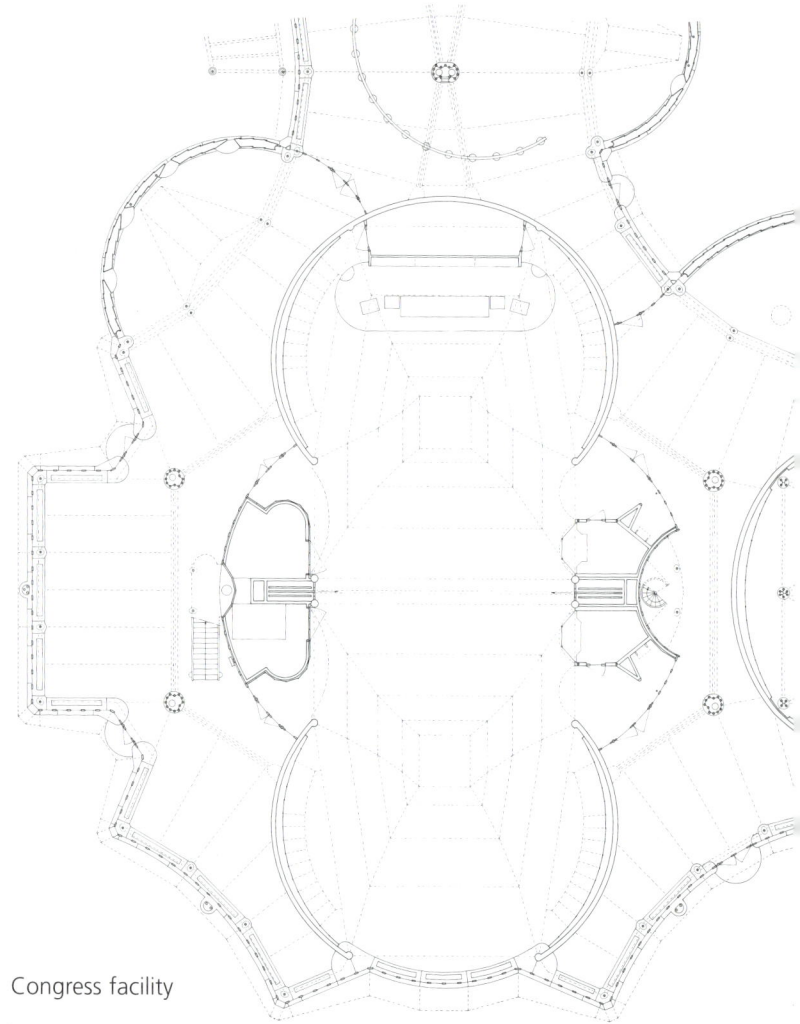
Congress facility

Daylight is first caught in a space of its own from where it spreads inwards.

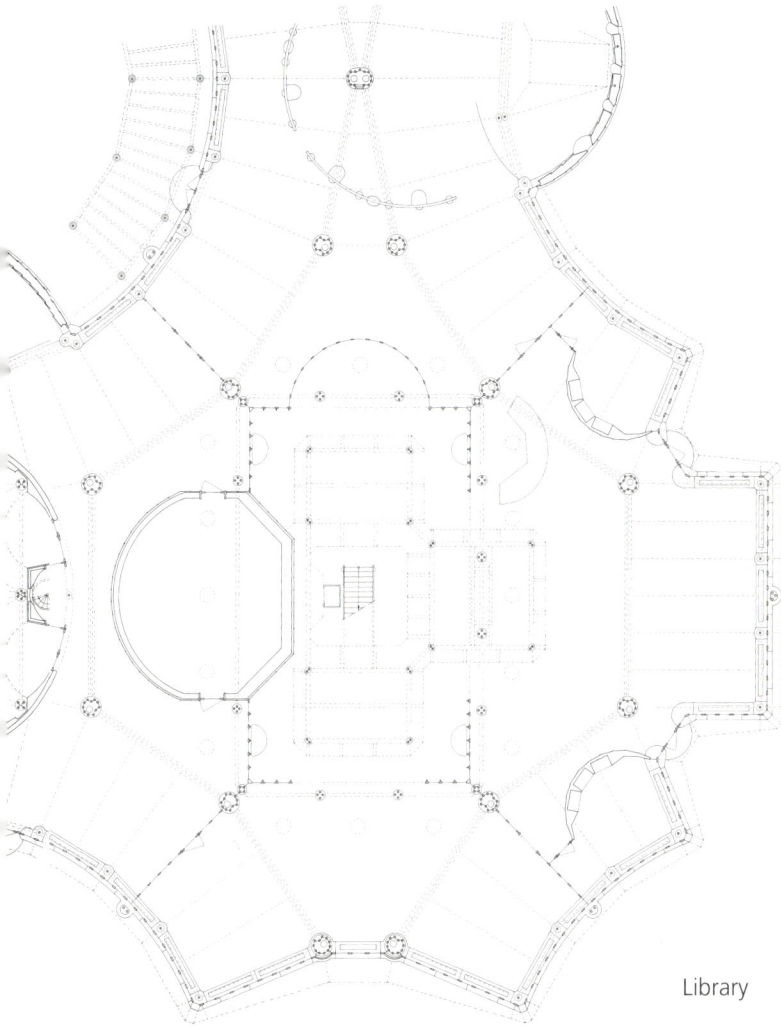

Library

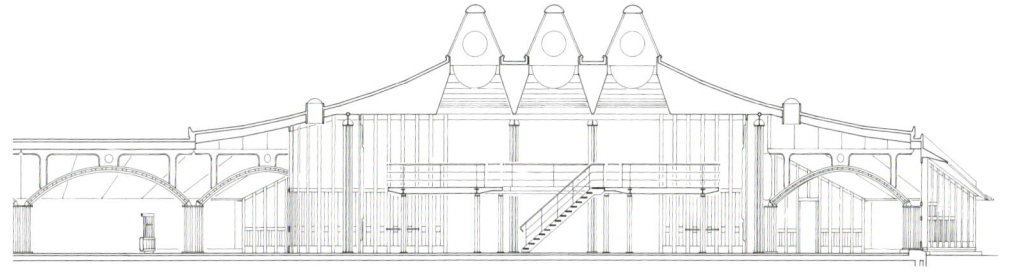

Longitudinal section library

243

Library entrance

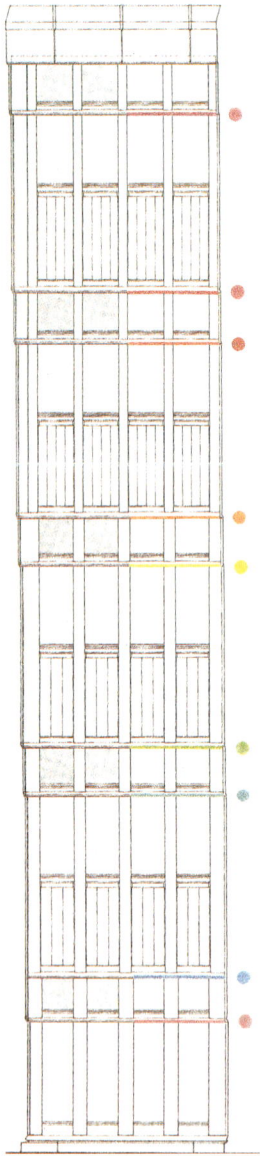

Externally the colour sequence is continued, though sparingly, on the painted metal strips underneath the overlapping timber elevation elements. Thus, whether the latter are wet or dry – hence dark, light or molted when half dry – the spectrum of thin horizontal lines retains its lustre. As the width of the vertical timbre members diminishes from ground floor upwards, the windows between them widen – and the height of the sill increases.

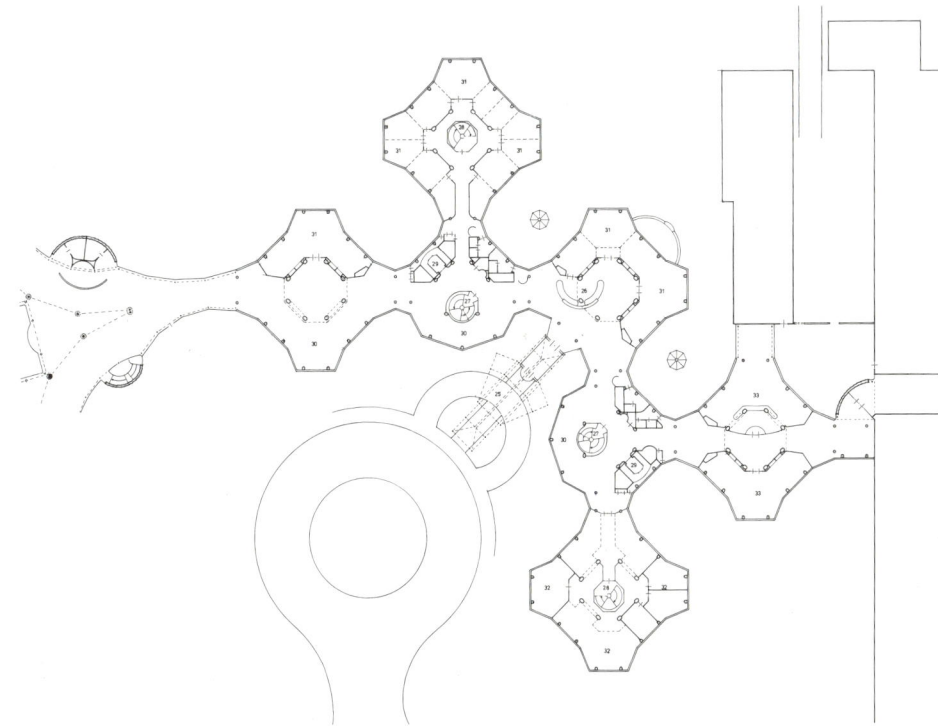

Entrance and reception

245

ESTEC offices

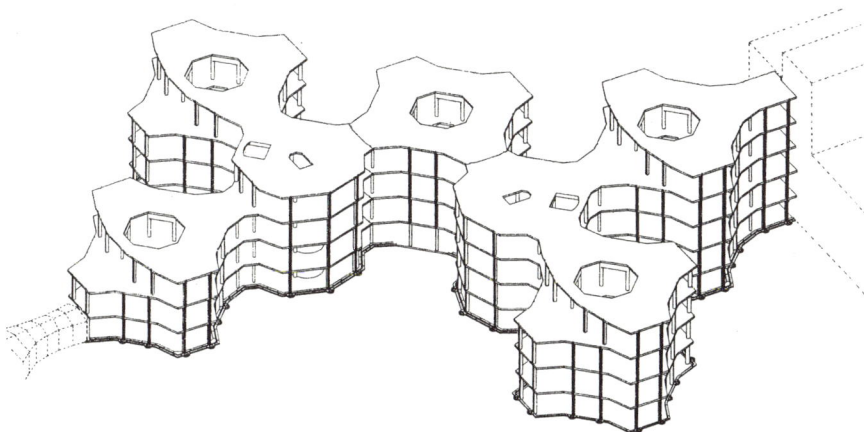

Sala de Notte, Benedictine Abbey, Catania, 1989 (conversion)
with Hannie van Eyck

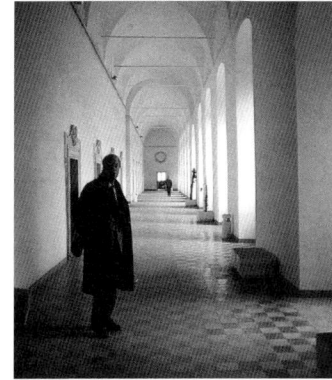

Giancarlo de Carlo, who was the architect in charge of the restoration of the Benedictine Abbey and its adaptation for future university use, suggested that we and Sverre Fehn should each do a specific part. This the university board accepted.

A vast complex for only 50 Benedictine monks! The architecture too is rather thin; at any rate we were not inspired. But it does offer endless footage for the multitudes of university students who will soon be accommodated there.

The Sala de Notte and the spaces around it – the part assigned to us – had at a later date all been crudely cluttered into the exterior triangle formed by the transept and nave of the church on two sides and a cloister on the third. It was our job to restore and refashion them into a central place for formal and informal student gatherings.

The first intervention was to open up the various spaces laterally so that, once interconnected, they could be used together as a single sequence of spaces around the Sala de Notte. This requires new openings in the thick interior walls, some low, some tall, some narrow and others very wide. All of them have a similar construction: steel lintels over steel tube columns painted white.

The second intervention was to expose as clearly as possible the massive, now completely obscured, exterior wall of the church inside the convent, by separating it from what was built against it and bringing light onto it from above through the roof where possible. Furthermore, through the use of active colours on this wall, it will stand out bit by bit in the background as one passes from space to space.

Orange and lemon groves are to bring shade to the two oversized cloisters and radiance to the cleared church wall once orange and yellow in combination (artist required!) have transformed it.

The third intervention concerns the exterior of the interior oval drum above the existing sacristy, which intrudes as an inaccessible mass into the very spaces we wish to open up. We hope its exterior can be made to approximate an

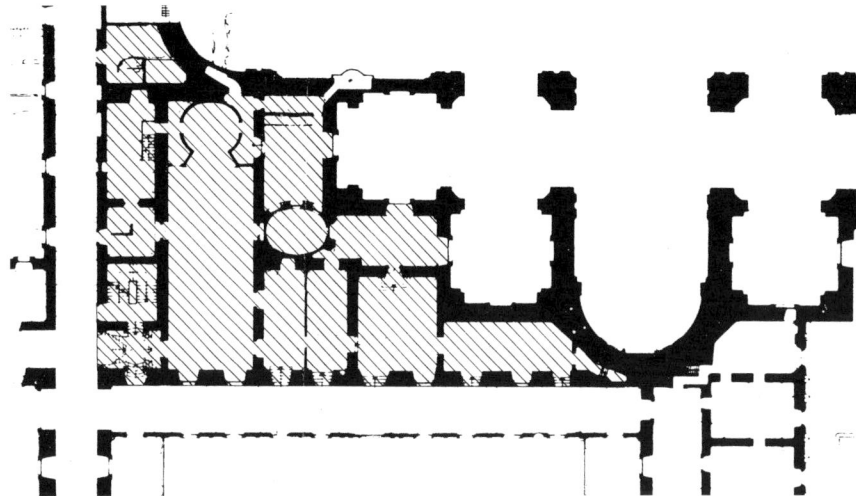

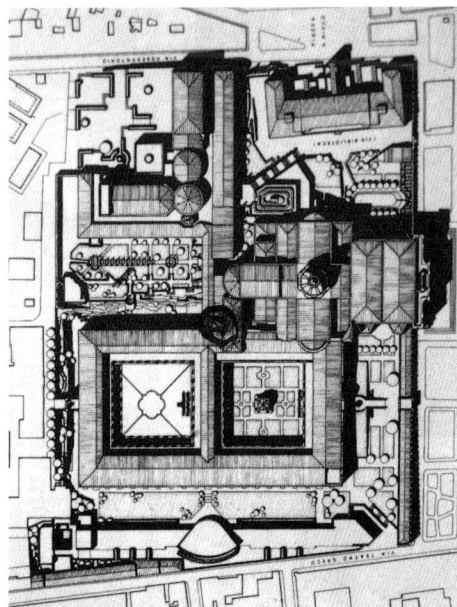

oval and that daylight can be brought in from above onto its actively coloured curvature.

Regrettably not all the proposed ingredients of the project were appreciated, e.g. the orange and lemon groves and orange and yellow as basic colours on the exterior of the church wall.

According to De Carlo, the idea is a mawkish one and would – like introducing clogs and windmills in Holland – he wrote, even irritate the local people.

It so happens that a friend and expert on Sicily told us that such lemon and orange groves within walls are actually a traditional feature in that part of the country and are called *Giardini*! Anyway for us it is the shade beneath the trees in those scorched oversized cloisters that counts; the foliage seen from above and the refreshing colours and smell. What we proposed was coherent and ought not to have been written off the way it was: so we withdrew.

1 void
2 balcony

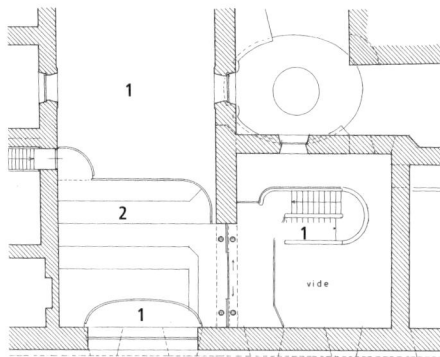

Sala de Notte

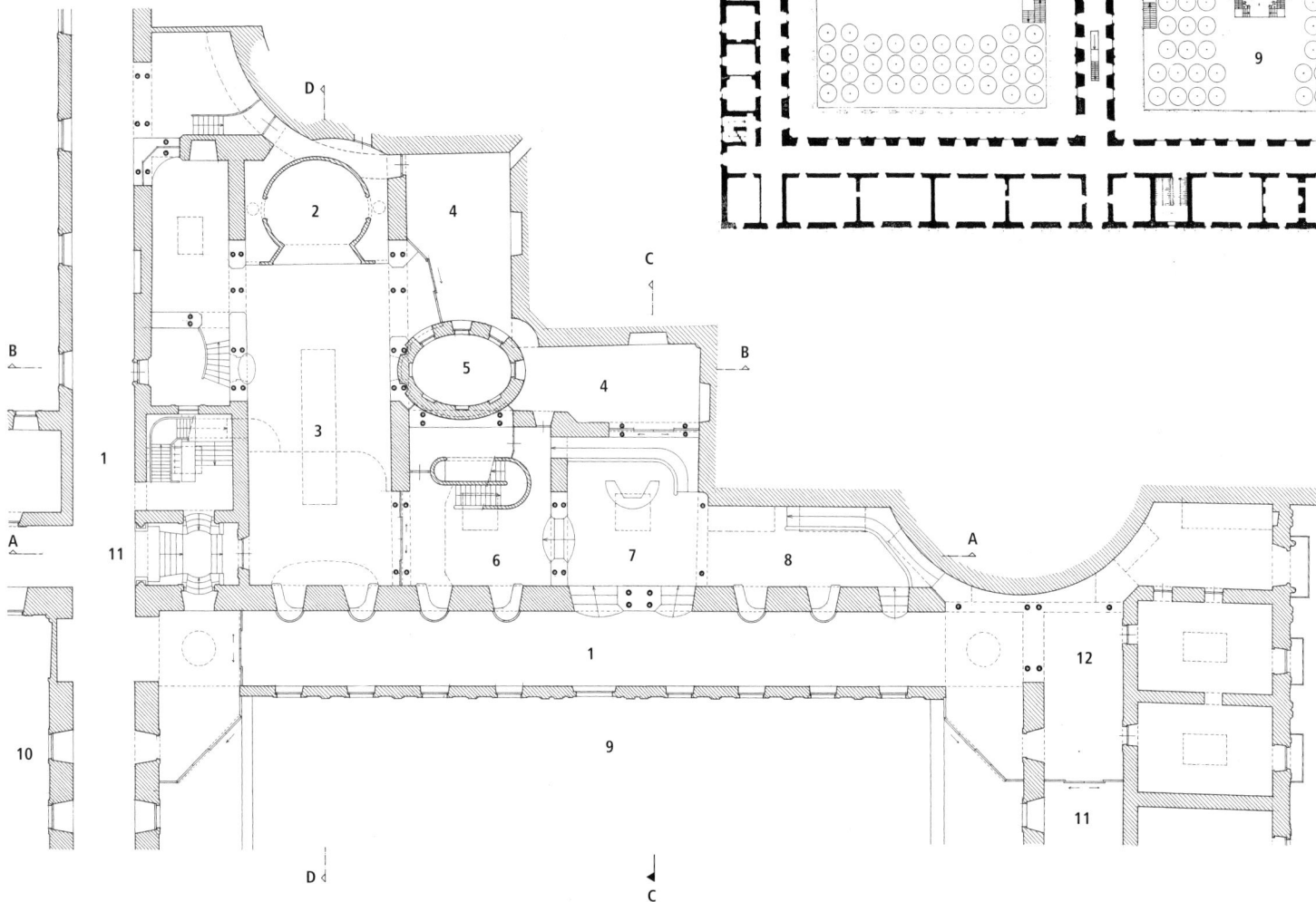

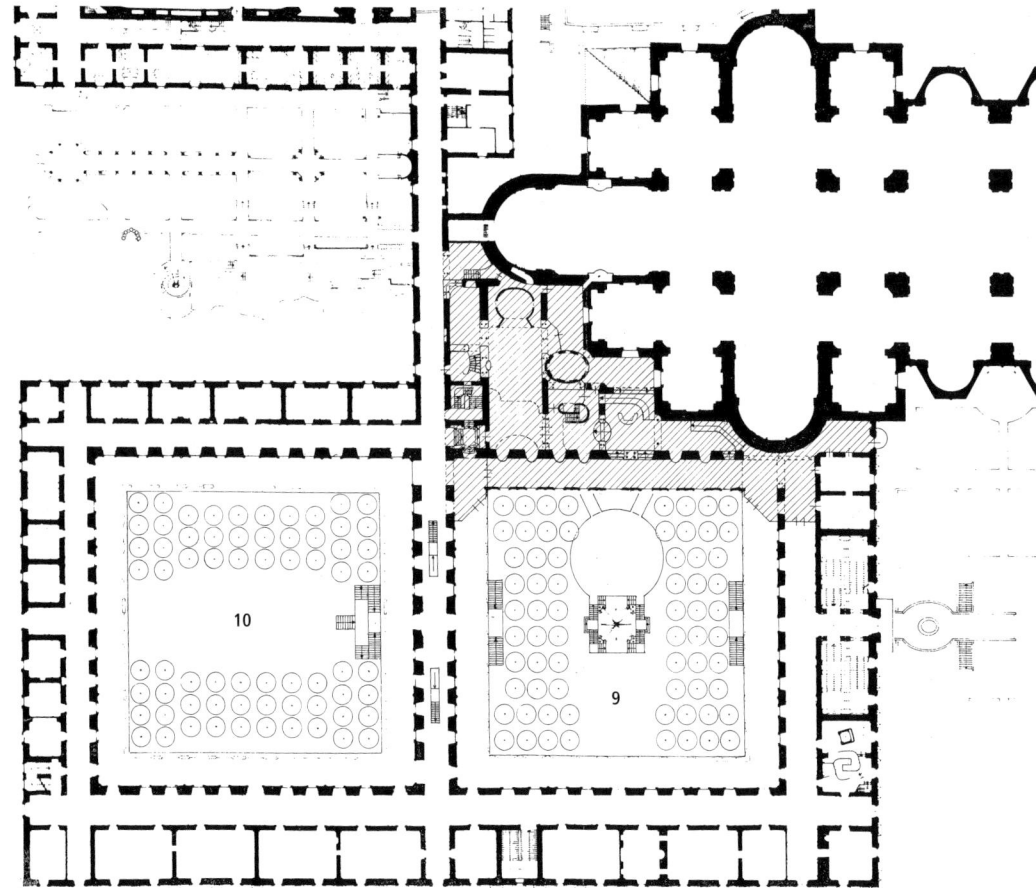

1 passage
2 platform
3 auditorium
4 terrace
5 void sacristy
6 reception room
7 buffet
8 hall
9 lemon grove
10 orange grove
11 entrance
12 lobby

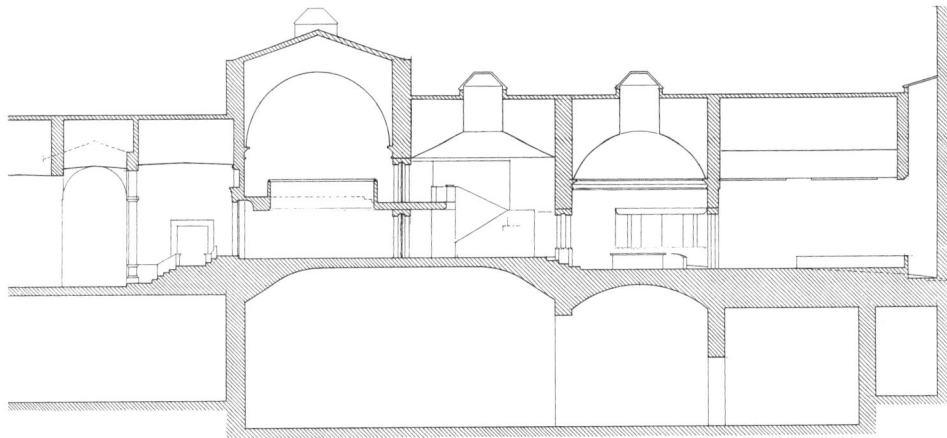

Section A-A

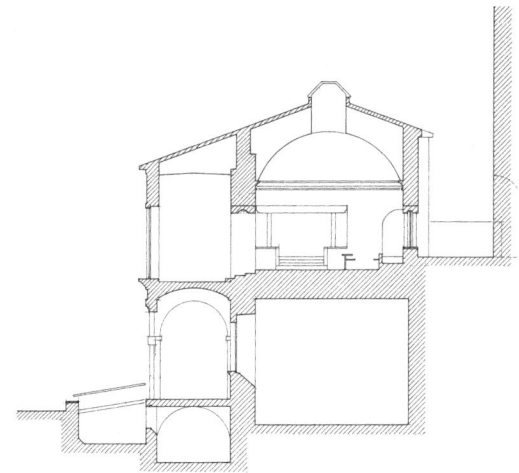

Section C-C

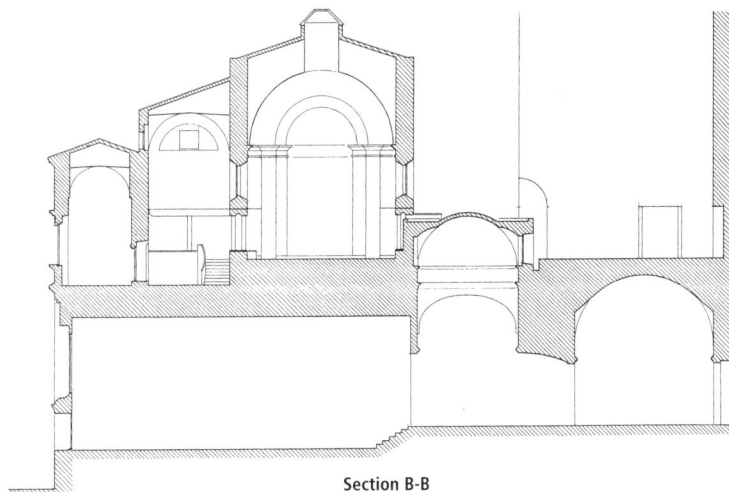

Section B-B

Section D-D

(White) steel lintels over cylindrical steel columns

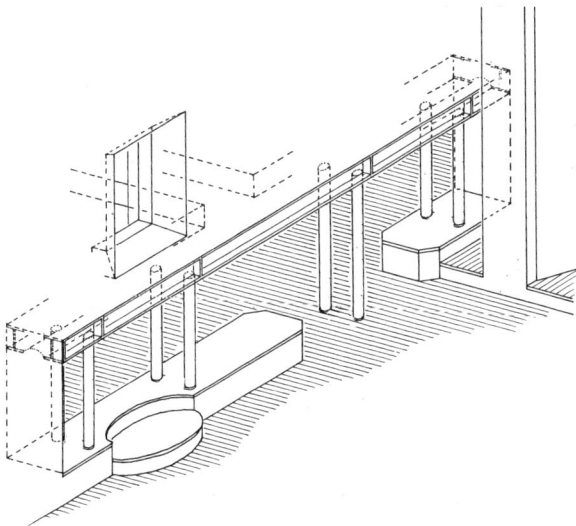

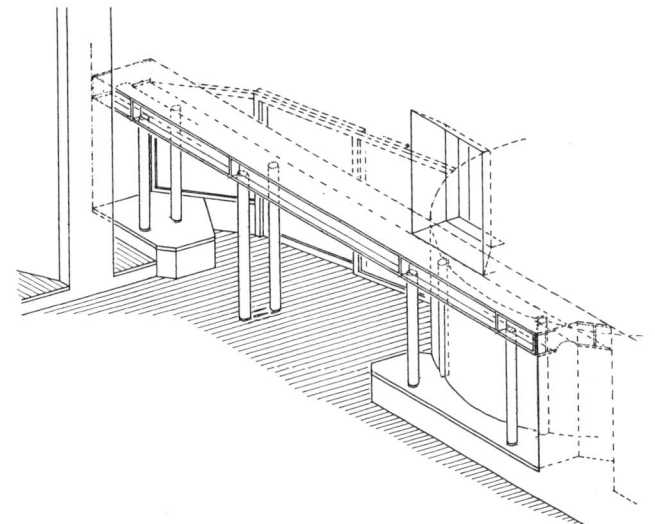

Carel Visser Exhibition, Kröller-Müller Museum, Otterlo, 1989
with Hannie van Eyck

Carel Visser, the sculptor, hoped that this museum's angular architecture could be subdued so that the impact of so much building material would not compete with that of his work. To achieve this a kilometer of tracing paper was introduced.

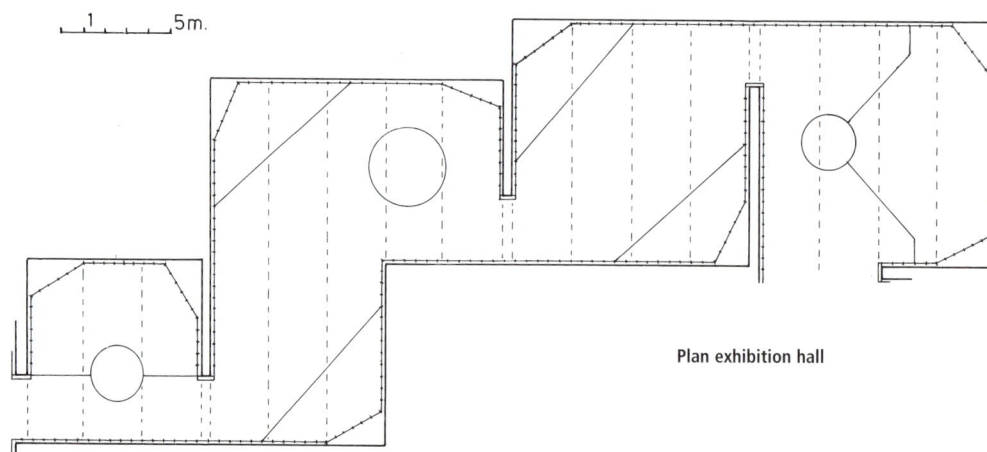

Plan exhibition hall

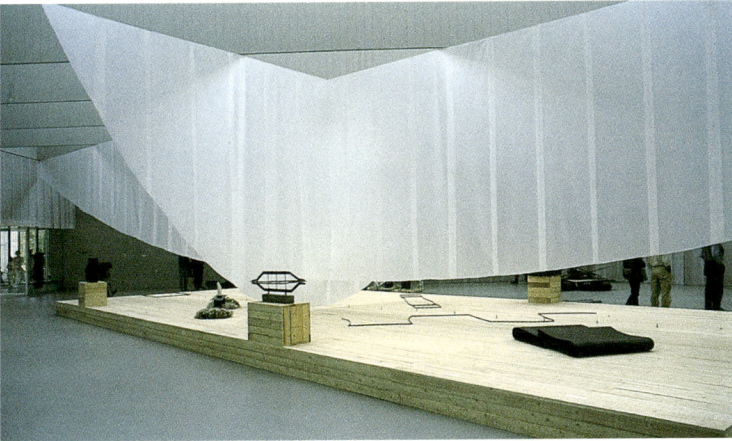

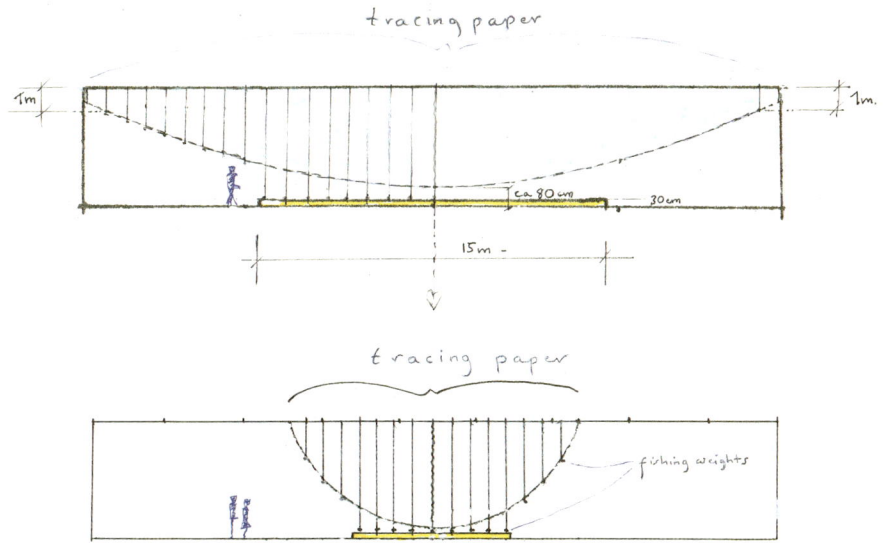

tracing paper

1m.   1m.

ca 80 cm   30cm

15m.

tracing paper

fishing weights

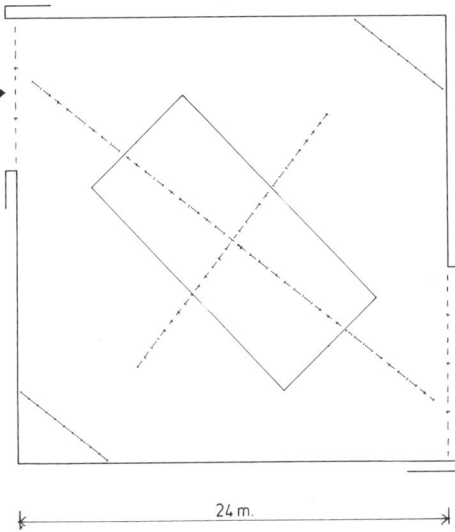

24 m.

Arts Centre, Middelburg, 1990
with Hannie van Eyck

The Maïsbaai, once the wharf of the historic East Indies Company, became an industrial area in the 19th century and remained so until quite recently. When that too belonged to the past, the time had come for an altogether new urban use, which this time was to be housing. As the planning advisor for the entire site I suggested the Amsterdam-based Lucien Lafour and Rick van Wijk as architects. Beyond that, as a link or intermediary between the old historic town and the Maïsbaai I proposed a public building with a social and/or cultural purpose relevant to the city as a whole – a focal point between old and new at the head of a new marina extension which we were to design.

Middelburg had for some time drawn the attention of the art world through its ambitious art exhibitions but it lacked suitably equipped premises. The municipal authorities therefore opted for the establishment of a centre for Contemporary Art, appointing us to draw up plans. That a building of this sort was actually to be built on this particular site between the old city and the new housing quarter was, in urban design terms, a crucial move. Beyond that it was to become our very first public building, moreover on an attractive site (one thus easily spoilt) which is conspicuously, and for once in a Dutch lifetime, not completely flat. Almost too good to be true. The considerable slope provided the main clue in that two floors were at ground floor level, both giving access from within to enclosed outdoor exhibition spaces. The building has three main floors and is entered on the middle level, which has no exhibition space, but serves as a mediator to a variety of rooms, the information desk, bookshop, library, reading room, restaurant and staff offices which are all situated on or around two semicircular balconies from which the entire interior space can be overlooked, thanks to the roof which slopes up and over all three levels in a single curve and provides both filtered daylight and artificial light from end to end. As to the building's exterior, it is as it were partially interiorized as a result of the outdoor enclosures which render it a larger, more expansive place than its modest bulk would suggest.

Beyond is the given contrast between the formal small-scale intricacy that goes with housing and the larger-scale closed surfaces and masses of an art building. It was clear to us that more was required to emphasize the distinctive public character/significance of the building on that somewhat peripheral site which was yet related to the city as a whole. With this in mind we decided that it should be timber clad diagonally in a single direction all round and painted in several variations of white. Although not a large structure it was to appear as a single homogenous shape, in fact rather like a large white shed or like the timber church on the Amstelveld in Amsterdam.

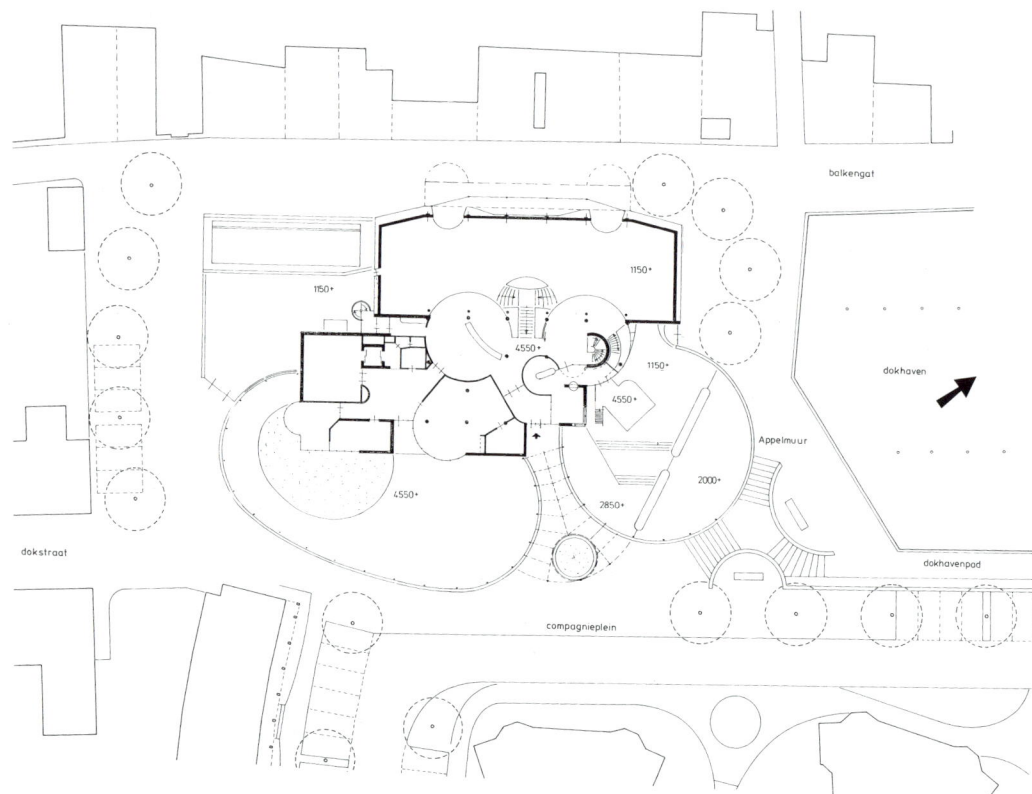

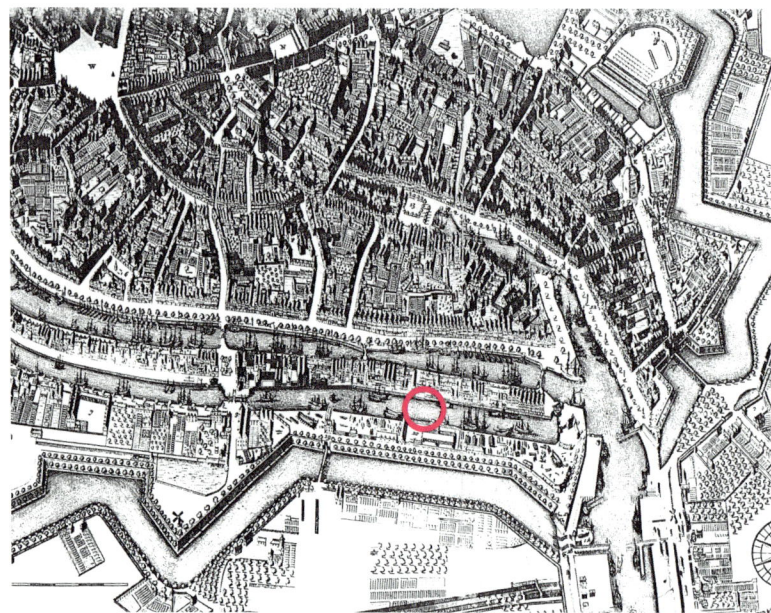

Location, Maïsbaai, Middelburg

The budget was approved by the town council by a vote of 13 for and 9 against. That is why the centre was called 'Centrum 13-9'. After the local elections the political balance changed and the funds were withdrawn just before building was about to start, despite numerous protests and extra financial support from the state.

Inside, reversing the contrast, all the walls are masonry with light grey rendering – neutral and solid and thus well-suited to receiving art exhibits. Basically the building is a two-part unity: i.e. a more or less continuously differentiated interior space on three main levels (with a minor fourth one) under a single roof, and two exterior open-air spaces enclosed within curved walls on the convex public-city-side – on which Karel Appel agreed to 'perform' in coloured ceramics (ceramics for durability and luminosity).

The idea was that Appel should not be obliged to cover the entire 124 metre wall or even 'complete' or finish the job in the accepted sense but that it should be open-ended – a work in progress with people saying 'Appel's at it again' and curious to see on another occasion what the next bit will be like and the one after that. It was to be a tribute to Holland's most outstanding living artist. This country produces astounding artists but treats them with indifference.

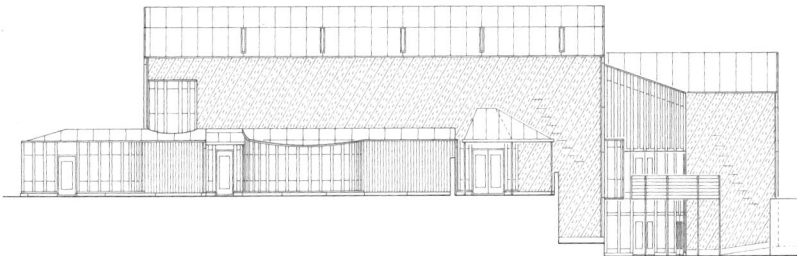

Entrance façade

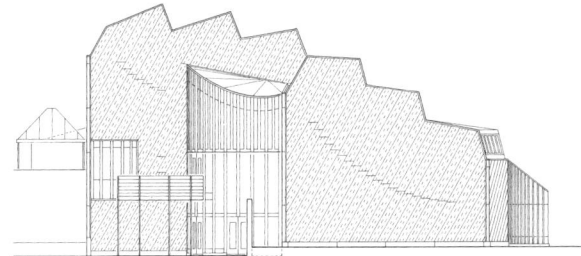

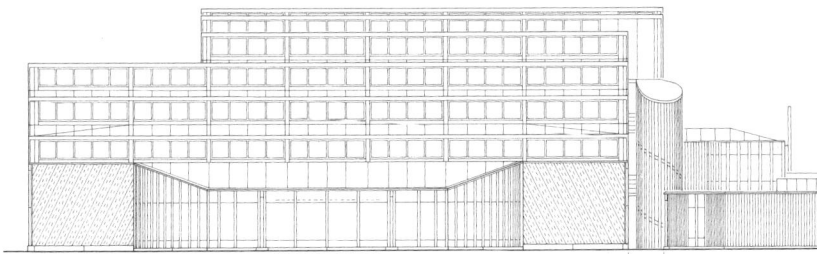

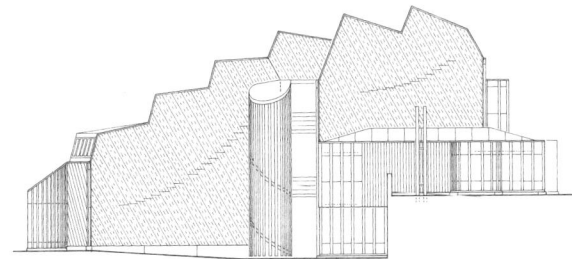

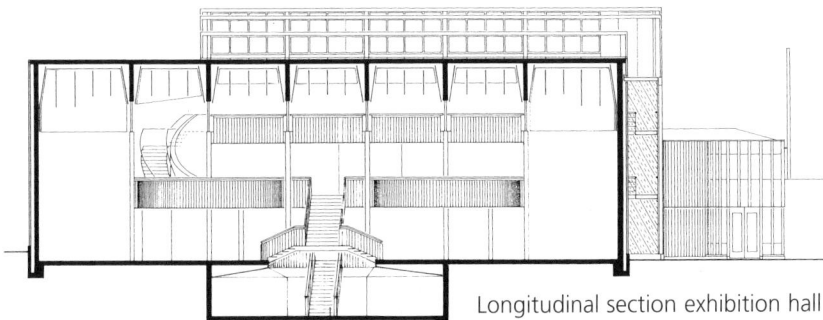

Longitudinal section exhibition hall

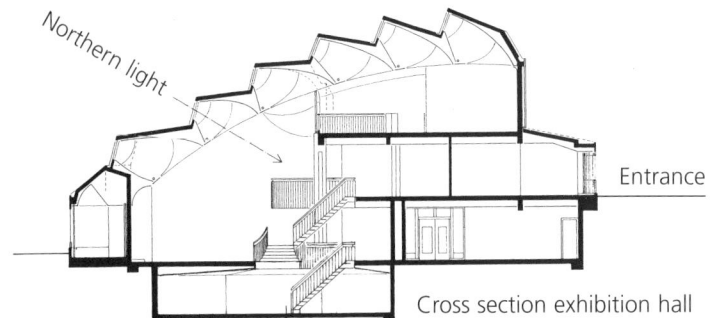

Northern light

Entrance

Cross section exhibition hall

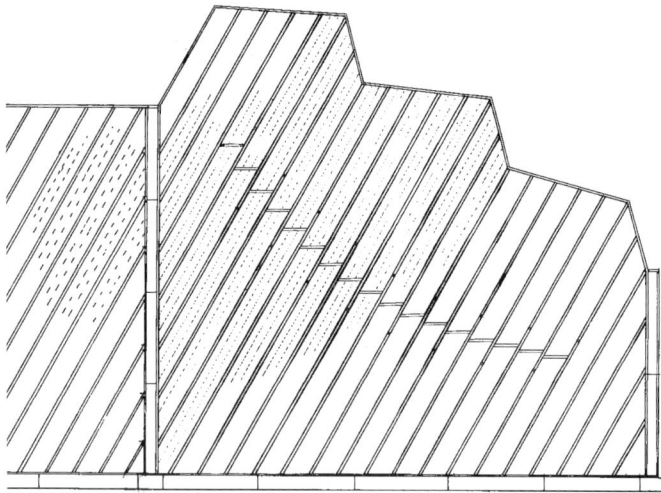

Wooden boards with a projecting semicircular batten at every third one and, diagonally round the corner, continuing in the same direction.

The curve in the middle of the façade created by the break in the boards is the result of the maximum length of board available.

254

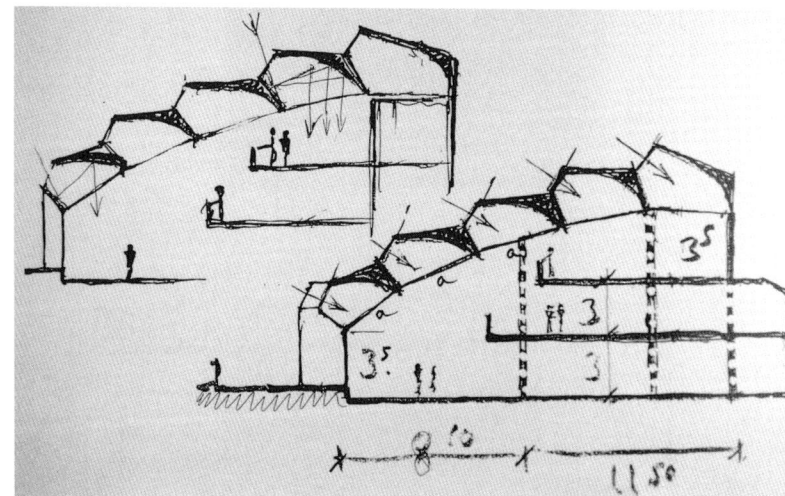

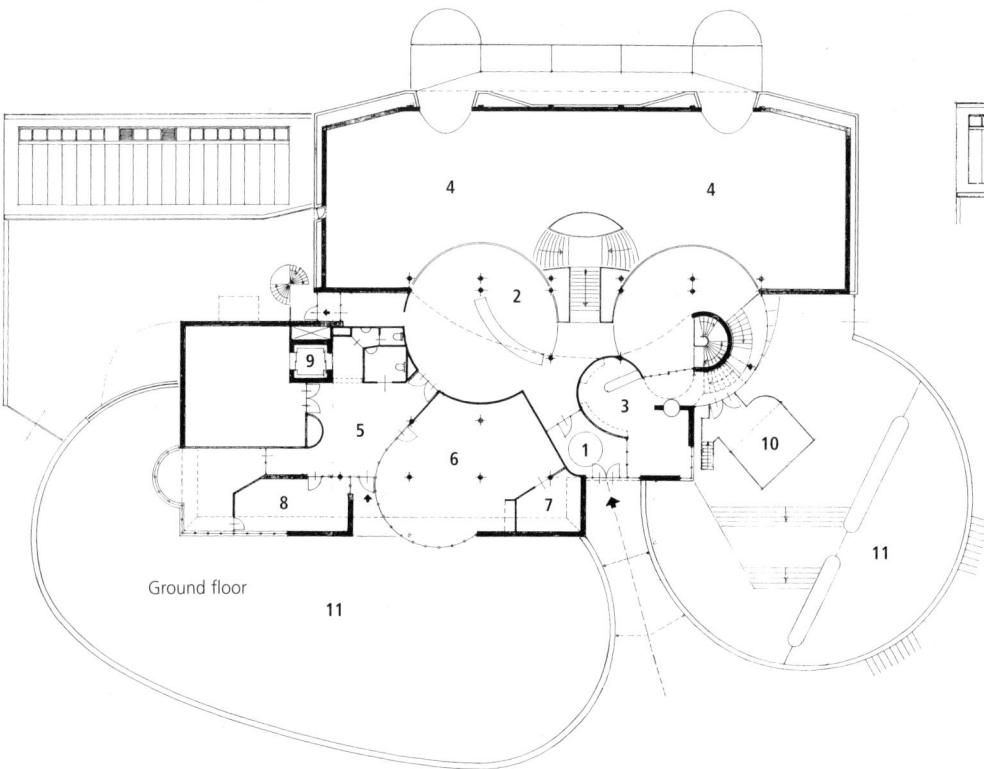

Ground floor

11

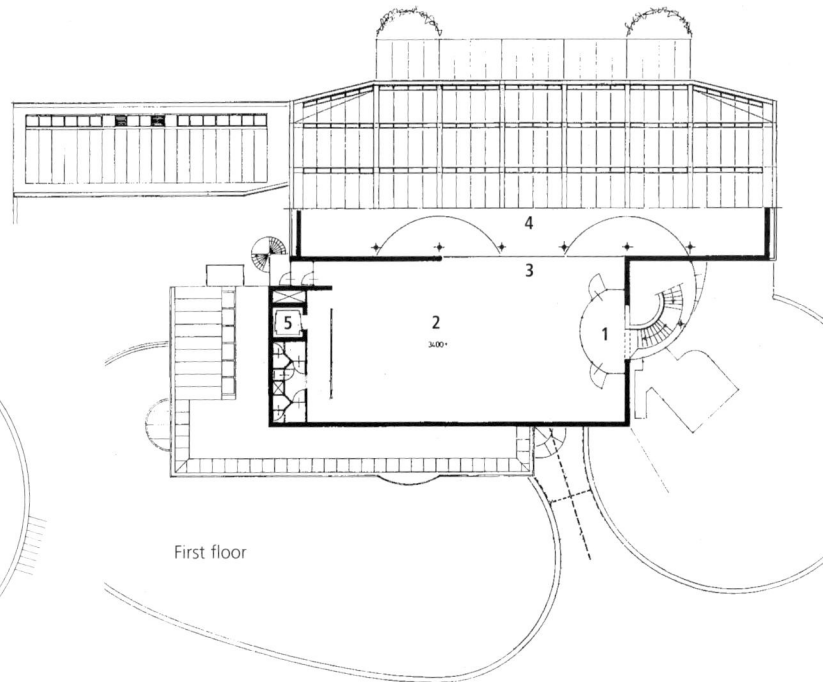

First floor

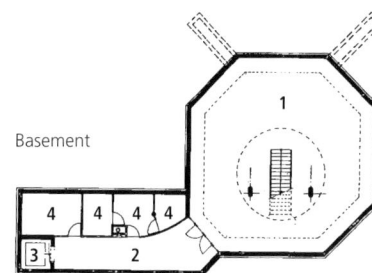

Basement

255

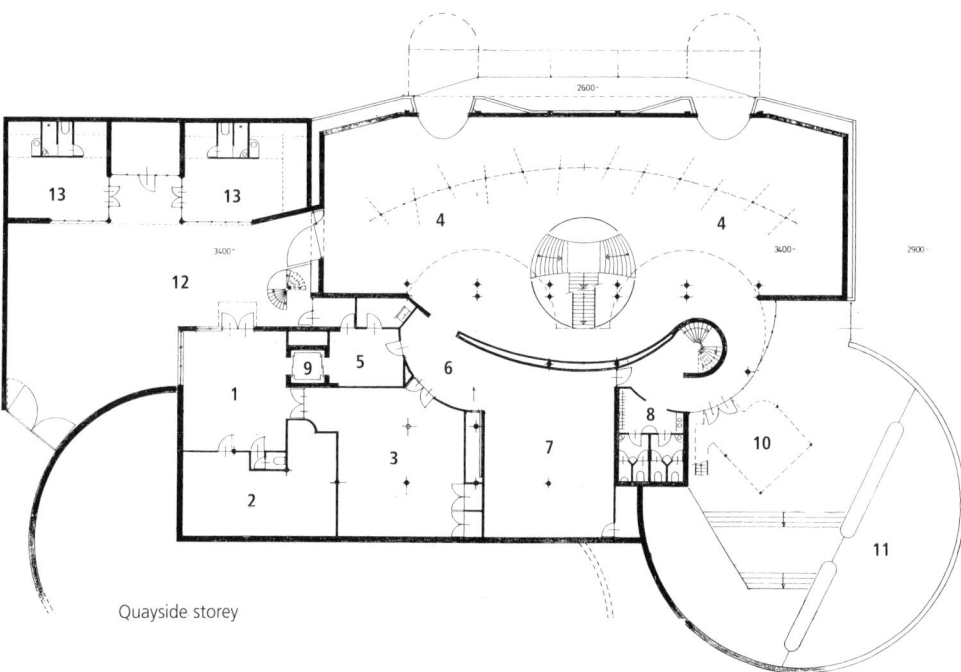

Quayside storey

Basement	Quayside storey	Ground floor	First floor
1 exhibition hall	1 technical service	1 entrance	1 entrance
2 lift entrance	2 air conditioning room	2 reception desk	2 'small' exhibition hall
3 lift	3 central depot	3 coffee corner	3 balcony
4 utility room	4 large exhibition hall	4 void in large	4 void
	5 entrance hall	exhibition hall	5 lift
	6 foyer	5 hall	
	7 lecture theatre	6 archives & library	
	8 cloakroom	7 video room	
	9 lift	8 office	
	10 terrace	9 lift	
	11 sculpture garden	10 terrace	
	12 dispatch	11 sculpture garden	
	13 studio		

Als alles goed gaat staat straks in Middelburg dit enorme
drie-tot-vier dimensionale spieraam voor jou klaar!

Doorlopend over beide gebogen
wanden heen, een ijl dak van
staal en glas. Vraag aan jou:
het geheel in kleur te beappelen...

Kan, wat de wanden betreft, ook
zwart, wit en grijzen betekenen

totale lengte dak 70m

globaal schema opstaande glazen friesen
niet getekend

stalen poten dubbel waartussen gekleurd glas →

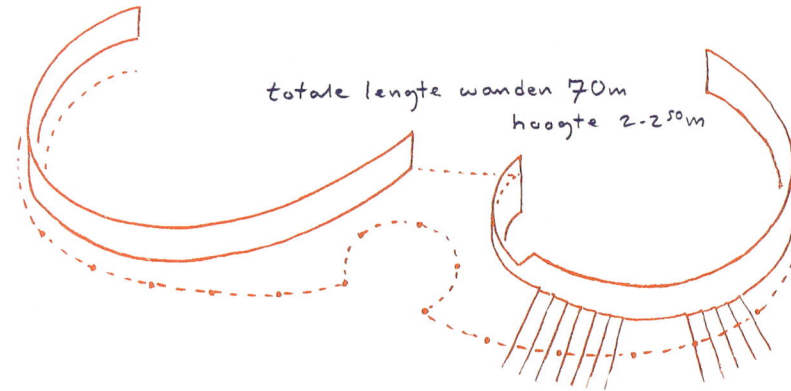

fries

totale lengte wanden 70m
hoogte 2-2,50m

maar ook de wanden aan de bolle buiten
(stadszijde) en wel in een "direkte" techniek
bv. grote hard gebakken ceramiek platen
door jou beschilderd en dan geglazuurd
(vlak, in reliëf, plastisch, met teksturen enz).

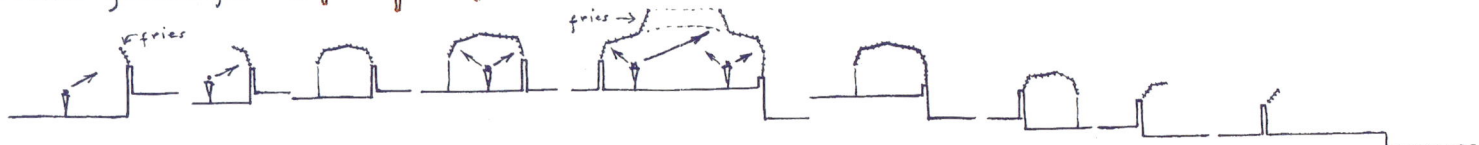

256

If all is going well in Middelburg this enormous three to four dimensional canvass will soon be ready for you!

Running over both curved walls,
a subtile roof of steel and glass.
You are requested to "Appel" the whole in colour
(which can, so far as the walls are concerned,
also mean black, white or gray),

Total length of walls 70 m,
2-2.5 m high

Total length of roof, 70 m
Global plan of upright friezes not drawn

Steel legs with coloured glass between them

but also to do the walls on the convex outer (city) side
in an "immediate" technique,
for instance, large hard-fired ceramic sheets painted
by you and then glazed
(flat, in relief, sculptural, textured, etc.).

[Fragment of a letter from Aldo van Eyck to Karel Appel]

Restoration of Orphanage, Amsterdam, 1990-4
with Hannie van Eyck

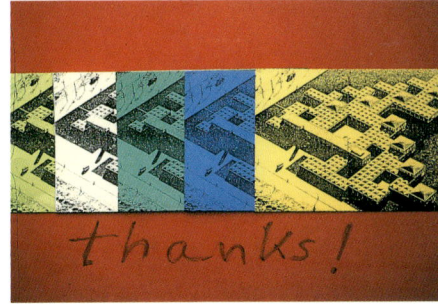

The preservation of the Orphanage – which was threatened with demolition in 1986 – resulted from an arrangement worked out by the Amsterdam city council. This meant that the project developer who took charge of the restoration was allowed to build an office complex on the former play area of the Orphanage.

As two tenants of the Orphanage – the Berlage Institute and Esprit – share the main entrance hall, the original plan, ranging all the departments along the 'interior street', could be retained only in the eastern part. Here at least the spatial continuity has survived. The remaining spaces, mainly on the western side, have been modified to suit the particular wishes of the five tenants without affecting the building's structure. It does however mean that the 'building street', if still present architecturally, no longer stitches the spaces together.

The small structures specially designed for children have been restored at three places. Likewise, the four loggias along Amstelveenseweg, once sealed off, are now back to their original state, as is the splash/paddling pool which had been demolished.

257

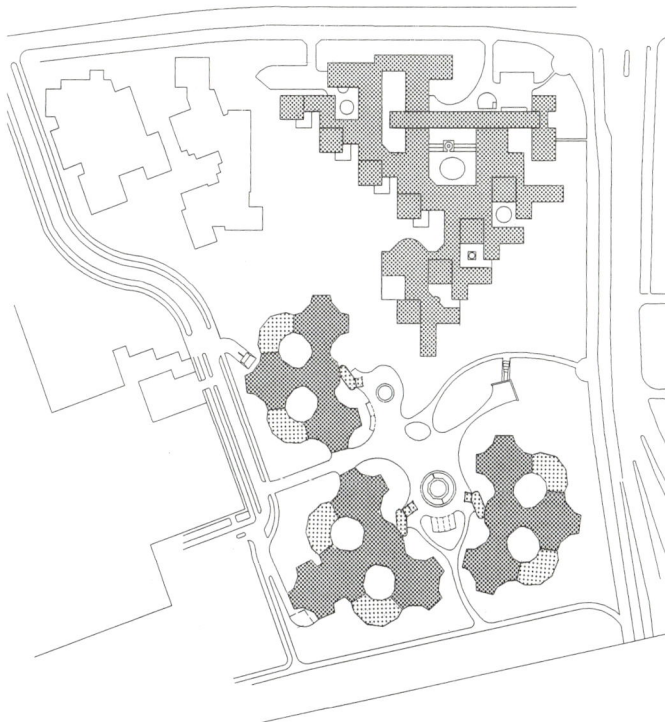

Tripolis Office Complex, Amsterdam, 1990-4 with Hannie van Eyck

Starting point in January 1990: 25,000 m^2 offices to be built in three buildings, of 10,870, 7790 & 6340 m^2, each with its own entrance on the ground floor and accessible from the 10,000 m^2 underground car park. The entire site including the grounds covers about 17,000 m^2. Building started in January 1992 and was completed in March 1994. The three buildings were built like a screen behind the Orphanage and from the height of that building rise to four storeys of offices, then to seven, then down to five again.

Each building is similar in intention; one enters the central tower through an asymmetrical intermediate entrance area. The tower contains a two-storey entrance hall, as well as the staircases, the lifts, the toilets and the service shafts, as well as the entrance from the underground car park.

Each building also has two multipurpose rooms on the ground floor, each of which encloses an inner court.

The exterior view of the building is formed solely by the course of the outline of the office towers, which in effect means by the repeated identical windows. There are no projecting or recessed elements, nor blind wall sections.

In addition to this nothing has been added or left out, it displays what it is, X m^2 of office space, toilets and vertical access. All one can see is where the vertical transport is, but only by the increased height of the vertical windows. The iroko elements, which are broader towards the ground (made of a single unglued section), and the *nero impala* granite parapet are deliberately of equal thickness and alternate as 'façade cladding' – they also both become equally dark when it rains (they do not dry out at the same rate, and react similarly to rain but differently to wind). So the rainbow colours (the aluminium frames) are the only constant! The columns consist of 'rainwater'.

The intended screen-like outline of the façade is emphasized by the façade components that are fixed both overlapping and adjacent to each other. In addition to homogeneity there is also a certain looseness, something loose yet fixed, on and next to each other – layered sheet on sheet.

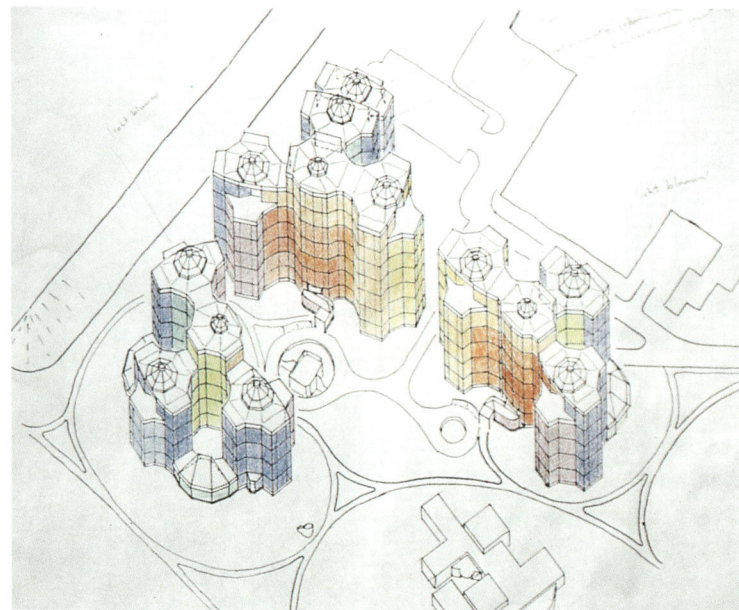

258

First floor

Fourth floor

Second floor

259

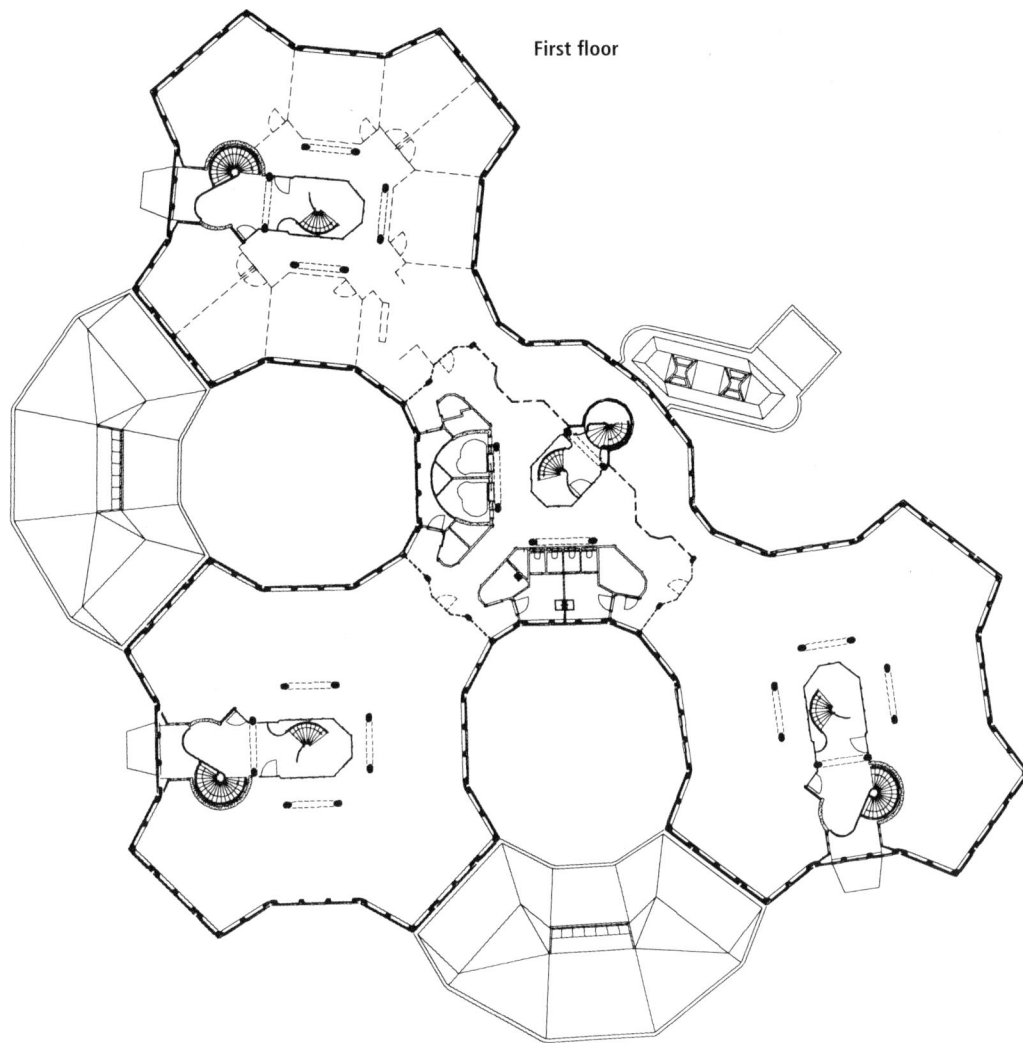

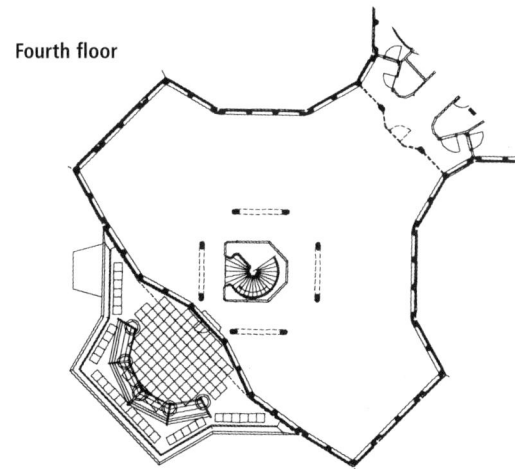

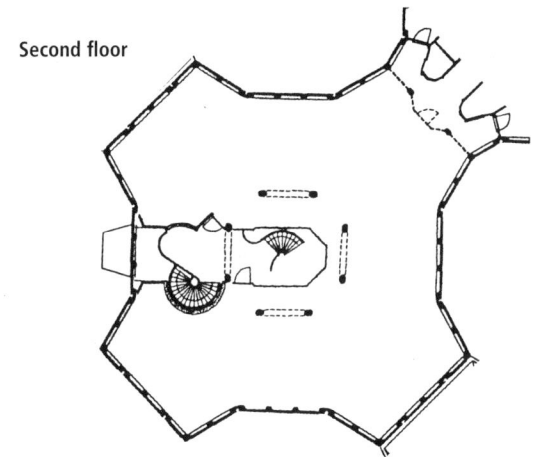

The office wings are accessible in three directions from the central towers, and each is provided with its own internal staircase with a glass roof above it to supply the middle of the building with daylight. On the lower floors the staircase has been shifted from the middle of the office towers towards the façade so as to compensate for the diminishing light from above by light from the side.

In addition there is a roof-terrace on top of each tower with pergolas and plants. This makes it clear, even from the street, that each office tower 'opens' up towards the top.

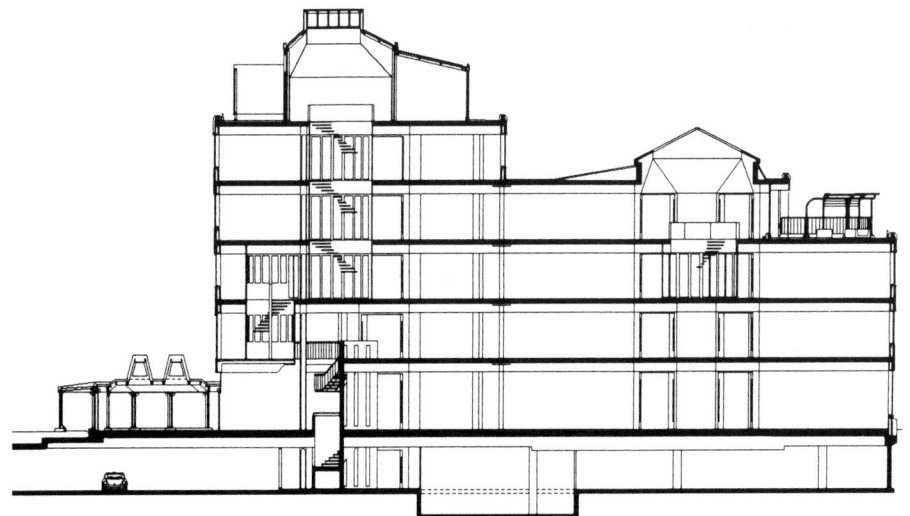

Entrance area

Green Area with Play Facilities, Apollolaan, Amsterdam, 1990
with Hannie van Eyck

Although the overall area is considerable, it is utterly flat and unadorned: there is nothing to obstruct the view across, so that the traffic-flow on the opposite side appears as though it is there in front of you. It is for this reason that the pedestrian path along the north side is raised 90 cm so as to obstruct the view across. The pedestrian is lifted above the traffic on one side and above the two oval fields on the other.

This main idea was accepted by all the authorities and advisory experts but execution was nevertheless disgracefully obstructed, for no defensible reason, by a few short-sighted local bureaucrats who had replaced the central authorities. The entire procedure took three years and scores of documents.

Having over the years executed hundreds of playgrounds without difficulty this final failure is inexcusable, demonstrating once again what the borough of Amsterdam-South is worth.

262

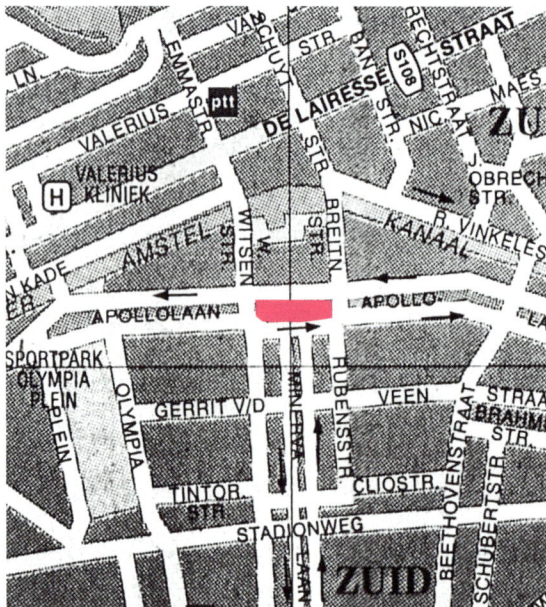

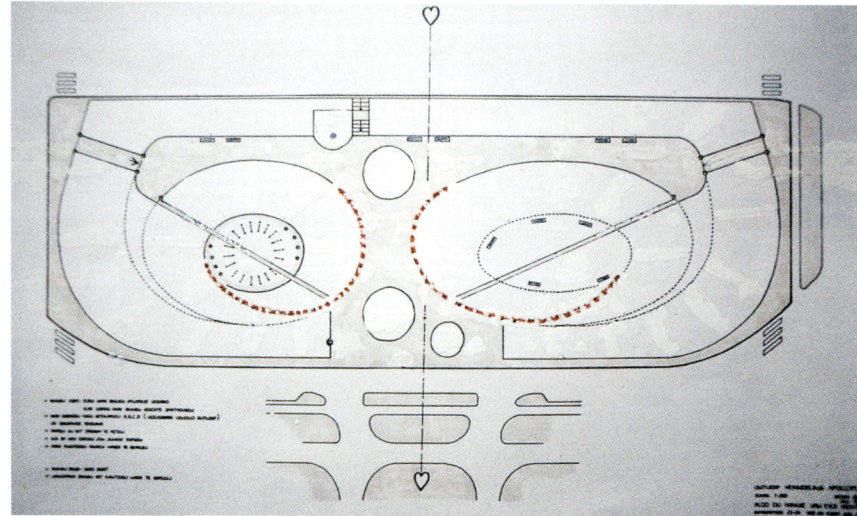

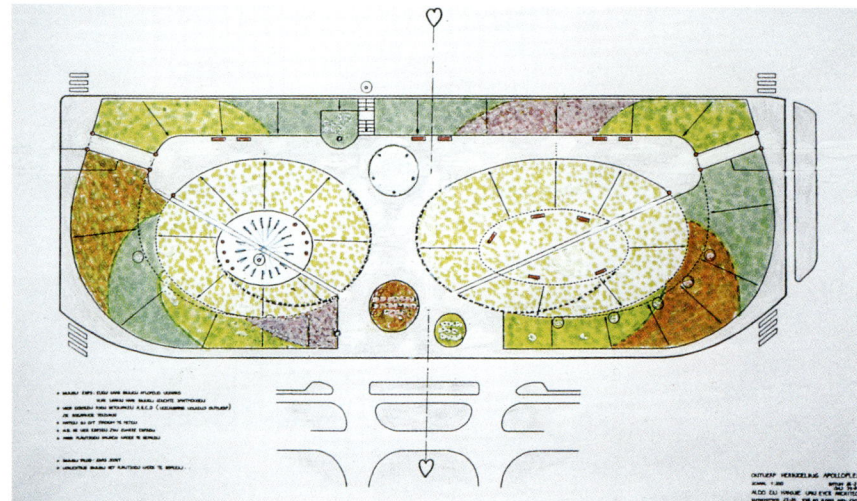

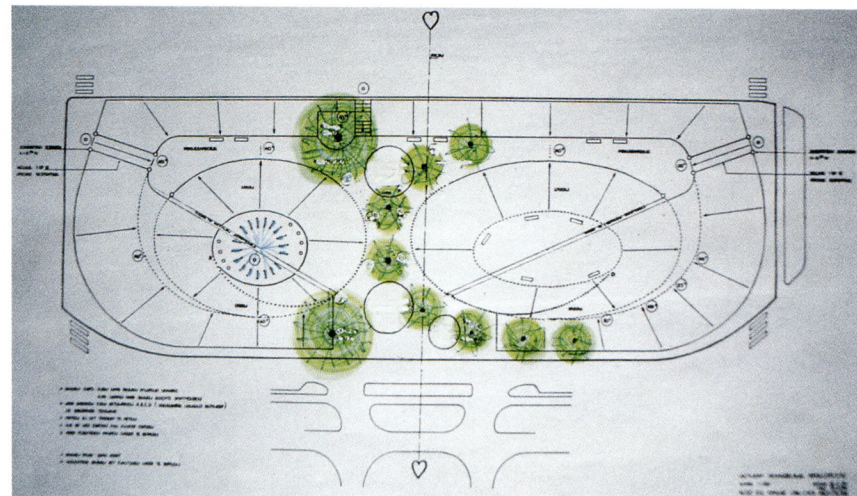

35m

50m

+100 +790

+190

variant indien groter

rval 18-19cm hoogte, 1.90m
hoog.
sm. Water
g zodat het
aleen dat plastiek
ler komen v.d. buizen
perontraining erater

as Minervalaan

blauwee

A

Ø0.11m   0.40 0.40 0.40

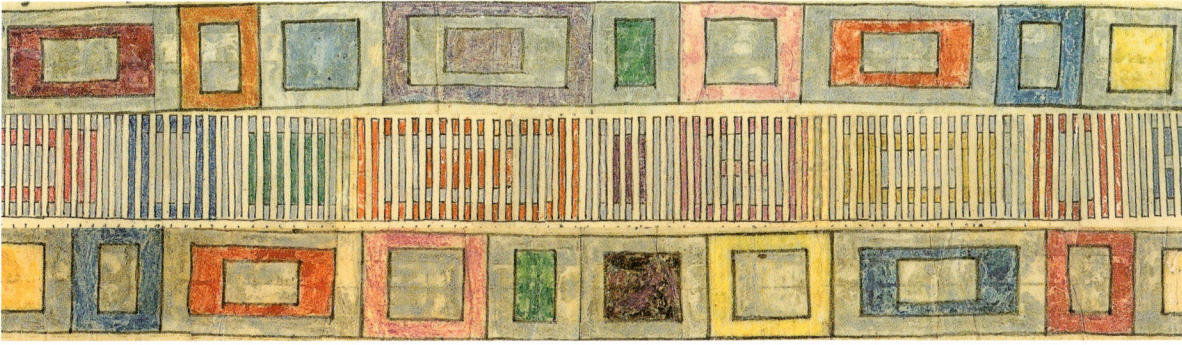

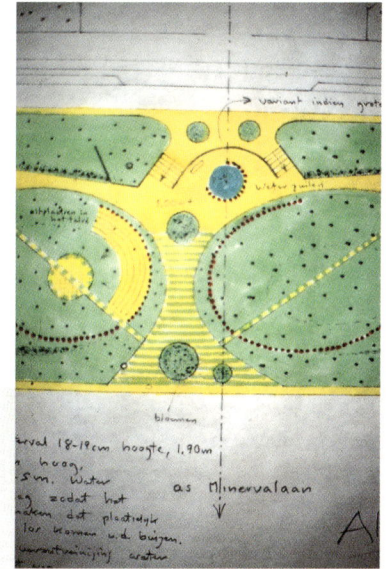

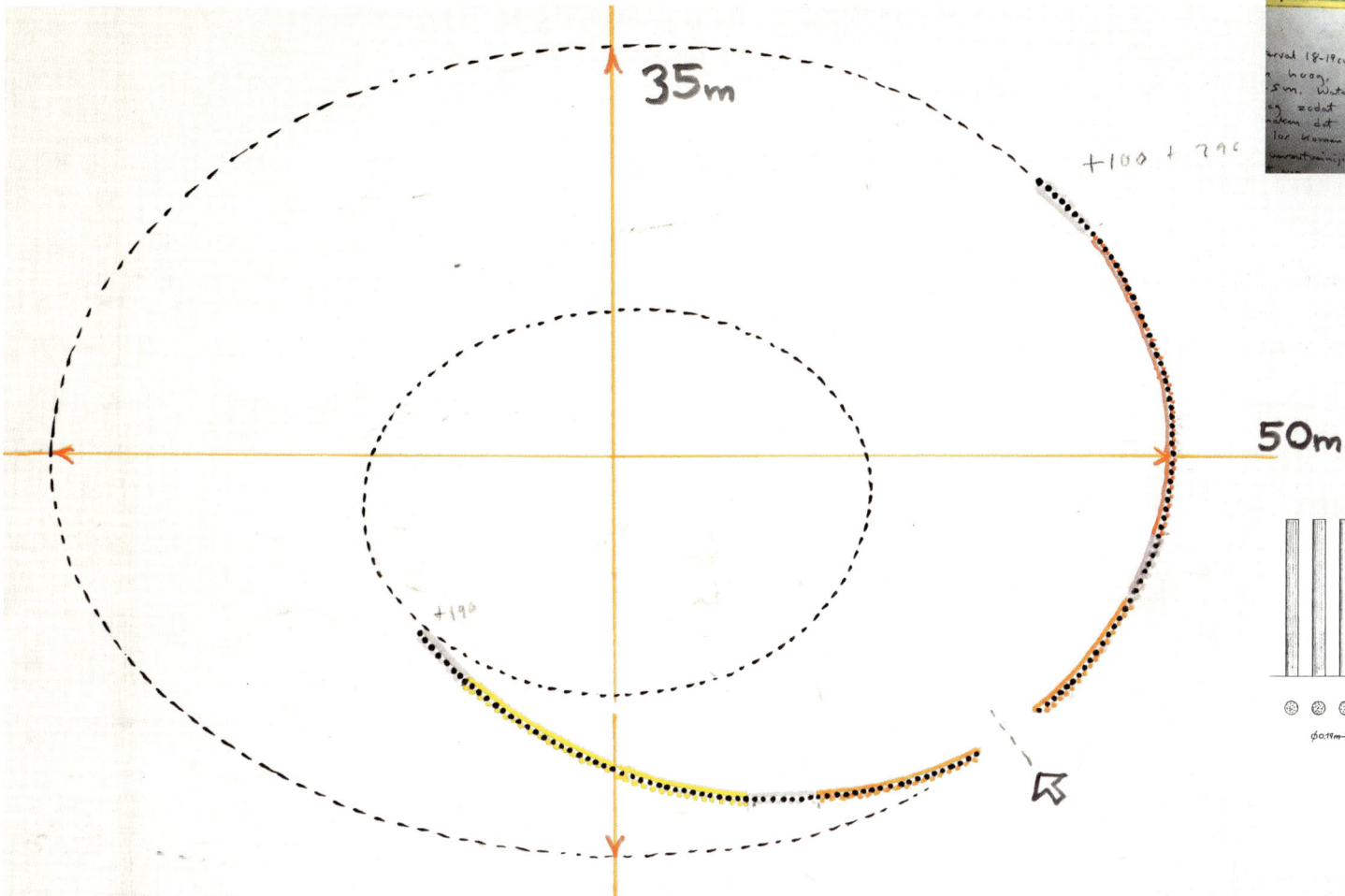

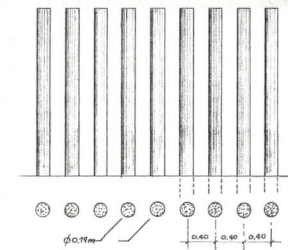

schokbetonnen palen volgens nog
te maken ontwerp veel kleurig
te schilderen en transparant te coaten.
palen exact loodrecht in
fundering (vergl. Theophil de Bockstr.)

263

The Netherlands Court of Audit, The Hague, 1992-7 with Hannie van Eyck

When the Government Building Department asked us to extend and refurbish the existing premises of the Court of Audit in The Hague – an 18th-century mansion along the city's noblest avenue – we were at first rather disappointed because it looked as though we were about to build something tucked away along backstreets behind the old building, but we soon saw that it might be possible to form a small public space, the new building wrapping around it, behind the old one and accessible through an old arched doorway along the main avenue. As you pass through it there is a spectacular 14th-century church nave on your left and another 18th-century house to your right. Straight ahead, we almost immediately visualised something definitely multicoloured (to replace, as it were, the tall stained glass windows the nave never had!) and, a little to the right: the main entrance.

As to the site itself, it was densely built up along a building line forming narrow back streets, an altogether impossible situation that conservative regulations obliged us to maintain, although originally there was a cloister and a cloister garden. Another negative was the way the nave was not freestanding but built-against on one side. To do away with all these negatives and instead build a multicoloured building with a free form set well back from the building line was certainly asking a lot – too much to be acceptable to the Department of Monuments, although their negative advice was finally overruled by the other municipal authorities: quite a feat. We made up for it by maintaining and restoring as a freestanding historical item a bit of the old cloister wall which was discovered inside one of the demolished buildings on the site.

As for the office spaces, they are all grouped round the central library and archives as well as round three hallways, two of which have circular staircases. The restaurant on the third floor has a panoramic view over the old city centre.

The exterior ceramic cladding: the choice of a blue/grey combination for the main tiled surface and vertical ribs is what we had to offer the artist Jaap Hillenius. It was up to him to come up with a colour 'score' for the narrow vertical strips between the ribs all round the building. The 15 spectral colours he selected as well as the blue and grey ones were made to order. Each column has a different colour scheme articulated vertically by means of concentric circles drawn over the elevations.

264

Engraving of Lange Voorhout with a view through Kleine Kazernestraat to the trees in the old monastery garden (18th century)

Reconstructional drawing of the monastery buildings in about 1560, by A. ter Meer Derval

The monastery church is the remnant of a Dominican monastery (1404). During the Reformation the States General of Holland sold the complex to private individuals, and it became the property of, among other things, a cannon foundry. The adjoining houses were fused together in the 17th century. Having been frequently converted and extended for the needs of the Court of Audit which they then housed, it was decided to demolish the non-functioning parts to make way for a new building.

Kazernestraat before the demolition

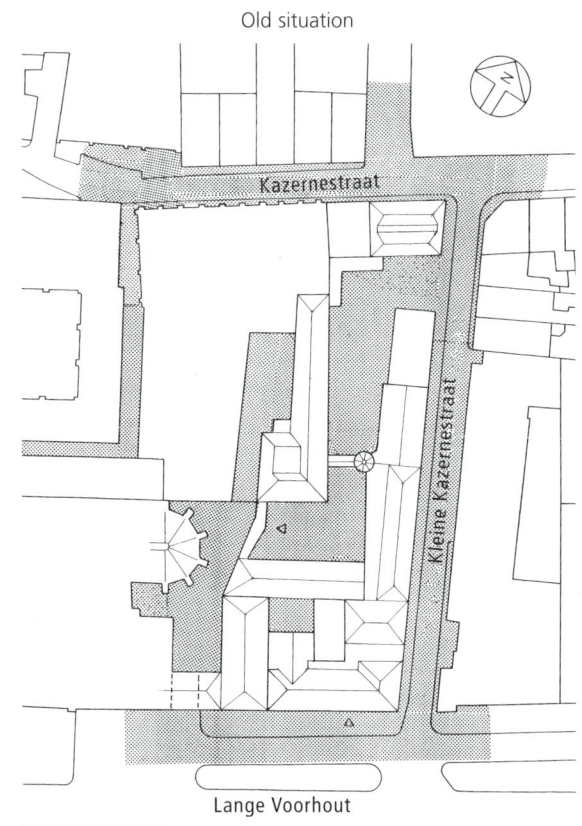

Old situation

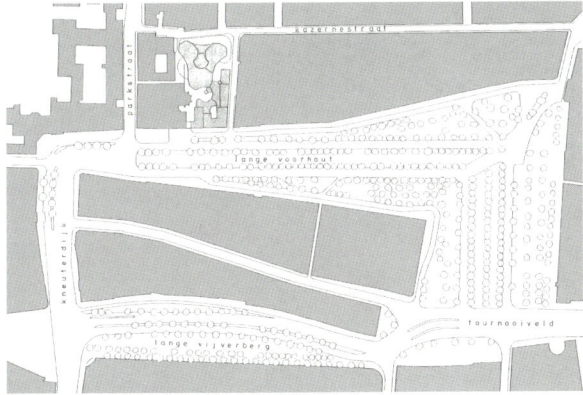

Looking for the 'right outline' for this building. This means one that creates sufficient space both inside AND OUTSIDE. After a lot of measurement and trying out, this outline ended up looking completely different from what would have resulted from simply building along the prescribed building line. It's true that the necessary square metres of floor space inside the building would have been provided (on each side of long corridors). On the outside, however, everything would have been wrong. The Department of Monuments appeared not to understand this very well and was therefore totally against our proposal. But also because there was an old monastery wall with traces of a gothic gate in one of the buildings to be demolished, outside the outline we proposed.

New situation

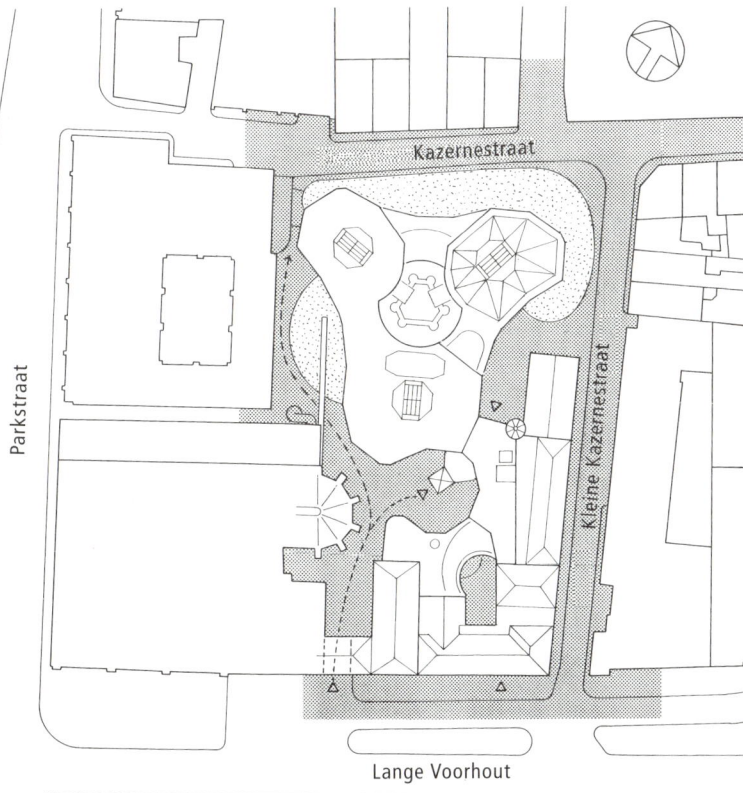

Parkstraat

Kazernestraat

Kleine Kazernestraat

Lange Voorhout

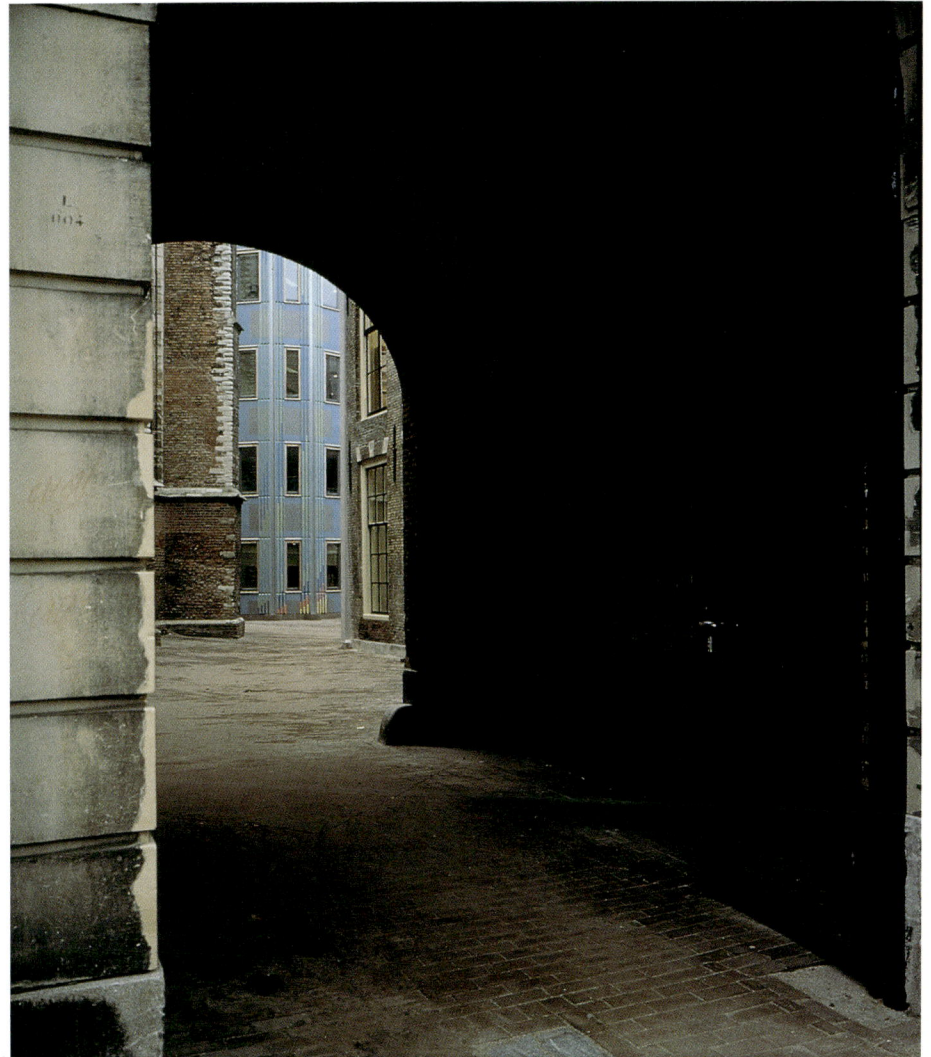

You come through the gate and then suddenly, by way of surprise, there is something magical. Opposite the medieval apse of the church there is now a small horseshoe-shaped square in front of the entrance. A round diphthong: the twentieth century opposite the apse from the Middle Ages. Concave and convex: the one is a hollow space and the other a round mass.

The entrance to the new Court of Audit

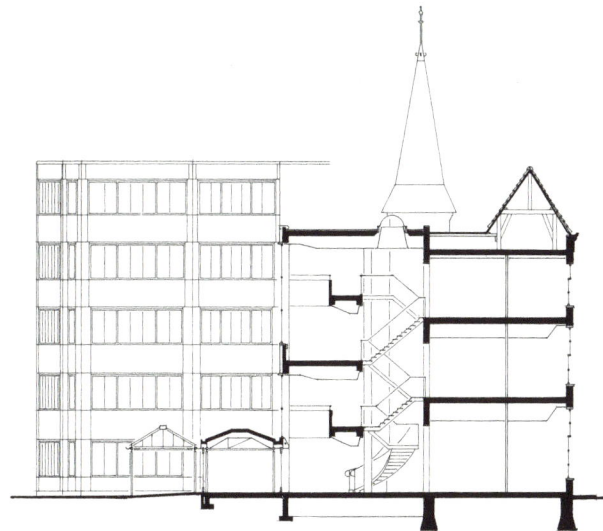

Entrance hall

Kazernestraat

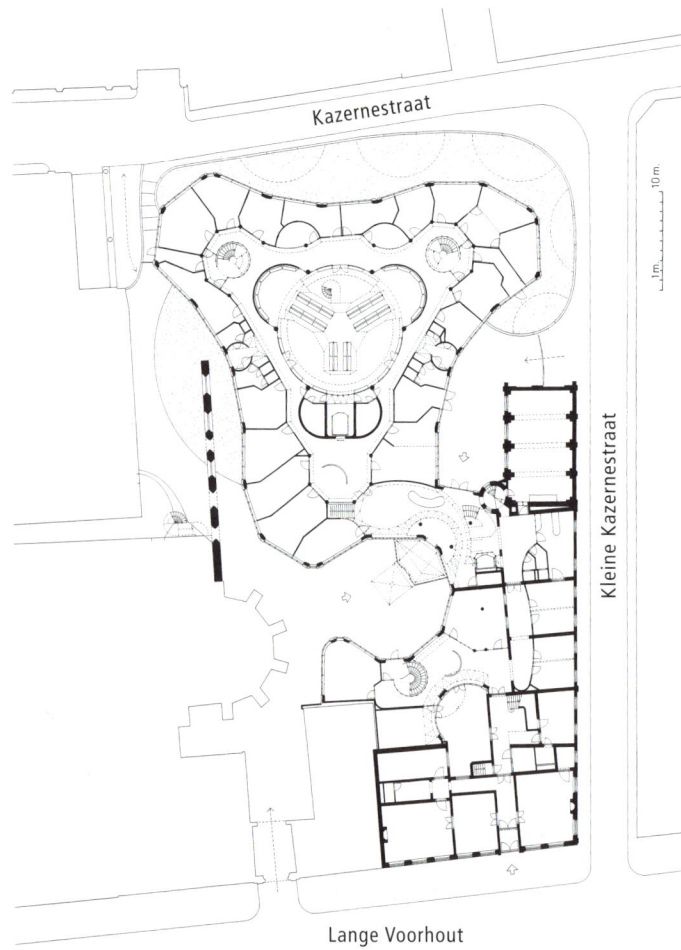

Kazernestraat

Kleine Kazernestraat

Lange Voorhout

Ground floor with entrance and library

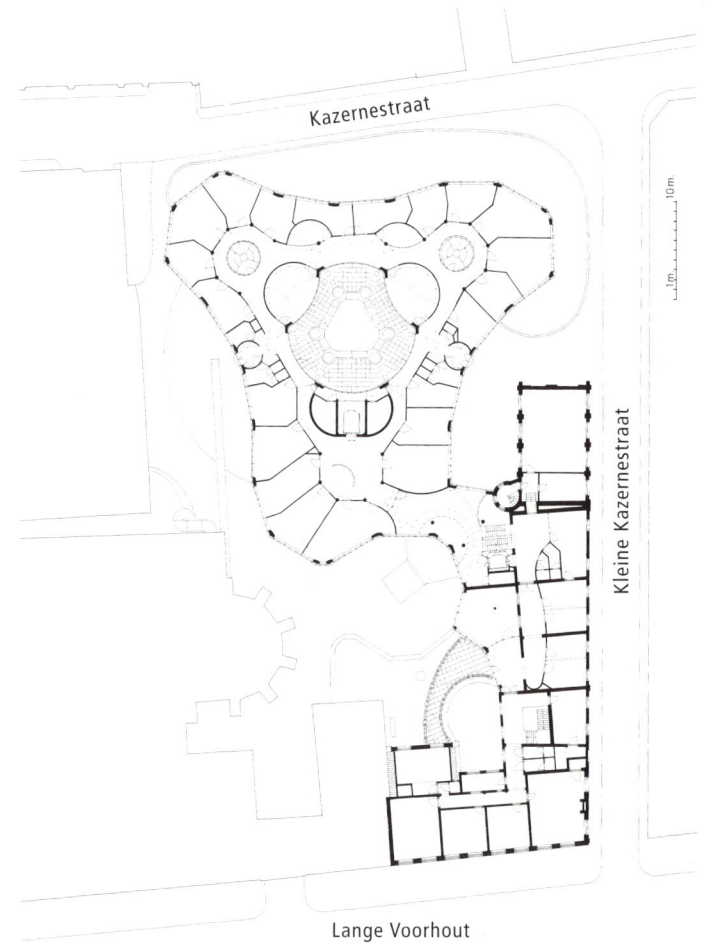

Kazernestraat

Kleine Kazernestraat

Lange Voorhout

Second floor with enclosed roof terrace

How do you create something like a blue building? In the end we got there: blue in grey round the outside and the reverse round the entrance square and the terrace above the library. As much blue as grey and both of equal intensity. In addition to these two basic colours, 16 active colours were specially made for the vertical and horizontal stripes, for which (this is where the painter Jaap Hillenius came in) a richly varied colour scheme was essential.

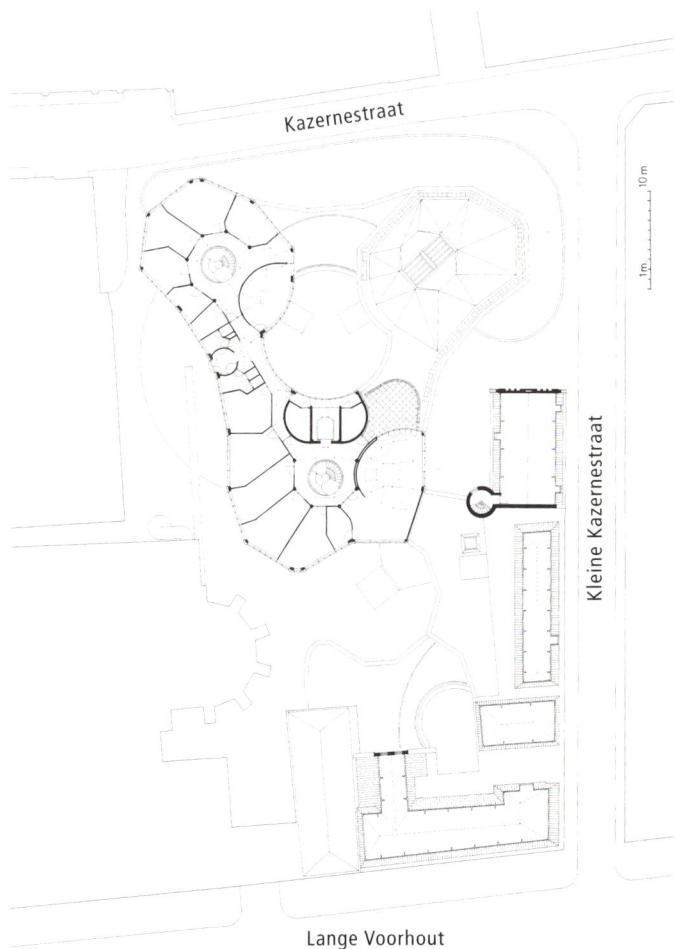

Kazernestraat

Kleine Kazernestraat

Fourth floor with roof restaurant

1m   10 m

Lange Voorhout

Corner Kazernestraat - Kleine Kazernestraat with access to rear entrance

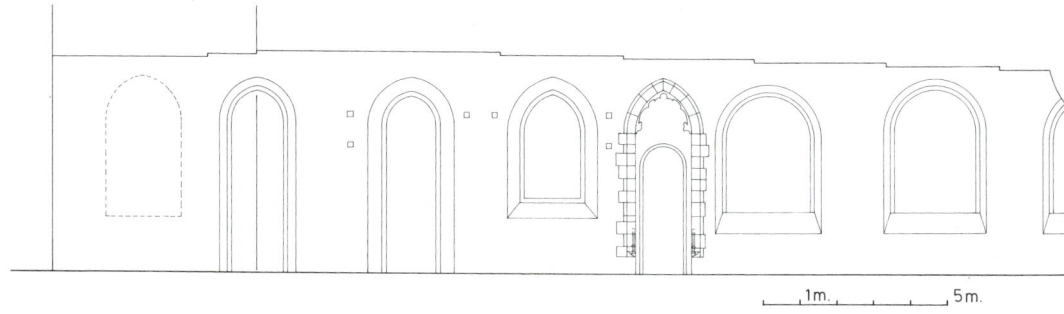

270

The old rough wall was capped with the same tiles used in the new building. To those in the Court of Audit who can see it, the old wall will have become more recognisable, more of this age.

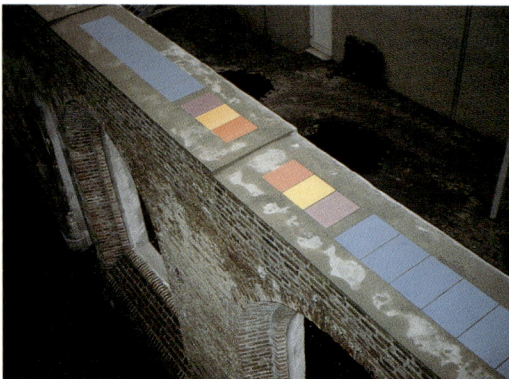

1m.   5m.

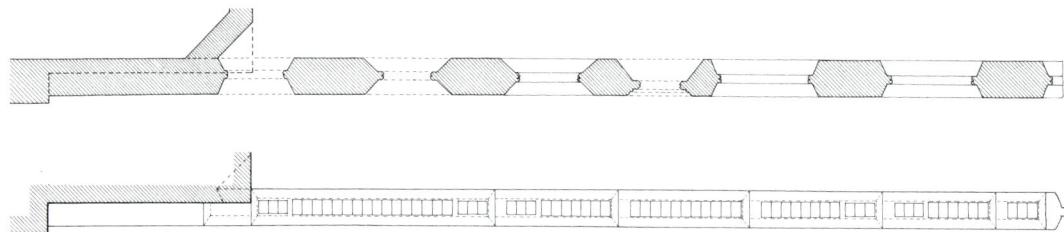

Roof terrace above library

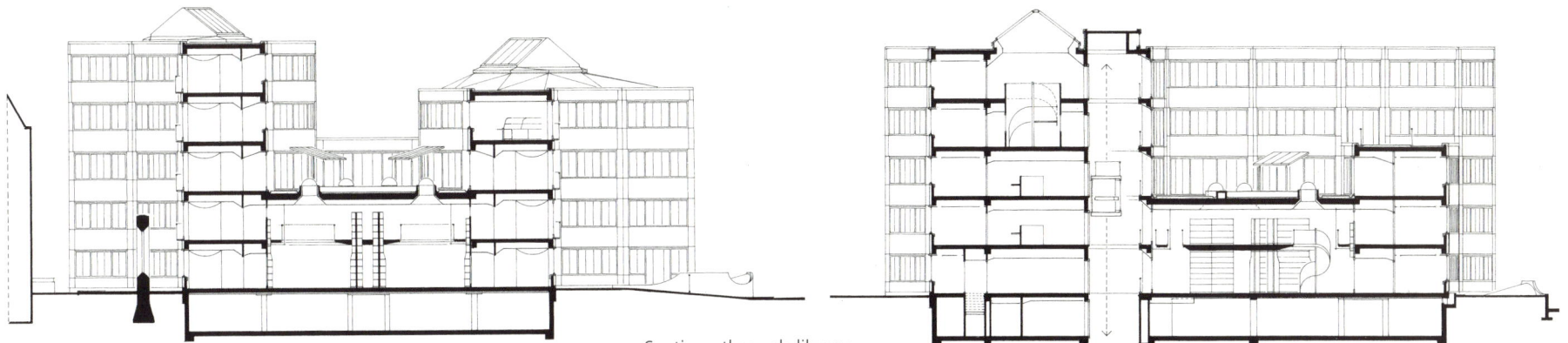

271

Sections through library
and roof terrace on top

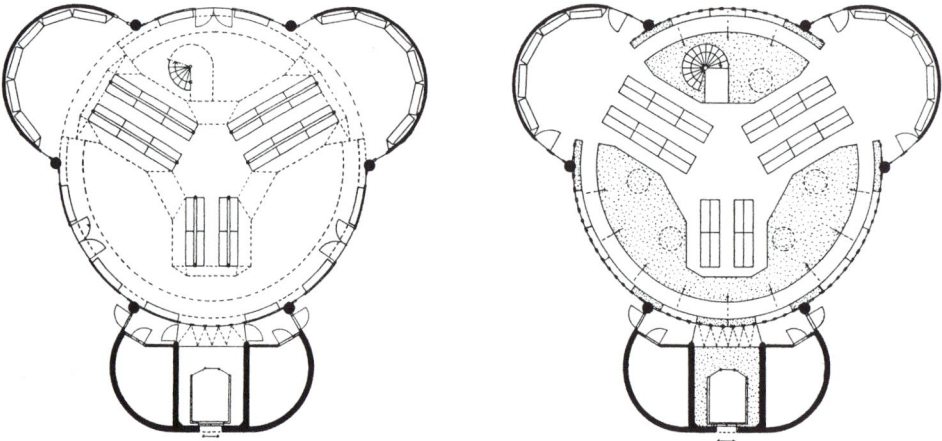

The library, the heart of the Court of Audit

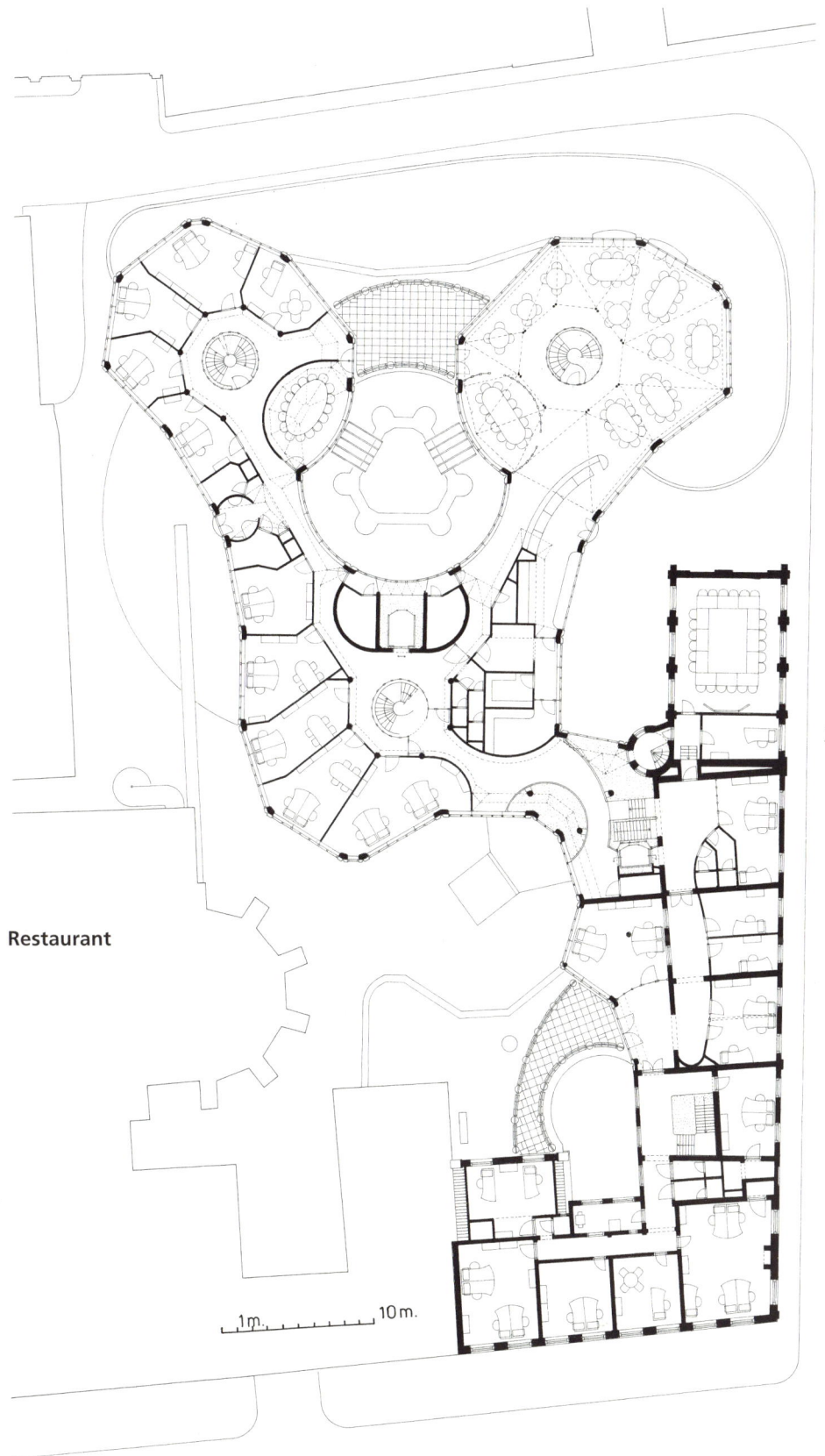

Restaurant

273

1 m. 10 m.

274

Jaap Hillenius had the idea of the circles to link the vertical and horizontal stripes.

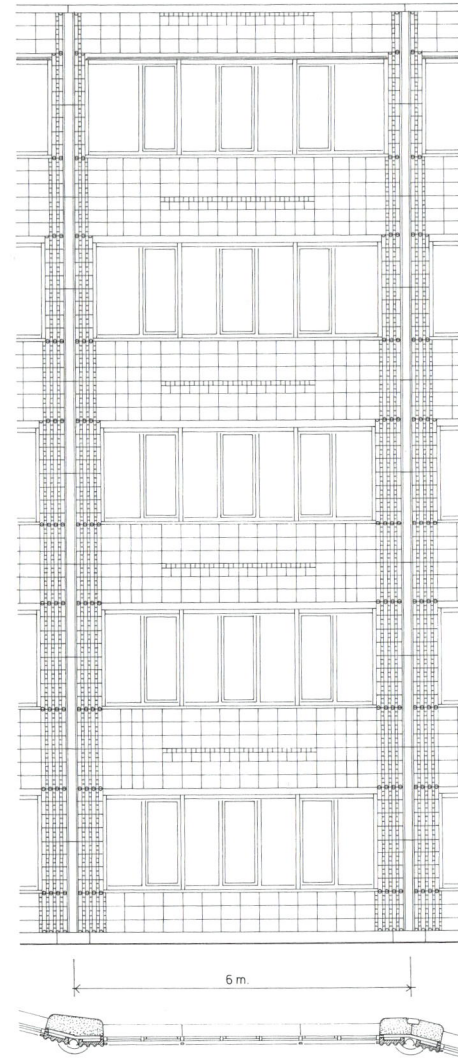

6 m.

It was with an eye to durability that glazed ceramic tiles and ribs were used, fixed to sheets and hung up.

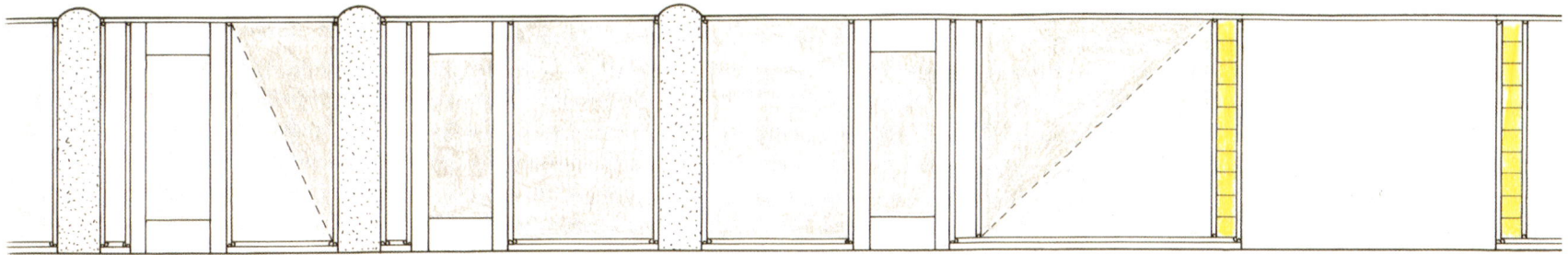

Angled corridor wall

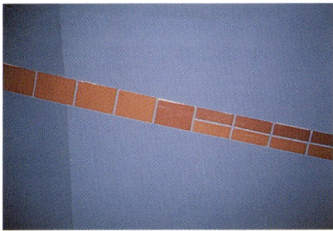

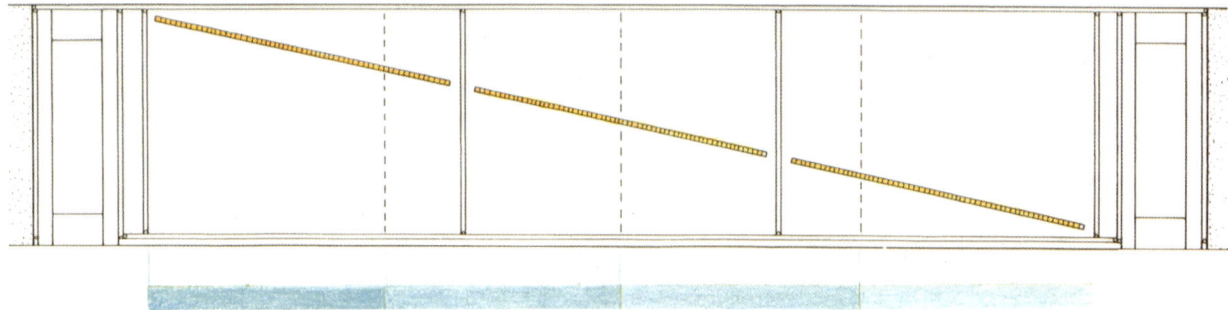

Round corridor wall

A blue building means blue inside too, but what, how much, where and which blue? What response did the exterior demand? On the outside of the round walls encircling both the reading rooms and the meeting rooms, strips of tile in three active colours, different on each floor. Around and on both sides of the lifts there are strips of tiles in three different active colours, again different on each floor. In the round coffee corners there are tiles with two active colours in each segment, with a different set of colours on each floor. There is a single diagonal

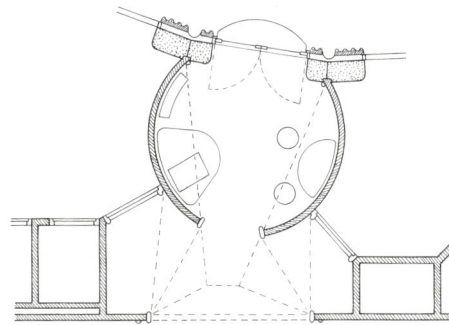

A coffee corner

strip of tiles in two active colours on each round wall: different colours for each strip of tiles.

As far as the wall surfaces between the doors of the rooms are concerned, they are the same height as the door frames and are finished in sprayed plaster. The division between light and dark grey here and there runs diagonally over the planes. Like the frames of the doors and side windows, all these planes are edged with semicircular wood. There are therefore no leftovers of wall between the doors, but restfully framed planes of differing widths.

275

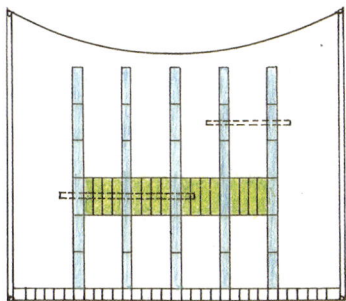

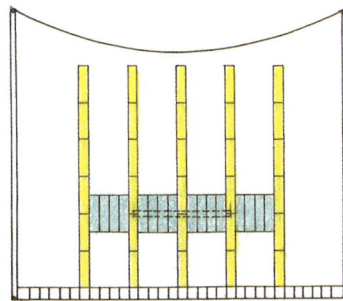

Walls of the coffee corner

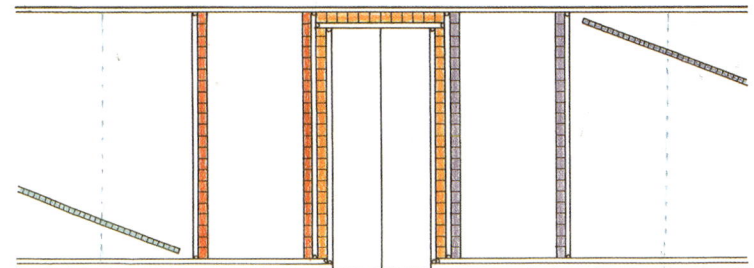

One of the lift entrances

Corridors with ceiling lamps grouped in series of different numbers

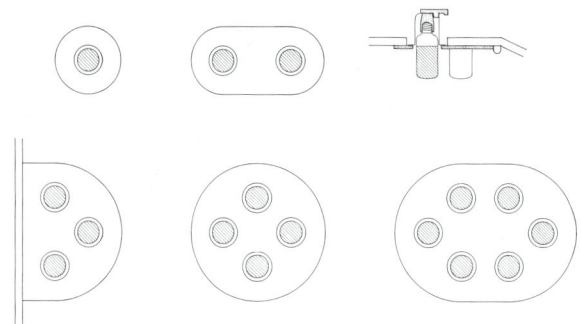

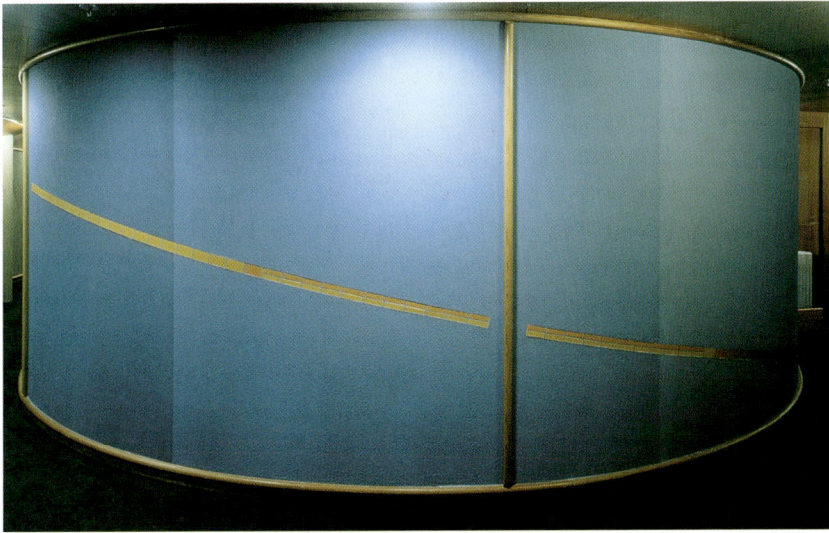

Court between old and new

277

Staircases in the new building

The yellow circle in the old staircase

Museum, Nijmegen, 1994 (competition) with Hannie van Eyck

An extensive, historically significant, open and partly wooded site in the city featuring remnants of a medieval castle and a raised earthen rampart on which a double row of splendid chestnut trees will form the backdrop to the museum, which is to be built adjacent to it along the broad end of a tapering urban space with to one side a spectacular view of the distant countryside.

The chestnut trees provided us with the right lead: how to build alongside them and how to open up the interior of the museum towards them. Everything was done to activate the difficult space 'behind' and between the building and the slope of the rampart.

Where the oval ground-floor exhibition spaces extend beyond the rectangular ones on the upper floor, light falls from above onto the concave curvature of the perimeter wall, from end to end. Both the oval and the exterior rectangular volumes are timber clad all round (30 cm panels). Note the fenestration: it will provide a gradual transition from closed to open as well as from scarce light to full light, by increasingly narrowing the aperture of the glazing on one or both sides.

Judging from their comments the jury failed even to read the plans properly.

278

First floor

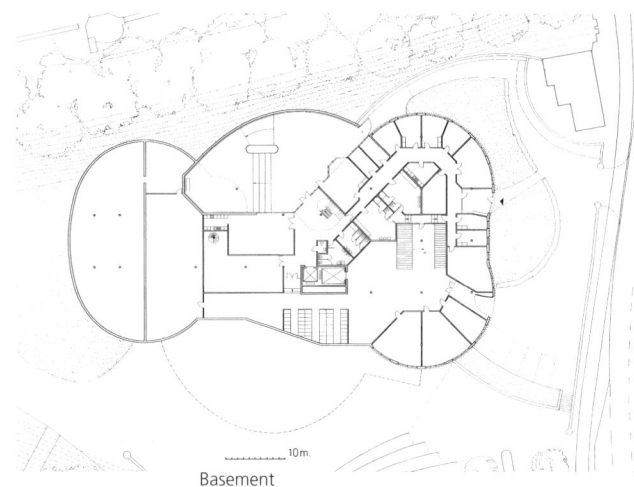

10 m.

Basement

Ground floor

10 m.

Basement
offices,
workshops
supplies

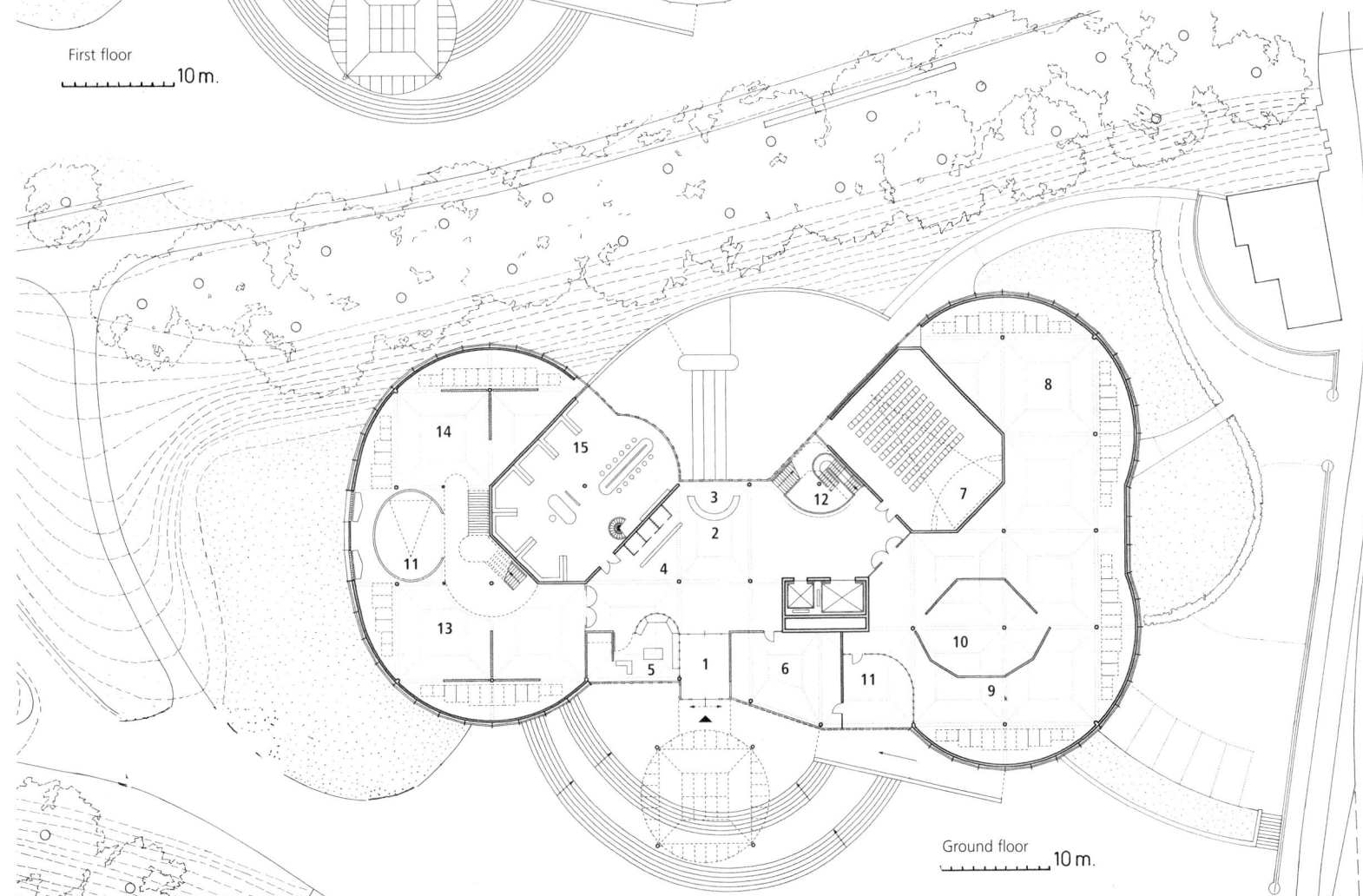

Ground floor
1 entrance
2 hall
3 reception
4 wardrobe
5 shop
6 service
7 auditorium theatre
8 historical art
9 modern art
10 vault
11 education
12 void
13 architecture of the
   Roman city
14 architecture of the
   Roman army
15 library

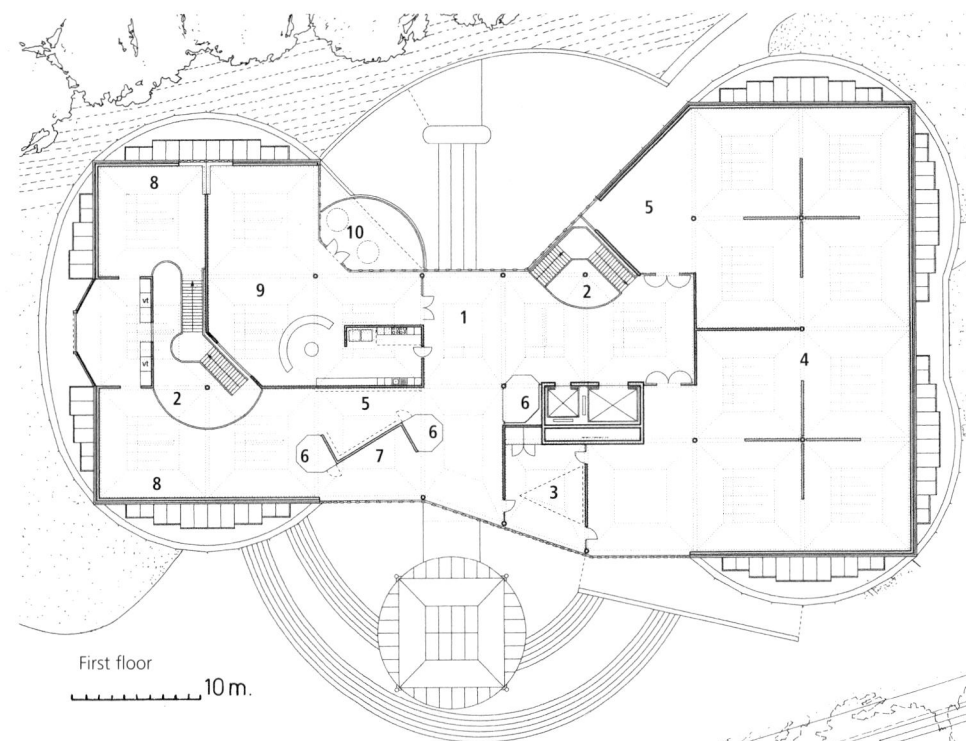

First floor
1 architecture, historical
   art and modern art
2 void
3 education
4 temporary exhibitions
5 vault
6 show case
7 Valkhof stronghold
8 architecture of the
   province of Gelderland
9 cafeteria
10 balcony

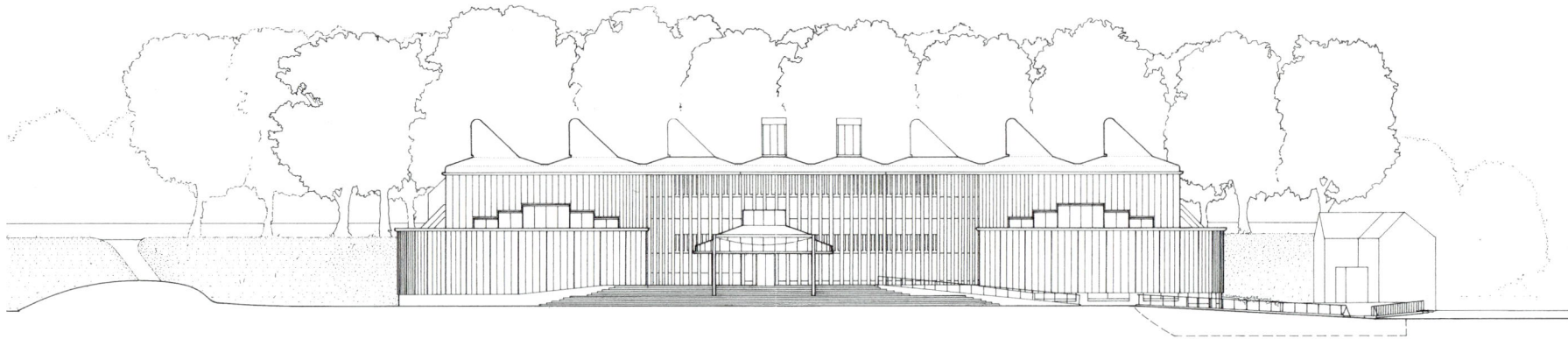

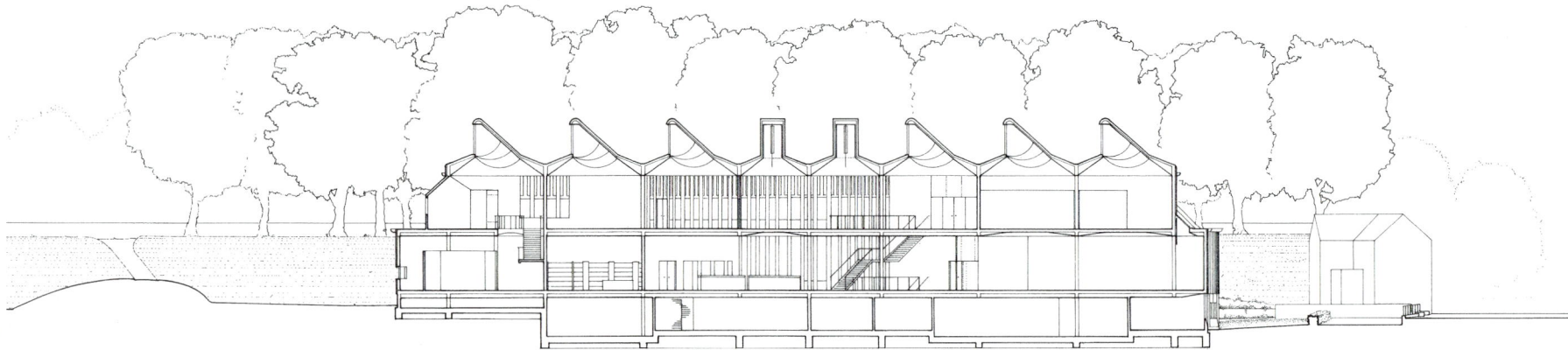

280

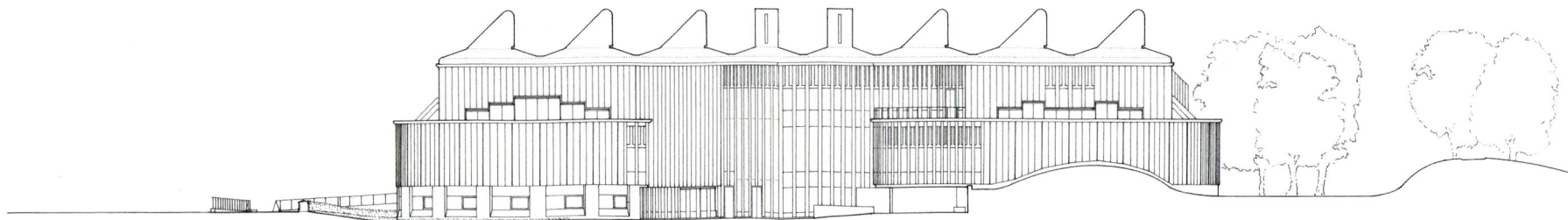

Considering the extent of the requirements, the size of the site available was very limited. Rather than come too close to the foot of the slope (a generous distance is impossible anyway) we would have the building emerge from the embankment – embed it in the embankment. In this way the curved incisions are positive 'encroachments' on the embankment, but do not breach it.

The gently sloping line from the square eastwards was reinforced by raising the museum by 1 metre. This gives the incisions in the embankment the right height.

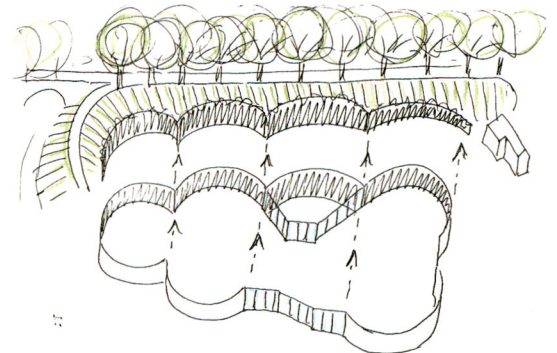

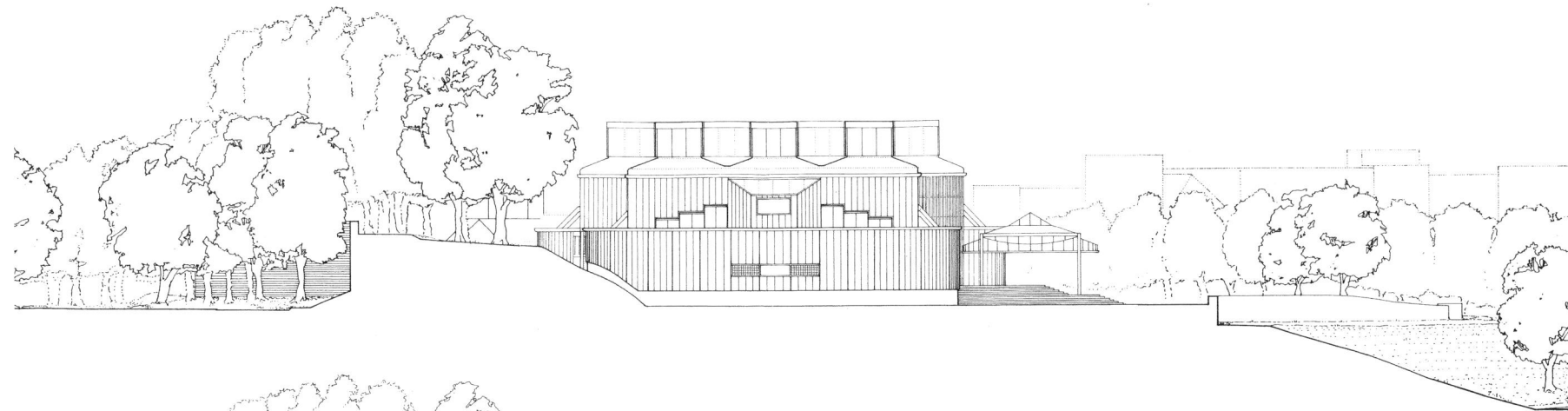

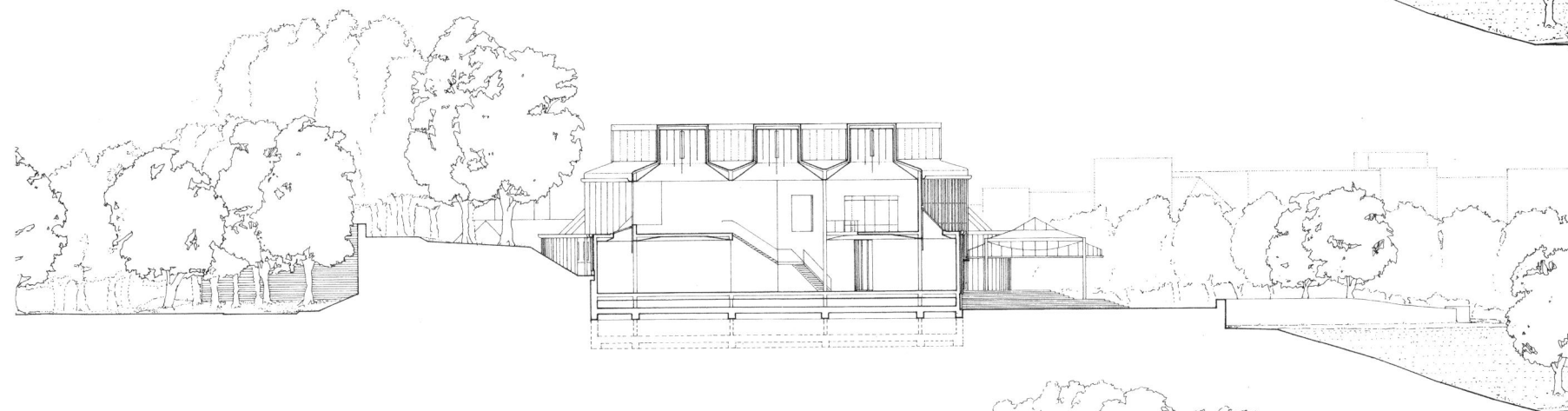

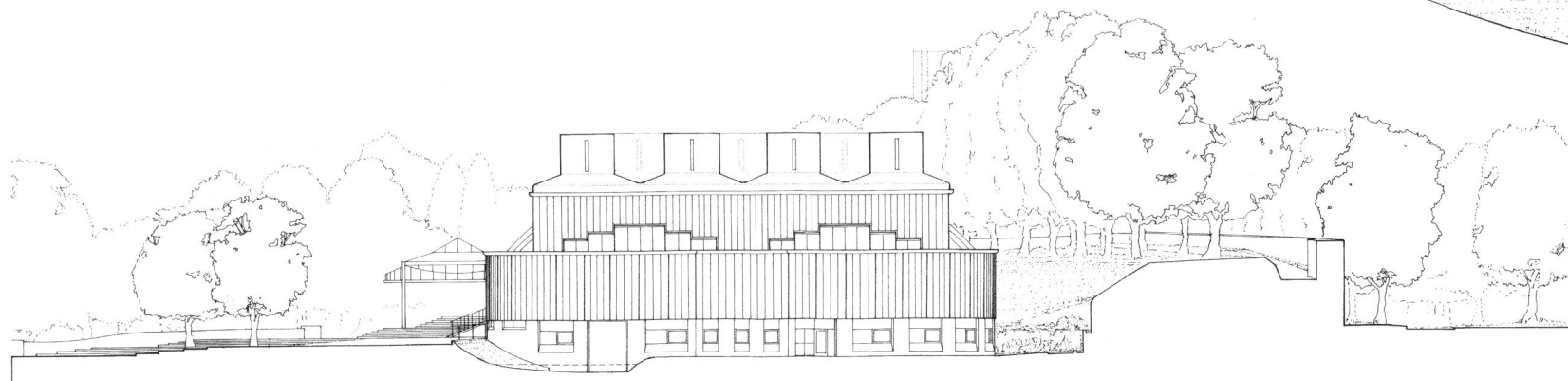

Closed walls for the exterior of a museum are always a problem, whereas for the interior it is the windows – not only because of the sudden bright light, but mainly because of the simultaneous presence of the outside world and the art inside. That's why there is here a different solution to the 'open-closed' and 'window-wall' opposites. The sketch shows a continuous wall that allows a variable degree of openness and closedness. Window widths increasing from 7 to 80 cm provide a gradual transition from light to dark.

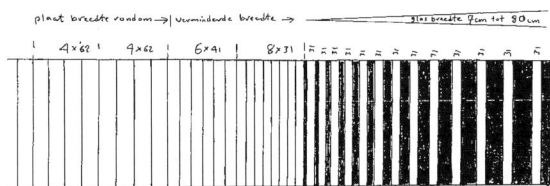

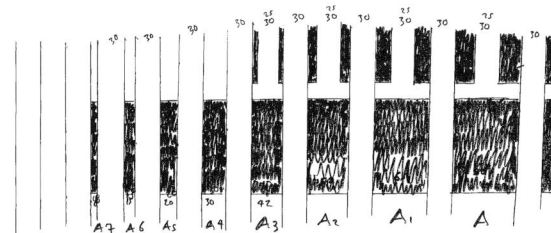

The Moscow House, 1994
with Hannie van Eyck

The idea of a house with two (twin) staircases has been in my mind for a long time. The opportunity afforded by Moscow to put it on paper – and possibly to even build it – was certainly gratifying.

Movement up and down, over and across, the entire house from end to end like an interior hill; *that* is what the two stairs will effectuate. They give access to the upper floor from both ends of the combined living spaces which span the entire width of the ground floor. Thus movement between the floors, instead of constantly referring back to a single central staircase, will encompass the whole house. I regard what is gained in this way as fundamental and valid beyond this incidental design and context.

All spaces are contained under a single pitched roof like a huge hat (a white dome in winter!). It could be of local slate combined with metal (zinc or copper) for low inclines. But I am not sure at this stage, since the nature of the actual locality (context) is still unfamiliar to me, as are the exact requirements of the future residents. The same applies to the principle construction and materials to be used. In some cases, however, I already have clear preferences: for example, the sturdy columns (stone or precast concrete drums – hollow for roof rain water). Also timber-frame construction for both exterior and interior walls. The roof construction could be either timber or steel and the floor construction timber or possibly concrete for lateral stability. As to detailing: since I wish the house to be both archaic and contemporary, colour and interior materials will be developed as I go along.

282

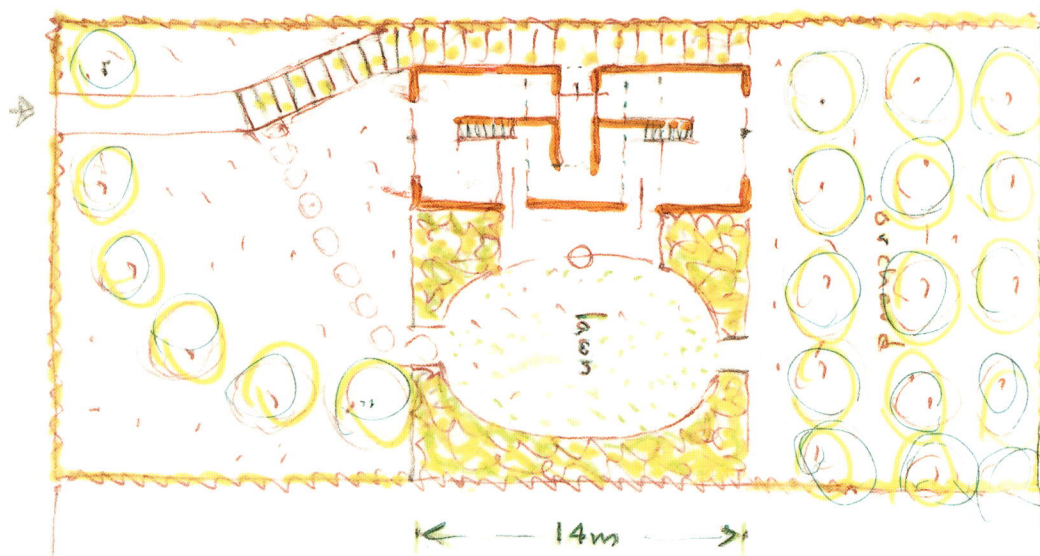

Rutger house, 1957, Loenersloot
first design of twin staircase

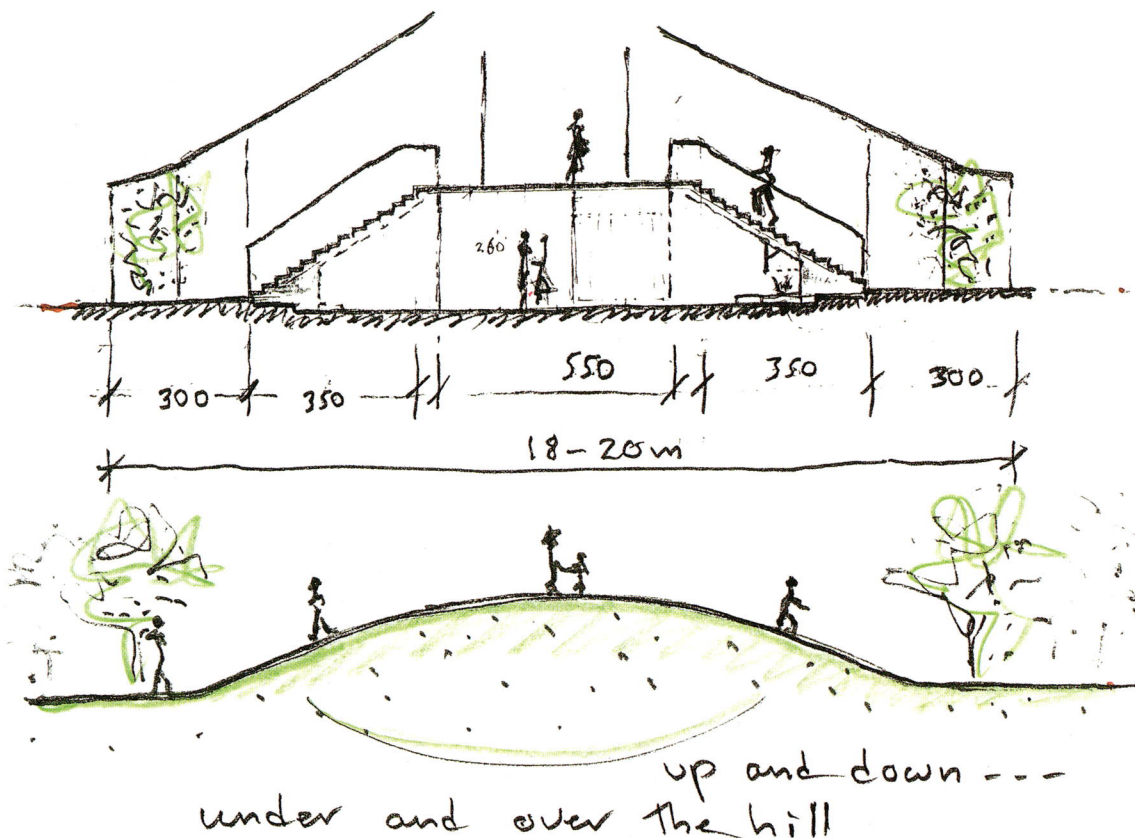

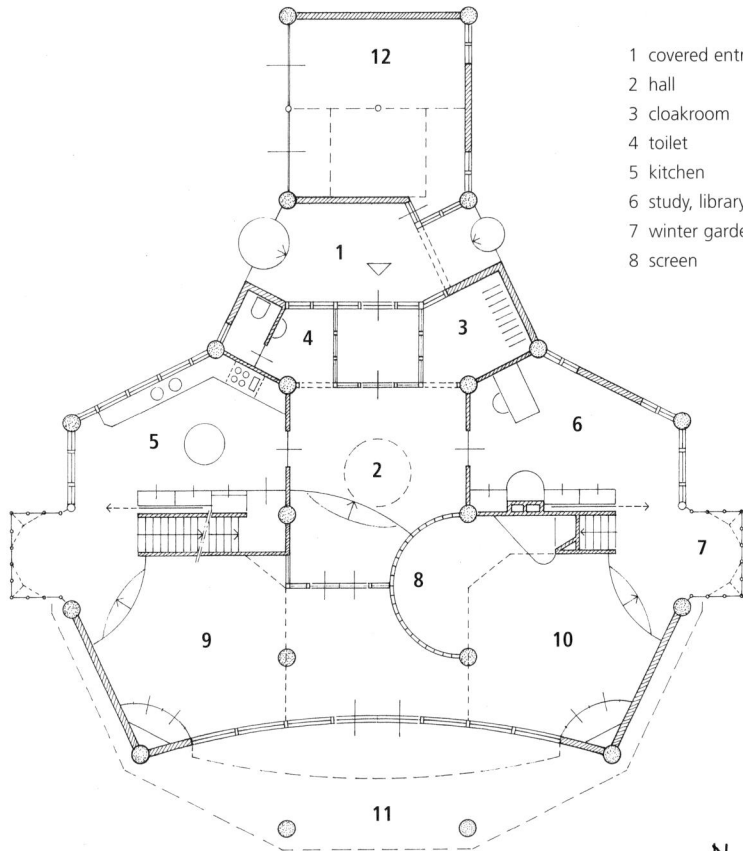

1 covered entrance
2 hall
3 cloakroom
4 toilet
5 kitchen
6 study, library or playroom
7 winter garden
8 screen

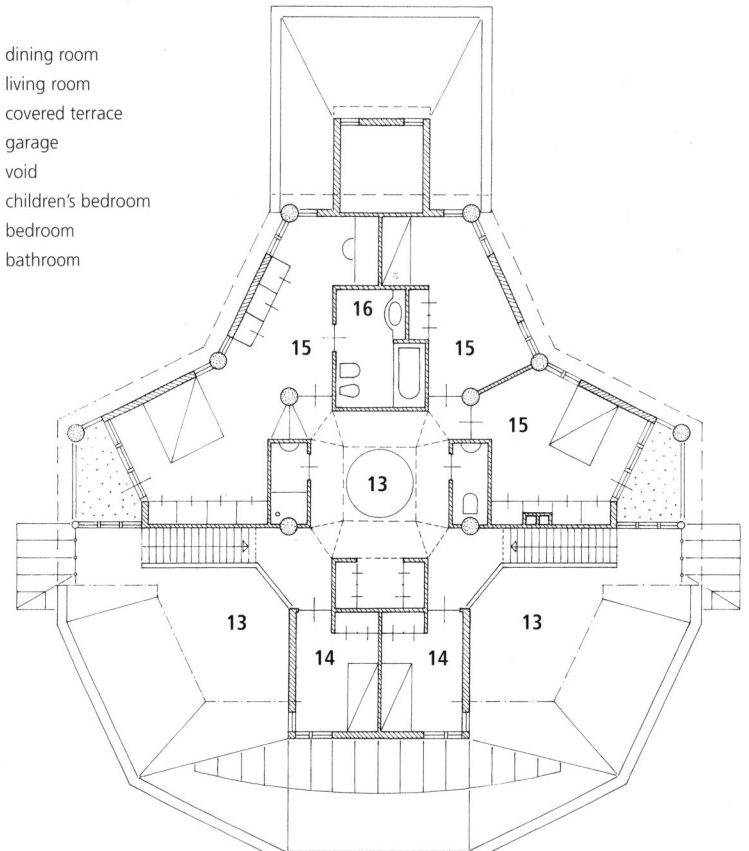

9 dining room
10 living room
11 covered terrace
12 garage
13 void
14 children's bedroom
15 bedroom
16 bathroom

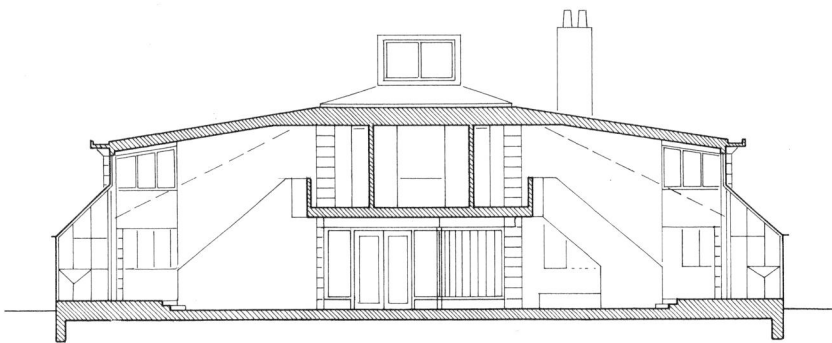

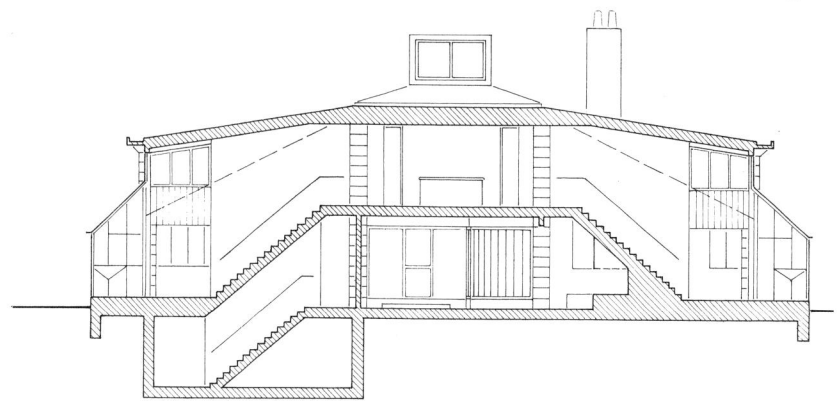

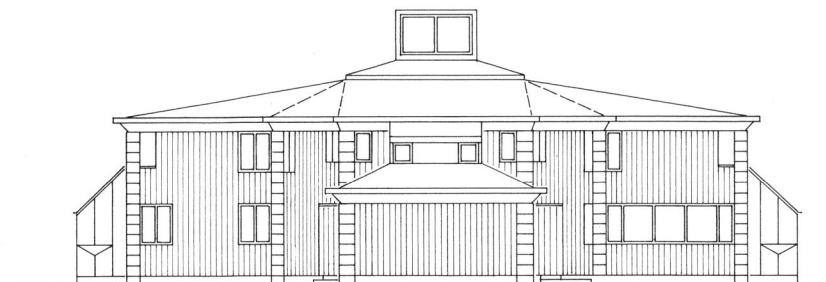

1m.   5 m.

N

N

283

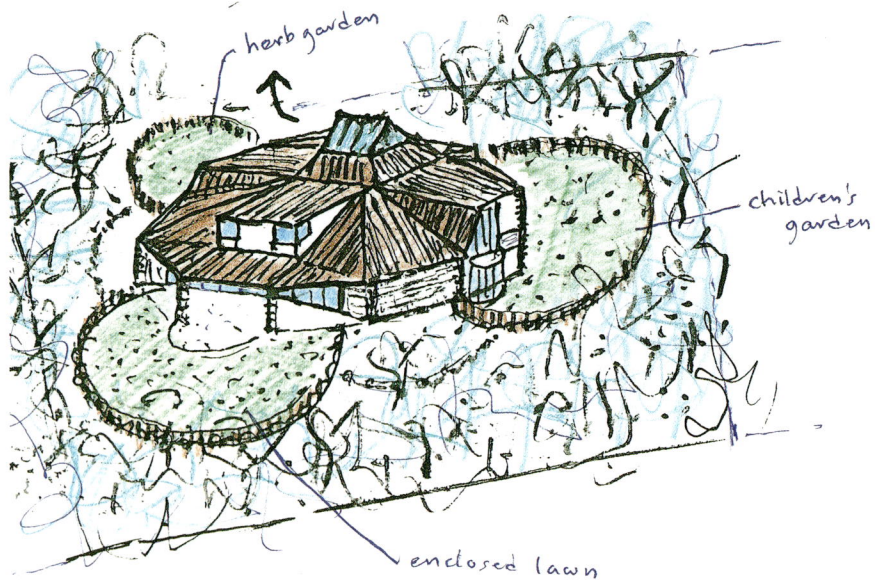

herb garden

children's garden

enclosed lawn

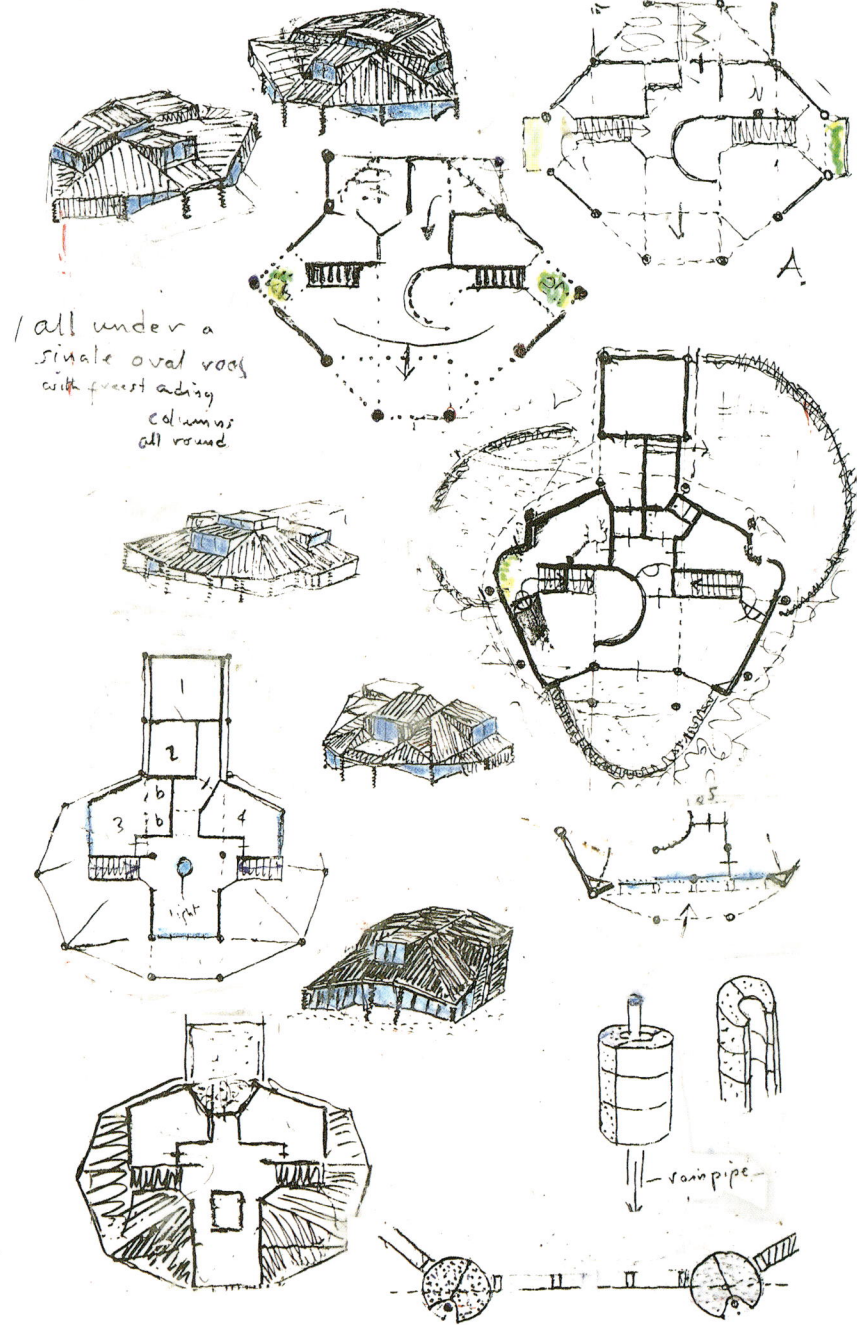

all under a
single oval roof
with forest acting
columns
all round

A

rainpipe

Terminal Pier, Thessaloniki Port, 1995
with Hannie van Eyck

Thessaloniki's sea front is certainly spectacular, although little has been undertaken in the past to enhance the beauty of the given location – no notable architecture save the White Tower, no properly designed coastal road adjusted to the needs of the city's pedestrian population. Nonetheless, the place designated for the boat terminal could still become emblematic vis-à-vis the city's sea-front location, if it acquires the urban quality it deserves, in other words if it is made to feel accessible by tying the rather isolated location of the terminal to the quay named Nikes, thus rendering its approach fluent. To achieve this, the abrupt right-angle turn at the last moment – with drifting refuse in the sea – is unacceptable. Hence the truncated corner and a platform with seats over the sea, sixty centimetres below quay-level, from which to enjoy the view.

To achieve the above we propose a screen of freestanding columns to follow the quay-side pavement around the truncated corner in a curve and finally pass right through the centre of the terminal.

Screen of free-standing columns

This screen of columns will accompany the pedestrian to and from the boat as a tangible intermediary between the distant horizon and the quay-side nearby. The idea is to interiorize, as it were, the final stretch of the sea front linking the terminal to the city. For a short distance you are clearly on the city-side with the sea on the other side, until you pass through the screen onto the semicircular pier under the large terminal roof which rests on sixteen columns arranged in a square at eight or nine-metre intervals. This is where the waiting room, coffee shop, kiosk, telephone and toilets are situated and on whose roof, accessible by means of two staircases, there is a partly covered roof terrace. Anything from shows by local artists to folk and popular music, as well as dancing, is possible here: a covered place for improvised public use at an attractive strategic point.

As to the columns, they should be of natural (local?) stone or glazed ceramics, the pieces stacked around a galvanized steel tube eight or ten centimetres in diameter, held in a reinforced concrete foundation. Ideally the low columns could be continued further along the quay as an effective balustrade, whilst the tall ones could be repeated at important places with, possibly, entries to more platforms with seats (and kiosks), sixty centimetres below street-level. Special street lights, trees and benches would thus enhance the entire quay-side from the terminal all the way to White Tower, making it really attractive: a comprehensible and unified urban entity from which thousands would benefit.

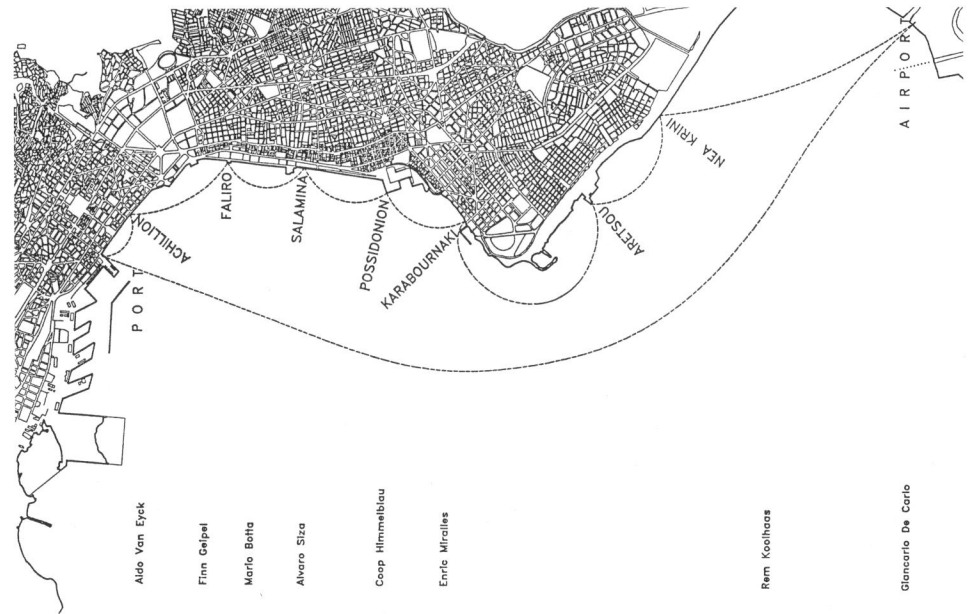

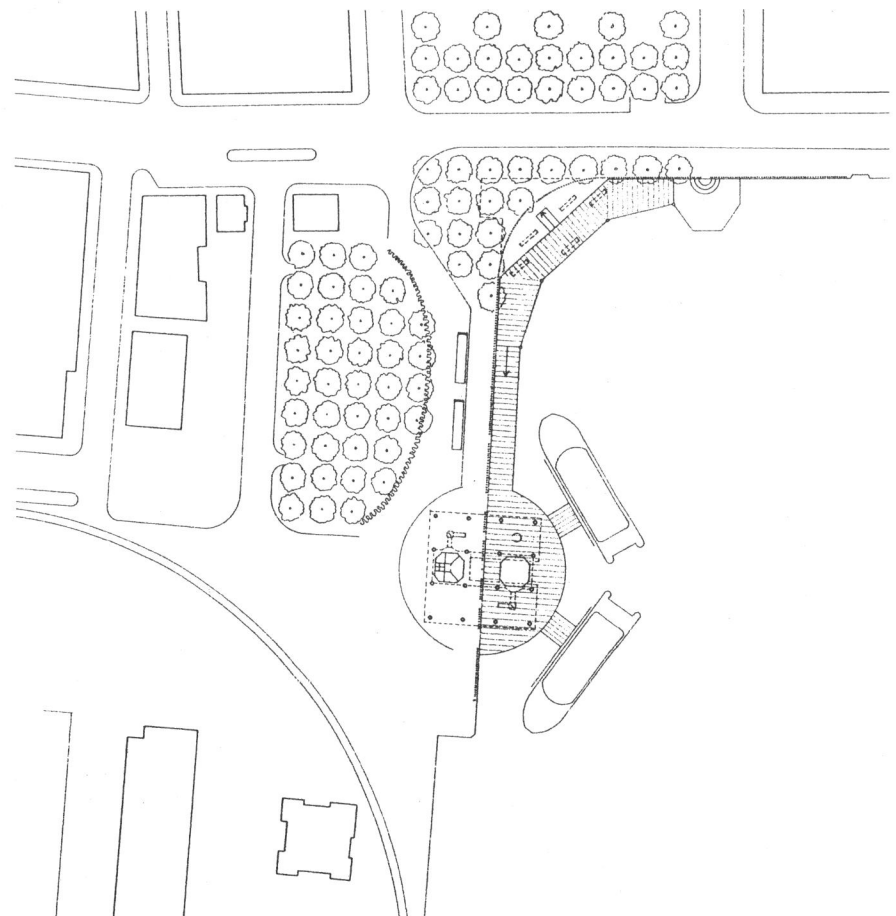

285

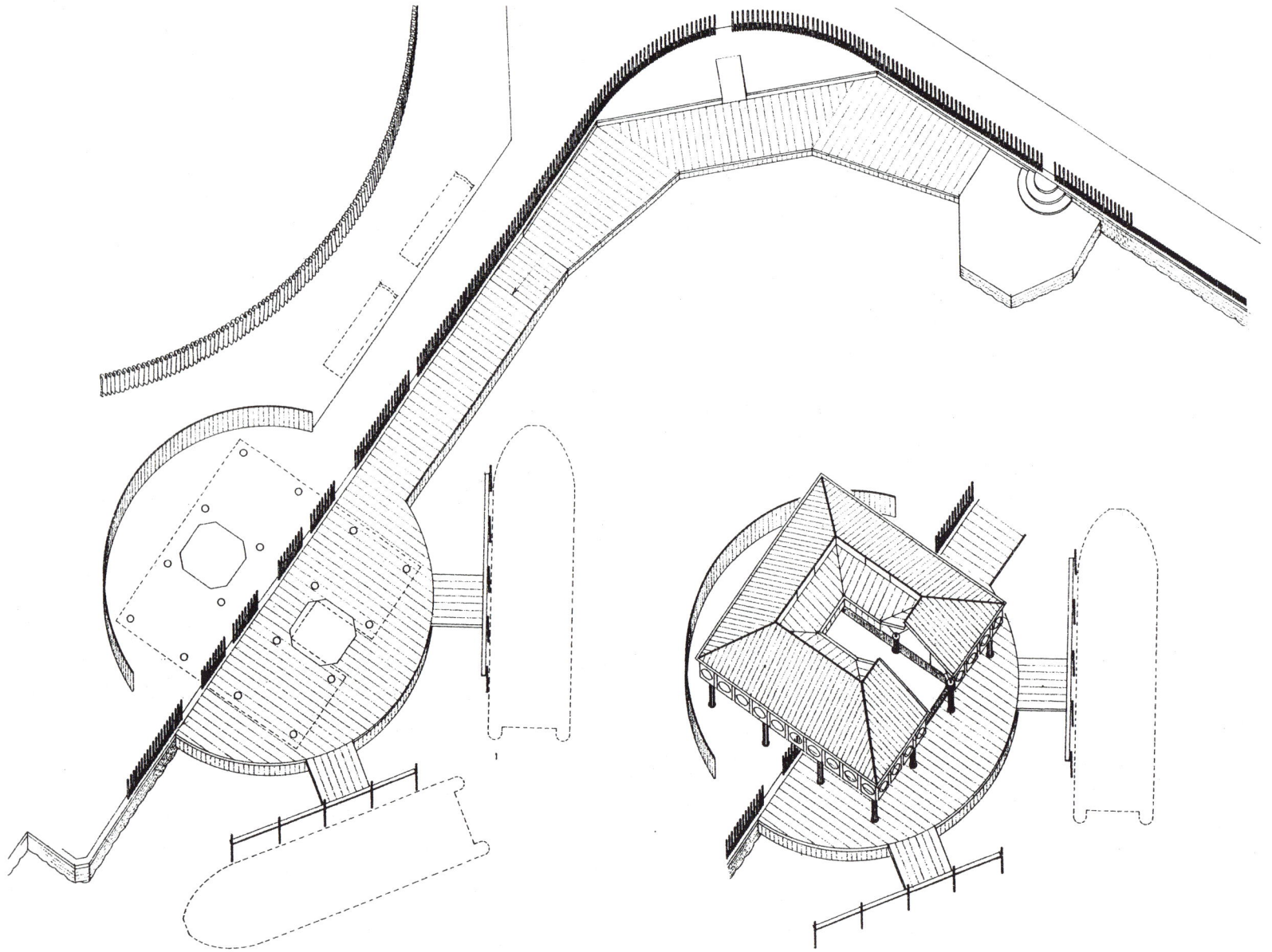

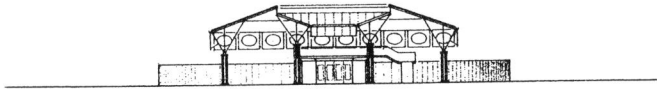

North-South section

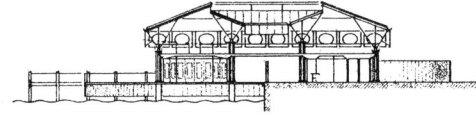

East-West section

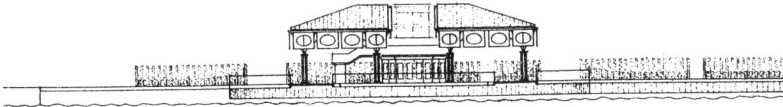

East elevation

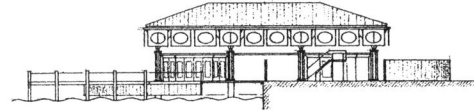

North elevation

Ground floor plan

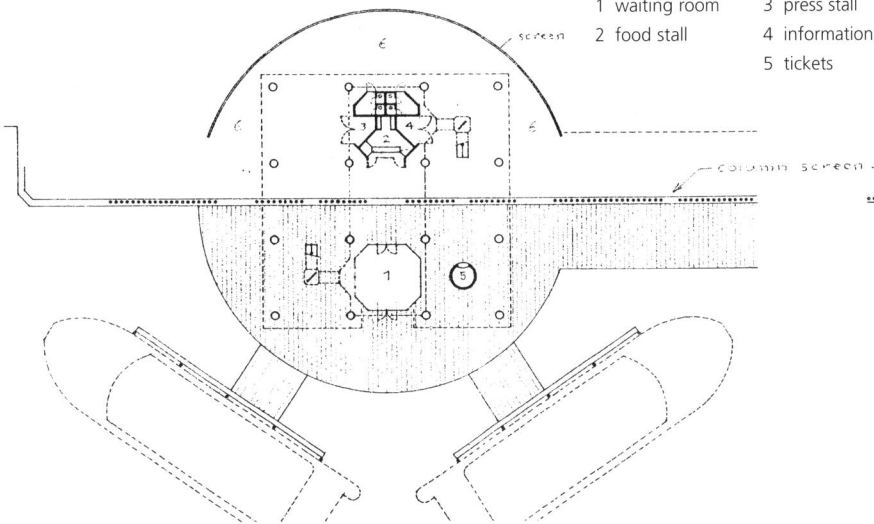

Upper floor plan

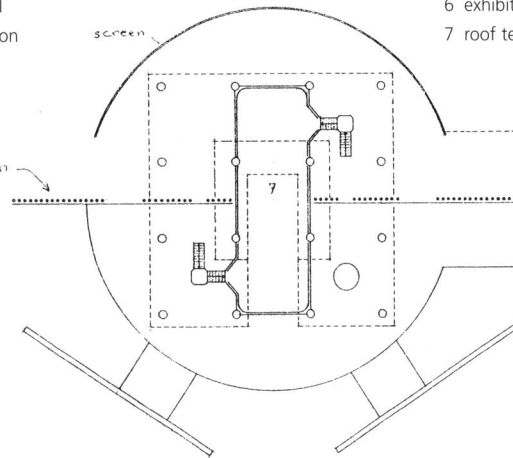

1 waiting room	3 press stall
2 food stall	4 information
	5 tickets

6 exhibition
7 roof terrace

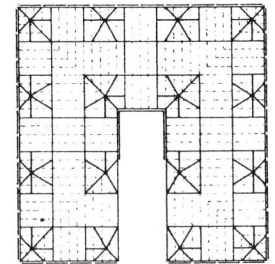

screen

screen

column screen

287

Roof seen from below

tiled roof

glass roof

875m+

575m+

605m+

360m+

500m+

3.25m+

3.00m+

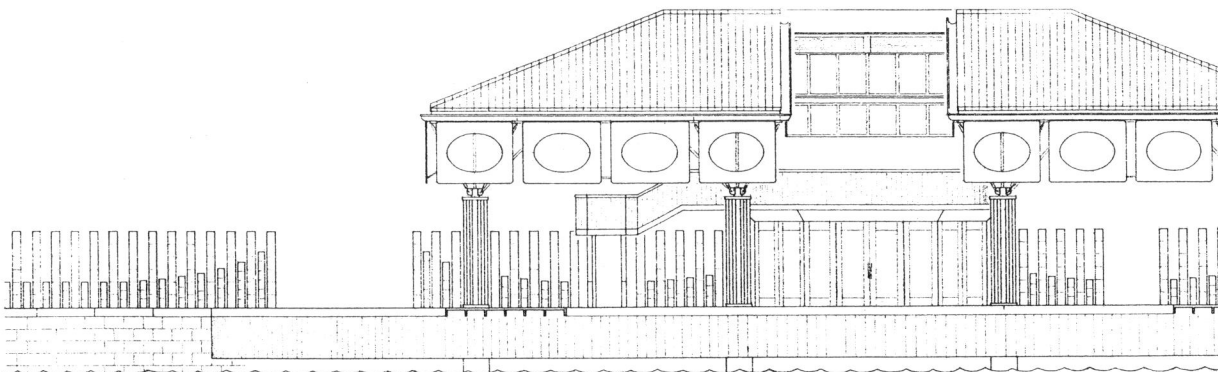

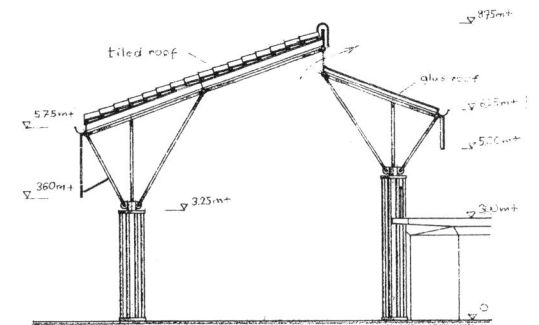

Port section, showing construction

φ 0,25

0.40m

steel pipe φ10cm

2,25m

0,65÷

gap – no balustrade ?

l.   c.   r.

low columns as balustrade

Terminal

A

+1,55

+2

+10
+15
+15
0,65÷

+0,20

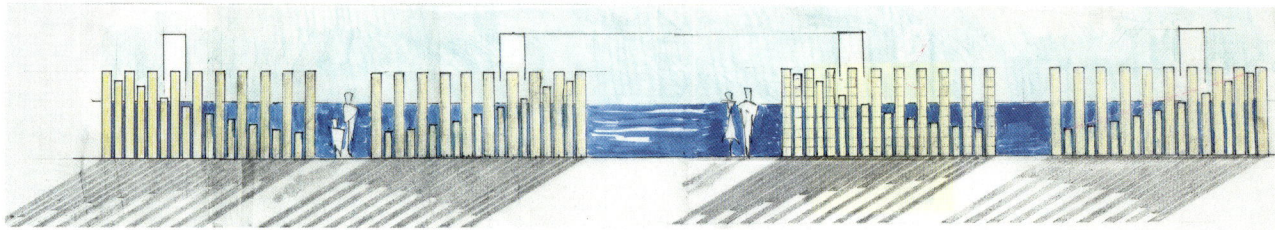

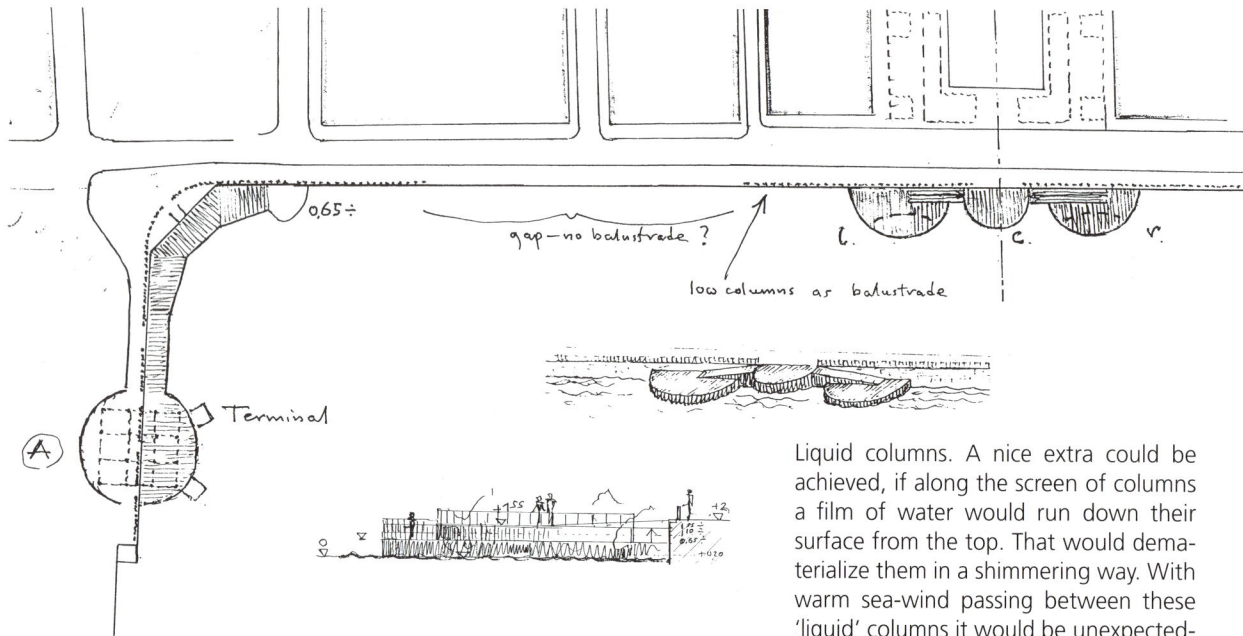

Saloniki's cultural year lies in the past and little headway has been made since then towards realization of the boat line.

Liquid columns. A nice extra could be achieved, if along the screen of columns a film of water would run down their surface from the top. That would dematerialize them in a shimmering way. With warm sea-wind passing between these 'liquid' columns it would be unexpectedly cool on the hot city-side of the column screen – touch such a column and water will pour over your hand.

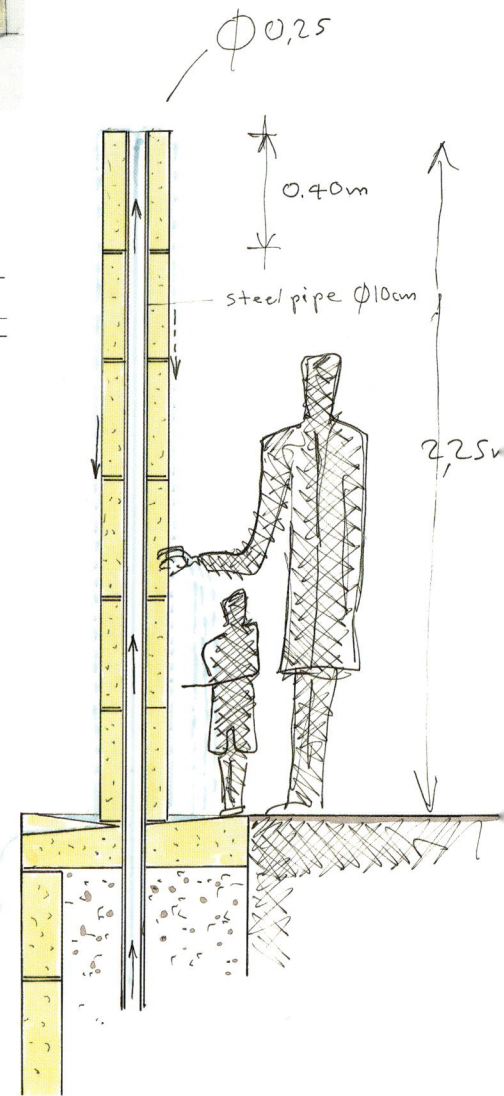

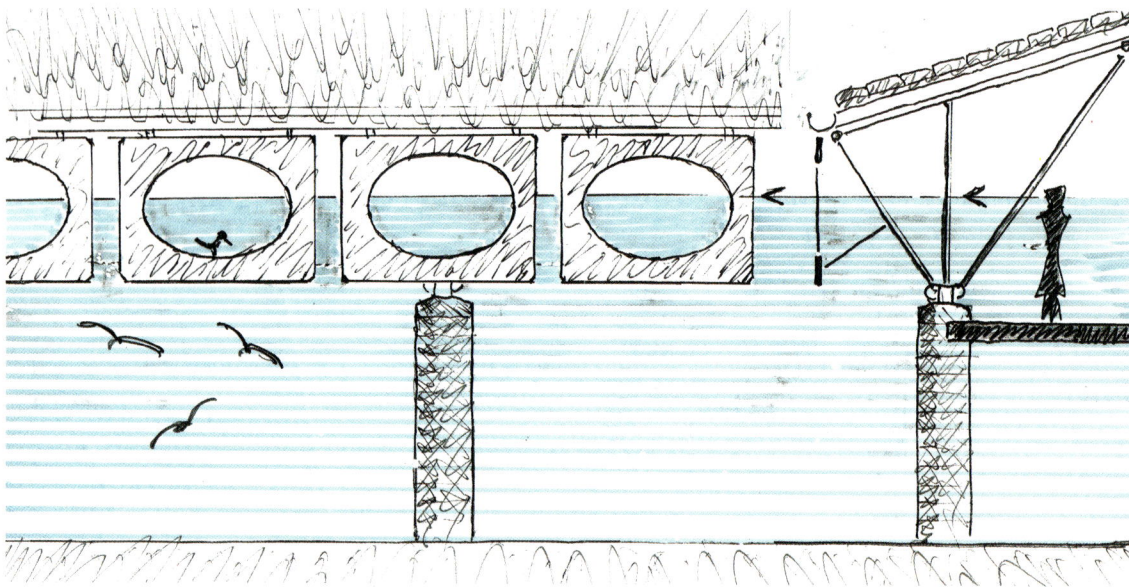

Exhibitions of Own Works and Ideas

Amsterdam, Berlage's Stock Exchange, 1989

It was the first time, strangely enough, that not only the immense central space of Berlage's great hall was used for exhibition purposes, but also the four aisles. Thus taking full advantage of the entire space. Transition from low to high as well as varying width was the reward.

The exhibition's principal item, perhaps more so than the actual subject matter shown, was the exhibition itself as an interior public space along the bustling main road. In fact down the centre there were no exhibits at all, just a few statements such as 'large hat – little roof', 'the enigma of size, and Dylan Thomas' 'the ball I threw whilst playing in the park had not yet reached the ground'. Beyond these, there were stools so that people could sit down and watch slides and TV clips whilst children chased round. All screens, open and closed, were painted dull aluminium so as not to interfere with Berlage's colour scheme. Evocative images from all over the world and all ages were shown along both aisles.

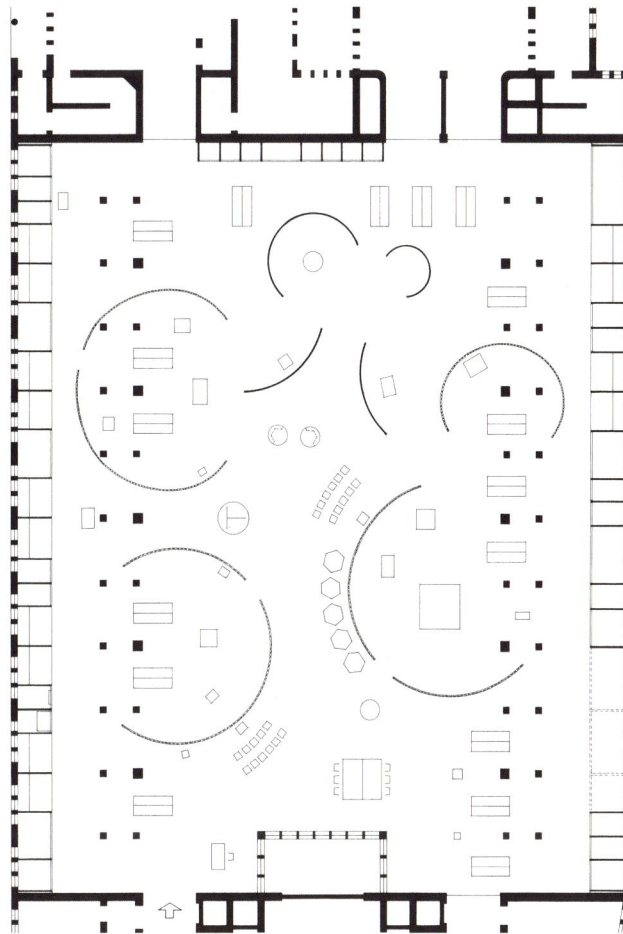

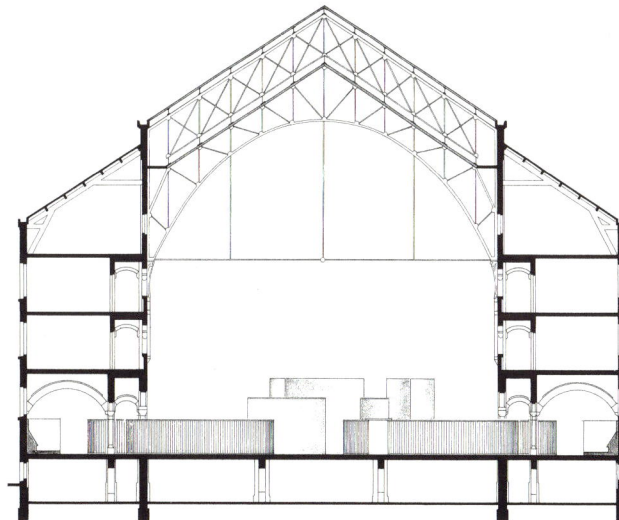

290

Amsterdam

1989

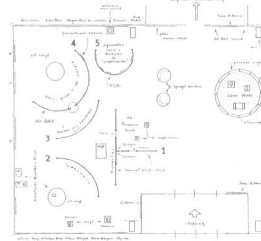

Athens 1983

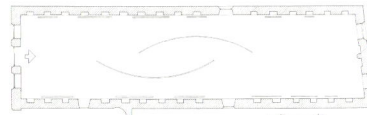

Middelburg 1990

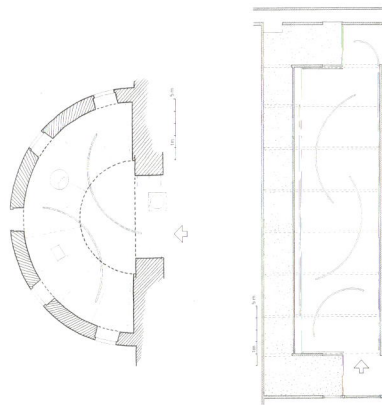

Kassel 1997   Rotterdam 1998

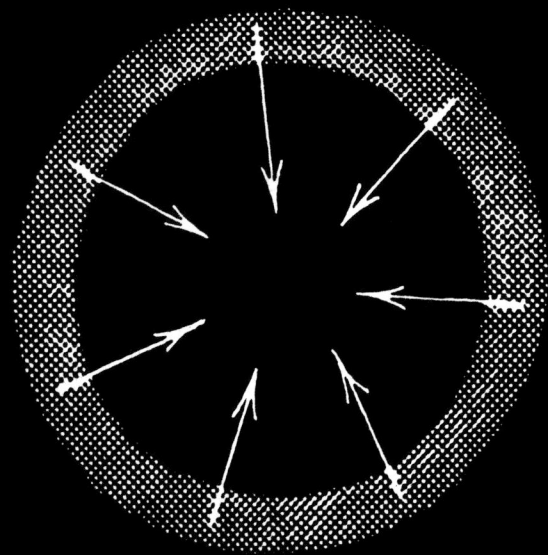

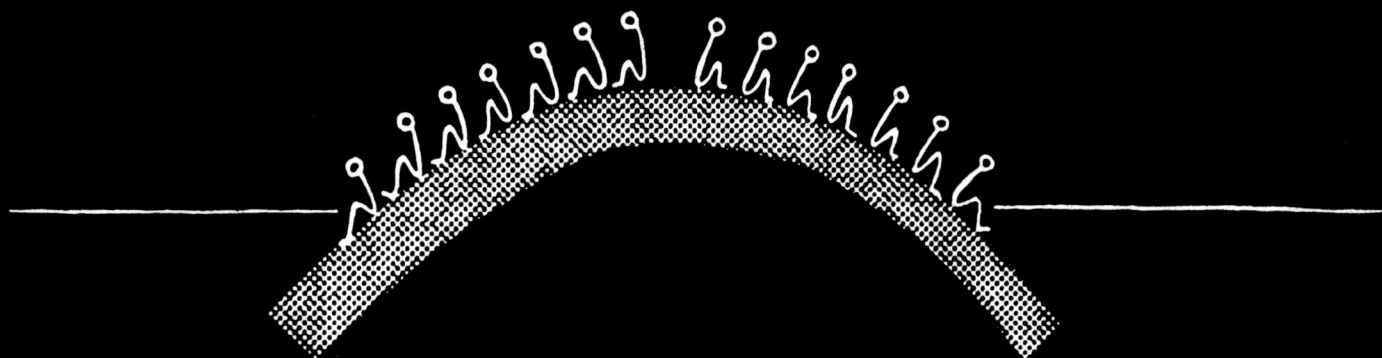

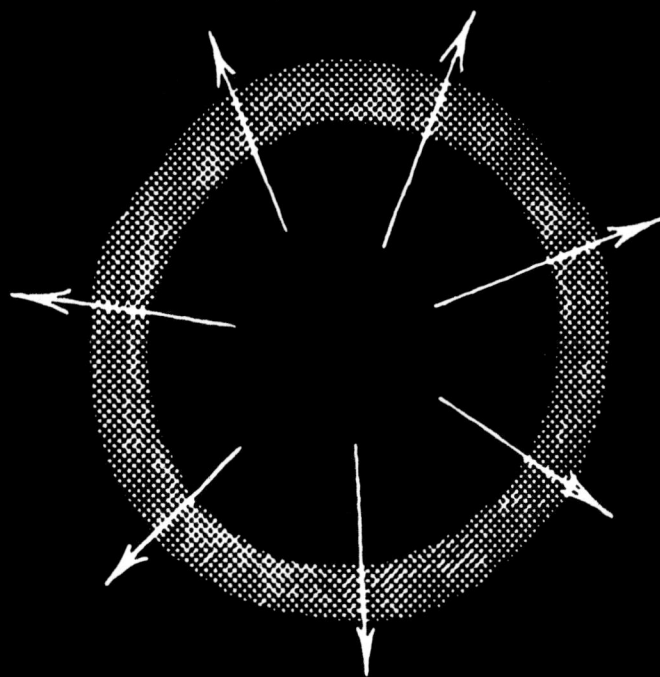

Richard Paul Lohse, Zurich

Aldo and I were always talking about the possible relations between art and architecture, about the question whether both involved analogous structures, and to what extent these structures can be made identical. It is not possible to transpose Lohse or Mondriaan directly into architecture. There is always the danger that this sort of transposition is limited to only the outer, visible picture. Nevertheless, the methods and systems a painter develops may contain possibilities for structural transference. This was the case in, among other places, Holland in the twenties, when there was a correspondence between the plastic principles of De Stijl painting and tendencies in architecture. There was an identity in the expression of painting and architecture, without Rietveld or Duiker having directly followed Mondriaan.

Van Eyck always pursued a logical dynamic. In the same way as this dynamic arises out of a cohesion of verticality and diagonality in my work. Diagonality was the determining force for Cézanne too, though he did not depict it as such. One can also recognise this sort of dynamic in the work of van Eyck.

Georges Candilis, Athens

After the Otterlo Congress in 1959, Aldo took me round the Orphanage, which at that time was under construction. Nothing had been finished yet, but he led me through the entire construction while clarifying his vision to me: how everything could be and how it could function. I learnt a tremendous architectural lesson from that.

He did not talk like most architects. He did not say: see this, or that, this finely finished detail, these well incorporated materials, or that room with its fine proportions and pleasant atmosphere. It was mainly the secret language of architecture he focused my attention on. He showed me a hidden corner in a large room, saying, 'See this? It's very important. The little boys can hide there to smoke a cigarette.' A bit further on he showed me a few mirrors he had laid in the floor so the boys could look up the girls' skirts. The way he talked about architecture was totally different from the norm. Not only had he created a superb space, but at the same time he had penetrated to the deeper meaning of architecture. And I found that more important than the question of whether something had been developed fully in accordance with the rules of modernism.

John Voelcker, Staplehurst

These playgrounds are significant at the present time for two reasons. Firstly because they reveal the importance of time to the urbanist, an empty plot of land is an inescapable reality; it must be used else the community in its immediate neighbourhood is, to some extent, deprived of their freedom of movement and right of expression; since it must be used it must be developed as the situation, social and economic, allows. All too frequently empty city sites lie idle, stagnating until 'the time comes and funds are available': such phrases reflect an utter contempt and disregard for the nature, the force, of time; citizens are inevitably deprived for a considerable period of large chunks of their city; in the end real time having acted, the site is absorbed into some hastily conceived and usually worthless development.

The second reason why these playgrounds are important is because they represent a particular scale of work essential to the urbanist for here he may come into personal contact with some of the more positive and vital elements at work in a community: he is able to combine in a single process both creative achievement and research. (The irresponsible presumption of the urbanist who relies upon the observations and statistics of a herd of non-creative research workers is unsufferable). Through a playground, and similar simple urban functions, existing urban associations, in hitherto isolated streets for instance, may be extended; the urbanist will achieve this extension through the clarity and relevance of the forms he makes; this is architecture. By observing the way in which this architecture is used the urbanist will be guided to future more extensive, socially more complex, and inevitably more expensive developments in that location, this is research.

Through a playground, and similar simple urban functions, existing urban associations (in hitherto positive qualities of a particular direction in Dutch architecture and beyond) have been interpreted in an attempt to reveal a structure of ideas common to a number of younger architects working in this country, Europe, and North Africa. The Amsterdam playgrounds, surgical operations within a densely populated city, express an attempt on the part of the architect to rediscover his identity through the re-integration of his techniques.

Carel Visser, Rijswijk

I saw Aldo at work at the time he was designing the Orphanage. He worked standing up at an ordinary flat table, so that he stood for hours literally bent over his work. He developed several spatial themes, and then stood endlessly trying them out and fitting them together. I saw the plan taking shape day by day, until it had a structure like a fugue by Bach. He was entirely deliberate in his use of the fugal principle. In fact at that time he often listened to Bach's organ music, the toccatas and fugues. And in the floor plan of the Orphanage you can see the motifs inserted into each other contrapuntally as in a fugue. The spaces unite into two groups, like two hands encountering each other in a large in-between area.

Richard Buckminster Fuller, U.S.

Dear Mr Aldo van Eyck, your orphanage is excellent! The understanding and logic of its design is in the supreme of economy which becomes a natural poetry. You have sacrificed nothing but instead have earned the undeniable right to include a good solution for every fundamental. You are thoroughly educated in the tools of our evolving moment. Am sorry not to have met you.

Shinkichi Tajiri, Los Angeles, Baarlo

Aldo's work always gives me auditive sensations. His buildings hum or sing, but never scream. They are modest and in their scale and proportions give the appearance of a profound respect for the dignity of the human individual. In 1967 he housed my spaceships in two enormous translucent cylinders stretching from floor to ceiling. As the autumn sun outside gradually faded as it set, the cylinders lit from inside slowly began to glow until they formed two monumental pillars of light. This natural metamorphosis had the poetic economy of a haiku.

Quotations

Peter Schat, Amsterdam

The Orphanage is clearly based on a series that recurs in changing transformations: the accommodation areas comprising the same basic elements, but which are subject to different variations each time. I visited the building with Boulez and Stockhausen and they were also greatly impressed by it. They saw in it an equivalent to the things they were doing themselves. That emancipation of the elements and at the same time that relativising way of thinking. It was an inspiring visit that definitely gave us a certain stimulus.

Constant, Amsterdam

Aldo was one of our first fans, one of the first who also bought our work: mine, Appel's, Wolvecamp's and the others, while at that time we were completely unknown. He bought our work simply because he liked it. When, in early 1950, Appel's mural in the coffee room at the town hall in Amsterdam was covered in wallpaper on the orders of the local authority, it was also Aldo who initiated the protest against this act. He wrote the manifesto 'an appeal to the imagination', which he had printed entirely at his own expense.

His admiration for Mondrian did not prevent him from being very open to our way of thinking and working. In his approach to art he did not appear to be at all ridden with any exclusive doctrine. He also recognised what was new in what we were doing: the collective aspect and the spontaneity of our work. He saw that in our work this was completely different from the Surrealists and Dadaists.

We found both Cobra exhibitions superb. We did not see a painting as something that had to be presented at eye-level. It was simply a gesture in space. No one had anything against their painting being hung at a height of two metres, or at the foot of the wall, against the skirting, or horizontally on a wooden pallet on the floor so that you had to bend over it to see it. We did that in our studios all the time!

Carola Giedion-Welcker, Zurich

Aldo does not cut himself off from the past. He does not say, 'now we are in the present and that's that,' he involves the whole of the past in the present. He does not conceive history or the world as a uniform or pyramidal structure, but as a spiral; as the sort of eternal recurrence Giambattista Vico proposed in his philosophy of history: the recurrence of things past, but which have not gone forever and are always ready to return.

He was amazingly conversant with English literature, both old and new, from Swift to Joyce, and he was able to point out passages from it that stimulated you to read. Everything he indicated was in one way or another substantial. He did not commend to you the sort of fleeting thing that vanishes as quickly as it appears, but handed you genuinely essential values. And that was even while there was a war on. We always said, 'Here in Switzerland we are living in the catacombs'. And that was really the case, with Hitler just next door. When we came together in the evenings, we were always happy when Aldo was with us, because his was the spirit behind the whole thing.

During the Second World War we always called him the Firebird. He functioned as a flame at our gatherings, because he is an exceptionally spontaneous person who was capable of assimilating and then reproducing all the events of the intellectual life, both in politics and in art, in an unprecedentedly personal way. It was really astonishing how he always hit the nail on the head.

Felix Schwartz, Zurich

I think that the quality of Aldo's work is connected to what I would like to call its 'deposits of poetic ore'. When I read a poem I cannot interpret it clearly or rationally either, but have to discover the various layers of the word. I am convinced that the ambiguity of Aldo's forms is linked to his multilingualism, to his hearing several languages internally, in which the words – by their timbre or something like that – acquire a shift of meaning.

I see Aldo as related much more to Loos than to Kahn. Loos was also a gripping personality, especially in his essays, someone able to combine things and at the same time discover new things. I find that though their work can hardly be compared, they were that much more akin in their complete personalities.

Giancarlo De Carlo, Milan

It must be at least thirty-five years since I met Aldo, perhaps at some international conference. But our acquaintance was renewed at Otterlo in 1959, where, though with different position, we both held the view that the CIAM's activity was to be discontinued because it has reached a dead end.

After this we met often, at least once a year, at Team X gatherings and we became friends. With Jaap Bakema, Shad Woods, Georges Candilis, Alison and Peter Smithson, Ralph Erskine, Jose Antonio Coderch, Jerzy Zoltan, Oscar Hansen and others who happened to be invited, we continued to debate architecture, using our projects as a starting point: we used to stick them up, each in turn, on the walls of wherever we happened to be and then go into them thoroughly, without holding anything back, with the frankness one owes to real friends.

At these meetings and many other times when we were able to get together and talk things over, three facets of Aldo's character always interested me. His mental openness, which led him to work and live without the least concession to commonplace. His intellectual honesty, so complete as to enable him to be irreverent and even uninhibited: real honesty, I mean, neither moralistic nor resigned.

And finally his surprising creativity which begets architectural forms that are always completely lucid yet also fraught with tensions: never in the least self-contemplative or indulgent. I have often been asked how much Aldo influenced my work and I his. Since I suppose that sooner or later I shall have to answer this ingenuous (when it comes from students) and childish (when it comes from critics) question, I shall try and do so now.

The members of Team X found themselves in a field of interconnecting influences, rather like the vertices of a polyhedron connected by a multitude of edges. The connections were direct but also indirect because they could run from one to another through a third, a fourth or even all the others together. There was never any attempt at a collective levelling because our reciprocal interest arose out of the way we were, and remained, different from one another. So Team X, unlike the postmodern groupings that formed later, never became either a sect or a kind of mafia. Aldo's possible influence on me or mine on his were transmitted along complex paths of curiosity, respect and friendship. They remain deep down, do not come to the surface, and so they elude description.

Concise Biography

1918

Aldo van Eyck was born in Driebergen, the Netherlands, on 16th March. When one and a half he moved to England with his parents. He lived in Golders Green in North London until 1935.

After going to school in England – at King Alfred School in Hampstead, London, and Sidcot School in Winscombe, Somerset – and architectural studies at the MTS (Senior Technical School) in The Hague, he continued to study architecture at the ETH in Zurich (1938-42).

1943

Married Hannie van Roojen, and had two children: Tess (1945) and Quinten (1948).

1944

His first design was executed: the interior of the tower room in Prof. W. Loeffler's house in Zurich.

1946

Returned to the Netherlands after the war. With references from Carola Welcker and Sigfried Giedion, Cor van Eesteren gave him a job as an architect-designer in the Urban Development section of the Department of Public Works in Amsterdam (1946-53). Having first worked on urban development designs, he was able to devote himself to the children's playground project initiated by Mrs Jakoba Mulder.

1947

As a member of the Dutch CIAM group 'de 8 en Opbouw', he worked on the Nagele project (1948-58) and he was the Dutch representative at the international CIAM congresses (1947-59). From 1948 to 1951 he took part in the Cobra movement with Alechinsky, Appel, Brands, Corneille, Constant, Jorn, et al.

1951

Started his practice in Amsterdam, from 1971 in association with Theo Bosch and from 1983 until his death with Hannie van Eyck.

1951-84

Lecturer in Art History at the Academy of Art and Industry, Enschede (1951-4). Lecturer at the Institute for Applied Art Education (1951-66) and the Academy of Architecture (1954-9) in Amsterdam. Professor at the Faculty of Architecture of the Delft University of Technology (1966-84).

1954

Co-founder of Team 10, with Bakema, Candilis, Erskine, Grung, A. & P. Smithson, Soltan, Voelcker, Woods.

1959

Member of editorial staff of *Forum*, with Apon, Bakema, Boon, Hardy, Hertzberger and Schrofer (1959-63 and 1967).

1982

Became member of the Jerusalem Town Planning Committee.

Prizes

Won the Sikkens Prize with Constant in 1960, with Joost van Roojen in 1961; the City of Amsterdam Architecture Prize for the Orphanage in 1964; first prize in the competition for the Protestant church in Driebergen in 1965; first prize for the town hall in Deventer in 1967; first prize for the Nieuwmarkt plan, Amsterdam, with Theo Bosch in 1970; first prize for the History Museum in Zwolle, with Hannie van Eyck, in 1973; the Rotterdam-Maaskant Prize in 1982; the Finnish International Wihuri Prize in 1982; the Royal Gold Medal, RIBA, London, in 1990; the Fritz Schumacher Prize, Hannover, in 1992; the Ikea Prize in 1992; and with Frei Otto the Israeli Wolf Prize in 1998.

Exhibitions

Dortmunder Architektur Ausstellung, Museum am Ostwall, Dortmund, 1976; Venice Biennale, Europe-America architecture exhibition, 1976; retrospective of his work, 'AX BAX', National Museum in Athens, 1983; major retrospective of his work on the occasion of Aldo's seventieth birthday, in Berlage's stock exchange in Amsterdam, 1989; retrospective, RIBA, London, 1990; retrospective, Vleeshal in Middelburg, 1992; selection of his work for Documenta X, Kassel, 1997; exhibition of images and his own work on the occasion of Aldo and Hannie's eightieth birthdays, NAi, Rotterdam, 1998.

Forthcoming

Retrospective of the work and ideas of Aldo and Hannie van Eyck, at the fourth São Paulo Biennale, November 1999.

Guest lectureships

At several institutions in the US, including Washington University in Saint Louis (1961-2); Harvard University in Cambridge, Mass. (1963); Tulane University in New Orleans (1965) and the University of Pennsylvania in Philadelphia (1980-2). Also at Trondheim University (1958); the AA School in London (1964); the Reid Hall in Paris (1966); the ETH in Zurich (1977-8); Singapore Polytechnic (1967 & 1985) and the Ecole d'Art Américaine de Fontainebleau (1989).

Honorary memberships, honours

Staatlichen Kunstakademie, Dusseldorf (1979); Royal Academy of Belgium (1981); American Institute of Architects (1982); Bund Deutscher Architekten (1982); Royal Incorporation of Architects of Scotland (1985); International Academy of Architecture (Sofia-Paris) (1987); Royal Institute of British Architects (1987); Officer in the Order of Oranje-Nassau (1990); Order for Science and Art of the Republic of Austria (1992); honorary member of the Association of Dutch Architects (1994); Commander in the Order of the Dutch Lion (1998).

Honorary doctorates

New Jersey Institute of Technology (1979); Tulane University, New Orleans (1979); University of Nova Scotia, Halifax (1985); University of Technology, Delft (1990).

Travels

From 1947 he travelled a lot to archaic cultures, from Tierra del Fuego to Iceland, from Christmas Island to Easter Island.

1999

Aldo van Eyck died in Amsterdam on 14th January.

Projects by Aldo van Eyck

1943-4
Furniture for his flat, Zurich.

1944
Interior design for the tower room in the house of W. Loeffler, Zürichberg-strasse, Zurich.

1947
First playground on the Bertelmanplein in Amsterdam, for the Department of Public Works. About 735 of them were built between 1947 and 1978.

1948
Interior design of his own apartment, Binnenkant 32, Amsterdam.

Nagele, plan for a rural village on re-claimed land. In association with the members of 'de 8 en de Opbouw' (Dutch CIAM Group). Design 1948-53; built 1954-8.

Alterations to the management offices at the Heldring & Pierson Bank, Korte Vijverberg, The Hague, 1948-9.

1949
Design for the first Cobra exhibition, Stedelijk Museum, Amsterdam, 3-28 November.

1950
Design for the jubilee exhibition of the Public Works Department, Stedelijk Museum, Amsterdam, 13 February-12 March.

'Landmark' at the entrance to the Ahoy' marine exhibition in Rotterdam.

Uhlman house, Utrecht. Not built.

Uhlman-Brakman double house, Utrecht, in collaboration with Jan Rietveld. Not built.

1951
Dutch entry for the ninth Milan Triennial, in collaboration with Jan Rietveld. Awarded a gold medal.

Conversion of Zwartjes shoe shop, Utrechtsestraat 125, Amsterdam.

Design for the second Cobra exhibition, Palais des Beaux Arts, Liège, 6 October-6 November.

64 houses for the elderly, Jan Bottema-straat, Amsterdam-Slotermeer, in col-laboration with Jan Rietveld. Design 1951-2; built 1953-4.

Damme house, Herman Gorterstraat 16, Amsterdam, in collaboration with Jan Rietveld. Design 1951-2; built 1953-4.

1952
The Blue-Purple Room with painting by Constant, for the 'Mens en Huis' exhibi-tion at the Stedelijk Museum in Amster-dam, 21 November 1952-5 January 1953.

1953
Design for the 'Ons Huis-Ons Thuis' fur-niture exhibition in the Bijenkorf, Amsterdam, February.

Holiday cottage, Schoorl, Terschelling. Not built.

Hexagonal table in teak, 1953; in purple-heart and greenheart, 1989.

Concept and layout for the 'Das neue Bauen in Holland' exhibition, Kunsthaus, Krefeld, in collaboration with Mart Stam.

1954
Charles Record Shop, Weteringschans 193, Amsterdam. Conversion of first-floor flat, 1959.

Three schools in Nagele, Noordoost-polder, in collaboration with H.P.D. van Ginkel. Design 1954-5; built 1955-6.

Draft design for conversion of lion's cage, Artis, Amsterdam. Design elabo-rated and built by the Public Works Department.

Bridge no. 356 over Zijkanaal 1, Klap-rozenweg, Amsterdam. Finished 1956.

1955
Bridge no. 21, Burg. Roëllstraat, Amsterdam-Slotermeer. Finished 1957.

'Nieuw Dordrecht' primary school (the so-called 'Greenhouse school of Drente'), Emmen. Not built.

Design for limited competition for the Open-Air School in Amsterdam. Not built.

Municipal Orphanage, Amstelveense-weg, Amsterdam. Design 1955-7; built 1957-60.
Plan for restoration and conversion, 1990, executed 1991-2.

1957
Rutgers house, Loenersloot. Not built.

1958
Congress Building, Jerusalem. Not built.

Project for own 'Four Tower House', Baambrugge. Design 1958-60; not built.

1959
War Memorial, in the vestibule of the Dutch Lower House, The Hague, 1959-60.

1960
Design for the Tajiri exhibition in the Stedelijk Museum, Amsterdam, 2 March-2 April. Built by Jurriaan Schrofer.

1962
Design for limited competition for urban expansion in Buikslotermeer. First design 1962; second design in collaboration with Jaap Bakema 1963. Neither plan built.

Design for Carel Visser and Joost van Roojen exhibition in the Zonnehof, Amersfoort, 2 November-9 December.

1963
Competition design for Modissa fashion shop in Zurich. Not built.

Design for limited competition for 'Wheels of Heaven', Protestant church in Driebergen. Prizewinning design, not built.

1964
Conversion of own house, Loenen aan de Vecht. Executed 1964-5.

Roman Catholic church, Aaltje Noorder-wierstraat 4, The Hague. Design 1964-6, built 1968-9.

1965
Layout of Oranjeplein, The Hague. Not executed.

Sculpture pavilion for Sonsbeek exhibition, Arnhem. Design 1965-6; built 1966.

1966

Scenery for the 'Labyrint' stage spectacular, Carré Theatre, Amsterdam.

Conversion of Maas house, Vreeland. Design 1966; executed 1967.

Limited competition, design for the town hall in Deventer. Prizewinning design, not built.

1967

Design for the Tajiri exhibition in the Stedelijk Museum, Amsterdam. 28 April-11 July.

Conversion of Martin Visser's Rietveld house, Eikendreef 2, Bergeyk. Design 1967; executed 1968-9.

Design for camp site in Mijnden, with two washing and toilet buildings. Design 1967-9; built 1969.

House with gallery for Alfred Schmela, Mutter-Eystrasse, Düsseldorf. Design 1967-9; built 1969-71.

Verberk house, Herungerweg, Venlo. Design 1967-70; built 1970.

1968

Villa for R. van Eyck, St-Paul-de-Vence. Not built.

'The greater number', an entry for the fifteenth Milan Triennial.

1969

Design for Joost van Roojen exhibition, Van Abbemuseum, Eindhoven. 7 March-20 April.

National Monument to Queen Wilhelmina, The Hague. Not built.

Limited competition for PREVI (Proyecto Experimental de Vivienda) housing in Lima. Design 1969; partially built 1972-6.

Conversion of house for the Marquis of Bute, London. Not executed.

1970

Magis house, Geldrop. Not built.

Limited competition for urban development project in the Nieuwmarkt area of Amsterdam. In association with Th. Bosch, P. de Ley, G. Knemeijer, D. Tuinman. Awarded a prize; built in modified form.

1971

The cube project, Stedelijk Museum, Amsterdam, 5 March-18 April. In collaboration with the composer Ton Bruynèl and the sculptor Carel Visser.

1972

Design for Carel Visser exhibition, Stedelijk Museum, Amsterdam, 18 March-30 April.

Limited competition for the extension of the Provincial Museum of Overijssel in Zwolle, in collaboration with Hannie van Eyck. Prizewinning design. Developed 1974-5; not built.

1973

The 'Hubertus House', a home for single parents and their children, Plantage Middenlaan 31, and alterations to old premises, Plantage Middenlaan 33 and 35, Amsterdam. Interior in collaboration with Hannie van Eyck. Design 1973-9, built 1976-81.

1974

House for G.J. Visser, Retie, Belgium. Design 1974-5, built 1975-6.

1976

De Jong house, Bergen. Not built.

1977

Alternative project for the 'Bouw-es-wat-anders' action group on the site of the former prison, Kleine-Gartmanplantsoen, Amsterdam. In collaboration with Hertzberger, van Klingeren, Klunder, Rietveld, Verster and Yap.

1979

Shop and house for Inez Stodel, Kerkstraat 195, Amsterdam. Built in 1980.

1980

'Padua' Psychiatric Clinic, Boekel, in collaboration with Hannie van Eyck. Built 1988-9.

1981

'Leefdael' addiction clinic, Helmond, in collaboration with Hannie van Eyck. Not built.

1982

Wilhelmina monument on Lange Voorhout in The Hague. Not built.

Overall urban development and organisational concept, as well as a draft design for a single unit, for the Siemens AG site Moorenbrunn, near Nuremberg. Design 1982-3, not built.

Van Eyck & Bosch Architects (1971-82)

1971

Design of building for KRO Broadcasting, Hilversum. Design 1970-2, not built.

75 dwellings and 21 commercial premises at Rode Torenplein, Zwolle. Design 1971-2, built 1974-5.

1972

50 dwellings and 22 commercial premises, Palmdwarsstraat, Amsterdam. Design 1972-4 and 1976, built 1979-80.

1974

83 dwellings for elderly residents, with central services, Rozenstraat 83-97, Amsterdam. Design 1974, built 1976-7.

1975

14 dwellings and one commercial space, Raamgracht-Moddermolensteeg; and 14 dwellings and 4 commercial premises, Sint-Antoniesbreestraat, Amsterdam. Design 1975, built 1976-8.

8 dwellings and 2 workshops, Korte Dijkstraat 9-23, Amsterdam; 4 dwellings, Korte Keizersstraat 20-26, Amsterdam. Design 1975, built 1977-8.

'Pentagon', 88 dwellings and 4 shops, near Nieuwmarkt, Amsterdam. First design 1975; second design 1978, built 1982-4.

15 dwellings, Oude Schans/Snoekjes-gracht, Amsterdam. First design 1975 and second design 1980, built 1981-2.

De Boogjes development, Dordrecht; design of 84 dwellings 1978-80, built 1981-3.

Building for the Faculty of Language and Literature, University of Amsterdam, Singel, Amsterdam. Design 1975-8, built 1981-4.

1977
Housing development project, Enkhuizen. Design 1977-8, not built.

Housing Koningsstraat, Amsterdam. First phase, design 1977-9, subterranean part of underground railway station built 1981; second and third phases, design 1978-81.

1978
Modified design for Deventer Town Hall, 1978; not built.

Housing development project, Burseplein, Deventer. Design 1978, not built.

21 dwellings with underground station entrance, Sint-Antoniesbreestraat/ Nieuwe Hoogstraat, Amsterdam. Design 1978-9 (underground part) and 1978-80, built 1981-3.

1979
Draft urban design for Binnengasthuis Site, Amsterdam, in collaboration with Werkgroep 'BG Terrein', 1979-80.

1980
New urban development scheme for Nieuwmarkt area, 1980-1.

Aldo & Hannie van Eyck Architects, from 1983

1983
Design for an exhibition of their own projects and ideas, National Museum, Athens, September.

Protestant church for the Moluccan community, Deventer. Design 1983-5, built 1991-2.

1984
Conference centre, library, restaurant and offices for ESTEC (European Space Research and Technology Centre), Noordwijk. Design 1984-6, built 1987-9.

Limited competition for the urban development scheme for the 'Campo di Marte', Giudecca, Venice. Prizewinning design, in collaboration with Julyan and Tess Wickham; not built.

1989
Design for the Carel Visser exhibition, Kröller-Müller Museum, Otterlo, March-April.

Design for an exhibition of their own work and ideas, Berlage Beurs, Amsterdam, 10 November 1989-2 January 1990.

Conversion of Sala de Notte of the Benedictine Abbey at Catania in Sicily. Not carried out.

1990
Restoration and alterations to the Orphanage in Amsterdam. Carried out in 1991-2.

Green area with play facilities for the Apollolaan, Amsterdam. Not carried out.

'Tripolis' office building in the grounds of the Orphanage, Amsterdam. Design 1990-1; built 1992-4.

Arts Centre at Middelburg. Murals by Karel Appel. Design 1990-1; not carried out.

Urban development scheme for the Vitrieten site in Middelburg. In collaboration with Lucien Lafour.

1992
Building for the Netherlands Court of Audit in The Hague. Design 1992-4; built 1996-7. Colour design for the façades by Jaap Hillenius.

1993
Extension for a travel agency at the ESTEC building in Noordwijk. Built 1994.

1994
Villa in Moscow. Not built.

Competition for the Valkhof Museum in Nijmegen. Not built.

1995
Extension of the kitchen at the ESTEC restaurant, Noordwijk. Built 1996.

Terminal pier at Thessaloniki. Not built.

1996
Design for memorial and park design in Houten. Not carried out.

1997
Design for exhibition of his own work and ideas, Documenta X at Kassel, 21 June-28 September 1997.

1998
Design for exhibition of his own projects and ideas, NAi, Rotterdam: 'Homage to Aldo and Hannie van Eyck'.

Writings by Aldo van Eyck (chronological order)

(The list of writings and the bibliography which are included here were for the greater part made out by Francis Strauven and with his admission taken from his monography *Aldo van Eyck. The Shape of Relativity*, published by Architectura & Natura in Amsterdam.)

1947

Architectuur-Schilderkunst-Beeldhouw-kunst en hun betekenis voor de Nieuwe Bewustwording – Report concerning the interrelation of the plastic arts and the importance of cooperation, report for CIAM 6, Bridgwater 1947.
'Statement against rationalism' (CIAM 6, Bridgwater 1947), in:
S. Giedion, *A decade of New Architecture* (Zurich, 1951), 37;
S. Giedion, *Architektur und Gemeinschaft* (Hamburg, 1956);
S. Giedion, *Architecture, you and me* (Harvard, 1958), 77-8.

1949

'Wij ontdekken stijl', *Forum* (1949, no. 2-3), 115-16.
'Inrichting van een torenkamer voor prof. W.L. te Zürich', *Forum* (1949, no. 2-3), 90.

1950

Een appèl aan de verbeelding, Amsterdam 12 Jan. 1950 (manifesto for the Experimental Group Holland Cobra).
'Bij het "teken" van de tentoonstelling', *Forum* (1950, no. 6-7), 202-3.
'Kind en stad', *Goed Wonen* (Oct. 1950, no. 10), 152-3.

1951

'Constant en de abstracten', opening speech for Constant exhibition in Galerie Le Canard, Amsterdam, stencil, 1 Feb. 1951.
'Over de Nederlandse inzending' (relating to Dutch contribution to Milan Triennale, 1951), *Forum* (1951, no. 9), 244-5; Italian translation *Domus* (Sept. 1951, no. 261), 6-7.

1952

'Kinderspielplatz in Amsterdam', *Bauen und Wohnen* (1952, no. 1), 28.
'Over Lohse', *Forum* (1952, no. 6-7), 186; and *Forum* (1959, no. 7), 223.
'P.W. en de kinderen van Amsterdam', *Forum* (1952, no. 6-7), 194-8.

1953

'Bouwen in de Zuidelijke Oasen', *Forum* (1953, no. 1), 28-38.
'Naar aanleiding van een weekendbij-eenkomst van de Nederlandse CIAM-groep ter bespreking van het probleem: Wapenfabriek Hispano Suiza', *Forum* (1953, no. 3), 91.
'Een ruimte door kleur begrensd', *Forum* (1953, no. 3), 92-3.
Voor een spatiaal colorisme (in co-operation with Constant) (Amsterdam, 1953).
'Enkele conclusies betreffende de structuur en realisering van het dorp Nagele', report of a three-day excursion to the Noordoost-Polder, 14, 15, 16 May 1953; stencil, in collaboration with D. van Ginkel.

1956

'Woningen voor bejaarden te Amsterdam' (Slotermeer), *Forum* (1956, no. 4), 130-3.
'Huis aan de Herman Gorterstraat te Amsterdam', *Forum* (1956, no. 4), 118.
'Over binnen- en buitenruimte', *Forum* (1956, no. 4), 133.
'Nagele, village in the N.E. Polder', grid presentation for the tenth CIAM Congress in Dubrovnik, 1956.
'The child and the city – problem of lost identity', grid presentation of the Amsterdam playgrounds at the tenth CIAM Congress in Dubrovnik, 1956.

1957

'A tribute to Carola Giedion-Welcker', introduction to a lecture by Carola Giedion-Welcker in the Stedelijk Museum, Amsterdam on 8 Feb. 1957, on the occasion of the opening of an exhibition of work by Paul Klee, *Forum* (1959, no. 9), 321-2.
'Scholen te Nagele', *Forum* (1957, no. 7), 243-5.
'Het kind en de stad', *Goed Wonen* (1957, no. 10), 207-12.

1958

'De bal kaatst terug', *Forum* (1958, no. 3), 104-11.
'Kwadraten met een glimlach', *De Groene Amsterdammer* (17 May 1958).
'Drei Schulhäuser in Nagele, Nordost-Polder, Holland', *Werk* (May 1958, no. 5), 170-3; English version: 'Three schools in Nagele', *Architects Year Book* (Aug. 1960, no. 9), 104.

1959

'Dag beeld', *De Groene Amsterdammer* (2 May 1959).
Statement on the relationship between architecture and art, *Forum* (1959, no. 6), 176.
'het verhaal van een andere gedachte' ('the story of another idea'), *Forum* (1959, no. 7, special issue).
Introduction to 5 projects, *Forum* (1959, no. 9).
'Kind und Stadt', in: A. Ledermann, A. Trachsel, *Spielplatz und Gemeinschaft-zentrum* (Teufen, 1959), 38-45.

1960

'Hello Shinkichi!', in: exhibition catalogue *Tajiri*, 2 March-2 April 1960, Stedelijk Museum, Amsterdam.
Assessment of design for Aquarium by J. Verhoeven, *Forum* (1960-61, no. 2), 69.
'There is a garden in her face', *Forum* (1960-61, no. 3), 107-17.
'Overwegend vuile was', *Forum* (1960-61, no. 4), 150-6.
Remarks on pictures of the old and the new Municipal Orphanage, *Goed Wonen* (Nov. 1960, no. 11), 319-31.

1961

'De milde raderen van de reciprociteit – The medicine of reciprocity tentatively illustrated', *Forum* (1960-61, no. 6-7, special issue).
'Visser is a winged digger', *Forum* (1961, no. 6-7), 238.
'Gensidighedens medecin forsgevis illus-tretet', *Louisiana Revy* (1961, no. 2), 25-7.
'Is architecture going to reconcile basic values?', in: O. Newman, *CIAM '59 in Otterlo* (Stuttgart, 1961), 26-35 and 216-17 (conclusion).
'Luogo e occasione', *L'architettura* (1961, no. 7), 395.
'Architecture of Dogon', *Architectural Forum* (Sept. 1961), 116-21.
'Waarom geen dierbaar stadhuis?', *De Groene Amsterdammer* (14 Oct. 1961).

1962

'Kinderhaus in Amsterdam', *Werk* (Jan. 1962), 16-22.
'Home for Children in Amsterdam', *The*

Indian Architect (Aug. 1962).

'The medicine of reciprocity tentatively illustrated', *Architects Year Book* (no. 10, London 1962), 173-8.

'The things that really matter', *Werk* (May 1962, no. 5), 108.

'The fake client and the great word "no"', *Forum* (Aug. 1962, no. 3), 79-80.

'Steps towards a configurative discipline', *Forum* (Aug. 1962, no. 3), 81-94. (Reprint in *Panorama van de avant-gardes* (Arnhem, 1981), 162; and in J. Ockman (ed.), *Architectural Culture in 1943-1968 – a documentary anthology* (New York, 1993.)

'The pueblos', *Forum* (Aug. 1962, no. 3), 95-114.

'Place and occasion', *Progressive architecture* (Sept. 1962), 155.

'Gensidigheden – menneskeligt og arkitektonisk', *Arkitekten* (1962, no. 24), 451-7.

Various passages in *Team 10 Primer*, *Architectural Design* (1962, no. 12, special issue, published by Alison Smithson), 559-60, 564-5, 570, 572, 574, 579, 590-1, 593, 594-5, 598, 601-2. Reprinted in paperback 1965. Hard cover edition with several additions (London 1968), 6, 12, 15, 20, 21, 22, 27, 30, 31, 32, 33, 35, 41, 43, 44, 45, 51-3, 59, 73, 83, 89, 95, 96, 98, 99, 100-4.

The Child, the City and the Artist, typescript of a book written on commission of the Institute of Urban Studies of the University of Pennsylvania, with a grant from the Rockefeller Institute, 1962.

1963

'The Pueblos', *Ecistics* (April 1963), 240-1.

Introduction to the prepublication of J. Rykwert, *The idea of a town*, *Forum* (1963, no. 3).

'Switch on the stars before the fuses go

– Organized Nowhere: The Boredom of Hygiene - Reconciling False Alternatives: The Inbetween Realm – Beyond Visibility', in: *Report '63, a record of the Pacific Congress organized by the students of the school of architecture* (University of Auckland, New Zealand, Sept. 1963).

'Beyond Visibility – About Place and Occasion – The Inbetween Realm – Right-size – Labyrinthian Clarity', *The Situationist Times* (Oct. 1963, no. 4), 79-85.

'Kindertehuis in Amsterdam', *Bouwkundig Weekblad* (1963, no. 1), 25-30.

1964

Contribution to symposium 'Gestaltungsprobleme der Gegenwart', *Werk* (March 1964, no. 3), 114.

'Het interieur van de ruimte', *Wijsgerig perspectief op Maatschappij en Wetenschap* (Sept. 1964, no. 1), 16-23.

1965

'Adolf Loos', introduction to exhibition held in Delft, *Delftse School* (April 1965, no. 12).

'The Wheels of Heaven', *Domus* (May 1965, no. 426), 2-3; and in: J. Donat, *World Architecture 3* (London, 1966), 121-9.

1966

'Labyrinthian Clarity', *World Architecture 3* (London, 1966), 120-9.

'University college in Urbino by Giancarlo de Carlo', *Zodiac* (1966, no. 16), and *Architects Year Book* (1968, no. 12), 151-160.

1967

Japanese translation of 'Place and Occasion, Labyrinthian Clarity, Otterlo Circles, Hill and Hollow Image,

Childrens Home, The Singular embracing the Plural, Protestant Church', *Kenchiku Bunka* (Jan. 1967, no. 243), 94-8.

'Paviljoen Sonsbeek 1966', *Forum* (July 1967), 24-5.

'Anna was, Livia is, Plurabelle's to be', *Forum* (July 1967), 28.

'Dogon: mand-huis-dorp-wereld', (in collaboration with P. Parin and F. Morgenthaler), *Forum* (July 1967), 30-50.

'Raadsel van de tijd' (1963), *Forum* (July 1967), 51.

'The sailor's nostalgia' (1960), *Forum* (July 1967), 52.

'Het interieur van de ruimte' (1964), *Forum* (July 1967), 54.

'De Spiegelmeester' (about Joost van Roojen), *Forum* (July 1967), 55-9.

'Paviljoen Arnhem, a place for sculpture and people', *World Architecture 4* (London, 1967), 59-60; and in: *Domus* (March 1968, no. 461).

1968

Open letter to the Hon. Eisaku Sato, Prime Minister of Japan, to save the Imperial Hotel of F.L. Wright, 12 Jan. 1968.

'Hello Shinkichi!' (2), *Domus* (March 1968, no. 461).

'*Kaleidoscope of the Mind*: Place and Occasion – The Interior of Space – The Interior of Time.' '*A Miracle of Moderation*: Design Only Grace, Open Norm; Disturb Order Gracefully, Outmatch Need – Basket, House, Village, Universe – The small brought about by the large – Some Comments on a significant Detour – Lacking the Spirit of Ecology' (in collaboration with P. Parin and F. Morgenthaler) and '*Image of Ourselves*: Another Miracle – The Snow Image again – The Boredom of Hygiene – The Fake Client and the

Great word "No"', in: *Via* (1968, no. 1), *Ecology in Design*, (University of Pennsylvania). Reprinted in 1976 at Eidgenössische Technische Hochschule, Zürich, under the title '*Miracles of Moderation*'.

'A Miracle of Moderation' was reprinted in: G. Baird, Ch. Jencks, *Meaning in Architecture* (London, 1969), 170-213; and in French translation in: *Le Sens de la Ville* (Paris, 1972). 'The Interior of Time' was reprinted in German translation under the title 'Das Innere der Zeit' in: G.R. Blomeyer, B. Tietze, *In Opposition zur Moderne* (Braunschweig-Wiesbaden, 1980) (Bauweltfundamente 52).

1969

'The Child, the City and the Artist', *Byggekunst* (1969, no. 1), 16-17.

'Bewoonbaar of onbewoonbaar', *Gemeentelijk Jaarboek 1969* (The Hague, 1969), 19-31.

'The Enigma of Vast Multiplicity – Mourn also for all Buterflies', *Harvard Educational Review* (1969, no. 4), 126-43. Reprinted in: *School House* (Delft, 1970.

'Juror's Statement', in: *Our Environment*, catalogue of the 59th Annual Exhibition of the Associated Artists of Pittsburgh, March-April 1969.

1970

'Footnote. – Who are we building for, and why?', *Architectural Design* (1970, no. 4), 189.

Description of own entry for Low Cost Housing competition, Previ, Lima, *Architectural Design* (1970, no. 4), 205.

'A propos: Jan Rietveld', *Wonen* (1970-71, no. 2), 5-8.

'Stadskern als donor' (in collaboration with G. Knemeijer), *TABK* (Sept. 1970, no. 20), 469-70; and *Forum* (Nov. 1970, no. 4), 20-7.

1971

'Waarborg voor behoud van verscheidenheid van functies en hun vervlechting' (in relation to Zwolle, in collaboration with Th. Bosch, P. de Ley, G. Knemeijer), *TABK* (1971, no. 22), 556-60.

1972

'Wonen in de binnenstad van Zwolle' (in collaboration with Th. Bosch, P. de Ley, G. Knemeijer), *Stedebouw en volkshuisvesting* (1972, no. 1), 18-22.

1974

'Enkele overwegingen die tot de gestalte van het huis hebben geleid', *Jaarverslag 1974 Hubertusvereniging*, 19-22.

Open letter to the Mayor and Aldermen of Amsterdam (8 July 1974, concerning Nieuwmarkt, with Th. Bosch), *Wonen-TABK* (1974, no. 15), 1-2.

1975

'In search of Labyrinthian Clarity' (comments regarding own work), *L'Architecture d'Aujourd'hui* (Jan.-Feb. 1975, no. 177), 14-30.

Open letter to the Mayor and Aldermen and Council of the City of Amsterdam (3 March 1975, with Th. Bosch, concerning Nieuwmarkt), *Wonen-TABK* (1975, no. 7), 2-3.

'Dank je wel, Pjotr', *B-nieuws* (1975, no. 34), 615.

1976

'Roman Catholic Church in The Hague', *Lotus International* (1976, no. 1), 109-14.

'Like that other gift', text for the architecture exhibit of the Venice Biennale,

July 1976. Published in Italian under the title 'Come l'altro dono', in: F. Raggi, *Europa/America. Architetture Urbane, alternative suburbane* (Venice, 1978), contribution to discussion, p. 179.

1978

Investigation of the effect of changes in climate and culture on the design process (in collaboration with F. Burke, S. Jhaveri), ETH Zurich, 1978.

1979

'Imagination and Competence: No Misplaced Suburbia – The Priority Jostle – The ironbound statement – Like that other gift – A Message to Mathias Ungers from a Different World – The Enigma of Size', *Spazio e Società* (Dec. 1979, no. 8), 43-78.

1980

'Errata corrige', *Spazio e Società* (March 1980, no. 9), 113.

'The Enigma of Size', *Signs and Insights* (Annual Report ILA&UD 1979) (Urbino, 1980), 42-53.

'Over het verhaal van een andere gedachte', *Wonen-TABK* (1980, no. 15), 7.

1981

'What is and what isn't architecture; à propos of Rats, Posts and Other Pests (R.P.P.)', *Lotus International* (1981, no. 28), 15-20. (Dutch translation in: *Forum* (1980-81, no. 3), 25-9, under the title 'Omtrent die massieve theepot'. In German translation partly included in: *Archithese* (1981, no. 5), 32-4, under the title 'Die Transparanz der Zeit'.)

'Over Bakema', *Forum* (1980-81, no. 3), 3.

'R.P.P. (Rats, Posts and Other Pests)', the RIBA Annual Discourse, prefaced by a letter to Dr. Papadakis, *AD News Supplement* (1981, no. 7).

'Zo iets bouw je toch niet voor mensen!', *Het Parool* (26 June 1981).

'Ex Turico Aliquid Novum', *Archithese* (1981, no. 5), 35-8.

'Transparancy and colours', *L'Architecture d'Aujourd'hui* (Oct. 1981, no. 217), 72-9.

1982

'En wel per definitie', on the work of Lucien Lafour, *Forum* (1981-82, no. 3), 27. English translation in: *AR* (Oct. 1984, no. 1052), 62; improved version in: *AR* (April 1985, no. 1058), 72.

'De bouw van een huis', in: H. Hertzberger, A. Van Roijen-Wortman, F. Strauven, *Aldo van Eyck* (Amsterdam, 1982), 38-95.

1983

'Ax Bax', in: collected documentation for the exhibition on A. van Eyck in the National Museum te Athens, Sept. 1983.

Pamphlet on the Elgin Marbles, *ibidem* and in: *Forum* (1983, no. 3), 8-9.

'Joop Hardy 1918-1983, herfstman tussen winters in', funeral address for Joop Hardy on 8 October 1983. Folder published by the Architecture Faculty, TH Delft 1986; also included in: J. Hardy, *Cultuurbeschouwing*, collected lectures given at the Technical University of Delft from 1981 to 1983 (Amsterdam, 1987), 313-17.

1984

'Un nouveau centre de gravité', comments on the design for a staff restaurant and conference facilities for ESTEC, Noordwijk; 'A propos de non espaces, de roses et de Codussi', comments on the design for a church for the Moluccan community in Deventer, *L'Architecture d'Aujourd'hui* (Oct. 1984,

no. 235), 18-23. English version in: *Architectural Review* (Jan. 1985, no. 1055), 14-17.

'Restaurant and conference facilities for ESTEC', *Architectural Design* (1984, no. 11-12), 80-3.

'Open brief aan het bestuur van de afdeling Bouwkunde', *B-nieuws* (24 Oct. 1984), 1.

1985

'Architetture e pensieri', *Casabella* (Oct. 1985, no. 517), 4-21.

1986

'A last Resort', programme for the international student competition held by the Royal Institute of British Architects, London, 1986.

'Toespraak bij de uitreiking van de Sikkensprijs 1962', 'Cobra (Luik en Stedelijk)', 'Avondje Limbo in de Lage Landen', 'Speelplaats Zeedijk', 'De Roze Po', 'Het project van Ton Bruynèl', 'Omtrent het aantal potloden', 'In de leegte gesproken', 'Kleine tafelspeech', and various other commentaries and reprints in: *Niet om het even – wel evenwaardig* (Rotterdam, 1986).

'Dylan Thomas', letter to the editor, *NRC Handelsblad* (Cultural Supplement, 26 Sept. 1986).

1989

'De architectuur van de gestolde toegankelijkheid', in: *Eikenheuvel* (house journal of Huize Padua, Boekel) (Aug. 1989).

'Padua', 'Local symmetry winking', in: *Aldo & Hannie van Eyck: recent work* (Amsterdam, 1989), 19, 27.

'En maar tuimelen tussen vandaag en gisteren', in: catalogue newspaper for the exhibition 'Aldo van Eyck in de Beurs van Berlage', 1989.

304

1990

'Verandert Delft voor of na Albanië?',
   Architectuur/Bouwen (1990, no. 11),
   45-50.

'Milano, Atene, Amsterdam', *Spazio e
   Società* (Oct.-Dec. 1990, no. 52), 6-17.

'Preface', in: P. Salomons and S. Door-
   man, *Jan Rietveld* (Rotterdam, 1990).

1991

'ESTEC', *Architecture and Urbanism*
   (April 1991, no. 247), 66-126.

1993

'Architectuur', letter to the editor in:
   Haagse Courant (21 Jan. 1993).

'Remembrance of a good friend' and
   'The Royal Gold Medal Address',
   Quaderns d'Arquitectes (1993, no. 3),
   110-45.

Statement on C.R. Mackintosh, *The Architects Architect* (London, 1993), 47-57.

1996

'Preface', in: Vincent Ligtelijn and Rein
   Saariste, *Josep M. Jujol* (Rotterdam,
   1996).

Letter to Vittorio Gregotti, *Casabella*
   (1996, no. 630-631), 116-17.

1997

A Superlative Gift – about Lina Bo Bardi,
   Sao Paulo Art Museum, Sao Paulo,
   1997.

1998

'Lured from his den', *Archis* (1998, no. 2),
   19-26.

Selected Bibliography

A selection of literature relating to Aldo van Eyck

1947

J.B. Bakema, 'Bridgwater 1947. Het 6e CIAM-congres, indrukken en feiten', *Bouw* (29 Nov. 1947), 389-97.

1950

C. Dotremont, 'L'Affaire Appel', *Le Petit Cobra* (no. 3, spring 1950).

1951

H. Salomonson, 'Bij het interieur van Aldo van Eyck', *Goed Wonen* (Feb. 1951, no. 2), 25-7.

H. Hartsuyker, 'Kinderspielplätze in Amsterdam', *Werk* (1951, no. 11), 335-6.

1952

R. Blijstra, 'Waar het kind zijn stad ontdekt', *Vrij Nederland* (23 Aug. 1952), 5.

S. Giedion, 'Historical Background to the Core', in: J. Tyrwhitt, J.L. Sert, E.N. Rogers, *The Heart of the City* (London, 1952), 17-25.

1955

Corneille, 'De mannen van de Hoggar', *Het Parool* (7 Jan. 1955).

J. Voelcker, 'Polder and Playground', *Architects Yearbook* (1955, no. 6), 89-94.

1958

P. Bakkum, 'Meervoudige opdracht tot het verkrijgen van een ontwerp voor de bouw van een openluchtschool voor het gezonde kind', *Bouwkundig Weekblad* (1958, no. 76), 437-48.

1960

J.J. Vriend, 'Verzet tegen materialistisch bouwen', *De Groene Amsterdammer* (27 Feb. 1960).

J. Weeks, 'The Children's House, Amsterdam', *Architectural Design* (May 1960, no. 5), 179-80.

M. van Beek, 'Verzoening tussen Palladio en Mies van der Rohe – Het nieuwe Burgerweeshuis te Amsterdam van Aldo van Eyck', *De Tijd-Maasbode* (2 July 1960).

H. Hartsuyker, 'Spielplatz Zeedijk in Amsterdam', *Werk* (Aug. 1960, no. 8), 293.

R. Blijstra, 'The Amsterdam Municipal Orphanage', *Delta* (autumn 1960, no. 3), 55-6.

J.J. Vriend, 'Het weeshuis van Aldo van Eyck', *De Groene Amsterdammer* (17 Sept. 1960).

J.B. Bakema, 'Gewoonte en gewoon – Nogmaals het weeshuis van Aldo van Eyck', *De Groene Amsterdammer* (8 Oct. 1960).

J.J. Vriend, 'Het ongewone is zeer gewoon' (answer to Bakema), *De Groene Amsterdammer* (15 Oct. 1960).

F. Oudejans, 'Het Burgerweeshuis nu in een nieuw tehuis onder 336 koepels', *Goed Wonen* (Nov. 1960, no. 11), 331-3.

1961

J.J.P. Oud, 'De melodie van de ruimte', *De Groene Amsterdammer* (18 March 1961).

B. Zevi, 'Convitto di Aldo van Eyck. Parlare con la propria eco non è dialogare', *L'Espresso* (3 Sept. 1961).

J.H. van den Broek, 'De Sikkensprijzen 1960 en 1961', speech delivered in the Stedelijk Museum, Amsterdam, Sept. 1961; stencil.

K. Wiekart, 'De duofenomenen van Aldo van Eyck', *Vrij Nederland* (7 Oct. 1961).

J. van Goethem, 'Casa dei Ragazzi ad Amsterdam', *L'architettura* (Oct. 1961, no. 72), 386-402.

1963

B. Kroon, 'Bruisend van ideeën? Niets nieuws bij! Laat mij maar bouwen, zegt Aldo van Eyck', *De Tijd* (16 Feb. 1963).

H.R. Hitchcock, 'A letter from Rome' (1 Sept. 1962), *Zodiac* (1963, no. 11).

S. Vinkenoog, *Karel Appel* (Utrecht, 1963), 56-61, 65-78, 167-9.

N. Kurakawa, 'New movements of Architecture and Urbanism in the World', *Kenchiki Bunka* (1963).

R. Maxwell, 'Frontiers of inner space', *Sunday Times Magazine* (29 Sept. 1963), 7-14.

1964

'Juryrapport meervoudige opdracht verleend door de Prof. dr. G. van der Leeuwstichting' (2 April 1964), *Mededelingen Prof. dr. G. van der Leeuwstichting* (1964), 1182-1211.

Mr. A.J. d'Ailly, 'Geef Aldo van Eyck een speciale uitnodiging om aan de open prijsvraag deel te nemen', *Het Vrije Volk* (10 Nov. 1964), 5.

1965

J. Schrofer, 'Een kwestie van verhoudingen', *Bouwkundig Weekblad* (18 June 1965, no. 12), 213-17.

An., 'Van Eyck kerk', *Architectural Review* (Aug. 1965, no. 822), 81-2.

J.A. Wells-Thorpe, 'Van Eyck Church', *Architectural Review* (Nov. 1965, no. 825), 318.

1966

R. Venturi, *Complexity and Contradiction in Architecture* (New York, 1966), 14, 19, 84 and 86.

W. Röling, 'Rond en recht in harmonie – beeldenpaviljoen in Sonsbeek door Aldo van Eyck', *Museumjournaal* (1966, no. 5), 127-9.

H. Hertzberger, W. Röling, 'Aldo van Eyck 1966', *Goed Wonen* (1966, no. 8), 11-15.

P. Fierz, 'Die AIA/ACSA Konferenz in Cranbrook USA', *Werk* (1966, no. 8).

1967

J.H. Mulder, 'Op de drempel', openbare les aan de Universiteit van Amsterdam, 8 Nov. 1966, *Bouw* (4 Feb. 1967).

Ch. Scheen, 'De Stedebouw en de Structuren', *Delftse School* (1967, no. 16).

M. van Regteren Altena-Zahle, 'Arkitekten Aldo van Eyck', *Arkitekten* (Denmark) (1967, no. 6), 133-7.

G. Bekaert, *In een of ander huis* (Tielt-The Hague, 1967), 90-2.

1968

L. van Marissing, 'Aldo van Eyck: "Ik zeg wel eens: een stad is een droom"', *de Volkskrant* (9 March 1968).

1969

'Meervoudige opdracht schetsontwerp nieuw stadhuis te Deventer', *Bouwkundig Weekblad* (1969, no. 18), 393-412.

G. Bekaert, 'De architectuur in Nederland aan de kunstgeschiedenis overgeleverd', *TABK* (1969, no. 15), 373-81.

1970

L. van den Bergh, 'Aldo van Eyck: "Een kind is geen economisch kwantum; er wordt een minimum aan zorgen aan besteed." Uit een duikelrek worden geen vlinders geboren', *Vrij Nederland* (27 June 1970).

P. Blom, 'Aldo moet het worden', *De Tijd* (9 Oct. 1970).

L. Schimmelpenninck, 'Het ontwerp van Van Eyck leent zich het best om uit te groeien tot een voor de buurt aanvaardbaar plan', *TABK* (1970, no. 22), 517-19.

1971

R. Brouwers, 'Woningbouw in de binnenstad van Zwolle door bureau Van Eyck & Bosch', *TABK* (1971, no. 22), 554-60.

1972

'Da vedere a Dusseldorf', *Domus* (Oct. 1972, no. 515), 30-4.

W.G. Overbosch, 'Aldo van Eycks Pastoor van Arskerk', *Mededelingen Prof. dr. G. van der Leeuwstichting* (no. 43, Amsterdam 1972).

306

1973

R. Brouwers, 'Een mirakel in de Jordaan. Een plan voor de bouw van woningen en winkels van Aldo van Eyck, Theo Bosch, Lucien Lafour en G. Knemeijer', *Wonen-TABK* (1973, no. 1), 9-21.

M. van Rooy, 'De bewoonbaarheid van Nederland hangt af van een lijstje telefoonnummers', *NRC Handelsblad* (Cultural Supplement, 2 March 1973).

F. Strauven, 'Symboliek in het werk van Charles Rennie Mackintosh', *Wonen-TABK* (Oct. 1973, no. 20), 5-21.

Ch. Jencks, *Modern Movements in Architecture* (Harmondsworth, 1973), 311-18.

1974

A. Smithson, 'How to read and to recognize Mat Building', *Architectural Design* (Sept. 1974).

R. Brouwers, 'Begint in Zwolle binnenstadsvictorie?', *Wonen-TABK* (1974, no. 22), 1-3.

W. Stokvis, *Cobra, geschiedenis, voorspel en betekenis van een beweging in de kunst van na de Tweede Wereldoorlog* (Amsterdam, 1974), 114-23, 130 et passim.

1975

B.B. Taylor, 'Songs of Innocence and Experience', *L'Architecture d'Aujourd'hui* (Jan.-Feb. 1975, no. 177).

K. Frampton, 'The Vicissitudes of Ideology', *L'Architecture d'Aujourd'hui* (Jan.-Feb. 1975, no. 177).

P. Gonggrijp, 'Open brief aan Aldo van Eyck', *B-nieuws* (Architecture Faculty newspaper, Technical University of Delft) (1975, no. 30), 532.

P. Smithson, 'Aldo van Eyck's church at the Hague', *Architectural Design* (June 1975, no. 6), 344-50.

A. Smithson, 'Team 10 at Royaumont', *Architectural Design* (Nov. 1975), 664-89.

Ch. Jencks, 'The Rise of Post Modern Architecture', *Architectural Association Quarterly* (Oct.-Dec. 1975), 3-9.

1976

A. Luchinger, 'Strukturalismus – eine neue Strömung in der Architektur', *Bauen und Wohnen* (1976, no. 1), 5-11.

'Aldo van Eyck', in: catalogue *Dortmunter Architekturausstellung*, 12 May-7 June 1976.

P.L. Nicolin, 'Aldo van Eyck, la trama e il labirinto', *Lotus International* (1976, no. 1), 105-8.

J. Roos, 'Praten met Aldo van Eyck', *Het Parool* (11 Nov. 1976).

T. Neelissen, *De vuurvogel*, NOS TV broadcast, prod. Max Appelboom, recorded in winter 1976-77.

O. Bohigas, 'Once Arquitectos', in: *La Gaya Ciencia* (Barcelona 1976).

1977

O. Bohigas, 'Aldo van Eyck or a New Amsterdam School', *Oppositions* (1977, no. 9), 21-36.

P. Gonggrijp, 'Dank je wel Aldo', *B-nieuws* (1977, no. 27), 638-9.

1979

H. van Dijk, 'Vertrouwen op de regenboog', *NRC Handelsblad* (Cultural Supplement, 20 April 1979), 3.

P. Goulet, 'Une bouffée d'air frais – Foyer pour des enfants et leurs mères', *Architecture Intérieure* (Nov.-Dec. 1979, no. 147), 121-4.

G. De Carlo, 'Questioni – Questions', *Spazio e società* (Dec. 1979, no. 8), 46-7.

1980

J. Taylor, 'The Dutch Casbahs', *Progressive Architecture* (1980, no. 3), 86-96.

F. Strauven, 'Plaats voor wederkerigheid', *Wonen-TABK* (1980, no. 8), 11-32. Published in Italian and English translations in *Lotus International* (1981, no.

28), 20-40.

J. Maule McKean, 'Rainbow House', *Building Design* (13 June 1980), 24-6.

U. Barbieri, 'Labyrinth and Square. The architectural story of Aldo van Eyck', *DA + AT* (1980, no. 7), 33-42.

J. de Heer, K. Vollemans, 'Postscriptum of Voorbij het laatste woord over de laatste stad (ook andere formaties kunnen dat)', *Raster* (1980, no. 12), 129-45.

A. Luchinger, *Structuralism in Architecture and Planning* (Stuttgart, 1980).

A.M. Vogt, *Architektur 1940-1980* (Munich, 1980), 72-3.

K. Frampton, *Modern architecture; a critical history* (London, 1980), 271-9.

G.R. Blomeyer & B. Tietze, *In Opposition zur Moderne – Aktuelle Positionen in der Architektur* (Braunschweig, 1980).

J. Furse, 'Aldo van Eyck', in: M. Emanuel, *Contemporary Architects* (London, 1980), 843-5.

1981

J. van de Beek (ed.), *Aldo van Eyck, projekten 1948-1961* (Groningen, 1981).

P. Blundell Jones, 'I'm just a hardboiled functionalist', *Architects' Journal* (18 Feb. 1981), 293.

A.M. Vogt, 'Mutmassungen über Aldo van Eyck', *Archithese* (1981, no. 5), 31-2.

I. Salomons, 'Het moederhuis: licht en ruimte', *Forum* (1980-81, no. 3), 20-4.

G. Broadbent, 'The Pests strike back', *RIBA Journal* (Nov. 1981), 31-4.

1982

H. Hertzberger, 'Het 20ste-eeuwse mechanisme en de architectuur van Aldo van Eyck', *Wonen-TABK* (1982, no. 2), 10-19. English and Italian translations in *Spazio e Società* (Dec. 1983, no. 24), 80-97.

R. Brouwers, 'Moderne Beweging zet met Van Eyck in Finland de tegenaanval in', *Wonen-TABK* (1982, no. 22), 2-3.

P. Buchanan, 'Mothers' house, Amsterdam', *Architectural Review* (March 1982, no. 1021), 25-34.

S. Doubilet, 'Weaving chaos into order', *Progressive Architecture* (March 1982), 74-7.

H. Hertzberger, A. van Roijen-Wortman, F. Strauven, *Aldo van Eyck*, (Amsterdam, 1982).

1983

J. van de Beek (ed.), *Aldo van Eyck, projekten 1962-1976* (Groningen, 1983).

E. Boesch-Hutter, 'Aldo van Eyck: Turmzimmer, 1946', *Archithese* (1983, no. 1), 25-6.

J. van Geest, 'Een roepende in de polder', *Forum* (1983, no. 3), 9-16; English version ('Assaulting grimness') in collected documentation for the exhibition on Aldo van Eyck, Athens, 1983.

G. Candilis, S. & D. Antonakakis, G. De Carlo, contributions on A. van Eyck, in collected documentation for the exhibition on Aldo van Eyck in the National Museum, Athens, Sept. 1983.

Th. Noviant, *Une Eglise catholique à La Haye* (dissertation Unité Pédagogique 8, Paris, 1983).

1984

H.M. Tromp, 'The essential architect: Aldo van Eyck', *Holland Herald* (1984, no. 4), 14-22.

C. Mathewson, 'Multiple Meaning in Equipoise', *Dichotomy* (Detroit Students' Journal) (1984, no. 1), 1-15.

C. Mathewson, 'Defining Space as the Appreciation of Space Entered', *Dichotomy* (Detroit Students' Journal) (1984, no. 2), 33-61.

H. Klotz, *Moderne und Postmoderne – Architektur der Gegenwart 1960-1980* (Braunschweig, 1984).

1985

F. Strauven, 'Aldo van Eyck als ontwerp-leraar', *Wonen-TABK* (1985, no. 1), 19-24.

P. Buchanan, 'Aldo van Eyck', *Architectural Review* (1985, no. 1), 14-17.

O. Laser, E. Vargas, 'Ein Grundriss ist keine Autobahn', *Arch+* (1985, no. 1), 56-60.

C. Mathewson, 'The Architecture of Aldo van Eyck', *Crit* (1985, no. 15), 5-64.

J. Burney, 'Taking a leap in the dark', *Building Design* (25 Oct. 1985), 9.

V. Gregotti, 'Un amico indisciplinato' – 'A rebellious friend', *Casabella* (Oct. 1985, no. 517), 6.

S. Brandolini, 'La semplicità dell'avan-guardia' – 'The simplicity of the avant garde', *Casabella* (Oct. 1985, no. 517), 16-18.

Questions (CERAA, Brussel), Oct. 1985, no. 7, special edition on Amsterdam and A. van Eyck, with contributions by B. Vellut, R. Matthu and F. Parmentier.

B. Baines, 'La quadrature de Aldo', *Parallèles* (no. 2 – supplement to *Questions*, no. 7 – Oct. 1985), 16-21.

A. Schimmerling, 'Amsterdam, modestie et audace – note sur la rénovation des quartiers Nieuwmarkt et Jordaan', *le carré bleu* (1985, no. 3-4), 7-16.

C. Magnani, 'Il Concorso dello IACP di Venezia per Campo di Marte alla Giudecca', *Casabella* (Nov. 1985, no. 518), 5-16.

1986

L. Lefaivre, 'Order in the Children's Home', *Forum* (1986, no. 1), 3-7 (with Dutch trans-lation).

P. Blundell Jones, 'Modernism betrayed' (report on Van Eyck's Tanner lectures in Cambridge on 21 and 22 April 1986), *Architects' Journal* (7 May 1986), 24-5.

F. Strauven, interviews about Aldo van Eyck with Felix Schwarz, Richard P. Lohse, Hein Salomonson, Jan Rietveld, Constant, Corneille, Alechinsky, Tajiri, Carel Visser, Dick Cassée, Peter Schat, Martin Visser, Georges Candilis, Peter Smithson, Piet Blom, Joop van Stigt, Jan Verhoeven, Herman Hertzberger, Theo Bosch, Lucien Lafour, Pjotr Gonggrijp, Gerrit Smienk, Joseph Rykwert, Yap Hong Seng, Hannie van Eyck and Jaap Hillenius, in: *Niet om het even – wel evenwaardig* (Amsterdam, 1986).

1987

H. Hertzberger, *Bewaar het weeshuis*, protest newspaper demanding preserva-tion of the Municipal Orphanage, with contributions from all over the world, Amsterdam 1987.

F. Strauven, *Het Burgerweeshuis van Aldo van Eyck, een modern monument* (Amsterdam, 1987).

1988

P. Buchanan, 'Nederlandse architectuur is spoor bijster', *Architectuur-Bouwen* (June-July 1988), 63-7.

G. Bekaert, 'Entre pragmatisme et radical-isme, une tradition moderne à la fois solide et mouvante', *L'Architecture d'Aujourd'hui* (July 1988, no. 257), 96-105.

I. Salomons, 'Architectuur van ongekende dimensies', *Het Parool* (11 August 1988).

1989

J. de Heer, 'Het centrumloze labyrint', *Oase* (1989, no. 23), 10-21.

J. van de Beek, reply to de Heer in *Oase*, 1989, no. 25, 22-3.

E. Mik, 'Aldo van Eyck: ruimte moet blij-moedig zijn', interview in *De Tijd* (3 March 1989), 30-6.

H. Selier, 'Berlage Instituut in Burger-weeshuis', interview with H. Hertzberger, *De Architect* (Oct. 1989), 46-9.

E. Koster, 'Alternatief functionalisme in low-tech en barok' (about ESTEC and Padua), *De Architect* (Dec. 1989), 42-54.

H. van Dijk, 'The demise of structuralism', in: *Architecture in the Netherlands-Yearbook 1988-1989* (Deventer, 1989).

I. Salomons, 'Estec under construction', in: *Architecture in the Netherlands – Yearbook 1988-1989* (Deventer, 1989).

F. Strauven, 'Aldo van Eyck: An outline of his ideas, the meaning of his work', in: catalogue newspaper for the exhibition 'Aldo van Eyck in de Beurs van Berlage' (Amsterdam, 1989).

P. Buchanan, 'Architect Ludens – The archi-tecture of Aldo and Hannie van Eyck', in: *Aldo en Hannie van Eyck: recent werk* (Amsterdam, 1989), 3-14 (with Dutch translation); and *Architectural Review* (Feb. 1990, no. 1116), 35-57.

L. Lefaivre & A. Tzonis, 'Dragon in the Dunes', *Aldo en Hannie van Eyck: recent werk* (Amsterdam, 1989), 22-6, with Dutch translation; French version in *le carré bleu* (1990, no. 1).

1990

J. Molenaar, 'Architectuur achter de zin-tuigen van de waarnemer – ESTEC en Padua, twee nieuwe werken van Aldo en Hannie van Eyck', *Archis* (1990, no.1), 32-41.

'Verbeelde Orde', *Oase* (1990, no. 26-27), special edition on Aldo van Eyck, with contributions by G. Hoving, E. Terlouw, H. Engel, E. van Velzen and J. Meuwissen.

P. Buchanan, 'Forum Fellowship', *Architectural Review* (Feb. 1990, no. 1116), special edition on recent work by A. & H. van Eyck, H. Hertzberger, Th. Bosch, P. de Ley, L. Lafour and R. Wijk.

1991

Liane Lefaivre and Alexander Tzonis, 'Dragon in the Dunes – Aldo and Hannie van Eyck's ESTEC', *Architecture and Urbanism* (April 1991), 70-4

1992

C. Davies, 'Window to another world', *Architectural Review* (April 1992, no. 1142), 46-50.

Aldo en Hannie van Eyck met Karel Appel in Middelburg, brochure published for presentation of the project Centrum Beeldende Kunst Middelburg, with contri-butions by K. Appel, A. van Eyck and I. Salomonson (Middelburg, 1992).

W.J. van Heuvel, *Structuralisme in de Nederlandse Architectuur* (Rotterdam, 1992).

S. Lebesque, 'Rietveld, Van Eyck, Koolhaas', *Vrij Nederland* (28 Nov. 1992), 56-8.

H. van Bergeijk, 'Architectuur van de bewustwording', *De Architect* (Dec. 1992), 52-61.

J. Bosman, 'CIAM after the War: a Balance of the Modern Movement', *Rassegna* (Dec. 1992), no. 52, 6-21.

F. Strauven, 'The Dutch Contribution: Bakema and Van Eyck', *Rassegna* (Dec. 1992), no. 52, 48-57.

1993

F. Strauven, 'Shifting Symmetry', *Archis* (Febr. 1993), no. 2, 17-25.

H. van Dijk, 'Laugier's garden', *Architecture in the Netherlands – Yearbook 1992-1993* (NAi, Rotterdam, 1993), 58-9.

P. De Santis, *Aldo van Eyck* (dissertation, Università La Sapienza, Rome, 1993).

J.R. Pratley, *Relativity and Architecture* (dis-sertation, Plymouth School of Architec-ture, Plymouth, 1993).

M. Pawley, 'Money, time and details', *World Architecture* (March 1993, no. 22), 22-3.

S. Brandolini, 'Passionate Practitioner', *World Architecture* (March 1993, no. 22), 24-7.

P. Pragnell, 'Cerchi magici e foreste incan-tate' – 'The extraordinary familiarity of ESTEC', *Spazio e Società* (Jan.-March 1993), 18-27.

S. Brandolini, 'La chiesa blu di Deventer di Aldo van Eyck', *Casabella* (Oct. 1993, no. 605), 60-70.

M. Casciato, 'Forum: architettura e cultura nei primi anni sessanta', *Casabella* (Nov. 1993, no. 606), 48-53.

1994

F. Strauven, *Aldo van Eyck. Relativiteit en verbeelding* (Amsterdam, 1994).

1995

F. Wildschut, 'Juryrapport prijsvraag uitge-schreven door de gemeente Nijmegen en de provincie Gelderland', *Vijf ontwerpen voor een nieuw museum in Nijmegen* (Nijmegen, 1995).

1996

Thomas Barrie, *Sacred Place – Myth, Ritual and Meaning in Architecture* (Boston & London, 1996), 97-102.

Barbara Jean, *Fata Morgana*, with contribu-tions by Kristien Feireiss, Gerrit Schoen-maker, Aldo and Hannie van Eyck, Max van Rooy, Anton van Gemert, Lex ter Braak, Leon Riekwell, Leo de Kraker, W.T. van Gelder, H.J. van Hunnik and Adri Duivesteijn (Venlo, 1996).

Bert Struijk, *Van Burgerweeshuis tot Garden Court – Ontstaan, betekenis, ver-val en de enerverende renovatie van een modern monument* (Ede, 1996).

F. Strauven, 'L'orphelinat d'Aldo van Eyck – un monument moderne' *eaV (Revue de l'Ecole d'architecture de Versailles)* (1996, no. 2), 68-81.

F. Strauven, *Aldo van Eyck's Orphanage – A Modern Monument* (Rotterdam, 1996).

1997

I. Salomons, *Met kleur gebouwd – De Alge-mene Rekenkamer in Den Haag* (Den Haag, 1997).

B. Colenbrander, 'A tradition resumed – rethinking Aldo van Eyck', *Archis* (Nov. 1997, no. 11), 42-9.

Max van Rooy, 'Een sluipende kat in de regenboog', *NRC Handelsblad* (4 July 1997).

Ursul Schaap, *Kleurrijk en veelvormig – de Nieuwbouw van de Algemene Rekenkamer* (Den Haag, 1997).

1998

F. Strauven, *Aldo van Eyck. The Shape of Relativity* (Amsterdam, 1998).

1999

Max van Rooy, 'Humaan en poëtisch bouwmeester – Aldo van Eyck (1918-1999)', *NRC Handelsblad* (15 Jan. 1999).

Hilde de Haan and Ids Haagsma, 'Aldo van Eyck volgde de menselijke maat', *de Volkskrant* (15 Jan. 1999).

Umberto Barbieri and Henk Engel, 'In memoriam Aldo van Eyck (1918-1999)', *Delta* (21 Jan. 1999, no. 2).

Izak Salomons, 'Mijn lievelingskleur is de regenboog', *Vrij Nederland* (23 Jan. 1999).

Izak Salomons, *Built with Colour – The Netherlands Court of Audit / Met kleur gebouwd – De Algemene Rekenkamer in Den Haag* (Rotterdam, 1999).

Joop van Stigt, Vincent Ligtelijn and Herman Hertzberger, 'Tot Besluit', over het Burgerweeshuis van Aldo van Eyck, *Eigen Huis & Interieur* (July 1999, no. 7).

309

Index of Persons

310

Source of the Quotations

Excerpts from interviews with Francis
    Strauven, published in: Aldo van Eyck (ed.),
    *niet om het even... wel evenwaardig –
    van en over Aldo van Eyck*, (Amsterdam,
    1982); Felix Schwartz: p. 17, Carel Visser:
    p. 63, Peter Schat: p. 71, Richard Paul
    Lohse: p. 18, Constant: p. 38, Shinkichi
    Tajiri: p. 54, John Voelcker p. 32-3.
Excerpt from the television programme
    'Aldo van Eyck', by Tom Neelissen,
    Markant, NOS, 1976-7: Carola Giedion-
    Welcker.
From the catalogue of the exhibition on
    the work of Aldo van Eyck, 'AX BAX'
    (Athens, 1983): Georges Candilis and
    Giancarlo De Carlo.
From a letter to Aldo van Eyck (23.7.1959),
    after a visit to the Orphanage, which was
    under construction: Richard Buckminster
    Fuller.

Photographic Credits

Most of the photographs and drawings are made by Aldo van Eyck,
with the exception of the following illustrations.

Associated Correspondents: 247 (above)

Maria Austria: 144

Kors van Bennekom: 179

Alexander van Berge: 211 (above),
   213 (right), 214 (above), 215 (top right),
   235 (under), 236 (above), 237 (under),
   246 (under)

Abel Blom: 80 (under)

Pieter Boersma: 70 (top left)

Foto Bräm: 52, 53 (right)

Wim Brusse: 75

Petra ten Cate: 172 (under), 173 (under),
   222 (top right), 223 (top left)

Violette Cornelius: 62, 63, 67 (left,
   top right), 69, 80 (centre), 97 (right),
   105 (left, centre right)

Jan Derwig: 238 (bottom right), 239 (above),
   240 (above), 241, 242 (bottom left),
   244 (bottom right)

Herman van Doorn: 222 (left), 223 (left)

ESA/ESTEC: 235

Bob Fleumer Aerial Photography: 258 (under)

Fotografische Dienst TU Delft, Faculteit der
   Bouwkunde: 131 (left)

Leonard Freed: 148 (bottom right)

Gemeentelijke Archiefdienst Amsterdam:
   70 (under), 71 (left), 73, 74, 79, 80 (left), 81

P.H. Goede: 88 (above), 92 (bottom left),
   96 (above), 109 (bottom left)

Tom Haartsen: 120, 205, 216, 217

Leo Klatser: 87 (right)

Teo Krijgsman: 265, 266 (above), 267
   (bottom left), 269 (under), 270 (right),
   271, 276 (left), 277 (left, bottom right)

Leith-Air Ltd.: 177

Harry van Liempd: 211 (bottom left)

Vincent Ligtelijn: 66, 67 (bottom right), 130,
   151 (top right), 153, 155, 157 (top right,
   bottom right), 158 (top left), 159, 161

(top left, bottom left), 170, 171,
   172 (above), 173 (above)

Jannes Linders: 266 (top left)

Sandra Lousada: 132 (top right)

J.J. van der Meyden: 90, 93 (top right),
   93 (top left, top right, centre right),
   96 (bottom right), 98, 101 (bottom left),
   103 (top centre), 106 (top right),
   108 (above), 109 (top left)

Maarten d'Oliviera: 86 (right), 87 (left)

Cas Oorthuys: 68

Har Oudejans: 72

Louis van Paridon: 71 (right), 92 (top left,
   top right), 93 (bottom right), 103 (bottom
   left)

Picture Report: 231

Wim Riemens: 254

Izak Salomons: 237 (above), 273 (bottom
   centre), 277 (top right)

Stedelijk Museum Amsterdam: 60

Francis Strauven: 53 (top left), 65 (top left),
   215 (bottom right)

J. Versnel: 54, 55, 56, 57, 58 (bottom right),
   59, 64, 65 (top right), 77, 82 (right),
   83 (right), 151 (above), 152 (top left, right)

Ger van der Vlugt: 184

Koen Wessing: 136 (top left)